ECONOMIC DEVELOPMENT

Handbook of Comparative Economic Policies

1. National Economic Policies
   Dominick Salvatore, editor
2. National Trade Policies
   Dominick Salvatore, editor
3. Monetary Policy in Developed Economies
   Michele U. Fratianni and Dominick Salvatore, editors
4. Economic Development
   Enzo Grilli and Dominick Salvatore, editors

ECONOMIC DEVELOPMENT

EDITED BY
ENZO GRILLI
AND
DOMINICK SALVATORE

HANDBOOK OF COMPARATIVE ECONOMIC POLICIES
VOLUME 4

GREENWOOD PRESS
Westport, Connecticut · London

Library of Congress Cataloging-in-Publication Data

Economic development / edited by Enzo Grilli and Dominick Salvatore.
     p.   cm.—(Handbook of comparative economic policies, ISSN
1054–7681 ; v. 4)
  Includes bibliographical references and index.
  ISBN 0–313–28047–9
  1. Developing countries—Economic policy. 2. Economic
development. I. Grilli, Enzo R. II. Salvatore, Dominick.
III. Series.
HC59.7.E277 1994
338.9'009172'4—dc20   93–30449

British Library Cataloguing in Publication Data is available.

Library of Congress Catalog Card Number: 93–30449
ISBN: 0–313–28047–9
ISSN: 1054–7681

First published in 1994

Greenwood Press, 88 Post Road West, Westport, CT 06881
An imprint of Greenwood Publishing Group, Inc.

Printed in the United States of America

The paper used in this book complies with the
Permanent Paper Standard issued by the National
Information Standards Organization (Z39.48–1984).

10 9 8 7 6 5 4 3 2 1

CONTENTS

ILLUSTRATIONS

TABLES

PREFACE

The present volume is the fourth in a series of comparative economic handbooks. It presents an overview of the development problems and experiences of developing countries. Volume 1 presented an overview of national economic policies, Volume 2 dealt with national trade policies, and Volume 3 examined monetary policies in the United States and in the world's leading industrial countries. Future volumes will deal with macroeconomic, tax, and environmental policies.

This volume examines the problems faced by developing countries and the progress achieved in overcoming development problems during the postwar period. It focuses not on development economics per se but rather on the problems faced by developing countries and the way they sought to overcome them.

After a brief introduction by the editors, the volume is divided into four parts. Part I of the volume (chapters 1 and 2) deals with development theory and economic development strategies. Part II (chapters 3–7) deals with the aggregate and sectoral record of economic development. Part III (chapters 8–14) deals with regional development experiences. Part IV (chapter 15) summarizes the main development lessons.

The chapters in this volume have been written by some of the world's most renowned experts in the field of development economics and present the most comprehensive and current comparative studies of the development experience on the market today. Thus, the handbook can be of great use to students of development economics in general and to economists, policymakers, and the general informed public as a very useful source of reference and comparison. The references at the end of each chapter and the selected bibliography at the end of the volume identify the most important sources of additional information and detail about the postwar development experience throughout the world.

INTRODUCTION

In his "State of Development Theory," W.A. Lewis (1984) defined development economics as the study of the economic structure and behavior of poor countries. Development economics, thus, refers to the study of how traditional societies can increase their productive capacity, change the structure of their economies, increase real per capita incomes, reduce poverty, and increase the health and education of the population. Viewed from this perspective, development economics is at once one of the oldest and one of the newest fields of economics. It is one of the oldest fields of economics because Adam Smith began, after all, with an inquiry into the nature and causes of the wealth of nations. It is one of the newest because interest in development economics was revived with the collapse of European-based empires after World War II and the emergence of about a hundred new Third World nations facing deep poverty and instability.

During the postwar period, development economics was confronted with controversies over balanced versus unbalanced growth, industrialization versus agriculture, import substitution versus export promotion, and planning versus reliance on the market. Although these controversies have not been entirely resolved, there is much agreement today that the development process by its very nature involves for the most part unbalanced, rather than balanced, growth; the choice between industry and agriculture is now regarded as a false choice—both industry and agriculture are important to the development process; import substitution may be important to large developing countries during their early stages of development, but export promotion and freer markets become essential for development to continue to proceed successfully; the same is generally true for planning versus reliance on markets.

Although many of these early controversies have been to a large extent resolved, development economics is today characterized by competing paradigms rather than a universally accepted theory or orthodoxy. Perhaps this is inevitable since the process of economic development involves not only economics but also history, psychology, sociology, and politics. Economists do agree, however, that the development process must inevitably involve capital accumulation, the introduction of new technologies, human resource development, the development of institutions and markets, and a permissive international framework.

In the absence of a dominant orthodoxy, the experience of individual and groups of countries becomes paramount in the study of the problems faced by different developing countries and in the ways in which they have dealt with them. Here, the experience has been most varied and uneven—not only in growth rates but also in the way different countries have dealt with their development problems and in the degree of success they had in resolving them.

The development successes of many of the Pacific Rim countries must be juxtaposed with worsening economic conditions in other regions, mainly Africa and parts of South Asia. Successful economic reforms in many Latin American countries must be viewed against the perspective of lack of success, so far, of the reform process in many African countries. Private sector development is by now generally recognized as a key prerequisite for a transition to an efficient economy and rapid growth. Yet, the forms of such development can vary a great deal from country to country, as the economic success of China shows us. State intervention in the economy has often been harmful, as shown by the experience of most of Africa and much of Latin America, but it can also help in the growth and development process, as demonstrated by several cases of countries in Southeast Asia. The various experiences in the ever-changing universe of development provide, therefore, a most useful avenue for understanding what works and what does not in the development process. This is the main reason for, and, we hope, the main contribution of, this handbook.

This book's unifying theme is that strategies and policies, more than factor endowment, geographical location, size, and international context, matter and make a large difference in growth and development outcomes. This is by now borne out by the experience of such a wide range of countries, in so many different parts of the developing world, that it should be part of the development "acquis."

The contributions to this handbook examine the record of, and reasons for, economic development in the main developing regions. Their focus is on the development experience of the component countries in light of the economic strategies followed by them over time. Development theories constitute the background for ordering facts, understanding outcomes, and comparing them across time and space, but they are not the main concern of this book, which concentrates instead on the record of development. For these reasons the title speaks of economic development rather than development economics, a subject covered extensively and authoritatively in other recent publications.

The volume begins with two introductory chapters (Part I) on the roots of development theories and the strategies of economic development that developing countries can follow. These survey chapters deal with the theories and strategies as we have known them during the postwar period and set the stage for the central focus of the volume, which is the record of economic development in the aggregate (Part II) and by major geographical area (Part III). The volume ends with a chapter (chapter 15 in Part IV) relating development policies to development performance. Structured in this way, the volume has the logic and perspective of a "state of the arts and facts" on economic development and can be seen as a complement to the existing literature on the economics of development.

REFERENCE

Lewis, W.A. 1984. "The State of Development Theory." *American Economic Review* 74 (March): 1–10.

PART I

DEVELOPMENT THEORY AND ECONOMIC DEVELOPMENT STRATEGIES

1

THE CLASSICAL ROOTS OF DEVELOPMENT THEORY

Paolo Sylos Labini

WHY WE SHOULD GO BACK TO THE CLASSICAL ECONOMISTS

Joseph Schumpeter used to distinguish between growth and development and defined the former as a gradual process in which all quantities—wealth, saving, population—increase slowly and continuously and the latter as a discontinuous process propelled by innovations (Schumpeter, 1939). Similar, though not identical to Schumpeter's distinction, is the one put forward by those economists—such as Robert Lucas (1988)—who define growth as the increase of income proportional to the increase of population and define development as the process in which income increases more rapidly than population. In other words, growth would not presuppose technical changes; development would. Recently it has become common to speak of growth with reference to advanced countries and of development with reference to Third World countries. In this conception development theory has become a specialized branch of economic theory, the main body of which is fundamentally static. In fact, the analytical tools used in the neoclassical theory, such as marginal productivity of factors, belong to the static approach, and growth is introduced with the device of an exogenous trend: techniques do not change. In any case, the conception that growth could go on without technical change simply as a consequence of the gradual increase of the factors of production cannot be accepted, since in the long run decreasing returns from agriculture and from mining would bring the growth of production gradually to a halt. Even with a stable population, per capita income would remain stable only if there were some kind of technical progress in mining capable of offsetting the tendency toward gradual depletion in this sector.

If we recognize that the difference between growth and development is theoretically unfounded, we could use the two terms as synonyms. However, not to upset the common usage, I will continue to use *growth* either as a general term or when referring to a country in which the increase of production is relatively slow and subject only to minor discontinuities—something that is true, in certain periods, for all countries—or when referring to mature industries, whose expansion is near or below the average rate.

What I cannot accept is the separation between growth, conceived as a process from which innovations, major or minor, are excluded, and development, conceived as a process in which innovations are instead admitted. Even more, I object to the separation between growth conceived as a process affecting advanced countries and development conceived as a process affecting the relatively backward countries. It is true that in the latter countries discontinuities are—or can be—a significant feature of the process; but this can be true also in the case of advanced countries. In economics we have already several kinds of artificial separations between static and dynamic analysis, between macroeconomics and microeconomics, between theoretical and empirical analysis, and, finally, between growth and development. We have to try to overcome them, reduce existing schizophrenias, and make all possible efforts to bring our discipline to unity again. To do this in the area of growth we have to go back to the classical economists, in particular to Adam Smith.

To be sure, when analyzing an underdeveloped economy, we make certain assumptions that are different from those that we introduce in analyzing a developed one. But we have to modify our assumptions also when we analyze different economies, developed or underdeveloped, or when we consider a given economy in different periods, since all theoretical models are historically conditioned and a theory that claims to be valid independently of time can be logically correct, but, except by chance, its interpretive power will not normally be too different from zero. Adam Smith was fully aware that his theoretical models were historically conditioned; in his great work historical facts, comparative analyses, and theory are harmoniously combined. Thus, what we may call the ''Adam Smith method,'' that is, integrated analysis of economic development, is necessary in all types of societies but is absolutely essential for underdeveloped countries.

The purpose of this chapter is to illustrate this view as well as to show that the price of not adopting such a method is often superficiality and, in any case, a waste of efforts in rediscovering conclusions that could have been found much earlier by simply adapting and developing certain insights of Adam Smith and other classical economists. In other words, I do not intend to describe here the evolution of development theory; this would be a tremendous task, and fortunately, it has been largely fulfilled by others in recent times. I limit myself to recalling the efforts of Chenery and Srinivasan (1989), Stern (1989), and Oman and Wignaraja (1991). These are first-rate efforts, even if limited to development theory in the narrow sense—and thus unacceptable to me in scope. In a broader context, we also have the recent important work of Rostow (1990).

The case of Rostow is very interesting. This author points out that the evolution of economic theory has suffered a "chasm" since 1870, when economic growth ceased to be the central problem of our discipline. I fully agree with this position, which is common among other economists and which I have tried to emphasize since my beginnings as an economist. I have often spoken of a "cleavage" and offered an explanation that, though not coinciding with that of Rostow, does not necessarily contradict it either. I do not elaborate here on my explanatory hypothesis but simply recall that in one of my writings I pointed to the paradox that "the static approach has come to dominate economic theory precisely in the historical period when technological change and economic growth have become the characteristic features of an increasing number of societies" (Sylos Labini, 1985).

Rostow's position is nonetheless puzzling because, after having explained at length the extreme difficulty, if not the impossibility, of reconciling the analysis of technological and economic development with "post-1870 formal theory" and having emphasized "the incompatibility of conventional equilibrium analysis and the rigorous treatment of the case of increasing returns" (Rostow, 1990, p. 454), he presents in the Appendix of his volume two formal Adam Smith models of growth that appear instead very much neoclassical and un-Smithian, if not in the method, certainly in the assumptions. It is true, as Schumpeter observes, that in his deeds the preacher can well enter into contradiction with his own sermon. Nevertheless, the "sin" of this particular preacher remains particularly striking.

Until 1870, when the marginal revolution broke out and the new paradigm emerged, directly or indirectly the problem of economic development was the main concern of the economists. This was unquestionably true in the case of the founder of modern economic theory, if perhaps less obvious in the case of David Ricardo. At a first reading, Ricardo's *Principles* seems to consider as the central problem of economic theory, not growth but the distribution of income and the effects of its variations on relative prices. Formally, this is so. Yet, the problem of income distribution for Ricardo was important precisely in relation to the problem of accumulation, that is, economic growth.

As Arthur Lewis has correctly pointed out in our time (Lewis, 1955), in many underdeveloped countries two distributive shares have a crucial role in economic growth: rents and profits. When the share going to rents increases to the detriment of that going to profits (there is in fact little scope for a reduction of the share going to wages, since they are very near the subsistence level), accumulation is discouraged. Accumulation is, on the contrary, stimulated when the share going to profits increases: in fact, "renters" have a low propensity to save and to invest, whereas this propensity is very high in the case of profit earners. Thus, in the case of underdeveloped countries, where agriculture is still important, the questions of the relations between income inequality and the aggregate propensity to save and of how to reconcile growth with a reduction of income inequality have to be considered. The classical—here I should say the Ricardian—problem must be faced.

Karl Marx attributes paramount importance to the problem of accumulation.

Some of his main theses—such as the progressive proletarianization of modern societies and the increasing misery of the masses—have turned out to be hopelessly wrong; the main theoretical proposition—the labor theory of value—has been shown to be logically untenable: this is the conclusion that we have to draw after the critical appraisals of a number of economists, among whom I mention only von Bortkievicz (1971) and Sraffa (1960). Yet, other theses have turned out to be analytically fruitful. First, at first approximation, the movement of the economic system is to be analyzed by considering two sectors, what we now call consumption and investment. Second, the process of capitalist accumulation is driven by innovations and assumes a cyclical form. Third, the creation of bank money plays an essential role in the process of cyclical accumulation. The trouble with Marx is that his huge analytical work is conceived as an instrument of his revolutionary program, which he intends to assert at all cost. Thus, we have to consider with the highest suspicion those Marxist theses that are directly tied up with his revolutionary program. In *Das Kapital* Marx, apart from the chapter on the theory of colonization, where he propounds views already found in Smith, says very little about underdeveloped countries. Yet, a number of Marxists, starting from Marx's analyses and observations—including the fragmentary ones in various short writings—and from Vladimir Lenin's theory of imperialism, have tried to develop an analysis of Third World countries intended, like Marx's, to form the basis for one kind or another of revolutionary programs concerning those countries.

The works of Marxist writers, for instance, generally emphasize the mischiefs and crimes of the European countries that carried out processes of colonization in various parts of the world. Here I wish to point to only two sophisms found in their argument. There can be no doubt that colonial countries are responsible for appalling mischiefs and crimes: massacres of natives; natives reduced to slaves or serfs and deprived of their land; men and women living in primitive, but free, communities forcibly transformed into wage earners. The first sophism here is that all the mischiefs of capitalism or imperialism do not automatically imply that "socialism" (in the Marxist sense) is necessarily economically and morally superior. The second sophism lies in the contention that capitalism, however defined, is cruel and wicked by definition and that it remains always the same, that is, that capitalism is irreformable. This is obviously not so: already in a given period we see that there are different types of capitalism; the differences appear even clearer when we look at the historical evolution of the capitalist countries.

NEOCLASSICAL THEORY AND THE THEORY OF GROWTH

Since the neoclassical theory still represents the dominating paradigm, it is fitting to explain why in this chapter I make little use of this theory.

Neoclassical theory includes, first of all, marginal theory, embracing both general and partial analysis—Walras and Marshall can be considered the leaders of the two schools. In a broad sense, neoclassical theory includes also a number of macroeconomic growth models, among which we find the Harrod-Domar and the Cobb-Douglas-Solow types of models—the former directly, the latter indirectly, related to the Keynesian theory. In the Marshallian theory growth is recognized but not studied; in the Walrasian theory growth is wholly neglected. For Harrod and Domar, on the one side, and Cobb-Douglas and Solow, on the other, growth is instead the central problem. Such models, however, are useful only in a preliminary approximation, since they neglect or assume as an external datum, without trying to explain it, the essential force of growth, namely, technical progress. Consistently, structural change, that is, a change that implies a nonproportional increase of productions and variations in the price system, is wholly neglected. Yet, structural change is a necessary feature of growth, due to technical progress (Schumpeter, 1939; Sylos Labini, 1962, 1991) and to changes in the composition of demand that the increase in per capita income necessarily entails (Pasinetti, 1981).

To be sure to understand the process of growth, we need, whenever possible, to use all the theoretical tools that neoclassical theory provides us. But it remains true that traditional marginal analysis is essentially static and that neoclassical growth models have a limited utility for the reasons just mentioned. It also remains true that development theory, conceived in the narrow sense, that is, related to Third World countries, has met with so many difficulties because the analytical tools of the dominating paradigm have been worked out to discuss the problems of equilibrium positions of prices and quantities, not to interpret growth processes. As a further consequence, in recent times the main progress made in growth economics—in the broad sense—is mainly empirical, like the great works by Kuznets and by several other economists. It is high time—I fully agree with Rostow—to try to develop also (and again) the theoretical aspects of growth.

To show that the separation between the analysis of advanced economies and the analysis of underdeveloped economies in principle is seriously misleading, I consider the following problems, which are clearly relevant in this area. (1) Why did the English colonies in America—particularly the regions that later on became the United States and, more particularly, the northern regions—grow more rapidly than the Spanish and the Portuguese colonies, although all of them had plenty of good land and other natural resources? (2) What are the factors regulating productivity growth? How can we explain the recent slowdown of productivity growth that was particularly pronounced in the United States and that has puzzled American economists so much? (3) What are the reasons for the changes in the terms of trade in the last two centuries? What are the reasons for their short-run variations?

Let us start with the problems of productivity growth.

PRODUCTIVITY GROWTH IN THE EUROPEAN COLONIES IN AMERICA

In the opening sentence of the first chapter of his *Wealth of Nations* Smith ([1776] 1961) presents, as the fundamental subject of his whole analysis, the "improvements in the productive powers of labour," or precisely what we now call the productivity of labor. For Smith the division of labor is the focus of all factors promoting the increase of productivity. Among such factors we find, first of all, culture, education, and knowledge—in brief, human capital; soon after, we find institutional factors that are shaped by history and include those that guarantee freedom and an orderly government; only in the third place do we find natural resources, conceived in a broad sense. The following quotations illustrate the point; three are from Smith, two from Alexis de Tocqueville:

The English puritans, restrained at home, fled for America, and established there the four governments of New England (they fled for freedom, we may add, and not to escape hunger or misery or, as adventurers, rapidly to enrich themselves). (Smith [1776] 1961, p. 102)

The colonies owe to the policy of Europe the education and the great views of their active and enterprising founders: and some of the greatest and most important of them, so far as concerns their internal governments, owe to it . . . to the policy of Europe . . . scarce anything else. (Smith [1776] 1961, p. 103)

Almost all colonies have had as their early inhabitants men with no education and no resources, that were pushed by misery or misconduct out of their native countries, or else greedy speculators and adventurers. (Tocqueville [1835] 1951, p. 44)

The emigrants who settled down on the shores of New England all belonged . . . instead . . . to the relatively well-to-do classes of their mother country. Their meeting in the American land presented straight from the beginning the singular phenomenon of a society without very wealthy men and lower classes, with no poor and no rich people. (Tocqueville, [1835] 1951, p. 45; Tocqueville himself emphasized that this was not the case for Virginia and other southern regions of the United States)

The colonists . . . coming from a civilized nation . . . carry with them a knowledge of agriculture and other useful arts . . . , some notion of the regular government . . . , of the system of laws which support it, and a regular administration of justice. (Smith [1776] 1961, p. 76)

Smith ([1776] 1961) also writes:

In the American colonies land is plentiful and free—the cost of a piece of land consists almost exclusively in the operations necessary for making it suitable for cultivation. [As a result,] every colonist gets more land than he can possibly cultivate. . . . He is eager, therefore, to collect labourers from all quarters and to reward them with the most liberal wages. But those most liberal wages, joined with the plenty and cheapness of land, soon make those labourers leave him in order to become landlords themselves, and to reward, with equal liberality, other labourers. (pp. 76–77)

(The availability of free land and the consequent difficulty of keeping dependent workers for long is the foundation of Marx's theory of colonization: Marx, however, who strained Smith's observations to the extreme, reached conclusions that have been shown to be utterly wrong.) For the reasons just explained, landlords, to keep them as dependent workers at least for a period, have "to treat the inferior with . . . generosity and humanity" and to pay high and increasing wages.

Thus, we can infer, a virtuous circle emerges in which increasing wages stimulate the increase of productivity and such an increase enables landowners to pay increasing wages. This occurs inside and outside agriculture, since wages tend to move together in all branches of the economy. Such process is put into motion by the availability of free land, not simply the physical, but also the institutional, availability of land. During the second part of the last century free land practically disappeared in the United States. However, once put into motion, this process of productivity enhancement went on, stimulated by a number of other factors, already in operation in the preliminary stages of growth and then becoming more and more important, among which we have to include the increase in income. To be sure, due to the gradual disappearance of free land and the large influx of poor European immigrants, average wages increased more slowly during the last two decades of the nineteenth century and the first decade of the present century than in the previous period, and productivity growth lost this stimulus.

In the Spanish and Portuguese colonies of America the virtuous circle described above was largely hampered not by physical limitations such as lower availability of good land—indeed, the quantity of good land was comparable, or even superior, to that of the English colonies of North America—but by institutional limitations in a broad sense, including such legal and fiscal aspects as the possibility of engrossing uncultivated land, the right of primogeniture, and heavy taxation. These limitations were rendering land artificially scarce and expensive in South and Central America. As a result wages of dependent workers could remain at low levels for relatively long times, a situation aggravated by the fact that in the large estates of the "conquistadors" slaves and feudal serfs were allowed. Slaves were also allowed in the southern regions of the United States, where the colonists were people of much inferior culture compared with those of the northern regions. A situation not much different from this is found in Asia and in Africa, that is, in the tropical colonies of several European countries, including England. In these colonies a kind of capitalistic sector was formed to produce agricultural and mineral raw materials, whereas a traditional (subsistence) sector continued to exist, organized in primitive communities. The traditional sector, essentially for lack of "knowledge of agriculture and other useful arts," was incapable of making improvement in production, and productivity in these communities remained stagnant. In the capitalist sector wages were somewhat higher than the incomes prevailing in the traditional one, so that some labor could be lured into moving into the capitalist sector. But these wages could be only moderately higher than those in the traditional sector and could remain only relatively stable in the face of an expansion in the capitalist sector as long as the potential laborers in the traditional sector were numerous enough and, if necessary, as long as they could be supplemented by small tradesmen and peddlers from the towns and by increases of population.

The above represent the main features of the situation identified in tropical areas by Arthur Lewis in his famous article on "Economic Development with Unlimited Supply of Labour" (Lewis, 1954). In his analysis Lewis considers himself (rightly) to be in the tradition of the classical economists, in particular, Adam Smith. Lewis's proposition that "the wage to be paid in the capitalist sector is determined by what people can earn outside this sector" is perfectly consistent with the Smithian analysis recalled previously, with the proviso that, in the latter, the existence of a subsistence sector outside the capitalist sector is not postulated. What is instead assumed is the availability of free lands, where dependent workers can easily move if they are not treated in a satisfactory way in the capitalist sector. However, in the Smithian analysis, dependent workers in the capitalist sector possess a non-negligible "knowledge of agriculture and other useful arts."

FACTORS REGULATING THE GROWTH OF PRODUCTIVITY

Probably the best way to discuss this complex problem is to start with a simplified version of the productivity equation that I put forward in 1982 and developed in subsequent writings (Sylos Labini, 1982, 1990). This equation summarizes the main factors affecting productivity, in particular, productivity in industry.

$$\hat{\pi} = a + b\hat{Y} + cW/Pma_{-m} + d\hat{I}_{-n} \tag{1}$$

where Y is income, W/Pma the ratio between wages and the price of machines, I is investment, and m and n lags, and the cap over the variable represents a rate of change. From the theoretical standpoint the rationale of the first variable can be traced back to Adam Smith, while that of the second to David Ricardo. Throughout his writings Smith insists on the thesis that division of labor is what allows all sorts of improvements and that division of labor is in turn "limited by the extent of the market." The following statement is the most directly relevant to the problem that we are considering:

The increase in the demand . . . , though at the beginning may sometimes raise the price of goods, never fails to lower it in the long run. It encourages production, and hereby increases the competition of the producers, who, in order to undersell one another, have recourse to new division of labour and new improvement of art, which might never otherwise have been thought of. (Smith, [1776] 1961, pp. 271–72)

Developing Smith's observations, we can say that an increase in income stimulates productivity growth, both in the short run and in the long run. In the short run, productivity grows when income rises because labor can be more efficiently organized and several inputs can be saved in various ways. In the long run, a sustained economic expansion stimulates the introduction of new machines, which as a rule are more efficient than those already in operation.

In the previous equation the first two variables are expressed in terms of yearly rates of change, and a year is usually considered as a short run. However, with the introduction of lags (of two or three years) in it, the equation does not simply refer to the short run. One may also note that the idea underlying this equation is that a rise in the W/Pma ratio stimulates labor-saving investment, which, in turn, pushes up productivity. The lag concerning this ratio is thus somewhat longer than that concerning investment. The rationale of the second variable in this equation is to be found in the analyses put forth by Ricardo in his *Principles*. Two quotations may suffice to justify this statement: "Machines would not rise in price in consequence of a rise of wages" (Ricardo, p. 41), and "Every rise of wages will have a tendency to determine the saved capital in a greater proportion than before to the employment of machinery. Machinery and labour are in constant competition, and the former can frequently not be employed until labour rises" (p. 395).

Empirical estimates of the productivity equation, in its simplified, as well as in its more complex, versions, have yielded clearly satisfactory results (Sylos Labini, 1984, 1990). It is worth noting that, soon after the observations just quoted, which I consider both correct and fertile, Ricardo writes: "In America and in many other countries, where the food of man is easily provided, there is not nearly such great temptation to employ machinery as in England" (p. 395).

Here Ricardo was wrong, since the "temptation," as historical evolution has made clear, was greater in America than in England. In fact, this statement reflects the subsistence theory of wages that Ricardo was adopting without qualifications. Adam Smith, who was writing forty years earlier, was better advised; his theory of wages was much superior to the theories of Ricardo and Marx, who were considering as exceptional an increase in wages above the subsistence level; Smith, on the contrary, considered perfectly possible a systematic increase in wages, hand in hand with an increase in productivity.

Recently a number of economists have, in a way and only very partially, rediscovered the Smithian as well as the (correct) Ricardian proposition. Among them we find, Romer (1987), and De Long and Summers (1991). This rediscovery can bear good fruit if, after so long a time, we also recover with it the classical approach.

This is not, however, an inevitable, or perhaps even a probable, outcome, since many contemporary economists have a propensity to read the classical economists that is close to zero and are often not even aware of the contributions of their peers just outside the "mainstream" of the profession. Thus none of the modern economists who have worked in this field seem to be aware of the analyses on productivity conducted by Melman (1983, p. 165) and by me (1982, 1984, 1990). These studies can help explain both the variety of productivity levels among different countries and the behavior of productivity growth in the course of time. As far as the latter is concerned, the slowdown in productivity growth that has taken place in the last fifteen years in the United States, but especially from 1977 to 1982—a puzzle for so many American economists—becomes relatively clear when the behavior of the variables included in the equation previously presented is considered.[1] In the years 1977–1982 variations in the first and the second explanatory variables were strongly contributing to said slowdown.[2]

It is appropriate to point out that our equation aims at explaining the variations of labor productivity in industry, which is the most dynamic sector of the economy. These variations are induced by impulses generated within the economic system: income, the W/Pma ratio, and investment can be considered as such. But productivity can increase also as a result of investment made for profit in research and development and as a consequence of discoveries made by nonprofit institutions, such as the universities. In the latter case the ensuing innovations cannot be directly related to economic factors and are to be considered exogenous. Exogenous innovations can be, and often are, even more important, from the scientific viewpoint, than the endogenous ones. From the economic viewpoint, however, endogenous innovations, often consisting of adaptations and improvements, are more important for the continuity and the speed of the process of growth.

After a painstaking cross-section analysis, De Long and Summers conclude that the relative prices of machines—which they conceive as the ratio between the said prices and the gross domestic product (GDP) deflator—can greatly help to explain the different levels of productivity in a relatively large number of countries. Their basic idea is well founded, even though the prices of machines should be related to wages, and the possible explanatory variables are not one, but several. Yet, we have to reflect on the meaning of the aggregate saving share when the relative price of machines is pushed up at artificially high levels, for example, by tariff protection. Thus, from a purely accounting standpoint, we see that, given the saving share, with lower prices for machines, saving employed in machines could be considerably higher, even twice as high. This hypothesis is not so far-fetched: the ratio just mentioned is not far from that given for India by De Long and Summers, who quote Krueger on this point. From the dynamic standpoint, if the price of machines is pushed up, the process of productivity growth is slowed down.

VARIOUS TYPES OF INVESTMENT

In the previous section we considered investment in equipment and only hinted at investment in research and development carried out by firms with a view to profit. There are other types of investment, like those—private and public—in structures. Considering the essential role played by investment in equipment for productivity growth, it is fitting to present here an equation that can explain the behavior of this type of investment I (Sylos Labini, 1974):

$$I = a + b\,U + c\,G + d\,G^*/K^* + e\,i \qquad (2)$$

where U, the degree of used capacity, that is, the ratio between real and potential output, expresses the principle of the capital stock adjustment (a variant of the principle of acceleration); G represents current total profits, which are the source of self-financing; G^*/K^* indicates the expected rate of profit; and i is the interest rate, that is, the price of external finance.

Investment in equipment has the effect of increasing both capacity and productivity. However, certain investments are mainly capacity-increasing; others are instead mainly productivity-increasing. When, to give an example, in a certain period, the ratio W/Pma increases at a sustained rate, whereas Y increases slowly or not at all, we can presume that the weight of the second type of investment tends to increase in the total.[3]

INTERNATIONAL RELATIONS: GROWTH AND CYCLES

It is accepted by many that the pace of growth in all countries of the world depends in some ways on that of advanced economies, which act as the "locomotives" of growth. Even countries that do not grow or that decline are affected by the behavior of the economies of the advanced countries. Let us remember that the United States represents 16 percent of total world imports, Germany 9 percent, Japan 7 percent. If we add the other advanced countries, their overall share exceeds 60 percent, though the population of all these countries taken together represents less than 20 percent of the world total. Thus, it is in the interest of underdeveloped countries that the advanced ones grow, though the kind of growth and the type of international trade policy followed by these countries count for no less, and possibly more, than the pace of growth.

At this point we have to recall that Marx and Schumpeter were right: growth and cycles are to be considered not as two distinct phenomena but as the expression of one and the same process, that is, the process of cyclical development. In analyzing this process we have, therefore, to single out, starting from advanced countries, the industries that lead in the growth process, which as a rule are also the innovating industries. At the same time, due to the great importance that nowadays, for good or bad, the state has reached in the economy, we have to examine the type of economic policy that is followed. In fact, the main impulses to growth come from innovations and from economic policy, and these impulses interact with one another. When we consider the growth process on the world scale, we have to compare the rates of change in industrial production of each individual country with those of the overall index of advanced countries—the deviations deserve careful scrutiny. As for the underdeveloped countries, we can assume that, as a rule, they play only a passive role in the world cycles.

Yet, these countries can profit to a greater or lesser extent from the impulses coming from the advanced countries. Therefore, the analysis of both the leading industries and the types of economic policy followed in the major countries is also relevant to the interpretation of cyclical developments in underdeveloped countries. It should be emphasized that a macroeconomic approach for this kind of problem is justified only in the first approximation. In successive approximations we should work on the basis of disaggregated multisector models, characterized by nonproportionality in the variations of output, prices, and incomes.

Leading industries as a rule are innovating industries, and innovations are the essence of growth. Innovations, however, which are to be distinguished from inventions, are such with reference to the particular situation of a given country. Thus, the installation of a railroad in a backward country in Central Africa is certainly, from an economic viewpoint, an innovation. To be sure, major innovations, which are directly related to new inventions and represent a novelty on the world scale, play the most dynamic role both internally and internationally. In general, the innovating industries are also those in which productivity rises more rapidly than the average. Thus the prices of the goods produced in these industries decline relative to the average price level—sometimes they even decline absolutely. Wages, on the other hand, increase more rapidly than the average in these industries. Thus, the explanation of productivity growth refers to the average increase, which, no doubt, indirectly depends on the impulses coming from the innovating industries but originates directly from the introduction of new machines that affect, to different degrees, all, or almost all, industries.

TRENDS AND CYCLICAL VARIATIONS IN THE TERMS OF TRADE

The problem of the terms of trade has absorbed the energies of a considerable number of economists. It represents the leitmotiv, so to speak, of the recent book by Rostow (1990). The main reason for this attention to terms of trade changes is probably that both economic and political questions are at stake. Among the former, we find the policy of import-substitution or export-promotion and, among the latter, the thesis that the trend of the terms of trade, apparently unfavorable to the underdeveloped countries for the last several decades, is to be considered the consequence of the power that the advanced capitalist countries use to exploit the underdeveloped ones.

Preliminarily, it is important to point out that the terms of trade of underdeveloped countries do not coincide with the ratio between the prices of primary commodities and those of manufactured goods, since a great number of those countries produce and export non-negligible amounts of industrial goods, whereas several advanced countries also produce and export considerable quantities of primary commodities.

The important distinction to make is still between primary commodities and industrial goods. Most primary commodities are traded in international markets;

and since, as a rule, they are homogeneous goods and very few of them are controlled by a limited number of firms, the prevailing market mode form for primary commodities can be assumed to be competition (in the classical sense, i.e., markets characterized by free entry). The situation of industrial products is different: here the processes of concentration and differentiation that have occurred in most industrial markets during the last hundred or so years have given rise to oligopolistic market forms. This means that, in the case of primary commodities, we can adopt the Ricardian view and assume that in the short run prices depend on demand and supply, whereas in the long run they depend on costs. In the case of industrial commodities, instead, we can assume that in the short run prices depend on variable costs, whereas in the long run they depend on average total costs.

The demand for primary commodities depends mainly on the world industrial output, which is, in turn, mainly influenced by the behavior of the economies of industrial countries. As for supply, I simply point out that the yearly output of agricultural commodities depends largely on weather, whereas the yearly output of mineral products normally does not vary very much. All things considered, the short-run variations in the prices of primary commodities will be influenced principally by demand variations, that is, by the variations of world industrial output. Industrial managers make their decisions concerning investment and production on the basis of the orders they receive and the stocks of finished goods and raw materials that they have. Thus, as a rule it is not misleading to consider the current variations of raw material prices as an anticipation of what is going to happen in the relatively near future to industrial output. All this refers to the short-run variations of the prices of primary commodities, be they produced in underdeveloped or in advanced countries. However, in practice advanced countries, due to their superior organization can (and do) introduce measures capable of reducing the downward flexibility of those prices. This applies, above all, to agricultural products.

In the long run, costs of production regulate the price behavior of primary commodities. But here we find very important differences among countries. In economically backward countries the mechanism described by Lewis (1954) seems to be at work. In such countries wages are relatively stable or increase very slowly, at least as long as the supply of labor is "unlimited." Thus, in the long run the cost will increase if only the prices of the means of production rise; and even in this case, the overall cost of production will not increase or will even decrease if the cost of labor decreases due to a sustained increase in productivity.

The prices of manufactured goods, however, tend either to remain stable or, more often, to increase, because wages tend to increase even more than productivity. This depends either on the strength of organized labor or on the market power that workers have gained in advanced countries because of differentiation of products and jobs. The market power of the firms also increases on the average, owing to the processes of concentration and differentiation that are at work. The combination of the two market powers have given rise to a situation in which both wages and prices are flexible in the upward direction but rigid in the downward direction. When productivity increases more than wages or when raw material prices go down, industrial prices diminish, but only in a very limited fashion. This asymmetry, plus the very slow increase in productivity in retail trade, has imparted an upward bias to all prices. At the wholesale level, this tendency applies also to the prices of raw materials, owing to the upward trend of the prices of manufactured goods employed in their production. All things considered, however, the mechanism applies to raw materials produced in tropical countries, and terms of trade thus tend to move unfavorably for the countries that mostly rely on them.

Lewis's mechanism can be formalized in the following way:

$$Ppc = a + b \, Wpc/npc + cPi$$
$$Pi = a' + b'Wi/ni + c'Ppc \tag{3}$$

where Ppc is the price index of primary commodities, Pi the price index of industrial goods, and W and n the wage rate and labor productivity in the two countries considered. I assume that the producers of primary commodities use, as means of production, industrial goods and that the producers of these goods use, as means of production, primary commodities. I take the tropical commodities as representative of all primary commodities produced in underdeveloped countries. Let us suppose that Wpc remains stable, that npc increases moderately, and that Wi increases more than ni. Under such conditions, the Ppc/Pi ratio tends to decline. In fact, with a number of refinements and qualifications, this seems to be the trend of the terms of trade of primary producing countries. The deterioration, however, appears to be moderate: this is the conclusion reached by Grilli and Yang after painstaking empirical and theoretical inquiries (Grilli and Yang, 1988). In spite of the heated debate over the long-term deterioration in the terms of trade of primary commodities, I think that the main practical problems for producers arise not from that side, but out of the great short-run variability of the commodity prices: a problem already considered, first, by Keynes (1980) and, then, by Kaldor (1983), who proposed stabilization plans that are still worth studying.

THE ROOTS OF WORLDWIDE INFLATIONARY PRESSURES

In the first table of the yearly *World Development Report* of the World Bank we find, for the 125 countries listed there, a column devoted to the "average rate of inflation." As a rule, two pluriannual periods are covered. We find almost invariably a positive sign for inflation in all countries. The cases of a negative sign are absolutely exceptional, and the negative figures are very low in absolute value.

If we try a mental experiment and imagine that a similar report with a similar table were available in the last century, the title of that column would have been "Average Rate of Deflation," since the long-run trend of prices was then very strongly in the downward direction—in the United Kingdom the price index of finished goods fell by almost 80 percent from 1800 to 1897. In my judgment, the reason is that in most of the last century the "Smithian mechanism" was at work; that is, money wages were either stable or moderately increasing, whereas productivity was increasing more rapidly. Since productivity was increasing more rapidly in industrial countries than in primary commodity-producing countries, the terms of trade for a good part of the last century were moving against, not in favor of, industrialized countries, especially the United Kingdom, which epitomized dependency on industrial goods (Sylos Labini, 1991).

The change in the direction of the terms of trade occurred toward the end of the last century (though before 1897), when the spread of collective bargaining and the relative scarcity of a rapidly increasing number of workers imparted an upward bias to wages. Prices of finished goods then became more and more rigid with respect to demand—during the Great Depression they fell almost exclusively as a result of the drastic fall in the prices of primary commodities, where competitive conditions still prevailed. With increasing per capita income the weight of services in the national product have also become more and more important; and the price of services has tended to increase hand in hand with wages, since in the service sector, productivity, however measured, increases very slowly.

These changes impart an upward bias to all prices at the wholesale and, even more, at the retail level. These changes have imparted an upward push also to prices in underdeveloped countries, which after World War II have often experienced high and, in certain cases, even explosive rates of inflation. To concentrate the explanation of inflation on money supply is thus superficial and ill-fitting of reality. This is true of both industrial and developing countries. Under certain conditions the increase in the money supply can actually represent the main source of inflation, although it is always necessary to inquire of the reasons for such an increase, once sheer stupidity or gross incompetence of monetary authorities is put aside. If we look carefully at the roots of inflation, we find, depending on countries and periods, a variety of causes, including wage increases, increases in the cost of nonlabor inputs, a policy of frequent devaluations, and fiscal policy. I come back in the next section to the impulse coming from fiscal policy.

INSTITUTIONAL REFORMS

The analytical approaches to the problems of economic growth—of both the advanced and the underdeveloped countries—are four: the classical, the neoclassical, the structuralist, and the Marxist. However, a large number of the economists who have studied the problems of underdeveloped countries have concentrated their efforts not so much on the analytical aspects but on the means to promote development. According to political preferences, the main groups of economists are the conservatives, the reformists, and the Marxists. Among the first group we find the extreme conservatives, who disapprove of all sorts of state intervention, and the moderate conservatives, who accept certain types of interventions that are supposed to improve the functioning of the market. In the second group, which includes the so-called structuralists, we find the economists who favor certain reforms and a more pronounced state intervention. In the third group we find those Marxists who are in favor of changes much more radical than those advocated by the economists of the second group. Among them are those who can be considered revolutionaries only with reference to the very long run and those who believe instead that a revolution is both necessary and possible in a relatively short run. In any case, both groups show deadly enmity toward capitalism and advocate only actions that can damage it.

Analytical approaches and political preferences overlap only limitedly. Thus, in general, neoclassical economists are critical of state intervention, but, looking carefully, they oppose certain state interventions, not others; they are rather skeptical of institutional reforms but do not oppose them in principle. Certainly, neoclassical economists are against revolutionary programs, but reformists are equally opposed to such programs. Among classical economists Adam Smith is depicted as a conservative. In my view such a definition is questionable. Indeed, if we take into account Smith's struggle against the feudal system and the mercantilistic regulations of trade, it would be correct to classify him as a radical or as a liberal (in the American sense). In any case, according to contemporary standards, Smith can be classified among "moderate," not "extreme," conservatives. In fact, he is on record with the view that "the sovereign," in addition to the duties concerning, first, defense and, second, justice has "the duty of erecting and maintaining certain public works and certain public institutions, which it can never be in the interest of an individual, or small number of individuals, to erect and maintain, because the profit could never repay the expense to any individual or small number of individuals, though it may frequently do much more than repay it to a great society" (Smith, [1776] 1961, p. 209). The third duty he attributes to "the sovereign" can open the door to a great variety of state interventions. These have been judged excessive, for example, by Milton Friedman, who, unlike Smith, can very rightly be included in the first group of conservatives—the extreme ones. In fact, "on the occasion of Adam Smith's bicentenary, Friedman suggested that the master may have gone too far with his definition of the third legitimate function of government" (quoted by Rostow, 1990, p. 49, who, by mentioning Smith's bicentenary, refers to the bicentenary of the *Wealth of Nations*).

Reforms intended to favor development of underdeveloped countries have been advocated particularly in two fields: agriculture and education. Land reforms in underdeveloped countries have long been advocated, at least since the end of World War II. At present, discussions of land reform, conceived as a redistribution of land, are generally considered "out of date," for mainly two reasons. First, most economists have realized that the redistribution of land, as such, is not enough—credit, technological change, and technical assistance are no less, and even more, important; second, the weight of agriculture in the total economy has been declining even in most underdeveloped countries. Yet, it is also widely accepted that a land reform, conceived in a broad sense, that is, duly supplemented by the previously mentioned measures, is still important in many underdeveloped areas today. The debate has been revived by the thesis recently put forward that an inverse relationship exists between farm size and output per acre (Berry and Cline, 1979).

Again, we must recall here that Smith had already pointed out that "great proprietors are seldom great improvers," whereas "a small proprietor . . . is generally of all improvers the most industrious, the most intelligent, and the most successful" (Smith, [1776] 1961, pp. 410, 441). Thus Smith was clear about that inverse relationship. He went further, since he insisted also—unlike most contemporary economists—on the importance of the types of agricultural contracts and institutions in agricultural development. Lasting and secure contracts, which give the farmers a credible guarantee that they can enjoy the fruits of the improvements that they introduce in the land, are the best, whereas extremely precarious contracts, like those of the "tenants at will," are the worst. As for institutions, we have to be fully aware even today that those institutions that put a brake on subdivision and exchange of land and make difficult "the multiplication of small proprietors" (e.g., certain laws of succession, such as the law of primogeniture, and the legal possibility of engrossing uncultivated land) discourage agricultural development.

Of course, Smith did not advocate land reforms. But I do think that a modern economist who advocates both a redistribution of land and a reform of agricultural laws and contracts is not at all against the spirit of Adam Smith. It is also perfectly in the spirit of Adam Smith to maintain that technological progress in agriculture can be stimulated or hindered depending on the legal framework that is adopted in any given country. Even the action of those experimental stations, recommended by certain modern agricultural economists, can be more or less effective depending on the institutional setup. In general, in those countries in which institutions hindered "the multiplication of small proprietors"—as was often the case in most Spanish and Portuguese colonies—the multiplication of entrepreneurs and managers outside agriculture was also made difficult. Urbanization and the growth of tertiary activities there reached very early pathological dimensions in these countries.

It is worthwhile to devote a few observations to three additional types of reforms: fiscal, credit, and reform of the public administration. If we exclude, on one side, the extreme conservatives, according to whom everything is to be left to the market—except perhaps defense and justice—and, on the other, those Marxists who advocate a revolution in the short run, the great majority of economists, though fully recognizing the importance of the market mechanism, are in favor of some state intervention in the economy, particularly to stimulate the development of underdeveloped countries.

To finance public works and infrastructures and, today, certain public institutions for social welfare, the state needs the necessary means. The main internal sources are given by taxes on incomes of families and firms and taxes on production and consumption of goods and services. The discussion over taxation in advanced countries has been mostly focused on the question of equity: income taxes are supposed to be more equitable than taxes on goods since the former can, whereas the latter cannot, be progressive. This is largely true, even if, when it is pushed too far, progressiveness can blunt the spirit of initiative; and excessive progressiveness should be avoided in both advanced and developing countries. But there is another aspect that for many underdeveloped countries is even more important than the previous one: income taxes cannot be shifted onto prices, whereas taxes on goods can. In both cases there are naturally exceptions to this rule, but it is the rule that matters. This means that an increase of taxes on goods is often inflationary—indeed, it is not the level of taxes that matters, but their variation.

The trouble is that inefficient fiscal administrations find it easy to collect taxes on goods, whereas they find it very difficult to collect income taxes. Thus, when, to obtain a loan from an international organization, the government of a developing country has to guarantee that it will resort not to issuing bank notes, but to taxation, this means that it will tend to raise taxes on goods or public services. This type of danger has been systematically underestimated by the officials of those international organizations that accept the simplistic view that inflation can be determined only by an excessive expansion of the quantity of money.

The truth is that inflation can instead be put into motion by a variety of impulses, one of which is taxation. Once prices increase as a result of a tax increase, a price-wage spiral can set in. Moreover, to avoid damaging exports by loss of competitiveness, devaluation of the nominal exchange rate can be decided, sometimes repeatedly. This adds fuel to the fire, unless appropriate downward adjustments are made to real aggregate demand. Sometimes, therefore, at the origin of this process we have a "fiscal inflation," and this is not simply a theoretical curiosity or a rare event.

To avoid such a process being put into motion, there seems to be no alternative but to carry out a fiscal reform capable of increasing both the amount and the share of the revenue of the government coming from direct (as opposed to indirect) taxation. Since the taxes on international trade have negative effects on the balance of payments and social security contributions have negative effects on the expansion of employment, fiscal reform should aim to reduce or, better, to cancel out taxes on international trade and at least not to increase social contributions. A fiscal reform, moreover, cannot be introduced and become functional in one or two years. It takes much longer. This means that the government of a country in the conditions just described needs "structural adjustment assistance" from the international community. The main criticism that can be raised about the leading international financial institutions is that they have devoted too much attention to short-run, and too little effort to long-run, problems. It is high time that the balance be reversed. It is true, however, that this state of affairs is a reflection of the fact that contemporary economic theory itself, in contrast with the classical theory, gives much more importance to the short run than to the long run.

A second reform, to be considered together with the fiscal, is that of the credit system. Putting the question in terms that would have been approved by classical economists, it is only from net revenue that "any deductions can be made for taxes, or for savings"; and both taxes and savings—which are, respectively, compulsory and voluntary deductions—are in various ways necessary for accumulation. Thus, the fiscal and the credit reform should go together and be conceived of as complementary. Suggestions concerning these reforms have been made several times by the structuralists. However, I think that these suggestions have been fragmentary; it is necessary to concentrate great intellectual and practical efforts on this issue.

Fiscal reform, which should take into account the famous four "maxims" put forward by Adam Smith ([1776] 1961, vol. 2, book 2, chap. 5), presupposes, in turn, the reform of the fiscal administration. This poses the more general, and even more difficult, problem of the reform of the public administration and of the code of public law. To this purpose a systematic cooperation between economists and jurists becomes necessary (let us recall here that the "Lectures on Jurisprudence" appear among the works of Adam Smith). Today, such cooperation also seems necessary for the economic reconstruction of the Eastern European countries and of those that emerged out of the dissolution of the Soviet Union, where, as an understandable reaction to the stifling and bureaucratic system of central planning, many economists became supporters of the extreme laissez-faire policies.

If central planning turned out to be a great failure, mainly because it proved to be incapable of innovating, extreme laissez-faire policies are by no means the remedy: the market requires a complex legal framework, capable of stimulating the initiative and the innovating capacity of individuals. In those countries, the reconstruction of such a framework, which is of paramount importance first of all in agriculture, should be the result of a systematic cooperation between jurists and economists. It is fitting to emphasize that, of the three essential factors of growth pointed out by Smith—education, proper institutions, and resources—the countries that emerged from the dissolution of the Soviet empire badly need the second: in most of them culture and resources are not lacking. This implies that, if their governments are able to introduce the proper institutions, their recovery will not be too difficult.

An important problem, which I mention because it can illustrate certain relations between economic factors, on one hand, and institutional and political aspects, on the other, is the question of whether growth and the reduction of income inequality can be reconciled. Kuznets thought that inequality in income distribution increased in the first stage of economic growth; then, after a number of years, it tended to decrease: this path assumes the shape of an arch. The findings of subsequent inquiries, among which I mention Adelman and Robinson (1988) and Grilli (chapter 3 in this book), on the whole are consistent with Kuznets's findings but emphasize that the exceptions are so numerous that we can hardly speak of a regularity. To be sure, in the initial stage of growth an increase in inequality is inevitable, since the growth process is necessarily uneven, but any further tendency is more and more influenced by policy choices. In short, the degree of indeterminateness is very important, as is made clear by the painstaking study by Grilli; and this applies to most social phenomena. Thus, in my 1983 book on underdevelopment I related the level of per capita income— a proxy of the stage of growth—to several social indicators, like life expectancy, birthrate, and income distribution, and I found that a certain correlation does emerge but that the "deviations" are also remarkable. These are to be explained by referring to noneconomic factors as well as to policy choices.

It is worth emphasizing that the policies intended to reduce income inequalities cannot be simply neutral with respect to growth: they can favor it, because they can increase the physical and intellectual efficiency of the persons belonging to the low stratum of income receivers. This is particularly true in the case of policies specifically aimed at satisfying basic needs (Streeten, 1981). However, it is becoming increasingly clear that the best policy is to reduce subsidies to the minimum and to supply goods or services in kind and to create jobs in productive or socially desirable activities.

CONCLUSIONS

More than once in the last forty years economists—particularly those who have given the most significant contributions—have expressed disappointment about the state of development theory, conceived in the narrow sense that I have criticized in the first section of this chapter. Some economists went so far as to speak of a crisis of development theory. I think that this is due mainly to two factors. First, development theory in the narrow sense is a very recent specialization of economic theory and therefore has, and cannot but have, superficial roots. Moreover, the main body of mainstream economic theory is static and thus provides a poor basis for development theory, both in the narrow sense and in the broad sense. Second, as the result of the situation just mentioned, development theory in the narrow sense is largely normative rather than analytical.

In this chapter I argue that, to remedy these serious shortcomings, we have to rediscover and revalue the roots of development theory, going back to the classical economists, first of all to Adam Smith and to his methodological approach, based on a combination of theory, history, and international comparisons, from a quantitative, as well as a qualitative, standpoint. Here I show how much has been lost up to now because of the habit—so common among economists, even among those whose propensity to read the works of the classics is considerably greater than zero—of looking at Smith and other economists of the past with purely historical, not theoretical, interest. In this chapter I concentrated my attention on a few problems that I consider particularly important; by necessity several others, for which the classical approach would be particularly fruitful, could not be mentioned. Let me at least hint at two such problems in these concluding remarks: the question of the relations between the market and the state and the very important and complex question of human capital.

In recent times a tendency has emerged among economists to pit state intervention against the market mechanism. A particular aspect of this tendency has been the contraposition between Keynesians and monetarists. Monetarism can to some extent be justified as a reaction to the excesses of which the supporters of state intervention—politicians and economists alike—have been guilty. As far as the problem of economic growth is concerned, a sober study of countries that have a very successful record of growth, like Japan and Korea, shows that in those countries coexistence between the state and the market has been not only possible but fruitful both in general areas and in specific areas (from sectoral policies to applied research). Moreover, the hatching of the "economic miracles" of Japan and Korea was facilitated by radical reforms, among which land reform was very important (in the case of Japan some of the most important growth-conducive reforms were carried out during the MacArthur administration).

Another example of this contraposition is the one between free trade and protectionism. Smith was in favor of free trade on the basis of the argument that the expansion of the markets, internal and external, stimulates growth. On a more limited plane, Ricardo was in favor of free trade of agricultural products, especially cereals, to prevent an increase in the price of such products and the consequent increase in rents, which, as we have seen, is an obstacle to growth. Nowadays several economists tend to differentiate between the short run and the long run and among periods, countries, and sectors and consider the cost-benefit balance between the two lines of policy. As in all economic questions, here, too, there is a problem of optimum, although a presumption in favor of free trade seems to be justified. The presumption is particularly strong in the case of machinery and equipment, for the reasons discussed previously.

We all agree that "human capital" plays an essential role in the process of economic growth; this is very clearly recognized by Adam Smith. Here I wish only to point out that from a welfare point of view "human capital" is important not only because it fosters the growth of total income but also because its increase tends to slow down the rate of increase of population. When income increases too slowly and population too rapidly, economic welfare necessarily deteriorates. It seems clear that the decline in the birthrate—which is under way in many underdeveloped countries—as a rule is quicker in those countries in which the rate of female illiteracy is declining more rapidly. In demographic trends the factors in play are many, but the one just mentioned seems to be particularly important. It is thus important to promote the increase in education of women in shaping policies aimed at containing population growth.

The main conclusions of this chapter are as follows:

1. On productive growth: the fundamental factors regulating productivity growth are the expansion of real demand and the increase in the ratio between wages and the price of machines. The first factor can be traced back to Smith, the second to Ricardo. Both factors must be considered—and this is the main lesson of Smith—by taking into account the institutional context. In the neo-classical theory productivity growth—the essential phenomenon of the overall growth process—is not explained but is taken as an external datum.

2. On investment: with reference to a growth process, we have to explain not the equilibrium position of investment but the determinants of its variation, that is, the changes in total profits (the course of self-financing), in the expected rate of profits, and in used capacity as well as those in the rate of interest. At the same time, it is important to study the variations in the composition of investment and the reasons for such variations.

3. On the variations in the terms of trade: in the study of the short run and the long run, traditional theory on the variations of the terms of trade, which refers to the general level of prices, is of little help. We have, instead, to distinguish between at least two categories of prices, whose variations follow different logics, and consider technical progress and market forms in both the product and labor markets.

4. On inflationary pressures: the study of inflation requires an even greater disaggregation of prices, and at least wholesale prices of raw materials and of manufactured goods and retail prices of goods and of services must be considered. In studying inflation it is necessary to be aware that it is wrong to look for a single cause, such as excessive supply of money. Behind inflation we find a multiplicity of impulses—the quantity of money can be seen as an impulse only in special circumstances; among the others we find costs, demand, the exchange rates, and fiscal measures. The long-run inflationary pressure of our time, which can be observed in all types of countries and which acquires a particular intensity in several Third World countries, is to be attributed to the changes in the wage and price mechanism that have emerged in our century as a consequence of deep structural changes that occured in labor and product markets.

5. On institutions and institutional reforms: the analysis of institutions and of their changes must be seen as an integral part of the theoretical analysis of the growth process—the above-mentioned analysis of productivity growth is an example of this. At the same time institutional reforms are to be seen as the long-run measures of economic policy intended to promote growth. To this purpose the cooperation between jurists and economists seems to be of fundamental importance. Similarly, if we recognize that the market itself is an institution and the state is a kind of organization endowed with coercive power, then we must also study the relations between the market and the state from the institutional point of view; for the economists the central problem concerns the way in which the state can improve the performance of the market.

6. On organizational reforms in agriculture: in those countries in which mal-

nutrition often becomes starvation, reforms should concern, first of all, agriculture and consist mainly of organizational reforms, based on technical assistance and original legal structures. Economists, agronomists, and jurists should prepare projects to be carried out on the basis of agreements between national governments and institutions such as the Food and Agriculture Organization (FAO) and the World Bank. This, not financial aid, is the main way to foster economic growth at a sustained rate in these countries, which is both in their interest and in our own, since it is becoming more and more difficult and painful in advanced countries to accept the immigration coming from them. Said agreements should be underwritten by international institutions on condition of substantial reductions in military expenditures. In many Third World countries such expenditures often represent even higher shares of the gross national product (GNP) than in advanced countries!

7. On human capital: we have seen that the improvement in the education of women can contribute to the reduction of the birthrate—which is a positive factor in present conditions—in most Third World countries. This is only one of the many positive effects stemming from improvements in human capital that represent key conditions of both economic and social growth. However, the increase of human capital should be seen not simply with reference to the degree of illiteracy and school enrollment, but in a much broader context. I think that it is not far-fetched to assert that the United States would not have reached the very high level of technological and economic growth that it did if originally the states of New England had been colonized by people mainly interested in escaping misery in their mother countries or driven by thirst of quick wealth— as was indeed the case in most European colonies—and not by people endowed with a good store of knowledge who had left their mother countries mainly for ideal reasons, in search of freedoms not enjoyed there.

NOTES

1. Regulations enforced in the 1970s to protect the environment were (wrongly) considered among the factors contributing to explain the slowdown of productivity growth. This is one of the reasons the United States, which until a few years ago was among the leaders in environment protection, is now to be reckoned among the laggards. A wrong diagnosis can have, in practice, very negative side effects.

2. In those years income was stagnating, mainly due to ill-advised restrictive monetary and financial policies, and money wages were stagnating due to several factors, among which one should consider the large influx of immigrants and the rapidly increasing number of women entering the labor force.

3. In a forthcoming paper, in which I propose an interpretation of the Cobb-Douglas production function radically different from the traditional one and I use the simplified version of that function, where we are left with only one exponent, I try to show that the variations of this exponent can indicate the shifts in the weights of the two types of investment here mentioned.

REFERENCES

Adelman, I., and Robinson, S. 1988. "Income Distribution and Development." In *Handbook of Development Economics,* edited by H. Chenery and T.N. Srinivasan. Amsterdam: North-Holland.

Berry, R.A., and Cline, W.R. 1979. *Agrarian Structure and Productivity in Developing Countries.* Baltimore: Johns Hopkins University Press.

Chenery, H., and Srinivasan, T.N., eds. 1989. *Handbook of Development Economics.* Vol. 2. Amsterdam: North-Holland.

De Long, J.B., and Summers, L.H. 1991. "Economic Growth in a Cross Section of Countries." *Quarterly Journal of Economics* (May).

Grilli, E.R., and Yang, M.C. 1988. "Primary Commodity Prices, Manufactured Goods Prices and the Terms of Trade of Developing Countries: What the Long Run Shows." *The World Bank Review* 2, no. 1.

Kaldor, N. 1983. "The Role of Commodity Prices in Economic Recovery." *Lloyds Bank Review* (July).

Keynes, J.M. 1980. "Activities 1941–1946. Shaping the Post-War World. Bretton Woods and Reparations." *The Collected Works of Keynes,* Vol. 28. London: Macmillan.

Kuznets, S. 1955. "Economic Growth and Income Inequality." *American Economic Review* 45, no. 1.

Lewis, W.A. 1954. "Economic Development with Unlimited Supplies of Labour." *Manchester School* 22:

———. 1955. *The Theory of Economic Growth,* Homewood, Ill.: Richard Irwin.

Lucas, R.E. 1988. "On the Mechanics of Economic Development." *Journal of Monetary Economics,* no. 22.

Oman, C., and Wignaraja, G. 1991. *The Postwar Evolution of Development Thinking.* London: Macmillan in association with the OECD Development Centre.

Pasinetti, L. 1981. *Structural Change and Economic Growth.* Cambridge: Cambridge University Press.

Romer, P. 1987. "Growth Based on Increasing Returns Due to Specialization." *American Economic Review Papers and Proceedings* (May).

Rostow, W.W. 1990. *Theorists of Economic Growth from David Hume to the Present: With a Perspective on the Next Century.* New York: Oxford University Press.

Schumpeter, J.A. 1939. *Business Cycles.* Vol. 2. New York: McGraw-Hill.

Smith, A. 1776. *An Inquiry into the Causes of the Wealth of Nations.* London: Methuan, 1961.

Sraffa, P. 1960. *Production of Commodities by Means of Commodities.* Cambridge: Cambridge University Press.

Stern, N. 1989. "The Economics of Development: A Survey." *Economic Journal* (September).

Streeten, P., with the collaboration of Burki, S.J., Haq, M.U., Hicks, N., and Stewart, F. 1981. *First Things First—Meeting Basic Human Needs in Developing Countries.* New York: World Bank, Oxford University Press.

Sylos Labini, P. 1962. *Oligopoly and Technical Progress.* Cambridge: Harvard University Press.

———. 1974. *Trade Unions Inflation and Productivity.* Lexington, Mass.: Lexington Books.

————. 1976. "Competition: The Product Markets." In *The Market and the State*, edited by T. Wilson and A. Skinner. Oxford: Oxford University Press.

————. 1982. *Lezioni di Economia*. Vol. 2. Rome: Edizioni dell'Ateneo.

————. 1983. *Il Sottosviluppo e l'Economia Contemporanea*. Roma-Bari: Laterza.

————. 1984. *The Forces of Economic Growth and Decline*. Cambridge: MIT Press.

————. 1985. "La spirale e l'arco." *Economic Politica* (June).

————. 1990. "Technical Progress, Unemployment and Economic Dynamics." *Structural Change and Economic Dynamics* (June).

————. 1991. "The Changing Character of the So-Called Business Cycle." *The Atlantic Economic Review*, no. 3.

————. 1992. "Long-Run Structural Changes, Change in the Price and Wage Mechanism and the Process of Economic Growth." In *Essays in Honor of Luigi Pasinetti*. London: Macmillan.

Tocqueville, A. de. 1835. *De la democratie en Amerique*. Paris: Genin, 1951.

von Bortkiewicz, L. 1971. "La teoria economica di Marx e altri saggi." In *Bohm-Bawerk, Walras e Pareto*, a cura di L. Meldolesi, Torino: Einaudi.

The World Bank. Various years. *World Development Report*. New York: Oxford University Press.

2

STRATEGIES OF ECONOMIC DEVELOPMENT

James Riedel

Under the title of this chapter it would be logical to focus on the various schemes devised by governments to achieve economic development. Strategy is the art of devising plans or stratagems toward an end, and governments are the ones that set national economic development goals. This approach to the subject would, however, bypass the central issue, which is whether a strategy is necessary or even useful for achieving economic development in the first place. There is no question that government has an important role to play in a market economy and as such has an important influence on the rate of a nation's economic progress. But whether that role should include devising strategies to achieve development is a matter of great debate. Underlying that debate are fundamental differences of view about how the world works or, more precisely, what causes, and what hinders, economic growth in developing countries. Explaining the different viewpoints and what they imply about the role of government and explaining how and why the consensus view has changed over time are the aim of this chapter.

It is commonplace to begin any discussion of economic development by explaining that development is more than gross domestic product (GDP) growth and that there may be trade-offs between growth and other objectives of development. I accept that to be true but leave it to others to consider its implications. In this chapter, the focus is solely on growth—what causes it and what hinders it and what role government plays in both.

GROWTH THEORY

All growth theories explain the long-term rate of growth by the growth of inputs and by technological progress. Where the various theories differ is in the assumptions they make about key parameters and about what determines input growth and technological change.

Harrod-Domar Model

The usual place to start in surveying growth theory is with the Harrod-Domar model. It is one of the earliest, simplest, and most influential models. The key assumptions of the model are that technology is unchanging, that input-output coefficients are constant, and that capital is either the only input or the only scarce input (all other required inputs being in excess supply). From these assumptions it follows that a change in the level of output (ΔY) depends on a change in the capital stock (ΔK), the impact of the latter on the former being determined by the capital-output ratio ($K/Y = k$).[1] In a closed economy, investment ($I = \Delta K$) is equal to domestic saving (S), and thus the rate of growth of output ($\Delta Y/Y = g$) depends on the average propensity to save ($s = S/Y$) and the capital-output ratio:

$$g = s/k \tag{1}$$

The model can easily be amended to allow for international capital flows. Expressing the net inflow of foreign capital (F) as a proportion of GDP ($f = F/Y$), the Harrod-Domar growth equation for an open economy becomes:

$$g = (s + f)/k \tag{2}$$

However, since a net inflow of foreign capital (foreign savings) constitutes an increase in net external debt (D), which eventually must be repaid by generating an excess of savings over investment sometime in the future, what matters over the long haul is a country's ability and willingness to save. All that international finance does is allow a country to separate the *timing* of saving and investment, but only within the limits of its ability to service its external debt and remain creditworthy. If the rate of foreign capital inflow (f) is set so as to keep the debt-output ratio ($d = D/Y$) constant at some level that is, if not optimal, at least manageable, then (2) becomes:[2]

$$g = s/(k - d) \tag{3}$$

As expressed in (3), the rate of GDP growth will be higher, the higher the average propensity to save, the lower the capital-output ratio, and the higher the debt-output ratio that a country can maintain.

Even though government does not enter the Harrod-Domar growth equation per se, the model suggests a powerful role for government, since all three of the variables on the right side are highly subject to government influence, directly and indirectly, positively and negatively. The domestic savings rate, of course, depends on macroeconomic policy; the efficiency of investment depends on incentive measures and regulations affecting resource allocation; and the amount of debt a country can service and maintain depends on, among other things, the ability to earn foreign exchange, which in turn largely hinges on trade policy.

The Harrod-Domar model figured prominently in the development economics literature in large part (as will be explained presently) because it suggests that government can be instrumental in raising a country's growth rate. However, in the theoretical literature the model came under criticism. One obvious short-coming of the model is its unrealistic assumption that only capital accumulation matters to growth. If an additional factor of production is introduced, for example, labor, it turns out that the full-employment equilibrium rests on a knife-edge. With fixed input-output coefficients, full employment requires that output grow at the same rate as labor (n), which implies that the average propensity to save must equal the product of the rate of growth of labor and the capital-output ratio, a condition that holds in the model only by accident.[3]

Solow-Swan Model

The solution to this problem, presented in Solow's (1956) seminal contribution to growth theory, was to specify a production function that allows for continuous substitution between capital and labor.[4] Assuming constant returns to scale and diminishing marginal productivity to each factor of production, with technological change assumed to be labor-augmenting and exogenously determined, the rate of growth of output is given by:

$$g = \alpha (\Delta K/K) + \beta n + a \qquad (4)$$

where a is the rate of labor-augmenting technological change and where α and β, under constant returns to scale ($\alpha + \beta = 1$), are the income shares of capital and labor, respectively. Assuming the savings rate is constant, the rate of capital accumulation is equal to s/k, as in the Harrod-Domar model, but with k no longer held constant.

The Solow model is illustrated in Figure 2.1. The long-run, or "steady-state," equilibrium is at E, where the output and the capital stock grow at a uniform rate equal to the rate of growth of "effective labor," the sum of the exogenously given rates, labor force growth, and labor-augmenting technical change (n + a). If the output-capital ratio were initially greater than its long-run equilibrium level (e.g., at J), growth of capital and output would exceed the long-run equilibrium rate, (i.e., $g_1 > g_0 = n + a$), but by the fact that capital expands faster than effective labor, the average product of capital (Y/K) declines, lowering the rate of growth of capital and hence of output, until the long-run equilibrium is reached at E in Figure 2.1.

One important implication of the Solow model is that government can do little to affect the *long-term* rate of growth, since it depends solely on labor force

Figure 2.1
Solow-Swan Growth Model

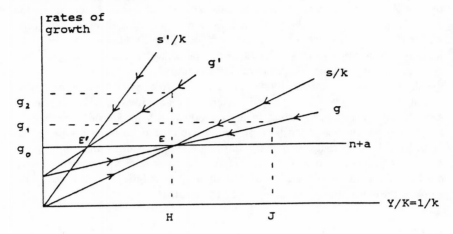

growth and technological change, both of which are assumed to be determined exogenously. An increase in the rate of saving, for example, is illustrated by a leftward rotation of the capital accumulation line and the growth line in Figure 2.1. Thus a rise in the saving rate from s to s' immediately raises the growth rate from g_0 to g_2, but at the same time diminishing returns set in, and gradually the growth rate settles back down to the steady-state rate (n + a) at E'. Similarly, policy measures that raise the efficiency of investment, such as might be expected from a liberalization of trade policy, for example, have only a transitory effect on growth (Corden, 1985). If a change in policy were to raise the output-capital ratio from H to J, the growth rate would immediately rise to g_1, but it would then gradually fall back to g_0 as the return to capital diminishes. Thus, in the Solow model the effect on growth of policies that affect the rate of saving and the efficiency of investment is transitory, albeit that the transition to steady state may take a long time. It is also important to note that policies that only temporarily raise the *growth rate* of output permanently increase the *level* of output. Therefore, the Solow-Swan model implies not that government policies are ineffective in raising wealth and prosperity, only that they cannot affect long-term growth.

The importance of government policy for economic growth has been brought into question not so much by Solow's model as by its empirical application as a growth accounting framework. Of the three variables on the right-hand side of equation (4), the one over which government presumably exerts the most influence, investment, turns out to have been the least important in explaining growth in the United States and in other countries where the method has been applied (Solow, 1957). What turns out to have been the most important was technological change, which the theory treats as exogenous, like manna from heaven.[5]

Figure 2.2
The Relation Between the Level and Rate of Growth of Per Capita Income

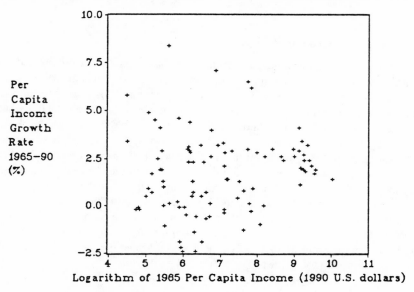

Source: World Bank, *World Development Report* (1992).

The Solow-Swan model is, however, itself called into question by at least two basic and related stylized facts about growth. One fact, which later will be reviewed in some detail, is that major shifts in economic policy, especially those affecting international trade, are closely associated with large and sustained changes in rates of economic growth, especially in developing countries (Reynolds, 1983; Riedel, 1990). Related to this is that there is no apparent tendency for either the level or the rate of growth of income across countries to converge, as the model would predict. If capital is subject to diminishing returns, then the productivity of capital in poor countries with low capital-labor ratios should be higher than in rich countries with high capital-labor ratios. In the context of Solow's model, with output per worker in the United States fifteen times that in India, the return to investment in India should be fifty-eight times that in the United States.[6] Therefore, with similar rates of investment, India and other poor countries should grow faster than the United States and other rich countries, a tendency that should only be reinforced by international capital flows in response to international differences in rates of return to investment. However, as Figure 2.2 shows, there is no apparent inverse relationship between the level and rate of growth of per capita income across a wide sample of ninety-seven developed and developing countries (all for which data were available). Instead of converging, international differences in growth performance seem to persist over long periods of time.[7] The neoclassical growth model is in need of repair, or an alternative should be found.

Endogenous Growth Models

Efforts to repair the model in recent years have spawned a growth industry within the economics discipline itself, known as "endogenous growth theory," the term *endogenous* denoting a property of these models that long-term per capita growth occurs in the absence of exogenous increases in productivity such as those associated with technological progress in Solow's model. Naturally, theorists approach the problem of fixing a model by overhauling its assumptions. The assumptions responsible for the neoclassical model's erroneous implications that (1) long-term per capita income growth is zero in the absence of exogenous technological progress and that (2) poor countries grow faster than rich ones are constant returns to scale and diminishing returns to reproducible capital.

It has long been recognized that implication (1) of the Solow model does not hold under increasing returns to scale. Long-term per capita growth ($g - n$) under increasing returns to scale ($\alpha + \beta > 1$) is positive in the Solow model even without technological progress (i.e., $a = 0$), since:

$$g - n = [(\alpha + \beta - 1)/(1 - \alpha)]n > 0 \qquad (5)$$

Postulating increasing returns to scale does not, however, suggest that policy can influence long-term growth or explain the absence of convergence. Moreover, the assumption of increasing returns to scale creates problems of its own in that either it does not support a competitive equilibrium or, if one obtains, because increasing returns apply only at the aggregate level and not the firm level due to some kind of externality, the equilibrium that obtains is not efficient.

The main contribution of endogenous growth theory is to show that it is not necessary to postulate increasing returns to scale to get endogenous growth; all that is needed is to assume constant returns to capital, broadly defined (Romer, 1986; Rebelo, 1991). This amounts to assuming $\alpha = 1$ in equation (4), which implies increasing returns to scale ($\alpha + \beta > 1$) when nonreproducible inputs (e.g., labor) play a role. One solution to this problem is to assume away non-reproducible inputs, for example, physical labor. It is sometimes argued that what is important for growth is not the number of people working, but rather the amount of "human capital" (skills and know-how) embodied in them, which is reproducible. If capital is redefined as a composite of different kinds of reproducible inputs, such as physical capital, human capital, the stock of knowledge, social infrastructure, and so forth, and if raw labor is dropped from the model, and if it is further assumed that the return to investment is constant ($\alpha = 1$), then what emerges is:

$$g = \alpha \, (\Delta K/K) = (I/K)(Y/Y) = s/k \tag{6}$$

In (6) growth is "endogenous" in the sense that it can occur indefinitely at a high or a low rate depending on the proportion of income invested (s) and the efficiency of investment (k), as in the Harrod-Domar model. Policy can play a major role, and there is no implication of convergence in levels or rates of growth of income, again as in the Harrod-Domar model.

This is not exactly the Harrod-Domar model, however, because the problem with which Harrod and Domar were concerned, the tendency for growing unemployment, is moot since physical labor plays no role. Another difference is that instead of taking the savings rate as given, the endogenous growth theories assume that savings are derived endogenously by individual consumers maximizing their utility over time. The growth equation obtained from this procedure is:

$$g = (r - \delta)/\sigma \tag{7}$$

where $r = (1/k)$ is the constant average and marginal return to capital, δ is the discount rate (measuring consumers' preference for present over future consumption), and σ is the elasticity of substitution between consumption in one period and the next (measuring consumers' preference for a smooth consumption profile over time). What is gained from this analytical sophistication is questionable, however, since the optimal savings rate in steady state is, in any case, constant and the conditions required to obtain an optimum savings rate (e.g., a perfect capital market and no distortions) simply do not exist, especially in developing countries.

Even though the assumption of increasing returns to scale is not necessary to get endogenous growth, a number of influential contributions to this literature postulate it anyway, but with increasing returns external to the firm (e.g., Romer, 1986; Lucas, 1988). As already noted, if increasing returns are external, a competitive equilibrium exists, but it is inefficient. This version of the endogenous growth model implies not just that government can play a role but that it must play a role if a country is to achieve all the growth and prosperity that it can. How government should intervene to achieve an optimal rate of growth depends, of course, on the nature of the externality, and the literature has offered a number of different hypotheses. For example, Romer (1986), following Arrow (1962), postulates a growth externality deriving from the accumulation of knowledge (learning by doing, to use Arrow's terminology). Lucas (1988) suggests that there are externalities from human capital accumulation, arguing that people are more productive when surrounded by other educated people. Another strand in the literature focuses on research and development (R&D) and the spillovers from R&D to other sectors of the economy (Grossman and Helpman, 1990). Additionally, in the context of an endogenous growth model with externalities it can be shown that openness to international trade can result in lower growth than under autarky (Stokey, 1991; Young, 1991) and that tariffs and other barriers to trade can raise a country's growth rate (Grossman and Helpman, 1991). Endogenous growth models have also been designed to illustrate "poverty traps," which result when certain forms of capital, such as human capital or infrastructure capital, are below a certain threshold level, which provides theoretical justification for large public investment programs (Murphy, Schleifer, and Vishney, 1989; Easterly, 1991).

To anyone familiar with the development economics literature of forty to fifty years ago, the themes emerging from the endogenous growth theory sound very familiar. The importance of saving and investment, the failure of markets in the presence of externalities, the potential "immiserazing" effects of international trade, and the need for "big-push" industrialization programs are the bread and butter of traditional development economics. It is, of course, useful to have old ideas formalized in a mathematical model, especially when such ideas hold sway over policy-making in vast regions of the globe. It is misleading, however, to suggest that the validity of many of these hypotheses is an open question. Most, if not all, have been thoroughly tested in the laboratory of economic history, and a fairly solid consensus about their validity exists (and is reviewed later).

Scott's New View

Rather than trying to repair orthodox growth theory, Maurice Scott (1989b) offers an alternative, what he calls "a new view of economic growth." The main problem with orthodox theory, according to Scott, is that it takes too narrow a view of investment, defining it as additions to a homogenous capital stock.[8] Instead, Scott argues that it is both more logical and more practical to define investment as the "cost, in terms of consumption foregone, of improving economic arrangements" (Scott, 1989b, p. 19). These may consist of "changes in the numbers and quality of the work force and changes in the physical environment in which they work, including changes in buildings, machines, vehicles, stocks of goods, etc." (Scott, 1991, p. 259). In Scott's view there is no need to consider the rate of technological change separately from the rate of investment; indeed, it cannot be done, and it does not make sense to try. The reasons are twofold: first, technological progress does not occur costlessly, and the cost, in terms of consumption foregone, of changing technology is investment, as investment is conventionally defined; second, investment rarely, if ever, takes the form of simply reduplicating the stock of capital. Instead, when firms invest, it is usually because they need *better* machines in order to remain competitive and profitable. When investment is viewed as "the cost of changing economic arrangements," rather than simply adding more of the same to the capital stock, there is no longer any reason to suppose that the return to investment diminishes with cumulative investment.

If investment is the main source of growth, as Scott contends, why have studies using the neoclassical growth accounting framework not attributed more importance to capital accumulation, leaving less to the residual, which they attribute to advances in knowledge? The answer, according to Scott, is in their erroneous treatment of depreciation. Scott presents evidence that capital depreciation results mainly from relative price changes that reduce the economic value of capital assets (obsolescence) rather than from physical deterioration. Neoclassical theory and its empirical application as a growth accounting framework make no distinction between depreciation from obsolescence and that from physical deterioration, nor do they consider the distinction valid (Denison, 1991). This implies that no matter what the source, a dollar of capital depreciation reduces output as much as a dollar of gross investment increases it. Scott argues, however, that insofar as depreciation results from price changes, it does not reduce output at all and therefore should not be deducted, as it is, in measuring the contribution of investment to growth.

Scott's reasoning is given by reference to the example of a firm that remains physically unchanged and employs a constant labor force to produce an unchanged output over a period of years. If the economy in which the firm operates is growing and, as a consequence, real wages are rising, then the quasi-rent earned on the firm's capital declines over time and eventually falls to zero, at which point the firm goes out of business, and its employees go elsewhere to work. Throughout the period, from the time the firm starts up until it shuts down, capital depreciates, but output remains constant. Even when the firm goes out of business, output does not fall if the firm's workers find employment elsewhere at the same wage, since at the point of zero profit all of the value of output is attributable to labor. The depreciation in the value of the firm's capital (to the extent that it is due to economic obsolescence) is just matched by the appreciation in the value of labor. Therefore, depreciation is not a social cost and represents no loss of output; rather, it is an income transfer between owners of capital and labor. Subtracting depreciation from gross investment therefore understates the contribution of investment to growth and, according to Scott, accounts for the large residual attributed to technological progress. If investment is defined more broadly as the cost of changing economic arrangements, then there is no residual to explain.

The foregoing example also illustrates Scott's view of why firms invest, which is to forestall the decline in profits that otherwise occurs from rising real wages and other relative price changes. At any given time, a firm is aware of the set of investment opportunities available to it that will either increase revenues or reduce labor costs and will select from that set those investments that it expects will maximize the present value of the firm. After the investment is made and after other investments are made simultaneously by other firms, a whole new set of investment opportunities is opened up that did not exist before. Scott argues that there is no reason to suppose that the new set of opportunities is any worse (or better) than what preceded it. In other words, there is no reason to suppose that there are diminishing returns to cumulative investment. Indeed, once the residual in neoclassical growth accounting is explained away as a mistake, there is no empirical evidence of diminishing returns to cumulative investment.

Scott's model leads to a simple linear equation to explain growth:

$$g = aQs + bn \qquad\qquad (8)$$

where a and b are constants and Q is an index of investment quality. The growth rate will be higher if proportion of income is saved and invested ($s = I/Y$), given the efficiency of investment, or if a given rate of investment becomes more efficient, the latter being all the more important since improvements in investment quality do not sacrifice consumption and since they are likely to stimulate increases in the quantity of investment (Scott, 1989b, p. 19). As for what determines the quality of investment:

> The knowledge, intelligence, originality, common sense, and effort of businessmen, inventors, and scientists are all highly relevant, as are the economic institutions that influence their perceptions and choices, including the degree of competition, taxes, and subsidies, the credit system, and product and factor markets generally. Learning from others' investments will be easier and quicker if communications and travel are easier and quicker. Decision-makers' motives are obviously important. Are they seeking to maximize present values, as we have assumed thus far, or are they pursuing other goals which may conflict with economic efficiency? How free and how decentralized are decisions to invest? (Scott, 1989b, p. 177)

In short, policy can play a major role, positively or negatively, in determining a country's growth rate.

Scott's view is similar to endogenous growth theory in that both explain why the return to investment has not fallen despite centuries of accumulation. However, they differ in that the endogenous growth models achieve this by introducing the cumulative stock of knowledge as a separate, endogenously determined primary input in a neoclassical production function, while Scott denies that advances in knowledge and investment can be separated. Indeed, he argues that advances in knowledge are the result of investment, and he presents empirical evidence to buttress this argument.

Scott's view is also similar to endogenous growth theory in that it suggests that significant positive externalities flow from investment and that, in consequence, actual rates of investment and growth in most countries are far below the optimum rates. Scott and the endogenous growth theorists differ, however, in what they suggest this implies for policy. In the tradition of neoclassical equilibrium theory, the endogenous growth models offer up first-best policy responses to each kind of market failure. Scott, however, is much more circumspect, recognizing as he does that "investment at any given time is undertaken in a state of ignorance about the future.'' For that reason he suggests that an industrial policy of trying to pick winners and avoid losers is unlikely to succeed. For as he stresses (1989): ''We can only choose current investments in the light of what we already know, and by changing the world we alter what is known and reveal hitherto unknown opportunities'' (p. 457). In Scott's view, policy should mainly aim at creating an environment conducive to good investment decision making and should avoid taxes and other measures that discourage saving.

DEVELOPMENT ECONOMICS

In examining the role of government from the perspective of ''development economics,'' I follow Hirschman (1981) and Sen (1983) in identifying development economics with ''a given body of beliefs and themes rather than with a collection of subject matters and problems to be tackled'' (Sen, 1983, p. 745). I can afford to be concise, since development economics has recently been thoroughly surveyed and critiqued from various perspectives by a number of authors.[9]

Diagnosis and Prescription

The main problem besetting developing countries, which is the cause of their poverty, as portrayed in traditional development economics, is too much labor in agriculture and too little capital in industry. The persistence of rural unemployment and the failure of industry to grow and absorb the rural unemployed (and underemployed) were interpreted as evidence that markets did not work in developing countries and could not be made to work, for several stated (or implied) reasons: (1) because entrepreneurship, an essential ingredient of a well-functioning market system, was missing in developing countries (Hirschman, 1958); (2) because markets in developing countries are rigid and unresponsive to price signals (Myrdal, 1958; Nurkse, 1953); (3) because industrialization involves increasing returns, externalities, and indivisibilities, which preclude the market from working efficiently (Rosenstein-Rodan, 1943; Scitovsky, 1954); and (4) because developing countries were seen to be essentially under siege from the developed countries through international trade (Prebisch, 1950; Singer, 1950). Traditional development economics views the world as inhospitable to growth and development, which must, therefore, be nurtured by government's following an appropriate strategy.

The lack of faith in markets and the corresponding enthusiasm for planning were in part a product of the times. The Great Depression, still a recent memory when development economics came into being, was often interpreted as a failure of capitalism; on the other hand, planning appeared to be successful in generating rapid growth in the Soviet Union and in mobilizing resources in wartime Britain (Little, 1982). This was also the heyday of the Keynesian revolution, with its emphasis on market rigidities and call for government activism. In developing countries after World War II there was a tide of nationalism that carried with it a natural inclination toward *etatism*.

The leading economists writing on economic development in the 1940s and 1950s were in tune with the tenor of the times and provided theoretical arguments supporting a heavy role for government in the industrialization of developing countries. One of the most influential was Rosenstein-Rodan (1943), who argued for a "big push" of public and private investment, his specific interest being South and Southeast Europe. He believed that any one industrial investment was doomed to fail because of insufficient demand; however, if a large number of investments were undertaken simultaneously, together they would generate enough complementary demand to make them all profitable.[10] The argument for a "big push" was developed further by Scitovsky (1954), who asserted that (pecuniary) externalities were common in industry, with investment in one industry leading to lower costs in another industry. Since individual investors are generally unable to foresee the long-term cost and price effects of their investments or those of others, they tend to underinvest. The solution, as he saw it, was for government to coordinate investment planning under the strategy of "balanced growth."

The concept of balanced growth, however, soon came under criticism from another one of the pioneers of development economics, A.O. Hirschman, who argued that "its application requires huge amounts of precisely those abilities (namely, entrepreneurship) which we have identified as likely to be very limited in supply in underdeveloped countries" (Hirschman, 1958, pp. 52–53). Instead, Hirschman called for a strategy of "unbalanced growth," in which government would promote growth "through forward thrusts that are meant to create incentives and pressures for further action, and then stand ready to react to, and to alleviate, these pressures in a variety of ways" (p. 202).

The arguments for big-push, balanced-growth industrialization apply, if they apply at all, to closed economies. Effective domestic demand and pecuniary externalities in traded goods industries are of little importance in an open economy that can sell its output and buy its inputs in world markets. The prospects for international trade after World War II, however, did not appear favorable for understandable reasons: the collapse of trade, in particular, commodity prices, in the 1930s; and the widespread application of quantitative restrictions and exchange controls in the 1940s.

The hostility toward international trade that became imbedded in development economics ran much deeper, however; it arose from a fundamental belief that developing countries (the "periphery") were exploited by the developed countries (the "center") through the mechanism of international trade. The main proponents of this view, Prebisch (1949) and Singer (1950), argued that because the goods developing countries export are produced under competitive conditions and face inelastic demand, while the goods developed countries export are produced under monopolistic competition and face elastic demand, the terms of trade inexorably turn against the developing countries. According to this view, the effect of trade is to transfer the benefits of growth in the primary sector of developing countries to the developed countries and to preclude any opportunity for growth in the industrial sector of developing countries. To overcome this constraint, it was asserted, industrialization should be fostered behind trade barriers and should aim to be import-substituting, initially in consumer goods and later extended to intermediate and capital goods branches.

The diagnosis of too much labor in agriculture and too little capital in industry led naturally to a central role for physical capital accumulation. Indeed, Lewis (1955) went so far as to state:

> The central problem in the theory of economic development is to understand the process by which a community which was previously saving and investing 4 or 5 per cent of its national income or less, converts itself to an economy where voluntary saving is running at about 12 to 15 per cent of national income or more. This is the central problem because the central fact of economic development is rapid capital accumulation (including knowledge and skills with capital). We cannot explain any "industrial" revolution (as the economic historians pretend to do) until we can explain why saving increased relatively to national income. (p. 155)

The target savings rate of 12 to 15 percent was derived by direct application of the Harrod-Domar growth equation, in which a target growth rate for per capita income of 2 to 3 percent, with population growing at 2 percent, requires a target GDP growth rate of 4 or 5 percent, with the average capital-output ratio of about 3 to 1.

Subsequently, the analysis was extended to shift the emphasis from domestic to foreign savings (Chenery and Bruno, 1962). The argument was that because of two peculiarities of developing country economies—(1) an inordinate dependence on imported capital goods and (2) external limitations on the ability to expand exports—the binding constraint on growth in developing countries was not domestic savings, but instead foreign savings (i.e., foreign exchange).

It is useful to spell out the logic of this idea, known as the "two-gap" model, since it became an important planning tool in developing countries. Suppose a growth target (g_T) is chosen; then the required investment ($I^* = g_T kY$) will be constrained by saving if $I^* \geq (S + F)$ and will be constrained by foreign exchange if $I^* \geq (X + F - M_0)/m$, where X is exports of goods and services, F is foreign savings inflow, M_0 is imports of goods and services (including factor services) other than capital goods, and m is the proportion of investment that is required to be imported ($M_I = mI$).[11] The binding constraint on growth is, therefore, the lesser of either $(S + F)$ or $(X + F - M_0)/m$, that is, savings or foreign exchange. If the constraint is foreign exchange, then raising domestic savings will have no effect on growth; on the other hand, an increase in foreign savings, which in the 1960s mainly took the form of aid, would be doubly effective because it would both supplement domestic savings and increase the availability of foreign exchange.

The crucial assumption of the two-gap model is that exports are strictly determined by external demand. The single emphasis on foreign savings also requires that there is little scope for substituting imports of consumer goods for capital goods, but that assumption became self-fulfilling under the import-substitution strategy. That exports are demand-determined is crucial to the model because if this were not the case, a country that increased its savings rate could always increase its growth rate by transforming savings into foreign exchange by taking appropriate measures to expand exports. Export pessimism is, therefore, essential to the two-gap model, indeed, to most of the main propositions of traditional development economics.

Success and Failure

Development economics started out, Hirschman (1981) contends, "[with] the implicit idea that it could slay the dragon of backwardness virtually by itself or, at least, that its contribution to this task was central. . . . [It] was taken for granted that progress of these countries would be smoothly linear if only they adopted the right kind of integrated development program!" (pp. 23–24). At the outset, developing countries did, by and large, adopt the strategy prescribed by development economics, but progress was not linear. There was progress, nonetheless, in fact, far more than was expected.

In summarizing the growth record over the first quarter-century of economic development by design, David Morawetz (1977) points out: "In average per capita income the developing countries grew more rapidly between 1950 and 1975—3.4 percent a year—than either they or the developed countries had done in any comparable period in the past. They thereby exceeded both official goals and private expectations" (p. 67). However, Morawetz further noted: "This impressive average growth and development performance masks a wide diversity of experience" (p. 68). As Table 2.1 shows, on average per capita income growth in developing countries remained high after 1975, but the variance in growth performance across regions (and even more across countries) became even greater.

The key to growth, according to the development economics paradigm, is raising saving and investment rates and expanding industrial output, especially in manufacturing. As Figures 2.3 and 2.4 show, these objectives were accomplished with astounding success. By 1965 the saving and investment rates for developing countries, in aggregate, were already well above anything ever dreamed of by the pioneers of development economics. Moreover, the share of industrial value-added in GDP has grown steadily to levels that currently exceed those of the advanced "industrial countries." Studies of the pattern of economic development across countries indicate that developing countries typically reach an investment rate of almost 21 percent by the time they reach a per capita

Table 2.1
Per Capita GNP Growth by Region

	Rosenstein-Rodan's Projection of 1976 Per Capita GNP		Chenery Strout's Estimates of GDP Growth Rates: 1962-75		Capita GNP in 1990
	1974 US$	Percent Realized	Estimate	Realized	US$
India	213	65	5.3	3.4	340
Pakistan	174	75	5.3	6.0	370
Sri Lanka	289	46	5.0	4.2	430
Taiwan	258	316	7.0	9.4	8000
Hong Kong	488	324	-	-	10350
South Korea	250	201	5.0	10.1	4400
Singapore	859	269	-	-	10450

Source: World Bank, *World Development Report* (1991, 1992).

Figure 2.3
Average Saving and Investment Rates in Developing Countries

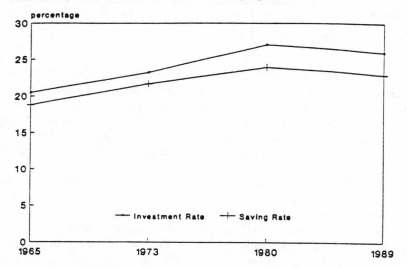

Source: I.B.R.D., *World Development Report* (1991).

income of $500, and by the time they reach $1,000 the investment rate is as high as 23 percent, and the share of manufacturing value-added in GNP is slightly over 18 percent (Syrquin and Chenery, 1989, pp. 152–53).

The average investment rate for developing countries, like average per capita growth rate, masks wide differences among regions and countries (see Table 2.2). However, growth rates exhibit more variation across regions and countries

Figure 2.4
The Share of Industry in GDP in Developed and Developing Countries

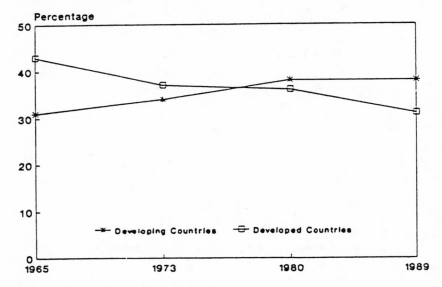

Source: I.B.R.D., *World Development Report* (1991).

than do investment rates, which implies that the efficiency of investment varies widely across regions and countries of the Third World. Most developing countries have managed to raise savings and investment well beyond Lewis's target of 12 to 15 percent, but not all get the same amount of growth for the same amount of sacrifice. This suggests that while investment is necessary for growth, it alone is not sufficient. The quality of investment clearly matters as much as the quantity.

The differences among developing countries in the return to investment have been thoroughly analyzed, and some of the findings are discussed later. At this point, it is interesting to explore how the relative prospects for growth of developing countries looked in the early 1960s when the import-substitution strategy was in full bloom. This is revealed in the forecasts of growth in developing countries done separately by two of the pioneers of development economics. In 1960, Rosenstein-Rodan (1961) forecast the 1961–1976 per capita growth rates of sixty-six developing countries, and a few years later Chenery and Strout (1966) forecast the 1962–1975 GNP growth rates for forty-five developing countries. Neither of these forecasts anticipated the success that developing countries were to achieve in the 1960s. Two-thirds of Rosenstein-Rodan's countries surpassed his forecast of GNP per capita in 1976 by more than 10 percent; three-fourths of Chenery-Strout's countries grew faster than projected.

There were, however, cases of overestimation of growth prospects, the most

Table 2.2
Investment and Growth by Region

	1965/73	1973/80	1980/89
East Asia			
g	8.1	6.6	7.9
I/Y	24.8	28.8	32.3
I/ΔY	3.1	4.3	4.1
South Asia			
g	3.6	4.2	5.1
I/Y	16.9	19.5	21.8
I/ΔY	4.7	4.6	4.2
Sub-Saharan Africa			
g	4.8	3.2	2.1
I/Y	15.8	18.9	17.5
I/ΔY	3.3	5.9	8.3
Latin America			
g	6.5	5.0	1.6
I/Y	20.8	22.8	20.3
I/ΔY	3.2	4.6	12.6
Middle East & N. Africa /a			
g	7.7	3.9	2.9
I/Y	23.8	28.1	30.1
I/ΔY	3.1	7.2	10.3
LDCs			
g	6.5	4.7	3.8
I/Y	21.8	25.1	26.5
I/ΔY	3.4	5.3	6.7
DCs			
g	4.7	3.0	3.0
I/Y	19.7	22.4	21.9
I/ΔY	4.2	7.4	7.3

Source: World Bank, *World Development Report* (1991).
[1]Also including developing European countries.

striking of which, in both sets of forecasts, were the South Asian countries, which because of their large domestic markets and relatively well developed infrastructure were, according to the logic of the import-substitution strategy, expected to have very good prospects for growth.[12] The most striking cases of underestimation of growth were for Taiwan, South Korea, Hong Kong, and Singapore, which because of their superlative performance subsequently earned the epithet the "gang of four." These countries were not expected to go far because their domestic markets were too small to allow them to capture economies of scale from industrialization, and, of course, foreign markets were assumed to be closed to developing countries. As Table 2.3 shows, Rosenstein-Rodan expected the South Asian countries to reach a per capita income in 1976 roughly

Table 2.3
Growth Projections in the Early 1960s

	Rosenstein-Rodan's Projection of 1976 Per Capita GNP		Chenery Strout's Estimates of GDP Growth Rates: 1962-75		Capita GNP in 1990 US$
	1974 US$	Percent Realized	Estimate	Realized	
India	213	65	5.3	3.4	340
Pakistan	174	75	5.3	6.0	370
Sri Lanka	289	46	5.0	4.2	430
Taiwan	258	316	7.0	9.4	8000
Hong Kong	488	324	-	-	10350
South Korea	250	201	5.0	10.1	4400
Singapore	859	269	-	-	10450

Source: Morawetz (1981).

equivalent to Taiwan and South Korea; instead their per capita income in 1976 was only about a quarter of that of Taiwan and Korea, and by 1990 it was less than one-tenth. Chenery and Strout did no better, forecasting that India would grow faster than Korea, when in fact Korea grew three times faster than India.

False Premises

These projections reveal two false premises underlying the import-substitution strategy: (1) that scale economies and externalities would allow developing countries to achieve high levels of efficiency in industries in which they lacked comparative advantage; and (2) that prospects for expanding exports were severely limited by deficient external demand.

If the first premise were valid, infant industries would exhibit relatively high rates of productivity growth, as scale economies are realized and positive externalities begin to pay off. Moreover, infant industries, after a period of time, should be able to stand on their own without the protection they required during the maturation phase. These are, however, only necessary, not sufficient, conditions for justifying infant industry protection. An additional requirement is that the initial costs of protecting an infant industry should be exceeded by the benefits that flow to the economy from the existence of a grown-up infant industry. Since the costs and benefits that accrue over time from protection and promotion of uncompetitive industries are all but impossible to measure precisely, it is difficult to make or refute a case for infant industry protection on economic grounds; decisions on these matters, therefore, almost always come down to politics. It is, however, easier to evaluate, after the fact, whether the necessary conditions for successful infant industry protection were met.

Is productivity growth higher in industries receiving infant industry protection than in other sectors where scale economies and externalities are supposedly less important? What evidence there is, is negative. Krueger and Tuncer (1982) examined the case of Turkey in the 1960s and 1970s, a country as committed as any to the import-substitution strategy, and found no systematic relation between the level of protection afforded an industry and its rate of productivity growth. Another study, which surveyed the literature on the performance of firms receiving infant industry protection in developing countries, concluded that "few of the infant enterprises studied in less developed economies appear to have demonstrated the high and continuous productivity growth needed to achieve and maintain international competitiveness" (Bell, Ross-Larson, and Westphal, 1984, p. 114). There is no doubt that protection from international competition and direct subsidies "worked," bringing into existence industries that otherwise would not have existed; but it is also apparent that in many cases the costs of import-substituting industrialization outweighed the benefits.

The second premise, that exports of developing countries are strictly determined by external demand, is even more obviously false than the first. If it were true, exports would grow at about the same rate in every country—namely, at the rate that external demand allowed. As Table 2.4 shows, however, export growth rates vary widely. Nor is there any obvious tendency for the terms of trade of developing countries to decline, when adjustment is made for quality changes (Grilli and Yang, 1988).

Initially, export pessimism arose from a belief that the developed countries were increasingly substituting domestic production for imports of primary commodities from developing countries. Nurkse (1959) pointed to the introduction of synthetic materials, an industrial structure in developed countries that was changing in favor of heavy industry with a low content of imported raw materials, the rising share of services in total expenditures, and economies in the use of raw materials through reprocessing of scrap. On these grounds he argued that while trade served as an "engine of growth" for countries in the periphery in the nineteenth century, it could not be relied upon by developing countries in the twentieth century.[13] Two decades later, Lewis resurrected the notion of trade as an engine of growth, only to argue that while it worked for developing countries in the postwar period up until 1973, it could be relied upon no longer because the industrial countries were slowing down.

The idea that developing country exports can grow no faster than income grows in developed countries rests on either of two assumptions: (1) that the demand for LDC exports is price-inelastic; or (2) that penetration of developed country markets automatically triggers protectionism. If these assumptions were valid, an acceleration of export growth would lead to falling export prices (because of price inelasticity in demand) and to a protectionist backlash in developed countries that would forestall further export expansion.

There have been many examples of rapid acceleration in export growth, usually following a major liberalization of trade policy in the countries concerned, with-

Table 2.4
Export Volume Growth Rates by Region

	1965/73	1973/80	1980/87
East Asia			
Primary	8.4	5.0	4.6
Manufactures	28.3	17.1	13.8
South Asia			
Primary	-1.9	2.1	3.7
Manufactures	1.1	6.3	6.2
Latin America			
Primary	-1.9	0.2	2.3
Manufactures	16.7	9.5	6.1
Africa			
Primary	14.7	-0.8	-2.0
Manufactures	5.8	9.7	2.4
Middle East			
Primary	--	} -0.6	} 4.8
Manufactures			
Developing Countries			
Primary	4.0	1.2	2.8
Manufactures	10.9	13.0	7.0
Developed Countries			
Primary	5.7	6.4	4.1
Manufactures	10.6	5.2	3.7

Source: World Bank, *World Development Report* (1991).

out either of these outcomes occurring. Given developing countries' minuscule shares in most of the world markets in which they compete, individually they resemble "price-takers" facing extremely price-elastic demand for most of their products, especially manufactures that now account for almost 70 percent of developing countries' nonfuel exports.[14] Collectively, developing countries may influence prices in some export markets, which (if ignored) could impose limits on their ability to gain collectively from trade. This is the core of the much-discussed "fallacy of composition argument," which is often invoked to dismiss the relevance of the East Asian super-exporters—what worked for a few small countries in East Asia cannot work if practiced by many developing countries. The logic of this argument seems valid enough as long as we think in partial equilibrium terms, with everything staying the same except that all developing countries suddenly begin exporting on a level comparable to that of Hong Kong. However, once one recognizes that nothing could possibly stay the same were developing countries universally to adopt an export promotion strategy, the fallacy of the composition argument becomes patently obvious. Indeed, it has been shown in a global general equilibrium model that the welfare benefits from export expansion are greater, not less, when all developing countries expand simultaneously (Martin, 1992). As for the threat of protectionism, it must never be taken lightly; but based on the export performance of developing countries in manufactured goods, it is difficult to infer that industrial country protection was a binding constraint (Balassa, 1990).

A NEW CONSENSUS

Export Promotion Strategy

Development economics in the 1950s provided intellectual justification for the dirigisme course that political leaders in developing countries began to chart at the end of World War II; in the 1960s, that course was altered in a number of countries with unexpected success, and true to form, "academic scribblers" came forward to demonstrate that what works in practice also works in theory. Taiwan, South Korea, and thereafter, a growing number of countries demonstrated that removing some, but not all, trade restrictions and other impediments to exporting led to higher growth rates. What Taiwan and Korea discovered by trial and error became christened the "export promotion strategy," and since then it has achieved the status of orthodoxy in development policy circles.

The new consensus that emerged from the relative success of countries pursuing the export promotion strategy has been characterized by Ian Little (1982) as a "neo-classical resurgence" and more vividly by Deepak Lal (1988) as a victory of "markets over mandarins." Certainly the price mechanism is given more prominence under the export promotion strategy, but it is anything but laissez-faire or even free trade. The export promotion strategy does not rule out import-substitution as an appropriate strategy in the early phase of industrialization, and it is consistent with *selective* import-substitution in later phases.

What constitutes an export promotion strategy, according to Jagdish Bhagwati, one of its leading proponents, is simply the equality of the *average* effective exchange rate for exports (EER_X) and the *average* effective exchange rate for imports (EER_M). This Bhagwati (1988) calls a "trade-neutral or bias-free" strategy. In contrast, the import-substitution strategy is defined as a system of incentives in which $EER_M > EER_X$, while $EER_M < EER_X$ is termed the "ultra-export promotion" strategy. The export promotion strategy is not to be confused with a free trade strategy, which implies equality of effective exchange rates for each and every branch of industry, not just equality on average for broad aggregates of import-competing and exporting industries. As Bhagwati (1988) notes:

We also need to remember always that the average EER_X and EER_M can and do conceal very substantial variations among different exports and among different imports. . . . Thus, within the broad aggregates of an [export promotion] country case, there may well be

Figure 2.5
Alternative Trade Strategies

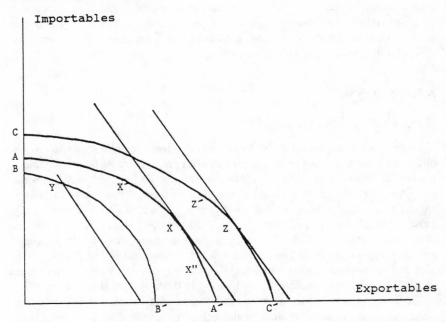

activities that are being import substituted (i.e., their EER$_M$ exceeds the average EER$_X$). Indeed, there often are. (p. 93)

The export promotion strategy is illustrated and contrasted with alternative trade strategies in Figure 2.5. The condition that, on average, EER$_X$ = EER$_M$ is shown at point X on the production possibility set AA′, where the opportunity cost of producing exports in terms of foregone production of import-competing goods is equal to the average relative price of exports and imports in world markets, shown by tan θ. At point X′ the average EER$_X$ < EER$_M$, which is the hallmark of the import substitution strategy, while at X″ the average EER$_X$ > EER$_M$, which is in the case of the ultra-export promotion strategy.

The import substitution strategy is associated not only with a high average EER$_M$ but also with relatively high dispersion of EER$_M$s around the average. This results from the way the import substitution strategy has been implemented, relying extensively on quantitative import restrictions and other exchange controls associated with an overvalued exchange rate. The consequence has been a chaotic pattern of differential protection for thousands of import-competing activities and, as a result, the creation of valuable rents accruing to those who get licenses to import. In such circumstances, the premiums on imports are often worth more than the imports themselves, which leads to widespread "rent-seeking," in which resources are diverted from producing goods and services into activities aimed at acquiring licenses, reducing the country's production possibilities (Krueger, 1974; Bhagwati, 1982).

Rent-seeking takes place everywhere, but there is reason (and some empirical evidence) to believe that it is more widespread under the import substitution strategy than under the export promotion strategy. The first step in implementing an export promotion strategy is usually a unification and devaluation of the exchange rate, which reduces to some extent the premiums on imports and foreign exchange that accrue under the import substitution strategy. The export promotion strategy also requires a certain amount of trade liberalization, resulting in a lower overall level of protection and often the substitution of tariffs for quantitative restrictions, which also reduce or eliminate rents.

Since rent-seeking is likely to be more extensive and costly under the import substitution strategy than under the export promotion strategy, the contrast between the two, as illustrated in Figure 2.5 by comparing points X and X', understates the difference, since in practice the entire set of production possibilities is likely to be lower under the import substitution strategy. Therefore, the contrast is better illustrated by comparing point X on AA' (under the export promotion strategy) with point Y on BB' (under the import substitution strategy).

Moreover, given that the export promotion strategy is consistent with a substantial amount of policy-induced distortions, the notion that the strategy is "trade-neutral or bias-free" is valid only in a limited sense. A free trade strategy, which is associated with a still larger set of production possibilities (illustrated by point Z on CC' in Figure 2.5), could lead to a larger volume of exports and a larger proportion of output in the export sector than would obtain under the export promotion strategy. Indeed, an import substitution policy whose only instrument was the exchange rate or, equivalently, a uniform tariff cum export tax that creates a divergence between a *uniform* EER_M and a *uniform* EER_X (e.g., Z' on CC') could be associated with more exports and a more export-oriented economy than would result from an export promotion policy in which there were substantial policy-induced distortions.

Openness and Growth

The case for an export promotion strategy rests not so much on principles of theory as on what works in practice. Of all the stylized facts about development, by far the most robust is the empirical relation between overall economic growth and export growth. Nurkse, it will be recalled, argued that exports were the "engine" of growth in the United States and other "regions of recent settlement" in the nineteenth century. The experience of contemporary developing countries during the century prior to 1950 also indicates that transitions from extensive growth (where output growth just keeps up with population growth, i.e., $g = n$) to intensive growth (rising per capita income, i.e., $g > n$) were almost invariably export-led (Reynolds, 1983). The relation between export expansion and economic growth in developing countries is even stronger and better documented for the period since 1950.

The evidence for the recent period is of two kinds: (1) studies of trade and industrialization in individual countries over time;[15] and (2) cross-country studies of the determinants of growth.[16] The former are by far more persuasive, since there are so many fewer "other things" that need to be held constant in analyzing growth of a single country. Unfortunately, recent contributors to the literature on economic growth have generally ignored the wealth of information and knowledge contained in the country studies of trade and development. The country studies have received less attention than they deserve also because their results are difficult to summarize. Nonetheless, they do clearly establish that *changes* in policy, especially policies affecting a country's ability to participate in international trade, lead to changes in economic performance. The validity of these findings has sometimes been denied on grounds that protectionism is pervasive even in fast-growing, export-oriented countries, like Korea (Wade, 1988). This has led to an endless debate about whether the protectionism cup in export-oriented countries is half full or half empty, which is entirely beside the point since all that the empirical evidence purports to show is that *reducing* the level of protection and elevating the role of trade *raise* the rate of growth. It could be inferred that going further toward a policy of free trade would yield an even higher growth rate, but that is not necessary to make the point that classical cum neoclassical principles, especially that of comparative advantage, are relevant to developing countries.

Even though cross-country studies encounter serious methodological problems and data limitations, collectively they present a convincing argument for a positive relationship between openness and growth, since it seems no matter what method or data set is used in cross-country analysis, the relationship reveals itself.

The key problem is how to measure a country's openness to trade. The level of protection is impossible to measure precisely when quantitative restrictions are used alongside tariffs. Attempts have been made to classify countries as relatively open or relatively closed according to various criteria, but they are inevitably arbitrary (World Bank, 1987). Cross-country differences in level of traded-goods prices have been interpreted as a measure of openness, but there is always doubt that the goods whose prices are being compared internationally are sufficiently similar to make the comparisons meaningful (Dollar, 1990; Barro, 1991). The alternative is to use an ex post facto performance measure, such as the share of trade in gross national product (GNP) or the rate of growth of exports, as a proxy for openness, but this approach inevitably encounters an identification problem. A country that experiences rapid export growth certainly cannot be closed, but if that country's rapid export growth is associated with relatively rapid GDP growth, can one be sure that exports drive GDP and not the reverse?

The method used in most cross-country studies is to estimate a neoclassical

Figure 2.6
Trade Regime and Rates of Return in the Public and Private Sectors of LDCs

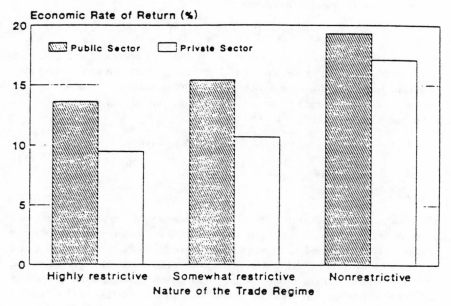

Source: Kaufmann (1991).

growth equation with some proxy for openness introduced as an additional explanatory variable:

$$g = a_0 + a_1 (I/Y) + a_2 n + a_3 \text{(openness)} \qquad (9)$$

If the coefficient for openness is found to be positive and significantly different from zero, then the hypothesis that more open countries grow faster is confirmed. A problem with this formulation is that it offers no insight as to how openness influences growth; indeed, it suggests implausibly that a country grows from being open even it does not invest or raise employment. It is likely, however, that one of the main reasons more open countries grow faster is that the return to investment is higher in more open countries where there are fewer distortions and less rent-seeking activity. This is, in fact, the finding of a recent study of economic rates of return on a set of about 1,200 projects undertaken by the World Bank and International Finance Corporation over the past twenty years in the public and private sectors in fifty-eight developing countries (Kaufmann, 1991). As shown in Figure 2.6, economic rates of return on investments in countries with nonrestrictive trade regimes were considerably higher than in countries with highly restrictive trade regimes.

This channel between openness and growth can be readily incorporated into the above regression model. If a linear relationship is assumed between openness and the return to investment, and if we take export growth (g_x) as a proxy for openness, then (9) can be rewritten as:

$$g = b_0 + [b_1 + b_2 g_x](I/Y) + b_3 n \tag{10}$$

where b_1 is the return to investment independent of openness and b_2 is the elasticity of the return to investment with respect to export growth. Fitting (10) to World Bank data for seventy-five developing countries (all for which data were available), with each variable expressed as a period average from 1965 to 1986, we obtain (t-statistics in parentheses):

$$g = [0.07 + 1.17 g_x](I/Y) + 0.75n$$
$$\qquad (3.05) \quad (7.00) \qquad\qquad (4.56) \tag{11}$$
$$R^2 = .61$$
$$F = 58.26$$

The constant term was omitted in (11) after it was found not to be significantly different from zero, thus confirming Scott's view that investment and labor force growth provide a complete explanation of growth, leaving no residual to be attributed to exogenous changes in technology. These results suggest that the return to investment rises about 1 percent for every percentage point increase in the rate of export growth. Thus, a country investing 20 percent of GNP whose labor force grows at 2 percent per annum and whose exports grow at 10 percent per annum will achieve an overall growth rate of slightly more than 5 percent, of which about half is attributable (according to the logic of this model) to openness. We hasten to caution that, given the limitations of the model and the data used to estimate it, these results are only suggestive of the effect of openness on growth. However, when considered together with the enormous weight of corroborating evidence, they leave little doubt about the importance of openness to international trade for growth in developing countries.

PERSPECTIVES ON THE ROLE OF GOVERNMENT

When Adam Smith wrote *An Inquiry into the Nature and Causes of the Wealth of Nations* ([1776] 1937), the world had produced very few instances of intensive growth (i.e., rising per capita income). The epoch-making British Industrial Revolution was only just getting under way, and looking backward at that time, one would have found only few, brief exceptions to the rule of economic stagnation throughout history. Yet Smith was extraordinarily optimistic about the world's potential for growth, as the following oft-cited quote attests:

Little else is requisite to carry a state to the highest degree of opulence from the lowest barbarism, but peace, easy taxes, and tolerable administration of justice; all the rest being brought about by the natural course of things (p. 60).

Smith's optimism proved correct, but his suggestion that growth comes naturally, provided the state takes care of its responsibilities, is widely disputed, to say the least. According to traditional development economics growth is not a plant that flourishes in nature, but rather is a hybrid that must be nurtured by government and protected from unfettered market forces. The "neoclassical resurgence" that emerged from the successes of the Asian NICs gives more scope to the market, but it largely retains the notion of growth as something that needs to be promoted by governments, rather than simply given a conducive environment, this despite the fact that most of what constitutes an export promotion policy is removing, or offsetting, obstacles that government itself put in the way of exporting.

After sifting through the accumulated historical evidence on 100 years of growth in forty-two contemporary developing countries, Lloyd Reynolds (1983) concluded, "My hypothesis is that the single most important explanatory variable is political organization and the administrative competence of government" (p. 976). On the face of it, this would seem to stand at odds with Smith's view of growth as doing what comes naturally. It is not a contradiction, however, since Smith's proposition carries the clearly stated caveat that everything follows naturally *provided that government plays its proper role,* which as set out by Smith ([1776] 1937) is not insubstantial:

According to the system of natural liberty, the sovereign has only three duties to attend to; three duties of great importance, indeed, but plain and intelligible to common understandings: first, the duty of protecting the society from the violence and invasion of other independent societies; secondly, the duty of protecting, as far as possible, every member of the society from the injustice or oppression of every other member of it, or the duty of establishing an exact administration of justice; and thirdly, the duty of erecting and maintaining certain public works and certain public institutions, which it can never be for the interest of any individual, or small number of individuals, to erect and maintain, because the profit could never repay the expense to any individual or small number of individuals, though it may frequently do much more than repay it to a great society. (p. 120)

Were Smith writing today, he would no doubt add a fourth duty of the sovereign: maintaining a stable macroeconomic environment.

Keeping the peace, operating a system of justice, supplying public goods, and maintaining macroeconomic stability are enormous responsibilities, which would strain the competence and administrative ability of the best of governments. Yet most, especially those in the developing world, undertake additional and even more complicated duties, including managing the system of incentives that guide private economic activity and directly producing nonpublic goods, such as steel, chemicals, and the like.

Failures to achieve an adequate rate of growth in developing countries have often been attributed to governments' all too obvious failures in the fifth area of involvement, but there is an identification problem here. Often the more ambitious a country's industrial policy, the less well it fulfills one or another of the first four duties of government, which is not surprising given limited resources and capabilities of most governments, especially in developing countries. Likewise, the developing countries that have grown fastest, in particular, the East Asian NICs, are often observed to be doing many of the same things that account for failure elsewhere, which then leads to an endless debate about whether industrial policy interventions are justified or not, when possibly the more relevant point is that if a country does a reasonably good job of supplying infrastructure, providing education, meting out justice, and maintaining macroeconomic stability, it can afford some unwise industrial policies without sacrificing too much growth. Reynolds is right, therefore, to give the credit for growth to government, if only because it can destroy the impulse for growth by failing to create an environment in which it can succeed.

The crucial importance of government does not invalidate the proposition that growth comes about "by the natural course of things." In order to refute this, one would have to find instances where government provided a conducive environment but where growth failed to occur, perhaps because of cultural impediments or other obstacles. This suggests that in trying to understand growth it might be more fruitful to look for the causes of failure rather than for the causes of success, which the literature indicates are many and vary from time to time and place to place.

This is precisely the approach advocated by the economic historian E.L. Jones (1988), who looked back at the apparent stagnation of most of history and found, beneath the surface, a persistent propensity for growth, but one that managed to assert itself on only a few occasions, as in Sung China (A.D. 960–1126) and Tokugawa Japan (A.D. 1603–1868). The negative force that suppressed the tendency for growth throughout the vast history of China, India, and the Middle East, according to Jones, is found "not in the absence of desire or effort but in grasping by rulers and governments and the secondary consequences of their acts, as well as their failure to create institutions conducive to change" (p. 189). As Jones sums it up, "Economic history may be thought of as a struggle between a propensity for growth and one for rent-seeking, that is, for someone improving his or her position, or a group bettering its position, at the expense of the general welfare" (p. 1).

Growth won out in this struggle only briefly a few times in premodern history. Its greatest triumph was the Industrial Revolution and the spread of industrialization subsequently throughout the world. These successes were possible only after limits were imposed on the power of rulers and governments, dispersing their power and allowing market forces to develop. Nevertheless, in every country, developed and developing, the struggle between the propensities for growth and for rent-seeking goes on, each having the potential to crowd the other out, with the outcome determined for the most part in the realm of politics rather than economics.

NOTES

Thanks are due to Mr. Luis Terrassa for research assistance and to Max Corden, Judy Dean, Isaiah Frank, Morris Morkre, and Enzo Grilli for helpful comments and suggestions on an earlier draft.

1. This assumes no capital depreciation, an issue that is taken up later.

2. Setting $\Delta d/d = f/d - g = 0$, we get, $f = gd$, which, when substituted into (2), gives (3).

3. Full employment of both labor and capital requires $g = n = s/k$, or $s = nk$. Since n, s, and k are independently fixed, the model is dynamically unstable.

4. For a survey of the development of the theory, see Hahn and Matthews (1964).

5. This result is inevitable when the growth accounting framework is applied to a country with steady growth of per capita output and a relatively large share of value added going to labor, which is the case for most developed countries at least. When growth is steady, output and capital grow at the same rate. Under this condition (i.e., $g = \Delta K/K$), equation (4) simplifies to $g = n + (1/\beta)a$, which implies that $a/(g - n) = \beta$, that is, the proportion of income growth attributable to technical change is equal to labor's share of value-added.

6. Lucas (1990) uses this example to illustrate this anomaly of the Solow model.

7. There is evidence of convergence among industrial countries, but not among a broader set of countries. See Baumol (1986); Abramovitz (1986); and Dowrick and Gemmell (1991).

8. Attempts have been made within the neoclassical growth framework to differentiate capital assets according to their vintage. However, these models turn out to have the very same properties as the standard version of the Solow-Swan model.

9. For a detailed discussion of the content and origins of development economics, see Hirschman (1981); Lal (1983); Sen (1983); Riedel (1987); Chenery and Srinivasan (1988, 1989); Ranis and Schultz (1988); Stern (1989); and World Bank, *World Development Report* (1991).

10. This idea has been formulated in the context of an endogenous growth model in Murphy, Schleifer, and Vishney (1989).

11. Ex post, these are the identities of national income accounting $(I - S - F = 0)$ and balance of payments accounting $(X - M + F = 0)$.

12. Growth in the two other large countries that launched ambitious import-substitution industrialization programs, Brazil and Mexico, was slightly underestimated by both authors. However, both Brazil and Mexico made major policy shifts in the late 1960s and early 1970s, while the South Asian countries adhered more faithfully to the import-substitution strategy.

13. Kravis (1970) convincingly refutes this argument, showing that trade was more like a "handmaiden" than an "engine" of growth in the nineteenth century and that demand conditions for LDC exports were even more favorable in the twentieth century than they were in the nineteenth century.

14. Most econometric estimates of the demand parameters facing LDC exports are misleading: indeed, the conventional estimation procedure rules out finding evidence of price-taking in export markets. If the inverse export demand function is estimated, coun-

tries that appear to face a price-elastic demand schedule are often found to be price-takers in world markets. See Riedel (1984, 1988a, 1991).

15. See, for example, Little, Scitovsky, and Scott (1970); Balassa (1971); Donges and Riedel (1977); Bhagwati (1978); and Krueger (1978).

16. See, for example, Balassa (1978); Barro (1991); Dollar (1990); Feder (1983); Jung and Marshall (1985); Michaely (1977); Ram (1985); Salvatore (1983); and Tyler (1981).

REFERENCES

Abramovitz, M. 1986. "Catching Up, Foreigners Ahead and Falling Behind." *Journal of Economic History* 46: 385–406.

Arrow, K.J. 1962. "The Economic Implications of Learning by Doing." *Review of Economic Studies* 29: 155–73.

Athukorala, P., and Riedel, J. 1991. "The Small Country Assumption: A Reassessment with Evidence from Korea." *Weltwirtschaftliches Archiv*, Band 127, Heft1: 138–51.

Balassa, B. 1971. *The Structure of Protection in Developing Countries*. Baltimore: Johns Hopkins University Press.

———. 1978. "Exports and Economic Growth: Further Evidence." *Journal of Economic Development* 26: 181–89.

———. 1990. "U.S. Trade Policy Toward Developing Countries." In *The Direction of Trade Policy*, edited by C. Pearson and J. Riedel. Oxford: Basil Blackwell.

Barro, R.J. 1991. "Economic Growth in a Cross-Section of Countries." *Quarterly Journal of Economics* 70: 407–43.

Baumol, W.J. 1986. "Productivity Growth, Convergence and Welfare: What the Long-Run Data Show." *American Economic Review* 76: 1072–85.

Bell, M., Ross-Larson, B., and Westphal, L. 1984. "Assessing the Performance of Infant Industries." *Journal of Development Economics* 16: 101–28.

Bhagwati, J.N. 1978. *Anatomy and Consequences of Trade Control Regimes*. New York: National Bureau of Economic Research.

———. 1982. "Directly Unproductive Profit-Seeking (DUP) Activities." *Journal of Political Economy* 90: 988–1002.

———. 1988. "Export-Promoting Trade Strategy: Issues and Evidence." *World Bank Research Observer*, 2: 27–57.

Chenery, H.B., and Bruno, M. 1962. "Development Alternatives in an Open Economy: The Case of Israel." *Economic Journal*, 72: 519–529.

Chenery, H., and Strout, A. 1966. "Foreign Assistance and Economic Development." *American Economic Review* 56: 679–733.

Chenery, H.B., and Srinivasan, T.N., eds. 1989. *The Handbook of Development Economics*. Amsterdam: North-Holland.

Corden, W.M. 1985. "The Effect of Trade on the Rate of Growth." In *Trade, Balance of Payments and Growth*, edited by J.N. Bhagwati et al. Amsterdam: North-Holland.

Denison, E.F. 1985. *Trends in American Economic Growth: 1929–1982*. Washington, D.C.: Brookings Institution.

———. 1991. "Scott's *A New View of Economic Growth:* A Review Article." *Oxford Economic Papers* 43: 224–36.

Dollar, D. 1990. "Outward Orientation and Growth: An Empirical Study Using a Price-Based Measure of Openness." World Bank, Washington, D.C. Mimeo.

Donges, J.B., and Riedel, J. 1977. "Expansion of Manufactured Exports in Developing Countries: An Empirical Assessment of Supply and Demand Issues." *Weltwirtschaftliches Archiv* 113: 58–87.

Dowrick, S., and Gemmell, N. 1991. "Industrialization, Catching Up and Economic Growth: A Comparative Study Across the World's Capitalist Economies." *Economic Journal* 101: 263–75.

Easterly, W. 1991. "Economic Stagnation, Fixed Factors and Policy Thresholds." World Bank, Washington, D.C. Mimeo.

Feder, G. 1983. "On Exports and Economic Growth." *Journal of Development Economics* 31: 35–74.

Grilli, E.R., and Yang, M.C. 1988. "Primary Commodity Prices, Manufactured Goods Prices, and the Terms of Trade of Developing Countries: What the Long Run Shows." *World Bank Review* 2: 1–48.

Grossman, G.M., and Helpman, E. 1990. "Comparative Growth and Long-Term Growth." *American Economic Review* 80: 796–815.

———. 1991. "Growth and Welfare in a Small Open Economy." In *International Trade and Trade Policy*, edited by E. Helpman and A. Razin. Cambridge: MIT Press.

Hahn, F.H., and Matthews, R.C.O. 1964. "The Theory of Economic Growth: A Survey." *Economic Journal* 74: 37–49.

Hirschman, A.O. 1958. *The Strategy of Economic Development*. New Haven, Conn.: Yale University Press.

———. 1981. *Essays in Trespassing: Economics to Politics and Beyond*. Cambridge: Cambridge University Press.

Hughes, H., and Krueger, A.O. 1984. "Effects of Protection in Developed Countries on Developing Countries." In *The Structure and Evolution of Recent U.S. Trade Policy*, edited by R. Baldwin and A. Krueger. Chicago: University of Chicago Press.

Lewis, W.A. 1954. "Economic Development with Unlimited Supplies of Labor." *Manchester School* Vol. 22.

Jones, E.L. 1988. *Growth Recurring: Economic Change in World History*. Oxford: Clarendon Press.

Jung, W., and Marshall, P. 1985. "Exports, Growth and Causality in Developing Countries." *Journal of Development Economics* 18: 1–12.

Kaufmann, D. 1991. "The Forgotten Rationale for Policy Reform: The Productivity of Investment." Background Paper for 1991 World Development Report. World Bank, Washington, D.C.

Kravis, I.B. 1970. "Trade as the Handmaiden of Growth: Similarities Between the Nineteenth and Twentieth Centuries." *Economic Journal* 80: 850–70.

Krueger, A.O. 1974. "The Political Economy of the Rent-Seeking Society." *American Economic Review* 64: 291–303.

———. 1978. *Liberalization Attempts and Consequences*. New York: National Bureau of Economic Research.

———. 1990. "Government Failures in Development." *Journal of Economic Perspectives* 4: 9–24.

Krueger, A.O., and Tuncer, B. 1982. "An Empirical Test of the Infant Industry Argument." *American Economic Review* 72: 1142–52.

Lal, Deepak. 1983. *The Poverty of Development Economics*. London: Institute of International Affairs.

———. 1988. "Markets, Mandarins and Mathematicians." *Cato Journal* 8: 225–39.

Lewis, W.A. 1955. *The Theory of Economic Growth*. London: Allen and Unwin.

———. 1980. "The Slowing Down of the Engine of Growth." *American Economic Review* 70: 555–64.

Little, I.M.D. 1982. *Economic Development: Theory, Policy and International Relations*. New York: Basic Books.

Little, I.M.D., Scitovsky, T., and Scott, M.F.G. 1970. *Industry and Trade in Some Developing Countries*. Oxford: Oxford University Press.

Lucas, R. E., Jr. 1988. "On the Mechanics of Economic Development." *Journal of Monetary Economics* 19: 3–42.

———. 1990. "Why Doesn't Capital Flow from Rich to Poor Countries?" *American Economic Review* 80: 92–96.

Martin, Will. 1992. "The Fallacy of Composition and Developing Country Exports of Manufactures." World Bank, International Trade Division, Washington, D.C.

Michaely, M. 1977. "Exports and Growth: An Empirical Investigation." *Journal of Development Economics* 25: 49–53.

Morawetz, D. 1977. *Twenty-Five Years of Economic Development: 1950 to 1975*. Washington, D.C.: World Bank.

Murphy, K., Schleifer, A., and Vishney, R. 1989. "Industrialization and the Big Push." *Journal of Political Economy* 97: 1003–26.

Myrdal, G. 1958. *Economic Theory and Underdeveloped Regions*. London: Duckworth.

Nurkse, R. 1953. *Problems of Capital Formation in Underdeveloped Countries*. Oxford: Basil Blackwell.

———. 1959. *Patterns of Trade and Development*. Stockholm: Almquist and Wicksell.

Prebisch, R. 1950. *The Economic Development of Latin America and Its Principal Problems*. New York: United Nations.

Ram, R. 1985. "Exports and Economic Growth: Some Additional Evidence." *Economic Development and Cultural Change* 12: 59–74.

Ranis, G., and Schultz, T. P. 1988. *The State of Development Economics*. Oxford: Basil Blackwell.

Rebelo, S. 1991. "Long-Run Policy Analysis and Long-Run Growth." *Journal of Political Economy* 99: 500–521.

Reynolds, L.G. 1983. "The Spread of Economic Growth to the Third World: 1850–1980." *Journal of Economic Literature* 21: 941–80.

Riedel, J. 1984. "Trade as an Engine of Growth, Revisited." *Economic Journal* 94: 56–73.

———. 1987. *Myths and Reality of External Constraints on Development*. London: Gower, for the Trade Policy Research Centre.

———. 1988a. "Demand for LDC Exports of Manufactures: Estimates from Hong Kong." *Economic Journal* 98: 138–48.

———. 1988b. "Economic Development in East Asia: Doing What Comes Naturally?" In *Achieving Industrialization in East Asia*, edited by H. Hughes. Cambridge: Cambridge University Press.

———. 1989. "Demand for LDC Exports of Manufactures: A Rejoinder." *Economic Journal* 99: 467–71.

———. 1990. "The State of Debate on Trade and Industrialization in Developing Countries." In *The Direction of Trade Policy,* edited by C. Pearson and J. Riedel. Oxford: Basil Blackwell.

Romer, P.M. 1986. "Increasing Returns and Long-Run Growth." *Journal of Political Economy* 94: 1002–38.

———. 1990. "Endogenous Technical Change." *Journal of Political Economy* 98: S71–S102.

Rosenstein-Rodan, P. 1943. "Problems of Industrialization of Eastern and South-Eastern Europe." *Economic Journal* 53: 202–11.

———. 1961. "International Aid for Underdeveloped Countries." *Review of Economics and Statistics* 43: 107–38.

Salvatore, D. 1983. "A Simultaneous Equations Model of Trade and Development with Dynamic Policy Simulations." *Kyklos* 36: 66–90.

Scitovsky, T. 1954. "Two Concepts of External Economies." *Journal of Political Economy* 62: 143–51.

Scott, M.F.G. 1989a. "Can Short-Term Macroeconomic Policy Affect Long-Term Economic Growth?" Nuffield College Oxford. Mimeo.

———. 1989b. *A New View of Economic Growth.* Oxford: Clarendon Press.

———. 1991. "A Reply to Denison." *Oxford Economic Papers* 43: 237–44.

Sen, A. 1983. "Development: Which Way Now?" *Economic Journal* 93: 745–62.

Singer, H.W. 1950. "The Distribution of Gains Between Investing and Borrowing Countries." *American Economic Review* 2: 473–85.

Smith, A. 1776. *An Inquiry into the Nature and Causes of the Wealth of Nations.* Toronto: Random House Edition, 1937.

Solow, R.M. 1956. "A Contribution to the Theory of Economic Growth." *Quarterly Journal of Economics* 70: 65–94.

———. 1957. "Technical Change and the Aggregate Production Function." *Review of Economics and Statistics* 39: 312–20.

Stern, N.H. 1989. "The Economics of Development: A Survey." *Economic Journal* 99: 597–685.

———. 1991. "Public Policy and the Economics of Development." *European Economic Review* 35: 241–71.

Stokey, N.L. 1991. "Human Capital, Product Quality, and Growth." *Quarterly Journal of Economics* 96: 587–616.

Syrquin, M., and Chenery, H. B. 1989. "Three Decades of Industrialization." *World Bank Economic Review* 2: 145–82.

Tyler, W.G. 1981. "Growth and Export Expansion in Developing Countries." *Journal of Development Economics* 9: 121–30.

Wade, R. 1988. "The Role of Government in Overcoming Market Failure: Taiwan, South Korea and Japan." In *Achieving Industrialization in East Asia,* edited by H. Hughes. Cambridge: Cambridge University Press.

World Bank. 1987. *World Development Report.* Washington, D.C.

———. 1991. *World Development Report.* Washington, D.C.

———. 1992. *World Development Report.* Washington, D.C.

Young, A. 1991. "Learning by Doing and the Dynamic Effects of International Trade." *Quarterly Journal of Economics* 96: 367–405.

PART II

THE RECORD OF ECONOMIC DEVELOPMENT: AGGREGATE AND SECTORAL

3

LONG-TERM ECONOMIC GROWTH, INCOME DISTRIBUTION, AND POVERTY IN DEVELOPING COUNTRIES: THE EVIDENCE

Enzo Grilli

In his book on the economic evolution of the Third World, one of the first systematic attempts to look at the long-term growth and development of less-developed countries,[1] Paul Bairoch observed that at the time there was not a study "which might help to single out the various characteristics of economic development . . . over a long enough period" (1967, p. 1). If by "long enough period" one means a century or more, this is still largely the case today, notwithstanding the efforts made by many researchers to clarify at least the evolution of some of the main economic variables: real output, population, and external trade.[2]

Apart from the countries of Latin America, which gained independence earlier than most others in the developing world, and a few in Africa (e.g., Egypt, Liberia, and South Africa) and in Asia (e.g., China and Thailand), which, owing to special circumstances, either escaped outright colonization or maintained a larger than usual degree of autonomy under it, the comparative record of development is still incomplete in many important aspects up to the middle of the present century. Even such basic indicators as aggregate output and population are often unavailable or subject to wide margins of error. Social conditions remain largely undocumented, except for the past thirty or so years.

In this chapter, I assemble the available evidence on economic growth in the developing world for over a century. A particular effort is made to integrate existing and consolidated knowledge about the basic evolution of the main developing economies in Asia and Latin America since 1870[3] with old and new information concerning economic growth in Africa, the region with the poorest statistical record and the largest remaining gaps even for such basic economic indicators as the size of the indigenous population and the rate at which it increased over time (Munro, 1976, p. 20). In addition, the chapter brings together what is known about the distribution of income and the evolution of poverty since about 1960 and examines them in the light of the growth experience of the developing countries to which they apply.

Despite its main focus on output, the chapter does not address specifically such important issues as the reasons for the differentials in the timing and speed of growth between industrial and developing countries (the convergence/divergence problem) or the determinants of the growth of either group in "a neoclassical" or "new growth theory" framework. Its aims in these areas are more documentative and analytically basic, namely: (1) to set out the record of long-term output growth in developing countries and relate it to that of the rest of the world; (2) to order and compare the growth record of individual developing countries and groups; (3) to show the broad correlations among the rates of output growth in developing countries, their economic structures, and some of the basic policy strategies that they followed; and (4) to examine the relationship among economic growth, the distribution of income, and poverty in a large sample of them. Neither systematic growth accounting nor formal testing of alternative growth hypotheses is attempted here.

LONG-TERM OUTPUT AND POPULATION GROWTH IN DEVELOPING COUNTRIES: THE BROAD PICTURE

The International Context

The main economic tendencies in the countries now considered industrialized, roughly those of Western Europe, North America, Japan, and Australia-New Zealand, during the last hundred years are now reasonably well known. The painstaking work of Maddison (1982, 1989) has shed considerable light on global long-term trends: real output, measured as gross domestic product (GDP), increased in these countries at 2.7 percent a year between 1870 and 1913 (what we may call, with some approximation, the "Victorian" period); at 2.1 percent a year between 1913 and 1950 (the years of the world wars and reconstruction); at nearly 4.4 percent a year between 1950 and 1973 (the "golden" period); and at 2.7 percent a year in the period 1973 to 1990 (the "post-oil shock," or adjustment, years) (Figure 3.1).

Expansion of output in industrial countries, moreover, was remarkably steady during the "Victorian" period and again in the "golden" decades of the 1950s and 1960s but fluctuated a lot more in the middle period, when two world wars and the post-1929 Great Depression interrupted much of the normal flows of world trade and finance (Kindleberger, 1973) and industrial production became mostly driven by the war needs of the key military contenders in Europe and North America. Output also fluctuated considerably between 1973 and 1990, when three successive oil shocks (two negative and one positive for most of these countries) caused large changes in their terms of trade. Yet, the data show that the underlying long-term trend of real output in industrial countries has

Figure 3.1
Real GDP Growth in Industrial and Developing Countries, 1870–1990

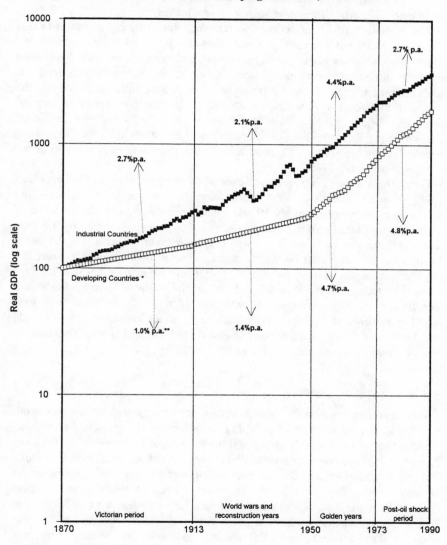

Sources: Maddison (1991); Table A 3.1.
*Growth for the periods 1870–1913 and 1913–1950 is represented only at end points as data for
   each intervening year are not available.
**Rough estimate.

remained around 2.5 percent per year since 1870, with the exception of the "golden" years, the only major phase of their recent growth during which rates were achieved and maintained. Quite striking, as observed by Boltho (1987, p. 18), is the return of industrial economies after 1973 to what appears to be their long-term growth trend in aggregate production.

The trend of growth of population remained fairly steady in industrialized countries, at around 1 percent per year, between 1870 and 1970 (Figure 3.2).[4] The main tendencies of per capita real output and income were thus determined by the evolution of overall production. Per capita real output growth declined, in fact, from 1.6 to 1.3 percent per year between the Victorian period and the period of the world wars and accelerated to 3.4 percent per year in the twenty-year span following World War II. Since the early 1970s, instead, continued decline in the rate of expansion of population contributed to offset the strong deceleration in the growth of output in industrial countries, maintaining it above 2 percent per year.

Given the absolute preponderance exerted by the economies of the industrialized (or rapidly industrializing, to be historically more precise) countries in the world economy since the early 1900s, what happened to them can be taken as a close approximation of the external economic environment faced by the less-developed ones in the following years. The semideveloped countries of Eastern Europe and Russia were in actuality either too small or too closed to exert any large effect on the rest of the world. Moreover, when they became socialist (Russia by the end of the World War I and much of Central Europe after World War II), they uniformly pursued a growth strategy of state-based, heavy-industry-led development in a close-economy framework, which kept to a minimum trade and financial relations with the world outside the socialist block. The same is true of China from the early 1950s to the late 1970s.[5]

The Developing Countries

It is, therefore, against this background of economic growth in the industrialized world that the record of developing countries must be evaluated and understood. Many of them were still colonial possessions of European states for more than half of the period under review[6] and did not emerge as autonomous economic and political entities until the late 1950s. Some of the developing countries, as we know them today, were not even precisely identified during substantial portions of both the past and current centuries, having been parts of larger and changeable colonial aggregations, often drawn up (and redrawn) for the convenience of the colonial powers that administered them. This is true of numerous countries in Africa (e.g., French West Africa and British East and Southern Africas), but the phenomenon was by no means limited to that continent. In Asia, Indochina was also largely a French colonial aggregation.

For these and other reasons, reconstructing even the basic economic features of the economies of many developing countries before their independence is

Figure 3.2
Population Growth in Industrial and Developing Countries, 1850–1990

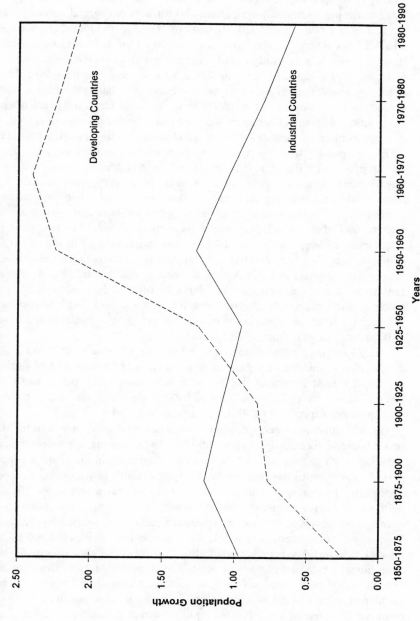

Sources: McEvedy and Jones (1978) for the period 1850–1950; Table 3.4 for the period 1950–1990.

quite difficult, and some subjective judgment in doing so is inevitable. Colonial records, generally adequate for tradable goods (agricultural and mining exports), usually developed by metropolitan capital, are most often wholly inadequate for subsistence (or traditional) agriculture and for noncommercial services that remained in the domain of local populations. For most colonial administrators, what did not emerge in the "modern" sector of the territorial possessions of their countries was generally not of great interest and thus not worth measuring. Even population data are very unreliable for many colonial territories. In most cases, censuses of population were not conducted until late in the current century; when taken, the pollings of residents in the colonial territories were often unsystematic, and results from them were often unreliable. As a consequence, most population figures available for Africa (and most of Asia as well) until the early 1900s are so shaky that experts consider them guesses at best (see, e.g., Durand, 1967a, pp. 19–20; Bairoch, 1967, p. 6). While these limitations are well known, they become particularly relevant to any attempt to survey growth in the developing world over the long term and are thus worth emphasizing at the outset.

From the available evidence, real output appears to have expanded at a positive rate in most of the developing world between 1870 and 1913 (Figure 3.1), if much more slowly than in industrial countries and not significantly above that of population. The only notable and statistically credible exception to this tendency is to be found in Latin America, where political stability was achieved a few decades after independence and large inflows of European capital spurred output growth, especially in agriculture during this period.[7] An optimistic guess is that real output per capita in the whole of developing countries may have risen at 0.4 percent a year from 1870 to 1913 (Table 3.1).

Overall output continued to advance between 1913 and 1950, but a strong acceleration in the rate of expansion of population and a concomitant slowdown in that of output in two of the largest economies of Asia (India and China), largely caused by political-military turmoil, appear to have nearly halted the growth of per capita real GDP in the developing world at large.[8]

The first episode of general, high, and sustained output growth in the developing countries occurred between 1950 and 1973, starting when decolonization went into high gear in Africa and Asia and continuing in the postindependence period roughly until the first oil shock. Real output growth during this period exceeded 5 percent a year in Asian countries and was nearly 4 percent a year in those of Africa. Continuation of growth in Latin America caused overall output in the developing world to expand at 5 percent per year during this period. Despite a further substantial acceleration in the rate at which population expanded, as mortality rates dropped almost everywhere with improving health conditions, a typical behavior in periods of demographic transition, such fast growth of real output was sufficient to sustain an overall rate of increase in per capita real income of 2.6 percent a year (Table 3.1). If not as fast as in industrial countries (because of a much more rapid growth of population), the increase in per capita real income achieved in most developing countries meant that for

Table 3.1
Industrial[a] and Developing[b] Countries: Growth of GDP,[c] Population, and Per Capita GDP, 1870–1990

	1870-1913	1913-1950	1950-1973	1973-1990
	(----------Average Annual Rates, %----------)			
Real GDP				
Industrial Countries	2.69	2.12	4.43	2.70
Developing Countries	1.05	1.42	4.75	4.79
Population				
Industrial Countries	1.10	0.86	1.06	0.62
Developing Countries	0.63	1.22	2.19	1.89
Real GDP Per Capita				
Industrial Countries	1.59	1.26	3.37	2.08
Developing Countries	0.42	0.20	2.56	2.90

Sources: Maddison (1982, 1992); OECD, *Main Economic Indicators* (various issues); and Table A 3.1.
[a]Countries now belonging to OECD (excluding Yugoslavia).
[b]The total is for a sample of countries accounting for 71 percent of developing countries' overall output in 1950. See Table A 3.1 for its composition.
[c]Growth rates for the two early periods were calculated using end points; for the latter two periods, using three-year average end points.

many of them outside East Asia and Latin America the transition to what Reynolds (1983, p. 843) calls "intensive growth" finally occurred.[9]

For the developing countries as a whole the years between 1973 and 1990 saw a further acceleration in the growth of their per capita output—to 2.9 percent a year, an average performance superior for the first time since 1870 to that of industrial countries (Table 3.1). However, as shown in greater detail in the next section, the variance in the growth performance of the various regions increased considerably during this period, and the weighted average reported here is largely the result of exceptional expansion of output in Asia, while much of the rest of the developing world stagnated or experienced economic stagnation or decline.

On the whole, the correlation between per capita real output growth in industrial and developing countries appears to have been quite strong since 1870. Fast growth in the industrial world during the "Victorian" period probably corresponded to a phase of reasonably good growth in developing countries (or at least in those for which economic records are available and credible). The slower pace of per capita growth in the most industrialized parts of the world, especially in Europe, in the periods subsequent to the two world conflicts, as well as during the Great Depression years, was also apparently paralleled by a deceleration in developing countries (even though one must consider that the base period from which their growth is measured is subject to a wide margin of error). With less uncertainty about the statistical record,[10] one can also observe

Table 3.2
Growth of Real Per Capita GDP in Developing Countries[a] by Main Geographical Regions

		1870-1913	1913-1950	1950-1973	1973-1990
		(----------Average Annual Rates, %----------)			
AFRICA		0.68	1.14	2.30	0.02
of which:	North Africa	0.65	0.74	2.08	2.15
	South of Sahara	0.95	1.36	2.38	-0.95
ASIA		0.30	-0.36	2.20	4.72
LATIN AMERICA		1.13	1.33	2.88	1.12

Source: Table A 3.1.
[a]Based on the same sample of developing countries as Table 3.1 and calculated by the same method.

how the strong acceleration in the pace of per capita output growth that occurred between 1950 and 1973 in industrial countries corresponded to an even stronger surge in the developing world (Figure 3.1). The "golden" years did witness very favorable economic performance in both industrial and developing countries. If these years did not appear "golden" to many people in developing nations, when compared with the starting economic and social conditions,[11] they constituted nonetheless a period of unprecedented output growth, in both overall and per capita terms, for much of the developing world (Table 3.2 and Table A3.1).

The correlation of the growth trend of per capita real output between industrial and developing countries seems to have weakened considerably during the past two decades. If the 1973–1990 period is considered as a whole, apparently corresponding to the growth slowdown in industrial economies that started after the first oil shock is a modest increase in the pace of growth of economic activity in the developing world. But variance in the growth of the three main developing regions was high during these years, as sharp slowdowns in output occurred in at least two of them.[12] This indicates that the correlation between the worsening economic performance in industrial countries and that of developing countries in the 1973–1990 period is still more important than what aggregate trends show.

The broad empirical regularities observed in the growth performance of industrial and developing countries since 1870, interesting as they may appear in themselves and also nicely fitting into a center-periphery economic dependence framework, should nonetheless be viewed with some caution. Not only is their factual basis somewhat shaky until the 1950s, but even in the most recent periods, the differences that have emerged in the growth performance of the main developing regions over the past hundred or so years, as well as the wide range of outcomes among the countries of each region, counsel prudence in drawing general conclusions about causalities.[13]

In the interwar period, for example, the economic performance of various developing areas seems to have been connected in no small way to specific conditions, including geographical location. Africa and Latin America, which escaped the direct effects of the last two major wars among the main developed nations, did better economically than Asia, where the second world conflict, as well as its antecedents and aftermath, negatively affected economic outcomes. In the 1970–1990 period, moreover, growth in the developing world varied across countries depending on the effects exerted by external factors such as the rise in the prices of petroleum (and the terms of trade consequences that they generated, obviously different for oil-exporting and oil-importing countries), as well as by internal policy decisions such as those concerning external borrowing in the 1970s and macroeconomic adjustment in the 1980s. The consequences of the debt crisis, which in itself was not unconnected to the economic policies and performance of the major industrialized nations, were much more severe for the more highly exposed and debt-service-laden developing countries of Latin America than for their generally less exposed and less heavily saddled counterparts in East Asia.[14] Here, too, however, policies affected actual performance. The Asian countries grew much faster also because they adjusted earlier and more rapidly to their debt difficulties and the changing external environment than the countries of Latin America and Africa.

Growth patterns in the developing world became particularly differentiated during the 1980s, with the two largest economies of Asia—China and India—doing well (and much better than in the previous decades)[15] and the export-oriented smaller economies of East Asia continuing to expand at a very fast pace, while growth of output nearly collapsed in South Saharan Africa and in much of Latin America and also decelerated drastically in Southern Europe and North Africa.

Aggregations, in other words, hide many important differences in economic performance, due to both external forces, such as the differential effects exerted by growth in industrial countries and exogenous terms of trade shocks, and internal factors, such as the different policies implemented in each developing nation. Neither set of conditions can be subsumed by the other, even though during the past twenty years the policy-performance nexus has become an increasingly apparent and accepted factor in explaining differences in country economic outcomes.

LONG-TERM GROWTH IN DEVELOPING COUNTRIES: A MORE DISAGGREGATED VIEW

Marked differences in the economic performance of developing nations are evident from the available statistics covering the past 120 years. Some of them have already been mentioned. Yet, in the variety of country experiences, one finds the most interesting aspects of the economic growth record. To say that developing countries represent a very composite reality is almost commonplace.

Differences among them are as wide in natural endowments, economic structures, and social systems as in growth strategies and specific policies pursued and, of course, in results obtained over time. Sector performance has also varied a great deal from country to country and region to region, as, for example, the differences in the growth of food output between South Asia and Africa or in the pace of industrial development between East and South Asia. No matter how evident and important these differences are, even the best-known students of economic development have shown at one time or another how easily they can be overlooked.

The very complexity of the universe of developing countries forces us to aggregate and generalize so as to be able to transmit some summary view or, even more basically, to convey factual pictures that can be grasped without undue difficulty. But much of the interest that arises from this universe lies precisely in the variety of situations and outcomes that it contains. One must, therefore, always try to strike a balance between the requirements of significance and precision in the proposed facts (or interpretations) and those of usefulness and intelligibility of what is being conveyed. To keep such a balance against the multiplicity of situations that make up the aggregate of developing nations and the speed at which these situations change over time is indeed very difficult.

Beginning with the geographical breakdown of the long-term growth record of the developing world, the first important differentiation that needs to be made is between Latin America, on one side, and Asia and Africa, on the other. Latin America's growth performance between 1870 and 1950 mirrors closely that of the industrial world. In fact, because of their income levels and the pace of economic growth that they attained, many South American nations would have qualified as advanced by the economic standards of the time, on par with many in Western Europe. The fact that South American countries attracted a vast immigration from Europe during much of this period witnesses the economic success that they had gained and the appeal that they exerted as lands of economic opportunity. Rich in agricultural land, endowed with a favorable climate and much mineral wealth, Latin America attracted not only European labor but also capital, first from Europe and then from the United States (Furtado, 1970; Stallings, 1987). These resource inflows contributed powerfully to its economic transformation and rapid growth in the post-independence period. Even when, after World War II, the Latin American model of growth changed from agriculture-based and moderately outward-oriented to industry-led and strongly inward-oriented, the rate of growth of per capita real output continued to rise (Table 3.2). This trend lasted until the end of the 1970s, despite heavy losses in the terms of trade, connected in part with the negative tendency in the relative prices of primary exports and in part with domestic policies, factors that reduced economic well-being in many of its country components.

Developing Asia, on the other hand, heavily colonized by European nations in its south and eastern parts, and with China saddled by ineffective and decaying government, grew at less than one-third the pace of Latin America until 1913 (in terms of per capita GDP) and stopped growing at all in the subsequent forty years, practically until the early 1950s. The negative impact of political-military events felt by this region in the 1930s and 1940s has already been mentioned. World War II, the civil war in China, and ill-conceived attempts by the Netherlands and France to restore colonial rule in Indonesia and Indochina after the end of the second world conflict conjoined to make this period particularly difficult for much of Asia, where large economic dislocations occurred and stagnation came to prevail (Table 3.2). Growth did not start again until the first half of the 1950s in the aftermath of the revolution in China and of the independence-cum-partition of India.[16] Economic performance has since improved dramatically, first in East Asia, where several countries began to industrialize rapidly, and subsequently in the large economies of South Asia (and in Indonesia), which finally began to open up to the outside world in earnest, paving the way for domestic economic reform. In the 1980s the Asia region at large became the "star performer" in the developing world with average per capita real income growth in the neighborhood of 5 percent a year.

Africa's economic record was probably also quite weak and uneven until 1913. What can be deduced from the scant evidence available points only to very limited growth in per capita real income, with the indigenous economy (outside the relatively small modern sector) producing enough food to barely keep up with its growing population. Population trends, moreover, are highly uncertain, and available data are probably biased downward. The evidence on economic activity between 1913 and 1950 is somewhat better than in the previous forty years but still quite incomplete. Stronger performance in the modern sector— especially in colonial agriculture—in much of the continent and particularly good growth in West Africa and in the Southern Cone, spurred in part by expanding European demand for tropical products and minerals, seem to have generated at least some appreciable increment in average per capita real output during this period (Table 3.2).

Point estimates of actual outcomes, however, still need to be taken as highly tentative. Even today the measurement of both real output and population is subject to large margins for error in most of Africa. Growth of per capita real income may have averaged at about 1 percent a year between 1913 and 1950, if population figures do not badly understate the increase that occurred during this period. Under less benign assumptions (or guesses) about population and output growth in key countries, the rate of increase of real GDP per capita drops to between zero and 0.5 percent a year.

Intensified growth efforts, made first by European administrations in the 1950s (just before most African colonies reached independence), then continued and renewed by the national governments of many newly independent states in the 1960s, often with sizable outside help,[17] produced a period of solid economic performance throughout much of Africa, with real GDP per capita increasing at over 2 percent a year between 1950 and 1973.

A variety of problems—ranging from bad weather and two oil shocks in the

1970s to the debt problem of the 1980s, in addition to political and social instability, inappropriate economic policies, and often incompetent governance—helped plunge most of Africa south of the Sahara first into near stagnation and then into negative growth during the past twenty years, making it the only region of the world that seriously regressed, on the whole, for an extended period of time. Africa north of the Sahara, on the contrary, boomed in the 1970s, with oil-led growth in many of its component countries, but experienced a drastic slowdown in the 1980s, when terms of trade worsened drastically for its oil-exporting countries and external debt accumulated in the previous decade became a heavy burden for all of them. In these circumstances, growth became more difficult, and the cost of previous misuse of resources became quite clear.

Within each of the main geographical areas there remained a fairly wide variance in country growth experiences. These are important to notice, since starting points and growth paths have often differed considerably even within geographically contiguous and similarly endowed countries. Growth in Latin America began earlier than elsewhere in the developing world and quickly spread to most of the nations of the hemisphere. Within-region variance seems to have been relatively small since at least 1913 (Table A3.1). Beginning in the 1950s, when coefficients of variation of country growth within each region can be computed on the basis of a large sample, uniformity of outcomes within Latin America was also strong. The same tendency continued in the 1960s, during which exceptions to fast growth were limited to two countries (Haiti and Uruguay). Strong and relatively stable growth prevailed also in the 1970s. In the 1980s, however, some serious reversals occurred, and country outcomes varied more widely. Per capita real GDP growth became strongly negative in Bolivia, Nicaragua, Peru, Venezuela, El Salvador, Guatemala, Guyana, Haiti, Panama, and Mexico. It stagnated in several others, while remaining appreciably positive only in Chile, Colombia, and Costa Rica.[18] Overall, the coefficient of variation of country growth in the region increased by a factor of five with respect to the previous decade (Table A3.2).

The picture of Latin America as an early starter in the process of intensive growth is confirmed by the analysis of Reynolds's "turning points"—the points in the growth path of a country at which per capita real gross national product (GNP) begins to rise.[19] As shown in Table 3.3, the approximate "turning points" of all the most important Latin American countries are centered around the middle of the nineteenth century, with Chile as the first intensive grower (1840) and Colombia the last (1885). While the specific years are inevitably somewhat arbitrary, the clustering of the "turning points" in the periods during which these countries attained political stability after the turbulence of the immediate postindependence era and during which vigorous export growth began seems to be significant, aside from being intuitively appealing.

The available country details show that, unlike Latin America, growth did not start easily and become quickly sustained in Asia (Table A3.1). Three of the four large economies in the region—India, Pakistan, and Indonesia—did not

Table 3.3

Turning Points in the Growth of Selected Developing Countries

Countries	Approximate Year of Turning Point	Source /b	Comments on the Date of Turning Point
Latin America			
Chile	1840	R	
Argentina	1860	R	
Mexico	1876	R	
Brazil	1880	R	
Peru	1880	R	
Jamaica	1880	A	
Colombia	1885	R	
Asia			
Malaysia	1850	R	
Thailand	1850	R	
Philippines	1900	R	
India	1947	R	
Pakistan	1947	R	
China	1949	R	(Growth trend reversed in later years)
Korea	1955	A	(Reynolds places it in 1970)
Taiwan /a	1955	A	
Indonesia	1970	A	

Table 3.3 (continued)

Countries	Approximate Year of Turning Point	Source /b	Comments on the Date of Turning Point
<u>Africa</u>			
Nigeria	1890	R	(Could be later, around 1910)
Cote d'Ivoire	1895	R	
Kenya	1895	R	
Ghana	1895	R	(Growth trend reversed in later years)
Tunisia	1915	A	
Morocco	1920	R	
South Africa	1920	A	(Could be as early as 1900)
Algeria	1925	A	
Ethiopia	1950	A	
Malawi	1950	A	
Sudan	1950	A	
Zaire	1950	A	
Egypt	1952	R	(First turning point was in 1886)
Tanzania	1960	A	
Togo	1962	A	
Cameroon	1962	A	
Upper Volta	1965	A	
Congo	1968	A	

Sources: Reynolds (1985) and own estimates.

[a]GDP per capita was positive during the 1920s, but the trend was reversed and GDP per capita became negative during the 1930s, turning positive again in 1955.

[b]R = Reynolds; A = Author's estimates.

experience a prolonged rise in real GDP per capita until the "golden" years in the aftermath of World War II (which coincided with the postindependence era for all of them), while in the fourth—China—growth did not become clearly positive and sustained in per capita terms until the 1970s, though temporary spurts were attained in earlier periods. As in many other cases, only after a modicum of internal political stability was reached following the turmoil of Maoism and some openness to the outside world was accepted by a slowly reforming national leadership did growth begin in earnest in China as well.

The "miracle growers" of East Asia—Korea, Taiwan, and Thailand—showed much of the same path as the large economies in going from extensive to intensive growth. In these countries the rise in per capita real output became sustained during the 1950s and 1960s, when they began to industrialize. What most strongly characterizes the performance of these smaller and more outward-oriented economies of Asia (subsequently joined by Malaysia and Sri Lanka) in the four decades after World War II are both the speed of growth that they achieved (which was roughly twice that of the other small-to-medium-size economies of the region) and its stability over time. With per capita GDP growing at between 3 percent and 6 percent a year for three or four consecutive decades, these countries not only became the highest performers in the developing world but outdistanced all the major industrial economies in speed of growth (with Japan the only partial exception). They also made enormous progress in reducing once widespread poverty and improved substantially their internal distribution of income. It is again noteworthy that economic growth became sustained and steady in both Korea and Taiwan after these countries achieved political stability, in the wake of sizable political-military shocks affecting both of them—forced separation from mainland China in Taiwan and partition plus civil war in Korea.[20] Over the past forty years, average output growth in Asia was not only faster than in all the other regions, with the exception of the Middle East, but also the most stable (Table A3.2).

Analysis of "turning points" confirms that intensive growth in most of Asia began only after World War II. With the possible exceptions of Malaysia, Thailand, and the Philippines, where the passage from extensive to intensive growth apparently occurred around 1850 and 1900, respectively, the changeover years for most other nations in this region can be identified in the late 1940s and early to mid-1950s. A latecomer appears to have been Indonesia, which after reaching positive per capita real income growth in the mid-1950s, fell into a prolonged economic crisis from which it emerged only in the late 1960s after political stability was restored. There is also considerable doubt about the time at which China's "turning point" actually occurred.[21] Reynolds dates it in the late 1940s, when positive per capita real income growth occurred. But since gains were subsequently reversed and output growth did not become again positive and sustained until the 1970s, it may not be incorrect to place the crossover of China into intensive growth only in the mid-1970s.

As previously noted, documenting and assessing growth in Africa are even more difficult than in Asia. There is information going back in time to the beginning of the current century or slightly before on Egypt (Hansen and Marzouk, 1965; Hansen, 1979), Algeria (Amin, 1966), South Africa (Frankel and Herzfeld, 1944; Franzsen, 1954; Krogh, 1960), Ghana (Szereszewski, 1965), and Nigeria (Helleiner, 1966), but very little else is known with any reasonable certainty about other countries until World War I. Even for the subsequent years, quantitative evidence on economic performance remains scarce and often of dubious value at least until World War II. Growth of North African nations is only partially documented. There are assessments regarding Tunisia and Morocco (Amin, 1966, 1970),[22] but only a dearth of information on the countries of the Mashreq (with the already noted exception of Egypt). As for Sub-Saharan Africa, aside from Ghana, South Africa,[23] and (in part) Nigeria, there exists some evidence on the growth of Mali (Amin, 1965), Zimbabwe (Barber, 1984), Zambia (Baldwin, 1966), and Kenya (Swainson, 1980), plus some aggregate indicators of economic activity in the modern sector of French West Africa (Maldant, 1973).

Between 1913 and 1950 real per capita income growth seems to have been positive and sustained in Ghana, South Africa, Kenya, Zambia, and Zimbabwe but much slower in Mali and Nigeria (Table A3.1). Judging from trade figures, real tax receipts, and investment in construction in the cities, economic activity seems to have increased at a fairly rapid pace also in French West Africa (at least in the modern sector of the economies of these countries). Yet, neither real output nor population estimates are firm enough to allow more than mildly informed guesses about per capita output growth in the whole of Sub-Saharan Africa during this period.[24] More certain is the widespread expansion of output and incomes that occurred in Africa after the end of World War II and lasted until the early 1970s. For most of the countries in this region these were the years immediately preceding or following independence. This relatively good period of economic growth, however, did not last long. A massive and generalized reversal of the positive, postindependence trend occurred between 1973 and 1990, affecting most of Sub-Saharan Africa. The only significant country exceptions were Burundi and Kenya and apparently Mali, Botswana, Chad, and Burkina Faso. These were the few countries where the growth of per capita real income remained positive (if barely so in most cases) during both the 1970s and 1980s. That the nations of Sub-Saharan Africa generally shared both the relatively good and bad economic fortunes is confirmed by the analysis of country growth. The coefficients of variation of within-region growth remained remarkably similar during both the good decades (the 1950s and 1960s) and the bad one (the 1980s) (Table A3.2).

Analysis of "turning points" also confirms that most of Sub-Saharan Africa was a latecomer to intensive growth. Apart from South Africa, Zimbabwe, Zambia, Côte d'Ivoire, Kenya, Ghana (a country that suffered, nonetheless, a serious and sustained reversal beginning in the late 1960s), and possibly Nigeria,[25] per capita real income growth did not become clearly positive in most of the other countries surveyed here until the 1950s and 1960s (Table 3.3). In some of them (e.g., Madagascar and Mauritania), intensive growth has not yet been reached. The picture for North Africa is also quite varied. The "turning points" of Algeria, Tunisia, and Morocco can be seen as having occurred between 1915 and 1925, while Egypt did not surely move into intensive growth until the early 1950s.[26]

GROWTH PATTERNS IN THE LAST FORTY YEARS

The achievement of nationhood for many former European colonies in Africa and Asia in the period after World War II, the associated stronger focus on growth and development as a matter of national policy, the enlargement of international cooperation on behalf of developing nations, and greater recognition of the importance of indicators capable of tracking domestic economic progress all contributed to the establishment of better economic records and improved monitoring systems in developing countries. The efforts of the United Nations to develop, for example, standardized national income accounts and a common trade reporting system and to encourage member countries to report regularly according to preset models, were reasonably successful. They helped improve the coverage and international comparability of national economic data. Similarly, technical assistance, extended by bilateral donors and international organizations to developing countries in the area of national income accounts and economic statistics in general, also helped to improve their quality.

From 1950 onward, available population and GDP data cover practically all developing nations, even though perceptible problems of reliability and comparability of data remain.[27] Country economic records are at least virtually complete, and available data allow more extensive comparisons of outcomes across countries and regions over a period spanning four decades,[28] the first two characterized by fast growth and relative stability in the international economy, and the last affected by a general slowing down of growth and by increasing instability in the economic performance of the main industrial nations.[29]

The Main Tendencies

In the aggregate, developing countries did very well in terms of output growth between 1950 and 1980. The trends that can be calculated for practically the entire population of them mirror closely those obtained from the sample utilized here to track growth since 1870.[30] Until 1980 real GDP apparently expanded on average at about 4 percent a year in Africa, at about 5 percent in Asia and Latin America, and even more rapidly in Southern Europe and in the oil-exporting countries of the Middle East (at nearly 6 percent and 8 percent per year, respectively). Output growth, moreover, was remarkably stable in developing countries. The coefficient of variation of country GDP growth remained virtually unchanged at about 0.5 over the three decades beginning in 1950 (Table A3.2).

Within Africa, the countries located north of the Sahara grew more rapidly than those to their south, especially between 1970 and 1980, when increased oil revenues directly or indirectly buoyed non-oil output in most of them (Algeria, Tunisia, Egypt, Morocco, and apparently also Syria). Within Sub-Saharan Africa, the eastern countries performed significantly better than those located in the western part until 1970 (Table 3.4). In the subsequent ten years, aggregate growth performance improved instead in the latter group and worsened in the former, mirroring the effect of the terms-of-trade shock on each group: negative for all East African countries and positive for several West African countries that exported oil (Nigeria, Congo, Gabon, and Cameroon).

In Asia, the very large and relatively more closed economies—India and China—did not do as well, until the 1980s, as their smaller counterparts in the region, among which the East Asian countries were particularly successful. The first generation of the newly industrializing countries (NICs)—Korea, Taiwan, Singapore, and Hong Kong—led the way in growth starting in the 1950s, followed by a second generation, made up of Malaysia, Thailand, Indonesia, and Sri Lanka, in the 1960s and 1970s.

In Latin America both the large economies and the smaller ones performed well in terms of growth until the early 1980s: Mexico and Brazil led the way, followed by Colombia, Ecuador, Paraguay, Costa Rica, and Honduras. Growth was thus widespread throughout the continent. There were some exceptions to this pattern, such as Uruguay for most of the period and Argentina and Chile for part of it. But on the whole, real output grew relatively fast throughout Latin America from the early 1950s to the onset of the debt crisis at the start of the 1980s (Table 3.4).

Growth continued strong in Asia during the 1980s, while a dramatic downturn occurred in all other developing regions. Latin American developing countries, aside from being the most heavily indebted at commercial terms and thus more susceptible to the negative effects of the interest-rate shock that occurred in the early 1980s, were also, generally speaking, slow to begin macroeconomic adjustment. The African nations had, in addition to high debt, the weakest economic structures and faced very adverse climate conditions. Asian countries, instead, managed to grow despite high real interest rates and the reduced pace of economic activity in industrial countries. The smaller ones, many of which were also highly indebted, adjusted early and successfully to both the higher cost and reduced availability of external (especially banking) credit, while the very large countries, which were relatively less indebted externally, reaped strong benefits from the beginning of fundamental economic reform and the increased outward orientation.[31] Growth also slowed drastically in Southern Europe, in North Saharan Africa, and in the Middle East (Table 3.4), where the collapse of oil prices reversed the terms of trade gains of many of the oil-exporting countries in this region and also severely reduced revenues in those most dependent on labor remittances from the Gulf.[32] On the whole, GDP growth in the 1980s became

Table 3.4
Growth of GDP and Per Capita GDP in the Main Developing Regions,[a] 1950–1990

	Real GDP				Population				Real GDP Per Capita			
	1950-60	1960-70	1970-80	1980-90	1950-60	1960-70	1970-80	1980-90	1950-60	1960-70	1970-80	1980-90
					---Average Annual Rates /b, %---							
AFRICA	4.12	4.20	4.19	1.83	2.24	2.54	2.66	2.99	1.88	1.66	1.53	-1.16
North of Sahara	4.59	4.48	6.52	3.52	2.33	2.52	2.45	2.71	2.26	1.96	4.07	0.81
South of Sahara	4.13	4.13	3.53	1.22	2.21	2.54	2.72	3.06	1.92	1.59	0.81	-1.84
East Africa	4.31	5.16	2.56	1.77	2.36	2.62	2.88	3.03	1.95	2.54	-0.32	-1.26
West Africa	3.69	3.02	4.39	0.54	2.03	2.44	2.51	3.10	1.66	0.58	1.88	-2.56
ASIA	4.45	4.77	5.38	7.39	2.14	2.35	2.10	1.85	2.34	2.43	3.28	5.53
China & India	4.38	4.28	4.35	8.20	2.03	2.28	1.98	1.73	2.35	2.00	2.37	6.47
East Asia	5.12	6.00	7.72	6.27	2.45	2.57	2.37	1.95	2.67	3.43	5.35	4.32
Other Asia	2.93	5.01	4.28	4.77	2.30	2.58	2.69	2.70	0.63	2.43	1.59	2.07
LATIN AMERICA	5.16	5.36	5.52	1.62	2.89	2.76	2.42	2.09	2.25	2.61	3.10	-0.47
SOUTHERN EUROPE	5.74	6.15	5.28	2.48	1.71	1.52	1.69	1.43	4.03	4.63	3.59	1.05
MIDDLE EAST	7.20	8.55	7.38 /c	1.16	2.68	3.34	3.41 /c	3.36	4.52	5.21	3.97 /c	-2.20
TOTAL DEVELOPING COUNTRIES	4.89	5.48	5.31	4.00	2.22	2.41	2.23	2.06	2.67	3.07	3.08	1.94
INDUSTRIAL COUNTRIES	4.10	5.10	3.21	3.03	1.21	1.02	0.78	0.59	2.89	4.08	2.43	2.44

Source: Table A 3.2.

[a] All developing countries. See Table A 3.2 for country details.

[b] Least square growth rates.

[c] For period 1970–77 only. In the last three years of the 1970s the overall growth rate of this region is profoundly influenced by the events affecting Iran, the largest economy in its midst.

also much more unstable than in the previous three decades. The coefficient of variation of country growth more than doubled in value (Table A3.2).

Population trends differed significantly across developing regions throughout the entire post–World War II period (Figure 3.3). In Latin America, the rate of growth of population slowed progressively during this period: from 3 percent a year in the 1950s to little over 2 percent in the 1980s. In Asia it peaked between 1960 and 1970 and fell below 2 percent a year for the region as a whole in the 1980s. The rate of expansion of population in the Middle East also reached a maximum in the 1960s, but the subsequent deceleration was more gradual there than in either Latin America or Asia, as annual growth remained at about 3 percent. In Africa population is still growing at an increasing rate, at or above 3 percent a year, with few exceptions. Before a turnaround is attained, around the turn of the century, the yearly rate of increase in population is expected to reach 3.5 percent.

The combined result of output and population growth is again illustrated in Table 3.4 for the major developing regions. Real output per capita is shown to have increased at a healthy pace in all of them until 1980, if more rapidly in the Middle East and Southern Europe than in Asia, Latin America, and especially Africa, where it grew at only around 1.7 percent a year between 1950 and 1980, roughly one-half the average for all developing countries. With population still expanding at an increasing rate and real output slowing drastically, Africa experienced an average decline of 1.2 percent a year in real GDP per capita during the 1980s. In Sub-Saharan Africa the decline was even faster: about 2 percent a year on average (over 2.5 percent in West Africa). Per capita real output also fell on average at 0.5 percent a year in Latin America, notwithstanding the much slower rate of growth of population that occurred in this region. Per capita growth during the 1980s was barely positive in Southern Europe and negative in the Middle East, while it increased strongly in Asia, especially in India and China, where it averaged 3.4 percent and 8.1 percent a year, respectively. In the smaller Southeast Asian economies per capita real income growth ranged between 3 percent a year in Malaysia and Sri Lanka and 5 percent to 6 percent a year in Thailand, Hong Kong, and Taiwan. The record was Korea's, with 8.2 percent a year.

What emerges from the regional trends of output and population in the developing world during the past four decades is, therefore, a highly composite picture. Most of the Asia region, long the object of Malthusian worries, seems instead to have "taken off" and to have vastly surpassed the industrialized world in speed of growth.[33] Africa, on the contrary, appears to be progressively falling behind, not only vis-à-vis the industrial world, but also with respect to the rest of the developing countries. There are exceptions to this trend—notably Kenya, Upper Volta, and more recently, Ghana and Uganda—but collectively Africa is performing much less well than one could have expected, even under the difficult circumstances it faced. Latin America—long the "middle class" of the developing world—stumbled badly in the 1980s, after three decades of reasonably

Figure 3.3
Population Growth in Developing Countries by Region, 1850–1990

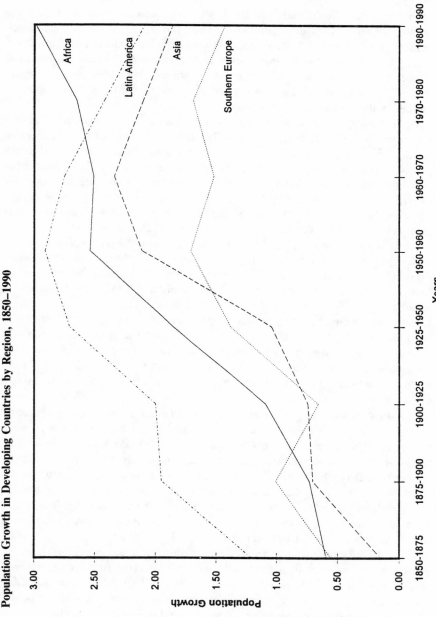

Sources: McEvedy and Jones (1978) for the period 1850–1950; Table 3.4 for the period 1950–1990.

fast (if still below-potential) growth. The poor economic performance of Brazil and Mexico set the trend, but difficulties were widespread and severe throughout the region. However, the problems faced by most of Latin America in what has been called the "lost decade" of the 1980s also spurred radical changes in the growth strategies previously followed—from inward-looking, state-led development (national or regional) to more outward-oriented, market-based growth— and signs of renewed economic vitality and resumption of output growth have already become evident in several of its countries: Chile, Mexico, and Argentina.[34] The region as a whole now appears ready to catch up, not only with Asia, but also with the industrial economies.

Until the 1970s the economies of those developing countries where income per capita had already reached relatively high levels seemed to expand more rapidly (in the aggregate) than those of their poorer counterparts. Growth appeared to proceed along two divergent tracks, faster in the middle-income countries of Latin America and Southeast Asia than in the lower-income countries of Africa and South Asia (Table 3.5). The middle-income–low-income divide, however, began to break down in the 1980s, when low-income South Asia grew even faster than both the rest of the Asia region and Latin America.

What emerged most clearly in the past decade were the profound differences in the growth performance of Africa with respect to other low-income developing economies (especially in Asia) and in that of the Asian NICs with respect to their middle-income counterparts in Latin America and the growth leadership assumed by Asia as a region. The overall differentials in growth between low-income and middle-income countries have thus become progressively blurred. Real GDP per capita increased on average much faster in low-income countries during the 1980s than in both middle-income and oil-exporting, high-income developing countries. Actually, average growth was higher even in "other low-income countries" (the total minus China, India, and Indonesia) than in the rest of the developing world.[35]

A positive relationship between output growth and starting levels of per capita GDP, with countries beginning at a higher level of per capita income growing faster than their poorer counterparts, can be hypothesized resorting to both neoclassical growth theory and (for a given saving propensity) to the Harrod-Domar framework. If capital were subject to diminishing returns, the return to investments in relatively capital-scarce (poorer) countries should be greater than in relatively capital-abundant (richer) countries. Health and education levels may be better in higher than in lower-income countries, thus tending to positively affect the productivity of human capital as well.

Cross-country analysis also reveals some positive (if weak) correlation between growth of domestic output and per capita income levels (measured at international prices) at the start of the two decades that began in 1950. Amidst considerable variance, countries with higher per capita income at the beginning of this period seem to have grown somewhat faster than those exhibiting lower starting income. But even this weak correlation can be seen to have broken down in the next

Table 3.5
Growth Differentials Between Groups of Developing Countries Classified by Income Levels, 1950–1990[a]

	GDP					GDP Per Capita				
	1950-60	1960-70	1970-80	1980-90	1950-90	1950-60	1960-70	1970-80	1980-90	1950-90
ALL LOW INCOME COUNTRIES	4.19	4.22	4.58	7.14	4.61	2.11	1.90	2.44	5.17	2.46
of which:										
China	5.05	4.73	5.05	9.55	5.18	2.97	2.48	3.27	8.09	3.32
India	3.41	3.71	3.28	5.44	3.85	1.46	1.39	1.00	3.35	1.63
Indonesia	4.64	3.80	7.46	5.29	5.57	2.52	1.56	5.14	3.26	3.31
Other Low Income	3.37	4.19	3.90	3.65	3.82	1.07	1.65	1.19	0.82	1.16
MIDDLE INCOME COUNTRIES	5.23	5.94	5.33	2.76	5.12	2.55	3.30	2.93	0.51	2.57
HIGH INCOME OIL EXPORTERS	7.06	7.30	7.31	-0.32	5.65	3.97	3.86	3.13	-4.38	1.82
TOTAL DEVELOPING COUNTRIES	4.89	5.48	5.31	4.00	4.80	2.67	3.07	3.08	1.94	2.52

Source: Table A 3.2.

[a]See Table A 3.3 for country classifications and criteria used.

twenty years, when total domestic output growth no longer appears to have been positively influenced by starting income in a sample of seventy developing countries (Figure 3.4).[36] The relationship between output growth and starting levels of income in the years between 1950 and 1990 is not much different if it is considered in terms of per capita (instead of total) output. It remains positive and weakly significant between 1950 and 1970 and positive but totally insignificant in the next twenty years.[37]

Specific reasons for many of the changes that occurred in the speed and basic traits of growth of many countries during the postwar period can be identified ex post. However, in order to compare meaningfully the economic growth performance of a large number of countries and capture key common characteristics of such growth over a significantly long period of time, one must resort to broad and meaningful ex ante categories, transcending as much as possible ad hoc explanations. At a minimum one must be able to order (or reorder) available evidence according to relevant factors that can be thought to be associated in a certain way to output performance, to see if common patterns emerge from the available data. At a higher and more meaningful level, one should test different, well-defined hypotheses concerning the observed growth outcomes.

Here I pursue the minimum objective and attempt only some reclassifications of country growth results according to such general criteria as size, economic structure, and trade orientation in order to illustrate some of the key patterns and characteristics of developing countries' growth over the medium term, without any pretense of accounting even for the most important factors, let alone establishing causalities.[38]

Growth and Size

The size of a country, measured by the available land, may have something to do with its growth potential. A large physical size, for example, may increase the probability of a favorable natural endowment, in terms of either land suitable for agricultural production or mineral resources. Other things being equal, large (and, on average, better resource-endowed) countries could be expected to grow faster than small (and generally less well endowed) ones. Large countries—in size and/or population—may also provide for better and more secure market opportunities for newly established enterprises at least in a closed economy context and thus encourage more strongly the development of local productions.

Obviously, complications can (and do) arise when using simple classification criteria such as this one. The growth of an economy will depend on more factors than size and natural endowment. Larger countries, for example, by virtue of size may tend to be more inward-looking and be prone to "go it alone" in economic strategies. A large economic size (and a favorable natural endowment, when associated with size) may thus not be fully exploited, or its exploitation may be inefficient. Smaller countries, on the contrary, have by necessity to be more outward-looking and to seek external opportunities through trade and capital

Figure 3.4
Country GDP Growth and Starting Levels of Per Capita Income

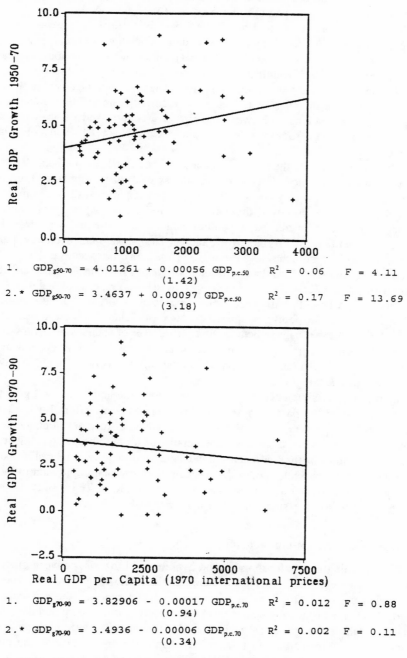

1. $GDP_{g50-70} = 4.01261 + 0.00056\ GDP_{p.c.50}$ $R^2 = 0.06$ $F = 4.11$
                (1.42)

2.* $GDP_{g50-70} = 3.4637 + 0.00097\ GDP_{p.c.50}$ $R^2 = 0.17$ $F = 13.69$
                (3.18)

1. $GDP_{g70-90} = 3.82906 - 0.00017\ GDP_{p.c.70}$ $R^2 = 0.012$ $F = 0.88$
                (0.94)

2.* $GDP_{g70-90} = 3.4936 - 0.00006\ GDP_{p.c.70}$ $R^2 = 0.002$ $F = 0.11$
                (0.34)

* With three outliers excluded from the sample.

flows. In doing so, they can tap external resources (and thus transcend the limitations of physical endowment), accumulate knowledge more easily, and become more efficient in the use of their domestic endowment.

But size may have other and more direct negative effects on growth. Large underdeveloped economies may have to shoulder much higher costs (per capita) of delivering basic infrastructure (physical and administrative) and public services (such as education and health) than more compact ones and be, therefore, relatively more disadvantaged in terms of growth. The public management problem may also be more complex and binding in larger, than in smaller, countries. The sign of the relationship between the size of a country and its growth possibilities—quite apart from the effects of policy choices actually made—is thus not clear a priori.

As previously noted, the available data show that, at least until the 1980s, the very large economies of Asia performed less well than many small ones in Asia and elsewhere. But, witness to the importance of policies, the performance of India and China improved dramatically in the 1980s, when steps toward economic reform and increased outward orientation of production were taken in both these countries. Brazil, moreover, another large developing economy, performed well at least until the early 1980s, when the debt crisis occurred. Nigeria's performance alternated considerably through the years, with the dominant effects exerted by economic strategies actually followed and by political stability (or lack thereof). Among the small economies, moreover, many in Central America and Africa did quite poorly, while others in East Asia, South America, and North Africa performed much better. Different degrees of openness explain some of the differences in growth outcomes, but structural traits (such as dependency on production and exports of primary commodities) can also be thought to have been important factors of growth.

The lack of any simple, direct relationship between country size and growth performance over the past forty years emerges rather clearly from Figure 3.5, where average growth rates over the period are plotted against developing countries' size, measured in both physical and population terms. The lack of statistical significance shown by the coefficients of the regressions of growth against country dimensions and minuscule size of the R^2s confirm the visual impression of lack of any simple correlation between the two sets of values. The results do not change if growth is measured in per capita terms.

Growth and Economic Structure

More meaningful relationships can be hypothesized to exist between growth and the basic economic structure of countries than between growth and undifferentiated physical size. Among relatively open economies,[39] those more dependent on the production and export of non-oil primary commodities, for example, can be thought of as having faced less favorable world demand conditions and thus lower growth possibilities than those specializing in the pro-

Figure 3.5
Growth and Country Size

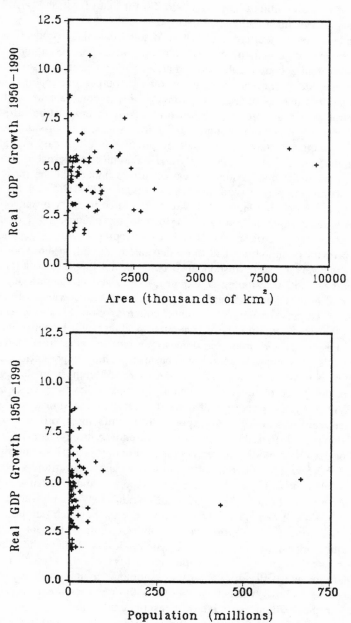

duction and export of oil and manufactures. The former group of products faces a foreign demand that is less income-elastic than that of the latter, where the difference is between values of less than 1.0 for the income elasticity of import demand of non-oil commodities, of 1.5 to 2.0 for that of oil, and of 3.0 to 4.0 for the demand of manufactures (Balassa, 1987).[40]

Dependence on agriculture and, within it, on "colonial" productions (i.e., agricultural primary commodities) and on mining was a fairly common condition in many developing countries before and after independence. Yet, some of these countries succeeded in diversifying their domestic output and export structures, while others did not. With few exceptions, the low-income countries of Africa and Central America were less successful in their diversification efforts than many of the middle-income countries of Latin America and Asia.[41] Defining economic structure in terms of reliance on production of primary commodities versus manufactures is thus historically and economically justifiable. However, given that within primary commodities, oil prices underwent the most drastic changes within the period (with huge increases in 1973–1974 and 1979–1980 and a drastic decline in 1985–1986), which translated in every instance in large terms of trade changes for oil-exporting developing countries,[42] it would also seem appropriate to differentiate between developing countries dependent on non-oil primary commodities and those dependent instead on oil exports.

Given the very close correspondence between the topologies of production and export in most developing economies, export and production dependence can be used almost interchangeably in highlighting the relevance of economic structure on country growth. Developing countries more highly dependent on exports of primary commodities, generally speaking, will be those where the share of agriculture and mining in domestic production is relatively higher.

Aggregation of countries according to basic structural categories at mid-period and comparison of outcomes indicate significant differences in the aggregate growth performance of the various country groups in the forty years after the end of World War II. Exporters of non-oil primary commodities, for example, grew on average less rapidly than exporters of manufactures, oil, or services for most of this period. Partial exceptions to this trend occurred in the 1970s, when non-oil primary commodity prices boomed, allowing countries exporting them to import, borrow, and grow at par with the rest, and again in the 1980s, when oil prices collapsed and income growth in oil-exporting and remittance-dependent countries declined strongly. The growth differentials between the various groups of countries do not depend too heavily on the way in which output growth is measured. During the past forty years countries most dependent on primary commodities appear to have done, in general, less well than the other main groups in either aggregate or per capita terms (Table 3.6). Moreover, the differential in growth between exporters of commodities and exporters of manufactures seems to have widened over time, with only a temporary break of this tendency in the 1970s irrespective of measurement mode.[43]

Overall growth in oil-exporting countries can also be seen to have depended

Table 3.6

Growth Differentials Between Groups of Developing Countries Classified by Economic Structure,[a] 1950–1990

| | Real GDP | | | | Real GDP Per Capita | | | |
	1950-60	1960-70	1970-80	1980-90	1950-90	1950-60	1960-70	1970-80	1980-90	1950-90
	(------------------------------Average Annual Growth Rates, %------------------------------)									
Exporters of Non-Oil Primary Commodities	4.43	5.26	5.52	2.50	4.78	1.82	2.58	2.99	0.06	2.16
Exporters of Manufactures	5.80	6.86	5.90	4.95	6.02	3.34	4.42	3.59	2.80	3.57
Oil Exporters /b	6.01	6.07	6.68	1.94	5.54	3.56	3.49	4.01	-0.77	2.89

Source: Table 3.2.

[a]See Table A 3.3 for country classifications. India and China are excluded from the classification.

[b]Growth for oil exporters is measured in terms of real GNP.

importantly on terms of trade developments, aside from export volume. Income growth is fastest in periods of rising oil prices and slowest when oil prices are falling (relative to those of imports). The differences in the average annual growth of real GNP for this group of countries between the 1960s (and 1970s) and the 1980s are cases in point. A similar tendency is shown by the aggregate economic performance of developing countries most dependent on non-oil commodities. Their growth accelerated in the 1970s, when terms of trade improved, and decelerated in the 1980s, when commodity terms of trade fell. Yet, since all other things affecting economic performance (e.g., external factors and domestic policies) were not the same between the 1970s and the 1980s, caution should be used in attributing growth differentials to movements in terms of trade alone. The relevance of sustained changes in relative export prices, which have been shown as capable of affecting growth in industrial economies,[44] should, nonetheless, not be dismissed too cursorily in the case of developing countries.

Aside from the broad relationships emerging from the comparison between aggregate growth of output and export structures of different groups of developing countries, the importance of the structural linkages with the outside world can also be highlighted by cross-country analysis. Figure 3.6 shows, for example, a definite inverse correlation between real output growth in 1950–1990 and dependence on non-oil primary commodity exports for all but the most closed developing economies.[45] The fastest growing countries over the past forty years have generally been those relatively less dependent on exports of primary products,[46] a relationship that, ceteris paribus, one would expect to find since the growth in a country's export volume depends on external demand conditions and growth of domestic output should be positively related to growth of exports.[47] The correlation between average growth between 1950 and 1990 and dependence on non-oil commodities at mid-period is found to be statistically significant in a sample of sixty-two developing countries, irrespective of whether dependence is measured in terms of the incidence of commodities in total exports, commodity exports in GDP, or agricultural and mining production in GDP.

Growth and Trade Orientation

Trade orientation refers to a country's attitude toward trade and thus to the role played by trade in the economy. To determine whether a country is outward- or inward-oriented, such a role must be related to a theoretical, or a priori, standard. When this is done, trade orientation can be gauged in terms of deviations of actual from expected outcomes.

Given that trade orientation will presumably depend on such factors as the physical, economic, and human attributes of a country (size and endowments of land, capital, and labor) and the relevant policies being followed (trade regimes and incentives pro or against tradable output), the standard that should logically be used to evaluate a country's trade orientation (and to compare it with others) is the trade expected on the basis of its factor endowment and size, under

Figure 3.6
Country GDP Growth and Dependency on Primary Commodities and Structure of Production

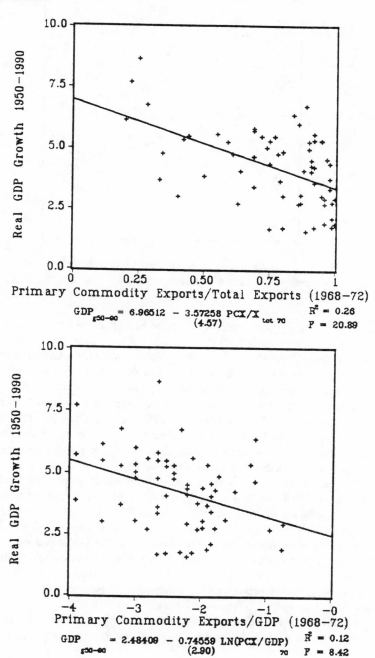

GDP$_{g50-90}$ = 6.96512 − 3.57258 PCX/X$_{tot\ 70}$ $\quad$ $\bar{R}^2$ = 0.26
$\quad\quad\quad\quad\quad\quad$ (4.57) $\quad\quad\quad\quad\quad\quad$ F = 20.89

GDP$_{g50-90}$ = 2.48409 − 0.74559 LN(PCX/GDP)$_{70}$ $\quad$ $\bar{R}^2$ = 0.12
$\quad\quad\quad\quad\quad\quad$ (2.90) $\quad\quad\quad\quad\quad\quad$ F = 8.42

Figure 3.6 (continued)

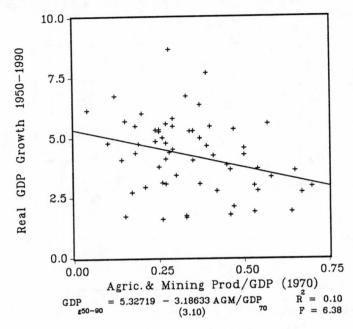

$$GDP_{g50-90} = 5.32719 - 3.18633 \, AGM/GDP_{70} \quad R^2 = 0.10$$
$$(3.10) \qquad\qquad F = 6.38$$

conditions of free trade and neutrality of price incentives to the production of goods.

Trade orientation, therefore, is not the same as openness. Any measure of openness that simply conveys the actual weight of trade in the economy of a country is, strictly speaking, an inadequate indicator of trade orientation. It is an ex post measure and does not differentiate between the determinants of trade orientation. Openness indicators cannot therefore characterize accurately and unambiguously the attitude of a country toward trade.[48] For these reasons the standard openness ratios[49] cannot be used to adequately classify countries into more or less outward-oriented at any given time.

The widespread utilization of such openness measures as proxies for trade orientation largely reflects their ready availability. More rigorous measures of outward orientation are much harder to obtain and thus less used.[50] Among those that are available, most focus on trade regimes and exchange rates, at the exclusion of other factors that are indicative of trade orientation (Greenaway, 1986; World Bank, 1987; Greenaway and Nam, 1988). Some focus on real exchange rate distortions (Dollar, 1992). A few are based on deviations of actual, from predicted, exports (or imports), where predictions are based on estimated export functions (Balassa, 1985; Colombatto, 1992).[51]

On the basis of the available measures, the developing countries can be partitioned into various groups representing more or less outward orientation. The

Table 3.7
Growth Differentials Between Groups of Developing Countries[a] Classified by Trade Orientation[b]

	1965-73		1973-84	
	GDP	GDP Per Capita	GDP	GDP Per Capita
	(------Average Annual Growth Rates, %------)			
Greenaway & Nam Classification /b				
Strongly Inward Oriented	4.05	1.65	2.59	0.22
Moderately Inward Oriented	6.58	3.88	5.00	2.54
Moderately Outward Oriented	8.21	5.65	4.15	1.89
Strongly Outward Oriented	8.69	6.61	7.88	6.20

	1976-85		1970-90	
	GDP	GDP Per Capita	GDP	GDP Per Capita
Dollar Classification /b				
Most Inward Oriented	0.82	-2.22	2.16	-0.89
Moderately Inward Oriented	0.02	-2.70	1.62	-1.10
Moderately Outward Oriented	3.50	1.25	4.35	2.10
Most Outward Oriented	3.83	1.61	4.32	2.08

	1970-90	
	GDP	GDP Per Capita
Colombatto Classification /b		
Most Inward Oriented	3.96	1.64
Neutral	3.92	1.52
Most Outward Oriented	7.78	6.04

Source: World Bank, *Economic and Social Database* (BESD).
[a]Least square growth rates.
[b]The composition of the country samples is shown in Table A 3.3.

aggregate growth outcomes for the various groups can then be examined. Comparisons of growth and outward orientation based on different standards (the Greenaway/World Bank categories, the Dollar index, and the Colombatto regression results) are shown in Table 3.7. Almost regardless of the classification chosen, developing countries considered more outward-oriented appear to have grown in the aggregate more rapidly than those seemingly less so oriented during much of the postwar period, a result that one would expect on at least two grounds: (1) the reduction of internal distortions and thus the greater efficiency that outward orientation should generate and (2) the faster rate at which developing countries that are outward-oriented should absorb foreign knowledge (or more simply, foreign technology).[52]

At the single-country level, the positive relationship between trade orientation and growth is not as easy to see, even though it is documented in numerous in-depth country studies. Obviously, there is more to output growth than trade orientation, in the same way that there is more to growth than country size and export structure. Even core relationships can become obscured by other factors, and simple correlations do abstract from most of them. Trade orientation, moreover, cannot be precisely and unambiguously measured. It is difficult to map countries along a continuum indicating higher or lower outward orientation at a given time.

Relating exchange rate distortions, as measured by the Dollar index, and GDP growth over the 1971–1986 period, for a sample of fifty-six developing countries, reveals a statistically significant negative correlation between the two variables. The less distorted the real exchange rate, the faster was growth for the countries included in the sample. Similarly, a positive and significant relationship is found to exist between growth in real GDP over the 1980–1990 period and outward orientation, as measured by the Colombatto index, in thirty-eight developing countries (Figure 3.7). The higher the outward orientation, the faster seems to have been output growth.[53]

INCOME DISTRIBUTION, INEQUALITY, AND POVERTY

The distribution of income on a world scale appears to have largely favored the developed and semideveloped countries since 1870. As real incomes in poorer countries grew more slowly than in richer ones and base income was already considerably larger in the latter than in the former group, what we may call "worldwide inequality" increased substantially until the 1960s. The record shows, moreover, that even when able to catch up collectively with the higher-income countries in terms of growth and to increase their share of world GDP, as in the last decades of the current century, low-income countries made gains that remained concentrated in only one region. Relative inequality, though declining between developing and industrial countries considered as groups, seems, in fact, to have widened substantially across developing areas during the past ten to fifteen years.

Internal distribution of income in developing countries does not appear to have changed much during the past thirty years, if available evidence is to be believed. The fears of those who thought, on the basis of a priori reasoning, that income in developing countries would progressively become less evenly distributed in the early stages of economic growth have probably not come true, but there also appear to have been only few instances of unambiguous improvement in income distributions during this period.

"Domestic inequality," that is, what happens to the distribution of income among different categories of recipients inside a country, and its changes over time are important indicators of how the benefits of economic growth are shared. Over significant periods of time domestic inequality indexes carry important information on the characteristics of the growth that was actually achieved. They may also convey important indications about the social sustainability of a given growth strategy and the need to improve on it through policies specifically aimed at reducing maldistribution of income and wealth.

Figure 3.7
Country GDP Growth and Trade Orientation

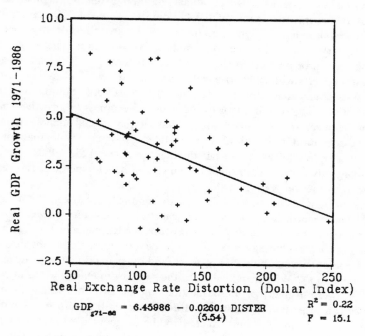

$$GDP_{g71-86} = 6.45986 - 0.02601 \text{ DISTER} \qquad R^2 = 0.22$$
$$(5.54) \qquad F = 15.1$$

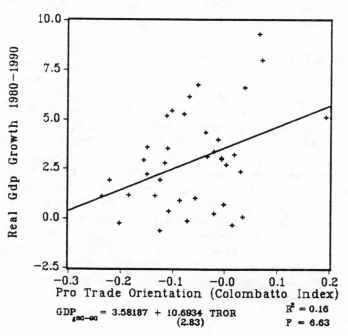

$$GDP_{g80-90} = 3.58187 + 10.6934 \text{ TROR} \qquad R^2 = 0.16$$
$$(2.83) \qquad F = 6.63$$

Finally, with constant income, changes in its distribution will directly affect poverty, making it better or worse, depending on the sign of this change. What happens to the income shares of the bottom 10 percent to 20 percent of the population should have a significant impact on the growth or decline of poverty in any country. Yet, as incomes do not stay the same, an important question is how the growth of income affects its internal distribution. If it leads to greater inequality, poverty will tend to rise in the process of growth, unless this "natural" tendency is counteracted by specific (and sustained) policies aimed at skewing the allocation of income in favor of the poor. Latecomers to growth—and thus most of the developing countries—would have to pay special attention to internal income distribution in the initial stages of their economic development process. This was a widely held tenet of development policies in the 1960s and 1970s, when many advocated redistributional policies in developing countries, even at the cost of some foregone growth.

These are important issues, giving rise to important questions. What has been the distribution of income on a world scale? Has inequality between rich and poor countries grown or diminished over time? What happened to income distribution inside developing economies? Has poverty increased in the developing world despite domestic output expansion (and other important improvements in social indicators)? Who benefited from the output growth achieved in most of them? Answers to many of these questions on the basis of available empirical evidence can often be only tentative. But they are still necessary, as without a "reality check," however imperfect, hypotheses about the benefits of growth become easily influenced by subjective beliefs and sociopolitical preferences.

International Income Distribution

Since data on income and population are now available not only for all the developed countries but also for the most important developing countries and the formerly centrally planned economies going back several decades, it would seem possible to draw a fairly representative map of the distribution of income in the world and to trace its changes over time. Pioneering computations made by Kuznets (1958) were expanded and updated, first by Kuznets himself (1966), then by Berry, Bourguignon, and Morrison (1983), and finally by Summers, Kravis, and Heston (1984) and Summers and Heston (1991). Kuznets's data showed that worldwide income distribution had favored the industrial countries from the 1930s to the 1950s. Subsequent estimates by Berry, Bourguignon, and Morrison indicated less conclusive trends for the following two decades: the share of world income going to the bottom quintile of world population appeared to have further decreased in the 1960s and 1970s if socialist countries were excluded from the total but to have remained constant if they were instead included in it. Only in the 1980s did the estimates of Summers, Kravis, and

Heston show a significant improvement in the developing countries' share of world income.

However, a main problem in the calculations covering the early periods was the poor international comparability of income levels. Comparability does require a common money numeraire. Expressing the incomes of different countries in a common currency necessitates the use of exchange rates. Yet, their values can differ substantially from equilibrium, even for extended periods of time, or can be otherwise distorted by commercial policy and other measures used to constrain trade and capital flows. Using actual exchange rates to convert incomes from local currencies to a common numeraire can, therefore, seriously bias cross-country comparisons.

There are additional problems associated to the use of exchange rates to make international comparisons of incomes. Even when they represent equilibrium values, exchange rates can be taken to reflect the relative prices of tradable goods and services, but not those of nontradables. If the prices of the goods and services that do not enter international trade (e.g., housing, transport, communications, education, health, domestic services) differ across countries, the same average incomes (expressed in a common currency) may have widely different purchasing powers in different countries. If prices of nontradables are higher in rich, than in poor, countries, even average incomes converted into the same currency using equilibrium exchange rates will overstate the purchasing power of recipients in richer countries and understate that of recipients in poorer countries. To properly compare the purchasing powers of average national incomes across countries, one needs to correct for the price differentials existing in nontraded goods.

The necessary corrections to per capita incomes expressed in a common numeraire on the basis of official exchange rates were impossible to make for a long time, especially in the case of developing countries. Exchange rates in many of them were highly distorted by protective trade regimes and were often differentially applied to various classes of goods (multiple exchange rates). Prices of nontradable goods were also not known with sufficient precision to allow meaningful intercountry comparisons of per capita incomes. The simplification of exchange rate regimes and the profound realignments that occurred in the 1980s in many developing countries, coupled with extensive trade liberalizations, alleviated some of the most acute problems connected with the use of exchange rates in arriving at internationally comparable income levels for them. Exchange rates, in other words, became more meaningful for many developing countries. Purchasing power ratios were also calculated for a progressively larger group of countries, making possible more accurate comparisons of the purchasing power of incomes both among developing nations and between developing and developed ones.

The more recent estimates of worldwide income distribution are based on GDP/GDY in constant dollars at international prices (i.e., converted using purchasing power parity or PPP factors). These much improved estimates, however,

Table 3.8
Shares of World GDP by Region[a]

	1870	1913	1950	1973	1989
	(--------------percent---------------)				
Industrial and Industrializing Countries:	55.1	70.2	75.6	74.5	65.5
North America	13.2	28.0	37.2	30.4	27.2
Western Europe	30.0	28.5	22.9	23.0	19.2
Asia & Pacific	3.1	3.9	4.2	9.0	9.6
Eastern Europe and Russia	8.8	9.8	11.4	12.1	9.5
Developing Countries:	44.9 /b	29.8	24.4	25.5	34.5
Africa		2.8	3.4	3.3	3.0
Asia		22.9	14.3	14.1	23.9
Latin America		4.2	6.7	8.1	7.6
TOTAL	100.0	100.0	100.0	100.0	100.0

Sources: Maddison (1992); UNDP (1992); World Bank, *Economic and Social Database* (BESD);
    Table A 3.1.
[a]Expressed in 1989 US dollars (at international prices).
[b]Regional breakdown not reliable for 1870.

cover only three decades, and in the case of the former, centrally planned economies (Eastern Europe, the USSR, and China) relied until quite recently[54] on less than fully satisfactory PPP converters, with the associated risk that stronger than average measurement biases are present in them.

Table 3.8 contains a computation of worldwide distribution of real income going back to 1913 made on the basis of (1) the most recent and complete set of estimates of purchasing-power-adjusted national GDPs (in U.S.$) prepared by Summers and Heston (1991); (2) the growth rates of real GDP provided by Maddison (1992); and (3) the additional ones that were assembled in this chapter. Not all developing countries are covered in our computation, but the sample includes 80 percent of all developing countries' total GDP in 1988. Subject to this caveat regarding country coverage, the figures shown in Table 3.8 confirm the tendency, first noted by Kuznets, toward growing inequality in the distribution of world income between industrial and developing countries in the early periods. Throughout the ''Victorian'' era and the inter-war years the share of world income accruing to industrialized and industrializing countries continued to increase from 55 percent in 1870 to 75 percent in 1950, while the share of developing countries decreased correspondingly.[55]

The data, however, also show a tendency for the imbalance in world income distribution to be corrected in the course of time. Between 1950 and 1989 international inequality first stopped widening, then diminished significantly. The share of world GDP accruing to industrial and industrializing countries (then all centrally planned economies) remained virtually stationary from 1950 to 1973 and thereafter declined by nine percentage points to the advantage of developing countries. The gains registered by developing economies vis-à-vis both industrial and formerly centrally planned economies in the 1973–1979 period, however, were limited to the Asia region. The shares of both Africa and Latin America in world real GDP did, in fact, decrease slightly during these years.

Income Distribution in Developing Countries

The developing countries of Africa, Asia, and Latin America, despite their much larger populations, not only account for a much smaller share of world income than Japan, the European countries, and their "overseas descendants" in North America, Australia, and New Zealand taken together but also have incomes that are less evenly distributed internally than those of the more developed countries.[56]

The question that arises immediately after this "recognition of facts" is whether the relatively greater inequality in the size distribution of income in developing countries is a "normal" state of affairs, reflecting differences in stages of development and standard evolution of the distributive process through the various phases of growth, or instead is the result of differences in the type of growth achieved by the two classes of countries. This question boils down to whether income inequality inside a country normally increases with economic growth and whether such tendency is automatically corrected (or reversed) as growth continues.

It was again Kuznets (1955) who, examining a cross-section of countries at different stages of economic development, first noted the relatively greater inequality in the income distribution of the poorer ones. He also put forward the hypothesis that such greater inequality was the result of the relatively higher concentration of income in the top and bottom groups of income recipients in developing, than in industrial, countries.[57] Partially modified by Kuznets himself (1963) in its motivations,[58] the hypothesis found statistical confirmation in subsequent work (Kravis, 1960; Paukert, 1973; Kakwani, 1980).[59]

On the actual profile of internal inequality during the growth process, Kuznets was only able to observe, from the available time series of income distribution in four developed countries, that it appeared to remain relatively constant until World War I and then to decline slightly (Kuznets, 1955, p. 5). Economic growth seemed to lead to some decline in inequality in the distribution of income over the long term. Kuznets's data did not yield any other evident pattern.

However, on the basis of observations of the structural shifts that normally occur in the process of growth (in particular, the reduction in the relative share of agriculture in total production) and the levels and distribution of incomes in rural and urban sectors (lower, but less unevenly distributed in the former than in the latter), plus some assumptions concerning constancy of sectoral income distributions, Kuznets was able to arrive, with the help of a numerical example, at the known hypothesis of increasing income inequality in the initial stages of economic growth of a country, followed by decreasing inequality in the sub-sequent stages, that is, to the "inverse-U" hypothesis (pp. 12–18).

Verification of such a hypothesis for the developing economies on the basis of actual time series data has so far remained impossible, given that measurements of income distributions in most of them did not begin until the 1950s and spread at a very slow pace. Even cross-section analysis of size income distribution in these countries could not be performed until the 1970s, when more observations on internal allocation of income became available. Ahluwalia (1976), using data assembled by Jain (1975), found statistical evidence of a parabolic pattern in the relationship between the shares of different groups of income recipients and the logarithms of per capita GNPs in both a sample of sixty developing and developed countries and a subsample of forty developing countries, which he interpreted as providing "a substantial measure of support" to Kuznets's hypothesis.

Despite their popularity, Ahluwalia's conclusions did not go unchallenged. First, the hypothesis that inequality raises in the early stages of growth and then diminishes as the process continues, should be tested using intertemporal (and not cross-section) data, since it represents a statement about changes over time. But neither pure time series tests nor the pooling of cross-section and time series of income distribution in developing countries is possible, given the paucity of country observations available.

Second, the essentially atheoretic test conducted by Ahluwalia has been crit-icized on grounds of inconsistent data and insufficient statistical stringency. Anand and Kanbur (1981, 1984) not only have cast doubts on Ahluwalia's statistical results but have shown that by using the more internally consistent income distributions from his own set and a nonlogarithmic parabolic function, one can arrive at exactly the opposite conclusion: a statistically significant shaped (instead of an inverted U-shaped) relationship between income distri-butions and per capita income growth in a cross-section of thirty-four developing countries. Saith (1983) also showed that the estimates of Ahluwalia for the income shares of the bottom 20 percent of income recipients in his sample of countries were unstable and lost significance when the socialist countries were removed from it and the dummy variable was also omitted, a result confirmed by Campano and Salvatore (1988) on the basis of a larger and more up-to-date data set. These authors, nonetheless, found in favor of Ahluwalia in all other percentiles of the population. The cross-section evidence is, therefore, far from conclusive, even for what it can be worth in testing Kuznets's hypothesis.

New data have become available on internal income distributions during the 1970s and 1980s, especially for Asian and Latin American countries. Yet, even taking this new evidence into account, not many firm generalizations seem possible. The conclusions that can be derived from the most recent data gathered in this study (generally regarding the 1980s) (Table 3.9) are that (1) income still seems to be in general more unevenly distributed in developing, than in industrial, countries; (2) the variance in income inequality between developing countries is

Table 3.9

Distribution of Household Income in Industrial and Developing Countries in the 1980s[a]

Country	Years	Income Shares of Quintiles					Top 10%	Ratio of Top 20% to Bottom 40%	Gini Index
		First	Second	Third	Fourth	Fifth			
Industrial Countries									
United States	1985	4.7	11.0	17.4	25.0	41.9	25.0	2.7	0.38
Canada	1987	5.7	11.8	17.7	24.6	40.2	24.1	2.3	0.35
United Kingdom	1982	5.8	11.0	17.6	24.7	41.0	24.8	2.4	0.36
Germany, Fed. Rep.	1984	6.8	12.7	17.8	24.1	38.7	23.4	2.0	0.32
France	1979	6.3	12.1	17.2	23.5	40.8	25.5	2.2	0.34
Italy	1986	6.8	12.0	16.7	23.5	41.0	25.3	2.2	0.34
Netherlands	1983	6.9	13.2	17.9	23.7	38.3	23.0	1.9	0.31
Denmark	1981	5.4	12.0	18.4	25.6	38.6	22.3	2.2	0.34
Sweden	1981	8.0	13.2	17.4	24.5	36.9	20.8	1.7	0.29
Norway	1982	5.0	12.0	17.9	25.1	40.0	23.7	2.3	0.35
Australia	1985	4.4	11.1	17.5	24.8	42.2	25.8	2.7	0.38
New Zealand	1981-82	5.1	10.8	16.2	23.2	44.7	28.7	2.8	0.39
Japan	1979	8.7	13.2	17.5	23.1	37.5	22.4	1.7	0.29
Average		6.1	12.0	17.5	24.3	40.1	24.2	2.2	**0.34**
Developing Countries									
Higher Income (above $4,500 per caput in 1990 /b)									
Brazil	1980	3.2	6.5	9.9	17.1	63.2	47.8	6.5	0.58
Peru	1981	---7.4---		9.7	19.8	63.0	43.8	5.9	0.57
Mexico	1984	4.1	8.0	12.9	21.2	53.7	37.0	4.4	0.49
Chile	1985	4.4	8.7	12.9	19.9	54.0	37.4	4.1	0.48
Colombia	1988	4.0	8.7	13.5	20.8	53.0	37.1	4.2	0.48
Venezuela	1987	5.2	10.0	15.2	22.8	46.8	30.2	2.0	0.41
Thailand	1988	4.5	8.1	12.3	20.3	54.9	37.8	4.4	0.48
Malaysia	1984	4.2	8.6	13.2	20.8	53.2	36.6	4.2	0.48
Korea	1988	4.9	10.7	16.2	22.6	45.5	29.2	2.9	0.40
Taiwan	1987	8.2	13.5	17.5	22.8	38.0	n.a.	1.8	0.31
Intermediate Income (between $2,000 and $4,500 per caput in 1990 /b)									
Indonesia	1976	6.6	7.8	12.6	23.6	49.4	34.0	3.4	0.44
Sri Lanka	1981-82	5.7	9.6	13.4	19.4	51.8	37.3	3.4	0.45
Philippines	1985	5.2	9.1	13.3	20.3	52.1	36.4	3.6	0.46
Egypt	1981	6.7	12.2	16.5	22.4	42.2	n.a.	2.2	0.35
Lower Income (below $2,000 per caput in 1990 /b)									
India	1975-76	5.8	9.9	14.2	20.8	49.3	33.9	3.1	0.43
Pakistan	1979	7.6	11.4	15.2	20.5	45.3	30.9	2.4	0.36
Bangladesh	1985-86	7.0	11.2	15.0	20.7	46.1	31.5	2.5	0.37
Cote d'Ivoire	1985-86	2.4	6.2	10.9	19.1	61.4	43.7	7.1	0.54
Botswana	1985-86	2.5	6.5	11.8	20.2	59.0	42.8	6.6	0.56
Average		5.1	9.2	13.5	20.8	51.6	36.9	3.9	**0.45**

Sources: United Nations (1985) and World Bank, *World Development Report* (1992), for industrial countries; Table 3.10 for all developing countries except Indonesia, for which household income distribution is taken from World Bank *Handbook* (1982).

[a]Data relate to total household income; coverage of household income data is national.

[b]Income measured in international prices.

very wide; and (3) this variance appears at first sight to be unrelated to income classes.

As already noted, the first of these conclusions concerning inequality in countries at different income (and development) levels is now generally accepted. The data in Table 3.9 clearly illustrate it. Gini coefficients[60] for industrialized countries have values ranging between 0.3 and 0.4, indicating low inequality. Similarly, ratios between the income accruing to the top 20 percent of households and that of the bottom 40 percent (another inequality measure often used) range between the values of 1.7 and 2.8, lowest in Japan, Sweden, and the Netherlands and highest in the United States, Australia, and New Zealand. With few exceptions, in low-income Asia[61] and in the Asian NICs, Gini coefficients in developing countries generally assume, instead, values between 0.4 and 0.6, indicating moderate to high income inequality. Similarly, with the same exceptions, the values of the ratio between the incomes of the top 20 percent and the bottom 40 percent of recipients typically range between 3.5 and 7.0, lowest in Sri Lanka and Indonesia and highest in Brazil, Botswana, and Côte d'Ivoire.

The existence of wide differences in the internal income distributions of developing countries also emerges quite clearly from Table 3.9. Aside from the range in the values of Gini coefficients and of the ratios between top and bottom sizes of income recipients already mentioned, one can notice the variety of country situations that exists across geographical regions as well as inside each of them. Generally speaking, internal income distributions appear to be more skewed in Africa and Latin America than in Asia. But among Latin American countries diversity abounds: income, for example, is relatively better distributed in Venezuela, Chile, and Colombia than in Brazil and Peru. There are also striking differences between internal distribution of income in North African countries and Sub-Saharan ones, with the latter being much more skewed. Finally, a few high-income developing countries, such as Taiwan and Korea, have already reached internal distributions of incomes that closely resemble those of mature industrial countries.[62]

More controversial, instead, is the relationship between per capita income levels and inequality in income distribution across developing countries. The standard view is that there is no apparent relationship between these two variables (Todaro, 1977). The classification of developing countries by broad income groups presented in Table 3.9 would appear to support this view. In many lower-income Asian countries, internal distributions of income appear to be considerably more equitable than in most higher-income countries of Latin America. Conversely, in the Sub-Saharan African countries for which recent data are available, income seems to be as unevenly distributed as in the worst of the higher-income countries of Latin America. There are, in addition, cases, such as those of Korea, Taiwan, and Singapore, in which per capita income levels are high and incomes are rather evenly distributed among households.

The variety of relations between income levels and income distributions also emerges quite clearly when the size distributions of income for the twenty-four developing countries shown in Table 3.9 (as synthesized by either simple inequality ratios or Gini coefficients) are systematically related to those countries' per capita incomes (measured in PPP equivalent) around 1980. No clear correlation is discernible at first sight, and the statistical estimates of the relationship between inequality and income levels in these countries emerge as weak and insignificant, irrespective of the inequality measure that is used (Figure 3.8).

The empirical evidence that we have been able to gather about the "secular" tendency of income distribution in developing countries allows even fewer conclusions than the examination of cross-country patterns at a given time. There are only a limited number of countries for which information on income distributions is available over a sufficiently long time period and is roughly comparable over time and across countries. There are even fewer country cases in which estimates of internal income distribution can be taken at face value. What emerges from the set of minimally consistent income distribution data[63] shown in Table 3.10 is that in five out of twenty country cases, the tendency was for overall income distribution to clearly worsen after the 1960s or early 1970s, while in nine other cases the tendency was toward improvements; in the remainder it was ambiguous.[64] Considering the cases where trends changed in time, these findings are not inconsistent with those obtained by Fields (1991b) in a sample of twenty-two developing countries during seventy growth spells. This author found a roughly even split between instances in which inequality increased and instances in which it decreased.

Poverty in Developing Countries

The time behavior of income shares going to the bottom 20 percent of recipients in developing countries reveals as mixed a record as that of overall income distributions. The sense that this subset of data conveys is one of overall stationariness in the relative income situation of the poorer groups: in nine out of twenty countries for which data are available for a long enough period, the share of income going to the bottom 20 percent of recipients seems to have consistently increased; in five cases it has consistently worsened, while in the rest it either seems unchanged or exhibits an indeterminate tendency.

Therefore, in only few of the developing countries for which information is available have the poor "unambiguously" increased their shares of income during the past four decades, even though the most pessimistic predictions about the "inevitable" worsening of their income and welfare in the process of growth (Adelman and Morris, 1973) do not seem to have materialized.[65] Moreover, even with unchanged internal distributions of income and thus unchanged relative incomes, the growth achieved in most developing countries should have contributed to a reduction of absolute poverty, at least until the late 1970s, as absolute incomes grew for the poor as well. In the 1980s the reduction of absolute poverty may have become less uniform across developing countries and regions than in previous decades. While further declines should have occurred in much of Asia,

Figure 3.8
Internal Inequality and Average Levels of GDP Per Capita

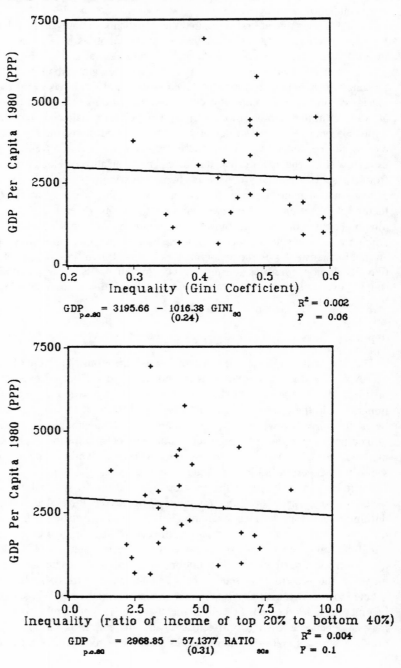

Table 3.10
Minimally Consistent Income Distributions in Individual Developing Countries,* 1960s, 1970s, and 1980s

Region/Country	Years	Income Shares of Quintiles					Top 10%	Gini Index	Income Unit	Source
		First 20%	Second 20%	Third 20%	Fourth 20%	Fifth 20%				
ASIA										
India	1960	4.1	9.5	14.1	20.6	51.7	36.7	0.47	HHY	JAIN
	1967-68	4.7	8.4	13.0	20.8	53.1	36.7	0.48	HHY	BHALLA & VASHISTHA
	1975-76	5.8	9.9	14.2	20.8	49.3	33.9	0.43	HHY	BHALLA & VASHISTHA
Pakistan	1963-64	6.9	11.6	15.7	21.9	43.9	28.6	0.36	HHY	MAHMOOD
	1969-70	7.9	12.2	16.1	21.5	42.3	27.7	0.33	HHY	MAHMOOD
	1979	7.6	11.4	15.2	20.5	45.3	30.9	0.36	HHY	MAHMOOD
Indonesia	1976	--19.6--		--38.0--		42.5	n.a.	0.34	PCE	TJONDRONEGORO et al./BPS
	1984	8.1	12.3	16.2	21.8	41.6	26.7	0.33	PCE	WB COUNTRY STUDY/BPS
	1990	8.6	12.2	15.8	21.2	42.2	27.5	0.33	PCE	BPS (prelim.)
Bangladesh	1966-67	8.7	10.9	14.6	21.7	44.1	29.5	0.34	HHY	WB HANDBOOK
	1973-74	7.0	10.3	15.1	22.8	44.8	28.4	0.36	HHY	BBS
	1981-82	6.6	10.7	15.3	22.1	45.3	29.5	0.39	HHY	BBS
	1985-86	7.0	11.2	15.0	20.7	46.1	31.5	0.37	HHY	BBS
Sri Lanka	1963	5.4	9.2	13.8	20.2	52.3	36.8	0.45	HHY	BRUTON
	1978-79	5.7	10.3	14.3	19.8	49.8	35.8	0.44	HHY	BRUTON
	1981-82	5.7	9.6	13.4	19.4	51.8	37.3	0.45	HHY	BRUTON
Thailand	1962-63	7.9	8.6	12.1	21.6	49.8	n.a.	0.41	HHY	DOWLING
	1975-76	6.1	9.7	14.0	21.0	49.3	n.a.	0.43	HHY	KRONGKAEW et al.
	1981	5.4	9.1	13.4	20.6	51.5	35.4	0.45	HHY	KRONGKAEW et al.
	1988	4.5	8.1	12.3	20.3	54.9	37.8	0.48	HHY	KRONGKAEW et al.
Korea	1965	5.7	13.6	15.5	23.3	41.8	25.8	0.34	HHY	SUH/KDI
	1976	5.7	11.2	15.4	22.4	45.3	27.5	0.39	HHY	SUH/KDI
	1988	4.9	10.7	16.2	22.6	45.5	29.2	0.40	HHY	KWON/KDI
Taiwan	1968	7.8	12.2	16.3	22.3	41.4	n.a.	0.36	HHY	TSDB
	1974	8.8	13.5	17.0	22.1	38.6	n.a.	0.32	HHY	TSDB
	1980	8.8	13.9	17.7	22.8	36.8	n.a.	0.30	HHY	TSDB
	1987	8.2	13.5	17.5	22.8	38.0	n.a.	0.31	HHY	TSDB

Table 3.10 (continued)

Region/Country	Years	First 20%	Second 20%	Third 20%	Fourth 20%	Fifth 20%	Top 10%	Gini Index	Income Unit	Source
Hong Kong	1963-64	4.4	8.9	12.2	17.8	56.7	n.a.	0.46	HHY	LIN
	1973-74	4.1	10.9	15.9	22.1	47.0	n.a.	0.40	HHY	LIN
	1979-80	6.2	10.9	15.1	21.3	46.5	n.a.	0.37	HHY	LIN
Malaysia	1960	3.2	6.4	10.7	18.5	61.2	45.7	0.57	HHY	JAIN
	1970	3.8	8.0	12.4	19.6	56.2	41.1	0.52	HHY	JAIN
	1984	4.2	8.6	13.2	20.8	53.2	36.6	0.48	HHY	BRUTON
Philippines	1961	4.2	7.9	12.1	19.3	56.5	41.0	0.51	HHY	NEDA
	1971	3.6	8.1	13.3	21.0	54.0	37.1	0.49	HHY	NEDA
	1985	5.2	9.1	13.3	20.3	52.1	36.4	0.46	HHY	NEDA
LATIN AMERICA										
Brazil	1960	3.5	8.0	13.8	20.3	54.4	39.7	0.50	HHY	LANGONI
	1970	3.2	6.9	10.8	16.9	62.2	47.8	0.56	HHY	LANGONI
	1980	3.2	6.5	9.9	17.1	63.2	47.8	0.58	HHY	CAMARGO
Mexico	1963	3.5	6.8	11.0	19.8	58.9	41.9	0.54	HHY	ASPE & BERISTAIN
	1968	3.4	7.2	11.6	19.6	58.2	42.0	0.54	HHY	ASPE & BERISTAIN
	1977	2.9	7.4	13.2	22.0	54.5	36.7	0.51	HHY	ASPE & BERISTAIN
	1984	4.1	8.0	12.9	21.2	53.7	37.0	0.49	HHY	LUSTIG
Colombia	1971	3.6	7.1	11.4	19.2	58.6	42.4	0.53	HHY	VAN DE WALLE
	1978	4.3	8.7	13.6	21.0	52.5	36.4	0.48	HHY	VAN DE WALLE
	1988	4.0	8.7	13.5	20.8	53.0	37.1	0.48	HHY	VAN DE WALLE
Chile	1968	4.4	9.0	13.8	21.4	51.4	34.8	0.45	HHY	VAN GINNEKEN & PARK
	1985	4.4	8.7	12.9	19.9	54.0	37.4	0.48	HHY	VAN DE WALLE
Peru	1971-72	1.5	5.2	10.8	21.1	61.4	43.2	0.57	HHY	BERRY
	1981	--7.4--		9.7	19.8	63.0	43.8	0.57	HHY	BERRY
Venezuela	1962	3.3	6.3	11.2	20.2	59.0	41.2	0.54	HHY	JAIN
	1970	3.0	7.3	12.9	22.8	54.0	35.7	0.49	HHY	VAN GINNEKEN & PARK
	1987	5.2	10.0	15.2	22.8	46.8	30.2	0.41	HHY	VAN DE WALLE

110

	Year							Gini		Source
Argentina	1961	6.9	9.7	13.3	19.2	50.9	37.0	0.44	HHY	JAIN
	1970	4.4	9.7	14.1	21.5	50.3	35.2	0.44	HHY	VAN GINNEKEN & PARK
AFRICA										
Egypt	1964-65	4.6	9.5	14.6	22.9	48.4	31.1	0.43	HHY	JAIN
	1974	5.8	10.7	14.7	20.8	48.0	33.2	0.40	HHY	WDR88
	1981	6.7	12.2	16.5	22.4	42.2	n.a.	0.35	HHY	WB Country Study
Kenya	1976	2.6	6.3	11.5	19.2	60.4	45.8	0.59	HHY	WDR82
Zambia	1959	5.4	7.6	11.1	17.7	58.2	44.0	0.52	HHY	JAIN
	1976	3.4	7.4	11.2	16.9	61.1	46.4	0.56	HHY	WDR88
Cote d'Ivoire	1985-86	2.4	6.2	10.9	19.1	61.4	43.7	0.54	HHY	WDR87
Botswana	1985-86	2.5	6.5	11.8	20.2	59.0	42.8	0.56	HHY	WDR92
Senegal	1970	5.5	7.8	10.5	15.3	60.9	45.4	0.51	HHY	LECALLION
Zimbabwe	1969	3.0	4.8	7.2	17.0	68.0	55.5	0.63	HHY	LECALLION

Sources: Aspe and Beristain (1984); Bangladesh Bureau of Statistics, BBS (1988); Biro Pusat Statistik, BPS (1970, 1984, 1990 preliminary); Berry (1990); Bhalla and Vashistha (1988); Bruton (1992); Camargo (1987); Dowling (1984); Jain (1975); Krongkaew, Tinakorn, and Suphachalasai (1992); Kwon (1990); Langoni (1973); Lin (1985); Lustig (1992); Mahmood (1984); National Economic and Development Authority, NEDA (1989); Suh (1985); Tjondronegoro, Soejono, and Hardjono (1992); Van De Walle (1991); Van Ginneken and Park (1984); World Bank Country Study, *Egypt, Alleviating Poverty During Structural Adjustment* (1991), *Indonesia, Strategy for a Sustained Reduction in Poverty* (1990); World Bank, *World Development Reports* (WDR), various issues; World Bank, *Handbook* (1982).

*Coverage is national, unless otherwise specified.

HHY = household income; PCE = per capita expenditure.

111

as a consequence of very fast growth in this region, the trends in Latin America and Africa are much more difficult to predict a priori. Income distribution may have worsened in some parts of these regions, and concomitant declines in per capita income and consumption in many of their component countries can be expected to have led to increases in poverty.

Poverty is a very real phenomenon, if one that is neither easy to conceptualize nor easy to measure. The key difficulty lies with the nature of poverty, as an absolute or a relative condition. Divisions of views on this point are long-standing, not only among economists but among social scientists in general. The "hard" scientific (mostly medical) evidence concerning the levels of absolute poverty—those at which continuation of life is endangered—is also less than conclusive. While poverty may very well be an absolute phenomenon, its definition in terms of income necessary to satisfy minimum nutritional requirements does not seem to be independent of time, geographical location, and cultural influences.[66]

Economists have dealt with the concept of absolute poverty pragmatically, trying to define it in a way that would ensure its adaptation to changing circumstances in time and places. This approach has made measurement of poverty easier over time (since subsequent "poverty levels" could be explicitly specified) but comparison across countries at any given time much more difficult, as poverty standards are not uniform among them.

By one of the standard methods of poverty measurement—head count[67]—absolute poverty appears to have decreased, from the 1960s to the 1970s, in most of Asia and also in much of South America (Table 3.11). Not only the share of total population living in poverty but also the total number of poor seem to have fallen in many of these countries during this period. In the 1980s, however, poverty trends became mixed. While absolute poverty continued to decline in Asia, it remained practically unchanged in Latin America and increased in Sub-Saharan Africa. In a few African countries the percent of population living below the national poverty lines has remained virtually stationary, while in most others it has increased substantially, meaning that the total number of poor has increased during this period, as total population grew by nearly 30 percent.

At the country level, there seems to be a fairly clear inverse relationship between growth of per capita income over one or two decades and poverty reduction, with countries experiencing fast and sustained economic growth (Asia throughout most of the period, and Latin America until the early 1980s) showing declines in the shares of their population living in poverty. Given that income distribution did not change much in most developing countries, one would generally expect to find this relationship under these circumstances.

Improving trends are most striking and general in Asia, where per capita income growth was above average throughout the post–World War II period. Fast-growing countries such as Korea, Taiwan, Malaysia, Thailand, and Pakistan (and more recently, China) often experienced dramatic reductions of poverty

Table 3.11

Population Below Poverty Level in Individual Developing Countries[a]

Years (approx.) Region/Country	1960	1970	1980	1990	Source
Asia					
India	38.4	44.2	41.9	33.1	WB
Pakistan	54.0	42.7	29.9	32.4	WB
Bangladesh	n.a.	82.9	73.8	51.7 /c	Hossain & Sen
Indonesia /b	n.a.	57.6	28.6	17.0 /c	WB & Tjondrenegoro
Sri Lanka	59.0	41.0	27.0	n.a.	Fields & WB
Thailand	57.0	39.0	24.0	22.0	Meesook, Krongkaew & WB
Malaysia	n.a.	18.0	9.0	2.0	WB
Philippines	n.a.	35.0	30.0	21.0	WB
Taiwan	35.0	10.0	5.0 /d	n.a.	Fields & Rao
Korea /b	40.9	23.4	9.8	5.0	Chung-Oh & WB
China	n.a.	33.0	28.0	9.0	WB
Singapore	19.2 /e	7.0	1.5	0.3	Rao
Latin America /f					
Guatemala			71 (40)	73 (49)	CEPAL
Brazil	56	52 (30)	45 (22)	45 (23)	CEPAL
Mexico	53	42 (15)	40 (14)	37 /g (13)	CEPAL
Colombia		47 (19)	42 (17)	42 (19)	CEPAL
Peru		56 (30)	53 (25)	60 (30)	CEPAL
Venezuela		28 (12)	25 (9)	32 (11)	CEPAL
Argentina		9 (2)	10 (3)	16 (5)	CEPAL
Uruguay		12* (5)	15 (4)	20 (5)	CEPAL
Costa Rica		26 (7)	24 (7)	27 (9)	CEPAL
Africa					
Egypt			23.3	24.0	WB
Morocco	50.0	42.6	38.0	30.0	WB
Tunisia			17.5	16.1	WB
Tanzania			53.0	n.a.	WB
Kenya			48.0	46.0	WB
Malawi			80.0	77.6	WB
Rwanda			n.a.	87.2	WB
Ghana			n.a.	44.0	WB
Ivory Coast			n.a.	28.6	WB
Zambia			58.6		WB
Madagascar			50.0	52.0	WB
Somalia			61.7	71.6	WB
Mali		44.5	n.a.	48.5	WB

Sources: Hossain and Sen (1992); Tjondronegoro, Soejono, and Hardjono (1992); Rao (1989); Fields (1989); Meesook (forthcoming); Krongkaew, Tinakorn, and Suphachalassi (1992); Chung and Oh (1992); CEPAL (1991); and World Bank, *Social Indicators of Development* (various years).
*Partially estimated.
[a]Data refer to total population unless otherwise indicated. Poverty levels are nationally set and thus comparable over time, but not across countries.
[b]Proportion of households with incomes below a certain amount (in real terms).
[c]Data are for 1985/1986.
[d]Data are for 1975.
[e]Data are for 1953/1954.
[f]Figures in parentheses are for percentages of population living in extreme poverty.
[g]Data are for 1984.

among their populations.[68] Growth (especially in the agricultural sector and of food production within it) also seems to have helped reduce poverty during the past twenty to thirty years in India, Bangladesh, and Indonesia, countries at the very bottom of the income ladder in Asia, and to have, as well, supported poverty reduction in Sri Lanka, where active redistributional policies were concomitantly used to obtain a reduction in the country's poverty.

In Latin America, the region at the middle of the growth spectrum, the inverse relationship between economic growth and poverty is only slightly less evident than in Asia, because the reductions in the share of poor were less dramatic, if still quite evident. Until 1980, while most countries managed to maintain good growth, reductions in relative poverty were widespread, even if they occurred at different speeds in different places. Only in countries such as Uruguay and Argentina, where growth faltered, did a worsening of the poverty situation occur. This, however, was still the expected outcome on the basis of the poverty-growth relationship that should exist in the presence of (roughly) constant internal distributions of income. Moreover, during the 1980s, when economic performance worsened throughout Latin America, declines in poverty came to a halt, and in several countries the situation worsened substantially (Argentina, Peru, Venezuela, and Uruguay). Only Mexico managed to reduce relative poverty, at least until the mid-1980s.[69]

While the poverty experience of Latin America during the economic adjustment years of the 1980s is still debated (CEPAL, 1991; Van de Walle, 1991; Fields, 1991a), and its complexity should not be overlooked, it does still seem to conform to the expectation that growth and reduction of poverty normally go hand in hand: a slowing down of economic growth over a relatively long period of time tends to worsen the poverty situation of any country, while a quickening in the pace of growth tends to generate improvements, as emphasized, among others, by Fields (1988, 1991b) on the basis of results from detailed country studies.

If some significant long-term trends in poverty can be observed from the available data, comparisons of poverty levels or poverty shares across developing countries are much more difficult to make, not only conceptually but also computationally. The shortcut most often used is to define absolute poverty at some arbitrary level of income per capita, mutated from a specific country or from the estimated costs of acquiring the minimum amount of calories necessary to continued life. Then this overall poverty standard is used for all countries after it is translated into local currency equivalents using exchange rates. Finally, the number of people living in each country below that minimum income level is estimated. Even leaving aside the difficulties connected with the identification of an appropriate international standard and its translation into local ones, this approach allows only "snapshots" of the poverty situation in the world at a given time. The fact that standards used in these calculations vary over time and from one study to another makes it impossible to rigorously compare worldwide poverty distributions based on this method.

There are several such estimates of the distribution of world poverty made at different times (Ahluwalia, Carter, and Chenery, 1979; Kakwani, 1980; World Bank, 1980, 1990; Ravallion et al., 1991). Though not strictly comparable, these estimates nonetheless convey one broadly consistent picture: absolute poverty, though possibly declining, is still very large and quite widespread in the developing world. According to the most recent estimates (Ravallion et al., 1991), about 30 percent of the world population (or 1.1 billion people) still live in extreme poverty (Table 3.12). Regionally, most poverty is concentrated in Asia, with India accounting for 35 percent of the total, and in Africa. Yet, deep pockets of absolute poverty exist in Central and South America as well. There also appears to be a broad correlation between the geographical distribution of the stock of poor and average income levels prevailing in the various regions and countries. Much of the world poverty is concentrated in South Asia (India, Bangladesh, Nepal) and Sub-Saharan Africa, where per capita incomes are lowest.

While the existence of a systematic, negative relationship between per capita income and poverty at the country level has at times been denied (Griffin, 1989), such a simple relationship appeared instead to exist and to have been statistically significant at the end of the 1980s in a sample of thirty-four developing countries for which a common measure of poverty was available and judged to be representative of the actual situation (Figure 3.9).[70] Developing countries with higher per capita income (measured on a PPP basis) generally exhibited lower levels of poverty than countries with lower per capita income. There were exceptions to this empirical "rule," but their existence was not enough to invalidate it. There were also a significant negative relationship between per capita income growth in the 1980–1990 period and poverty reduction in a sample of twenty-four developing countries for which changes in poverty at the national level could be measured.[71]

CONCLUSIONS

Economic growth in the developing world is not a totally recent phenomenon. Some positive growth in real output per capita seems to have already occurred in the 1870–1913 period, at least in two of the major developing regions: Latin America and Asia. What happened in Africa during this period is more difficult to ascertain. On average, moreover, growth in developing countries also seems to have remained positive in per capita terms in the subsequent thirty years, if probably less so than between 1870 and 1913. A strong and general pickup in the tempo of economic activity did occur after the end of World War II and the completion of decolonization, when average growth of per capita real income was nearly 3 percent a year in the developing world as a whole, a rate roughly similar to that experienced by industrialized countries. In the most recent years, the average rate of growth of real per capita income in developing countries exceeded that of industrial countries. Though mostly driven by Asia, this reversal in long-standing aggregate tendencies represents a notable and historically significant event.

At the aggregate level, the medium-term growth spells registered by developing countries since 1870 appear to be roughly in line with those of the in-

Table 3.12
Poverty in the Developing World, 1990

Country Groups	Higher Poverty Line /a			Lower Poverty Line /b			Social Indicators		
	Number of Poor (million)	Headcount Index (%)	Contribution to Total Poverty (%)	Number of Poor (million)	Headcount Index (%)	Contribution to Total Poverty (%)	Life Expectancy at Birth (years)	Infant Mortality (x 1000)	Adult Literacy (%)
South Asia (of which India)	562 (448)	49.0 (52.8)	49.8 (39.7)	287 (226)	25.0 (26.6)	44.7 (35.2)	58 (59)	92 (92)	47 (48)
East Asia (of which China)	169 (128)	11.3 (11.3)	15.0 (11.3)	74 (63)	5.0 (5.6)	11.5 (9.8)	68 (70)	34 (29)	76 (73)
Africa South of Sahara	216	47.8	19.1	152	33.6	23.7	51	107	50
North Africa & Middle East	73	33.1	6.5	53	24.0	8.3	61	80	53
Latin America	108	25.2	9.6	76	17.8	11.8	68	47	84
All Developing Countries	1,128	29.7	100.0	642	16.9	100.0	63	62	64

Source: World Bank data files.
[a]Based on a poverty line of $370 (in 1985 international prices).
[b]Based on a poverty line of $275 (in 1985 international prices).

Figure 3.9
Income Levels, Income Growth, and Poverty

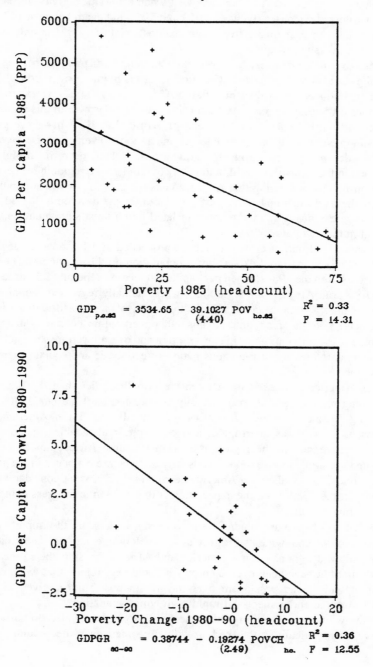

$$GDP_{p.o.85} = 3534.65 - 39.1027\ POV_{ho.85}$$
$$(4.40)$$

$R^2 = 0.33$
$F = 14.31$

$$GDPGR_{80-90} = 0.38744 - 0.19274\ POVCH_{ho.}$$
$$(2.49)$$

$R^2 = 0.36$
$F = 12.55$

dustrialized countries: the pace of output growth in the developing world quickened when economic activity expanded most rapidly in the industrial world (e.g., between 1950 and 1973) and slowed when economic activity decelerated in industrialized countries (between 1913 and 1950 and again between 1973 and 1990, at least in four of the five major regions). Naturally this is only a very aggregate, average linkage.

These overall tendencies, however, hide significant differences between developing regions and countries. The process of economic growth consolidated earlier in Latin America than in Asia or Africa. Asia, moreover, experienced enormous difficulties in reaching "intensive growth." Growth in this region did not become fairly general until the end of World War II. It has since gained strong momentum and has proceeded at much-above-average rates. Over the past two decades per capita income growth has, in fact, been much higher in Asia than in the industrial world, and most countries in the region have partaken of this growth. Considering that Asia accounts for the bulk of world population and for the overwhelming portion of population in the developing world, economic progress made by this region translated into a most significant improvement in human welfare.

Per capita real output growth in Africa proceeded at a reasonable pace until the 1970s, given the rapid expansion of population on this continent. The trend reversed itself in the 1980s, when per capita real income generally fell, especially in Sub-Saharan Africa. This region as a whole actually regressed economically for more than a decade and is still in the midst of a very difficult period of adjustment. With income regression absolute poverty almost certainly increased, and some of the previous gains in consumption and overall welfare were nullified. All this exemplifies the still-tenuous nature of economic and social progress in this region.

Latin America embarked upon intensive growth earlier than the other two developing regions, and its pace steadily accelerated until the late 1970s. The following decade, however, was very difficult also for Latin America. The process of growth was interrupted, and per capita real income expanded at a barely positive rate in the region as a whole. Unlike Africa, however, what happened in Latin America in the 1980s appears to be more a pause in the growth process than a reversal. Latin American economies underwent considerable adjustment in the 1980s, and the expectation is that economic progress could start again in this region.

The record of the past hundred years does not underscore the importance of natural resource endowments for growth in developing countries. The relatively better endowed regions—Latin America and Africa—did start their process of growth first but have been overtaken by Asia, the very region that was long the object of widespread pessimism over its growth possibilities, given its poor overall resource endowment and rapidly growing population.

On the whole, cross-country differences in income levels also do not appear to have systematically influenced growth outcomes over the medium term.

Growth in per capita real income was neither favored nor hampered by either relatively high or low starting income bases. For a while in the post–World War II period, "middle-income" developing countries grew more rapidly in aggregate, and especially in per capita, terms, than "low-income" countries, but a reversal of this trend occurred in the 1980s, when low-income Asia reached a faster than average growth tempo. However, if a low starting level of income does not prevent fast growth from occurring, it also does not ensure favorable growth results, as witnessed by most of the Sub-Saharan African countries during the 1970s and 1980s. Conversely, the slowdown in the fast growth trend of middle-income Latin America indicates that a relatively high income base does not ensure per se continuation of favorable growth conditions.

Size also seems to have had little importance in influencing growth outcomes over the past century. No systematic pattern relating growth to physical or economic size is evident from the economic performance of developing countries. In addition, size in itself does not appear to have any discernibly positive or negative influence on the timing of intensive growth. The large economies of Asia, for example, were relatively late starters, but Brazil was an early one.

Country experience, at least in the past forty years, shows instead the importance of economic structures in influencing economic performance. There was, in general, an inverse relationship between reliance on the production and export of non-oil primary commodities (as opposed to manufactures or fuels) and growth—a relationship that one would expect, given the lower productivity growth in agriculture than in industry. The countries more dependent on primary products or, better, those that remained for a longer time dependent on them generally experienced slower growth than those that relied instead on manufactures.

Trade orientation is also shown to have been a factor significantly correlated with economic growth in many developing countries, an important illustration of the role of economic strategies and policies in the process of growth. More outward-oriented countries have grown faster than less outward-oriented ones. This relationship, generally exemplified by the growth experience of the Asian NICs, is by no means limited to any given group of countries. It encompasses a much wider spectrum of country situations and appears to be, broadly speaking, an incremental one.

Country experience points, in addition, to the importance of political stability as a necessary, but by no means sufficient, condition for initiating and maintaining economic growth. In a large number of cases the start of intensive growth occurred just after a minimum of political stability was reached after a large shock or deep internal turmoil. This is the case of China after the victory of the socialist revolution in 1949, of India after independence from Great Britain, of Korea, Taiwan, and Singapore after partition or separation, and of much of South America after the prolonged turmoils of the postindependence era. Conversely, phases of political instability in the life of many countries have coincided with noticeable deteriorations of economic performance, as in the cases of China at the time of the Cultural Revolution, Indonesia in the last period of Sukharno's presidency, and Nigeria in much of the postindependence period. There is also evidence that drastic changes in political regimes—what one may call large political shocks—have constituted turning points in a country's growth process.

The pace of economic growth in developing countries has caught up with that of industrial countries and in the most recent period has been even higher. This does not mean that the absolute income gap between developed and developing countries is already getting smaller, given the vastly different bases to which rates of growth apply, but it certainly foreshadows this possibility for at least some countries. Developing countries have already reversed the trend in world income inequality that had been adverse for them since at least the 1870s. In the past twenty or so years the percentage share of world income going to developing countries, especially those in Asia, has substantially increased. The barycenter of world economic growth seems to be moving toward Asia, where the process started with Japan, spread to the smaller countries of East Asia, and now appears to be reaching its most significant extension in China and India.

Income remains less evenly distributed in developing, than in industrial, countries. The variance in income distribution is also higher in the former than in the latter. However, income distribution in developing countries does not seem to have worsened during the early stages of their development as some had hypothesized and many had feared. Nonetheless, cases of unambiguous improvements are few. In many cases trends in internal income distributions were mixed during the past thirty years. No significant relationship between income distribution and per capita income levels is discernible in developing countries at a given time.

If economic growth did not significantly affect income distribution in one direction or another in most developing countries, it seems to have benefited the poor. The benefits of growth may have been lower for the poor than those that accrued to higher-income groups but appear nonetheless to have been appreciable in size. Given that internal income inequality does not seem to have changed appreciably in most developing countries, growth of income contributed at a minimum to a substantial reduction of absolute poverty in many of them. Declining poverty was a relatively clear and well documented tendency in most of Asia and much of Latin America until the early 1980s, but much less so in Africa.

Despite much economic progress, in income as well as social conditions,[72] poverty is still an enormous problem in developing countries, where nearly 30 percent of the total population lives in conditions of extreme poverty. The hopeful part of the poverty distribution picture is that much of it is concentrated in Asia, where economic progress has been fast and growth has gained a very strong momentum. Much less reassuring seem to be the prospects for poverty reduction in Africa, a region that is still suffering from a profound economic crisis and where resumption of intensive growth still appears quite problematic, if indispensable to allow gains in the fight against poverty.

NOTES

The very helpful assistance of Stefania Scandizzo, Parita Suebsaeng, and Giovanni Zanalda in assembling and elaborating the statistical evidence on which the paper is based and the comments provided by Ram Agarwala, Piero Alessandrini, Desmond McCarthy, and James Riedel on previous drafts of the paper are gratefully acknowledged.

1. Throughout this chapter I distinguish—if somewhat loosely—between growth (which refers mostly to output) and development (which also encompasses income distribution, social progress, fulfillment of basic human needs, and other "desirable" structural changes).

2. On output growth in developing countries, the contributions of Zimmerman (1962), Mitchell (1982), Reynolds (1985) and Maddison (1989, 1991, 1992) are particularly noteworthy. On population growth, those of Durand (1967a) and the population office of the United Nations are to be mentioned. On trade, the League of Nations (1942, 1945), Bairoch (1967), and UNCTAD (1969 and later years) have provided vital information. Comprehensive reviews of the economic evolution of developing countries, if for different periods and areas, can be found in Kuznets (1966), Bairoch (1967), UNCTAD (1969 and subsequent years), Morawetz (1977), Cassen (1981), Mitchell (1982), and World Bank *World Development Report* (1991).

3. Previous work on growth in individual developing countries was recently systematized by Mitchell (1982), Reynolds (1983, 1985), and Maddison (1989, 1991, 1992).

4. Since most of the migration occurred within the industrial world, these global population growth figures are not invalidated by the vast movements that occurred from Europe to North America and Australia, especially between 1870 and 1913. The main population leakage not captured here, which in some measure contributes to the downward bias of the overall growth rate of industrial countries, is represented by the European migration to South America.

5. China, however, by virtue of its low income and relative economic backwardness in the period under review is considered throughout as a developing country.

6. The main exceptions were the Latin American republics, most of which gained independence in the first half of the nineteenth century, and a few other countries, such as Egypt, Ethiopia, South Africa, Liberia, and Thailand, which were not (or not fully) colonized. China also represents a partial exception, having been able to escape complete colonial domination even during the years of foreign occupation of its coastal areas by Western nations and of Manchuria by Japan.

7. Discussed later in the chapter.

8. The main exception to the overall stagnation of per capita income in the developing world during this period was again Latin America, where real output growth exceeded population growth by 1.3 percent a year. Actually real per capita GDP growth in Latin America, untouched by world wars, was almost as high as in the industrial world throughout this period.

9. According to this author, until real output expands at the same rate as that of population, growth is simply "extensive." When real output expands faster than population, growth becomes "intensive." Growing per capita real output is thus the hallmark of "intensive" growth.

10. This is still a strongly relative statement: it applies to the improvement in the quality and reliability of data between the periods of 1913–1950 and 1950–1970. In

absolute terms, the measurement of real output is difficult and unprecise even in economically advanced countries (Fua', 1993). It is even more so in many developing ones.

11. Available data on per capita income, measured in a common currency using PPP converters (Summers and Heston, 1988, 1991), show that in 1950 the average per capita GDP in the main countries of South America (the richest in the developing world) was $2,380, or about half that of the industrial countries. Average per capita GDP was around $1,620 in Asia, about one-fourth that of industrial countries. In the six African countries (excluding South Africa) for which data are available on a common PPP basis, per capita GDP was $680, about one-fourth that of Latin America and one-eighth that of the industrial countries. Roughly 60 percent of the world population living in Asia and Africa, therefore, accounted for less than 20 percent of world income in 1950.

12. This is clearly shown in Table 3.2.

13. The developed-to-developing countries' growth causality was again recently expounded by Lewis (1979), who in his Nobel lecture observed: "For the past hundred years the rate of growth of output in the developing world has *depended* on the rate of growth of output in the developed world. When the developed world grows fast, the developing world grows fast, and when the developed slow down the developing slow down" (p. 1; emphasis added). Lewis lamented on the same occasion the "breaking down" of the "engine of growth," that is, the positive pull exerted by industrial countries. Revisiting this critical linkage, Riedel (1984) concluded instead that "the economic relationship between developed and developing countries [cannot] be defined adequately in terms of simple mechanical linkages. . . . The theory of trade as an engine of growth in developing countries is, as its name suggests, highly mechanistic." He also said, "Measures of linkage obtained by regressing LDC exports on [industrial countries'] income prove far too unstable to be interpreted reasonably as mechanical gears of an engine of growth" (p. 71).

14. India and other large South Asian countries, such as Pakistan and Bangladesh, were also highly exposed, if one considers standard stock of debt to GNP or export indicators. Yet, the concessional terms at which very large portions of its debt had been contracted limited the debt-service burden of South Asia quite considerably, when measured against export capacity. The same applied to most of Sub-Saharan Africa.

15. The economic performance of China from the late 1940s to the late 1960s is subject to much uncertainty. Official estimates of growth do not appear to be believable, and private estimates are tentative at best. This point is discussed later in the chapter.

16. The notable exception to this trend was Indochina, where war did not stop for any significant amount of time until the 1980s.

17. Fostering economic growth became one of the main objectives of the newly independent countries, whose governments assumed direct responsibility for it. These governments received substantially increased amounts of external assistance from the international community. Such assistance included technical inputs as well as means to finance the imports of capital goods necessary to increase investment rates. Between 1950 and 1960, for example, Western aid to Sub-Saharan Africa increased from about 1 percent to 1.9 percent of the region's GNP. It rose to almost 3 percent between 1960 and 1970 and to 4.5 percent in the next ten years (OECD, 1985).

18. Chile and Colombia were early adjusters to the oil and external debt shocks.

19. Reynolds finds that "turning points are almost always associated with some significant political event" and "usually associated with a marked rise in exports" (1983, p. 903).

20. The same is true in the case of Singapore, where the local economy boomed after separation from Malaysia.

21. Growth of output was apparently very strong between 1952 and 1958 and again in the late 1960s, but official data are unreliable for both the years of the "great leap forward" and those of the "cultural revolution." China, moreover, was for a long time an exceptionally closed economy, with exports accounting for only 3 percent of GNP and imports for an equivalent amount as late as 1970 (IMF, 1990). For a discussion of China's postwar growth, see chapter 12. Liu and Yeh (1965) provide some estimates of growth in the early postwar period, while Perkins (1980) discusses and compares various unofficial estimates of China's GDP growth until 1970.

22. Reynolds, however, calls into question even Amin's estimates (Reynolds, 1985, pp. 192, 199) but seems to have based his judgment on Amin (1970), instead of Amin (1966), which contains much more detail on sources and methods used and on assumptions made by the author.

23. Estimates of per capita real income growth in South Africa are plagued by the lack of appropriate price deflators. This seems to be a particularly serious problem, beginning in the early 1930s, when growth of nominal output recovered strongly and continued at a very fast rate until the Korean War, with the possibility of considerable overestimates of real income.

24. One should treat the country estimates for the 1913–1950 period presented in Table A3.1 and the aggregates contained in Tables 3.1 and 3.2, which were derived from it, as "educated" guesses.

25. Reynolds puts the "turning point" of Nigeria in 1890, but this is little more than a guess.

26. Actually Egypt seems to have experienced significant increases in real per capita incomes between 1886 and 1898 (Hansen, 1979, p. 33). Reynolds dates the turning point of Algeria in 1880 (1985, p. 32), but this seems far too early. The years between 1920 and 1930 are probably a better estimate. Little is known about Jordan and Syria.

27. There remains considerable differences in the quality and reliability of available statistics across developing countries. All improvements that occurred in this area are relative to the previous period.

28. The first twenty-five years of growth and development of the post–World War II period have already been extensively reviewed by Morawetz (1977).

29. The years between 1950–1951 and 1972–1973 can be thought of as the heydays of the post–World War II economic order, ushered in by the United States and based on fixed exchange rates (the so-called Bretton Woods System), progressively freer trade under the General Agreement on Tariffs and Trade (GATT), reemerging international capital mobility, and generalized commitment to full employment of resources. The years between 1974 and 1990 can instead be thought of as those in which this order was dealt several setbacks: first the adoption of floating exchange rates by the main industrial countries in the early 1970s, then the emergence of high inflation rates in the late 1970s, and finally the resurgence of trade protectionism in the 1980s. The commitment to full employment, through active government intervention, also waned during the 1970s and was substituted by a much greater reliance on spontaneous market outcomes.

30. Tables 3.1 and 3.2 are based on a sample of developing countries for which long-term growth could be tracked. Table 3.4 is instead based on nearly the universe of developing countries. Aside from differences in methods used to compute the average annual growth rates (interpolations of growth trends at end points in Tables 3.1 and 3.2

and least-square regressions in Table 3.4), the discrepancies in the regional aggregates and in the totals computed for all developing countries are, therefore, due to different country coverage.

31. See chapters 11 and 12.

32. Egypt and Jordan are highly dependent on exports of labor services.

33. The laggard nations in Asia are mostly Bangladesh, Nepal, and those of Indochina, afflicted by wars throughout most of this period and slower than their neighbors in implementing fundamental structural reform (of prices, other incentives to production and export, organization of markets, trade, and financial regimes).

34. This characterization of the 1980s as a "lost decade" applies to output growth and social progress. Economic policies in many Latin American countries were changed drastically in the 1980s, and structural reforms were initiated in many of them: the antitrade bias of many commercial and exchange-rate regimes was reduced or eliminated, financial systems were reformed, direct government participation in production activities was cut back, and tax systems were transformed and modernized in many Latin American countries. In terms of policy reforms, the 1980s were thus far from being a "lost decade." In fact, important and, at times, fundamental change was introduced in the economic structure of the region. See chapter 8.

35. This is obviously true only on average or, to be more precise, for the weighted average of the various income groups, whose growth is computed after summing up the real GDP of all their components. Individually, most of the middle-income developing countries of Asia grew faster (in per capita terms) than the low-income countries of this region (with the exception of China).

36. Barro (1991) also finds a weak, if statistically insignificant, positive relationship between per capita GDP growth from 1960 to 1985 and 1960 GDP per capita in a sample of ninety-eight countries (which include industrial countries). He shows, however, that after accounting for such factors as the "quality" of human capital and the ratios of government consumption to GDP, the relationship between per capita GDP growth and starting levels of GDP per capita becomes significantly negative in his sample of countries.

37. There is, however, another possible interpretation of the empirical relationship between output growth and starting levels of per capita income in our sample of developing countries. As shown in Figure 3.4, below a certain level of per capita income ($2,000 in the 1950–1970 period and $2,500 in the 1970–1990 period), the relationship between total output growth and per capita income at the start of the period may have remained positive, while a negative relationship may have persisted between these two variables above these levels of per capita income.

38. Many recent studies of the main "determinants" of growth in developing countries are based on either traditional growth theory (mostly neoclassical) or new formulations of the growth relationship (the so-called endogenous growth). See Lynn and McCarthy (1989) and Riedel in chapter 2 of this volume for examples of the former type and Romer (1989) and Barro (1991) for examples of the latter. Renelt (1991) provides an exhaustive survey of recent literature and empirical results. Results from traditional models generally highlight savings or investments as the main factors behind country growth. Results from the new growth models point instead to the importance of factors such as human capital.

39. Growth in large and relatively closed economies such as China, where exports until recently accounted for 3 percent of GDP, can hardly be thought of as influenced by exports and their structure.

40. As a consequence of lower income elasticity of foreign demand, the growth in

the volume of exports of the non-oil primary exporting countries for any given positive change in foreign income can be expected to have been lower than that of countries exporting manufactures or oil, even at unchanged relative prices of non-oil commodities. Export growth can relax a key constraint to economic expansion through the possibility that it offers to augment imports of capital expansion and of intermediate products. Thus higher export growth should be associated with faster output growth, other things being equal (especially productivity of investments). To make things even worse for exporters of non-oil primary commodities, the prices of their exports slowly declined over the years with respect to those of manufactures (Grilli and Yang, 1988) causing a further decline in the purchasing power of these exports. One can arrive at a similar conclusion regarding the relative disadvantage of exporters on non-oil primary commodities compared with exporters of manufactures by considering that price elasticities of demand are higher for manufactures than for primary products. For a given growth in their supply capacity, developing countries that export manufactures can more easily make volume gains without (or with less) price loss than those that export primary commodities. Thus the purchasing power of exports of the former can increase faster than that of the latter.

41. This tendency has by now created a close identification between low-income and primary-commodity-dependent developing countries.

42. The first two were obviously positive, at least in the sense that they represented a considerable improvement in the relative prices of exports. The last one was negative: the price of the main export product—oil—fell drastically relative to the prices of imported goods.

43. There is some ambiguity in the classification that we just proposed and used. We have classified countries depending on export structure in 1970, the first year for which export data by product are uniformly available. Having used dependency coefficients at mid-period to classify countries as more or less reliant on primary commodity exports, we have implicitly reflected in the classification the effects of diversification policies previously followed. The countries less dependent on commodity exports are, in fact, the countries that began their export diversification earlier and were more successful in doing so. The 1970 commodity ratios, in other words, reflect the export structure of countries as modified by policy. However, since the number of developing countries that by then had already succeeded in diversifying into manufactures was quite limited, the ambiguity carried by the commodity export ratios as indicators of economic structure should not be too large.

44. Terms of trade changes affect, inter alia, the profitability of firms producing for exports, thus influencing investments and, through them, future growth of output. Their importance in explaining the growth of transformation economies such as Italy is shown in Grilli, Kregel, and Savona (1982).

45. Excluded from the sample were countries, such as Albania and China, for which trade to GDP ratios were not available with any degree of confidence and city-states, such as Singapore and Hong Kong, that because of lack of land do not produce non-oil primary commodities. For these countries even a loose attribution of growth consequences to the structure of such small external sectors would be contrived.

46. The notable exceptions were Thailand, Malaysia, and Brazil, where high dependence on primary commodity exports did not prevent the achievement of high growth (above 6 percent a year) in the 1950–1990 period.

47. Conceptually, at least, the reasons for the positive effects of faster exports on output growth should be clear even when economies are not foreign-exchange constrained

(the case previously mentioned in note 36). Greater production for exports directly increases income in the exporting economy. This enlarges the "size" of the market for producers and allows them to exploit economies of scale. If the marginal propensity to consume of the exporting country is less than one, greater exports will also mean greater investments and a permanent rise in the capacity to produce. Investment efficiency is also likely to increase, because of improved resource allocations and greater access to imported technology. Positive knowledge externalities can also be gained. The empirical evidence on the matter is less clear-cut, but on the whole, supportive of a positive relationship between trade and growth. For a recent survey of the evidence, see Edwards (1989).

48. Openness, for example, may be large because factor endowments allow in practice the production of only one tradable good, whose proceeds go to finance all needed imports, regardless of the trade regime, which can be restrictive, and of price incentives, which can be nonneutral. A small, oil-based economy with high import (and export) duties for revenue purposes and an overvalued real exchange rate would approximate this situation. Similarly, openness may be small despite a country's varied factor endowment and liberal trade regime, if production of tradables does not receive sufficient incentives from prices. In both cases the trade orientation of the country would, strictly speaking, be inward-looking, despite high opennness in the first and low openness in the second.

49. There are several measures of trade openness, from trade to GDP (X/Y, M/Y, X + M/Y), to trade to total domestic supply ratios (X + M/Y + M), to trade intensity ratios across industries ($\Sigma_j |X_j - M_j|/GDP$). This last measure, which is the ratio of the sum of absolute net exports to GDP, was recently proposed by Leamer (1988).

50. For a comparative view of measures of trade orientation in developing countries, see Pritchett (1991).

51. Balassa's specification of the per capita export function, for example, contains only per capita income and a variable representing the availability of mineral resources in the countries included in the sample. Colombatto's specification is more comprehensive. His export and import functions include income per capita, proxies for size, trade regimes, export composition, the trade balance, and price elasticities of demand in major importing countries.

52. Because of greater efficiency induced by outward orientation, countries would eventually produce on their production possibility frontier, instead of remaining inside it. These gains would ultimately become exhausted. But in developing economies, where there exist extensive distortions, these gains could be quite large. There is also mounting evidence that higher openness to trade leads to faster rates of technological development (Romer, 1989).

53. The same was found by Salvatore and Hatcher (1991) using the World Bank/Greenaway definition of outward orientation.

54. The 1991 estimates of Summers and Heston represent the exceptions to this tendency, as they are based on the latest and improved set of PPP conversion indexes.

55. The sharp drop in the share of world GDP accounted by Asia between 1913 and 1950 and by the developing countries as a whole between 1870 and 1913 seems to be primarily related to the poor growth performance of India and China, which have a large relative weight in the regional total.

56. Throughout the chapter internal distribution of income refers to personal or size distribution, that is, to the allocation of income to distinct groups (or sizes) of individuals or households. There are several indicators of size distribution of income that are com-

monly used by economists and statisticians: ratios between the shares of income accruing to various classes or sizes of recipients (e.g., bottom 40 percent to top 20 percent), Lorenz curves (the shape of the relationship between the percentage of income recipients and the percentage share of total income that they actually receive), and inequality coefficients (such as those proposed by Gini and Theil). For a review of statistical measures of inequality see Sundrum (1990). An in-depth analysis of measurement problems can be found in Kakwani (1980).

57. This also meant that recipients in intermediate income groups would get a smaller share of income in developing, than in industrial, countries.

58. In his 1963 article, Kuznets, using a larger sample of countries and income distributions than in 1955, concluded that greater inequality in developing countries was primarily the result of higher concentration of income in the top classes of recipients. The shares of lower-income groups did not seem to differ significantly across developed and developing countries. Nonetheless, the conclusion that middle-income groups did relatively better in developed, than in developing, countries still stood.

59. Oshima (1962) questioned the possibility of making generalizations about inter-country income patterns in the presence of vast differences, not only economic but historical, social, and political, existing among them. Adelman and Morris (1973), on the basis of data covering a large sample of countries and a statistical analysis of their income distributions, concluded instead that differences in income levels did not appear to have a particularly strong influence on internal income distributions: income levels did not belong to the set of factors identified statistically as most significantly related to income distributions.

60. These coefficients, first elaborated by Gini (1912), constitute a measure of the deviation between the cumulative proportions of income received by the various classes of recipients and perfect equality (i.e., the situation in which each percentage group of recipients receives the same percentage share of total income). Their values range from zero (perfect equality) to one (perfect inequality). Though not the only or even the most generally consistent indicators of inequalities in the incomes on different classes of population, the values of the Gini coefficients are sufficient to support the observations and broad conclusions that are drawn here.

61. These are the cases of India, Pakistan, and Bangladesh. The income distributions of these countries, especially those of Pakistan and Bangladesh, nonetheless, appear surprisingly even.

62. Hong Kong and Singapore fall within the same category of developing countries with internal income distributions already roughly similar to those of industrial countries.

63. The data are minimally consistent as far as income concept (household income), income recipient unit (household), and coverage of the distribution (national). Pretax consistency could not be ensured.

64. Improvements or worsenings of income distributions were deduced from the comparison of Gini coefficients. These are only broadly indicative measures, but considering the weakness of the basic data, more rigorous measurements of changes in size distributions of income in the developing countries included in the sample would convey only a sense of spurious accuracy. Improvements were judged from systematic reductions in the values of the Gini coefficients over time. The opposite tendency was considered a worsening. Taken as ambiguous results were either the cases where trends in the value of the Gini coefficients changed during the period covered or the cases where no definite tendencies in these values were detectable. Despite best efforts to check, compare, and

validate data in size distributions of incomes in the countries included in the sample, some "surprises" remain (e.g., the improvement in the size distributions of income in the Philippines).

65. Numerous indicators of welfare—life expectancy at birth, caloric intakes, availability of health services (and education levels)—confirm that widespread improvements have taken place over time in most developing countries, particularly in those containing the largest populations. See any of the recent World Development Reports of the World Bank or the recent UNDP's Human Development Report.

66. As noted by Griffin (1989, p. 13), in the classical tradition poverty was considered a relative concept, determined by custom, a view subsequently shared by British humanitarian thinkers as well as by modern economic anthropologists (the idea of socially defined poverty). The opposite view, that poverty is ultimately an absolute notion, is instead common among both nutritionists and modern welfare economists (see, e.g., Sen, 1983, p. 153). Nutritionists, in particular, have stressed that there are minimum nutritional requirements (measured in caloric intake) necessary for productive life. The debate is on whether such a minimum standard is fixed or variable, depending not only on climatic and other environmental conditions but also on the capacity of the human body to adjust to lower intakes of calories and thus to a lower "minimum."

67. Once a poverty line is defined, the degree of poverty relative to it can be measured in different ways: (1) by a *head count index*, which gives the proportion of the population with a living standard that lies below the poverty line; (2) by a *poverty gap index*, which measures across all poor households the average gap between their individual standards of living and the poverty line; or (3) by a *poverty severity index*, which measures the distribution of living standard among the poor. Head count simply tells us who is below the poverty line. The poverty gap provides, instead, an indication of the depth of poverty. The poverty severity measurement captures, as the name indicates, the severity of poverty and the effects of income changes within the group of poor.

68. China obtained a significant reduction in poverty even before its growth process consolidated, through the application of strong measures aimed at directly improving the living standard of the poor.

69. The last available statistic for the percentage of total population living below the poverty line in Mexico refers to 1984, but data on the percentage of households living in poverty show that in 1986 the share of such households was two percentage points below 1980 and four percentage points below 1970 (CEPAL, 1991, p. 75).

70. See Table 3.11 for the country sample and values.

71. These are the countries for which data on poverty for both 1980 and 1990 are shown in Table 3.9, excluding Singapore and Korea, which can be considered to be poverty-free countries.

72. See chapter 4.

REFERENCES

Adelman, I., and Morris, C.J. 1973. *Economic Growth and Social Equity in Developing Countries*. Stanford, Calif.: Stanford University Press.

Ahluwalia, M.S. 1976. "Inequality, Poverty and Development." *Journal of Development Economics* 3, no. 4: 307–42.

Ahluwalia, M.S., Carter, N.G., and Chenery, H.B. 1979. "Growth and Poverty in Developing Countries." *Journal of Development Economics* 6, no. 3: 299–341.

Amin, S. 1965. *Trois Experiences Africaines de Developpment, Le Mali, la Guinée et le Ghana*. Paris: Presses Universitaires de France.

——. 1966. *L'Economie du Maghreb*. Paris: Les Editions de Minuit.

——. 1970. *The Maghreb in the Modern World: Algeria, Tunisia, Morocco*. Harmondsworth: Penguin Press.

Anand, S., and Kanbur, R.S.M. 1981. "Inequality and Development: A Critique." St. Catherine's College, Oxford. Mimeo.

——. 1984. "Inequality and Development: A Reconsideration." In *Towards Income Distribution Policies*, edited by H.P. Nissen. Tilburg: EADI.

Aspe, P., and Beristain, J. 1984. "Toward a First Estimate of the Evolution of Inequality in Mexico." In *The Political Economy of Income Distribution in Mexico*, edited by P. Aspe and P.E. Sigmund. New York: Holmes and Meier.

Bairoch, P. 1967. *Diagnostic de L'Evolution Economique du Tiers-Monide*. Paris: Gautheir-Villard.

Balassa, B. 1985. "Export Policy Choices and Economic Growth in Developing Countries After the 1973 Oil Shock." *Journal of Development Economics* 18 (May-June): 23–35.

——. 1987. "The Importance of Trade for Developing Countries." *Banca Nazionale del Lavoro Quarterly Review*, no. 163: 437–70.

Baldwin, R. 1966. *Economic Development and Export Growth: A Study of Northern Rhodesia*. Berkeley: University of California Press.

Balisacan, A. 1992. "Rural Poverty in the Philippines: Incidence, Determinants and Policies." *Asian Development Review* 10, no. 1: 125–63.

Bangladesh Bureau of Statistics. 1988. *Report of the Bangladesh Household Expenditure Survey 1985–86*. Dacca.

Barber, W.J. 1984. *The Economy of British Central Africa*. Westport, Conn.: Greenwood Press.

Barro, R.J. 1991. "Economic Growth in a Cross-Section of Countries." *Quarterly Journal of Economics* 106, no. 2: 407–43.

Berry, A. 1990. "The Effects of Stabilization and Adjustment on Poverty and Income Distribution: Aspects of the Latin American Experience." *World Development Report Background Paper*. No. 21, World Bank, Washington, D.C. Mimeo.

Berry, A., Bourguignon, F., and Morrison, C. 1983. "Changes in the World Distribution of Income Between 1950 and 1977." *Economic Journal* 93 (June): 331–50.

Bhalla, S.J., and Vashistha, P.S. 1988. "Income Distribution in India: A Reexamination." In *Rural Poverty in South Asia*, edited by T.N. Srinivasan and P.K. Bardhan. New York: Columbia University Press.

Biro Pusat Statistik. 1970, 1984, 1990. National Socio-Economic Surveys (SUSENAS), Jakarta.

Boltho, A. 1987. "Can We Return to Rapid Growth?" *Economic Analysis and Prospects Division Working Paper*. No. 1987-4. World Bank, Washington, D.C. Mimeo.

Bruton, H.J. 1992. *The Political Economy of Poverty, Equity and Growth: Sri Lanka and Malaysia*. Oxford: Oxford University Press (for the World Bank).

Camargo, J.M. 1987. *Brasil: Ajuste Estructural y Distribucion de Ingreso*. Santiago: Oficina Internacional del Trabajo, PREALC.

Campano, F., and Salvatore, D. 1988. "Economic Development, Income Inequality and Kuznet's U-Shaped Hypothesis." *Journal of Policy Modeling* 10, no. 2: 265–80.

Cassen, R. 1981. "The Record of Development." In *The Brandt Commission Papers*. Geneva: IBIDI.

Choo, H. 1985. "Estimation of Size Distribution of Income and Its Sources of Change in Korea, 1982." *Korean Development Institute Working Paper*, No. 8515, Seoul.

Chung, K.W., and Oh, N.W. 1992. "Rural Poverty in the Republic of Korea: Trends and Policy Issues." *Asian Development Review* 10, no. 1: 91–124.

Colombatto, E. 1990. "An Analysis of Export Growth in LDCs." *Kyklos* 43, no. 4: 579–97.

———. 1992. "Openness and Trade Orientation: Where Do We Stand?" *Quaderni dell'Istituto di Economia Politica G. Prato*, No. 3, University of Torino, Torino. Mimeo.

Comision Economica Para America Latina de Las Naciones Unidas (CEPAL). 1991. *Magnitud de la Pobreza en America Latina en los Años Ochenta*. Santiago de Chile: CEPAL.

Council for Economic Planning and Development. 1991. *Taiwan Statistical Data Book, 1991*. Taipei.

Crosswell, M.J. 1981. "Growth, Poverty Alleviation and Foreign Assistance." In *Basic Needs Approach to Development*, edited by D.M. Leipziger. Cambridge, Mass.: Oelgeschlager, Gunn, and Hain.

Dollar, D. 1992. "Outward Oriented-Developing Economies Really Do Grow More Rapidly: Evidence from 95 LDCs, 1976–85." In *Economic Development and Cultural Change* 40: 21–35.

Dowling, J.M. 1984. "Income Distribution and Poverty in Selected Asian Countries." *Asian Development Bank Economic Staff Paper No. 22*, Asian Development Bank, Manila.

Durand, J.D. 1967a. "The Modern Expansion of World Population." In *Proceedings of the American Philosophical Society, III* (cited in Munro, p. 20).

———. 1967b. "World Population Estimates, 1750–2000." In *World Population Conference, 1965*. New York: United Nations.

Edwards, S. 1989. "Openness, Outward Orientation, Trade Liberalization and Economic Performance in Developing Countries." *Policy, Planning and Research Working Paper*. No. 191, World Bank, Washington, D.C. Mimeo.

Eisner, G. 1961. *Jamaica 1830–1930: A Study in Economic Growth*. London: Manchester University Press.

Fields, G. 1980. *Poverty, Inequality and Development*. Cambridge: Cambridge University Press.

———. 1988. "Income Distribution and Economic Growth." In *The State of Development Economics*, edited by G. Ranis and T.P. Schultz. Cambridge: Basil Blackwell, 459–81.

———. 1989. "Changes in Poverty and Inequality in Developing Countries." *World Bank Research Observer* 4, no. 2: 167–85.

———. 1991a. *Changing Poverty and Inequality in Latin America*. Cornell University, Ithaca, N.Y. Mimeo.

———. 1991b. "Growth and Income Distribution." In *Essays on Poverty, Equity and Growth*, edited by G. Psacharopoulos. Oxford: Pergamon Press (for the World Bank).

Frankel, S.H., and Herzfeld, H. 1944. "An Analysis of the Growth of the National

Income of the Union in the Period of Prosperity Before the War." *South African Journal of Economics* 12, no. 1: 112–38.

Franzsen, D.G. 1954. "National Accounts and National Income in the Union of South Africa Since 1933." *South African Journal of Economics* 22, no. 1: 115–26.

Fua', G. 1993. *Crescita Economica: Le Insidie delle Citre.* Bologna: Il Mulino.

Furtado, C. 1970. *Economic Development of Latin America.* Cambridge: Cambridge University Press.

Gini, C. 1912. *Variabilità e Mutabilità.* Bologna: il Mulino.

Greenaway, D. 1986. "Characteristics of Industrialization and Economic Performance Under Alternative Development Strategies." Background Paper to the 1987 *World Development Report,* Washington, D.C. Mimeo.

Greenaway, D., and Nam, C.H. 1988. "Industrialization and Macroeconomic Performance in Developing Countries Under Alternative Trade Strategies." *Kyklos* 41, no. 3: 419–35.

Griffin, K. 1989. *Alternative Strategies of Economic Development.* New York: St. Martin's Press.

Grilli, E., Kregel, J., and Savona, P. 1982. "Terms of Trade and Italian Economic Growth: Accounting for Miracles." *Banca Nazionale del Lavoro Quarterly Review* no. 143 (December): 395–416.

Grilli, E., and Yang, M.C. 1988. "Primary Commodity Prices, Manufactured Goods Prices, and the Terms of Trade of Developing Countries: What the Long Run Shows." *World Bank Review* 2, no. 11: 1–47.

Hansen, B. 1979. "Income and Consumption in Egypt, 1886/1887 to 1937." *International Journal of Middle East Studies* 10, no. 1: 24–47.

Hansen, B., and Marzouk, G. 1965. *Development and Economic Policy in the UAR (Egypt).* Amsterdam: North-Holland.

Helleiner, G. 1966. *Peasant Agriculture, Government and Economic Growth in Nigeria.* Homewood, Ill.: Richard D. Irwin.

Hossain, M., and Sen, B. 1992. "Rural Poverty in Bangladesh: Trends and Determinants." *Asian Development Review* 10, no. 1: 1–34.

International Monetary Fund (IMF). 1990. *International Financial Statistics Yearbook.* Washington, D.C.: IMF.

Issawi, C. 1982. *An Economic History of the Middle East and North Africa.* New York: Columbia University Press.

Jain, S. 1975. *Size Distribution of Income: A Compilation of Data.* Washington, D.C.: World Bank.

Jastram, R. 1977. *The Golden Constant: English and American Experience 1560–1976.* New York: Wiley.

Jones, S., and Muller, A. 1992. *The South African Economy, 1910–1990.* London: Macmillan Academic and Professional.

Kakwani, N.C. 1980. *Income Inequality and Poverty.* New York: Oxford University Press (for the World Bank).

Kindleberger, C. 1973. *The World in Depression: 1929–1939.* Berkeley: University of California Press.

Kravis, I.B. 1960. "International Differences in the Distribution of Income." *Review of Economics and Statistics* 42, no. 4: 408–16.

Kravis, I.B., Heston, A.W., and Summers, R. 1978. "Real GDP Per Capita for More Than One Hundred Countries." *Economic Journal* 88, no. 350: 215–42.

Krogh, D.C. 1960. "The National Income and Expenditure of South West Africa, 1920–1956." *South African Journal of Economics* 28, no. 1: 3–22.

Krongkaew, M., Tinakorn, P., and Suphachalasai, S. 1992. "Rural Poverty in Thailand: Policy Issues and Responses." *Asian Development Review* 10, no. 1: 199–225.

Kuznets, S. 1955. "Economic Growth and Income Inequality." *American Economic Review* 45, no. 1: 1–28.

————. 1958. "Regional Economic Trends and Levels of Living." In *Population and World Politics*, edited by M. Hauser. New York: Free Press. Reprinted in S. Kuznets, *Economic Growth and Structure: Selected Essays*. New York: Norton, 142–75.

————. 1963. "Quantitative Aspects of the Economic Growth of Nations." *Economic Development and Cultural Change* 11, no. 2: 1–80.

————. 1966. *Modern Economic Growth: Rate, Structure and Spread*. New Haven, Conn.: Yale University Press.

Kwon, S. 1990. "Korea: Income and Wealth Distribution and Government Initiatives to Reduce Disparities." *Korea Development Institute Working Paper*, No. 9008, Korea Development Institute, Seoul.

Langoni, C.G. 1973. *Distribuicao da renda e Desenvolvimento Economico do Brasil*. Rio de Janeiro: Expressao e Cultura.

League of Nations. 1942. *The Network of World Trade*. New York.

————. 1945. *Industrialization and Foreign Trade*. New York.

Leamer, E.E. 1988. "Measures of Openness." In *Trade Policy Issues and Empirical Analysis*, edited by R.E. Baldwin. Chicago: University of Chicago Press, 147–200.

Lecallion, J., 1984. *Income Distribution and Economic Development*. Geneva: International Labor Organization.

Lewis, W.H. 1979. "The Slowing Down of the Engine of Growth." *American Economic Review* 70, no. 4: 555–64.

Lin, T. 1985. "Growth, Equity and Income Distribution Policies in Hong Kong." *Developing Economies* 23, no. 4: 391–413.

Liu, T.H., and Yeh, K.C. 1965. *The Economy of the Chinese Mainland: National Income and Economic Development, 1933–1959*. Princeton, N.J.: Princeton University Press.

Lustig, N. 1992. *Mexico: The Remaking of an Economy*. Washington, D.C.: Brookings Institution.

Lynn, R., and McCarthy, F.D. 1989. "Recent Economic Performance of Developing Countries." *Policy, Planning and Research Working Paper*, No. 228, World Bank, Washington, D.C. Mimeo.

McEvedy, C., and Jones, R. 1978. *Atlas of World Population History*. New York: Facts on File.

Maddison, A. 1982. *Phases of Capitalist Development*. Oxford: Oxford University Press.

————. 1983. "A Comparison of Levels of GDP Per Capita in Developed and Developing Countries, 1700–1980." *Journal of Economic History* 43, no. 1: 27–41.

————. 1989. *The World Economy in the Twentieth Century*. Paris: OECD Development Center.

————. 1991. *Dynamic Forces in Capitalist Development*. London: Oxford University Press.

————. 1992. "Explaining Divergence in the Economic Performance of Nations, 1820–

1989." Paper presented at the Conference on *Historical Perspectives on the International Convergence of Productivity*, New York University. Mimeo.

Mahmood, Z. 1984. "Income Inequality in Pakistan: An Analysis of Existing Evidence." *Pakistan Development Review* 23, nos. 2, 3: 365–76.

Maldant, B. 1973. *Croissance et Conjoncture dans l'Quest Africain*. Paris: Presses Universitaires de France.

Meesook, O.A. Forthcoming. *The Political Economy of Thailand's Development: Poverty, Equity and Growth 1850–1985*. Washington, D.C.: World Bank.

Mitchell, B.R. 1982. *International Historical Statistics: Africa and Asia*. New York: New York University Press.

Morawetz, D. 1977. *Twenty-Five Years of Economic Development, 1950 to 1975*. Washington, D.C.: World Bank.

Munro, J.F. 1976. *Africa and the International Economy: 1800–1960*. London: J.M. Dent.

National Statistical Coordination Board. 1989. *Philippines Statistical Yearbook*. Manila.

Organization for Economic Cooperation and Development, Development Center. 1968. *National Accounts of Less Developed Countries 1950–1966*. Paris: OECD.

Organization for Economic Cooperation and Development. 1985. *Twenty-Five Years of Development Cooperation*. Paris: OECD.

Oshima, H.T. 1962. "The International Comparison of Size Distribution of Family Incomes with Special Reference to Asia." *Review of Economics and Statistics* 44, no. 4: 439–45.

Paukert, F. 1973. "Income Distribution at Different Levels of Development: A Survey of Evidence." *International Labour Review* 108, no. 2–3: 97–125.

Perkins, D. 1980. "Issues in the Estimation of China's National Product." In *Quantitative Measures of China's Economic Output*, edited by A. Eckstein. Ann Arbor: University of Michigan Press, 246–73.

Pritchett, L. 1991. "Measuring Outward Orientation in Developing Countries: Can It Be Done?" *Policy, Research and External Affairs Working Paper*, No. 566, World Bank, Washington, D.C. Mimeo.

Psacharopoulos, G., ed. 1991. *Essays on Poverty, Equity and Growth*. New York: Pergamon Press (for the World Bank).

Rao, V.V.B. 1989. "Income Inequality and Poverty in East Asia: Trends and Implications." *Indian Economic Journal* 37, no. 2: 57–64.

Ravallion, M. 1992. "Poverty Comparisons: A Guide to Concepts and Methods." *Living Standards Measurement Study Working Paper*, No. 88, World Bank, Washington, D.C. Mimeo.

Ravallion, M., Datt, G., Van de Walle, D., and Chan, E. 1991. "Quantifying the Magnitude and Severity of Absolute Poverty in the Developing World in the Mid-1980s." *Policy, Research and External Affairs Working Paper*, No. 587, World Bank, Washington, D.C. Mimeo.

Renelt, D. 1991. "Economic Growth: A Review of the Theoretical and Empirical Literature." *Policy, Planning and Research Working Paper*, No. 678, World Bank, Washington, D.C. Mimeo.

Reynolds, L.G. 1983. "The Spread of Economic Growth to the Third World: 1850–1980." *Journal of Economic Literature* 21, no. 3: 941–80.

———. 1985. *Economic Growth in the Third World: 1850–1980*. New Haven, Conn.: Yale University Press.

Riedel, J. 1984. "Trade as an Engine of Growth in Developing Countries, Revisited." *Economic Journal* 94 (March): 56–73.

Romer, P.M. 1989. "What Determines the Rate of Growth and Technological Change." *Policy, Planning and Research Working Paper*, No. 279, World Bank, Washington, D.C. Mimeo.

Saith, A. 1983. "Development and Distribution: A Critique of the Cross-Country U-Hypothesis," *Journal of Development Economics* 13, 367–382.

Salvatore, D., and Hatcher, T. 1991. "Inward Oriented and Outward Oriented Trade Strategies." *Journal of Development Studies* 27, no. 3: 7–25.

Sen, A. 1983. "Poor, Relatively Speaking." *Oxford Economic Papers* 35 (July): 153–69.

South Africa Bureau of Census and Statistics. 1960. *Union Statistics for Fifty Years 1910–1960*. Pretoria.

South African Reserve Bank. 1991. *South African National Accounts 1946–1990*. Supplement to Quarterly Bulletin (June).

Stallings, B. 1987. *Banker to the Third World*. Berkeley: University of California Press.

Suh, S.M. 1985. "Economic Growth and Change in Income Distribution: The Korean Case." *Korea Development Institute Working Paper*, No. 8508, Korea Development Institute, Seoul.

Summers, R., and Heston, A. 1988. "A New Set of International Comparisons of Real Product and Prices: Estimates for 130 Countries; 1950–1985." *Review of Income and Wealth* 34, no. 7: 1–25.

———. 1991. "The Penn World Table (Mark 5): An Expanded Set of International Comparisons, 1950–1988." *Quarterly Journal of Economics* 106, no. 2: 327–68.

Summers, R., Kravis, I.B., and Heston, A. 1984. "Changes in the World Income Distribution." *Journal of Policy Modeling* 6, no. 2: 237–69.

Sundrum, R.M. 1990. *Income Distribution in Less Developed Countries*. London: Routledge.

Swainson, N. 1980. *The Development of Corporate Capitalism in Kenya, 1918–77*. London: Heinemann.

Szereszewski, R. 1965. *Structural Changes in the Economy of Ghana, 1891–1911*. London: Weldenfeld and Nicolson.

Tjondronegoro, S., Soejono, I., and Hardjono, J. 1992. "Rural Poverty in Indonesia: Trends, Issues and Policies." *Asian Development Review* 10, no. 1: 67–90.

Todaro, M.P. 1977. *Economic Development in the Third World*. New York: Longman.

United Nations. 1985. *National Accounts Statistics: Compendium of Income Distribution Statistics*. New York: United Nations.

United Nations Conference on Trade and Development (UNCTAD). 1969. *Handbook of International Trade and Development Statistics*. New York: United Nations.

United Nations Development Program (UNDP). 1992. *Human Development Report 1992*. New York: Oxford University Press.

United Nations Statistical Office. *Demographic Yearbook*. Various years. New York: United Nations.

Van de Walle, D. 1991. "Poverty and Inequality in Latin America and the Caribbean During the 1970s and 1980s: An Overview of Evidence." Technical Department, Latin America and the Caribbean Region, World Bank, Washington, D.C. Mimeo.

Van Ginneken, W., and Park, J., eds. 1984. *Generating Internationally Comparable Income Distribution Estimates.* Geneva: International Labor Office.

Van Zwanenberg, R.M.A., and King, A. 1975. *An Economic History of Kenya and Uganda 1800–1970.* Englewood Cliffs, N.J.: Humanities Press.

World Bank. 1980, 1982, 1983, 1987, 1988, 1990, 1991. *World Development Report.* New York: Oxford University Press (for the World Bank).

———. 1982. *Handbook on Income Distribution Data.* Development Policy Staff, World Bank, Washington, D.C. Mimeo.

———. 1990. World Bank Country Study. *Indonesia: Strategy for a Sustained Reduction in Poverty.* Washington, D.C.

———. 1991. World Bank Country Study. *Egypt: Alleviating Poverty During Structural Adjustment.* Washington, D.C.

———. Various years. *Social Indicators of Development.*

———. Various years. *Economic and Social Database* (BESD).

Zimmerman, L.J. 1962. "The Distribution of World Income: 1860–1960." In *Essays on Unbalanced Growth: A Century of Disparity and Convergence,* edited by E. Vries. Mouton, Netherlands: Gravenhage.

Table A 3.1

Long-Term Growth of Real GDP and Population in a Sample of Developing Countries

------ Average Annual Growth Rates, % /a ------

	Real GDP Growth				Population Growth				GDP Per Capita Growth			
	1870-1913	1913-1950	1950-1973	1973-1990	1870-1913	1913-1950	1950-1973	1973-1990	1870-1913	1913-1950	1950-1973	1973-1990
AFRICA	2.46	2.58	4.64	2.66	1.78	1.44	2.34	2.64	0.68	1.14	2.30	0.02
A. North Africa	2.53	2.31	4.39	4.67	1.88	1.57	2.31	2.52	0.65	0.74	2.08	2.15
Algeria	2.01	1.95	4.79	3.93	1.70	1.31	2.30	2.91	0.31	0.64	2.49	1.02
Egypt	3.09	1.61	4.77	6.20	1.96	1.40	2.24	2.46	1.13	0.21	2.53	3.74
Morocco	-	3.56	3.14	4.62	-	2.27	2.61	2.35	-	1.29	0.53	2.27
Tunisia	-	2.46	4.85	4.39	-	1.63	1.95	2.32	-	0.83	2.90	2.07
B. South of the Sahara	2.05	2.71	4.74	1.76	1.10	1.35	2.36	2.71	0.95	1.36	2.38	-0.95
Ghana	2.05	3.23	3.62	0.93	1.10	2.08	2.49	2.58	0.95	1.15	1.13	-1.65
Kenya	-	2.37	5.32	4.29	-	1.89	3.06	3.61	-	0.48	2.26	0.68
Mali	-	1.80	3.42	3.42	-	1.09	1.95	2.22	-	0.71	1.47	1.20
Nigeria	-	1.44	4.67	1.15	-	0.80	2.17	2.70	-	0.64	2.50	-1.55
South Africa	-	3.55	4.82	2.25	-	2.19	2.41	2.17	-	1.36	2.41	0.08
Zambia	-	3.91	4.44	0.85	-	1.98	2.64	3.18	-	1.93	1.80	-2.33
Zimbabwe	-	6.07	6.19	2.34	-	2.60	3.28	3.02	-	3.47	2.91	-0.68

ASIA	_0.84_	_0.77_	_4.31_	_6.50_	_0.54_	_1.13_	_2.11_	_1.78_	_0.30_	_0.36_	_2.20_	_4.72_
China	0.77	0.54	3.96	7.44	0.50	1.10	1.99	1.41	0.27	-0.56	1.97	6.03
India	0.75	0.68	3.39	4.56	0.44	0.97	2.10	2.07	0.31	-0.29	1.29	2.49
Pakistan	-	1.41	4.85	5.79	-	1.72	2.79	2.93	-	-0.31	2.06	2.86
Indonesia	1.86	0.88	4.82	5.88	1.40	1.12	2.20	2.04	0.46	-0.24	2.62	3.84
Korea	-	1.67	6.71	8.35	-	1.89	2.36	1.32	-	-0.22	4.35	7.03
Philippines	-	1.82	4.83	3.36	-	2.08	2.96	2.38	-	-0.26	1.87	0.98
Taiwan	-	2.66	8.82	7.85	-	2.24	3.07	1.52	-	0.42	5.75	6.33
Thailand	1.35	2.21	6.42	6.91	0.96	2.22	2.91	2.05	0.39	-0.01	3.51	4.86
LATIN AMERICA	_2.99_	_3.28_	_5.59_	_3.14_	_1.86_	_1.95_	_2.71_	_2.02_	_1.13_	_1.33_	_2.88_	_1.12_
Argentina	5.43	2.96	3.71	0.38	3.43	2.21	1.60	1.40	2.00	0.75	2.11	-1.02
Brazil	2.36	4.16	6.49	3.85	2.07	2.15	2.86	2.13	0.29	2.01	3.63	1.72
Chile	-	3.25	3.32	2.63	-	1.51	2.12	1.53	-	1.74	1.20	1.10
Colombia	-	3.74	5.00	3.81	-	2.19	2.93	1.79	-	1.55	2.07	2.02
Jamaica	1.62	1.71	5.52	-0.30	1.20	1.41	1.49	1.27	0.42	0.30	4.03	-1.57
Mexico	2.25	2.61	6.35	3.35	1.13	1.65	3.13	2.22	1.12	0.96	3.22	1.13
Peru	-	2.81	4.78	1.22	-	1.43	2.51	2.31	-	1.38	2.27	-1.09
TOTAL	1.05	1.42	4.75	4.79	0.63	1.22	2.19	1.89	0.42	0.20	2.56	2.90

Sources: Amin (1965, 1966, 1970); Baldwin (1966); Barber (1984); Eisner (1961); Hansen (1979); Hansen and Marzouk (1965); Helleiner (1966); Issawi (1982); Jastram (1977); Maddison (1983, 1989, 1992); OECD Development Center (1968); Swainson (1980); South African Reserve Bank (1991); UN Demographic Yearbook (various years); Union Statistics (1960); Van Zwanenberg and King (1975); World Bank Economic and Social Database (BESD).

[a]Growth rates for the two early periods were calculated using end points, for the latter two periods using three-year average end points.

Table A 3.2
GDP Growth and Variation in Developing Countries, 1950–1990

	REAL GDP GROWTH					REAL GDP PER CAPITA GROWTH				
	1950-60	1960-70	1970-80	1980-90	1950-90	1950-60	1960-70	1970-80	1980-90	1950-90
	(---------------- Average Annual Growth Rate, % ----------------)									
AFRICA										
NORTH OF THE SAHARA										
ALGERIA	6.48	4.23	6.77	2.59	4.95	4.33	1.77	3.71	-0.44	2.28
EGYPT	4.94	5.29	7.04	4.63	5.79	2.59	2.79	4.76	1.98	3.39
MOROCCO	1.32	4.31	5.39	4.19	4.10	-1.24	1.52	3.08	1.57	1.50
TUNISIA	2.82	4.98	6.64	3.40	5.25	0.74	2.85	4.44	0.96	3.07
S.D./MEAN	0.58	0.10	0.11	0.24	0.14	1.49	0.29	0.19	1.04	0.33
SOUTH OF THE SAHARA										
CAMEROON	1.70	1.78	6.92	2.23	4.04	-0.20	-0.23	3.99	-0.76	1.59
CAR	2.48	1.67	1.97	1.58	1.76	0.92	0.03	-0.17	-1.11	-0.16
CONGO	1.09	3.39	4.97	3.20	4.74	-1.34	0.99	1.97	-0.14	1.98
COTE D'IVOIRE	3.58	8.52	6.08	0.07	5.34	0.04	4.74	2.07	-3.66	1.55
ETHIOPIA	3.75	4.36	2.41	1.91	3.33	1.78	1.84	-0.27	-0.71	0.88
GHANA	4.41	2.13	-0.10	2.93	2.10	1.74	-0.08	-2.23	-0.45	-0.41
KENYA	4.08	5.68	6.23	4.38	5.28	1.10	2.47	2.54	0.62	1.85
MADAGASCAR	2.27	2.82	0.58	1.10	1.58	-0.29	0.42	-1.98	-1.83	-1.03
MALAWI	3.85	5.20	5.60	3.01	4.55	1.62	2.78	2.85	-0.57	1.72
MALI	4.24	3.29	4.66	2.70	3.60	2.24	1.21	2.75	0.20	1.48
MAURITANIA	-1.81	6.69	1.35	2.02	2.69	-3.86	4.61	-1.07	-0.35	0.47
NIGERIA	3.66	2.60	4.59	-0.12	3.68	1.78	0.11	2.16	-3.24	1.19
SENEGAL	6.29	2.46	2.12	3.04	3.05	4.21	-0.20	-0.75	0.14	0.37
SOUTH AFRICA	4.38	6.14	2.92	1.43	4.06	1.93	3.59	0.62	-0.89	1.65
SUDAN	4.94	0.72	5.14	1.16	2.77	2.35	-1.40	2.15	-1.79	0.23
TANZANIA	2.77	5.71	3.08	2.79	3.85	0.84	2.74	-0.20	-0.70	0.62
TOGO	1.38	8.42	3.84	1.50	4.27	-0.29	5.54	1.45	-1.96	1.61
UGANDA	3.36	5.28	-2.11	2.78	1.68	0.96	2.91	-4.68	-0.38	-0.68
UPPER VOLTA	1.89	2.97	3.70	3.91	3.05	-0.13	1.01	1.58	1.32	0.68
ZAIRE	3.85	3.45	-0.36	1.61	1.73	1.59	0.94	-3.58	-1.58	-1.09
ZAMBIA	5.34	4.27	1.28	1.01	2.94	2.68	1.48	-1.77	-2.56	0.00
ZIMBABWE	6.72	4.66	1.41	3.01	4.64	3.58	1.02	-1.43	-0.37	1.34
S.D./MEAN	0.55	0.50	0.79	0.53	0.34	1.63	1.10	8.30	1.28	1.32
ASIA										
BANGLADESH	1.51	3.62	3.61	3.60	2.99	-0.60	1.02	0.92	0.90	0.37
CHINA	5.05	4.74	5.05	9.55	5.18	2.97	2.49	3.27	8.09	3.32
HONG KONG	8.69	8.59	8.80	6.77	8.56	4.23	6.11	6.40	5.31	5.98
INDIA	3.41	3.71	3.28	5.44	3.85	1.46	1.39	1.00	3.35	1.63
INDONESIA	4.64	3.60	7.46	5.29	5.57	2.52	1.56	5.14	3.26	3.31
KOREA	5.25	7.85	9.06	9.31	7.69	2.68	5.42	7.29	8.19	5.64
MALAYSIA	3.50	6.29	7.53	5.10	6.05	0.64	3.63	4.97	2.53	3.40
MYANMAR	5.11	2.56	4.49	1.02	3.79	2.64	0.36	2.29	-1.15	1.55
PAKISTAN	3.48	6.98	4.60	6.18	5.48	0.62	4.23	1.51	3.10	2.51
PHILIPPINES	4.94	5.05	6.17	1.12	4.51	1.93	1.60	3.48	-1.22	1.64
SINGAPORE	n.a.	8.32	8.03	6.25	8.36	n.a.	6.00	6.53	4.07	6.48
SRI LANKA	3.82	4.48	4.55	4.00	4.38	1.10	2.11	2.90	2.56	2.39
TAIWAN	7.76	9.48	9.05	7.95	8.66	4.05	6.45	7.13	6.65	6.14

	S.D. MEAN									
THAILAND	4.86	8.04	6.90	7.24	6.60	1.90	4.98	4.23	5.41	4.07
	0.40	0.36	0.32	0.46	0.32	0.89	0.82	0.55	0.81	0.57
LATIN AMERICA										
ARGENTINA	3.29	4.28	2.36	-0.32	2.69	1.41	2.81	0.73	-1.65	1.11
BOLIVIA	-0.47	5.03	4.54	-0.62	2.75	-2.34	2.46	2.01	-3.34	0.21
BRAZIL	5.53	5.30	7.75	2.70	8.00	2.30	2.52	5.40	0.55	3.36
CHILE	3.04	4.29	1.39	3.13	2.92	0.69	2.07	-0.18	1.44	0.99
COLOMBIA	4.49	4.95	5.28	3.53	4.77	1.29	1.59	3.30	1.70	2.23
COSTA RICA	4.86	6.20	5.57	2.99	4.84	0.83	3.01	3.08	0.68	1.92
DOMINICAN REPUBLIC	5.45	4.56	6.23	1.93	5.32	1.91	1.41	3.71	-0.34	2.45
EL SALVADOR	4.40	5.63	4.07	0.49	3.42	1.64	2.16	1.78	-1.01	0.83
ECUADOR	4.66	4.32	9.05	1.95	5.58	1.63	1.15	8.11	-0.77	2.54
GUATEMALA	4.04	5.42	5.60	0.70	4.35	0.98	2.62	2.64	-2.17	1.51
GUYANA	4.16	3.71	1.54	-2.03	1.87	1.21	2.14	0.25	-2.51	0.31
HAITI	1.89	0.21	3.67	-0.02	1.68	0.20	-1.54	1.99	-1.89	-0.05
HONDURAS	3.48	5.12	5.76	2.37	4.24	0.55	2.08	2.44	-1.01	1.05
JAMAICA	7.76	4.33	-1.18	1.40	2.73	6.49	2.64	-2.67	0.08	1.21
MEXICO	6.05	7.13	6.15	0.90	5.69	2.90	3.85	3.28	-1.11	2.75
NICARAGUA	5.10	7.07	1.09	-1.48	3.10	2.14	3.90	1.87	-4.82	-0.01
PANAMA	5.09	7.53	4.32	0.30	5.48	2.22	4.64	5.21	-1.75	2.87
PARAGUAY	3.08	3.96	8.14	2.48	4.97	0.89	1.15	0.87	-0.60	2.14
PERU	4.52	5.04	3.59	-0.23	3.76	2.27	2.11	3.45	-2.44	1.15
TRINIDAD & TOBAGO	8.48	4.18	4.63	-4.67	3.65	5.62	2.11	3.45	-6.21	1.77
URUGUAY	1.83	1.68	3.12	0.37	1.71	0.37	0.87	2.85	-0.18	0.97
VENEZUELA	7.85	4.87	3.47	0.93	3.67	4.02	1.48	-0.04	-1.79	0.29
S.D./MEAN	0.46	0.34	0.56	2.53	0.35	1.09	0.58	1.04	1.42	0.69
MIDDLE EAST										
IRAN	7.53	10.59	2.19	3.20	6.07	5.28	7.24	-0.78	0.20	3.19
IRAQ	9.42	5.90	8.00	-7.04	4.04	8.46	2.76	5.27	-10.56	0.75
ISRAEL	9.85	7.90	4.63	3.22	6.74	5.42	4.49	2.01	1.57	3.78
KUWAIT	8.33	5.81	2.08	2.05	3.95	-1.21	-4.50	-4.04	-2.27	-3.39
OMAN	6.32	18.26	6.36	8.19	10.74	4.02	15.63	2.22	3.64	7.33
SAUDI ARABIA	6.33	8.93	10.09	0.05	7.52	3.57	5.57	5.20	-4.65	3.36
SYRIA	3.97	4.52	9.37	0.43	5.47	1.05	1.38	5.98	-3.14	2.19
S.D./MEAN	0.29	0.52	0.54	3.19	0.37	0.77	1.32	1.62	2.15	1.33
SOUTHERN EUROPE										
GREECE	5.77	7.00	4.37	1.54	5.00	4.82	6.44	3.41	0.20	3.28
MALTA	3.86	5.13	11.12	3.33	6.14	3.44	5.09	9.84	4.02	5.81
PORTUGAL	4.19	6.12	4.25	2.71	4.77	3.86	5.97	3.05	2.46	4.28
TURKEY	4.98	5.94	5.58	5.19	5.27	2.17	3.45	3.20	2.95	2.79
YUGOSLAVIA	5.48	5.73	5.99	0.28	5.01	4.31	4.70	5.07	-0.40	4.07
S.D./MEAN	0.17	0.11	0.45	0.71	0.10	0.27	0.23	0.58	0.64	0.25
TOTAL DEVELOPING COUNTRIES										
S.D.	2.13	2.56	2.73	2.76	1.80	1.96	2.59	2.80	3.02	1.89
MEAN	4.44	5.28	4.76	2.44	4.49	1.88	2.68	2.24	0.00	1.96
S.D./MEAN	0.48	0.48	0.57	1.13	0.40	1.04	0.96	1.25	n.t.	0.97

Sources: World Bank Economic and Social Database (BESD); OECD Development Center (1968); UN Demographic Yearbook (various years).

[a]Least square growth rate.

139

Table A 3.3
Country Classification for Developing Countries by Groups and Regions

INCOME GROUPS

	AFRICA: North of Sahara	AFRICA: South of Sahara	ASIA	LATIN AMERICA	MIDDLE EAST	SOUTHERN EUROPE
Low Income Countries (countries with per capita GNP of US$300 or below in 1976).	Egypt	Cameroon Central Afr. Rep. Ethiopia Kenya Madagascar Malawi Mali Mauritania Sudan Tanzania Togo Uganda Upper Volta Zaire	Bangladesh China India Indonesia Myanmar Pakistan Sri Lanka	Haiti		
Middle Income Countries (countries with per capita GNP above US$300 in 1976).	Algeria Morocco Tunisia	Congo Cote d'Ivoire Ghana Nigeria Senegal South Africa Zambia Zimbabwe	Hong Kong Korea Malaysia Philippines Taiwan Thailand	Argentina Bolivia Brazil Chile Colombia Costa Rica Dominican Rep. El Salvador Ecuador Guatemala Guyana Honduras Jamaica Mexico Nicaragua Panama Paraguay Peru Trinidad & Tobago Uruguay Venezuela	Iran Israel Syria	Greece Malta Portugal Turkey Yugoslavia

MAJOR EXPORTS

Exporters of Non-Oil Primary Commodities (countries whose exports of primary commodities [excluding oil] constitute 50% or more of total exports during 1970-72).	Egypt Morocco Tunisia	Cameroon Central Afr. Rep. Cote d'Ivoire Ethiopia Ghana Kenya Madagascar Malawi Mali Mauritania Senegal Sudan Tanzania Togo Uganda Upper Volta Zaire Zambia Zimbabwe	Bangladesh Malaysia Myanmar Philippines Sri Lanka Thailand	Argentina Bolivia Brazil Chile Colombia Costa Rica Dominican Rep. El Salvador Guatemala Guyana Haiti Honduras Mexico Nicaragua Paraguay Peru Uruguay	Iraq Kuwait Oman Saudi Arabia	Turkey
Exporters of Manufactures (countries whose manufacturing exports constitute 50% or more of total exports in 1975).		South Africa	China Hong Kong India Korea Pakistan Taiwan	Jamaica	Israel	Yugoslavia
Oil Exporters	Algeria	Congo Nigeria	Indonesia	Ecuador Trinidad & Tobago Venezuela	Iran Iraq Kuwait Oman Saudi Arabia Syria	

Table A 3.3 (continued)

	AFRICA: North of Sahara	AFRICA: South of Sahara	ASIA	LATIN AMERICA	MIDDLE EAST	SOUTHERN EUROPE
COLOMBATTO CLASSIFICATION						
Most Inward Oriented		Cameroon Ethiopia Ghana Madagascar Sudan Tanzania	Bangladesh India Philippines	Bolivia Colombia Dominican Rep. Peru Uruguay		Turkey
Neutral	Tunisia	Cote d'Ivoire Kenya Nigeria Senegal Zambia	Hong Kong Indonesia Pakistan Sri Lanka Thailand	Argentina Brazil Chile Costa Rica El Salvador Guatemala Honduras Mexico Nicaragua	Israel	Yugoslavia
Most Outward Oriented			Korea Malaysia Singapore			
DOLLAR CLASSIFICATION						
Most Inward Oriented	Algeria Egypt	Ghana Mauritania Nigeria Tanzania Uganda Zaire Zambia		Bolivia El Salvador Guyana Haiti Honduras Nicaragua Paraguay	Iraq	
Moderately Inward Oriented		Cameroon Central Afr. Rep. Congo Cote d'Ivoire Malawi Senegal Sudan Zimbabwe		Argentina Dominican Rep. Ecuador Guatemala Jamaica Trinidad & Tobago Venezuela	Iran	

142

Moderately Outward Oriented	Morocco Tunisia	Ethiopia Kenya Madagascar Mali Togo Upper Volta	India Indonesia Myanmar Philippines	Brazil Chile Costa Rica Panama Uruguay	Syria	Greece Turkey
Most Outward Oriented		South Africa	Bangladesh Hong Kong Korea Malaysia Pakistan Taiwan Thailand Sri Lanka	Colombia Mexico Peru		Malta Portugal Spain

GREENAWAY & NAM CLASSIFICATION /a

Strongly Inward Oriented		Ethiopia Ghana Sudan Tanzania Zambia	Bangladesh India Pakistan Sri Lanka	Argentina Chile Dominican Rep. Peru Uruguay		Turkey
Moderately Inward Oriented	Tunisia	Kenya Madagascar Nigeria Senegal	Philippines	Bolivia El Salvador Honduras Mexico Nicaragua		Yugoslavia
Moderately Outward Oriented		Cameroon Cote d'Ivoire	Indonesia Malaysia Thailand	Brazil Colombia Costa Rica Guatemala	Israel	
Strongly Outward Oriented			Korea Hong Kong Singapore			

aCountries as classified for the 1965–1973 period. Country classification for the 1973–1984 period differed slightly from the earlier period.

4

THE SOCIAL DIMENSIONS OF DEVELOPMENT

Paul Streeten

Involuntary poverty is an unmitigated evil. All development efforts aim at eradicating it and enabling people to develop fully their potential. Yet, all too often in the process of development, the poor shoulder the heaviest burden. Development itself interferes with human and social development. In the transition from subsistence-oriented agriculture to commercial agriculture, poor women and children are sometimes hit hardest. In the transition from a traditional society, in which the extended family takes care of its members who suffer misfortunes, to a market society, in which the community has not yet taken on responsibility for the victims of the market struggle, the fate of these victims can be cruel. In the transition from rural patron-client relationships to relations based on the cash nexus, the poor suffer by losing one type of support without gaining another. In the transition from an agricultural to an industrial society, the majority of the rural people are neglected by the public authorities in favor of the urban population.

Technical considerations of the means to achieving social development and statistical aggregates of national income and its growth occasionally obscure the fact that poverty reduction is a primary objective of development, partly because these aggregates do not show the components, pattern, composition, and beneficiaries of national income and its growth and partly because poor people set store by achievements that do not show up at all, or not immediately, in higher income or growth figures. Among these are better education for their children, better nutrition and health services, safe water at hand, cheap transport to their places of work, and more secure livelihoods. This chapter is concerned with people, their communities, and their needs. It is about human and social development. By this is meant the provision of opportunities to improve the human condition. It covers, in the first place, access to productive assets, the creation of productive and remunerative jobs, the provision of social services such as health and education, subsidies to essentials such as food and water where these cannot be afforded without subsidies, and transfer payments to supplement inadequate incomes. It also includes nonmaterial aspects, to be discussed later. Human development might be a better term for the central concern of this chapter, but *social* has come to be the accepted word.

Social and human development is thrice blessed: it is an end in itself; it makes for higher productivity; and it contributes to lower reproductivity. Above all, it is the ultimate purpose of all development efforts, and to promote human well-being needs no further justification. In addition, a healthy, alert, vigorous, well-nourished, well-educated population is also a source of production and productivity. It thereby contributes to the improvement of living conditions now and in the future. Third, by reducing the number of infant deaths and hence the size of the desired family, it contributes to reduced population growth and to a better quality of life. This may, at first, seem paradoxical, for improved social services can be expected to lead to lower mortality rates and therefore to higher population growth. But the evidence from some countries, especially those in East and South Asia, shows that reduced infant mortality soon leads to a reduction in the desired size of the family (which previously had led to an overinsurance against children's deaths in order to secure enough surviving children). Although the evidence is not entirely conclusive, education, especially women's education, also tends to lead to smaller families.

Some contributions to social development, such as education, have five distinct aspects. The process of being educated, insofar as it is enjoyable and satisfying in itself, resembles a nondurable consumption good (like apples) that is used up in the process of education. It also resembles the production of a product that uses up resources in the process and therefore a nondurable producer good (like coal). The subsequent state of being educated has the characteristics of both a durable consumption good and a durable investment good. In the former capacity it enables people to improve the quality of their lives, to enjoy books, music, the arts, and participation in the cultural and political activities of their community. (In this respect it resembles, as well as contrasts with, a durable consumer good, such as a television set or a stereo system.) In the latter capacity it raises the productivity of the worker in employment, generating incomes and output both for the worker and for others. (In this respect it is like a machine.) It also raises the productivity in nonmarket activities, such as work inside the household for self and family (like an automobile or a washing machine).

Conflicts may, of course, arise between pursuing these different aspects and objectives. Policies aiming at improvement as an end will pay equal attention to the unemployables, the disabled, the aged, the chronically ill, who can make no contribution to production. Even here, however, the knowledge that society will look after the disabled, handicapped, and old will remove one important motive for having a large family, will reduce population growth, and will thereby contribute indirectly to higher incomes per head. In the absence of social services it is important to have many children, for the surviving sons are expected to look after their parents, should they become disabled.

Other conflicts may arise about the specific groups for whom programs are designed or about the content of these programs. General education will equip people to widen their horizons and develop their faculties, while vocational training will make them more efficient workers. Even here, however, a general education may contribute more to the adaptability and flexibility that a modern society requires than a narrow vocational one. There may be conflicts about the role of women: should they be encouraged to choose their activities freely or to be good wives and mothers?

Plutarch tells the story of three Spartan women who were sold as slaves. Their captors asked them what they had learned to do. The first replied, "How to manage a household well." The second said, "How to be loyal." The third said, "How to be free." The story raises the perennial question about the education, status, and role of women. Should they perform well in a distinct women's sphere, the household, should they be loving wives, or should they become free and autonomous citizens, equal to men? In Plutarch's version, the third woman manages to commit suicide (Nussbaum, 1986, p. 7). But such choices do not make the need for human development less important: on the contrary, the fact that it is both an end and a means, both a process and a product, makes it imperative to advance more rapidly, so as to reduce the force of the dilemmas when they do arise.

The purpose of this chapter is not to attach blame and find fault for the neglect of the poor. Many positions are possible on this subject. John Iliffe, in his book *The African Poor* (1988), writes, "The eager hope of Independence conspired with current economic theory to direct development policy towards unbalanced growth through urban industry and infrastructure, which bred unprofitable enterprises, heavy recurrent costs, unpayable debts and exploited villagers." War and civil disorder also contributed their share to poverty, and the combination of violence and famine has been in the past, as it is still, one of the most seriously impoverishing conditions. High rates of population growth have strained the resources and the ecological base. Others blame bloated urban-biased government, paid for by buying peasant crops at a fraction of their market value; others blame climate and soil and natural disasters.

It is equally possible to attribute the crisis in the developing countries to violently fluctuating and deteriorating terms of trade; the slowing down of the growth of demand for exports; the rapid rise in, and unprecedentedly high, interest rates; the drying up of public and private sources of finance; the uncoordinated and often inconsistent ways of the donor community; outside shocks such as the fluctuating price of oil; and the neglect of creating the human infrastructure by the ex-colonial powers. Some success stories indicate that rapid progress in industry showed up agriculture as the lagging sector; that the much-deplored high rates of population growth mean that more children survive, surely a welcome phenomenon; and that rapid aggregate growth is impossible while agriculture constitutes a large part of national income and employment and when institutions, skills, and attitudes have to be built for future growth.

External and domestic causes are interdependent. Poor terms of trade, though caused by declines in external demand, are also the result of domestic rigidity and inflexibility; they reflect an inability to move into more remunerative exports. Nor is there a one-way relation between causes and remedies. External causes call for domestic remedies if foreign assistance or improved trading conditions are not forthcoming. Searching for causes is much less important than discovering remedies.

Living conditions in some parts of the Third World, especially Africa and Latin America, are poor and have been deteriorating. Too many people live in abject poverty, degradation, and misery. Undernutrition, malnutrition, and hunger have been increasing; roads are crumbling, and infrastructure is deteriorating; the shelves in village shops are empty; fuel is becoming increasingly scarce; hunched-over women lug loads of wood on their backs over ever longer distances; clinics have no medicines; factories are idle for want of materials; unemployment and underemployment are rising; schools are without textbooks, chalk, and other teaching equipment; mothers' and children's health is deteriorating.

In many parts of Asia the situation is much better. The growth of real income between 1960 and 1987 has outstripped that in the industrial countries, and the poor have benefited from this. Since the bulk of the world's population lives in Asia, the notion that the 1980s were a "lost decade" is wrong, if we count people rather than countries.

Developing countries as a whole have made progress in improving the social conditions of their people (see Table 4.1). Their populations are healthier and better educated. Average life expectancy increased between 1960 and 1990 as a proportion of the level in the North from 67 to 84 percent. The daily supply of calories per head increased between 1964–1966 and 1984–1986 from 72 to 80 percent of the level in the North. Infant and child mortality rates more than halved between 1960 and 1990, an achievement that took over a century in the industrial countries. Adult literacy increased from 46 to 64 percent between 1970 and 1990, narrowing the literacy gap between North and South from 49 to 34 percent.

People in the developing countries now live longer, and more have acquired a rudimentary education than three decades ago. But even where these successes are registered (and averages conceal wide disparities), the developing countries have been left behind in technological progress and the accompanying rises in productivity. The gap in informatics, technological research, and technical education is widening and disturbing.

The exact extent of the growing poverty and its composition, trend, and causes are difficult to assess, partly because data are not available or are unreliable. But action cannot wait for a full analysis and collection of reliable statistics. In this chapter an attempt is made to base judgments on the available evidence, to

Table 4.1
Life Expectancy, Infant Mortality, and Literacy, 1950–1990

	Life Expectancy at Birth (------years------)			Literacy Rate (-----percent-----)			Infant Mortality Rate /a	
	1950	1970	1990	1950	1970	1990	1965	1990
All Developing Countries	43	51	63	33	45	64	117	63
Low-Income	41	49	62	20	36	60	124	69
Middle-Income	46	57	66	51	65	78	94	48
High-Income	65	71	77	95	98	99	24	8

Source: World Bank, *World Development Report* (various issues).
[a]Per 1,000 live births.

identify the obstacles to the removal of poverty, to indicate where figures are unreliable, and to encourage, where necessary, the collection and management of better data for the purpose of reducing poverty and improving living conditions. The objective is to present the state of knowledge about living conditions, the trends of changes in these conditions, and the key policy issues. The impact on the poor of a range of policies, programs, and institutions not normally intended to reduce poverty but serving other purposes is also examined.

A concern for people is at the heart of this chapter. Development is (or should be) about, for, of, and by people—above all, the many poor people in the developing countries but also the people in the advanced countries whose sense of solidarity and humanity can be mobilized for a joint effort. The rise of private, voluntary organizations, debates in the legislatures of rich countries, discussions in the media, and the success of donor countries that have built their programs on this basis show that people's enthusiasm can be harnessed to a common effort to eradicate poverty.

THE POOR

The poor are a heterogeneous group. They may be identified by occupation, region, age, sex, or other characteristics. Unless this is understood, the remedies may be ill-chosen. In some parts of the world the bulk of the poor are small farmers who produce largely for their own and their families' consumption. There are the landless laborers who have nothing but their labor to sell. Then there are the urban poor with various links to their villages but often without any assets, either physical or human, or very low-yielding assets. Some of the poor are to be found within otherwise adequately endowed households: very hardworking women, carrying water over long distances or spending hours collecting firewood, in addition to cultivating crops, cooking meals, and bearing and nurturing children. Then there are the children themselves, too numerous, some of them unwanted and neglected, others required to contribute hard work from an early age. There are the handicapped, the sick, the disabled, the infirm, and the old. There are the poor who reside in distant regions or who belong to ethnic groups that have been persecuted or neglected by the development process. Above all, there are the breadwinners in the family, whether men or women, on whose precarious earnings food for the children and other members of the household depends.

Different policies are appropriate for these different groups. Expenditure on some of these groups can be a high-yielding form of investment, and on others, simply a manifestation of a civilized, caring society. But while the costs of investing in the poor may be high, the costs of failing to do so can be even higher. The economic, social, political, and cultural costs of a malnourished, diseased, illiterate, inert population can put an enormous burden on a society, and a compassionate policy can pay high dividends in the longer run.

OBJECTIVES

It is often said that the objective of development is economic growth with equity. A World Bank publication was entitled *Redistribution with Growth*. Professor Ali Mazrui has defined development as modernization (which involves growth) minus dependence. Common to all these definitions is an emphasis on economic growth as a necessary, though not sufficient, condition of development and poverty reduction. Yet, economic growth is simply the intertemporal dimension of income or, more precisely, of consumption. If the metaphor of a "takeoff into self-sustained growth" is accepted, the task for low-income countries is to lay the runway. Laying the institutional and human foundations for future increases in consumption is not immediately reflected in higher growth rates. This is particularly so for countries where many of the most important policies, such as institution building, controlling population growth, and raising savings ratios and productivity, are slowly gestating measures. High rates of growth are quite consistent with growing poverty, and low levels of income and its growth have been associated with rapid poverty reduction.

Since growth has increasing costs, it is not sensible to maximize growth. But "optimizing" growth does not tell us how much we should tighten our belts today in order to enjoy more tomorrow or to allow our children and their children to enjoy more in thirty or forty years. Growth is almost by definition limitless, or at least horizonless. Meeting basic needs and conquering poverty are limited objectives.

Any objective of policy must have a time frame, an intertemporal dimension. We may be ready to endure some poverty today in order to reduce that of a larger population in ten years; we may tolerate greater inequality today, if it permits us to reduce it, at a higher level of income, in the future; we may allow some unemployment resulting from labor-saving techniques if the plowed-back profits enable us to create more jobs for more job seekers after five years; and so on. At a minimum, the time frame must be such that the policy is sustainable. There is no point in eradicating poverty today, if the basis of this eradication collapses after a few years and mass poverty then increases. *Sustainability* is therefore an important minimum condition. It comprises at least maintaining physical and human capital (and increasing it for a growing population) and fiscal and administrative resources. Recently it has also come to refer to the need to maintain the physical environment, the biosphere, the soil, the forests, the water, and the air and to make provision for the replacement of exhaustible resources. But there is frequently a confusion between ends and means, between the constituents of well-being and its determinants. It is the end results, the constituents, that should be (at least) sustainable, not any particular resource base that serves as an input. Another difficulty with some of the formulations is that they allow neither for growing populations and rising living standards nor for technical progress. There is nothing sacrosanct about sustaining the present level of living (and even less about maintaining the resource base for the present level). We must provide for a growing population and higher living standards. At the same time we know that technical progress will provide substitutes for exhaustible materials. Even more recently, sustainability has come to cover political sustainability of policies, that is, both credibility and support for these policies.

Consumption or income is among the proper objectives of development. Growth, up to a certain point and properly composed and distributed, is the *result* (almost a by-product), not the *objective,* of a rational economic policy, in which dates are attached to the achievement of the increase in consumption (or income) of different groups and to the achievement of other development objectives, such as employment, improved health, nutrition and education, reduced inequality, increased leisure, and conservation of the physical environment.

Environmental concerns have recently moved out of the wings and onto the center of the political stage. Deforestation, desertification, soil erosion, nutrient depletion, higher levels of toxicity of land, poor land management, silting, and fresh water depletion are growing threats to development. It has been estimated that we are losing 10,000 species a year—plants, insects, birds, fish, mammals, microorganisms. The current mass extinction of plants and animals is comparable, in terms of its destructive effects on the diversity of life on earth, to earlier mass extinctions, such as the end of the dinosaurs. Sustainability in the sense of conserving the environment can, of course, (though it need not) conflict with equity, just as there can, but need not, be conflicts between growth and equity. Particularly the concern for the global environment, mainly concentrated in rich countries, can deny access to resources to the people and their children in developing countries. The environmental problems of the poor countries are mainly about land and water and are local, regional, or national, rarely global.

A common minimum formulation of the objectives is sustainable growth (of consumption) with equity or, better, with rapid poverty reduction. Equity means that there should not be unfair discrimination between equals. Some poverty reduction may have to be inequitable, in the sense that not all the poor can become better off at the same time, so that some groups or some regions may have to be favored, at least for a time. This is particularly important if the selective policy unfairly favoring one group eventually helps to eradicate more speedily the poverty of those left behind.

There is also a distinction between inequality and inequity. If A, whose situation is in all relevant respects the same as B's, has more than B, that is inequality; if A has more *because B has less,* or if B has less *because A has more,* that is inequitable or iniquitous. But even where exploitative and iniquitous inequality is absent, we should still be concerned with the fate of the poor.

Raising production and productivity of the poor, although important, is not enough. Many productivity gains in the Third World have been passed on to foreign buyers (e.g., in lower prices of export crops), to large multinational corporations, or to the better-off groups at home. The gains must also be remunerative for the poor, as well as productive.

We may also wish to add the objective of security and stability: economic, political, and legal. Greatly fluctuating gains and insecure jobs are discounted, even if their average is larger than a more stable, though lower, level. So, as a first approximation, the objective is productive, remunerative, sustainable, stable, and equitable growth of consumption (or, to remove the ambiguities in *equity*, growth with rapid reduction of absolute poverty).

But this does not exhaust the range of objectives. Some of the most important contributions to poverty reduction, reflected in what poor people actually want, do not show up in growth figures and are not achieved by economic growth. Poverty is multidimensional and cannot be subsumed under one or two or a few indicators. We have already seen that adequate nutrition and safe water, better medical services, more and better schooling, cheap transport, adequate shelter, available cheap fuel, better access to public goods and to common property, continuing employment, and secure livelihoods do not register in higher income per head, at least not for some time. Some of these are provided free or at subsidized prices by the government; others, by private voluntary societies; still others, by groups of poor people themselves. They tend to be evaluated by national income accountants at the cost of the social services ministering to basic needs, or (as in the case of secure livelihoods or shorter queues at clinics) they are benefits that are not recorded at all in money income measures. In addition, poor people certainly also want a higher and rising level of measured real income, but this is not their only or even principal basic need.

Other nonmaterial benefits, often more highly valued by the people than material improvements, especially by poor, inarticulate, powerless people, only indirectly and, after a time lag, may or may not contribute to growing production. Some of these partake in the characteristics of rights, either positive or negative, and others, in those of states of mind. Some express the need to *do* certain things, and others, the need to achieve certain states of *being*. These aspects are obviously related. Among these objectives are good working conditions; freedom to choose jobs and livelihoods; self-determination and self-respect; independence; mobility; liberation from oppression, patronage, violence, and exploitation; security from persecution and arbitrary arrest; the assertion of traditional cultural and religious values (often the only thing a poor man or woman can assert); access to power, or empowerment; recognition; status; adequate leisure time and satisfying forms of its use; a sense of purpose in life and work; the opportunity to join and participate actively in the activities of a pluralistic civil society and in decisions that affect people's life and work, with institutions that are layered between the individual and the central government; and the opportunities to develop fully the personality of every human being born into this world.

All of these are important objectives, valued both in their own right and as means to satisfying and productive work. Many of these can be achieved in ways that do not increase the measured production of commodities, while a high and growing national income, even if fairly distributed, can leave these basic needs unsatisfied. No policymaker can guarantee the achievement of all, or even a majority of, these aspirations, but policies can create the *opportunities* for their fulfillment. In assessing successes or failures in the pursuit of these objectives, it is important not to fall victim to the twin fallacies that only what can be counted counts (or exists) and that any figure, however unreliable, is better than none.[1]

ADJUSTMENT AND SOCIAL DEVELOPMENT

In the 1970s and early 1980s, when the world economy experienced a series of violent shocks, in particular the large oil price rises, stabilization and adjustment problems occupied the center of the stage. About thirty-five Sub-Saharan countries are now pursuing structural adjustment programs. Among the key objectives of the stabilization loans of the fund are usually cited:

1. the reduction or elimination of a deficit in the balance of payments;
2. the resumption of higher rates of growth; and
3. the achievement of structural changes that would prevent future payments and stabilization problems.

Initially, the focus had been exclusively on the correction of the balance of payments, normally by devaluation and reduction of domestic demand through monetary and fiscal contraction. But it was soon noted that this should not be done at the expense of productive investment and economic growth. So growth had crept back into the adjustment objective.

The next step was to emphasize that the austerity imposed by the need to correct the balance of payments and reduce inflation should not be implemented on the backs of the poor. This led to a debate on whether adjustment measures had in fact been carried out by increasing poverty; on what the fate of the poor would have been without the adjustment measures; and on what types of expenditure should be cut if productive investment, mass consumption, social expenditure, and defense must not be touched.

These questions are not the concern of this chapter. Once it is agreed that malnutrition, illiteracy, ill health, inadequate shelter, and underemployment are evils, it does not matter whether they are caused by contractionist adjustment measures or by external shocks, by domestic misfortune or mismanagement, or by deep structural forces or misalignment of prices. Whatever their causes, top priority should be given to their elimination.

Gradually, almost all issues discussed initially under the headings of policy reform and "development" had been reintroduced into the adjustment debate: not only fiscal, monetary, and exchange rate policy but also international trade policy, industrial, agricultural, and regional policies, employment and labor policy, the performance of public enterprises, the management of the public sector and of social services, and others. Although the emphasis was now more on macroeconomic policy, it was clear that this has to be supported by sound micro- and meso-policies, as well as foreign assistance. At first, the meaning of "adjustment" had changed from responses to violent shocks, to general economic reforms; then it had become synonymous with development. From a once-for-all change it had come to mean a continuing process.

If we start with a situation in which a society uses more resources than it produces and can finance by borrowing, grants, and reserves, it follows that some expenditure must be cut. It is true that adding concerns about economic growth, poverty reduction, the physical environment, and political stability reduces the number of items that can be cut. But by changing the composition and pattern of some large macroeconomic magnitudes, by mobilizing underutilized resources, particularly the commitment, initiative, and enthusiasm of the people themselves, and by improving the productivity of human capital, an expansionary, sustainable, and equitable solution of the adjustment problem can be found. The human and social dimensions of adjustment have to be, from the very beginning, an integral part of adjustment programs. By mobilizing underutilized, largely local resources, by drawing on the capacities of the poor, by enlisting their participation in the design, execution, maintenance, and evaluation of projects and programs, by community-focused, low-cost approaches, by seeking expansionist solutions, and by raising the productivity of the poor, we find that, far from there being a conflict between social development and successful adjustment, the two can mutually support each other. Making poor people more productive and their work more remunerative is an integral part of a sound structural adjustment program.

When considering the impact of adjustment policies on the poor, four things should be clear to start with. First, any form of macroeconomic adjustment is bound to affect income distribution, if only because its purpose is to raise incomes in some sectors and reduce them in others. This means that there will be gainers and losers.

Second, the main concern should be the impact of adjustment on the poor, not on relative income distribution. If some groups benefit from the process without vulnerable groups being further hurt, this should not be a cause for complaint, although in fact conflicts over the division of benefits can be as serious as conflicts over absolute gains and losses.

Third, any cut in living standards, imposed by the need to correct a balance-of-payments deficit, is bound to hit some members of the community who consider themselves poor, if only because the poor are so numerous and average incomes in the poor countries are so low. This is particularly the case if productive investment that contributes to economic growth, to future adaptability, and to safeguarding future living standards; expenditure on conserving the environment and on defense; and expenditure for the benefit of politically powerful groups are all to be protected. Some austerity is therefore inevitable. In particular, employed wage earners in the formal, urban sector, including some of those in public enterprises, who are not normally among the poorest, may have to suffer temporarily.

But, fourth, in the adjustment process the poorest groups in the population can and should be protected against having to bear an excessive burden. In some cases their living standards can be improved. We try to show that expansionist solutions that raise supplies are possible, which, by encouraging the formation of human capital, by changing the composition and pattern of production and of social services, by adopting appropriate meso-policies, by utilizing existing resources more fully, and by mobilizing through participation underutilized manpower, can bring about adjustment while not only protecting, but actually benefiting, the poor.

The fate of the poor in adjustment programs is sometimes compared with their fate without such programs, sometimes with their position before the program. The proper hypothetical alternative situation to that of access to additional foreign funds should be neither the situation without additional funds nor the situation with funds provided on contractionist, deflationary, demand-reducing conditionality (in both of which the poor might fare worse) but the situation with additional funds and the expansionist solution.

The impact of adjustment policies on vulnerable groups will depend on how public expenditures on food subsidies and social services for the poor, the remuneration for their employment and livelihoods, their access to credit, and the prices and availability of essential goods are affected. In the past, austerity programs have sometimes harmed the poor (though perhaps not the poorest). Import liberalization has thrown people out of work in previously protected industries and raised the prices of imported essentials. Tighter credit has made it impossible for small businesses to borrow. Reductions in the civil service and in parastatal organizations have directly and indirectly caused hardships. Women who had to seek jobs had to neglect their children, some of whom became "street kids." Demand contraction reduced the demand for labor. The need to reduce the budget deficit led to reductions in food subsidies and subsidies to inputs of poor farmers, such as fertilizer, seeds, credit, and equipment. Reduced public services did not always lead to an increase in the supply from private sources, and the poor had to go without them. Where cost recovery was introduced, it reduced the access to health services and education of the poor. Devaluation raised the price of imported food and other necessities. There were offsetting benefits, but the haphazard incidence of these measures has, no doubt, caused deprivation.

Adjustment normally consists of two parts: expenditure reduction and expenditure switching. It is true that expenditure reduction in a poor country will tend to hit the poor, unless specific measures are adopted to protect or compensate them. But expenditure switching need not harm them. The reallocation from the domestic sector to tradables will tend to raise incomes in this sector. If traded goods are mainly agricultural products and if many poor are occupied in agriculture, they will benefit from the reallocation. On the other hand, some nontradables, such as construction, food for domestic consumption, and government services, are labor-intensive, and a switch to the production of tradables will then reduce employment and incomes of these people. Analysis of the impact of balance-of-payments adjustments on income and poverty is sometimes conducted in terms of a two-sector neoclassical model, in which tradables have different factor proportions from nontradables. A switch to tradables then benefits the owners of the factor of production that is used more intensively in the production of tradables, not only in the tradables sector but in both sectors. It also benefits the consumers of nontradables because their relative prices fall, while hurting the consumers of tradables, the prices of which rise. But the difficulty with this type of analysis is that incomes of people do not follow the neat functional lines of capital and labor. Most people supply both capital and labor, though in very different amounts and proportions.

Moreover, the two-sector model is of limited use. Within each sector there may be an informal, labor-intensive subsector, in which producers own a little capital and operate by themselves and with members of their families on a small scale, and a formal, capital-intensive, large-scale subsector, with wage employment. As expenditure is switched to the tradables sector, workers in the formal subsector may benefit but the poor in the informal subsector may be harmed. If there is substantial mobility between the two subsectors, this does not matter, for people will move from the informal into the formal subsector. But if mobility is limited, the distinction is crucial. In Côte d'Ivoire, for example, export croppers, who are among the poorer groups, would benefit from a rise in the price of tradable goods, but so would some processors and manufacturers in the formal sector, who are richer than the average. In addition, the model analyzes changes in *relative* prices and incomes, whereas what concerns us here is *absolute* poverty.

The higher prices of imported necessities caused by devaluation could be offset by subsidies targeted toward the poor, and the restrictions on investment could be on luxury housing, large-scale infrastructure, and durable consumer goods of the upper classes. In fact, however, many stabilization policies have hit the poor hard. The price increases that follow devaluation and the removal of controls frequently affect particularly the prices of necessities consumed by them. Reductions in government expenditure are frequently on labor-intensive public works, parastatal organizations that have provided jobs, food subsidies, and social services. The liberalization of financial markets and higher interest rates can encourage concentration of wealth if lenders are richer than borrowers (but this is not always so), though lower rates combined with credit rationing favoring the rich often do the same. Monetary and fiscal restrictions raise unemployment and reduce the bargaining power of unskilled labor. The poor tend to suffer more than they would in a situation of repressed inflation, where demand for labor is high, the prices of necessities are controlled, and social services are more generous. The price to be paid for these benefits is perhaps a less efficient allocation of resources.

A distinction is often drawn between adjustment policies that reduce demand

and those that increase supply. But this distinction ignores the fact that reductions in demand, by reducing incentives to produce and sell, also tend to reduce supply and that in the process of increasing supply, incomes are automatically generated that raise demand. What is required is either a reduction in demand without, or with a smaller, reduction in supply or an increase in supply without, or with a smaller, increase in demand, in other words, an increase in savings, without a corresponding reduction in output. Implicit in the advocacy of expansionary adjustment policies is the belief that the economic system generates savings as it expands, through higher personal savings, higher company savings, or higher tax collections unmatched by higher government expenditure.

Although normally both reductions in demand and increases in supply will be necessary in the process of adjustment, the emphasis should be on supply increases, with restraints on accompanying demand increases, even though supply increases take longer, so as to mitigate the need to contract demand. The relatively slower operation of supply increases is, or should be, one of the main reasons for international assistance, that is, the contribution of foreign savings, discussed more fully later. The removal of price distortions, both between sectors and within sectors, improvements in the efficiency of public enterprises, the breaking of bottlenecks, and the encouragement of competition will contribute to supply increases. Even if the poor do not directly benefit from the improvements in efficiency, the higher taxable capacity makes it possible to mobilize resources for their benefit.

An analysis confining itself to the changing demand for labor also neglects other ways of affecting the incomes of the poor. Among these are:

1. the impact on their access to productive assets such as land, credit, fertilizer;

2. the return on these assets—the impact on human capital formation, such as nutrition, health, education, that enables the poor to become more productive; and

3. the effect on transfer payments or of contributions in kind through social services, charity, or the extended family.

A rigorous model for assessing only the impact of adjustment policies on vulnerable groups, including women and children, is, however, not necessary if we are concerned with poverty reduction, whatever its causes. Certain guidelines for adjustment policies are useful. First, maintain a floor for minimum nutrition, health, and education expenditures aimed at the poor and do not permit cuts to affect these levels. Second, restructure production within the productive sectors—industry, agriculture, services, foreign trade—so that the producers in the small-scale, informal sector are not discriminated against but are made to complement the organized sector; give them access to credit, markets, sources of supply and information. More about this will be said. Third, restructure the social and public services—education, health, water, and sanitation—so that the poor are not deprived of minimum services. Fourth, provide international support for these types of adjustment, both financial and technical assistance. In particular, ease debt service conditions, so as to permit the flexibility and adaptability called for by these programs.

A serious difficulty with reducing more broad-based and more expensive welfare programs to more "targeted" ones is always that savings in government revenue are bought by excluding some of the poor beneficiaries. It is almost impossible to benefit *all* the poor and *only* the poor. "Leakages" can occur at both ends: excess coverage means that some nonpoor benefit, but reduced coverage means that some poor do not benefit. The case for erring on the side of excess coverage is that this also raises the taxable capacity of the nonpoor, so that at least some of the expenditure can be recovered, say, by a tax on tobacco, which helps to finance food subsidies. A further advantage is that it gains the political support of the nonpoor beneficiaries, who will tend to be more vocal and more powerful.

Special problems of protecting the poor arise for the period of transition from mistaken to correct policies. Consider a government that has kept agricultural prices too low and wishes to raise them so as to encourage production of food and raise the incomes of poor sellers of agricultural products. Once supply and employment in agriculture have increased and new technologies have been introduced, we may assume that most groups will benefit. If in the process supply curves have been lowered, prices may be even lower than before. But in the interim some may suffer. Poor buyers of food may starve while the adjustment to the reforms takes time. Policymakers embarking on a course of raising food prices must therefore pay special attention to protecting the poor in the transition.

Problems also arise when a government attempts to shrink its public sector and parastatal firms. The best people are the first to leave, and if, as is usual, the shrinking is done by not replacing staff who leave, the sector is left with the deadwood. If salaries are not adequate, there are incentives to seeking outside work, to corruption, and to slacking. Morale will be low. If those dismissed do not find alternative employment, a burden is thrown on the community. They may become a source not of productive but of rebellious activity.

The high cost, in terms of political constraints, such as the riots against the removal of food subsidies in Zambia, Tunisia, and Egypt, among others, and of economic and financial resources, is one of the biggest obstacles to reform. One solution is to increase the prices of food items gradually, in small steps. A second is to adopt selective subsidies to the poor. Subsidies can also be combined with rations, so that the poor are guaranteed a minimum of food. Fiscal and administrative constraints set limits to such programs. It is particularly difficult to reach poor food buyers, such as landless laborers, in rural areas. Experience has shown, however, that programs of subsidies aimed specifically at vulnerable groups can be quite effective, as long as the number of poor is not too large, say less than 30 percent of the population. We have seen that it is rarely possible to cover *all* the poor and *only* the poor, and we may have to accept some sacrifice of total food production in response to higher food prices for the sake of better nutritional standards of poor food buyers, safeguarded by lower food prices (and hence a smaller stimulus to production) in the transition period.

A CONCEPTUAL FRAMEWORK

The approach to improving the conditions of human and social well-being and of human capital can be considered under the headings of eight (or nine) *instruments*, some of them government *inter*ventions, or INs.

1. Incentives
2. Input
3. Innovation
4. Information
5. Infrastructure
6. Institutions
7. Initiative
8. Independence

It is sometimes said that a consistent macroeconomic framework is essential for good policy-making. But since the relation between these INs is uncertain, *inconsistency* the ninth IN, can be a virtue; it assists the learning process. Under each of these headings the composition and pattern are as important as the aggregate.

Setting the right *incentives,* by using prices as signals, incentives, and mobilizers, has rightly been much emphasized in the recent literature and has also been reflected in changes in policies. Little needs to be added, except to say that the task of the government is to organize efficient markets, not to expose them to the free play of laissez-faire and to carry out its own functions efficiently, not to minimize them. Incentives do not operate in a vacuum. The framework for their operation is set by the government, which can use prices and incentives as instruments of policy. Indirect taxes and subsidies, including pollution taxes, taxes on rents and subsidies to food, the introduction of insurance schemes, the encouragement of competition, whether among private or public enterprises or between the two, and similar interventions, can lead to more efficient and more equitable market performance.

Inputs are clearly important, both as primary and intermediate goods for the production of output and as consumption goods to provide incentives to producers. Their unavailability has in some countries held back agricultural production, which has further reduced foreign exchange earnings and imports, hence agricultural production, and so on in a vicious circle. Increasing the supply of some crucial inputs, both producer and consumer goods, can help to activate large, otherwise unused capacities.

Innovation, the introduction of new and appropriate technologies, is the primary condition for progress and improved living standards. It cannot be just "transferred" from advanced countries. An indigenous technological capacity is needed in order to adapt, maintain, repair, and improve imported technologies and to invent new ones where these are necessary. It is also needed in order to judge which technologies should be imported and how much should be paid for them. Much research has been concentrated on export crops that are in inelastic demand. Improvements and increased production by several countries are then reflected in lower prices and passed on to foreign buyers. Redirection of research to food crops domestically consumed would be desirable.

Other types of innovation have been wrongly transferred to Africa from the Asian experience. The combination of irrigation, fertilizers, and high-yielding seeds is appropriate for India and other parts of South Asia, where land is scarce and labor plentiful. Much advice given by Western experts was wrong (Binswanger and Pingali, 1988). As a result, staff was demoralized, farmers did not respond, and the projects failed. Emphasis in research should be on drought- and disease-resistant varieties, on staple food crops, on new cash crops, and on ways to improve quality.

Other research is directed at the food consumed by the better-off. A redirection of research to poor people's crops, such as cassava, sweet potatoes and other root crops, and cheap cereals, an increase in the critical mass of research institutes, particularly in Africa, reduction in the turnover of personnel, and reduced dispersal would show up in better results, without additional outlay. Here, as in the case of infrastructure, a change in the composition of activities is more promising than an increase in the total, if it were to follow conventional lines.

The results of the research and the technical innovations have to be disseminated through extension services and *information* centers. The generation and dispersal of information about markets, technologies, and labor are typically activities carried out better in the public sector. They are essential for the working of efficient markets, and they are normally among the contributions that the government can make better than private suppliers.

The design and construction of appropriate *infrastructure,* also normally carried out by the government, face a dilemma. Infrastructure, like innovation and information (and like foreign exchange earnings), is an essential ingredient for making investment in agriculture, industry, and services efficient; at the same time its call on resources deprives these sectors of resources. It therefore competes with directly productive investment and consumption. One way out of this dilemma is to eliminate wasteful, large-scale types of infrastructure investments that serve the consumption needs of the rich or the ostentation of public officials and to select only those that contribute to production: not four-lane highways but feeder roads for farmers; not large, publicly subsidized grain silos but on-farm storage facilities; not fully automated global telephone systems but those that link neighboring villages and market towns. Another way is to concentrate on maintaining existing useful projects rather than starting new ones: gasoline for cars to use existing roads rather than new roads that will not be properly maintained; breeding crop varieties that are less susceptible to delays rather than building new expensive ports and roads. Trade and exchange can be good ways of raising production, productivity, and incomes, but they can also be excessively subsidized, at the expense of production for local markets and neighborhoods. Much of policy amounts to excessive subsidies to trade with distant partners and to the consumption of the rich. Again, regional integration among African countries is desirable, but large-scale, expensive infrastructure for cooperation at the expense of small farmers and informal sector enterprises is a mistake. Small is not always preferable to large, but much of the potential strength of poor countries lies in building on the ability and capacity of small farmers and small entrepreneurs.

The creation and strengthening of *institutions* are another way of combining public sector activity with organizing markets. The impact on the poor of the conversion of communal land to private property titles in some countries is uncertain, and more research is needed. The need for land reform, that is, redistribution of land to those who cultivate it, especially in Latin America, is an institutional reform that reduces poverty and increases output.

A central theme of this chapter is that the exercise of our institutional imagination has lagged behind that of our scientific and technological imagination and that the design of appropriate institutions has an important part to play in reforms. The developing countries' most plentiful underutilized resource is their people. Participation from the earliest stages of a project by its beneficiaries meets a basic need to be a recognized and active member of one's community and can also greatly reduce the costs of constructing and maintaining the project. A centrally organized supply of piped water to all Indian villages would be extremely expensive. But the construction of standpipes or wells by the villagers would be substantially cheaper and achieve its purpose more effectively. Participation has too often been used as a slogan rather than part of a strategy. Local participation has often to be supported by money and management at the intermediate and central level. Decentralization can add to the oppressive strength of the local power elite. But in a correctly designed decision structure it has an important part to play. Nongovernmental organizations, both indigenous and international, can also draw on the enthusiasm and commitment of volunteers at low costs, but their efforts have often to be combined with those of governments and profit-oriented enterprises.

The correct policy is not to swing from one extreme to the other—from excessive government intervention to complete withdrawal, from encouraging the organized sector to promoting only the informal sector, from excluding all foreign enterprises to permitting all comers—but to combine judiciously large-scale and small-scale, formal and informal, domestic and foreign, public and private institutions and enterprises.

Credit institutions have an important part to play in giving poor people, including poor women, access to productive assets. At present, credit policy too often combines subsidized interest rates with credit rationing and the promotion of inequality. The richer farmers and the urban middle class benefit. The demand for credit by the poor, informal sector businesses and by the small farmers must first exist and must then be met by small loans. In view of the high rates of population growth, Africa can learn a good deal for its policy for the future from the overpopulated countries of South and Southeast Asia, where the landless rural and urban poor have no collateral to offer for their loans but where their repayment record is strikingly good, often much better than that of richer borrowers with substantial assets.

The market is, of course, another valuable institution, capable of harnessing the dispersed initiative and information of many individuals. Its encouragement and careful cultivation and its setting in a framework of law and order should be a primary task of government policy, not an alternative to government policy. Policy must aim at widening markets, both in the geographical dimension through regional cooperation and in the dimension of size, through raising productivity and incomes. The interaction of growing specialization and widening markets is the key to economic progress.

Social security provision can be made by the government, often pressured by organizations of poor people and a free press, by private voluntary societies, by unions of the poor themselves, by community- and family-based institutions, and by the creative use of markets, such as insurance schemes, public works programs, and other employment-creating projects (see Drèze and Sen, 1989; von Braun, 1989).

Various types of hybrid institutions (briefly discussed in the section on the informal sector) can draw on the initiative and enterprise of individuals in a free market and at the same time be publicly accountable and responsible. The challenge is not to get stuck in one-sided ideological commitments but to design institutions that are efficient, accountable, and equitable.

This points to the need to prevent the stifling of *initiative* and its careful nurturing. This is partly, but not entirely, a matter of the right incentives. Much of the discussion of human and social capital formation is concerned with education and the creation of skills and the use of aptitudes. But at least equally important is the creation of appropriate attitudes, though these are less easily measured and therefore tend to be neglected. The desire to earn money, it is now generally recognized, is pretty universal. Private enterprise and the initiative of small farmers and businessmen are among the developing world's most important potential assets. By exercising our institutional imagination and setting up appropriate organizations, this private energy can be combined with public concerns. But initiative is not confined to the private, profit-seeking sector and the public sector. It is also manifest in private, voluntary organizations that harness the enthusiasm of volunteers to social development.

Finally, *independence* and self-reliance are essential, both as ends (for basic needs without freedom can be well provided for in an efficiently run prison) and as a means to the cost-effective way of reducing poverty. Self-reliance must not be confused with self-sufficiency, for to attempt to rely wholly on domestic production can make a country truly dependent if, for example, the harvest fails. Independence means a diversified pattern of production for domestic consumption and foreign trade, diversified by sources of supply, by markets, and by commodities. It is consistent with interdependence. It means strengthening the educational system and building an indigenous scientific and technological capacity. It means teeth-gritting humility in being prepared to learn from foreign experts and capacity to adapt knowledge to local conditions.

We do not know enough about the interaction of these eight INs to prescribe priorities and phasing, and, in view of our uncertainty, some inconsistency, as was said, may be a virtue. It indicates the range of uncertainty and enables us to learn. The learning approach, rather than blueprints, can be built into program design. But the main lesson is the importance of the composition and direction of action under each heading, what may be called the intermediate or meso-policies, as well as an emphasis on the aggregates, and of the need to mobilize the poor themselves by drawing on their initiative, their participation, their enthusiasm, their skills.

DILEMMAS

In several contexts we have come across fundamental dilemmas, the need for choice, for an "either . . . or," while at the same time emphasizing complementarities, the need for a "both . . . and." There is the dilemma between short-term stabilization and long-term growth with equity. There is the dilemma in pricing policy between high food prices to encourage production and help for the poor food sellers and low food prices to prevent starvation of the poor food buyers. There is the dilemma between investment in infrastructure that would lower agricultural and industrial production functions and make them more elastic and devoting resources directly to more agricultural and industrial production. There is the dilemma between industrialization and promoting agriculture, between import substitution and exports.

There is always the dilemma between saving more for the future consumption of a rapidly growing population and raising current consumption, especially the nutritional and health status, of very poor people, a dilemma made somewhat less acute by the fact that in poor countries raising nutrition, health, and education of the poor, normally counted as increases in consumption, is a form of human investment that raises future output and reduces population growth. There is the dilemma between exporting more to earn foreign exchange for the purchase of inputs of fertilizer for more domestic food production and for a fuller utilization of existing industrial capacity and using these resources to raise domestic food and industrial production directly.

There is the conflict between the large outlays on agricultural research and the meager returns to them. There is the dilemma between devoting resources—savings, management, know-how, wage goods—to the organized modern sector with its high productivity and using them to encourage the creation of livelihoods in the informal sector, where productivity may be lower but the spread of benefits to the poor wider. There is the dilemma between devoting resources to the formation of physical capital—machines, buildings, roads—and devoting them to the formation of human capital—health, nutrition, skills—which is needed to use, maintain, and improve the physical capital.

At the same time, resources are scarce, and public institutions are weak, particularly in poor countries. The need to choose between priorities is therefore imperative. Proper phasing or sequencing of complementary measures is of the utmost importance, for advancing on one front without complementary advances on others can be ineffective or counterproductive.

Although economics and politics are about the necessity to choose, an important theme of this chapter is that many of these dilemmas present false choices and that the task is to combine components of one side with components of the other, to adopt "both . . . and" solutions and, by eliminating the less important components on both horns of the dilemmas, to draw on the strengths of both. Thus there is really no dilemma between agriculture and industry or between food for domestic consumption and export crops; the task is to cut across these distinctions and to choose the right agro-industrial projects, processing, and marketing crops; projects that create remunerative employment for poor people contribute to food production and foreign exchange earnings.

Another important theme is that the formation of human and social capital has to precede that of physical capital if waste is to be avoided and that the human capital formation at the same time raises the living standards of the poor. Within human capital formation, education should have a high priority, especially the education of women, for it can, initially, substitute for other components, whereas without it other components can be ineffective. Dropout rates in primary schools are reduced when the mothers of these children are educated. If people know when to boil water, the need for supplies of safe water is reduced. If they do not know about personal hygiene, safe water supplies are futile, if, after washing their hands, they dry them on dirty, infected towels.

A third theme that softens or eliminates some of the dilemmas is the need to encourage community-based institutions. Neither central government action by itself nor the free market by itself can solve any problems. Familial and community institutions are a potentially rich source of energy, if creatively combined with government action. Rural development, based on a combination of these four types of institution, can reduce the rate of urbanization and its high costs (von Braun, 1989).

THE INFORMAL SECTOR: A SOURCE OF EQUITABLE EFFICIENCY

There are four reasons for paying attention to the informal sector in a chapter on social development. These arise from the need to raise production, employment (and with it self-confidence and self-respect), and incomes and the need to avoid rebellion.

First, the informal sector represents a potentially large reserve of productivity and earning power. Although it is a heterogeneous collection of activities that have been sometimes romanticized and although some of these have very low or even negative productivity, while others are illegal, there are some potentially productive ones that are now constrained by government harassment, discrimination, and neglect and by unfair competition from large firms.

Second, the labor force in most developing countries is likely to grow rapidly in the next fifteen years, and neither modern agriculture nor the organized industrial sector is capable of absorbing even a fraction of it, to say nothing of the fate of the large number of already unemployed and underemployed. With population and the labor force growing at 3 percent per year (in many developing countries the rate of growth is even higher) and industry frequently employing at most 10 percent of the labor force, industrial employment would have to grow at 30 percent in order to employ merely the new entrants. Nowhere has industrial employment grown at anything like this rate. Population growth plus urbanization plus world recession have swollen the ranks of people seeking jobs in the urban, informal sector. Similarly, neither agriculture, though starting from a much larger base, nor the modern service sector can provide enough new jobs. The only opening then are the urban and rural informal sectors. Employment is important as a source not only of production and income but also of self-respect and social recognition.

Population pressures are unevenly distributed. In Africa, for example, in a little over one-third of the countries—Burundi, Kenya, Malawi, Mauritius, Nigeria, Rwanda, and Uganda—population densities will be high in thirty years. In much of the remainder there will still be surplus land, cultivation of which can absorb population growth rates of over 3 percent per year.

Third, although the members of the informal sector should not be equated with the poor (many people in the informal sector earn more than some in the formal sector), in this sector many poor people are to be found. By harnessing its potential, not only is efficient growth promoted, but poverty is also reduced. A source of earned incomes is created. If its productivity and remunerativeness can be raised without depriving the high-productivity sector of resources, there is no conflict between efficiency and equity.

Fourth, prolonged unemployment leads to alienation and can be, as we have seen, a source of rebellious, instead of productive, activity. Particularly, governments in power have an interest in not upsetting the existing order, and they should seek to use the informal sector as a vote bank.

The informal sector comprises three quite distinct groups. First, there are the self-employed. They are themselves a heterogeneous group, ranging from shoeshine boys, garbage collectors, petty thieves, prostitutes, drug traffickers, smugglers, self-appointed tourist guides, and bag carriers to jobbing gardeners and small-scale producers such as blacksmiths, carpenters, sandal makers, lamp makers, bricklayers, bus and taxi drivers, seamstresses, repairmen, cobblers, bakers, shopkeepers, street vendors, auto mechanics, and builders, some of whom are very productive and earn more than workers in the formal sector.

Second, there are the casual workers, hired on a day-to-day basis in the docks, construction, transport, and some services. If the criterion for being in the informal sector is the method of hiring, then some workers hired casually by quite large firms should be counted as being in the informal sector.

Third, there are workers employed on a regular basis by small-scale, labor-intensive, not bureaucratically controlled firms outside the regulated, income tax-paying formal sector. This is a source of potential leadership and a very dynamic element.

Another distinction is that between two quite different kinds of informal sector firms. First, there are the productive, entrepreneurial, often rapidly growing firms. Frequently they graduate to middle-sized firms. Second, there are the absorbers of the lame ducks thrown out of the formal sector or incapable of entering it: small firms of infirm, old, or otherwise unemployable people. They constitute a safety net for those thrown out of, or prevented from entering, the formal sector. The second type has been swollen in recent years by declining aggregate growth rates, austerity programs, and foreign exchange shortages. At the same time, the crisis also provided opportunities to expand for some firms that belong in the first category.

The task then is to make these small, informal sector enterprises complementary to the larger-scale, formal sector firms, including foreign multinational corporations. Now they are too often in competition with one another, and, aided by the government, the large firms often drive out the small ones. The success of the Japanese in combining a modern and a small-scale sector illustrate the possibility of successfully uniting the two sectors.

One model for such a symbiosis has been pioneered by the British Commonwealth Development Corporation, first in the Kulai oil palm project in Malaysia and then in the Kenya Tea Development Authority. A modern nucleus estate is responsible for management, processing, exporting, marketing, and extension services and provides the credit for a group of smallholders clustered round the estate. Activities best carried out on a large scale, with modern techniques, are done by the nucleus estate, while the growing of the crop is done by newly settled smallholders. The aim is not to maximize profits but to maximize development. Expatriate managers train local counterparts and give them control as soon as they are ready.

No similar type of arrangement exists as yet in manufacturing. One can easily imagine a large, modern manufacturing plant round which are clustered informal, small enterprises carrying out repairs, manufacturing components and spare parts, and providing ancillary services such as transport, handling, cleaning, packaging, and catering. Such institutional innovation would require changes in government policies. The first step would be to stop repressive regulation, harassment, and discrimination against the informal sector; the next step would be to adopt policies and create institutions for the provision of credit, information, and imported inputs. As to credit, innovative steps are needed for small loans against new types of collateral, such as inventories, an unlicensed bus, or plots of land in shantytowns. Or peer pressures can be used for repayments of loans, as in the Grameen Bank in Bangladesh, which has had successful imitators in many countries. A third step would be to remove legislation that gives the formal sector special advantages.

A second illustration of the symbiosis between formal and informal sector enterprises is to be found in a modern, nonexploitative version of the eighteenth-century putting-out system. Subcontracting by large firms to small, informal sector firms or cottage industries is quite common. But there is still considerable scope for importing houses or retail chains (independent of developed countries' producer interest) in advanced countries to subcontract to informal sector firms in developing countries. The large firm provides the material, design, credit, and marketing, while the informal sector firm produces the clothes, the sports equipment, the electronic components, the parts of a watch, the cloth and woodwork for handicraft, or the crops.

In addition, the political power of these retail chains can be used to counteract the political pressures for protection of the producer lobbies in the advanced countries. Their interest in low-cost, labor-intensive imports coincides with that of the poor producers in the developing countries. It is important to adopt institutional safeguards against exploitation, through policies, by legislation, or by setting up hybrid firms of the type of the Commonwealth Development Corporation whose purpose is, while covering their costs, to benefit the small enterprise.

Several measures are needed to implement such a policy.

First, a more favorable environment for the informal sector should be created. At present, policies discriminate against it. For example, investment incentives confine tax concessions to formal sector firms. Overvaluation of exchange rates combined with import restrictions, and low interest rates combined with credit rationing handicap access to inputs by informal firms.

Second, the access of the poor to assets should be improved. In agriculture the policy has worked for small farmers. In industry new forms of collateral for credit have to be explored. The International Fund for Agricultural Development has successfully experimented with lending without conventional collateral.

Third, the returns to these enterprises should be raised. It has already been said that productivity gains, by themselves, are not enough. The benefits may be passed on in the form of lower prices to buyers who are better-off. The focus should be earning power.

Fourth, employment opportunities should be improved. Even though the informal sector is sometimes defined as supply-driven and although, unlike in the formal sector, incomes are flexible downward, there are obstacles to entry, such as access to credit and information, capital equipment, and social or family connections, which should be reduced. The proposed complementarities of formal and informal sector enterprises would lead to the replacement of activities now carried out inside the formal sector firms in a capital-intensive way by efficient labor-intensive activities in the informal sector firms.

Fifth, the demand for the production of these firms should be raised. Since the poor tend, by and large, to buy the goods that the poor produce and produce the goods that the poor consume, policies that encourage production by poor people will also raise the demand for their products, and policies that generate demand by poor people will also stimulate their production.

Sixth, access to education, training, and health services should be improved, not only as an end in itself but also to raise productivity. Technical training and instruction in simple managerial techniques, such as simple accounting and bookkeeping, and marketing and technical know-how are important. The identification and provision of missing components, such as market information, information about technology, or simple forms of infrastructure can yield great benefits at little cost.

Transfer payments out of public funds are also required not only to provide a safety net for the unemployables but also to tide people over periods of no or too low earnings, failure of their businesses, or temporary inability to work. This can be regarded as a way of maintaining human capital in periods when it is not used.

In the manner just described, the informal sector can be made complementary to the formal, the small-scale to the large-scale firms, domestic to foreign businesses, public to private enterprises, and nongovernmental organizations to government, with respect to access to markets, inputs, information, and technology. Our knowledge of the informal sector is still rudimentary. The principal difficulty in analyzing it is the shortage and unreliability of data. This also makes comparisons between countries and periods difficult. In more market-oriented countries, with fewer regulations and taxes, the microenterprises of the informal sector will tend to surface and will show up in the statistics of employment and production. The same activities will appear as evasion of regulations, controls and taxes, black marketeering, smuggling, and so on, and therefore show up as semilegal or illegal in more regulated economies. The productive performance will therefore be understated in the official figures. What we need is both time-series and cross-country studies of informal sector activities to show at what income levels and with what policies, which activities, actually or potentially, contribute to employment, skill formation, productivity, earning power, production, and growth. These data collections should be carried out by local people who have the confidence of, and are in touch with, the men and women in the informal sector. Too many statistical data collections are examples of inappropriate, high-technology, bureaucratic projects, conducted by visitors from advanced countries.

The encouragement of complementarities should not be done at the expense of the growth of the high-productivity, modern sector. On the contrary, the small units should contribute to raising the productivity of the large ones. Nor should there be any form of exploitation, such as child labor, inhuman working conditions, sweated labor, or monopolistic overpricing of the intermediate products supplied by the formal sector as inputs to informal sector enterprises. Such overpricing could be the result of import restrictions or other barriers to entry. In Sierra Leone, for example, a large-scale flour mill, which supplies flour to small-scale bakers, is protected by an exclusive import license and therefore can sell its flour at prices over twice those of potential imports (Chuta and Liedholm, 1985). The policies should be designed to mobilize the energies of the small-scale firms and to make use of their lower costs, more labor-intensive techniques, longer application of labor hours, greater employment creation, and wider dispersion of technology, without, on one hand, sacrificing efficiency and innovation and, on the other, depriving the informal sector, by underpricing outputs or overpricing inputs, of adequate rewards and humane working conditions.

INTERNATIONAL IMPLICATIONS

If a country intends to switch from a set of mistaken policies to reforms that promote social development, it will create for itself transitional problems. To these the literature has paid relatively little attention. They may take the form of heavy burdens on the budget and the administration, even if the ultimate objective is to reduce the role of government in the economy. Or they may take the form of political discontent and the threat of riots. If there is redistribution of income to the poor, there is the possibility of added inflationary pressures from the sectors producing goods (especially food) on which the poor spend their money, but the supply of which is inelastic in the short run. At the same time, there will be unemployment in the luxury goods trades, as the expenditure of the better-off on luxury housing and durable consumer goods is reduced. There may be balance-of-payments problems caused by additional food imports, and there may be additional capital flight. If the reformist government replaces a repressive dictatorship, previously oppressed groups will assert their claim to higher incomes, with further inflationary results. If groups become disaffected, they may organize strikes, sabotage, or even coups d'état. All these are familiar troubles of reform-minded governments that wish to change the direction of policy. Yet, we do not have manuals or even rough guidelines for such reform-minded presidents or prime ministers who, faced with these trials, wish to know what to do. On the contrary, such situations are sometimes confused with mismanagement (which, of course, may contribute to the troubles), and international aid tends to be withdrawn.

In the critical situation just described, the international community can help in making the transition less painful and disruptive. It can assist in overcoming an important obstacle to reform—the fear that the economic and political cost of the transition to more human and social policies is too high. It can add flexibility and adaptability to otherwise inert policies set on a destructive course. Adjustment loans have come to be accepted in other contexts, such as the transition to a more rational international trade regime, to greater emphasis on agricultural growth, or to reduced government intervention. By a simple extension of the same principle, adjustment loans should be given for the transition to a more human and socially responsible regime. These could take the form of financial or technical assistance to a land reform, a tax reform, an educational reform, or administrative reforms involving the dismissal of excess labor or food aid or a scheme of international food stamps to tide over periods of excess demand for food. They would be truly structural adjustment loans, for they would reform the social structure of the society.

Another way in which donors could contribute to more self-reliant policies is for them to finance the food exports of one developing country to other, food-deficit countries. Such schemes could encourage production and trade on a regional basis and raise nutritional standards.

It is surely sensible and capable of mobilizing political support to reinforce domestic efforts for creating the conditions in which poor people can earn enough to feed themselves and their families and to provide the necessities of life. This type of new international economic order would call for support at the global level of domestic and regional efforts of self-help and poverty reduction.

ISSUES OF STRATEGY

In Nadine Gordimer's novel, *The Sport of Nature,* an African leader says: "We've taken all the things the world keeps in compartments, boxes, and brought them together. *A new combination, that's us.* That's why the world doesn't understand. We don't please the West and we don't please the East. We never will. We don't keep things separate. Isn't that what orthodoxy is—separation? *We make our own mess of things.* They interfere, we ask them to interfere—what else am I doing?"

Problems of technology, energy, the environment, and political representation tend to be discussed in separate compartments. Even the Africans have not succeeded in bringing them together. Yet, progress depends on seeing their connections. For example, women spend hours collecting firewood, often at the expense of looking after their children, having time to themselves, or participating in the activities of their communities. The resulting deforestation threatens the environment and sustainable agriculture. The devotion of resources to the design of simple stoves, using cheap alternative fuels, is not high on the agenda, because women are not represented on village councils and their concerns go by default. Their education, political representation, and empowerment would simultaneously contribute to the solution of the energy crisis, to conservation of the forests, soil, and air, to the improvement of the nurture of children, and to women's liberation. Other examples are the need for collaboration and coordination among governments, aid agencies, and NGOs; between foreign investors and domestic formal and informal sector firms; and between the public and the private sector. This need for a package transcends ideological and partisan disputes over the respective merits of the components.

The developing world's largest underutilized resource is its people. It is on them, for them, and by them that a successful strategy for renewal has to be built.

REFLECTIONS ON SOME QUANTITATIVE EVIDENCE

Most statistics have to be treated with great caution. According to what basis is used for making gross domestic product (GDP) per head figures comparable, Ethiopia's income per head, for example, varies between $110 (converting by the foreign exchange rate) and $310 (converting by purchasing power parity). For China the difference is a factor of ten. Not only the absolute figures but also the ranking of countries change according to the basis of conversion. For example, Zaire drops six places because its income per head, when calculated in purchasing power, rises only from $170 to $210 (Summers and Heston, 1988). It is therefore often better to give ranges of figures than a single figure. In addition, it is helpful to grade the degree of reliability of any given set of statistics, possibly awarding two grades, one according to the reliability of the source, the other according to its plausibility, in the light of impressions, context, and other evidence. A 1:5 would, for example, indicate a highly reliable source with an utterly implausible figure, a 5:1 a quite unreliable source but an entirely plausible figure.

In trying to reveal a portrait of human and social development, we may envisage the process as the removal of six veils. The removal of each veil gets us nearer the facts that we want to measure, but the outer veils are not therefore unnecessary. Each contributes something to the portrait.

First, there is money income, per head per household, or per consumer unit. It does not reveal anything about changes in the prices of the goods and services bought.

Second, there is real income, adjusted for changes in the general price level. General price indexes are useful for converting money values into average purchasing power, eliminating the influence of general inflation.

Third, there is real income adjusted for the region-specific and commodity-specific purchases of the relevant income group, say, the poor, if we are interested in measuring poverty. It also should allow for the nonavailability of important items. Relatively little work has gone into calculating price indexes for the commodities consumed by different income groups. These are important, because the poor consume the same commodities in different proportions (e.g., a much higher proportion is spent on food) and consume different commodities, and the prices of these items move in different ratios from the general price index.

But even the measure of real income has certain defects. It ignores the welfare derived from leisure. Attempts to estimate the value of leisure run into problems as to what value to attach to it. The concept often does not include nonmarketed and nonpriced subsistence income, such as that from crops grown and consumed within the household, or the services of housewives. Sometimes attempts are made to impute these. It fails to account for free social services and the benefits from pure public goods. If presented as an average for an income group (the nation, a province, a region, or a household), it fails to account for distribution. To some extent this deficiency can be overcome for national figures by using not the mean, which is biased upward by the few very large incomes, but the median or the mode. Unfortunately, reliable figures for these are rarely available.

Nor do income figures show how efficient people are in converting expenditure into welfare. Assuming that longevity is one important dimension of welfare, it can be incorporated in the income measure by giving not average annual income but average lifetime income. Two societies or two income groups may enjoy the same average annual income, but in one people live, on the average, to age fifty, and in the other, to age seventy-five. On the other hand, critics may regard it as wrong to trade off life against money, for a society in which average incomes were $30,000 and people lived thirty years would be regarded as good as one in which average incomes were $15,000 and people lived sixty years.

While some of these distributional, social, and demographic considerations can therefore, in principle, be incorporated in average real income per head of the income group or the socioeconomic group, there are many important aspects that remain concealed. Some of these are revealed as the next veils are lifted.

Fourth, there are direct measures of physical inputs or of services to meet basic needs, such as calories consumed, yards of cloth bought, cubic feet of house room occupied, hospital beds available, school enrollment, years of schooling, number of teachers, letters posted. These are still instruments or means, but they penetrate behind the veil of money and identify characteristics of commodities and services that are regarded as contributing to social achievements. A measure of dietary energy intake relative to requirements (not easily determined) would be a good scalar measure of nutritional status, if supplemented by the type of impact indicator of basic needs discussed under the fifth heading, such as infant mortality, literacy, and morbidity. "There is a strong case for using adequate food as the scalar indicator, at least for the presence of ultra-poverty. That is not because people, children or households 'live by bread alone.' It is because access to adequate sources of nutrition turns out to be a very good and in a sense self-weighting *summary* of what most people mean by absence of ultra-poverty: health, shelter, education, even mobility, all are reflected in nutritional status, although not in a linear or otherwise simple way" (Lipton, 1988, pp. 6–7).

This measure of adequate access to food is a particularly good indicator of ultrapoverty, of the standard of living of the poorest of the poor. They spend about 80 percent of their income on food, and this proportion does not decline when their income rises, as it does for those above the ultrapoverty line. The Engel curve, namely, the declining proportion of income spent on food as income rises (and the Bennett curve, namely, the declining proportion of food consisting of starchy staples, such as cereals and roots), begins to register only above the range of ultrapoverty.

Fifth, there are impact measures of health, mortality, literacy, and morbidity, which register, in A. K. Sen's (1987) terminology, as "capabilities" or "functionings." Weight for age or height for age (in children) and weight for height (in adults) are anthropometric measures trying to get at one purpose of nutrition: the full, healthy development of the body. These measures look behind income and what it is spent on, at the inputs in relation to requirements and the skills and abilities of people of converting goods and services into human "functionings," such as a long and healthy life. One may have more money and more food than another but be more undernourished because she has parasites in her stomach, is pregnant or lactating, has to work harder collecting water and wood, lives in a colder climate, or has a higher metabolic rate or a larger body. Or, having less education, she may marry earlier, produce more children, and thereby raise the food requirements of the household. The impact is, moreover, determined not only by income and the ability to convert what it buys into nutritional status but also by social services, provided free of charge, which do not appear in figures for income.

Not only are figures of average income (or expenditure) per head (or per consumer unit) not very closely correlated to these human indicators, so that quite low-income countries perform well, while some higher-income ones perform poorly, but a good deal of research has been done on how specific groups of small farmers change their nutritional status as their incomes rise. In some cases nutritional status drops as households enter into commercial transactions and their incomes increase, while they produce less of the subsistence crops. (In Great Britain during World War II nutritional status rose in spite of a substantial decline in real consumption.) On the other hand, by and large, different basic needs indicators are fairly highly correlated with one another, so that recording the composition of poverty is less important than its level.

The nexus between income (or expenditure) per head and nutritional status is weaker in Africa than it is in South and East Asia. Income distribution apart, the precise reasons for this are a matter for research, but it is plausible to assume that factors such as education (particularly in health and hygiene), infrastructure, such as safe water and sewerage, and the distribution of power within the household among men, women, and children are important components of any explanation. Clearly, this is very important for policy because the answer to the question of the nexus will determine whether opportunities to earn income or the provision of public services should have priority.

Sixth and finally, much of the information on income and consumption and their impact is based on the household as the unit of observation. Removal of the sixth veil would reveal the distribution of the benefits from basic necessities and services *within* the household and show the impact on specific individuals: adults and children, men and women, able-bodied and disabled. Consumption per head (or better, per adult equivalent[2]) is a better measure than consumption per household, where such figures are available.

The human impact indicators have some advantages over income or consumption indicators, but they are useful as complements rather than replacements. Specific human and social indicators make, for some purposes, better sense than average income. The reason is that income distribution can be highly skewed, while, for example, life expectancy (in spite of the marvels of modern medicine) or literacy has a definite maximum—say, 100 years or 100 percent. Any increase in life expectancy or literacy can therefore be welcomed, although the incidence of these indicators between different groups (e.g., men and women, rich and poor, urban and rural residents) can throw light on the allocation of resources in a society.

A second advantage is that it makes sense and is realistic to attempt to reduce international gaps (between rich and poor, men and women) in life expectancy, literacy, and infant mortality, while it makes less sense to reduce gaps in income per head.

A third advantage is that impact measures sift "goods" from items that should be counted as costs, regrettable necessities, or "anti-bads." Food consumed to meet excess food requirements or, resulting from unwanted pregnancies, children that die, and long walks to collect water or fuel wood, in search of jobs, or between unconsolidated plots of land show up not as increases in welfare but as regrettable, though possibly avoidable, hardships. So do the higher housing and transport costs that urban dwellers incur but that are counted as higher incomes, giving the false impression of higher levels of welfare.

A fourth advantage is that impact indicators for education, health, and nutrition are less subject to reflecting relative deprivation than income per head. Negative externalities, which can be strong in an inegalitarian society, do not apply with the same force to social achievements.

A fifth advantage is that they register "overdevelopment" or maldevelopment, as well as underdevelopment. There are diseases of affluence and problems of overeating and an idle life, which are not caught in income measures.

It is, however, a drawback that there is no easy and clear way of aggregating these human indicators into a composite one. Gross national product (GNP) appears to have great attractions of precision and simplicity by comparison. But, as Sen asks, "Why must we reject being vaguely right in favour of being precisely wrong?" (1987). GNP figures are not, of course, "precisely wrong," as long as we bear in mind their limitations and do not ask them to bear a heavier burden than they can.

Indicators reflect our vision of a certain style of development. Development as perceived by the people who are its beneficiaries goes substantially beyond economic values, although these are part of it. Development should meet the basic material and nonmaterial human needs of all; it should also be socially just, equitable, sustainable, and ecologically sound; and it should be self-reliant in the sense of making the fullest use of national and local capabilities.

Indicators obviously reflect our shifting concerns. A decade ago we should have wanted indicators of energy consumed per head, but we would perhaps not have wanted indicators of women's participation. Awareness of the inadequacy of relying solely or largely on GDP or GNP indicators has grown. They often take no or only inadequate account of nonmonetary transactions, such as household work, and make inadequate allowance for environmental damage and resource depletion. They do not show income distribution or the impact of production on well-being.

We are very short of environmental indicators, such as areas of forest, grazing, and crop land destroyed or lost to deserts. One would also like to see more human rights indicators, especially on basic civil rights, such as torture or imprisonment without trial. The United Nations Development Programme has pioneered with a Human Freedom Index in its 1991 *Human Development Report.* More detailed figures of the informal sector would also be useful.

In the recorded statistics on Africa, life expectancy gently but steadily rises, and infant mortality gently but steadily falls. Since these are indicators of impact or achievement, this, at face value, is clearly splendid news. On the other hand, all the instruments normally used to bring about these results are recorded to be deteriorating: down is calorie intake per head; down is food production per head; down are education and health expenditures as percentages of government expenditure or as a proportion of GDP; down are female participation rates; down are export values; up are debt service ratios; terms of trade deteriorate; and so on.

There are four possible explanations for this discrepancy between inputs into the social welfare function and results. First, there could have been a massive redistribution of wealth and income and access to social services from the better-off to the poor. Second, without such a redistribution, social achievements have a ratchet effect. Once people, especially mothers, know how to keep themselves and their children healthy, their incomes may fall, but the knowledge remains, at least for some time. Third, the miserable life of the poor might just have been extended. Thomas Hobbes said that in the state of nature, man's life was ''nasty, brutish and short.'' In the African countries life might have become nasty, brutish, and long. This interpretation may gain confirmation from the fact that progress in reducing infant mortality and extending life expectancy can be made cheaply, for example, by oral rehydration, and that it contains a momentum, for example, because this knowledge is spread and children of parents who can read are more likely to be able to read too. But the evidence suggests that at very low levels of living, illness fairly quickly leads to death, so that it is not plausible to say that while life expectancy has increased, all the other ills have gotten worse. Fourth, the credibility of the good news may be doubted. The even and smooth trend of these figures suggests, in any case, that they are simply extrapolations from a happier past or interpolations of wishful thinking, not related to what is actually happening. Many censuses were taken in the late 1970s, and it is likely that these figures are just projections from these census figures.

This conclusion is reinforced when we observe that in Mozambique and Angola (since 1960) and Ethiopia (since 1982) the infant mortality rate has steadily declined, and in all three countries life expectancy has steadily increased (with only a brief and small setback between 1980 and 1982 in Ethiopia), through droughts, wars, civil wars, invasions, and major errors in policy. According to the figures, in Mozambique food production per head between 1970 and 1986 declined by over 40 percent, and calorie intake per head declined by 20 percent, while infant mortality over the same period also declined by 20 percent.

Although debt service ratios for African countries have risen, official development assistance has also risen, at least in money terms. But the figures for life expectancy, infant mortality (for what they are worth), and official development assistance nearly exhaust the good news.

There is, however, one more item of good news. The life expectancy of females is higher than that of males, where figures are available. (The one exception is Nigeria.) Sen has suggested that India could learn from Africa how to reduce the "gender-bias" against women, which produced "30 million missing Indian women," who would be living now if African attitudes to women prevailed in India (see Arrow, 1988).

Women in Africa are an important part of the labor force, although all countries, including Botswana, show a puzzling decline in the female participation rate. This could be explained by changes in counting methods. In the early years expatriate or United Nations personnel may have counted women's activities as part of the labor force that African accountants later excluded. Or it could mean that the recession and crisis drove women back into their homes, where they are not counted as part of the labor force.

Both food production per head and calorie intake per head have declined in most African countries. These figures, however, do not appear to be based on hard data but are extrapolations and intrapolations. It is now generally recognized that these figures, even if they were more reliable, would be poor indicators of hunger, malnutrition, and undernutrition. Food production per head may rise, but if the poor lack purchasing power or other forms of entitlements, they will starve in the midst of plenty. On the other hand, food per head may decline, as in wartime Britain, but the nutritional status of the population may improve, because special measures are adopted to ensure that everyone has enough to eat. But there is no reason to believe that African countries have adopted such measures in the face of declining food output.

It is noteworthy that countries that have reduced health and education expenditure as a proportion of government expenditure (or of GNP) less than others (and these figures seem somewhat more reliable), like Côte d'Ivoire or like Malawi and Botswana, have also performed better on other fronts, such as growth rates of GDP. It is, of course, not evident from the figures whether maintaining human capital by maintaining expenditure on health and education is the cause of economic growth, whether higher economic growth makes it possible to keep up these expenditures, or whether there is mutual causation. In all countries total government expenditure increased substantially during this period, and a decline in the ratio of expenditure on health and education is therefore entirely consistent with absolute increases in real expenditure, which seem to have occurred in some countries.

But health and education comprise many activities, from urban hospitals to rural preventive services, from the pay of surgeons to that of midwives, and from universities to primary schools. It is not clear how much the poor have benefited from any increases. Moreover, the proportion of government expenditure spent on wages has declined, while that on interest payments has increased. It is not known whether the reduction meant lower wage rates, a lower wage bill with more dismissals, or a combination of the two; whether dismissals were largely of low-paid workers or more highly paid bureaucrats; and whether those dismissed found alternative jobs in the private sector or in self-employment.

Military expenditure tends to be high, especially in view of the low incomes of these countries, though the variations are substantial. Mauritius spent less than 1 percent of government expenditure on defense, Angola (in 1982) 50 percent, Chad (in 1985) 32 percent, Somalia and Ethiopia nearly 30 percent, Mauritania 25 percent. On the whole, good performers tend to have a low military budget (Cameroon less than 10 percent, Botswana about 6 percent, Côte d'Ivoire 5 percent), while poor economic performance tends to go with high military expenditure.

One of the most striking features of all African countries is the rapid decline in the agricultural labor force. This reflects a worldwide transformation of profound significance. For millennia, the majority of the human race had cultivated the land. For the first time in history, fewer people are finding employment and incomes in agricultural production. This has profound implications not only for economics but also for the social and cultural life of a community.

It is also of great political importance. African policy has suffered for some time in the past from "urban bias." Not only were the terms of trade twisted against agriculture, by depressing the prices of agricultural crops and raising those of the industrial goods farmers bought, but also public resources in health, education, and infrastructure were concentrated on the towns, while rural areas were starved. According to Mancur Olson the smaller groups, which suffer less from the free rider problem of members' refusing to contribute and are in a better position to mobilize support through penalties and rewards, exercise stronger pressure on governments, and the larger groups lose—hence urban bias in the largely rural countries of Africa and rural bias in the advanced industrial countries of the North. Does the shift to larger urban populations in Africa then signal reduced urban bias?

Against this view is that of Jeffrey Sachs (1985), who has explained the differential impact of the debt burden in Latin America and East Asia by the fact that East Asia has larger rural populations and therefore discriminates less against agricultural exports than Latin America, with its larger urban populations. In Sachs's explanation the pull comes from the size of the group behind it. Insofar as Africa is showing reduced urban bias, this could, of course, be the result not of shifting populations but of pressure by the World Bank and other donors or of learning by mistakes.

Even if much greater reliance could be put on these statistics than appears warranted, we should still not know very much, because for many purposes they are too aggregated. Health expenditure can be on expensive, curative urban hospitals for the rich or on preventive rural health services for the poor; education can be on universities that create educated unemployables or on literacy and rural education. The content of the school curriculum is at least as important as enrollment ratios.

One important lesson is that the ability of the developing countries to collect data and to analyze them should be strengthened. What is needed is the reinforcement of existing sample surveys and the addition of microstudies, based on observations and impressions. Such partial and eclectic information, though clearly inconclusive by itself, would complement and give flesh and blood to the data from the general censuses and sample surveys.

Although many data are either not available or, if available, unreliable, their availability and reliability, in the future, are a function of the demand for such data by the research community, the international agencies, and policymakers. They are not a quantity given from the outside but are endogenously determined by the direction of interest and work.

This clearly does not mean that antipoverty action should or can wait until further data are collected. Historians still dispute whether the poor during the Industrial Revolution in England got better or worse off. Two hundred years hence there will, presumably, still be disputes about the current situation of the poor in the world. But, while action cannot wait for full information, the better informed the policies are, the more effective they are likely to be.

SOME SUCCESS STORIES

Africa has been regarded as the great development failure, while East Asia is held up as a model of success. But Africa also has its successes. Botswana, Kenya, and Zimbabwe started in about 1960 with low incomes, low levels of social development, poor social indicators, and unequal income distributions. Infant mortality rates were high, life expectancy short, and literacy rates low. In Kenya only one out of five females and 44 percent of males were literate in 1970.

On all these fronts, these countries have made substantial progress since then, although in Kenya female literacy is still below 50 percent. However, Kenya and Zimbabwe appear to have had difficulties in maintaining this progress through the mid-1980s, while Botswana has continued to improve consistently its social conditions.

Botswana has also registered spectacularly high economic growth rates, including the recent period, when many other African countries showed declines.

Economic growth was largely based on minerals, especially diamond exports, which more than compensated for the drought that hit agricultural production. Though this might have been expected to affect vulnerable rural groups unfavorably, the growing share of social expenditure provided these groups with a safety net. Until the end of the 1970s, economic growth produced the social achievements; but in the 1980s, social expenditures, especially drought relief measures after 1982, prevented a reversal. In addition, Botswana introduced a public works program and a supplementary feeding program for primary school children, pregnant and lactating women, and tuberculosis patients. Water systems were repaired, and emergency water supply was introduced when local sources dried up. Small farmers were also helped in other ways, such as the provision of free seeds, assistance in land clearing and cattle vaccination, and guaranteed markets. Botswana also introduced a successful nutritional surveillance system for children under five and an agro-meteorological early warning system, which contain important lessons for other countries. Policy responds rapidly to deteriorating nutritional indicators.

Kenya had a reasonable growth record in the 1960s and 1970s, but negative growth in the 1980s. The share of social expenditure in the budget has been remarkably stable at between 7 and 8 percent of GDP. Most of this went into education, which accounted for more than two-thirds of all social expenditure between 1973 and 1986. The rest was devoted to health. Voluntary self-help efforts (Harambee) also contributed to education. The principal lesson of the Kenyan experience is that the decline in human and social achievements in the 1980s was the result of declining economic growth, combined with a constant proportion of social expenditure. Kenya's human rights record is, however, deplorable.

Zimbabwe, like Kenya and Botswana, started from low levels of income and social development. It enjoyed neither vigorous economic growth nor income redistribution, initially quite unequal. After independence in 1980 the government increased social expenditure and restructured an initially quite unequal system toward the poorest people. Free health care was provided for those, constituting the majority of the population, who earned less than Z$150 per month. A program of immunization against the six major childhood infectious diseases was launched, as well as tetanus immunization of pregnant women. Rural health centers were built, and rural clinics and provincial hospitals were upgraded. A disease control program against diarrhea was launched in 1982, and a Department of National Nutrition was established, with responsibility for monitoring the growth of children, their nutritional status, and supplementary feeding. Similarly, there was a restructuring of education expenditure toward primary education. These measures, though not preventing a deterioration of the human condition, contributed to preventing a substantial reversal.

CONCLUDING REMARKS

The briefest way of summing up the social dimensions of development is to say that it is development *of* the people, *for* the people, *by* the people. *Of* the people means the provision of productive and remunerative jobs and incomes, *for* the people means social services, and *by* the people means participation. A thorough democratization, not only of the political process but also inside firms and voluntary organizations and even inside the family, is an important component, both as a means to effective and responsive administration and as an end in itself. The main obstacle to poverty eradication and social development is not economic or technical but the absence of political commitment. In this there is a message of hope.

NOTES

1. Perhaps the most vivid example of the failure of the "quantitative systems" approach was the Vietnam War, the American failure due largely to a tendency for computer-based quantitative analysis to disregard anything that cannot be quantified.

2. Normally it is assumed that the numerator of these indicators is total physical quantities and the denominator is the number of persons, so that we get the measure of food per head. But not all persons have the same requirements. The correct denominator is "adult equivalents," so that we can allow for the fact that children need less food than adults.

REFERENCES

Arrow, Kenneth J., ed. 1988. *The Balance Between Industry and Agriculture in Economic Development*. Vol. 1, *Basic Issues*. Basingstoke: Macmillan, for the International Economic Association.

Binswanger, Hans, and Pingali, Prabhu. 1988. "Technological Priorities for Farming in Sub-Saharan Africa." *World Bank Research Observer* 3, no. 1 (January).

Chuta, Enyinna, and Liedholm, Carl. 1985. *Employment and Growth in Small-Scale Industry*. Basingstoke: Macmillan.

Drèze, Jean, and Sen, Amartya. 1989. *Public Action for Social Security: Foundations and Strategy*. The Development Economics Research Programme, No. 20, London School of Economics.

Iliffe, John. 1988. *The African Poor, a History*. Cambridge: Cambridge University Press.

Lipton, Michael. 1988. "Who Are the Poor? What Do They Do? What Should We Do?" Center for Advanced Studies in International Development, Michigan State University, East Lansing, Mich. Mimeo, 6–7.

Nussbaum, Martha. 1986. *New York Review of Books* 33, no. 1 (January 30).

Sachs, Jeffrey D. "External Debt and Macroeconomic Performance in Latin America and East Asia," *Brookings Papers on Economic Activity* 2: 523–64.

Sen, A.K. 1987. *The Standard of Living*, edited by Geoffrey Hawthorn. The Tanner Lectures. Cambridge: Cambridge University Press.

———. 1988. *The Balance Between Industry and Agriculture in Economic Development*. Vol. 1, *Basic Issues*, edited by Kenneth Arrow. Basingstoke: Macmillan, for the International Economic Association.

Summers, Robert, and Heston, Alan. 1988. "A New Set of International Comparisons of Real Product and Price Levels Estimates for 130 Countries 1950–1985.'' *Review of Income and Wealth.*

von Braun, Joachim. 1989. *Social Security in Sub-Saharan Africa: Reflections on Policy Challenges.* The Development Economics Research Programme, No. 22, London School of Economics.

World Bank. various issues. *World Development Report.* Washington, D.C.: World Bank.

5

TRADE AND TRADE POLICIES OF DEVELOPING COUNTRIES

Dominick Salvatore

The relationship between international trade and economic development has long interested economists. There has been a great deal of controversy, however, with some asserting that international trade plays a crucial positive role in the development process and others believing that trade has often harmed development. This chapter reviews and evaluates the relationship between international trade and the various facets of the development process.

Specifically, in this chapter, I review the theoretical and empirical relationship between international trade and economic development in general, present basic background and trade data for major developing-country groupings and the most important countries in each group, evaluate the alternatives of industrialization through import substitution and export promotion, review the relatively recent process of trade liberalization in most developing countries, evaluate the harm that trade protectionism in developed countries inflicts on economic development in poor countries, discuss the effect on developing countries' trade resulting from the impasse reached in the Uruguay Round of trade negotiations and the tendency of the developed world to break up into three huge trading blocks, examine the relationship between strategic trade policies in developing countries and their economic development, and finally, analyze the effect of foreign debts and investments on economic development.

THE RELATIONSHIP BETWEEN INTERNATIONAL TRADE AND ECONOMIC DEVELOPMENT

During the nineteenth century, most of the world's industrial production was concentrated in Great Britain. Large increases in industrial production and population in resource-poor Britain led to a rapidly rising demand for the food and raw material exports of the so-called regions of recent settlement (the United States, Canada, Australia, New Zealand, Argentina, Uruguay, and South Africa). For example, during the century from 1815 to 1913, Britain's population tripled, its real gross national product (GNP) increased ten times, and the volume of its imports increased twenty times. This growth spread to newly settled lands through the familiar accelerator-multiplier process. Thus, according to Nurkse (1959), the export sector was the leading sector and operated as an "engine of growth" for these regions of recent settlement during the nineteenth century.

The regions of recent settlement were able to satisfy Britain's burgeoning demand for food and raw materials (and in the process grow very rapidly) because of several favorable circumstances. First, these countries were richly endowed with natural resources, such as fertile, arable land, forests, and mineral deposits. Second, workers with various skills moved in great waves from overpopulated Europe to these mostly empty lands, and so did huge amounts of capital. Though data are far from precise, it seems that from 30 to 50 percent of total capital formation (i.e., investments) in such nations as Canada, Argentina, and Australia were financed through capital inflows. The huge inflows of capital and workers made possible the construction of railroads, canals, and other facilities that allowed the opening up of new supply sources of food and raw materials. Finally, the great improvement in sea transportation enabled these new lands to satisfy the growing demand for wheat, corn, wool, leather, and a variety of other foods and raw materials more cheaply than traditional sources in Europe and elsewhere. Thus, all "ingredients" were present for rapid growth in these new lands: the demand for their products was rising rapidly; they had a great deal of unexploited natural resources; and they received huge amounts of capital and millions of workers from Europe.

The situation for the regions of recent settlement in the nineteenth century is in sharp contrast to that prevalent in the majority of developing countries today. This is due to less favorable demand and supply conditions. On the demand side, it is clear that the demand for food and raw materials is growing much less rapidly today than a century ago. There are several reasons for this:

1. The income elasticity of demand in developed nations for many of the food and raw material exports of developing countries is less (and sometimes much less) than 1, so that as income rises in developed nations, their demand for the agricultural exports of developing countries increases proportionately less than the increase in income. For example, the income elasticity of demand for coffee is about 0.8, for cocoa 0.5, for sugar 0.4, and for tea 0.1.

2. The development of synthetic substitutes has reduced the demand for natural raw materials; for example, synthetic rubber has reduced the demand for natural rubber, nylon, and cotton, and plastic has sharply reduced the demand for hides and skins.

3. Technological advances have reduced the raw material content of many products, such as tin-plated cans and microcircuits.

4. The output of services (with lower raw material requirements) has grown faster than the output of developed nations.

5. Developed nations have imposed trade restrictions on many of the temperate exports (such as wheat, vegetables, sugar, oils, and other products) as well as on simple manufactured goods produced by developing countries.

On the supply side, it is pointed out that today's developing countries are much less well endowed with natural resources (except for petroleum-exporting countries) than were the regions of recent settlement during the nineteenth century. In addition, most of today's developing nations are overpopulated, so that most of any increase in their output of food and raw materials is absorbed domestically rather than exported. Furthermore, the international flow of capital to developing nations is relatively much less than it was during the nineteenth century, and today's developing countries seem also to face an outflow rather than an inflow of skilled labor. Until recently, developing countries have also neglected their agriculture in favor of more rapid industrialization, thereby hampering their export (and growth) prospects.

A large number of empirical studies conducted during the past two decades found that while international trade (with few exceptions) has *not* operated as an engine of growth for today's developing countries as it did for the regions of recent settlement during the nineteenth century, it is has nevertheless contributed positively to the growth of most of today's developing countries (see Bahami-Oskooee, 1991; Boggio and Tirelli, 1989; Cline, 1984; Kravis, 1970; Ram, 1987; Riedel, 1984; Salvatore, 1983; Salvatore and Hatcher, 1991). There are several important ways by which international trade contributes to economic development even under today's changed international conditions. Trade can lead to the full utilization of otherwise underemployed domestic resources. That is, through trade, a developing nation can move from an inefficient production point inside its production frontier, with unutilized resources because of insufficient internal demand, to a point on its production frontier with trade. For such a nation, trade would represent a *vent for surplus,* or an outlet for its potential surplus of agricultural commodities and raw materials. This has indeed occurred in many developing nations, particularly those in Southeast Asia and West Africa.

In addition, by expanding the size of the market, trade makes possible division of labor and economies of scale. This is especially important and has actually taken place in the production of light manufactures in such economies as those of Taiwan, Hong Kong, Singapore, Korea, and other countries. International trade is the vehicle for the transmission of new ideas, new technology, and new managerial and other skills. Trade also stimulates and facilitates the international flow of capital from developed to developing countries. For example, in the case of foreign direct investments, where the foreign firm retains control over its investment, the foreign capital is likely to be accompanied by foreign skilled personnel to organize production. In several large developing nations, such as Brazil and India, the importation of new manufactured products has stimulated domestic demand until efficient domestic production of these goods becomes feasible. Finally, international trade is an excellent antimonopoly weapon (when allowed to operate) because it stimulates greater efficiency by domestic producers to meet foreign competition. This is particularly important to keep low the cost and price of intermediate or semifinished products used as inputs in the domestic production of other commodities.

Critics of international trade can match this impressive list of benefits with an equally impressive list of allegedly harmful effects of trade. However, since a developing nation can always refuse to trade if it gains nothing or loses, the presumption is that it must also gain from trade. It is true that when most of the gains from trade accrue to developed nations, there is a great deal of dissatisfaction and justification for demands to rectify the situation, but this should not be construed to mean that trade is actually harmful. One, of course, could always find cases where, on balance, international trade has actually hampered economic development. However, in most cases it can be expected (and the empirical evidence to date overwhelmingly seems to show) that international trade can provide invaluable assistance to the development process (see Bhagwati, 1978; Bliss, 1989; Chenery, 1961; Evans, 1989; Findlay, 1984; Greenaway, 1987; Grilli, 1990; Grilli and Yang, 1988; Helleiner, 1990; IMF, 1989; Krueger, 1978; Lal and Sarath, 1987; Salvatore, 1989, 1992b; Salvatore et al., 1992; Spraos, 1983; World Bank, 1991a).

BACKGROUND AND TRADE DATA FOR DEVELOPING COUNTRIES

In this section, we present some basic background and trade data for major developing-country groupings and the most important countries in each group. Table 5.1 shows GNP per capita in 1990 and its average annual percentage growth from 1965 to 1990, as well as the distribution of gross domestic product (GDP) among agriculture, industry, manufacturing, and services in both 1965 and 1990.

From Table 5.1, we see the huge disparities in per capita incomes between the high-income economies and the low-income countries, especially those of the Sub-Sahara. Even correcting for the well-known exaggeration in per capita income inequalities between rich and poor countries when expressed in the same currency would leave huge differences. Furthermore, while the growth of real per capita GNP of low-income countries as a group exceeded the growth of real per capita GNP in high-income economies between 1965 and 1990, this is due primarily to the very high growth experienced by the countries of East Asia and the Pacific. Sub-Saharan countries barely grew, and Argentina's real per capita GNP actually declined. Table 5.1 also shows that the percentage of GDP from agriculture declined from 1965 to 1990 for each group of countries and individual country listed (in Korea, it actually declined 38 percent to 9 percent); the percentage of GDP from industry increased for most groups and individual countries

Table 5.1

Gross Domestic Product and Economic Structure

	GNP per Capita 1990 (dollars)	GNP per Capita Growth 1965-1990 (percent)	GDP 1990 (billions of dollars)	Agriculture 1965	Agriculture 1990	Industry 1965	Industry 1990	Manufacturing 1965	Manufacturing 1990	Service 1965	Service 1990
				-------------------------------------percent-------------------------------------							
Sub-Saharan Africa	340	0.2	163	40	32	20	30	7	..	39	40
East Asia & Pacific	600	5.3	821	37	21	32	45	24	34	30	36
China	370	5.8	365	38	27	35	42	28	38	27	31
Indonesia	570	4.5	107	51	22	13	40	8	20	36	38
Korea, Republic of	5,400	7.1	236	38	9	25	45	18	31	37	46
Thailand	1,420	4.4	80	32	12	23	39	14	26	45	48
South Asia	330	1.9	346	44	33	21	26	15	17	35	41
Bangladesh	210	0.7	23	53	38	11	15	5	9	36	46
India	350	1.9	255	44	31	22	29	16	19	34	40
Pakistan	380	2.5	36	40	26	20	25	14	17	40	49
Low- & Middle-Income Europe	2,400	..	489	..	..	..	31	..	..	..	..
Greece	5,990	2.8	58	24	17	26	27	16	16	49	56
Portugal	4,900	3.0	57	..	..	..	..	..	..	..	..
Turkey	1,630	2.6	96	34	18	25	33	16	24	41	49
Middle East & N.Africa	1,790	1.8	..	20	..	38	..	10	..	40	..
Algeria	2,060	2.1	42	..	13	..	47	..	12	..	..
Egypt, Arab Rep.	600	4.1	33	29	17	27	29	..	16	45	53
Latin America & Caribbean	2,180	1.8	1,015	16	10	33	36	23	25	50	54
Argentina	2,370	-0.3	93	17	13	42	41	33	..	42	45
Brazil	2,680	3.3	414	19	10	33	39	26	26	48	51
Mexico	2,490	2.8	238	14	9	27	30	20	23	59	61
Low-Income Countries	350	2.9	916	41	31	26	36	19	27	32	35
Middle-Income Countries	2,220	2.2	2,438	19	12	34	37	20	..	46	50
Severely Indebted Countries	2,140	2.1	1,026	16	10	34	35	23	26	49	53
High-Income Economies	19,590	2.4	16,316	5	..	43	..	32	..	54	..

Source: World Bank, *World Development Report* (1992).

(especially for Indonesia, where it was financed from petroleum receipts); the same is generally true for manufacturing (a subdivision of industry) and services.

Table 5.2 shows the value of merchandise exports and imports in 1990 and their growth between 1965–1980 and 1980–1990, as well as the terms of trade (the ratio of export to import prices multiplied by 100) in 1985 and 1990. The table shows that the merchandise exports and imports of all developing countries as a group are only about one-quarter of the merchandise exports and imports of the high-income economies in 1990. The value of exports and imports of Korea is higher than that of China (a much larger country), while the exports and imports of Bangladesh, Pakistan, and Egypt are very small for their size. The growth of exports between 1965–1980 and 1980–1990 declined sharply for Sub-Saharan Africa (because of the serious drought in the 1980s), in the Middle East and North Africa and Indonesia (because of the decline in petroleum prices), and in Korea (where, however, it remained very high), but it increased sharply in Pakistan (because it became more trade-oriented). The striking thing about imports is their decline in the 1980–1990 time period in the Middle East and North Africa as well as in Latin America (which include the most severely indebted countries). Between 1985 and 1990, the terms of trade deteriorated for all groups of developing countries (especially for the Middle East and North Africa), except for low- and middle-income Europe and Brazil (which experienced a sharp increase) and for the high-income economies.

Table 5.3 presents the change in the structure of merchandise exports. It shows that the share of fuels, minerals, and metals exports increased for low-income countries and for the severely indebted countries but declined for middle-income countries and for high-income economies from 1965 to 1990. It declined sharply for Korea and Thailand and increased sharply for Argentina, Brazil, and Mexico. The share of the exports of other primary commodities declined (sometimes sharply) for every group of countries and individual countries listed. The share of machinery and transport equipment increased sharply for all groups and most individual countries, except for Indonesia and Pakistan (where it declined). The same is true for other manufactures, except for Sub-Saharan Africa, where it remained unchanged. While the share of textile and clothing increased for every group of countries, except for the high-income economies, the experience is very mixed within each group. It decreased significantly for India and Korea and sharply increased for Thailand, Indonesia, and probably Bangladesh. To be noted is that even though there has been a shift away from the export of primary commodities and toward the export of manufactured goods between 1965 and 1990, the exports of primary commodities remained substantial in 1990 in most cases.

Table 5.4 shows the share of total imports of food, fuels, other primary commodities, machinery and transport equipment, and other manufactures in 1965 and 1990. The table shows much more stability in the various categories of imports as compared with exports between 1965 and 1990 for most country groups and individual countries listed. As expected, however, the share of de-

Table 5.2
Merchandise Trade

	Merchandise Trade (billions of $)		Average Annual Growth Rate (percent)				Terms of Trade (1987=100)	
	Exports 1990	Imports 1990	Exports 1965-80	Exports 1980-90	Imports 1965-80	Imports 1980-90	1985	1990
Sub-Saharan Africa	34	32	6.1	0.2	5.6	-4.3	110	100
East Asia & Pacific	217	224	8.5	9.8	7.1	8.0	106	103
China	62	53	4.8	11.0	7.4	9.8	109	111
Indonesia	26	22	9.6	2.8	13.0	1.4	134	111
Korea, Republic of	65	70	27.2	12.8	15.2	10.8	103	108
Thailand	23	33	8.6	13.2	4.1	10.2	91	99
South Asia	28	38	1.8	6.8	0.6	4.1	101	95
Bangladesh	2	4	..	7.6	..	8.0	109	95
India	18	24	3.0	6.5	1.2	4.2	96	96
Pakistan	6	7	-1.8	9.0	0.4	4.0	90	95
Low- & Middle-Income Europe	94	126	..	..	..	..	94	103
Greece	8	20	11.9	3.8	5.2	4.3	94	105
Portugal	16	25	3.4	11.7	3.7	8.2	85	105
Turkey	13	22	5.5	9.1	7.7	7.0	82	98
Middle East & N.Africa	113	90	5.7	-1.1	12.8	-4.7	130	96
Algeria	15	10	1.8	5.3	13.0	-4.6	174	99
Egypt, Arab Rep.	3	10	-0.1	2.1	3.6	-1.7	131	76
Latin America & Caribbean	123	101	-1.0	3.0	4.1	-2.1	111	110
Argentina	12	4	4.7	1.4	1.8	-8.4	110	112
Brazil	31	22	9.3	4.0	8.2	-0.3	92	123
Mexico	27	28	7.7	3.4	5.7	-1.1	133	110
Low-Income Countries	141	144	5.1	5.4	4.8	2.8	107	100
Middle-Income Countries	491	486	3.9	3.8	6.1	0.9	110	102
Severely Indebted Countries	136	100	-0.5	3.4	6.6	-2.1	118	101
High-Income Economies	2,556	2,725	7.3	4.3	4.4	5.3	97	100

Source: World Bank, *World Development Report* (1992).

Table 5.3
Structure of Merchandise Exports

	Fuels, Minerals and Metals		Other Primary Commodities		Machinery and Transport Equipment		Other Manufactures		Textiles and Clothing	
	1965	1990	1965	1990	1965	1990	1965	1990	1965	1990
	(--- percentage share ---)									
Sub-Saharan Africa	23	63	70	29	0	1	7	7	0	1
East Asia & Pacific	21	13	48	18	5	22	27	47	13	19
China	10	15	20	16	9	17	56	56	29	27
Indonesia	43	48	53	16	3	1	1	34	0	11
Korea, Republic of	15	2	25	5	3	37	56	57	27	22
Thailand	11	2	86	34	0	20	3	44	0	16
South Asia	6	6	57	24	1	5	36	65	29	33
Bangladesh	..	1	..	25	..	1	..	72	..	60
India	10	8	41	19	1	7	47	66	36	23
Pakistan	2	1	62	29	1	0	35	70	29	58
Low- & Middle-Income Europe	10	9	21	16	33	27	32	47	8	16
Greece	8	14	78	32	2	4	11	50	3	27
Portugal	4	6	34	13	3	19	58	61	24	29
Turkey	9	7	89	25	0	7	2	61	1	37
Middle East & N.Africa	74	75	24	12	0	1	4	15	3	4
Algeria	57	96	39	0	2	2	2	2	0	0
Egypt, Arab Rep.	8	41	71	20	0	0	20	39	15	27
Latin America & Caribbean	45	38	48	29	1	11	6	21	1	3
Argentina	1	6	93	59	1	7	5	29	0	3
Brazil	9	16	83	31	2	18	7	35	1	3
Mexico	22	43	62	13	1	25	15	19	3	2
Low-Income Countries	17	27	52	20	3	9	28	45	17	21
Middle-Income Countries	38	32	39	20	11	17	14	33	3	9
Severely Indebted Countries	39	42	42	22	8	14	9	22	2	4
High-Income Economies	10	8	21	11	31	42	38	40	7	5

Source: World Bank, *World Development Report* (1992).

Table 5.4
Structure of Merchandise Imports

(--percentage share--)

	Food 1965	Food 1990	Fuels 1965	Fuels 1990	Other Primary Commodities 1965	Other Primary Commodities 1990	Machinery and Transport Equipment 1965	Machinery and Transport Equipment 1990	Other Manufactures 1965	Other Manufactures 1990
Sub-Saharan Africa	15	16	6	14	3	4	30	30	46	36
East Asia & Pacific	13	8	6	9	9	10	32	38	40	35
China	7	8	1	2	10	9	39	41	43	39
Indonesia	6	5	3	9	2	9	39	43	50	35
Korea, Republic of	15	5	7	16	26	15	13	34	39	29
Thailand	6	5	9	9	6	8	31	41	49	37
South Asia	25	13	4	16	11	10	34	20	27	41
Bangladesh	..	30	..	14	..	6	..	17	..	33
India	22	8	5	17	14	12	37	18	22	45
Pakistan	20	19	3	17	5	8	38	27	34	29
Low- & Middle-Income Europe	14	11	12	17	17	9	32	34	28	34
Greece	15	15	8	8	11	7	35	31	30	40
Portugal	16	11	8	11	19	6	27	37	30	35
Turkey	6	7	10	21	10	11	37	31	37	30
Middle East & N.Africa	24	17	5	6	7	6	24	33	40	37
Algeria	27	27	0	2	6	8	15	28	52	35
Egypt, Arab Rep.	26	31	7	2	12	10	23	23	31	34
Latin America & Caribbean	12	12	13	13	8	7	32	31	35	35
Argentina	6	4	10	9	21	11	25	33	38	44
Brazil	20	9	21	23	9	11	22	27	28	30
Mexico	5	16	2	4	10	7	50	36	33	37
Low-Income Countries	17	12	5	9	8	8	33	33	37	38
Middle-Income Countries	15	11	10	12	11	8	30	34	34	35
Severely Indebted Countries	14	15	9	11	10	9	32	31	34	35
High-Income Economies	19	9	10	11	19	7	20	34	32	39

Source: World Bank, World Development Report (1992).

veloping countries' imports of manufactured goods remained very high as compared with their share of primary commodity imports both in 1965 and 1990.

INDUSTRIALIZATION THROUGH IMPORT SUBSTITUTION VERSUS EXPORT PROMOTION

During the 1950s and 1960s most developing nations made a deliberate attempt to industrialize rather than continuing to specialize in the production of primary commodities (food, raw materials, and minerals) for export, as prescribed by traditional trade theory. Developing countries correctly believed that while continuing to specialize in the production of primary commodities would maximize welfare in the short run, the resulting pattern of specialization and trade would relegate them to a subordinate position vis-à-vis developed nations and keep them from reaping the *dynamic* benefits of industry and, therefore, from maximizing their welfare and growth in the long run. The dynamic benefits resulting from industrial production are a more trained labor force, more innovations, higher and more stable prices for the nation's exports, and higher income and employment for its people. If developing nations continued to specialize in primary commodities while developed nations specialized in manufactured products, all or most of the dynamic benefits of industry and trade would accrue to developed countries, leaving developing nations poor, undeveloped, and dependent. This belief was reinforced by the empirical observation that all developed nations are primarily industrial while all developing countries are primarily agricultural or engaged in mineral extraction.

During the 1950 and 1960s, most developing nations, particularly the larger ones, strongly opted for a policy of import substitution to industrialize. They protected their infant industries or stimulated their birth with effective tariff rates that rose sharply with the degree of processing. This was done at first to encourage the relatively simple step of assembling foreign parts, in the hope that subsequently more of these parts and intermediate products would be produced domestically (backward linkage). Heavy protection of domestic industries also encouraged the establishment of tariff factories in developing nations.

The policy of industrialization through import substitution generally met with only limited success or with failure. Very high rates of effective protection, in the range of 100 to 200 percent or more, were common during the 1950s and 1960s in such nations as India, Pakistan, Argentina, and Brazil. These led to very inefficient domestic industries and very high prices for domestic consumers. Sometimes the foreign currency value of imported inputs was greater than the foreign currency value of the output produced (negative value added). Furthermore, the highest priority was usually given to construction of new factories and the purchase of new machinery, with the result of widespread idle plant capacity for lack of funds to import needed raw material and fuel. Heavy protection to industry also led to excessive capital intensity and relatively little labor absorption. In fact, it was entirely unrealistic to expect that import substitution could have solved the unemployment and underemployment problem of developing countries. For example, even with 25 percent of the labor force in industry and 20 percent growth in industrial output per year, at most 0.5 percent (0.25 times 0.20) of the 2 or 3 percent annual increase in the labor force of developing nations could be absorbed into modern industry. The other workers had to be absorbed into agriculture and in the traditional service sector or remain unemployed. In addition, the hope of finding high-paying jobs in the modern sector attracted many more people to the cities than could find employment, leading to overurbanization and to an explosive situation (see Salvatore, 1988a, 1988b).

The effort to industrialize through import substitution also led to the neglect of agriculture and other primary sectors, with the result that many developing nations experienced a decline in their earnings from traditional exports, and some (such as Brazil) were even forced to import some food products that they had previously exported. Furthermore, the policy of import substitution often aggravated the balance of payment problems of developing nations by requiring more imports of machinery, raw materials, fuels, and even food. The overall result was that those developing countries (such as India, Pakistan, and Argentina) that stressed industrialization through import substitution fared much worse and grew at a much slower rate than the few (smaller) developing economies (such as Singapore, Taiwan, and Hong Kong) that followed from the early 1950s an export-oriented policy. It has been estimated that the policy of import substitution resulted in waste of up to 10 percent of the country's national income (see Chenery, 1986; Chenery and Syrquin, 1975; Little, Scitovski, and Scott, 1970; Pack 1989).

Starting in the early 1970s, an increasing number of developing countries began to pay more attention to efficiency considerations and to shift from an import substitution to an export orientation policy. Econometric research (including the author's—see Salvatore and Hatcher, 1991) showed that the economic performance of developing nations that followed or switched to an export-oriented policy was better than that for nations that continued to follow a policy of import substitution. As Table 5.5 shows, the average annual growth of real value added in manufacturing and agriculture, the average share of manufacturing value added in GDP, the average share of labor force in industry, and the average growth of employment in industry all grew or were much higher for the outward-oriented than for the inward-oriented countries, over both the 1963–1973 and the 1973–1985 periods. Table 5.6 shows the trade orientation for a large number of countries for which data existed and its change between 1963–1973 and 1973–1985.

TRADE LIBERALIZATION IN DEVELOPING COUNTRIES

Starting in the early 1970s, an increasing number of developing countries, especially those that had opted for an inward-oriented strategy for industrialization during the 1950s and 1960s, began to liberalize trade. This involved some

Table 5.5

Growth and Industrialization in Developing Countries Grouped by Trade Orientation

Trade Strategy	Average Annual Growth of Real Manufacturing Value Added		Average Annual Growth of Real Agricultural Value Added		Average Share of Manufacturing Value Added in GDP		Average Share of Labor Force in Industry		Average Annual Growth of Employment in Manufacturing	
	1963-73	1973-85	1963-73	1973-85	1963	1985	1963	1980	1963-73	1973-84
Strongly outward oriented	15.6	10.0	3.0	1.6	17.1	26.3	17.5	30.0	10.6	5.1
Moderately outward oriented	9.4	4.0	3.8	3.6	20.5	21.9	12.7	21.7	4.6	4.9
Outward oriented (average)	10.3	5.2	3.7	3.3	20.1	23.0	13.2	23.0	6.1	4.9
Moderately inward oriented	9.6	5.1	3.0	3.2	10.4	15.8	15.2	23.0	4.4	4.4
Strongly inward oriented	5.3	3.1	2.4	1.4	17.6	15.9	12.1	12.6	3.0	4.0
Inward oriented (average)	6.8	4.3	2.6	2.1	15.2	15.8	12.7	14.1	3.3	4.2

Source: World Bank, *World Development Report* (1987), 87.

The countries included and their trade orientation in each time period are given in Table 5.6.

Table 5.6
Composition of Trade-Orientation Country Groups, 1963–1973 and 1973–1985

PERIOD I: 1963-1973

Strongly Outward Oriented:
Korea, Rep. of, Singapore

Moderately Outward Oriented:
*Colombia, Israel, *Ivory Coast, Malaysia

Moderately Inward Oriented:
El Salvador, Honduras, Kenya, Mexico, Nicaragua,
*Nigeria, Philippines, Senegal, *Tunisia, Yugoslavia

Strongly Inward Oriented:
Argentina, Bangladesh, *Chile, Dominican Republic,
India, *Pakistan, Peru, *Turkey, *Uruguay, Zambia

PERIOD II: 1973-1985

Strongly Outward Oriented:
Korea, Rep. of, Singapore

Moderately Outward Oriented:
*Chile, Israel, Malaysia, *Tunisia, *Turkey, *Uruguay

Moderately Inward Oriented:
*Colombia, El Salvador, Honduras, *Ivory Coast, Kenya, Mexico,
Nicaragua, *Pakistan, Philippines, Senegal, Yugoslavia

Strongly Inward Oriented:
Argentina, Bangladesh, Dominican Republic,
India, *Nigeria, Peru, Zambia

Source: World Bank, *World Development Report* (1987), 83.
*Refers to countries that changed trade orientation between the two time periods.

mixture of reduction and simplification of import tariffs, import taxation, and quantitative restrictions, as well as attempts to reduce impediments to exports. These trade-liberalizing measures were intended to promote the more efficient use of resources in the country by eliminating the static costs of protection (such as the higher prices paid by domestic consumers of the product), overcoming X-inefficiencies (i.e., the cost associated with the "quiet life"), taking away the incentive for such unproductive activities as lobbying to retain or impose trade regulations, making economies of scale possible, and stimulating the flow of investments and advanced technology from abroad.

Some countries (such as Chile, Greece, Israel, Korea, New Zealand, Singapore, and Spain) consistently pursued liberalization during the past two decades. Others (such as Argentina, Brazil, Colombia, Mexico, Pakistan, Peru, the Philippines, Sri Lanka, Turkey, and Yugoslavia) were not as consistent, and their commitment to trade liberalization during some years wavered. In general, the majority of the more liberalizing countries were smaller, had a higher per capita income, and were more politically stable than those countries that were less consistent in their liberalizing efforts. In addition, while the shift from an inward-oriented to an outward-oriented strategy can best be accomplished by removing existing trade barriers and devaluing the nation's currency, many countries (mostly in the second group, which was less consistent in its liberalization efforts) used export incentives without eliminating or significantly reducing their import barriers or devaluing their currency. As a result, the growth of their exports was half as large as that for the more liberalizing countries. Furthermore, while exports grew at about the same rate as GDP in the less liberalizing countries, exports grew significantly faster than GDP in the more liberalizing countries and, therefore, behaved more like the leading sector in the latter than in the former group of countries.

Research conducted at the World Bank (1988) also showed that liberalization policies are more likely to be sustained in the long run if they are initiated in the midst of macroeconomic difficulties, carried out in a crisis atmosphere and under international pressure, and launched in a single bold move rather than with a number of small hesitant steps over time. There is also a consensus that the likelihood of success for a program of trade liberalization is much greater if trade liberalization precedes macroeconomic stabilization than if it follows it or if it is undertaken at the same time. Managing one type of stabilization at the time makes each more manageable. Furthermore, when macroeconomic stability has already been achieved and prices are playing their full signaling role, it is more likely that trade liberalization will achieve its desired results. As Sachs (1987) pointed out, prior macroeconomic stabilization was crucial to the success of the trade liberalization programs in Japan and Taiwan in the late 1950s and early 1960s. Empirical research by Nabli (1990) on the political economy of trade liberalization also showed that trade liberalization is more likely to succeed the greater the strength of the exporter group, the smaller the strength of the import-competing sector's opposition, the smaller the time for which the import-substitution measures were in place, the smaller the size of the country, and the stronger the political leadership and its commitment to a program of trade liberalization.

The World Bank has greatly facilitated the planning and the carrying out of trade liberalization programs with technical assistance and loans. The bank began its lending for structural adjustment in 1980, and by 1990 it had lent more than $15 billion to more than fifty countries for the purpose of implementing structural or sectoral reforms. The largest number of loans went to Sub-Saharan African countries, but since these loans were generally small, a much larger amount went to other developing countries. The purpose of the bank's loans also varied. In Sub-Saharan Africa, the loans went mostly to support agriculture (to increase producer prices and setting up or improve extension services and research) and to carry out institutional reforms in the public sector (to restructure production and finances and for divestiture). On the other hand, in other highly indebted

Table 5.7
Developing Countries' Export Growth, High and Low Scenarios, 1988–1995

	High-Growth Scenario	Low Growth Scenario
	(average annual percentage change)	
Merchandise Export Volume	5.1	4.1
Manufactures	7.4	5.7
Primary goods	2.8	2.7
Merchandise Import Volume	5.7	4.6

Source: World Bank, *World Development Report* (1989), 20.

countries, bank loans went mostly for trade (to remove disincentives for, and to encourage, exports) and for financial sector policies (such as reforming the banking system and establishing financial intermediaries).

The World Bank estimated (see Table 5.7) that with credible policy actions to reduce macroeconomic imbalances within and among industrial countries (such as reduction of the twin budget and trade deficits in the United States and trade surplus of Japan and Germany) and with continued structural adjustments (including trade liberalization) in developing countries, the total merchandise export volume of the developing countries as a group would increase at an average rate of 5.1 percent in the 1988–1995 period. This is the high-growth scenario. Without adequate effort in industrial countries to reduce their macroeconomic imbalances and in the absence of continued structural adjustments in developing countries (the low-growth scenario), on the other hand, the developing countries' total merchandise export volume would increase at an average of only 4.1 percent during the 1988–1995 period. For manufactures, the respective rates of growth would be 7.4 percent and 5.7 percent, while for primary commodities the rates of growth would be 2.8 percent and 2.7 percent, respectively. While the rates of export growth under the high-growth scenario are not spectacular, they are at least as high as during the 1980s and much higher than in the 1965–1980 period (World Bank, *World Development Report,* 1991). As in the past, these average rates of export growth will probably differ widely among the various groups of developing countries. As far as merchandise imports are concerned, they exceed the developing countries' export-based capacity to import only by the amount of foreign loans, investments, and aid (see Balassa, 1988; Bhagwati, 1988, 1989, 1991; Dornbusch, 1992; Edwards, 1991; Fischer, 1991; IMF, 1992a; Michaely et al., 1989, 1991; Meier, 1990; OECD, 1992; Roubini and Sala-i-Martin, 1991; Salvatore, 1991a, 1991b; Thomas and Chhibber, 1989; United Nations, 1992a, 1992b).

TRADE PROTECTIONISM IN DEVELOPED COUNTRIES AND DEVELOPING COUNTRIES' TRADE

Since the mid-1970s, developed countries, beset by slow growth and large unemployment, have increased the trade protection they provide to some of their large industries (such as textile, steel, shipbuilding, consumer electronic products, television sets, shoes, and many other products) on imports from developing countries. These are the very industries in which developing countries have gained or are gaining a comparative advantage. A great deal of this new protectionism has been directed especially against the manufactured exports of newly industrializing countries (NICs). These nations (Brazil, Hong Kong, Korea, Mexico, Singapore, and Taiwan) are characterized by rapid growth in GDP, in industrial production, and in manufactured exports. Over the past twenty years the ratio of the industrial exports of the NICs to the total imports of the developed countries has risen from 1 percent to 6 percent. However, the timing and the type of products exported by the NICs have led to increased trade restrictions by the developed countries.

This new protectionism by developed countries took such new forms as antidumping and countervailing duties and voluntary export restraints (VERs). The proliferation of these new forms of protectionism have more than neutralized the significant reduction in tariffs that resulted from successive rounds of multilateral negotiations concluded under the auspices of the General Agreement on Tariffs and Trade (GATT) during the postwar period. Developed countries thus substituted one type of trade barrier (tariffs) with another (nontariff barriers or new protectionism). Since antidumping and countervailing duty investigations allegedly serve either to rectify a wrong (dumping) or to prevent the collapse of an entire industry (countervailing duty) or are "voluntary," they do not violate the letter of GATT rules. Since they are abused and have in fact been used for protectionistic purposes (the simple filing of an antidumping complaint, e.g., discourages trade according the harassment thesis), however, they certainly violated the spirit of the law. It has been estimated that U.S. barriers on steel, automobiles, and textiles are equivalent to an additional import tariff of 25 percent, thus raising protection in the United States to the level of the early postwar years. The same is true for other developed countries. Nontariff barriers (NTBs) also affected more developing than developed countries' exports. The World Bank (1987) estimated that these new types of trade barriers affected 25 percent of the exports of developing countries, as compared with 21 percent of developed countries' exports. Furthermore, even though remaining tariffs on developed countries' imports are very low, they apply primarily to labor-intensive commodities that are of particular importance to low-income nations. Industrial country tariff protection also exhibits tariff escalation (i.e., tariffs rise with the degree of processing and thus favor the import of raw materials and discourage processing in developing nations).

Since textiles and clothing are relatively labor-intensive, industrial countries' trade restrictions on these products are particularly detrimental to developing countries. About one-half of world trade in textiles and clothing is now managed by export restraints under the aegis of the Multifiber Arrangement (MFA). MFA legitimizes bilaterally negotiated quotas designed to slow the growth of textile and clothing exports from low-cost suppliers in order to protect production and employment in developed countries. MFA has been in existence since 1959 and has become increasingly restrictive and inclusive over time. Despite MFA, the textiles and clothing exports of developing countries are now over $30 billion per year, but they could be much higher in the absence of MFA. To be noted is that MFA harms both developed and developing countries. It harms developing countries because it prevents or slows down their industrialization and full integration into the world trading system. As reported by Abreu (1989), the abolition of MFA would lead to welfare gains of $1.0 billion for Brazil, $1.4 billion for Taiwan, $2.3 billion for China, and $2.1 billion for Korea (but to surprisingly small gains for India and Sri Lanka and some losses to Pakistan, Singapore, Thailand, and Hong Kong since they would lose their quotas). MFA also harms developed countries because it leads to higher consumer prices and a misallocation of resources (i.e., it prevents the reallocation of resources to areas of developed countries' comparative advantage). World Bank estimates (1990) indicate that the cost of protecting each job in the textile industry in the United States is roughly four times the average employee's salary. MFA can be explained only by the political economy of protection in developed countries—that is, that the benefits or rents from protection accrue to relatively few producers and are very large (thus giving them a strong incentive and large financial resources to lobby for their retention), while the losses in the form of higher textile prices are spread over the more or less silent majority (where each family's losses are rather small and not widely known).

Developed countries' agricultural programs in the form of price support, direct payments, and supply management schemes also seriously distort production and trade in agricultural commodities and restrict developing countries' agricultural exports to developed countries. Assistance to farmers raises the domestic production and prices of temperate products in Organization for Economic Cooperation and Development (OECD) countries and results in agricultural surpluses and subsidized exports, which compete with developing countries' exports. Excise taxes on tropical products (coffee, tea, cocoa) and quantitative restrictions on imports of sugar, dairy products, fruits, groundnut, tobacco, and rice in developed countries also seriously restrict developing countries' exports of these products.

The increased protectionism has occurred in spite of the Generalized System of Preferences (GSP), negotiated by Western European countries and Japan in 1971–1972 and by the United States in 1976, which grants preferential access to the exports of developing countries into developed countries' markets. Currently more than twenty OECD countries operate GSP schemes with more than 140 beneficiaries. However, exception after exception to the GSP has been "voluntarily" negotiated by the United States and other developed countries for many "sensitive" products such as textile, clothing, and footwear, which are of great importance to developing countries. By 1990, more than 120 such exceptions had been negotiated by the United States and other developing countries. Furthermore, the U.S. Tariff and Trade Act of 1984 authorized the president of the United States to deny GSP privileges to NICs that did not curb their own unfair trade practices and restricted U.S. exports. The act also called for "graduation" or the removal of preferential access for the exports of the most advanced of the developing nations, such as Korea and Taiwan. These conditions were included in the face of the increase in the NICs' trade surplus with the United States from just over $2 billion in 1981 to more than $30 billion in 1990. It must, however, be pointed out that while most criticism for restricting developing countries' exports is usually directed at the United States, the United States absorbs more than half of developing countries' exports. The European Community (EC), which is now larger than the U.S. economy, absorbs less than one-third of developing countries' exports (down from one-half in 1965), while Japan, with an economy about half the size of that of the United States, takes in less than 10 percent, and this has remained practically unchanged since 1965 (Finger and Messerlin, 1989). Most studies indicate that the GSP has a very limited effect on increasing developing countries' exports. The World Bank (1990), for example, reports that the total imports of developed countries increased by only 0.5 percent because of the GSP, the exports of developing countries are only about 1–2 percent (about $6.5 billion) higher, and most of the benefits accrued to a small number of middle-income developing countries or NICs.

It has been estimated that removing all trade restrictions by developed countries would lead to a 10 percent increase in developing countries' exports (of which 40 percent would be in clothing and another 10 percent in food and food products). This would raise developing countries' GNP by about 3 percent and cost developed countries 0.7 percent of their GNP or roughly double the amount that they now provide in foreign aid (Finger and Messerlin, 1989). As Table 5.8 shows, most of the benefit from complete trade liberalization in developed countries would accrue to successful middle-income exporters, with some low-income (mostly Sub-Saharan African) countries actually losing because their existing trade preferences would disappear. Similar results are reported in United Nations (1992a) and the World Bank (*Global Economic Prospects,* 1992). See also Corden (1987); Grilli and Sassoon (1990); Laird and Yeats (1989); Mankiw, Romer, and Weil (1990); Salvatore (1987a, 1987b, 1988a, 1992a, 1992b, 1993b); U.S. International Trade Commission (1988); Winglee (1989).

THE URUGUAY ROUND, TRADING BLOCKS, AND DEVELOPING COUNTRIES' TRADE

Most of the present trade problems afflicting the world economy in general and developing countries in particular were taken up in the Uruguay Round (the

Table 5.8

Effect of Complete Trade Liberalization on Selected Developing Countries

Middle-Income Developing Countries	Percentage Change in Exports	Low-Income Developing Countries	Percentage Change in Exports
Hong Kong	25.9	Sri Lanka	20.9
Korea, Republic of	21.6	China	13.0
Yugoslavia	14.0	Pakistan	10.7
Dominican Republic	13.0	Haiti	9.3
Tunisia	11.4	India	8.6
Mauritius	10.5	Bangladesh	-1.0
Thailand	10.3	Tanzania	-3.3
Morocco	8.9	Burundi	-5.5
Singapore	7.2	Nepal	-9.6
Brazil	6.8	Somalia	-24.3

Source: World Bank, *World Development Report* (1990).

eighth round of multilateral trade negotiations that started in 1986 and was scheduled to be completed by December 1990). Its aim was to establish rules for checking the proliferation of the new protectionism and reverse its trend; bring services, agriculture, and foreign investments into the negotiations; negotiate international rules for the protection of intellectual property; and improve the dispute settlement mechanism by ensuring more timely decisions and compliance with GATT rulings. The Uruguay Round reached an impasse in December 1990 and remained stalled as of fall 1993. Successfully concluding the round would go a long way toward resolving the serious problems faced by the present international trade system, restore international confidence, and create a truly global trade regime under GATT. Negotiating rules of conduct to reverse the spread of the new protectionism is extremely difficult, however, because issues of national sovereignty are often involved. Furthermore, several of the leading developing countries, under the leadership of India and Brazil, object to bringing services into the negotiations because they fear that with foreign competition they will be unable to develop such service industries as telecommunications, data processing, banking, and insurance, which they regard as crucial to their national development. In agriculture, the European Community and Japan essentially killed the proposal that the United States presented at GATT to eliminate by the end of the century all farm aid programs that interfere with international trade.

The principal interest of developing countries in the Uruguay Round is to gain increased access for their textile and agricultural exports in the developed countries' markets. Indeed, developing countries have indicated that they will use this as the yardstick with which to judge its success. Developing countries seem willing to open their own markets to services from developed countries and accept rules to protect intellectual property on condition that developed countries dismantle their MFA restrictions against the textile exports of developing countries. To be sure, developing countries' interests are not uniform. For example, liberalization of textile trade would benefit mostly the NICs and China, but not India or most of the poorest developing countries. Similarly, liberalizing trade in agriculture would, for the most part, benefit only a few large developing countries, such as Argentina and Brazil. Exporters of tropical products that enjoy preferential access into developed countries' markets are less interested in liberalizing trade in these products since they would lose their preferences. Because different groups of developing countries have different interests, no strong coalition of developing countries has emerged. The closest that developing countries have come to presenting a united front in the negotiations is in demanding increased access for their textile and agricultural exports to developed countries' markets. It is politically unrealistic, however, to expect a speedy dismantling of MFA by developed countries. All that could be expected during the next few years, therefore, are a globalization of quotas across countries or products and a gradually scheduled liberalization. The minimum that the Uruguay Round must accomplish to be deemed moderately successful is reversing the spread of the new protectionism and reasserting the principle of an open multilateral trading system, strengthening the dispute settlement procedure of GATT, and achieving some liberalization in services and agriculture and setting up the framework and establishing the principle for subsequent trade liberalization in these sectors.

The formation of a unified market by the end of 1992 by the members of the EC is also likely to strongly affect world trade in general and developing countries' trade in particular. The EC has become the single largest unified market in the world and accounts for 30 percent of developing countries' exports. It has been estimated that EC growth will be 5 percent higher and that this would increase developing countries' exports by $4 billion (World Bank, *World Development Report*, 1990). This, however, depends on whether trade creation will exceed trade diversion. An excess of trade diversion from developing countries' manufactured exports is more likely if the EC sets up special trade arrangements with Eastern European countries to help them restructure their economies after the collapse of the communist regimes. Should that happen and trade be diverted from developing nations, there would surely arise a disillusionment with outward-oriented policies, which may lead to a revival of export pessimism and a return to inward-looking policies in developing countries during the 1990s. This would force second-best trade policies on developing countries (such as expanding trade with other developing countries only) and a return to relying more on import-substitution policies for growth (see Abreu, 1989; Finger and Olechowski, 1987; Hamilton and Whalley, 1988; Salvatore, 1993a).

STRATEGIC TRADE POLICIES AND ECONOMIC DEVELOPMENT

While trade liberalization is likely to stimulate the rate of economic development in general, the judicious use of strategic trade policies can also be useful.

The oldest and best-known argument for departing from free trade in the early stages of development in order to promote the establishment of a domestic industry is the infant industry argument. According to this, temporary protection is required in a developing country in order to overcome distortions in the economy and be able to capture the externalities and other dynamic benefits usually associated with industrial production. The argument that this is better achieved with a subsidy rather than with import tariff (because the former does not distort domestic consumption while the latter does) is usually answered by pointing out that subsidies are not feasible because they require revenues, which are difficult to raise through regular taxation in developing countries. Since the benefits of setting up an industry are only partially reaped by private firms (i.e., the industry gives rise to external economies), either the industry would not be established by the private sector or there would be underinvestment in the sector in the absence of tariff protection. In order to be justified, however, the protection must be temporary and generate enough extra return to also cover the cost associated with the higher domestic prices resulting from the tariff. But as Krueger (1984) pointed out, the entire manufacturing sector in a developing country is an infant. This implies that a uniform rate of protection should be applied to the entire sector. Such uniform protection would then lead to the establishment of those industries in which the developing nation has the greatest potential comparative advantage and thus avoid costly mistakes of possibly targeting the wrong industry or industries for development. Thus, imposing a uniform across-the-board tariff would minimize the cost of protection and the cost of industrialization for the nation.

During the period of their industrialization a century ago, today's developed countries enjoyed both a high degree of natural protection (because of high transportation costs) and high artificial protection through tariffs and quantitative restrictions imposed by national governments intent on fostering industrialization. During the postwar years, Japan, Korea, and Taiwan also industrialized behind a high protective wall. To be sure, other, more important internal factors were obviously also at work (such as a high saving and investment rate, an increasingly trained labor force, sound macroeconomic policies, and political stability) without which successful industrialization could not have occurred. But trade protection certainly played an important facilitating role. To be effective, however, trade protection must be temporary. The nation should establish a timetable for gradually reducing protection and strictly adhere to it. Of course, the domestic industries that are set up with protection are very likely to spend a great amount of time and effort lobbying the government to retain trade protection indefinitely and even to increase it over time. If these efforts succeed, the nation's industry will be unable to meet international competition, and, as a result, the entire industrialization process is likely to come prematurely to a halt. The classic example of this is Argentina. It is now more or less widely agreed that most developing countries provide excessive protection to their infant industries and retain it long after it should have been necessary.

Even the imposition of a uniform tariff on all manufactured imports by the developing country, however, leads to serious distortions in the economy because preferential treatment is provided to domestic producers of import-competing products but not to potential exporters. Ideally, equal incentives should be provided in production for domestic sales and for export. This can be accomplished by providing a subsidy to exporters (paid out of the tariff revenues collected on imports) equal to the effective tariff rate on imports. The export subsidy can be supplemented by organizing trade fairs, opening foreign trade offices, and sending trade missions abroad. A simpler alternative for providing the same degree of protection to producers for the domestic market and for export is keeping the exchange rate of the domestic currency undervalued by the same percentage as provided by a uniform import tariff and export subsidy. Such an undervalued exchange rate creates equal potential profit opportunities for all domestic producers. In fact, Edwards (1988) showed that nations that kept undervalued exchange rates over time have grown much faster than nations that kept overvalued exchange rates or mismanaged their exchange rates. The percentage of the undervaluation can then gradually be reduced to stimulate increased efficiency by domestic firms over time.

Even under recessionary conditions in developed countries and resulting slow growth or even declining aggregate demand for developing countries' exports, there is always room for one or a few countries to increase their exports rapidly if efficiency in the nation or nations increases faster than in other countries. This has certainly been the experience of the newly industrializing countries during the past two decades. Government officials should be careful, therefore, not to fall into the fallacy-of-composition trap and believe that since all developing countries could not rapidly expand their exports simultaneously in the face of sluggish growth for the world economy, one or a few of them could not do so. In particular, it should always be possible for a small, open economy to expand its exports rapidly if productivity increases more at home than abroad. It should also be clear that the country is not condemned to continue to export the same simple manufactures that it did at the beginning of its development process if the nation's firms reinvest a large proportion of their earnings efficiently and its government pursues policies to improve technical education, improve the nation's infrastructures, and maintain a low rate of inflation and successfully pursues other growth-related policies. According to strategic trade policy, a developing nation can, in this way, create a comparative advantage in increasingly sophisticated products over time and in the process increase its rate of growth and economic development. Again, the NICs provide an excellent example of this (see Ernst and O'Connor, 1989; Krugman, 1986; Rodrik, 1988).

FOREIGN TRADE, DEBT, INVESTMENTS, AND ECONOMIC DEVELOPMENT

During the 1970s, developing countries accumulated a huge international debt that they are now finding very difficult to repay or even service. The debt arose as many developing countries borrowed heavily from private banks in developed nations to finance their growing capital needs and to pay for sharply higher oil bills. By heavily borrowing abroad, developing countries continued to grow at a relatively rapid pace even during the second half of the 1970s. In the early 1980s, however, their huge and rapidly growing foreign debts caught up with them, and large-scale defaults were avoided only by repeated large-scale rescheduling and interventions by the IMF. Servicing the foreign debt now uses up a large proportion of the export earnings of most developing nations, leaving too little for new investments. It is now widely agreed that in order for the debt problem to be overcome and for rapid sustained growth to resume in developing countries, a large increase in the flow of *equity* capital in the form of direct investments from developed countries, as well as the opening of developed countries' markets more widely to developing countries' exports, is required.

Because of the debt problem and the precipitous decline in voluntary bank lending, developing countries are more ready to acknowledge today the benefits that can arise from foreign direct investments and are adopting policies to encourage such an inflow. Foreign direct investment can supply needed capital and technology, lead to the expansion of exports, and relieve the debt problem. Thus, foreign direct investments are closely related to trade and to the trade policies of developing countries. Foreign direct investments are more likely to flow to developing countries that have stable and predictable policies on foreign investments and do not impose many restrictions and conditions on its flow, are politically stable and have sound macroeconomic policies, have a reasonably educated and trained labor force, and have a large domestic market and/or are outward-oriented. Foreign direct investments still face many impediments in the majority of developing nations today. For example, because of the debt problem, many developing nations restrict the import of essential equipment and the repatriation of profits. Brazil restricts foreign direct investments in advanced technology, Mexico has compulsory local-content requirements, and India excludes foreign investments in its financial sector. Since 1985, foreign direct investments flowing to developing countries remained fairly stable at the level of $10–11 billion annually. This is far lower than the $16–18 billion that took place during the early 1980s. The distribution of foreign direct investments is also highly uneven, with 86 percent of the total going to only eighteen developing countries (China, Hong Kong, Taiwan, Thailand, Singapore, Malaysia; Brazil, Mexico, Argentina, Chile, Colombia, Venezuela, Trinidad and Tobago; Egypt, Nigeria, Tunisia, Oman).

Since the early 1970s, new forms of investments (NFI) have become widespread as traditional forms of foreign direct investments (FDI) in developing countries stagnated. NFI are foreign investments in which the host country retains majority or whole ownership of the project or enterprise. They include joint ventures, subcontracting, licensing, production sharing, franchising, management contracts, and turnkey projects. There are two reasons for this development. One is that many OECD-based corporations became hesitant to risk on expanding

FDI in many developing countries during the 1970s and 1980s and began to realize that, through NFI, they would be able to increase leverage on firm-specific (especially intangible) assets. That is, with local partners or international lenders supplying the start-up and working capital, the firm could concentrate on supplying only the truly unique services of the firm (and receive high returns for them), while reducing its exposure to the political risk in the host country, as well as the financial and commercial risks usually associated with traditional FDI. NFI also seemed to better fit the firm's strategy of global competition in high-tech oligopolistic markets in today's highly integrated world. The other reason for the spread of NFI during the 1970s and 1980s is that developing countries saw this as a way to have access to new technologies, export markets, and management skills without losing control over key natural resources and/or manufacturing industries, and also capture the rents that these industries generate. NFI became particularly attractive to the larger and the more advanced developing countries, such as Brazil, that already have a great deal of management and technical capacities and can, therefore, concentrate on acquiring only those assets that they cannot yet provide internally.

Not much hard data exist on NFI. The reason is that it is very difficult to assign monetary values on the tangible and intangible nonequity international asset flows represented by NFI in a form that is statistically comparable across industries and nations. Simply counting the number of NFI projects indicates that their importance has grown significantly both absolutely and in relation to FDI since the early 1970s in many, if not all, developing countries. For example, NFI are very important in the manufacturing sector in Brazil (though FDI still remain predominant) but are relatively insignificant in Singapore. Furthermore, many developing countries have come to more objectively appreciate the higher risks that accompany NFI in relation to traditional FDI. The possibility of NFI has also led many smaller OECD-based firms to go multinational by providing only the specific services in which they specialize and without the much greater capital commitment usually associated with FDI. This has increased the range of choice for developing countries and increased global interfirm rivalry, which developing countries can exploit. Be that as it may, developing countries will have to carefully evaluate the benefits and costs of the various forms of foreign investments and view them as an important and integral part of their overall trade and development strategy (see IMF, 1992b; OECD 1989; Oman 1989; United Nations, 1992c; Wallace, 1990; World Bank, *World Bank Debt Tables,* 1991b).

REFERENCES

Abreu, M. de Paiva. 1989. "Developing Countries and the Uruguay Round." In *Proceedings of the Annual Conference on Development,* edited by World Bank. Washington, D.C.: World Bank.

Bahami-Oskooee, M. 1991. "Exports, Growth and Causality in LDCs." *Journal of Development Economics* (October).

Balassa, B. 1988. "Subsidies and Countervailing Measures: Economic Considerations." *Journal of World Trade* (April).

Bhagwati, J. 1978. *Foreign Exchange Regimes and Economic Development: Anatomy and Consequences of Exchange Control Regimes.* New York: National Bureau of Economic Research.

———. 1988. "Export-Promoting Strategy: Issues and Evidence." *World Bank Research Observer* (March).

———. 1989. *Protectionism.* Cambridge: MIT Press.

———. 1991. *The World Trading System at Risk.* Princeton, N.J.: Princeton University Press.

Bliss, C. 1989. "Trade and Development." In *Handbook of Development Economics,* edited by H.B. Chenery and T.N. Srinivasan. Vol. 2. Amsterdam: North-Holland, chap. 23.

Boggio, L., and Tirelli, P. 1989. "Economic Growth, Exports and International Competitiveness." *Economia Internazionale* (February–March).

Chenery, H.B. 1961. "Comparative Advantage and Development Policy." *American Economic Review* (March).

Chenery, H.B. 1986. *Industrialization and Growth.* New York: Oxford University Press.

Chenery, H.B., and Syrquin, M. 1975. *Patterns of Development, 1950–1970.* London: Oxford University Press.

Cline, W.R. 1984. *Exports of Manufactures from Developing Countries.* Washington, D.C.: Brookings.

Corden, M.W. 1987. *Protection and Liberalization: A Review of Analytical Issues.* Occasional Paper 54. Washington, D.C.: International Monetary Fund.

Dornbusch, R. 1992. "The Case of Trade Liberalization in Developing Countries." *Journal of Economic Perspectives* (Winter).

Edwards, S. 1988. "Exchange Rate Misalignment in Developing Countries." In *Occasional Paper 2* (New Series).

———. 1991. "Trade Orientation, Distortions and Growth in Developing Countries." *NBER Working Paper No. 3716* (May).

Ernst, D., and O'Connor, D. 1989. *Technology and Global Economy: The Challenge for Newly Industrializing Economies.* Paris: Organization for Economic Cooperation and Development.

Evans, D. 1989. "Alternative Perspectives on Trade and Development." In *Handbook of Development Economics,* edited by H.B. Chenery and T.N. Srinivasan. Vol. 2. Amsterdam: North-Holland, chap. 24.

Findlay, R. 1984. "Growth and Development in Trade Models." In *Handbook of International Economics,* edited by R.W. Jones and P.B. Kenen. Vol. 1. Amsterdam: North-Holland, chap. 4.

Finger, M.J., and Messerlin, P.A. 1989. *The Effects of Industrial Countries' Policies on Developing Countries.* Washington, D.C.: World Bank.

Finger, M.J., and Olechowski, A., eds. 1987. *The Uruguay Round: A Handbook of Multilateral Trade Negotiations.* Washington, D.C.: World Bank.

Fischer, S. 1991. "Growth, Macroeconomics, and Development." *NBER Working Paper No. 3702* (May).

Greenaway, D., ed. 1987. *Economic Development and International Trade*. New York: St. Martin's Press.

Grilli, E. 1990. "Responses of Developing Countries to Trade Protectionism." In *The Direction of Trade Policy*, edited by C.P. Pearson and J. Riedel. Oxford: Basil Blackwell.

Grilli, E., and Sassoon, E., eds. 1990. *The New Protectionist Wave*. London: Macmillan.

Grilli, E., and Yang, M.C. 1988. "Primary Commodity Prices, Manufactured Goods Prices, and the Terms of Trade of Developing Countries; What the Long Run Shows." *World Bank Review* (January).

Hamilton, C., and Whalley, J. 1988. *Coalitions in the Uruguay Round: The Extent, Pros and Cons of Developing Country Participation*. National Bureau of Economic Research Working Paper 2751. Cambridge, Mass.: National Bureau of Economic Research.

Helleiner, G.K. 1990. *The New Global Economy and the Developing Countries*. Brookfield, Vt.: Edward Elgar.

International Monetary Fund. 1989. *Developments in International Exchange and Trade Systems*. Washington, D.C.: International Monetary Fund.

———. 1992a. *Issues and Developments in International Trade Policy*. Washington, D.C.: International Monetary Fund.

———. 1992b. *World Economic Outlook*. Washington, D.C.: International Monetary Fund.

Kravis, I.B. 1970. "Trade as a Handmaiden of Growth: Similarities Between the 19th and 20th Centuries." *Economic Journal* (December).

Krueger, A.O. 1978. *Foreign Trade Regimes and Economic Development: Liberalization Attempts and Consequences*. New York: National Bureau of Economic Research.

———. 1984. "Trade Policies in Developing Countries." In *Handbook of International Economics*, edited by R.W. Jones and P.B. Kenen. Vol. 1. Amsterdam: North-Holland, chap. 11.

Krugman, P., ed. 1986. *Strategic Trade Policy and the New International Economics*. Cambridge: MIT Press.

Laird, S., and Yeats, A. 1989. "Nontariff Barriers of Developed Countries, 1966–1986." *Finance & Development* (March).

Lal, D., and Sarath, R. 1987. "Foreign Trade Regimes and Economic Growth in Developing Countries." *World Bank Research Observer* (July).

Little, I., Scitovski, T., and Scott, M. 1970. *Industry and Trade in Some Developing Countries*. London: Oxford University Press.

Mankiw, N., Romer, D., and Weil, D. 1990. "A Contribution to the Empirics of Growth." *NBER Working Paper No. 3541* (December).

Meier, G.M. 1990. "Trade Policy, Development, and the New Political Economy." In *The Political Economy of International Trade*, edited by R.W. Jones and A.O. Krueger. Oxford: Basil Blackwell.

Michaely, M. 1989. *The Design of Trade Liberalization*. Oxford: Basil Blackwell.

———. 1991. *Liberalizing Foreign Trade*. Vol. 7, *Lessons and Experience in the Developing World*. Cambridge, Mass.: Basil Blackwell.

Nabli, M. 1990. "The Political Economy of Trade Liberalization in Developing Countries." *Open Economy Review*, no. 2.

Nurkse, R. 1959. "Contrasting Trends in the 19th and 20th Century World Trade." In *Problems in Capital Formation in Underdeveloped Countries, and Patterns of*

Trade and Development, edited by R. Nurkse. New York: Oxford University Press.

Oman, C. 1989. *New Forms of Investment in Developing Country Industries.* Paris: Organization for Economic Cooperation and Development.

Organization for Economic Cooperation and Development. 1989. *International Direct Investment and the New Economic Environment.* Paris: Organization for Economic Cooperation and Development.

————. 1992. *Integration of Developing Countries into the International Trading System.* Paris: Organization for Economic Cooperation and Development.

Pack, H. 1989. "Industrialization and Trade." In *Handbook of Development Economics,* edited by H.B. Chenery and T.N. Srinivasan. Vol. 1. Amsterdam: North-Holland, chap. 9.

Ram, R. 1987. "Exports and Economic Growth in Developing Countries: Evidence from Time Series and Cross-Sectional Data." *Economic Development and Cultural Change* (October).

Riedel, J. 1984. "Trade as an Engine of Growth in Developing Countries, Revisited." *Economic Journal* (March).

Rodrik, D. 1988. "Imperfect Competition, Scale Economies, and Trade Policy in Developing Countries." In *Trade Policy Issues and Empirical Analysis,* edited by R.E. Baldwin. Chicago: University of Chicago Press.

————. 1992. "The Limits of Trade Policy Reform." *Journal of Economic Perspectives* 6 (Winter).

Roubini, N., and Sala-i-Martin, X. 1991. "Financial Development, the Trade Regime, and Economic Growth." *NBER Working Paper No. 3876* (October).

Sachs, J. 1987. "Trade and Exchange Rate Policies in Growth-Oriented Adjustment Programs." In *Growth-Oriented Adjustment Programs,* edited by V. Corbo, M. Goldstein, and M. Khan. Washington, D.C.: International Monetary Fund and World Bank.

————. 1989–1990. *Developing Country Debt and Economic Performance.* 4 Vols. Chicago: University of Chicago Press.

Salvatore, D. 1983. "A Simultaneous Equations Model of Trade and Development with Dynamic Policy Simulations." *Kyklos* 36, no. 1: 66–90.

————. 1987a. "Import Penetration, Exchange Rates, and Protectionism." *Journal of Policy Modeling* (Spring).

————, ed. 1987b. *The New Protectionist Threat to World Welfare.* New York: North-Holland.

————. 1988a. *World Population Trends and Their Impact on Economic Development.* Westport, Conn.: Greenwood Press.

————, ed. 1988b. *Modeling Demographic and Economic Dynamics. Journal of Policy Modeling* (special issue) 10 (April).

————, ed. 1989. *African Development Prospects: A Policy Modeling Approach.* New York: Francis and Lewis for the United Nations.

————. 1991a. "Ethics and Increasing International Income Inequalities." *Journal of Regional Policy* (July/December).

————, ed. 1991b. *Handbook of National Economic Policies.* New York and Westport, Conn.: North-Holland and Greenwood Press.

————. 1992a. "Recent Trends in U.S. Protectionism." *Open Economies Review* (Spring).

————, ed. 1992b. *Handbook of National Trade Policies.* New York and Westport, Conn.: North-Holland and Greenwood Press.

————. 1993a. "Trading Blocks and Protectionism." In *International Trade and Finance in the 1990s,* edited by M. Kreinin. New York: Francis and Taylor.

————, ed. 1993b. *Protectionism and World Welfare.* New York: Cambridge University Press.

Salvatore, D., and Hatcher, T. 1991. "Export and Growth with Alternative Trade Strategies," *Journal of Development Studies* 27 (April): 7–25.

Salvatore, D., et al. 1992. "Modeling African Development Prospects." In *Policy Adjustment in Africa,* edited by C. Milner and A.J. Rayner. London: Macmillan.

Spraos, J. 1983. *Inequalizing Trade?* Oxford: Clarendon Press.

Thomas, V., and Chhibber, A. 1989. "Experience with Policy Reforms Under Adjustment." *Finance and Development* (March).

United Nations. 1992a. *Trade and Development Report.* New York: United Nations.

————. 1992b. *World Economic Survey.* New York: United Nations.

————. 1992c. *World Investment Report.* New York: United Nations.

U.S. International Trade Commission. 1988. *Foreign Protection of Intellectual Property Rights.* Washington, D.C.: U.S. International Trade Commission.

Wallace, C. 1990. *Foreign Direct Investments in the 1990s: A New Climate in the Third World.* Dordrecht: Martinus Nijhoff.

Winglee, P. 1989. "Agricultural Policies of Industrial Countries." *Finance & Development* (March).

————. 1987, 1989, 1990, 1991, 1992. *World Development Report.* Washington, D.C.: World Bank.

World Bank. 1988. *Trade Liberalization: The Lessons of Experience.* Washington, D.C.: World Bank.

————. 1991a. *Human Development Report.* Washington, D.C.: World Bank.

————. 1991b. *World Bank Debt Tables.* Washington, D.C.: World Bank.

————. 1992. *Global Economic Prospects and the Developing Countries.* Washington, D.C.: World Bank.

6

ECONOMIC INTEGRATION

Ali M. El-Agraa

The purpose of this chapter is to bring together the development experience of
the developing countries (LDCs) within the context of international economic
integration (hereafter, simply economic integration) in terms of theory, strategy,
and performance. As the editors of this volume have put it, this contribution
should provide a sort of "state of the arts and facts" on economic development
within the stated provisos. Thus, this chapter considers the potential that economic integration can provide for fostering economic development, the necessary
conditions for the realization of such positive growth effects, and the existence
of such conditions in the LDCs where integration has been tried. Obviously,
this task implies a comprehensive review of the experience in Africa and Central
and Latin America as well as in the poor Asian nations and, arguably, in some
of the countries of Eastern Europe that used to belong to the Council for Mutual
Assistance (CMEA, or COMECON, as it was generally known).

This is a very tall order to meet, especially when the subject is so important
yet confined to only one chapter. Therefore, I am highly selective and in some
cases almost dismissive; hopefully this does not result in either complete neglect
or superficial discussion of some of the issues.

The chapter comprises four main sections. The first introduces the schemes
of, and expected developments in, economic integration among the LDCs. The
second not only tackles the theoretical rationale for economic integration in the
LDCs but also examines the pragmatic and historical reasons for it. The third
provides analyses of the actual performance of these LDCs. The final section
simply states those conclusions that require particular attention and points out
some pertinent questions that have to be asked by any LDC seriously considering
membership of either an already existing or about-to-be-created scheme of economic integration.

However, before embarking on this, it is both appropriate and space-saving to start by pointing out that economic integration takes different forms:

1. *free trade areas* (FTAs), in which the member nations remove all trade impediments among themselves but retain their freedom with regard to the determination of their policies vis-à-vis the outside world (the nonparticipants);

2. *customs unions* (CUs), which are very similar to FTAs except that the members must conduct and pursue common external commercial relations; for instance, they must adopt common external tariffs (CETs) on imports from the nonparticipants;

3. *common markets* (CMs), which are CUs that also allow for free factor mobility across national member frontiers; that is, capital, labor, enterprise, and technology should move unhindered between the participating countries;

4. *complete economic unions* (EUs), which are CMs that ask for complete unification of monetary and fiscal policies; that is, a central authority is introduced to exercise control over these matters so that existing members effectively become regions of one nation; and

5. *complete political integration,* in which the participants become a single nation with one political authority, as happened recently with the Federal Republic of Germany and the German Democratic Republic.

It should be stressed that each of these forms of economic integration can be introduced in its own right: they should not be confused with *stages* in a *process* that eventually leads to complete political integration. Also, although other classifications are possible, the one adopted here is fully consistent with Article 24 of the General Agreement on Tariffs and Trade (GATT); one should not confuse economic integration with intergovernmental economic cooperation. It should also be noted that within each scheme there may be *sectoral* integration in particular areas of the economy, for example, the Common Agricultural Policy (CAP) of the European Community (EC), which started and developed when the EC was barely a CU. Strictly speaking, under GATT's Article 24, sectoral integration should not be introduced in its own right. This is because the article states that since economic integration is tantamount to the formation of "discriminatory associations," members may not pursue policies that increase the level of their discrimination beyond what existed prior to their formation and that tariffs and other trade restrictions (with some exceptions) are removed on substantially all the trade among the participating nations. The latter condition effectively condemns sectoral integration, unless one or two products form the sole basis of an economy, as is the case in some LDCs. All these issues are fully discussed in Ali El-Agraa (1989c).

SCHEMES OF ECONOMIC INTEGRATION IN THE LDCs

Almost every single LDC belongs to one arrangement or another, and some belong to more than one scheme. Tables 6.1–6.4 provide a fairly comprehensive and easily digestible picture for both the LDCs and the advanced countries (so that one can have a proper sense of perspective). Nevertheless, a few words may be in order.

The European experience must be mentioned not only because the EC and the European Free Trade Association (EFTA) have been the pioneers in terms of *voluntary* membership but also because the EC has a strong association with sixty-six LDCs in the form of the EC-ACP (African-Caribbean-Pacific) agreements as well as specific association treaties with individual countries, including Eastern European nations and LDCs (see El-Agraa, 1990, chaps. 20, 21). Table 6.1 depicts this experience. Note that although the EC and EFTA have just signed an agreement creating the European Economic Area (EEA), the agreement formalizes, with some extensions, what has been in existence between the two blocs since the mid-1970s.

Until recently, there were four schemes of economic integration in Latin America and the Caribbean. Under the 1960 Treaty of Montevideo, the Latin American Free Trade Association (LAFTA) was formed between Mexico and all the countries of South America except for Guyana and Surinam. LAFTA came to an end in the late 1970s but was promptly succeeded by the Association for Latin American Integration (ALADI) in 1980, renamed the Latin American Integration Association (LAIA) in 1990. The Managua Treaty of 1960 established the Central American Common Market (CACM) among Costa Rica, El Salvador, Guatemala, Honduras, and Nicaragua. In 1969, the Andean Group (or Andean Pact) was established under the Cartegena Agreement among Bolivia, Chile, Colombia, Ecuador, Peru, and Venezuela; the Andean Group forms a closer link between some of the least developed nations of LAIA. In 1973, the Caribbean Community (CARICOM) was formed among Antigua, Barbados, Belize, Dominica, Grenada, Guyana, Jamaica, Montserrat, St. Kitts-Nevis-Anguilla, St. Lucia, St. Vincent, Trinidad, and Tobago; CARICOM replaced the Caribbean Free Trade Association (CARIFTA). The experience of the Americas and the Caribbean is shown in Table 6.2.

Several points need mentioning regarding recent developments in economic integration in this region. First, the United States, Canada, and Mexico have signed the North American Free Trade Agreement (NAFTA). Second, the Enterprise for the Americas Initiative (EAI), launched by former President George Bush in 1990, aims for the creation of an FTA in the Western Hemisphere. However, in the meantime, the United States seems set to establish bilateral agreements with either single nations or groups thereof since twenty-nine countries (including, before the EAI, Bolivia and Mexico) have signed framework agreements with the United States. Third, in June 1990, members of the CACM revived their attempts to carry out a free trade agreement by 1992, and in December of the same year they started to draft an agreement for the creation of a CM. A year later (in July), they formally approved the schedule for the liberalization of their mutual trade, and Panama participated in the discussions as a full member for the first time. In January 1991, Mexico and the countries

Table 6.1
Regional Trade Arrangements in Europe

	Existing Arrangements						Prospective Arrangements				
	EC /b	EFTA /c	EFTA-East Europe /d	EC-Czechoslovakia /e	EC-Hungary /e	EC-Poland /e	EEA /f	EC-Israel /g	EC-Bulgaria /h	EFTA-Israel /i	EC-GCC /j
Founded: /a	1957	1960									
Objective: /a	CM	FTA	FTA	FTA	FTA	FTA	CU	FTA	FTA	FTA	FTA
Western Europe											
Belgium	•			•	•	•	•	•	•		•
Denmark	•			•	•	•	•	•	•		•
France	•			•	•	•	•	•	•		•
Greece	•			•	•	•	•	•	•		•
Ireland	•			•	•	•	•	•	•		•
Italy	•			•	•	•	•	•	•		•
Luxembourg	•			•	•	•	•	•	•		•
Netherlands	•			•	•	•	•	•	•		•
Portugal	•			•	•	•	•	•	•		•
Spain	•			•	•	•	•	•	•		•
United Kingdom	•			•	•	•	•	•	•		•
Germany	•			•	•	•	•	•	•		•
Austria		•	•				•			•	
Finland		•	•				•			•	
Iceland		•	•				•			•	
Norway		•	•				•			•	
Sweden		•	•				•			•	
Switzerland		•	•				•			•	
Eastern Europe											
Bulgaria									•		
Czechoslovakia			•	•							
Hungary			•		•						
Poland			•			•					
Romania											
Yugoslavia											
Israel								•		•	
GCC /j											•

Source: Torre and Kelly (1992).

[a]FTA: free trade area; CU: customs union; CM: common market.

[b]Years of accession to the EC: Denmark, Ireland, and the United Kingdom (1973); Greece (1981); and Portugal and Spain (1986). The single market program (EC 1992) is to be completed by the end of 1992.

Austria and Sweden currently have membership pending. Liechtenstein became a full EFTA member in 1991.

[c]Finland was an associate member until its accession in 1986.

[d]The countries concerned have agreed to examine conditions for gradual establishment of free trade areas.

[e]Association agreements, including the establishment of free trade areas between each of the countries and the EC, are being negotiated.

[f]The European Economic Area (EEA) is currently being negotiated.

[g]The EC may negotiate an agreement with Israel similar to the agreement it is negotiating with EFTA countries to form an EEA.

[h]Bulgaria has requested preliminary discussions toward negotiation of an association agreement involving establishment of a free trade area.

[i]Currently being negotiated.

[j]Gulf Cooperation Council (GCC) members include Bahrain, Kuwait, Oman, Qatar, Saudi Arabia, and the United Arab Emirates.

Table 6.2
Regional Trade Arrangements in the Western Hemisphere

Founded: Objective:/b	US- Canada 1988 FTA	US- Israel 1989 FTA	CACM /c 1961 FTA	El Salvador- Guatemala /d 1991 FTA	CARICOM /e 1973 CU	OECS /f 1991 CU	LAFTA/ LAIA 1960/80 FTA	MERCOSUR /g 1991 FTA	Argentina- Brazil 1990 FTA
North America									
Canada	•								
Mexico							•		
United States	•	•							
Central America									
Belize					•				
Costa Rica			•						
El Salvador			•	•					
Guatemala			•	•					
Honduras			•						
Nicaragua			•						
Panama /m			•						
Caribbean									
Antigua & Bermuda					•	•			
The Bahamas					•				
Barbados					•				
Dominica					•	•			
Grenada					•	•			
Jamaica					•				
Monserrat					•	•			
St. Kitts & Nevis					•	•			
St. Lucia					•	•			
St. Vincent					•	•			
Trinidad & Tobago					•				
South America									
Argentina							•	•	•
Bolivia							•		
Brazil							•	•	•
Chile							•		
Colombia							•		
Ecuador							•		
Guyana					•				
Paraguay							•	•	
Peru							•		
Uruguay							•	•	
Venezuela							•		
Other Countries									
Israel		•							

Table 6.2 (continued)

	Andean Pact /h 1969 FTA	Chile-Mexico 1991 FTA	NAFTA FTA	Prospective Arrangements					
Founded: Objective:/b				EAI (US) /i 1991 FTA	Mexico-Central America /j	Chile-Colombia-Venezuela	Colombia-Mexico-Venezuela /k	Venezuela-Central America /l	RIO Group
Canada			•						
Mexico		•	•		•		•		•
United States			•	•					
Belize				•				•	
Costa Rica				•	•			•	
El Salvador				•	•			•	
Guatemala				•	•			•	
Honduras				•	•			•	
Nicaragua				•	•			•	
Panama /m				•	•			•	
Antigua & Bermuda				•					
The Bahamas				•					
Barbados				•					
Dominica				•					
Grenada				•					
Jamaica				•					
Monserrat				•					
St. Kitts & Nevis				•					
St. Lucia				•					
St. Vincent				•					
Trinidad & Tobago				•					
Argentina				•					•
Bolivia	•			•					
Brazil				•					
Chile	•	•		•		•			
Colombia	•			•		•	•		
Ecuador				•					
Guyana				•					
Paraguay				•					
Peru	•			•					•
Uruguay				•					•
Venezuela	•			•		•	•	•	•
Israel									

Source: Torre and Kelly (1992).

[a] Does not include unilateral trade preferences and exclusive countries with no arrangements.

[b] FTA: free trade area; CU: customs union.

[c] Revived in 1990; aims to establish a common market by 1992.

[d] Effective in October 1991.

[e] Aims to achieve a common external tariff by 1994.

[f] Organization of East Caribbean States.

[g] Aims to establish a common market by 1995.

[h] Efforts are under way to revive AP and create a common market by 1994.

[i] The Enterprise for the Americas Initiative aims to achieve hemisphere free trade zone. As of October 1991, the United States had signed framework agreements with 29 countries including the 13 CARICOM countries, the 4 MERCOSUR countries, Chile, Colombia, Costa Rica, Ecuador, El Salvador, Honduras, Panama, Peru, Nicaragua, and Venezuela.

[j] These countries aim to form a Central American/Mexican free trade zone by 1996.

[k] Signature of the trade and investment agreement occurred in 1991, and trilateral limited free trade is expected by end-1993.

[l] The agreement aims to phase out tariffs on trade in the area.

[m] Panama participates in summits but is not ready to participate fully in regional integration.

of Central America agreed to form an FTA by 1996, but it is not very clear what effect NAFTA will have on this or on the Mexico-Chile free trade agreement signed between the two in September 1991. Venezuela has also signed a similar agreement with the countries of Central America. Fourth, in 1990, LAIA agreed to new reductions in mutual tariffs and to trade liberalization measures. In December 1989, the Andean Group set 1995 and 1997 as the respective years for the formation of an FTA and a CM. In November 1991, these targets were accelerated to, respectively, 1992 and 1993. Fifth, in July 1990, Argentina and Brazil opted for the creation of a CM by the end of 1994, and in March 1991, Paraguay and Uruguay signed to join them in 1995 in a similar association (MERCOSUR). Sixth, in 1991, Colombia, Mexico, and Venezuela agreed to liberalize trade and investment by the end of 1993, and in January 1991, Venezuela and the countries of Central America agreed to establish an FTA by 1996. Finally, in 1990, CARICOM agreed on a new timetable for the establishment of their CET: the phasing in was set to commence in January 1991 (later postponed), and the CET was to be fully operative by January 1994. They also agreed to remove all remaining barriers on mutual trade by July 1991, but this has not been achieved. The subgroup of CARICOM known as the Organization of East Caribbean States (OECS), comprising seven nations, agreed to implement CARICOM's CET ahead of schedule, but only Dominica and St. Vincent have managed to do so. In early 1991, OECS agreed to carry out the phased elimination of all quantitative restrictions on intrabloc imports.

In Africa, there are several schemes of economic integration. The Customs and Economic Union of Central Africa, generally known by its French name, Union Economique de l'Afrique Centrale (UDEAC), established by the Treaty of Brazzaville in 1973, comprises Cameroon, Central African Republic, Chad, the People's Republic of Congo, Gabon, and Equatorial Guinea (joined in 1985). The original aim of the bloc was to create a CU, a monetary union, and a common customs administration for trade with the outside world, but a year later, all aims were effectively abandoned and intrabloc trade in manufactures was confined to commodities produced by companies granted the so-called Taxe Unique system. The Communauté Economique de l'Afrique de l'Ouest (CEAO), which was formed under the Treaty of Abidjan in 1973, consists of Burkina Faso (formerly Upper Volta), the Ivory Coast, Mali, Mauritania, Niger, and Senegal; Benin joined in 1984. The members effectively form a common currency zone since they are all of the CFA Franc Zone, but that is all that is left because efforts to create a full CU have not succeeded. Member countries of the CEAO, except for Mauritania, plus Benin and Togo, are participants in a monetary union. In 1973, the Mano River Union (MRU) was established between Liberia and Sierra Leone, but they were joined by Guinea in 1980. The MRU is a CU that involves a certain degree of cooperation, particularly in the industrial sector. The Economic Community of West African States (ECOWAS) was formed in 1975 and now has sixteen members: it consists of all those countries who participate in UDEAC, CEAO, and MRU plus some other West African States.

Despite its name, ECOWAS is a CM with a Fund for Cooperation, Compensation and Development (FCCD) to assist the least-developed members of the bloc facing difficulties because of integration, but in reality, all this is no more than ink on paper. In 1969, the Southern African Customs Union (SACU) was established among Botswana, Lesotho, Swaziland, and the Republic of South Africa. The Economic Community of the Countries of the Great Lakes (CEPGL), a CM aiming at joint financing of projects by both domestic and foreign sources, was created in 1976 by Rwananda, Burundi, and Zaire. Until its collapse in 1977, there was the East African Community (EAC) among Kenya, Tanzania, and Uganda. In 1981, fifteen states from the Eastern and Southern African region adopted the Treaty for a Preferential Free Trade Area (PTA): Angola, Botswana, the Comoros, Djibouti, Ethiopia, Kenya, Lesotho, Malawi, Mauritius, Mozambique, Swaziland, Tanzania, Uganda, Zambia, and Zimbabwe. The aim is eventually to create an EU. In 1983, the Economic Community of Central African States (EEAC, abbreviation from French) was created by eleven nations in Equatorial and Central Africa. There are also many smaller subregional groupings such as the Kagera River Basin Organization (KBO), the Lake Tanganyika and Kivu Basin Organization (LTKBC), and the Southern African Development Coordination Council (SADCC).

As for North Africa, in August 1984, a treaty was signed by Libya and Morocco to establish the Arab-African Union, whose main aim is to tackle their political conflicts in the Sahara Desert. In 1989, the Arab-Maghreb Union (AMU) was formed among Algeria, Libya, Mauritania, Morocco, and Tunisia with the aim of eliminating all barriers to the free movement of people, goods, and services across the borders of the member states; the aim is to create an EC-type organization with EC-type institutions. Egypt participates in the Arab Cooperation Council (ACC), which was created in 1990 to encourage economic ties among the members and to boost "Arab solidarity"; other members are Iraq, Jordan, and the Yemen Arab Republic (discussed later).

Several other schemes were in existence in the past but have been discontinued while others never got off the ground. Hence, a unique characteristic of economic integration in Africa is the multiplicity and overlapping of the schemes. For example, in West Africa alone, there is a total of thirty-two schemes (and intergovernmental organizations), which is why a Benin Union (BU) consisting of Benin, Ghana, Nigeria, and Togo was recommended by the United Nations Economic Commission for Africa (see UNECA, 1984) in an attempt to rationalize economic integration and cooperation arrangements in West Africa. This approach has recently been applied to most African schemes by the Lagos Plan of Action (1980) for rationalizing and providing a unifying framework for existing schemes and for establishing a CM in Sub-Saharan Africa, and this seems to be succeeding since no new schemes have been formed since then. Table 6.3 provides most of the information on Africa.

Asia does not figure prominently in the league of economic integration, but this is not surprising given the existence of such large—either in population or

Table 6.3
Regional Trade Arrangements in Africa

	CEAO /b 1972 FTA	CEPGL 1976 FTA	EAC /c 1967 EU	ECOWAS 1975 FTA	MRU /b 1973 CU	PTA /d 1981 FTA	SACU 1969 CU	UDEAC /e 1964 FTA	Sene Gambia 1981 CON	Lagos Plan of Action 1980 EU
Angola	●					●				●
Benin	●			●						●
Botswana						●	●			●
Burkino Faso		●		●						●
Burundi			●			●				●
Cameroon								●		●
Cape Verde				●						●
C.A.R.								●		●
Chad								●		●
Comoros						●				●
Congo								●		●
Cote d'Ivoire	●			●						●
Djibouti						●				●
Equatorial Guinea										●
Ethiopia						●				●
Gabon								●		●
Gambia, The				●					●	●
Ghana				●						●
Guinea				●	● /f					●
Guinea-Bissau				●						●
Kenya			●			●				●
Lesotho						●	●			●
Liberia				●	●					●
Madagascar						●				●
Malawi						●				●
Mali	●			●						●

Founded:
Objective: /a

Table 6.3 (continued)

Founded: Objective: /a	CEAO /b 1972 FTA	CEPGL 1976 FTA	EAC /c 1967 EU	ECOWAS 1975 FTA	MRU /b 1973 CU	PTA /d 1981 FTA	SACU 1969 CU	UDEAC /e 1964 FTA	Sene Gambia 1981 CON	Lagos Plan of Action 1980 EU
Mauritania	•			•						•
Mauritius						•				•
Mozambique						•				•
Namibia							•			•
Niger	•			•						•
Nigeria				•						•
Rwanda		•				•				•
Senegal	•			•						•
Seychelles									•	•
Sierra Leone				•	•					•
Somalia						•				•
South Africa							•			•
Sudan						•				•
Swaziland						•	•			•
Tanzania			•			•				•
Togo				•						•
Uganda			•			•				•
Zaire		•								•
Zambia						•				•
Zimbabwe						•				•

Source: Torre and Kelly (1992).

a FTA: free trade area; CU: customs union; EU: economic union, CON: confederation.
b In effect since 1974.
c Dismantled in 1978.
d In effect since 1984.
e In effect since 1966.
f Joined in 1980.

gross national product (GNP) terms—countries as China, India, and Japan. The Regional Cooperation for Development (RCD) is a very limited arrangement for sectoral integration among Iran, Pakistan, and Turkey. The Association of South-East Asian Nations (ASEAN) comprises six nations: Brunei, Indonesia, Malaysia, the Philippines, Singapore, and Thailand. ASEAN was founded in 1967 in the shadow of the Vietnam War. After almost a decade of inactivity it was galvanized into renewed vigor in 1976 by the security problems that the reunification of Vietnam seemed to present to its membership. The drive for the establishment of ASEAN and for its vigorous reactivation in 1976 was both political and strategic. However, right from the start, economic cooperation was one of the most important aims of ASEAN; indeed, most of the vigorous activities of the group between 1976 and 1978 were predominantly in the economic field.

Recently, a number of proposals have been put forward for enhancing regional cooperation and, in some instances, for the liberalization of Asian trade. In December 1990, the Malaysian prime minister proposed the formation of an East Asian Economic Grouping (EAEG) to speak on behalf of the Asian countries in multinational organizations and negotiations. This was later transformed into the East Asia Economic Caucus (EAEC) to act as a consultative forum for the region on world trade problems. Other proposals have also been forthcoming; for instance, Thailand recommended the formation of an ASEAN FTA (AFTA) within fifteen years, and Indonesia suggested the establishment of common effective preferential tariffs on selected products; these were formally accepted by the ASEAN ministers in January 1992.

Since this area is closely intertwined with Australia and New Zealand, it should be added that about a decade ago, these two countries entered into an FTA arrangement (the New Zealand Australia Free Trade Area—NAFTA). NAFTA was later replaced by the more important Australia New Zealand Closer Economic Relations and Trade Agreement (ANZCERTA, now simply CER): not only have major trade barriers been removed, but significant effects on the New Zealand economy have been experienced as a result (see Mayes, 1988).

The experience of Asia and these two nations, together with the latest developments, is displayed in the top half of Table 6.4. One should add that for the Asia-Pacific region as a whole, there also exist some important institutions:

1. the Pacific Economic Cooperation Conference (PECC), which is a tripartite structured organization with representatives from governments, businesses, and academic circles and with secretarial work being handled between general meetings by the country next hosting a meeting;

2. the Pacific Trade and Development Conference (PAFTAD), which is an academically oriented organization;

3. the Pacific Basin Economic Council (PBEC), which is a private sector business organization for regional cooperation; and

4. the Pacific Telecommunications Conference (PTC), which is a specialized organization for regional cooperation in this field.

Table 6.4
Regional Trade Arrangements in Asia-Pacific and Middle East

	Existing Arrangements						Prospective Arrangements	
Founded: Objective: /a	ANZCERTA 1983 FTA	ASEAN 1967 FTA	ACM/a 1964 CU	ECO/b 1985	GCC 1981 CU	AFTA/c	EAEC/d/e	APEC/e
Australia	•							•
Brunei		•				•	•	•
China							•	•
Hong Kong								•
Indonesia		•				•	•	•
Japan							•	•
Korea, Republic of							•	•
Malaysia	•	•				•	•	•
New Zealand	•							•
Philippines		•				•	•	•
Singapore		•				•	•	•
Taiwan Prov. of China								•
Thailand		•				•	•	•

Middle East

Bahrain
Egypt
Islamic Rep. of Iran
Iraq
Jordan
Kuwait
Libya
Oman
Qatar
Saudi Arabia
Syria
United Arab Emirates
Yemen

Other Countries

Canada
Mauritania
Pakistan
Turkey
United States

Source: Torre and Kelly (1992).

[a]FTA: free trade area; CU: customs union.

[b]The purpose of this group is bilateral trade promotion and cooperation in industrial planning.

[c]Thailand proposal endorsed by ASEAN ministers in 1991.

[d]This grouping was initially proposed by Malaysia in 1990.

[e]Regional grouping to represent members' views in multilateral negotiating forums.

This leaves some of the satellites of the former USSR, the former USSR itself, and the Middle East. With regard to the former, some countries intend to join the EC, and agreements of association have already been reached—see the right hand side of Table 6.1. As for the former USSR countries, soon after the Soviet Union was dismantled, Russia and another sixteen nations formed the Commonwealth of Independent States (CIS), which is effectively a very involved type of EU. Turning to the Middle East, one should begin with a scheme that covers more than one continent: the Arab League (AL). The AL consists of twenty-one (twenty-two if one included Palestine) independent nations, extending from the Gulf in the East to Mauritania and Morocco in the West. Hence, the geographical area covered by the group includes the whole of North Africa, a large part of the Middle East, Somalia, and Djibouti. The aim of the AL is to strengthen the ties linking Arab states, to coordinate their policies and activities and direct them to their common good, and to mediate in disputes between them. The Arab Economic Council, whose membership consists of all Arab ministers of economic affairs, was entrusted with suggesting ways for economic development, cooperation, and coordination (see Sayigh, 1982, p. 123). The Council for Arab Economic Unity (CAEU), which was formed in 1957, had the aim of establishing an integrated economy of all members of the AL. In 1964, the Arab Common Market was formed among Egypt, Iraq, Jordan, and Syria. However, nothing really serious has resulted from any of these organizations. The Gulf Cooperation Council (GCC) was established among Bahrain, Kuwait, Oman, Qatar, Saudi Arabia, and the United Arab Emirates to bring together the Gulf states and to prepare the ground for them to join forces in the economic, political, and military spheres. The ACC and Arab-Maghreb Union have already been mentioned in the African context. These and recent developments in this area are shown in the bottom half of Table 6.4.

THE RATIONALE FOR ECONOMIC INTEGRATION AMONG LDCs

There is no general overall rationale for economic integration among the LDCs. For example, in the case of the EAC, Kenya, Tanzania, and Uganda were brought together into the scheme purely for the administrative convenience of the British colonialists. That is why the EAC cannot claim to be the world's first experience of economic integration; at the beginning, it was not a *voluntary* association. As we have seen, in the case of some West African blocs, the ties have been historical in the sense that the French left behind a number of shared institutions and the same official language and currency. In Southern Africa, SADCC (see Table 6.5) was established mainly to enable the member countries to break away from heavy reliance on the Republic of South Africa. Later, international organizations such as the United Nations (UN) thought of economic integration as a means of enhancing political stability among the LDCs, especially in Africa;

Table 6.5

Some Economic Indicators for Sub-Saharan Africa (1989 unless otherwise indicated)

Country	GDP		Population		GNP Per Capita	
	m. of US$	Annual % Growth Rate 1980-89	1000	Annual % Growth Rate 1980-89	US$	Annual % Growth Rate 1980-89
WEST AFRICA						
ECOWAS						
CEAO						
Benin	1,600	1.8	4,593	3.2	380	-1.8
Burkina Faso	2,460	5.0	8,776	2.6	310	2.3
Cote d'Ivoire	7,170	1.2	11,713	4.0	790	-3.0
Mali	2,080	3.8	8,212	2.5	260	1.0
Mauritania	910	1.4	1,954	2.6	490	-2.2
Niger, The	2,040	-1.6	7,479	3.5	290	-5.0
Senegal	4,660	3.1	7,211	3.0	650	0.0
MRU						
Guinea	2,750	...	5,547	2.5	430	...
Liberia	...	...	2,475	3.1	...	...
Sierra Leone	890	0.6	4,040	2.4	200	-3.2
OTHER ECOWAS						
Cape Verde	281	5.8	369	2.5	760	3.2
Gambia, The	196	2.2	848	3.3	230	-1.0
Ghana	5,260	2.8	14,425	3.4	380	-0.8
Guinea Bissau	173	3.4	960	1.9	180	1.5
Nigeria	28,920	-0.4	113,665	3.3	250	-3.6
Togo	1,340	1.4	3,507	3.5	390	-2.4

Table 6.5 (continued)

Country	GDP		Population		GNP Per Capita	
	m. of US$	Annual % Growth Rate 1980-89	1000	Annual % Growth Rate 1980-89	US$	Annual % Growth Rate 1980-89
CENTRAL AFRICA						
UDEAC						
Cameroon	11,080	3.2	11,554	3.2	1,010	0.7
CAR	1,050	1.4	2,951	2.7	390	-1.5
Chad	1,020	6.5	5,537	2.4	190	3.9
Congo	2,270	3.9	2,208	3.4	930	0.1
Equ. Guinea	149	...	334	5.1	430	...
Gabon	3,060	1.0	1,105	3.7	2,770	-2.6
CEPGL						
Burundi	960	4.3	5,299	2.9	220	1.6
Rwanda	2,170	1.5	6,893	3.3	310	-1.9
Zaire	9,610	1.9	34,442	3.1	260	-1.6
OTHER CEN. AFRICA						
Sao Tome & Prin.	43	-2.8	122	3.0	360	-5.7
EAST AND SOUTHERN AFRICA						
PTA						
Angola	7,720	...	9,694	2.5	620	...
Burundi	960	4.3	5,299	2.9	220	1.6
Comoros	209	3.1	459	3.7	460	-0.6
Djibouti	...	...	410	3.5	n.a.	n.a.
Ethiopia	5,420	1.9	48,861	2.9	120	-1.1
Kenya	7,130	4.1	23,277	3.8	380	0.4
Lesotho	340	3.7	1,722	2.7	470	-0.5
Malawi	1,410	2.7	8,230	3.4	180	-0.1
Mauritius	1,740	5.9	1,062	1.0	1,950	5.3
Mozambique	1,100	-1.4	15,357	2.7	80	-6.0
Rwanda	2,170	1.5	6,893	3.3	310	-1.9

Swaziland	683	4.1	761	3.4	900	0.6
Somalia	1,090	3.0	6,089	3.0	170	-1.3
-Sudan	...	1.1	24,423	3.0	...	-1.8
Uganda	4,460	2.5	16,772	3.2	250	-1.0
Tanzania	2,540	2.6	25,627	3.5	120	-1.6
Zambia	4,700	0.8	7,837	3.7	390	-3.8
Zimbabwe	5,250	2.7	9,567	3.6	640	-0.8
SADCC						
Angola	7,720	...	9,694	2.5	620	...
Botswana	2,500	11.3	1,217	3.4	1,600	6.7
Lesotho	340	3.7	1,722	2.7	470	-0.5
Malawi	1,410	2.7	8,230	3.4	180	-0.1
Mozambique	1,100	-1.4	15,357	2.7	80	-6.0
Namibia	...	...	...	...	...	...
Swaziland	683	4.1	761	3.4	900	0.6
Tanzania	2,540	2.6	25,627	3.4	120	-1.6
Zambia	4,700	0.8	7,837	3.5	390	-3.8
Zimbabwe	5,250	2.7	9,567	3.7	640	-0.8
				3.6		
SACU						
Botswana	2,500	11.3	1,217	3.4	1,600	6.7
Lesotho	340	3.7	1,722	2.7	470	-0.5
Namibia	...	...	...	...	...	...
Swaziland	683	4.1	761	3.4	900	0.6
South Africa	80,370	1.5	34,925	2.4	2,460	-0.8
Other East & South Africa						
Madagascar	2,280	0.8	11,174	2.8	230	-2.6
Seychelles	285	2.5	68	0.9	4,170	1.7
Total SSA	171k	2.1	480k	3.2	340	-1.2

Source: World Bank, *World Development Report* (1991), *World Bank Atlas* (1990).

227

hence it was conceived to be a good vehicle for promoting their economic development, especially when the economies concerned were so small and poor—see Table 6.4 for the basic data for the various members of economic integration schemes. The Economic Commission for Latin America (ECLA) preached economic integration during the late 1950s in that area on the understanding that the liberalization of intra-area trade was essential for the success of economic development based on a strategy of import-substitution. The UN Economic Commission for Africa (UNECA) had been openly preaching economic integration as the only sensible way to promote Africa's development.

It would be futile to continue along such lines, especially when the record of achievement is almost blank. Given the immense popularity of economic integration among the LDCs demonstrated in the previous section, this statement must come as a complete surprise. Indeed, it is tantamount to an outright paradox: very high popularity going hand in hand with very low effectiveness. However, there are obvious reasons for the lack of achievement, the most significant being the apparent mutual contradiction in objectives: the pursuit of fundamentally inward-looking national development strategies and the openness in trade inherent in regional economic integration. However, there are also practical implementation problems:

In most cases, initial deadlines for the removal of barriers to intraregional trade were postponed, often several times. Normally, a reduction in quantitative restrictions and import tariffs was contemplated. In a number of cases (for example, the LAFTA/LAIA and PTA), delays in liberalizing intraregional trade reflected a lack of automaticity in implementation timetables, with reciprocal tariff reductions made subject to periodic negotiating rounds and consensus, either on a product-by-product basis or on a request-and-offer basis. In addition, in many cases (for example, the ASEAN, Andean Pact, CEAO, LAFTA/LAIA, and PTA), reductions in trade barriers were not based on across-the-board reductions in tariff and non-tariff barriers but on a system of positive "lists" that gave participating countries considerable latitude to exclude sensitive products from the set of items subject to reciprocal trade concessions, and biased the selection of products in favor of those with limited potential for intraregional trade. In a number of cases (for example, the ASEAN, ECOWAS, and PTA) that aimed to create a [FTA]—permanently or as a precursor to a [CU]—the coverage of intra-area trade liberalization was also limited by fairly restrictive rules of origin; these narrowed the range of goods eligible for tariff preferences on the basis of value-added criteria, and in some cases (for example, the ECOWAS and PTA) also on the basis of enterprise ownership criteria. . . .

Where the establishment of a [CU] has been an operational target (and not only a statement of intent), the implementation of a [CET] has proven elusive. The initial deadlines were in most cases not met. For example, the CACM agreed in principle to a [CET] but [this] was rendered largely ineffective—mainly because of exemptions from external tariffs granted by some member countries for "necessary" imports from outside the region—over most of the period since the CACM was formed. The GCC adopted a minimum [CET] in principle—albeit with some delays—but exceptions have been applied for certain members, significant variations among countries remain, and non-compliance has persisted in some areas—particularly concerning luxury items. In most other cases, nonimplementation of the envisaged [CET] has been the rule. (Torre and Kelly, 1992, pp. 32–33)

Table 6.6 sets out the objectives and implementation records in a clear and easily digestible manner. All that needs adding is to state that similar observations can be made with regard to the official allocation of new manufacturing industries and free factor mobility. However, what is more important are the reasons behind such failure. Here, the answer lies in the contradiction stated above, as well as in the drive, especially in the past, for the establishment of import-competing industries, which by their very nature work against intrabloc trade liberalization, and the deteriorating economic conditions in the outside world during the 1970s and 1980s.

Further considerations along these lines are pursued later. At this juncture, it is more fruitful to consider the more fundamental question of whether or not there is a purely economic rationale for economic integration among the LDCs. Since a thorough discussion of this requires a book in its own right (see Robson, 1983; El-Agraa, 1989c), here I merely highlight the pertinent points.

Trade Creation and Trade Diversion

Viner (1950) and Byé (1950) were the first to challenge the proposition that economic integration was equivalent to a move to free trade by stressing that CU formation combined two contradictory elements: free trade between the partners and protection against the outside world. This combination could result in *trade creation* (TC) and/or *trade diversion* (TD). TC is the replacement of expensive domestic production by cheaper imports from a partner, and TD is the replacement of cheaper initial imports from the outside world by more expensive imports from a partner. They stressed the point that TC is beneficial since it does not affect the rest of the world (W) while TD is harmful, and it is therefore the relative strength of these two effects that determines whether or not CU formation is to be advocated. Hence, it is important to understand the implications of these two concepts.

Assuming perfect competition in both the commodity and factor markets, automatic full employment of all resources, costless adjustment procedures, perfect factor mobility nationally but perfect immobility across national borders, prices determined by cost, three countries—H (the home country), P (the potential CU partner) and W—plus all the traditional assumptions employed in tariff theory, one can use a simple diagram to illustrate these two concepts.

In Figure 6.1, S_W is W's perfectly elastic tariff-free supply curve for this commodity; S_H is H's supply curve while S_{H+P} is the joint H and P tariff-free supply curve. With a nondiscriminatory tariff imposed by H of AD (t_H), the effective supply curve facing H is $BREFQT$, that is, its own supply curve up to E and W's, subject to the tariff $[S_W(1 + t_H)]$, after that. The domestic price is therefore OD, which gives domestic production of Oq_3 and imports of q_2q_3. H

Table 6.6
Selected Regional Trade Arrangements in Developing Countries

NAME	OBJECTIVE/INSTRUMENT	IMPLEMENTATION RECORD
CACM	Customs union and joint industrial planning. Elimination of tariffs, QRs within region. Adoption of Common External Tariff (CET).	Initially on schedule; most restrictions lifted by early 1970s, but re-introduced 1980s. CET not effective in all members.
Andean Pact	Customs union and joint industrial planning. CET by end-1980. Modified: 1988. Revived: 1989. Establish FTA by 1992, common market by 1993, phase out exceptions by 1995. Harmonize macroeconomic policies.	Postponed several times.
LAFTA/LAIA	Free trade association and industrial planning; common lists of products to be implemented by 1972. Facilitation of bilateral cooperation.	Partial implementation in 1960s. Common lists not liberalized on schedule.
ECOWAS	Free trade area and customs union, development and policy harmonization. Original targets for liberalization and CET by 1990. New target to eliminate NTBs by 1995. Enhance labor and capital mobility.	Progress negligible.
PTA	Free trade area: harmonization of policies. Elimination of tariffs on all goods traded in the PTA by 2000; reduction of NTBs.	Some progress on tariffs.
SADCC	1. Reduce economic dependence (on South Africa); 2. foster cooperation for balanced growth; and 3. coordinate and secure external support.	Successful in achieving 2 and 3.
ASEAN	Regional industrial cooperation; free trade area (trade policy subordinate to regional import substitution).	FTA repeatedly postponed; industrial cooperation scarcely implemented.
GCC	Political coordination and customs union; harmonization of policies. CET and Customs Union originally by 1986, now by March 1993.	1982 -- Virtual elimination of customs tariffs. 1983 -- Unification of tariff schedules, liberalization of trade in services.

Sources: World Bank, *World Development Report* (1991); IMF, *Direction of Trade Statistics.*

Figure 6.1
Trade Creation and Trade Diversion

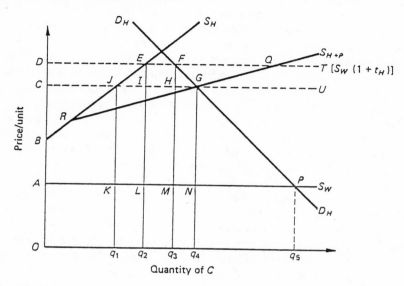

Quantity of C

pays q_2LMq_3 for these imports while the domestic consumer pays q_2EFq_3 with the difference (*LEFM*) being tariff revenue that accrues to the *H* government. This revenue can be viewed as a transfer from the consumers to the government with the implication that when the government spends it, the marginal valuation of that expenditure should be exactly equal to its marginal valuation by private consumers so that no distortions should occur.

If *H* and *W* form a CU, the free trade position will be restored so that Oq_5 will be consumed in *H* and this amount will be imported from *W*. Hence free trade is obviously the ideal situation. But if *H* and *P* form a CU, the tariff will still apply to *W* while it is removed from *P*. The effective supply curve in this case is *BRGQT*. Price falls to *OC*, resulting in a fall in domestic production to Oq_1, increase in consumption to Oq_4, and an increase in imports to q_1q_4. These imports now come from *P*.

The welfare implications of these changes can be examined by employing the concepts of consumers' and producers' (consumer/producer for short) surpluses. As a result of increased consumption, consumer surplus rises by *CDFG*. Part of this (*CDEJ*) is a fall in producer surplus due to the decline in domestic production and another part (*IEFH*) is a portion of the tariff revenue now transferred back to the consumer subject to the same condition of equal marginal valuation. This leaves the triangles *JEI* and *HFG* as gains from CU formation. However, before one concludes whether or not these triangles represent *net* gains, one needs to consider the overall effects more carefully.

The fall in domestic production from Oq_2 to Oq_1 leads to increased imports of q_1q_2. These cost q_1JIq_2 to import from P while they originally cost q_1JEq_2 to produce domestically. (Note that these resources are supposed to be employed elsewhere in the economy without any adjustment costs or redundancies.) There is therefore a saving of JEI. The increase in consumption from Oq_3 to Oq_4 leads to new imports of q_3q_4, which cost q_3HGq_4 to import from P. These give a welfare satisfaction to the consumers equal to q_3FGq_4. There is therefore an increase in satisfaction of HFG. However, the *initial* imports of q_2q_3 originally cost the country q_2LMq_3, but these imports now come from P costing q_2IHq_3. Therefore these imports lead to a loss equal to the loss in government revenue of $LIHM$ ($IEFH$ being a retransfer subject to the same condition of equal marginal valuation). It follows that the triangle gains ($JEI + HFG$) have to be compared with the loss of tariff revenue ($LIHM$) before a definite conclusion can be made regarding whether or not the net effect of CU formation has been one of gain or loss.

It should also be apparent that q_2q_3 represents, in terms of our definitions, TD, and $q_1q_2 + q_3q_4$ represent TC (it is now generally accepted that the consumption effect has to be included in TC—Viner and Byé were concerned with production effects only), or alternatively that area JEI plus area HFG are TC (benefits) while area $LIHM$ is TD (loss). It is then obvious that TC is economically desirable while TD is undesirable. Hence Viner and Byé's conclusion that the relative strength of these two effects should determine whether CU formation is beneficial or harmful.

It should also be apparent that if the initial price is that given by the intersection of D_H and S_H (due to a higher tariff rate in H), the CU would result in pure TC since the tariff rate is prohibitive. If the price is initially OC (due to a lower tariff rate in H), then CU formation would result in pure TD. It should also be clear that the size of the gains and losses depends on the price elasticities of S_H, S_{H+P}, and D_H and on the divergence between S_W and S_{H+P}, that is, cost differences.

However, this does not settle the question. Viner and Byé's conclusion was challenged by Cooper and Massell (1965a). They suggested that the reduction in price from OD to OC should be considered in two stages: first, reduce the tariff indiscriminately (i.e., for both W and P) to AC, which gives the same CU price and production, consumption, and import changes; second, introduce the CU starting from the new price OC. The effect of these two steps is that the gains from TC ($JEI + HFG$) still accrue while the losses from TD ($LIHM$) no longer apply since the new effective supply curve facing H is $BJGU$, which ensures that imports continue to come from W at the cost of q_2LMq_3. In addition, the new imports due to TC ($q_1q_2 + q_3q_4$) generate tariff revenue of $JILK$ plus $MHGN$. Cooper and Massell then conclude that a policy of *unilateral tariff reduction* (UTR) is superior to CU formation.

In economics, conclusions seem to have no permament validity, and the UTR proposition is no exception. In 1981b, Wonnacott and Wonnacott set out to prove that when transport costs and the trade restrictions exercised by the partners to the economic integration scheme as well as by the outside world are taken into consideration, it can be shown that CU formation is superior to UTR. However, El-Agraa and Jones (1983) and El-Agraa (1983) demonstrate that the Wonnacotts' conclusion is based on an analysis that is far removed from the economic integration context—see El-Agraa (1989c) for a summary—and Berglas (1983) shows that it can be valid in only one case out of a number of possible permutations, a conclusion endorsed by the Wonnacotts (1981a). The Berglas conclusion is, of course, encouraging for the LDCs, but it rests crucially on the ability of the partners to an economic integration scheme to exercise control over the terms of trade. This depends on the LDCs under consideration: the very poor who depend on the export of one or two basic raw materials or semimanufactured products stand no chance in this respect, but the newly industrializing economies (NIEs) and those with similar characteristics may do so. Hence, the level of development of the partners is of critical importance. However, I shall not pursue this point here simply because there are issues that are more pertinent for the LDCs, and to these I now turn.

Preference for Industrial Production

One would be perfectly justified in stating that the assumptions behind the previous analysis do not take the specific circumstances of the LDCs into account. Realizing this, but in completely different contexts, Cooper and Massell (1965b) and Johnson (1965) tried to incorporate a "public good" element into the analysis. Since Johnson's approach is conducted in a manner not far removed from my analysis, I confine my presentation to his contribution.

Johnson assumed that governments use tariffs to achieve certain noneconomic (social, political, and so on) objectives; actions taken by governments are aimed at offsetting differences between private and social costs and benefits—they are therefore rational efforts; government policy is a rational response to the demands of the electorate; and countries have a preference for industrial production. In addition to these assumptions, he makes a distinction among private and public consumption goods, real income (utility enjoyed from both private and public consumption, where consumption is the sum of planned consumption expenditure and planned investment expenditure), and real product (defined as total production of privately appropriable goods and services).

The assumption regarding the preference for industrial production has particular relevance to the LDCs. This is because many LDCs, especially in Latin America and Asia (e.g., India), gave early preference to industrialization as the touchstone of development. They also realized that the across-the-board preferences dictated by the GATT's conditions for the formation of CUs and FTAs were either not working or not enough to foster development in the early schemes that were tried out.

Johnson's assumptions have important implications. First, competition among political parties will make the government adopt policies that will tend to maximize consumer satisfaction from both private and collective consumption goods. Satisfaction is obviously maximized when the rate of satisfaction per unit of resources is the same in both types of consumption goods. Second, collective preference for industrial production implies that consumers are willing to expand industrial production (and industrial employment) beyond what it would be under free trade.

Tariffs are the main source of financing this policy, and protection will be carried to the point where the value of the marginal utility derived from collective consumption and industrial activity is just equal to the marginal excess cost of protected industrial production.

The marginal excess cost of protected industrial production consists of two parts: the marginal production cost and the marginal private consumption cost. The marginal production cost is equal to the proportion by which domestic cost exceeds world market cost. In a very simple model this is equal to the tariff rate. The marginal private consumption cost is equal to the loss of consumer surplus due to a fall in consumption brought about by the tariff.

In equilibrium, the proportional marginal excess private cost of protected production measures the marginal "degree of preference" for industrial production. This is illustrated in Figure 6.2, where S_W is the world supply curve; D_H is the free trade constant-utility demand curve; S_H is the domestic supply curve; and S_{H+u} is the marginal private cost of protected industrial production, including the excess private consumption cost. (FE is the first component of marginal excess cost—determined by the excess marginal cost of domestic production in relation to the free trade situation due to the tariff [AB]—and the area GED [$= IHJ$] is the second component, which is the deadweight loss in consumer surplus due to the tariff.) The height of VV above S_W represents the marginal value of industrial production in collective consumption, and its slope reflects the assumption of diminishing marginal utility.

The maximization of real income is achieved at the intersection of VV with S_{H+u} requiring the use of tariff rate BA/OA to increase industrial production from Oq_1 to Oq_2. Note that, in equilibrium, the government is maximizing real income, not real product: maximization of real income makes it necessary to sacrifice real product in order to gratify the preference for collective consumption of industrial production.

To make the model useful for the analysis of CU issues it is necessary to alter some of the assumptions. Let us assume that industrial production is not one aggregate but a variety of products in which countries have varying degrees of comparative advantage, that countries differ in their overall comparative advantage in industry as compared with nonindustrial production, that no country has monopoly/monopsony power (conditions for optimum tariffs do not exist), and that no export subsidies are allowed (GATT rules).

The variety of industrial production allows countries to be both importers and exporters of industrial products. This, in combination with the "preference for industrial production," will motivate each country to practice some degree of

Figure 6.2
Preference for Industrial Production

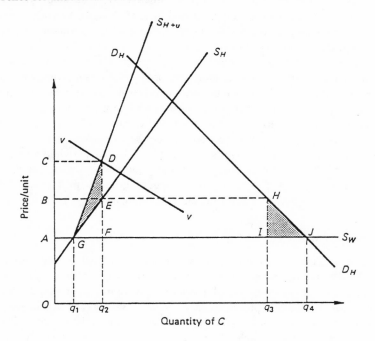

Quantity of C

protection. A country can gratify its preference for industrial production only by protecting import-competing industries. Hence the condition for equilibrium remains the same: $VV = S_{H + u}$. However, $S_{H + u}$ is slightly different because, first, the protection of import-competing industries will reduce exports of both industrial and nonindustrial products (for balance of payments purposes). Hence, in order to increase total industrial production by one unit it would be necessary to increase protected industrial production by more than one unit to compensate for the induced loss of industrial exports. Second, the protection of import-competing industries reduces industrial exports by raising their production costs (due to perfect factor mobility). The stronger this effect, ceteris paribus, the higher the marginal excess cost of industrial production. This marginal excess cost will be greater, the larger the industrial sector compared with the nonindustrial sector and the larger the protected industrial sector relative to the exporting industrial sector.

In the event of CU formation, if reciprocal tariff reductions are arrived at on a "most-favored nation" (MFN) basis, the reduction of a country's tariff rate will increase imports from *all* the other countries. If reduction is, however, discriminatory (starting from a position of nondiscrimination), there are two advantages: first, each country can offer its partner an increase in exports of industrial products without any loss of its own industrial production by diverting imports from third countries (TD); second, when TD is exhausted, any increase in partner industrial exports to this country is exactly equal to the reduction in industrial production in the same country (TC), hence eliminating the gain to third countries.

Therefore, discriminatory reciprocal tariff reduction costs each country less, in terms of reduction in domestic industrial production (if any) incurred per unit increase in partner industrial production, than does nondiscriminatory reciprocal tariff reduction. On the other hand, preferential tariff reduction imposes an additional cost on the tariff-reducing country: the excess of the costs of imports from the partner country over their cost in the world market.

The implications of this analysis are that both TC and TD yield a gain to the CU partners; TD is preferable to TC for the preference-granting country since a sacrifice of domestic production is not required; and both TC and TD may lead to increased efficiency due to economies of scale.

Economies of Scale

If one has no qualms about the assumptions made, Johnson's analysis provides a forceful argument in favor of economic integration, especially among the LDCs. However, instead of using valuable space to examine the realistic nature or otherwise of these assumptions, it may be more productive to consider other aspects of the economic integration issue. These relate to the so-called dynamic effects (Balassa, 1961), which relate to the numerous means by which economic integration may influence the rate of growth of GNP of the participating nations and which include the following:

1. scale economies made possible by the increased size of the market for both firms and industries operating below optimum capacity before integration occurs;

2. economies external to the firm that may have a downward influence on both specific and general cost structures;

3. the polarization effect, by which is meant the cumulative decline either in relative or absolute terms of the economic situation of a particular participating nation or a specific region within it due either to the benefits of TC becoming concentrated in one region or to the fact that an area may develop a tendency to attract factors of production;

4. the influence of the location and volume of real investment; and

5. the effect of economic efficiency and the smoothness with which trade transactions are carried out due to enhanced competition and changes in uncertainty.

Apart from economies of scale, the possible gains are extremely long-term in nature and cannot be tackled in orthodox economic terms: for example, intensified competition leading to the adoption of best business practices, an American-type attitude, and so on (Scitovsky, 1958) seems like a naive sociopsychological abstraction that has no solid foundation with regard to both the aspirations of

Figure 6.3
Economies of Scale and Customs Unions

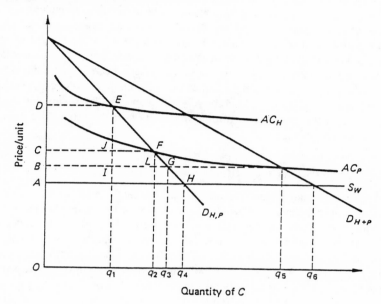

those countries contemplating economic integration (the EC aims to achieve unity within diversity) and its actually materializing.

Economies of scale that are internal to the industry can, however, be analyzed in orthodox economic terms. In Figure 6.3, $D_{H,P}$ is the identical demand curve for this commodity in both H and P, and D_{H+P} is their joint demand curve; S_W is again the world supply curve; AC_P and AC_H are the average cost curves for this commodity in P and H, respectively. Free trade is clearly the best policy, resulting in price OA with consumption satisfied entirely by imports of Oq_4 in each of H and P, giving a total of Oq_6.

If H and P impose tariffs, the only justification for this is that uncorrected distortions exist between the privately and socially valued costs in these countries (see El-Agraa and Jones 1981). The best tariff rates to impose are Corden's (1972) 'made-to-measure' tariffs, which can be defined as those that encourage domestic production to a level that just satisfies domestic consumption without giving rise to monopoly profits. These tariffs are equal to AD and AC for H and P, respectively, resulting in Oq_1 and Oq_2 in H and P, respectively.

When H and P enter into a CU, P, being the cheaper producer, will produce the entire union output (Oq_5) at a price OB. Note that this requires a CET of OB/OA, that is, a lower tariff than initially in the more efficient partner. This gives rise to consumption in each of H and P of Oq_3 with gains of $BDEG$ and $BCFG$ for H and P, respectively. Parts of these gains, $BDEI$ for H and $BCFL$

for P, are "cost-reduction" effects; that is, the initial cost of this amount has been reduced due to economies of scale. There also result a production gain for P and a production loss in H due to abandoning production altogether.

Whether CU formation can be justified in terms of the existence of economies of scale will depend on whether the net effect is a gain or a loss (in this example P gains and H loses), as the loss from abandoning production in H must outweigh the consumption gain in order for the tariff to have been imposed in the first place. If the overall result is net gain, then the *distribution of these gains* becomes an important consideration. Alternatively, if economies of scale accrue to an integrated industry, then the *locational distribution* of the production units becomes an essential issue.

The Specific Case of the LDCs

We have seen that certain of the assumptions that have led to the ambiguous results regarding the expected benefits from economic integration are particularly irrelevant to the LDCs in the sense that they are unlikely to be met under their conditions. For example, the first-best policies in the case of economies of scale cannot be carried out by the LDCs simply because their governments cannot possibly raise enough revenue to enable them to do so. Moreover, it was immediately realized (see Meade, 1955; Lipsey, 1960; Brown, 1961) that the static resource reallocation effects of TC and TD have little relevance for the LDCs. The theory suggested that there would be more scope for TC if the countries concerned were *initially* very competitive in production but *potentially* very complementary and that a CU or FTA would be more likely to be trade-creating if the partners conducted most of their foreign trade among themselves. These conditions are unlikely to be satisfied in the majority of the LDCs (see El-Agraa, 1969, for the case of the Arab Common Market; Robson, 1983, for West Africa; El-Agraa, 1989b, for the Arab League). Moreover, most of the effects of integration in the LDCs are bound to be trade-diverting, since most LDCs seek to industrialize at a time when practically all industrial products are imported from either the advanced nations or the NIEs.

On the other hand, it was also realized that an important obstacle to the development of industry in the LDCs is the inadequate size of their individual markets (see Brown, 1961; Hazlewood, 1967, 1975; Metwally, 1979; Robson, 1983). It is, therefore, necessary to increase the market size so as to encourage optimum plant installation; hence the need for economic integration.

Let me put this differently. The neoclassical approach to economic integration among a group of LDCs is based on an entirely different framework. It is built on the understanding that there is a rationale for protecting certain areas of economic activity (especially industry, which is why trade theorists have conceded the "infant industry" argument as the only exception to free trade, but only under very specific conditions—see El-Agraa, 1989a, for a full discussion of this issue) in these countries in order to raise their income levels or their rates of economic growth or to realize certain noneconomic objectives desired for their own sake. Hence, the quest for economic integration among the LDCs has to be seen in the much wider context of economies of scale, which cannot be achieved within single national markets, and divergencies between private and social costs because of distortions in both factor and commodity prices, which are the result of government policies.

Because economies of scale are seen in the context of economic development, their analysis is intimately connected with planned investment decisions. The coordination of investment and production program contributes to a more rational division of labor within the integrated bloc. It widens the scope for efficient investments through the reallocation of available funds within the integrated area together with inflows of capital, new technologies, and know-how from the outside world. This should make it possible to expand production in those industries where economies of scale are likely to occur and to coordinate planning for the large public services, such as transport and communications systems.

Moreover, it is increasingly realized that the industrialization of the LDCs is partly determined by the operations of the multinational enterprises (or transnational corporations—TNCs). These introduce new patterns of production that are largely determined by the differences in the price they charge different nations for technology, specialized intermediate inputs, and other factors imported from the parent enterprise. Furthermore, through their ability to transfer profits from one member country to another in order to take advantage of more liberal tax and profit repatriation policies, they can determine both the pattern and volume of production. Of course, this does not mean that TNCs are undesirable, particularly since they may have no influence on which policies a member nation of an integrated scheme may adopt. However, what is crucial is that the operations of TNCs do not point to the existence of market imperfections.

Since these issues have already been tackled, what needs discussion is the reality that the necessity to increase the size of the market so as to enable appropriate plant installations would result in industries' clustering together in the relatively more advanced of the LDCs under consideration—those that have already commenced the process of industrialization; this is the so-called backwash effect discussed by Brown (1961), Hazlewood (1975), and Robson and Lury (1969).

Brown, using a macroeconomic model, argued that even though the clustering together of industries might be a natural development, the other parties to the economic integration scheme would gain from such an association and that the benefits could be more equitably distributed if some arrangements were introduced for this purpose; this is the so-called spread or multiplier effect discussed by Brown (1961).

These developments have led economists to the conclusion that economic integration in the advanced world is a very different matter from that in the

LDCs (see Hazlewood, 1975; Robson and Lury, 1969; Kahnert *et al.*, 1969; and Robson, 1983). Before examining this conclusion, I need to consider a pertinent model, which is fully explained elsewhere (see El-Agraa, 1979, 1985).

The Model

Although the model is based on certain assumptions meant to simplify the analysis, it could be argued that they are very relevant to the LDCs under consideration. The assumptions are:

1. Factors of production are perfectly mobile within each country but lack the freedom to move across national borders. The economic integration scheme is, therefore, not allowed to introduce measures to divert resources to the industrializing partner. Hence the scheme is necessarily a CU, not a CM.

2. There is a plentiful supply of all factors of production.

3. The newly introduced industrial output is to be sold as a substitute for a product imported from W; hence the CU is purely trade-diverting. This product shall be sold at a price equal to the import price plus the customs duty—this amounts to assuming that the CU has a CET equal to the initial (assumed equal) tariff rate(s).

4. Each partner nation receives customs revenues from those commodities consumed within its territories as well as the revenue from direct and excise taxes collected accordingly.

5. The governments' budgets are to remain balanced throughout, so that any change in government revenue must bring about an equal change in government expenditure. This change in expenditure must fall on goods and services so that transfers are unaltered.

6. No change in investment takes place in any of the partner countries. This might seem a very strange assumption, particularly when a new industrial output is to be introduced. It will become apparent, however, that the relaxation of this assumption will reinforce the conclusions of the model rather than render them invalid.

The newly produced output of manufactured goods by the partner that has already commenced the process of industrialization will be indicated by Q. The tax-free value of the imports displaced by this new product is $Q(1 - t)$, where t is the ad valorem marginal rate of duty in the partner countries 1, 2, and 3. Country 1 is the partner that has already started industrializing; x_1 and x_2 of Q are consumed in 1 and 2, respectively, while the remainder $Q(1 - x_1 - x_2)$ is consumed in 3. Thus the consumption of Q in 2 and 3 together is equal to $Q(1 - x_1)$; m_1, m_2, and m_3 are the total marginal propensities to import (*mpis*) of 1, 2, and 3, respectively. These *mpis* are composed of three parts each: a_1, a_2, and $[m_1 - (a_1 + a_2)]$ are 1's *mpis* for imports from 2, 3, and W, respectively; a_3, a_4, and $[m_2 - (a_3 + a_4)]$ are 2's *mpis* for imports from 1, 3, and W, respectively; and a_5, a_6, and $[m_3 - (a_5 + a_6)]$ are the relevant *mpis* for 3 from 1, 2, and W, respectively, and t^* is the direct marginal tax rate and *mps* ($= 1 - c$) is the marginal propensity to save (s in Table 6.7).

Table 6.7
Representative Data

Variable	t_1	t_2	t_3	t_1^*	t_2^*	t_3^*	s_1	s_2	s_3	a_1	a_2	a_3	a_4	a_5	a_6	m_1	m_2	m_3	x_1	x_2	$1 - x_1 - x_2$
Case 1	0.2	0.2	0.2	0.1	0.1	0.1	0.15	0.15	0.15	0.05	0.05	0.05	0.05	0.05	0.05	0.03	0.03	0.03	0.75	0.125	0.125
	0.2	0.1	0.2	0.1	0.05	0.1	0.15	0.01	0.15	0.01	0.01	0.01	0.01	0.01	0.01	0.05	0.03	0.3	0.75	0.25	0.0
	0.3	0.2	0.2	0.2	0.1	0.1	0.2	0.15	0.15	0.05	0.05	0.05	0.05	0.05	0.05	0.3	0.35	0.3	0.5	0.25	0.25
	0.2	0.3	0.2	0.1	0.2	0.1	0.15	0.2	0.15	0.05	0.05	0.05	0.1	0.05	0.05				0.8	0.1	0.1
	0.3	0.3	0.3	0.2	0.2	0.2	0.2	0.2	0.2	0.05	0.05	0.0	0.05	0.05	0.05						
	Cases XIX-XXII			Cases XV-XVIII			Cases XI-XIV			Cases II-V						Cases VI and VIII			Cases VIII-X		

Note: Case I is the basic case; all other cases have the same values for their variables except for the variables specified. For each category, the case number is to be read from top to bottom.

Table 6.8
Results

Case	$Y_1 = Qx$	$Y_2 = Qx$	$Y_3 = Qx$	$\dfrac{Y_2}{Y_1}$	$\dfrac{Y_3}{Y_1}$	$\dfrac{Y_2}{Y_3}$
			Result			
I	1.999	0.195	0.195	0.097	0.097	1.000
II	2.225	0.590	0.590	0.265	0.265	1.000
III	2.022	0.198	0.198	0.098	0.098	1.000
IV	2.002	0.198	0.218	0.099	0.109	0.908
V	1.976	0.192	0.192	0.097	0.097	1.000
VI	1.787	0.167	0.167	0.094	0.094	1.000
VII	1.996	0.174	0.192	0.087	0.096	0.907
VIII	1.999	0.143	0.246	0.072	0.123	0.581
IX	2.102	0.143	0.143	0.068	0.068	1.000
X	1.978	0.205	0.205	0.104	0.104	1.000
XI	2.002	0.218	0.198	0.109	0.099	1.102
XII	1.806	0.170	0.170	0.094	0.094	1.000
XIII	1.996	0.176	0.192	0.088	0.096	0.915
XIV	1.802	0.151	0.151	0.084	0.084	1.000
XV	1.998	0.191	0.194	0.096	0.097	0.985
XVI	2.072	0.204	0.204	0.099	0.099	1.000
XVII	2.000	0.202	0.196	0.101	0.098	1.032
XVIII	2.074	0.213	0.213	0.103	0.103	1.000
XIX	2.003	0.224	0.198	0.112	0.099	1.130
XX	1.821	0.172	0.172	0.094	0.094	1.000
XXI	1.995	0.165	0.191	0.083	0.096	0.865
XXII	1.813	0.138	0.138	0.076	0.076	1.000

The resulting equations are too distracting for our purposes, but they are fully specified in El-Agraa (1989c, chap. 5). Here, it suffices to make deductions from them by inserting some hypothetical but representative values. The data are given in Table 6.7, and the resulting income changes are given in Table 6.8. These results lead to the following conclusions:

1. Y_1 is a multiple of the newly introduced industrial output (the results range from $2.225Q$ to $1.787Q$) while Y_2 and Y_3 are a small but positive fraction of this output (the results range from $0.59Q$ to $0.143Q$). These results are clearly indicated by the spillover ratios (the ratios of income changes in the two partners relative to Y_1, given in the last three columns), which range from 0.072 to 0.265 (7–25 percent).

2. Cases II–VII, considered together, clearly indicate that the higher the three countries' *mpis* from each other, the higher the income changes; and the higher the *mpis* from the rest of the world, the lower the resulting income changes (cases VI and VII).

Within this general conclusion one notices the following:

a. the higher the *mpis* of the three countries to import from each other, the higher the rates of change of the income changes for countries 2 and 3 (case II); that is, the net spillover ratios are at their highest;

b. the higher the *mpi* of country 2(3) to import from country 1, the higher the income change overall. This income change is, however, experienced equally by country 3(2)—(cases II and V). This suggests the results that one would expect: the most crucial factor is the *mpi* of country 1 to import from the other two partner countries; and

c. the higher country 2's *mpi* from country 3, the higher the income change in country 3 and the lower the rate of change of income change in country 1 (case IV)—this result is consistent with the previous conclusion and, of course, with the concept of the "multiplier" in general.

3. As one would expect, the higher the *mpis*'s, the lower the income changes (cases XI–XIV). Also the higher the income tax rates, the higher the income changes (cases XV–XVIII). This is clearly suggested by the definitional expressions; this is because any income tax revenue is spent by the government to counteract the effect of the difference between "earned" and "disposable" income on consumption, but it is well known that in such a highly simplified model government expenditure financed by equal taxation has a multiplier effect. Moreover, the higher the tariff rates, the lower the income changes—this follows from assumption (3): the higher the tariff rate, the greater the loss to countries 2 and 3 from such a scheme of economic integration.

4. The most significant conclusion is that the lower the proportion of the newly introduced industrial output consumed by a partner, the higher the country's income change (cases VIII–X).

All these are generally valid conclusions. However, since one is here concerned with only CU theory, the interpretation of these equations should be confined to answering the pertinent question, What happens to these income changes if one of the potential partner countries decides not to participate in the CU? In other words, what happens if country 2 or 3 decides to continue to import from W rather than consume any part of the newly introduced industrial product?

Suppose country 3 makes such a decision. It can then be shown that its income change is greater than previously by a multiple of $t_3Q(1 - x_1 - x_2)$—see El-Agraa (1989c). The point that needs emphasizing, therefore, is that the crucial consideration is not whether or not Y_2 and Y_3 would be negative or positive (Brown's, 1961, main conclusion) but whether or not they would have been greater had 2 and 3 decided to stay out of the CU. The results clearly indicate that 2 and 3 would be better off staying out of such a CU.

Could one then argue that since it is 1's *mpis* from 2 and 3 that are the most significant elements, then it is to the benefit of 2 and 3 to join a CU with 1? It is quite obvious that such an argument would be absurd—these "spread" effects are the outcome of the three countries' *normal relationships* (apart from the new industrial output), and unless country 1 suddenly decides to exercise some compulsion on 2 and 3, there is no reason why these normal relationships should not persist. Moreover, it is to the benefit of country 1 to have a market in which to dispose of its surplus industrial output, an output that is by definition not globally competitive.

Relevance of Integration Theory to the LDCs

Because of the above considerations, it has been claimed that the theory of economic integration as developed for the advanced world has very little relevance to the LDCs. Ignoring the subtle issues previously raised, there are three basic considerations for a *purely economic* justification for CUs: the static resource reallocation effects (TC and TD), provided they are on balance beneficial; the terms of trade (t/t) effects; and the so-called dynamic effects—economies of scale and external economies.

I have demonstrated here that with regard to the static resource reallocation effects there is no difference between CUs in the advanced world and in the LDCs: TD diversion is detrimental because the country concerned is bound to lose (a multiple of the loss of) its tariff revenue. Moreover, TC and TD are static concepts; their effects are practically once-and-for-all changes in the allocation of resources.

As for the t/t effects, these can materialize only if the CU partners can charge higher prices for their exports and/or bargain for lower prices for their imports. Here, one is thrown into the world of monopoly/monopsony or oligopoly/oligopsony, or whatever permutation of these, where any outcome is perfectly feasible, particularly if retaliation by the injured parties is allowed for. I cannot, however, see any difference between the advanced world and the LDCs in this particular respect, and, if the immediate past is anything to go by, the OPEC countries occasionally seem to have gained from such action, although OPEC is not a CU.

As for economies of scale, it should be equally obvious that there is more scope for them in a CU of LDCs than in such associations as the EC and EFTA; optimum plant size, hence economies of scale, lies at the very heart of the rationale for CUs among certain LDCs. Indeed, it has been argued quite coherently that the market size is an important hindrance to economic development— see Brown (1963), Hazlewood (1967, 1975), and Mikesell (1960). Moreover, Johnson (1957, 1958a, 1958b), Brown (1963), and Williamson (1971) have questioned whether there is great scope for scale economies in the EC, although Cecchini (1988), Emerson *et al.* (1988), and Digby, Smith, and Venables (1988) suggest that they are significant is such areas as car production.

When it comes to external economies, it should also be obvious that there is much more scope for them (and absolute necessity for them for development purposes, which is why international trade theorists have conceded the "infant industry" argument as an exception to free trade, but only in the case of certain very underdeveloped countries—see El-Agraa [1989a]) in the LDCs than in the advanced world: a pool of skilled labor and the provision of infrastructure and technology are the basic needs of industry, and they are lacking.

It therefore appears that the body of theory developed for economic integration in the advanced world is even *more appropriate* for the LDCs. Of course, the LDCs are very different in structure from the advanced world, which results in certain aspects of the theory being more relevant to them. But for the advanced world, too, some elements will be more relevant than others, depending on the nature of the economies under consideration. Hence, to conclude from the above that the theory of economic integration as developed for the advanced world is very different from that for the LDCs is to confuse broad theoretical generalizations with their specific application to a particular group of nations *whose structure is different from that of advanced nations:* different structures of economies should not be confused with different theoretical structures. The intrinsic differences between the LDCs and their advanced counterparts ensure that one is not referring to a *unified* approach.

Monetary Integration and Factor Mobility

Since some of the schemes of economic integration discussed here suggest that factor mobility may become an important consideration, it is also appropriate to examine the implications of this. However, in spite of the arrangements in some of the West African schemes, EUs are not a serious issue for the LDCs at present. This is because monetary integration does not lead only to an exchange rate union (i.e., permanently and irrevocably fixed exchange rates for the members) and capital market integration (i.e., permanent absence of all exchange controls for both current and capital transactions, including interest and dividend payments) but also to a common central bank in charge of members' monetary policies and a pool of their foreign exchange reserves. This is a tall order for the LDCs to meet so we need not go into the complicated analysis of economic and monetary unions here; those interested should turn to El-Agraa (1989c).

It should be apparent that the removal (or harmonization) of all barriers to labor (L) and capital (K) may encourage both to move across the borders of member nations. L may move to those areas where it can fetch the highest possible reward, that is, the highest "net advantage" since pecuniary rewards are not the only consideration: tax allowances, health benefits, housing allowances, and so on have to be taken into the calculations. This encouragement need not necessarily lead to an increase in actual mobility since there are sociopolitical factors that normally result in people staying near their birthplace—social proximity is a dominant consideration, which is why the average person does not move. However, recently, economic hardship and high unemployment have induced a considerable degree of factor mobility, but away from the LDCs to the advanced nations (see Panagariya, 1991). If the reward to K is not equalized—that is, if differences in marginal productivities (*mps*) exist before the formation of a CM—K will move until the *mps* are equalized. This will result in benefits that can be clearly described in terms of Figure 6.4, which depicts the production characteristics in H and P. M_H and M_P are the schedules that relate the K stocks to their *mps* in H and P, respectively, given the quantity of L in each country, assuming only two factors of production.

Figure 6.4
Economic Implications of Free *K* Mobility in *H* and *P*

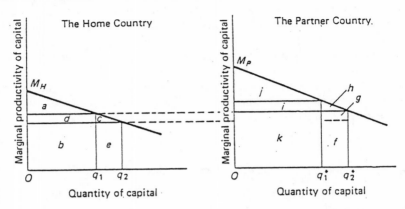

Prior to the formation of the CM, the *K* stock (which is assumed to remain constant throughout the analysis) is Oq_2 in *H* and Oq_1^* in *P*. Assuming that *K* is immobile internationally, all *K* stocks must be nationally owned, and, ignoring taxation, profit per unit of *K* will be equal to its *mp*, given conditions of perfect competition. Hence the total profit in *H* is equal to areas $b + e$ and $i + k$ in *P*. Total output is, of course, the whole area below the *Mp* curve but within Oq_2 in *H* and Oq_1^* in *P*, that is, areas $a + b + c + d + e$ in *H* and $j + i + k$ in *P*. Therefore, *L*'s share is $a + c + d$ in *H* and *j* in *P*.

Since the *mp* in *P* exceeds that in *H*, the removal of the barriers to *K* mobility or the harmonization of such barriers will induce *K* to move away from *H* and into *P*. This is because nothing has happened to affect *K* in *W*. Such movement will continue until the *mp* of *K* is the same in both *H* and *P*. This results in q_1q_2 ($= q_1^*q_2^*$) of *K* moving from *H* to *P*. Hence the output of *H* falls to $a + b + d$ while its *national* product, including the return of the profit earned on *K* in *P* ($= g + f$), increases (by *g* minus *c*). In *P*, *domestic* product rises (by $f + g + h$) while *national* product (excluding the remittance of profits to *H*) increases by area *h* only. Both *H* and *P* experience a change in the relative share of *L* and *K* in national product, with *K*-owners being favorably disposed in *H* and unfavorably disposed in *P*.

Of course, this analysis is too simplistic since, apart from the fact that *K* and *L* are never perfectly immobile at the international level (see McManus, 1972; Buckley and Casson, 1976; Dunning, 1977; Panagariya, 1991), the analysis does not take into account the fact that *K* may actually move to areas of low wages after the formation of a CM. Moreover, if *K* moves predominantly in one direction, one country may become a depressed area, hence the "social" costs and benefits of such an occurrence need to be taken into consideration, particularly if the CM deems it important that the economies of both *H* and *P* should be balanced. Hence, the above gains have to be discounted or supplemented by such costs and benefits.

PERFORMANCE

It follows from what has been said on economic integration among the LDCs that the estimation of the impact of economic integration on them must concentrate on the calculation and evaluation of the joint projects generated because of economic integration, their sources of finance, the achievement (or otherwise) of economies of scale, that is, the locational distribution of plant and equipment, and the distribution of the benefits. Only when such estimates are available should one expect to see calculations on the changes in intrabloc trade and the equitable distribution of benefits and costs. We have some information on some of these. For example, in Africa, the SADCC has been successful in developing the Beira corridor, a 300-kilometer strip running from Beira on the coast of Mozambique to the borders of Zimbabwe, with an electricity line, an oil pipeline, a port, a railway line, a road, and several development projects, but, as we have seen, the main drive behind this was to enable independence from the Republic of South Africa. In the CEAO, a Community Development Fund was established to compensate members of the bloc for the loss of tariff revenue due to the tariff preferences granted to the partners, and a Solidarity Fund, mainly provided for by the Ivory Coast and Senegal, was established to finance projects in the poorest regions. In the EAC, after a long and acrimonious debate, a compensation mechanism was established just before the EAC met its demise. We have already encountered the FCCD, which was created by ECOWAS to assist the least-developed countries within the bloc.

In Latin America, the Andean Pact introduced the Sectoral Program for Industrial Development (SPID) so as to rationalize industrialization by allocating plants in a way that would ensure optimal utilization in the context of even development. However, what is happening in reality is far removed from this noble ideal. For example, in the car and metalworking SPIDs, production was allocated to members where production facilities were already in existence. Indeed, allocations proved easier to make on a "regional" basis only with regard to industries that did not exist at all within the bloc, and little has actually materialized here. By mid-1980 production was in progress in more than 60 percent of units assigned, and this involved sixty-five firms, but these companies had been in existence well before the SPID. (See El-Agraa and Hojman, 1988, for a full list and discussion.)

Prior to the formation of the CACM, there was virtually no investment by TNCs in Central American industry, direct investment being restricted mainly to agriculture, transport, communications, and public utilities. The CACM changed this picture completely, and since 1960, there has been a clear increase in direct foreign investment, most of which has been marked for industry. That the formation of the CACM was the crucial incentive for investment by the

TNCs "cannot be doubted; out of 155 foreign manufacturing subsidiaries setting up after integration, only ten established plants in more than one country . . . suggesting that market size was the all-important determinant of investment flows. Much of this investment . . . would not have come at all had it not been for regional integration" (Bulmer-Thomas, 1988, pp. 304–5).

However, the empirical studies of the trade effects of integration not only are very scanty but also either deal entirely with the calculation of changes in the shares of intrabloc trade or apply the gravity model used by Linnemann (1966) and later adopted by Aitken (1973) and Pelzman (1977). Due to the argument in the previous paragraph and given space limitations, I consider only two representative studies.

Straubhaar's Trade Share Approach

Straubhaar (1987) tried to assess the changes in the trade shares in the ten most important blocs within the LDCs. To add a sense of perspective, he also included the EC, EFTA, and CMEA. Recall that Tables 6.1–6.4 and 6.6 list the integrated groups included in this study, briefly summarize their intended degree of cooperation, and show some of the problems and conflicts in achieving them.

Table 6.9 gives the share of intrabloc trade as a percentage of the total exports of the relevant bloc for the latest period for which information is available. Information along these lines but ending in 1983 led Straubhaar to conclude that for integrated groups of LDCs, intrabloc trade, as a share of the total exports of the bloc, was very modest in the best of cases (ASEAN 23.1 percent, down to 18.47 percent in 1990, and the CACM 21.8 percent, down to 15.81 percent in 1990) and insignificant (less than 10 percent, but note the slight improvement in the case of ALADI and CEAO) in the majority of cases, with the value of intrabloc trade exceeding $1 billion in 1983 only in the cases of ASEAN and ALADI. The table also shows that in comparison with the EC and the CMEA, intrabloc trade among the LDCs had clearly been less significant, as in both the EC and the CMEA it accounted for more than half of total trade.

The changes in the ratios of trade to GDP given in Table 6.10 provide further evidence in support of these conclusions since they clearly demonstrate that, on the whole, economic integration among the LDCs has not resulted in substantial or sustained increases in intrabloc trade—see Torre and Kelly (1992, pp. 28–32).

In order to give an estimate of the extent of the influence of the integration schemes, Table 6.9 also gives the (uncompounded) growth rates of intrabloc trade and compares them with the rates of external trade. Very briefly, for Straubhaar, these rates indicated that at the time of the formation of a new scheme, the elimination of trade restrictions increased the volume of intrabloc trade, with intrabloc trade growing much faster than external trade. In the case of ALADI, intrabloc trade rose from 7.7 percent in 1960 to 10.2 percent in

Table 6.9
Growth of Intrabloc and External Trade of Schemes of Economic Integration

Value of Intra-Trade, Millions of Dollars

	1960	1970	1980	1990
ASEAN	839	860	11918	26290
ALADI	564	1290	10270	11670
ANDEAN	25	109	955	1192
ECOWAS	17	61	1056	1280
CACM	33	299	1141	664
CARICOM	27	73	354	273
CEAO	6	73	296	575
UDEAC	3	33	200	180
CEPGL (from 1970)		2	5	7
MRU (from 1976)		2	2	6
EC ('60-'70 EC6)	10300	43400		
EC ('75, '85, '90 EC12)		161600	352300	820600
EFTA ('60-'70 total)	2900	9400		
EFTA ('75, '85, '90 manu)		8000	12000	24900
CHEA ('80=85)	8100	18400	98600	65900

Value of Exports, Millions of Dollars

	1960	1970	1980	1990
ASEAN	4210	6290	73080	142370
ALADI	7280	12730	80790	112540
ANDEAN	3520	5380	31300	31220
ECOWAS	1330	2960	32450	20850
CACM	440	1120	4880	4200
CARICOM	590	1140	10930	6800
CEAO	300	830	4740	4740
UDEAC	223	470	4668	4194
CEPGL		830	1816	1184
MRU		737	1183	893
EC ('60-'70 EC6)	29744	88743		
EC ('75, '85, '90 EC12)		307580	649810	1337409
EFTA ('60-'70 total)	7500	19710		
EFTA ('75, '85, '90 manu)		50900	109590	225100
CHEA ('80=85)	13000	31000	168600	172800

Intra-Trade as a % of Exports

	1960	1970	1980	1990
ASEAN	19.93	13.67	16.31	18.47
ALADI	7.75	10.13	12.71	10.37
ANDEAN	0.71	2.03	3.05	3.82
ECOWAS	1.28	2.06	3.25	6.14
CACM	7.50	26.70	23.38	15.81
CARICOM	4.58	6.40	3.24	4.01
CEAO	2.00	8.80	6.24	12.13
UDEAC	1.35	7.02	4.28	4.29
CEPGL		0.24	0.28	0.59
MRU		0.27	0.17	0.67
EC ('60-'70 EC6)	34.63	48.91		
EC ('75, '85, '90 EC12)		52.54	54.22	61.36
EFTA ('60-'70 total)	38.67	47.69		
EFTA ('75, '85, '90 manu)		15.72	10.95	11.06
CHEA ('80=85)	62.31	59.35	58.48	38.14

Intra-Trade Growth, % Per Annum

	1960-70	1970-80	1980-90
ASEAN	0.25	30.07	8.23
ALADI	8.63	23.05	1.29
ANDEAN	15.86	24.24	2.24
ECOWAS	13.63	32.99	1.94
CACM	24.66	14.33	-5.27
CARICOM	10.46	17.10	-2.56
CEAO	28.39	15.03	6.87
UDEAC	27.10	19.74	-1.05
CEPGL (from 1970)		9.60	3.42
MRU (from 1976)		0.00	11.61
EC ('60-'70 EC6)	15.47	8.10	18.43
EFTA	12.48	4.14	15.72
CHEA ('80=85)	8.55	11.84	-7.74

Export Growth, % Per Annum

	1960-70	1970-80	1980-90
ASEAN	4.10	27.80	6.90
ALADI	5.75	20.30	3.37
ANDEAN	4.33	19.26	-0.03
ECOWAS	8.33	27.06	-4.33
CACM	9.79	15.86	-1.49
CARICOM	6.81	25.36	-4.63
CEAO	10.71	19.03	0.00
UDEAC	7.74	25.81	-1.06
CEPGL (from 1970)		8.14	-4.19
MRU (from 1976)		12.56	-2.77
EC ('60-'70 EC6)	11.55	7.77	15.53
EFTA	10.14	7.97	15.48
CHEA ('80=85)	9.08	11.95	0.49

Difference

	1960-70	1970-80	1980-90
ASEAN	-3.85	2.27	1.33
ALADI	2.88	2.75	-2.08
ANDEAN	11.53	4.98	2.27
ECOWAS	5.30	5.93	6.27
CACM	14.87	-1.53	-3.78
CARICOM	3.65	-8.26	2.07
CEAO	17.68	-4.00	6.87
UDEAC	19.36	-6.07	0.01
CEPGL		1.46	7.61
MRU		-12.56	14.38
EC	3.92	0.33	2.90
EFTA	2.34	-3.83	0.24
CHEA	-0.53	-0.11	-8.23

Source: Handbook of International Trade and Development, 1991.

Table 6.10
Selected Developing Country Regional Arrangements: Changes in Trade to
GDP Ratios

		Total	External	Intra-Regional
Andean Pact	1970-80	9.7	8.8	0.9
	1980-85	-11.0	-10.5	-0.4
	1985-90	3.2	2.9	0.3
ASEAN	1960-70	9.4	3.6	5.8
	1970-80	27.6	23.6	4.0
	1980-90	23.9	19.3	4.5
CACM	1960-70	9.7	8.5	1.2
	1970-80	10.3	0.7	9.6
	1980-90	-10.6	-6.1	-4.4
CEAO	1970-80	9.5	2.0	7.4
	1980-90	-12.9	--	-12.9
CPGL	1975-90	0.4	0.2	0.3
ECOWAS	1975-80	2.1	--	2.1
	1980-85	-12.2	0.1	-12.3
GCC	1980-90	-15.6	1.0	-16.6
LAFTA/LAIA	1960-70	-3.3	--	-3.4
	1970-80	4.2	0.9	3.2
	1980-90	-2.5	-0.4	-2.1
MRU	1970-80	13.1	0.2	12.8
	1980-90	-27.4	-0.2	-27.2
PTA	1980-85	-9.8	-0.9	-8.9
	1985-90	12.2	0.9	11.3
SADCC	1980-85	-19.1	-0.4	-18.7
	1985-90	29.6	1.4	28.2
UDEAC	1965-75	-0.3	1.0	-1.3
	1975-90	-12.7	-0.1	-12.6

Sources: IMF, *Direction of Trade Statistics, International Financial Statistics; World Economic Outlook;* IMF staff estimates.

1970. For the CMEA, it increased from 7.5 percent in 1960 to 26.8 percent in 1970. This effect was also witnessed in the African schemes: in the case of the CEAO, intrabloc trade increased from 2.0 percent in 1960 to 9.1 percent in 1970, and in UDEAC it rose from 1.6 to 3.4 percent for the respective years. However, except for ASEAN, this momentum was greatly diminished, with intrabloc trade increasing only insignificantly more than external trade, with ALADI maintaining its 1970 rate in 1983 and UDEAC registering a negative difference by then.

It should be added that up-dating along the lines considered here is not likely to produce a different picture.

Straubhaar then emphasized three problems in connection with these results. First, in contrast to integration schemes among advanced nations, the estimates for the LDCs were heavily influenced by frequent and repeated fundamental economic, social and political changes within the integrated group since practically no single bloc was spared from multiple, and often violent, uprisings in one or more member countries within the group. Second, there were frequent changes in the composition of the individual blocs. Finally, there were also frequent changes in the degree of coordination within the individual blocs.

From the discussion in El-Agraa (1989c), which are too complex to go through here, it should be noted that estimates of simple changes in trade percentages do not form a solid basis for the analysis of economic integration effects. Moreover, and more fundamentally, since the aim of economic integration among a group of LDCs is to enable the establishment of optimum plant installations financed basically by imported investments, it follows that economic integration may actually result in increased trade with the outside (advanced) world, particularly since most of the capital equipment and intermediate products which are needed for plant installations and production are imported from the advanced world. Of course, sometimes such trade is a precondition for advancing the foreign technology, know-how, and finance that are desperately needed. In short, an estimate that fails to take these fundamental considerations into account should not be taken seriously.

The Estimates by Brada and Méndez

To date, the only rigorous estimate of the trade effects of economic integration among a group of LDCs has been made by Brada and Méndez (1985) for the CACM, LAFTA, and the Andean Group/Pact. For comparison purposes, they also included results for the EC and EFTA. They utilized Linnemann's gravitational equation as their starting point since they believed that it had a sound theoretical basis (see Bergstrand, 1985) and provided an empirically tractable general equilibrium framework for modeling bilateral trade flows. Hence, the careful reader is assumed to be familiar with that equation and its properties (see El-Agraa, 1989c, p. 211).

However, Brada and Méndez felt that the use of the variables in that equation to model the relationship among endowments, tastes, and trade with a sample that included both developed countries and LDCs raised some conceptual problems. First, it had to be assumed that all the countries included in the study were developing along similar lines and that the development process did not change their trade behavior in any manner that was not predicted by the Linnemann equation. However, they accepted Chenery's (1960) evidence, which had suggested that this assumption was acceptable. Second, aggregate measures of income varied between developed countries and the LDCs in terms of both their coverage of economic activity and the mix of commodities included. The biases generated by this tended to work in the same direction: incomes in the LDCs were likely to be understated, and each dollar of income included fewer tradables relative to incomes in the advanced nations. But they were convinced that the log-linear specification of the equation took care of such biases since the equation weighted each dollar of income in an LDC more than a dollar of income in a developed country. They also introduced measures to adjust for these differences—see later in chapter. Third, the distance variable indicating resistance to trade comprised an economic element (consisting of transport and information costs), a structural element (reflecting differences in consumption patterns and factor endowments), and a policy element, which included the impact of economic integration. Because the effects of the structural elements are ambiguous (differences in factor endowments promote trade while differences in consumption hinder it), they decided to focus their attention on the remaining factors by improving on the manner of specifying the impact of economic integration on resistance to trade. Finally, they felt that although both the procedures of introducing dummy variables (DVs) and selecting a preintegration period on the basis of which the equation is estimated for projection purposes were legitimate for measuring the trade-augmenting effects of economic integration among countries at the same level of development, or with similar size or economic system, they were not appropriate for the blocs they chose.

Some of these issues warranted elaboration. They stressed that the impact of economic integration on intermember trade was influenced by three sets of factors. The first was the *environment,* which they took to mean the physical and economic characteristics of the integrating group of countries and their economic relations with W. As an example, they hypothesized that countries closer to each other would experience, ceteris paribus, more trade augmentation after integration than countries far apart. The second was the *economic system* of the countries under consideration. Here they pointed to the literature that suggested that centrally planned economies tended to trade less, ceteris paribus, than comparable market-oriented economies. Third, was the *policy* element. Some schemes of economic integration lowered their intermember trade barriers to a greater extent than others; hence the former were expected to be more effective in augmenting interbloc trade. They concluded that when one dealt with a homogeneous group of nations, one could presume that the integration DVs or the difference between the actual and predicted trade flows did not reflect systematic differences. Also, one did not expect environmental factors to change drastically over time or differ greatly between integration schemes. Therefore, the coefficients of integration DVs or the differences between expected and actual postintegration trade could safely be attributed to economic integration as a policy variable. However, with a more heterogeneous group, the estimates of the impact of economic integration would become "tainted at best and swamped at worst by the differences in system and environment" (Brada and Méndez, 1985, p. 551) that prevailed among various schemes.

In order to allow for these problems, Brada and Méndez modified the gravity equation to include the environmental effects as well as the effectiveness of economic integration. Two environmental variables were modeled for the distance between members of the scheme and for their level of economic development. The distance hypothesis amounted to stating that if, for example, three countries decided to establish a form of economic integration, the two closest to each other would experience greater expansion in their mutual trade relative to the third. This could be partly due to the fact that it may be feasible to trade highly perishable products between geographically closer countries, but such trade might be uneconomic with distant nations. Also, the farther distance would place traders at a disadvantage in terms of evaluating reactions to opportunities in the partner's markets due to lack of more precise information and to less direct acquaintance with the culture and the economy of the place. Moreover, countries closer to each other are supposed to be more likely to have greater similarity in terms of culture and climate; thus they are more likely to have similar patterns of consumption and production. In short, the hypothesis is that a scheme of economic integration among geographically closer countries should stimulate interbloc trade more, ceteris paribus, than one whose member nations are far apart.

Brada and Méndez noted that, on one hand, the LDCs had a structural bias against trade since their production was mainly in subsistence agriculture and in services, neither of which entered into international trade. Thus, most of their trade tended to be conducted with the advanced nations, exchanging agricultural products and raw materials for manufactured goods. On the other hand, the advanced nations tended to have large manufacturing sectors that encouraged both complementary trade (manufactured products being exchanged for raw materials) as well as intraindustry trade, which is generally not available to the LDCs. Therefore, the hypothesis they advanced was that the level of economic development would also have a positive impact on economic integration.

In order to measure the impact of these environmental factors on trade flows, they respecified the Linnemann equation in a suitable fashion. Brada and Méndez then collected data for trade of the member countries of the EC, EFTA, CACM, LAFTA, and the Andean Pact with each other and with eighteen developed countries and LDCs that belonged to no scheme of economic integration. The trade flows for the CMEA countries were not used to estimate the parameters of their equation since the systemic differences between them and the rest of the groups implied that they could not be expected to follow the market-oriented regime depicted by the equation.

Because the observations could not be pooled over time, it was necessary to estimate parameters for their equation for each year. Due to space limitations, Brada and Méndez presented the parameter estimates for only the last year for which complete data were available (1976), together with 1970 and 1973. They drew attention to the fact that during this period all the schemes under consideration were in existence. They noted that the coefficients for income and population had the expected signs, and these together with the coefficient for distance were similar to those reported by Aitken (1973) and by Hewett (1976). Except for the constant term and one variable, they found all the coefficients to be relatively stable over time.

Their results point to certain conclusions: (1) economic integration tends to reduce the resistance to trade between member countries of an integration scheme; (2) economic integration among countries with high per capita incomes tends to increase trade more than integration among countries with low per capita incomes; and (3) the impact of economic integration on trade tended to diminish as the distance between members of an integrated scheme increased. With regard to (2), they pointed out that the value of this parameter falls over time and in 1976 was not significantly different from zero. Brada and Méndez attributed this to the global increase in the prices of fuels and raw materials, since they were of the opinion that these price increases then resulted in complementary trade in these goods among countries, with different per capita incomes being weighted more heavily in total trade relative to competitive trade flows among the advanced nations.

Also, they found that, altogether, the differences among the five schemes (EC, EFTA, LAFTA, Andean Pact, and CACM) are very small. This suggests that differences in per capita incomes do not explain much of the difference in the capability of an integration scheme to augment interbloc trade. However, the results indicate that differences in average intermember distance do explain these differences; the average distances vary from 306 miles for the CACM to 9,173 miles for LAFTA. Consequently, although the CACM consists of the least-developed countries in the study, it is expected to increase intermember trade by 500 percent, slightly more than for EFTA. They note that the decline in the value of the relevant parameter over time changes the relative influence of environment on economic integration. Given the decline in the significance of the level of development as a factor promoting intermember trade in their results for 1973 and 1976, it appears that integration schemes among the LDCs become less disadvantaged relative to schemes among advanced nations with the progress of time. Brada and Méndez thus conclude that it would seem more appropriate to consider the results as the *range* of likely environmental influences on economic integration rather than as point results. But they were quick to add that the results as a whole clearly indicate that the impact of environmental factors cannot be ignored.

Brada and Méndez then turned to the results regarding the policies by which economic integration was promoted. They drew attention to the significant differences in the integration policies of the five schemes under consideration. For example, some were FTAs while others were CMs, thus resulting in different types of scheme; there were differences in the extent to which nontariff trade barriers were lowered among the member countries; and there were differences in the height of their CETs. The procedure they followed in comparing the effectiveness of the integration policies pursued by the five schemes was to establish whether the actual increase in intermember trade was greater than that predicted by the results given earlier. Their justification for this procedure was that since the predicted increases in intermember trade reflected the environmental differences among the five groups when *identical integration policies* were adopted in all five schemes, it followed that any differences between the predicted and the actual increases in intermember trade indicated differences in the *effectiveness of the integration policies* of each integration bloc.

Allowing for these considerations, their results point to certain conclusions: (1) the integration policies pursued by the Andean Pact, the EC, and LAFTA show that the three blocs had less than average effectiveness; for example, the increases in trade obtained by the EC were only 60 percent of what could have been achieved had it pursued integration policies of average effectiveness; (2) the integration policies in Latin America were about as effective as those of the EC; (3) the differences in TC between the EC and the Latin American blocs reflected mainly environmental factors; and (4) to restore the average, the CACM and EFTA seem to have adopted integration policies of above average effectiveness, with the CACM faring better than EFTA. Brada and Méndez then advanced an explanation for these seemingly puzzling results: the CACM and EFTA pursued economic integration mainly for its possible economic benefits while the other three blocs included important noneconomic objectives as well, such as the protection of agriculture in the EC and the promotion of industry while limiting the power of the TNCs in Latin America (see El-Agraa, 1988, 1990, for a full coverage of the policies adopted by these schemes during the period under consideration).

CONCLUSION

Using my own model, I have demonstrated that within that limited framework there is no economic justification for a CU of LDCs based on protected industrialization, that is, a trade diverting association. However, one could argue that such a conclusion is unwarranted since the model does not include investment, but a careful consideration would reveal that the incorporation of investment would actually reinforce the conclusion. If the investment were provided by the three countries themselves, country 1 would get an extra boost to its income change (since it would receive investment from the potential CU partners) while countries 2 and 3 would incur losses (since they would have to divert their investments to country 1). If the investment came from outside the CU through foreign aid or cheaper-interest loans, the conclusion would remain intact because even if all the servicing of the investment were paid by country 1, the other two would still incur the specified losses, but, of course, the investment would be beneficial for country 1.

Nevertheless, it would be naive to conclude from this that there is no rationale whatsoever for CU formation among a group of LDCs. This is because this model implies that if such a union is to be formed, the benefits that accrue to country 1, which are a multiple of the pre-CU output, must somehow be equitably distributed so that countries 2 and 3 also get a share of the benefits. We have already examined the reasons for the formation of CUs among such countries: lack of sufficient markets; the need for economic development; market distortions; and so on. Hence the considerations tackled here plus the general rationale that has already been established for the formation of CUs among a certain group of LDCs reinforce each other such that the CU under consideration must incorporate explicit policies for dealing with the equitable distribution of the gains from economic integration.

Thus, given all these considerations, one has a clear case for economic integration among a group of LDCs, provided the stated conditions are met, especially those with regard to the distribution of the benefits. However, one has to warn the LDCs concerned that if they all try to maximize their share of the (expected) benefits, they all stand to lose; it is like the classical oligopoly case where profit maximization requires collusive action, but if each firm then goes for maximizing its own share of the profit, they will all incur losses instead.

However, the reality is very different. As we have seen, there is hardly any scheme of economic integration among LDCs that can claim to have been successful. This is not due to lack of seriousness of purpose; it is mainly due to the absence of the necessary preconditions that can provide hope for success and to less than whole-hearted commitment: countries that belong to more than one bloc and that change commitment at almost regular intervals (witness the overlapping and frequent movement in the schemes) cannot be that serious about economic integration. They seem to be on the lookout for whatever is going, irrespective of whether it suits their purposes, and, even worse, without knowing precisely what they are looking for: the clear guidelines for successful integration are either always dodged or are never carried out properly, if at all (witness the acrimony over compensation criteria and institutions to run them).

It is therefore wise to conclude by asking such LDCs to ask themselves some searching questions:

1. Are the members prepared to agree on a common system of fiscal incentives to encourage an acceptable distribution of investment among them and to prevent the competitive offering of concessions to investors?

2. Is a substantial degree of regional planning over such matters as the location of new industries and the pattern of industrial specialization essential to achieve an acceptable distribution of the benefits of integration? If so, are members prepared to accept the constraints imposed on them by such planning? How does such planning cope with the strong preferences by potential investors as to the location of production?

3. Are members willing to take a long-term view and to see the benefits from cooperation grow with the growth of trade among them, or do their assessments inevitably have a short horizon within which transactions among them, and hence the benefits from cooperation, are likely to be small?

4. If there are gains from the scheme for the members as a whole and for every member individually, can it be ensured that they all perceive the benefit and do not have incompatible perceptions of the distribution of the benefits?

5. Is it necessary only that all members of a bloc should benefit, must they benefit equally, or must the poorer or less developed members gain most so that the gap between the members in their wealth and level of development actually narrows over time? The last is a very strong requirement, because it is perfectly possible for the gap to widen, even though the integration arrangements themselves may have a strong equalizing element.

6. Are the expected benefits from industrialization to serve a protected regional market great enough to make the effort to surmount the difficulties worthwhile, given the possibilities for manufacturing for extra-bloc exports, including exports to advanced countries through TNCs? The expectation will differ from country to country according to the size of its domestic market and its international competitive ability. Is a strong affirmative from every member necessary for a grouping to have good prospects of success?

7. Is continuing political harmony among the members essential, and must it go beyond a minimum of goodwill without which cooperation would be impossible?

NOTE

When editing a book, I assume full responsibility for what goes into it. This approach sometimes leads to a rejection or a complete rewriting of invited contributions. Therefore, I never permit my contributors to thank me for my editorial commitments. However, there are those who think that all an editor does is simply to send off a few chapters to the publisher: the *Journal of Economic Literature* enters *Festschrifts* under the honoree's name! Due to these differing perceptions, I hope I will be allowed to express my gratitude to Dr. Enzo Grilli, not only for doing an excellent editorial job but also for providing me with articles and statistical and pictorial information that would otherwise have been beyond my reach.

REFERENCES

Aitken, A.D. 1973. "The Effects of the EEC and EFTA on European Trade: A Temporal Cross-Section Analysis." *American Economic Review* 63.

Balassa, B. 1961. *The Theory of Economic Integration.* Homewood, Ill.: Irwin.

Berglas, E. 1983. "The Case for Unilateral Tariff Reductions: Foreign Tariffs Reconsidered." *American Economic Review* 73.

Bergstrand, J.H. 1985. "The Gravity Equation in International Trade: Some Microeconomic Foundations and Empirical Evidence." *Review of Economics and Statistics* 67.

Brada, J.C., and Méndez, J.A. 1985. "Economic Integration Among Developed, Developing and Centrally Planned Economies: A Comparative Analysis." *Review of Economics and Statistics* 67.

Brown, A.J. 1961. "Economic Separatism Versus a Common Market in Developing Countries." *Yorkshire Bulletin of Economic and Social Research* 13.

———. 1963. "Common Market Criteria and Experience." *Three Banks Review* 57.

Buckley, P.J., and Casson, M. 1976. *The Future of the Multinational Enterprise.* London: Macmillan.

Bulmer-Thomas, V.G. 1988. "The Central American Common Market." In *International Economic Integration,* edited by A.M. El-Agraa. London: Macmillan.

Byé, M. 1950. "Unions douanières et données nationale." *Economie Appliquée* 3. Reprinted (1953) in translation as "Customs Unions and National Interests." *International Economic Papers,* no. 3.

Cecchini, P. 1988. *1992: The European Challenge.* London: Gower.

Chenery, H.B. 1960. "Patterns of Industrial Growth." *American Economic Review* 50.

Cooper, C.A., and Massell, B.F. 1965a. "A New Look at Customs Union Theory." *Economic Journal* 75.

Cooper, C.A., and Massell, B.F. 1965b. "Towards a General Theory of Customs Unions for Developing Countries." *Journal of Political Economy* 73.

Corden, W.M. 1972. "Economies of Scale and Customs Union Theory." *Journal of Political Economy* 80.

Digby, C., Smith, A., and Venables, A. 1988. "Counting the Cost of Voluntary Export Restrictions in the European Car Market." *CEPR Discussion Paper,* no. 249.

Dunning, J.H. 1977. "Trade, Location of Economic Activity and the MNE: A Search for an Eclectic Approach." In *The International Allocation of Economic Activity,* edited by B. Ohlin. London: Macmillan.

El-Agraa, A.M. 1969. "The Sudan and the Arab Common Market: A Conflict." *Eastern Africa Economic Review* 3.

———. 1979. "Common Markets in Developing Countries." In *Inflation, Development and Integration: Essays in Honour of A.J. Brown,* edited by J.K. Bowers. Leeds: Leeds University Press.

———. 1983. "A Generalisation of the CU vs UTR Analysis." *Leeds Discussion Papers,* no. 128.

———. 1985. "The Distributional Implications of Customs Unions in Developing Countries." *Kashmir Economic Review* 1.

———, ed. 1988. *International Economic Integration.* New York: St. Martin's. First edition, 1982.

———. 1989a. *International Trade.* London: Macmillan.

———. 1989b. "The Need for Rationalisation of Arab League Integration Attempts." *The Middle East Business and Economic Review* 2.

———. 1989c. *The Theory and Measurement of International Economic Integration.* New York: St. Martin's.

———, ed. 1990. *The Economics of the European Community.* New York: Simon and Schuster.

El-Agraa, A.M., and Hojman, D.E. 1988. "The Andean Pact." In *International Economic Integration,* edited by A.M. El-Agraa. London: Macmillan.

El-Agraa, A.M., and Jones, A.J. 1981. *Theory of Customs Unions.* Oxford: Philip Allan.

———. 1983. "On Unilateral Tariff Reduction Versus Customs Unions." *Leeds Discussion Papers,* no. 127.

Emerson, M. 1988. *The Economics of 1992: The EC Commission's Assessment of the Economic Effects of Completing the Internal Market.* Oxford: Oxford University Press.

Foroutan, F. 1992. "Regional Integration in Sub-Saharan Africa: Past Experience and Future Prospects." Paper presented at the World Bank and Centre for Economic Policy Research joint conference on "New Dimensions in Regional Integration," Washington, D.C., 3 April.

Hazlewood, A. 1967. *African Integration and Disintegration.* London: Heinemann.

———. 1975. *Economic Integration: The East African Experience.* London: Heinemann.

Hewett, E.A. 1976. "A Gravity Model of CMEA Trade." In *Quantitative and Analytical Studies in East-West Economic Relations,* edited by J.C. Brada. Bloomington: Indiana University Press.

Johnson, H.G. 1957. "Criteria of Economic Advantage." *Bulletin of the Oxford University Institute of Economics and Statistics* 13.

————. 1958a. "The Gains from Freer Trade with Europe: An estimate." *Manchester School* 73.

————. 1958b. "The Economic Gains from Free Trade with Europe." *Three Banks Review.*

————. 1965. "An Economic Theory of Protectionism, Tariff Bargaining and the Formation of Customs Unions." *Journal of Political Economy* 73.

Jones, A.J. 1980. "Domestic Distortions and Customs Union Theory." *Bulletin of Economic Research* 32.

Kahnert, F. 1969. *Economic Integration Among Developing Countries.* Paris: OECD, Development Centre.

Linnemann, H. 1966. *An Econometric Study of International Trade Flows.* Amsterdam: North-Holland.

Lipsey, R.G. 1960. "The Theory of Customs Unions: A General Survey." *Economic Journal* 70.

McManus, J.G. 1972. "The Theory of the International Firm." In *The Multinational Firm and the Nation State,* edited by G. Paquet. Ontario: Collier Macmillan.

Mayes, D.G. 1988. "Causes of Change in Manufactured Exports." In *Causes of Changes in the Structure of International Trade 1960–85,* edited by J. Black and A.I. MacBean. London: Macmillan.

Meade, J.E. 1955. *The Theory of Customs Unions.* Amsterdam: North-Holland.

Metwally, M.M. 1979. "Market Limitation and Industrialisation in Arab Countries." In *Inflation, Development and Integration: Essays in Honour of A.J. Brown,* edited by J.K. Bowers. Leeds: Leeds University Press.

Mikesell, R.F. 1960. "The Theory of Common Markets as Applied to Regional Arrangements Among Developing Countries." In *International Trade Theory in a Developing World,* edited by R. Harrod and D. Hague. Cambridge: Cambridge University Press.

Panagariya, A. 1991. "Explaining the Pattern of Factor Flows Between the North and South." *Osaka Economic Papers,* 40. An edited version has been published in *Public and International Economics: Essays in Honour of Professor Hirofumi Shibata,* edited by A.M. El-Agraa. London: Macmillan, 1993.

Pelzman, J. 1977. "Trade Creation and Trade Diversion in the Council of Mutual Economic Assistance." *American Economic Review* 67.

Robson, P. 1983. *Integration, Development and Equity: Economic Integration in West Africa.* London: Allen and Unwin.

Robson, P., and Lury, D.A. 1969. *The Economics of Africa.* London: Allen and Unwin.

Sayigh, Y. 1982. *The Arab Economy.* Oxford: Oxford University Press.

Scitovsky, T. 1958. *Economic Theory and Western European Integration.* London: Allen and Unwin.

Straubhaar, T. 1987. "South-South Trade: Is Integration a Solution?' *Intereconomics,* (January/February).

Torre, A. de la, and Kelly, R.M. 1992. "Regional Trade Arrangements." *Occasional Paper,* no. 93. Washington, D.C.: IMF.

United Nations Economic Commission for Africa. 1984. *Proposals for Strengthening Economic Integration in Africa.* Addis Ababa: UNECA.

Viner, J. 1950. *The Customs Union Issue.* New York: Carnegie Endowment for International Peace.

Williamson, J. 1971. "On Estimating the Income Effects of British Entry to the EEC."

Surrey Papers in Economics, no. 6. A revised version, "Trade and Economic Growth," is in *The Economics of Europe: What the Common Market Means for Britain,* edited by J. Pinder. London: Knight.

Wonnacott, G.P., and Wonnacott, R.J. 1981a. "How General Is the Case for Unilateral Tariff Reduction?" *American Economic Review* 74.

————. 1981b. "Is Unilateral Tariff Reduction Preferable to a Customs Union? The Curious Case of the Missing Foreign Tariffs." *American Economic Review* 71.

World Bank. 1991. *World Bank Development Report.* Washington D.C.: World Bank.

7

AGRICULTURE

John Mellor

The simple empirical evidence overwhelmingly demonstrates close association between high rates of growth in the general economy, in the agricultural, and in nonagricultural subsectors. Succeeding exposition explains the causality in that association, at least for poor countries in early stages of development. The case is made for acceleration in the agricultural growth rate as a means of accelerating overall economic growth, speeding the structural transformation of the economy from dominantly agricultural to dominantly nonagricultural, radically reducing absolute poverty through increased employment and higher real wages, and diffusing the pattern of urbanization, even while the rate of urbanization accelerates. In such a context, the private sector and market processes play the dominant role in accelerated growth. However, particularly for the agricultural sector, facilitative public policy, stimulation of the public institutional structure, and expansion of public expenditure on education and physical infrastructure are critical to accelerated growth.

Figure 7.1 graphs the rate of growth of the agricultural and nonagricultural sectors for the Asian countries for which the *World Development Report* (World Bank, 1988–1989) provides such data. Two broad points can be made from this figure. First, there is a clear relationship between the rate of agricultural growth and the rate of nonagricultural growth. Second, there are notable outliers from that line of relationship. If the four most prominent outliers are removed, the R^2 for the remaining observations is 0.92, and for each 1 percent acceleration in the rate of growth of the agricultural sector, there is a 1.4 percentage point acceleration in the rate of growth of the nonagricultural sector.

The presence of the outliers and of the variance generally indicates that there are forces affecting the nonagricultural growth rate in addition to the agricultural growth rate. Given the complexity of the processes at work, the closeness of

Figure 7.1
Growth Rates of Per Capita Agriculture and Nonagriculture GDP, Various Asian Countries and Years, 1960–1986

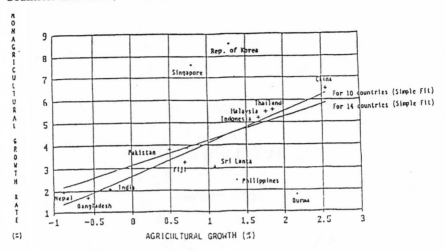

Source: World Bank, *World Tables* (1988–1989).
Descriptive variables for simple fit of 10 countries (excluding Burma, Philippines, Republic of Korea, and Singapore): R-square, 0.91; value of coefficient of agricultural growth rate, 1.43; T-stat. of agricultural growth rate, 9.33; and standard error of agricultural growth rate, 0.15.
Descriptive variables for simple fit of 14 countries: R-square, 0.23; value of coefficient of agricultural growth rate, 1.07; T-stat. of agricultural growth rate, 1.92; and standard error of agricultural growth rate, 0.56.
Constant 1980 price GDP at market prices in local currency.

the simple relationship must be surprising. The four principal outliers have important messages about the other forces, and since the remaining variance is small, they tell much of the story about the other forces. Of those four outliers, two represent success in the nonagricultural sector and poor performance in agriculture, and two represent the converse.

The Singapore story in this relationship is trivial. Agriculture in this city state is of inconsequential size and thus can have little effect on the nonagricultural growth rate. In contrast, virtually all low-income countries have economies that are initially dominated by agriculture.

South Korea is a nontrivial case. South Korea had a massive inflow of foreign capital, on private account in particular, which allowed a rapid expansion of the nonagricultural sector without an effective demand-driven stimulus from agriculture. Capital being less constraining to growth, the low capital-labor ratios associated with demand driven by expenditure patterns of small farmers were less important to the rate of labor force absorption. South Korea's period of rapid structural transformation was also one in which those few developing countries turning to foreign markets as the primary source of demand for an expanding nonagricultural sector faced unusually buoyant markets and little competition from other developing countries. Again, domestic demand from a prospering agriculture was less essential to expansion of the nonagricultural sector. Thus, South Korea stands out as an unusual case in which the nonagricultural sector was the leading sector and eventually pulled the agricultural sector into accelerated growth.

There are two outliers on the other side. Burma is a country that has had extraordinarily bad public policy for development generally. But Burma's agricultural resources are so highly productive that the record in agricultural growth was reasonably good, despite the poor public policy. When it came to the nonagricultural sector, however, for which Burma did not have unusually favorable resource endowments, the unfavorable macropolicy prevented an effective agricultural stimulus to the nonagricultural sector. We comment more on this later.

The Philippines is the most interesting outlier. The conditions of physical rural infrastructure and rural education were unusually propitious both for agricultural growth and for large multipliers from agricultural to rural nonagricultural growth. There were also positive public policies toward agriculture, particularly with respect to technology, that allowed that sector to grow rapidly despite relatively unfavorable macropolicy. Thus in the period 1965 to 1980 the agricultural sector grew at 4.69 percent per year, compared with the average for all developing countries of 3.1 percent. Despite all these favorable forces the nonagricultural sector of the Philippines has grown slowly even in periods of rapid agricultural growth, and the Philippines has experienced slow growth in employment, declining real wage rates, increasing absolute poverty, and increasing concentration of urbanization in metropolitan Manila, which is associated with agricultural failure (Bautista, forthcoming). We turn to macropolicy, generally, and trade and capital allocation policies, specifically, for explanation of the Philippine failure when we illuminate these relationships in later sections of this chapter. For now we should simply note the words of Romeo Bautista when writing on this issue—"rapid agricultural growth is not enough" (Bautista, forthcoming).

Figures 7.2 and 7.3 for Africa and Latin America tell a very different story. They show no relationship between the rate of growth in the agricultural and nonagricultural sectors. That lack of relationship cannot be remedied by simply removing a few outliers. The lesson, of course, is not that accelerated growth in agriculture does not, unlike Asia, stimulate accelerated growth in the nonagricultural sector. However, in Africa, economic growth generally has been pursued neither vigorously nor successfully. What growth has occurred has been random, with that in agriculture tending to be the short-run product of successive years of fortuitous weather and that in nonagriculture caused by the large flow of foreign aid or oil revenues into the major urban areas with stimulation of the government, service, and construction sectors. In Latin America, the economies have been structurally transformed, giving relatively less importance to agriculture, and generally unfavorable macropolicy has resulted in slow growth in

Figure 7.2
Growth Rates of Per Capita Agriculture and Nonagriculture GDP, Various Sub-Saharan African Countries and Years, 1960–1986

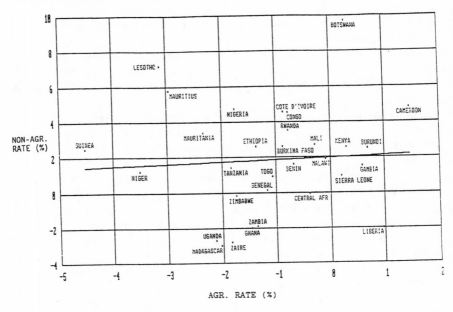

Source: World Bank, *World Tables* (1988–1989).
Note: Constant 1980 price GDP at market prices in local currency.
Descriptive Variables for Simple Fit: R-Square 0.0029;
Value of Coefficient of Agriculture Growth Rate 0.025;
T-Stat. of Agriculture Growth Rate 0.29;
Std. Error of Agriculture Growth Rate 0.085.

most periods and weak relationships among sectors. However, it should be noted that, as in Africa, the successful countries (e.g., Colombia, Costa Rica) have demonstrated concurrent rapid growth in both agriculture and nonagriculture.

Returning to successful growth, not only does accelerated growth in the agricultural sector generally stimulate acceleration in the nonagricultural sector, but it has both a direct and an indirect effect on poverty reduction. In general, when agricultural growth has accelerated, absolute poverty has declined rapidly (Mellor, 1990). The significant exception is the Philippines. There, agriculture did not significantly stimulate the nonagricultural sector. It follows that accelerated growth of the nonagricultural sector is crucial to expansion in employment sufficient to absorb the high rates of labor force growth inevitably associated with high rates of population growth. While technological change-driven increase in agricultural output typically demonstrates low elasticities of employment with

Figure 7.3
Growth Rates of Per Capita Agriculture and Nonagriculture GDP, Various Latin American Countries and Years, 1960–1986

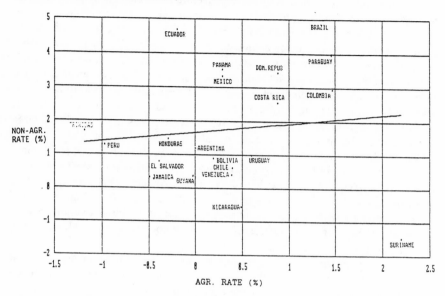

Source: World Bank, *World Tables* (1988–1989).
Note: Constant 1980 price GDP at market prices in local currency.
Descriptive Variables for Simple Fit: R-Square 0.0170;
Value of Coefficient of Agriculture Growth Rate 0.2714;
T-Stat. of Agriculture Growth Rate 0.57;
Std. Error of Agriculture Growth Rate 0.47.

respect to the agricultural growth rate (on the order of 0.3 to 0.6, as reported by Rao, 1975), effective stimulus to the nonagricultural sector combined with the large size of agriculture results in rapid overall increase in employment. The Philippines experienced substantial growth in agricultural employment, but that was not enough to raise real wage rates in the face of population growth and failure in the nonagricultural sector.

The most striking empirical evidence with respect to the relationship between agricultural growth and absolute poverty reduction comes from India. There, the five states (Punjab, Haryana, Andhra Pradesh, Gujarat, and Maharashtra) with the fastest growth rate in the agricultural sector, in a twenty-year period, 1963–1984, reduced the proportion of the rural population in absolute poverty by half or more (Dev, 1988). The Indian states for which agriculture stagnated, such as Bihar, actually experienced an increase in the proportion of the rural population in absolute poverty.

Kerala is the interesting exception to the generalization that absolute poverty reduction in poor states or countries with a large agricultural sector is closely related to accelerated agricultural growth. Kerala also reduced its proportion of the population in absolute poverty by more than half in the twenty-year period analyzed, but it had a relatively poor record with respect to the rate of growth in the agricultural sector. Once again, we draw the conclusion that it is possible to reduce poverty without moving the agricultural sector. However, the conditions are difficult to achieve. In the case of Kerala, the relatively high educational levels in the state facilitated out-migration. Historically that migration was to other parts of India, which did not dramatically reduce poverty in Kerala; but recently it was to the Gulf states, from which remittances have been very large and have played a major role in reducing absolute poverty.

Country data for Indonesia, Thailand, and Malaysia all confirm that accelerated agricultural growth reduces the proportion of the rural population in absolute poverty (Chernichovsky, 1984; Meesook, 1979; Anand, 1983). In each case, the proportions of the rural population in absolute poverty have dropped on the order of one-half within a ten- to twenty-year period of rapid overall growth. Furthermore, agricultural growth rates in all three countries were well above the average for developing countries.

It is implicit in the preceding that emphasis on agriculture in development does not slow the pace of urbanization. Indeed, one can say that the faster the agricultural growth rate, the faster the decline in the relative importance of the agricultural sector (Mellor, 1966). That relationship follows basically from Engel's law. However, it is notable that where the agricultural growth rate has been rapid, it has been associated with distribution of urban growth over a large number of geographically dispersed urban centers, rather than concentrating in a single megalopolis (Mellor, forthcoming). The Philippines's failure of agriculture to simulate accelerated nonagricultural growth has been associated with the concentration of urban growth in the single center of metro Manila, with associated major diseconomies of scale and environmental hazard (Bautista, forthcoming).

Finally, it should be noted that we have learned a great deal in the last twenty-five years, not only about the relationship between agricultural and nonagricultural growth but also with respect to the means of developing the agricultural sector. For issues on which we were only hypothesizing twenty-five years ago, we can now speak with considerable authority (e.g., Mellor and Mudahar, 1992; Eicher and Baker, 1992; Schuh and Brandao, 1992).

THE CONCEPTUAL FRAMEWORK

How agriculture grows and how it influences growth of the other sectors are now conceptually straightforward. The key to both processes is increasing factor productivity in the dominant agricultural sector, which initially contains the bulk of the factors of production in a low-income country. In the long run, that increase in factor productivity depends upon technological change, and if it is to proceed rapidly, that technological change must grow from the application of modern science. In the short run, expansion of the land area may be of importance. Change in the composition of agricultural output toward higher value commodities is also important.

The increased factor productivity in the dominant agricultural sector raises net national income. The expenditure of that incremental income stimulates growth of other sectors. Because one is dealing with an addition to income, consumption expenditure can be an important source of such stimulus concurrent with an increase in the savings and hence investment rate. Such a conceptualization is consistent with the theoretical work of Solow and the empirical work of Dennison with respect to the dominant role of increased factor productivity as the source of growth in contemporary developed countries (Solow, 1963).

The expenditure patterns of smallholder farmers are substantially on the order of a 40 percent incremental budget share for consumer goods produced in the rural nonagricultural sector (Hazell and Bell, 1980). There is also substantial incremental expenditure, on the order of a 20 percent incremental budget share, on labor-intensively produced agricultural commodities, such as livestock and horticultural commodities (Anderson and Hazell, 1989; Hazell and Röell, 1983). These expenditure patterns, providing increased demand for labor, document the causality between accelerated growth in agriculture and accelerated growth in the nonagricultural sectors.

The supply of the additional goods demanded from the incremental agricultural incomes tends to be highly elastic. In addition, it is likely that the cross-elasticities of demand for these rural-based, labor-intensive consumer goods will be relatively high so that an inelasticity with respect to any particular commodity can be met by expansion of a substitute commodity.

The elasticity of supply of the activity stimulated by expenditure of increased agricultural income is high because of the nature of both the labor and capital markets. In a low-income country, the supply of labor is highly elastic. This is significantly due to underemployment, as usually defined, of labor in the rural sector. There is substantial use of labor in activities that provide returns well below the average income and below its productivity in the activity stimulated by increased agricultural incomes (Mellor, 1976). With such a slack labor situation, it is also possible to increase labor productivity by very low cost changes in organization and technology (Mellor and Johnston, 1984; Johnston and Kilby, 1975; Mellor, 1976).

Savings tend also to be elastic in the rural sector with respect to the rate of return on investment (Desai and Mellor, forthcoming). Thus, the initial response to increased demand from rising rural incomes can easily be an increase in the savings rate and therefore of investable funds and investment. However, in the longer run, as will be clear in later exposition of the Philippine example, integrated national financial markets are important to expansion of the employment-intensive rural agricultural and nonagricultural activities. That is because a substantial amount of the expansion comes from increase in size of the more efficient of the rural producers. That increase in size is beyond what can be financed from retained earnings and increased savings at the individual household level.

There is one remaining potential constraint to expansion of the nonagricultural sector. In general, processes that are labor-intensive utilize substantial quantities of intermediate products that are capital-intensive (Mellor, 1976). These take the form of steel, aluminum, plastics, and related goods. In order to maintain low capital-labor ratios it is important that the capital-intensive intermediate products be imported. Thus, the demand for imports will rise as domestic demand for labor-intensive products increases. Fortunately, accelerated agricultural growth and market-oriented policies facilitate accelerated growth of exports. It is notable that in this context nontraditional agricultural exports expand rapidly (Mellor, forthcoming). That is because of the improvement in physical infrastructure associated with accelerated agricultural growth and consequent reduction in transaction costs, as well as an increase in sophistication in the labor force with increased education. Thus, agricultural exports are likely to be an important means of earning the incremental foreign exchange for increasing imports of the capital-intensive intermediate products associated with increased employment intensity. We expand later on the need for open trading regimes and complementary macropolicy to these aspects of agriculture-based growth strategy.

Potential Conceptual Shortcomings

The most important source of weakness in the application of the conceptual framework set forth is a highly skewed income distribution in the agricultural sector arising from either feudal systems or large-scale plantation agriculture. The high degree of concentration of wealth in such systems results in expenditure patterns that have a much more import-intensive or capital-intensive composition. As a result the stimulus from agricultural incomes is very weak with respect to mobilizing underutilized labor and domestic savings potentials, particularly in the rural sector. In the case of feudal systems, the land tenure weakness may also restrain the changes needed to achieve accelerated growth in agricultural output and factor productivity.

Historical examples of major land tenure weakness for achieving strong linkages between agricultural and nonagricultural growth are imperial Ethiopia and most of the Central American countries. Mixed situations arise in the case of the Philippines, Colombia, and Costa Rica, all of which have about half of their agricultures in the large-scale, wealth-concentrated systems. In the latter two cases, the land concentrations were not sufficient to prevent strong growth linkages between agricultural and nonagricultural growth, but they do seem to have weakened the relationship (Mellor, forthcoming). In the case of the Philippines, concentrated land ownership combined with unfavorable macropolicy, which itself probably arose in substantial part because of the stratified society associated with a history of concentrated land ownership, combined to prevent the linkages between agricultural and nonagricultural growth with all the unfortunate consequences previously indicated (Mellor, forthcoming).

Taiwan and Japan represent the ideal situations, at the other end of the land tenure spectrum, for strong multipliers between agricultural and nonagricultural growth. The countries of Africa are, in general, well placed from this point of view. South Asia is also well placed. Even though land distribution is somewhat skewed in that region, it is not skewed toward highly wealthy people with very different consumption patterns from those of the mass of rural people.

Land tenure weakness is difficult to cure. Conceptually, all that is needed is a land reform that redistributes land more equitably. Such a land reform was undoubtedly important to the success of Taiwan in pursuing an agriculture-led, high-employment strategy of economic growth (Mao, forthcoming). Productivity of resources tends to be higher in smallholder production (Mellor, 1966). But the political inhibitions are immense. In general, the major land reforms have occurred under outside pressure, such as the MacArthur Land Reform in Japan and the Chiang Kai-shek land reform in Taiwan. The very major land reforms in the mid-1950s in India were possible because the wealthy landed class had thrown in its lot substantially with the losers in the freedom movement. Short of radical political change of the types indicated before, land reforms seem to be rare occurrences.

The land reforms associated with radical change from feudal or semifeudal political systems to Marxist systems provide the redistribution of land necessary for the growth linkages to work, but Marxist governments seem rarely to understand what is needed to bring about accelerated growth in the agricultural sector. They tend to be heavily urban-oriented and to believe in major-scale economies in agricultural production and thus avoid assisting smallholder agriculture.

Deficiency in macropolicy is the second major weakness that may prevent strong multipliers from agricultural to nonagricultural growth. The Philippines exemplifies that weakness. The first deleterious macropolicy set is that leading to an overvalued exchange rate. High tariffs and quantitative restrictions on imports discriminate against growth of agricultural exports generally and nontraditional agricultural exports specifically. Large public budget deficits reinforce the tendency toward overvalued exchange rates as devaluation is abjured in the name of restraining inflation. Damage to nontraditional agricultural exports for which most developing countries in the low- to middle-income range have growing comparative advantage is particularly severe in such a regime. That damage is unlikely to be offset by subsidies and other assistance because, by definition, it is unlikely that government officials will correctly predict which nontraditional commodities will experience an export boom. The poor performance of nontraditional agricultural exports not only slows growth of the agricultural sector but also, through a foreign exchange constraint, weakens the linkages to rural nonagricultural growth.

The second macropolicy set deleterious to agriculturally led growth is that of policies that direct capital resources largely toward capital-intensive, large-scale, urban-based industries, thereby starving for capital the rural-based activities stimulated by agricultural growth. In the case of the Philippines, an overvalued exchange rate and related preferential licensing for capital-intensive industries directed capital away from the rural sector toward metropolitan Manila. The banking system was then used to siphon funds from rural areas toward the favored industries. These tendencies were reinforced by low interest rates to the favored borrowers (Bautista, forthcoming).

Many countries also engage in a physical allocation of capital resources to large-scale, capital-intensive industries. That was notably the case in India and China, where these industries were located largely in the public sector (Mellor, 1976). The result has been that the small- and medium-scale rural industries are starved for capital. They must expand entirely on retained earnings, which are adequate for getting started and for initial expansion but inadequate for rapid expansion of the more successful of such firms.

Alternative Strategies

Perhaps in part because of failure of smallholder agricultural strategies in specific circumstances, there is often a turn to alternative strategies. There may also be a turn to alternative strategies because of a lack of understanding of the agricultural sector or an urban bias in the political system that makes it politically inexpedient to develop the agricultural sector. The most common alternative strategy is to use tariff restrictions, trade quotas, and direct allocation of capital to foster large-scale, capital-intensive urban industry. Such efforts often start with import substitution toward industries in which a country has a comparative advantage, namely, the more labor-intensive consumer goods. Over time, the strategy becomes more and more capital-intensive. The result is soaking up capital resources in forms that provide relatively little employment and low rates of return to capital (Mellor and Johnston, 1984; Mellor, 1976). These development strategies virtually always grind to a halt with decreasing productivity of capital, high unemployment rates and often consequent civil disturbance, and slow overall growth rates, which further slow the rate of capital formation.

In recent years, another nonagricultural orientation has become fashionable: encouraging growth of what is often called the nonformal sectors. These are basically the small-scale enterprises that are substantially located in rural areas. This strategy is bound for failure if agriculture lags, primarily because the effective demand for such commodities comes largely from agricultural incomes. If agricultural incomes are stagnating, there cannot be growth in effective demand for the output, and growth will halt due to declining prices and profitability. Such efforts to stimulate the nonformal sector appear successful in pilot projects within which demand can be taken from other producers. However, as soon as they expand sufficiently to have an aggregate effect, the aggregate demand is deficient, and they fail. The Grameen Bank in Bangladesh, a success in lending to the poor, faces substantial problems from lack of expanding demand for output of goods and services produced by its borrowers (Hossain, 1988).

HOW AGRICULTURE GROWS

There are three principal means of agricultural growth: expansion of the land area, change in the product mix, and factor productivity increasing technological change. Historically, area expansion has been a principal source of agricultural growth. But, as can be seen from Table 7.1, population growth has gradually expanded onto most of the world's potentially arable area. Thus, area growth has been gradually displaced by yield growth as the principal means of increasing output. This shift, not surprisingly, came first in high-population-density Asia. But, even in Africa, the contribution of area grants to output increase has been declining.

Land Area Expansion

A number of developing countries that have done well in agriculture and, through that, stimulated accelerated growth in the nonagricultural sector have expanded substantially through area expansion. Thailand is an excellent case (Siamwalla, forthcoming). Costa Rica (Celis and Lizano, forthcoming) and Colombia (Berry, forthcoming) both substantially expanded this way.

It is important to note that increased factor productivity is essential if growth in agriculture is to stimulate other sectors of the economy. This requirement means that the land area must be expanded by bringing land into production that is of higher average productivity than what is already in production. That becomes feasible where diminution of disease, such as malaria, makes it possible to bring new high productivity areas into production. It also becomes feasible with introduction of physical infrastructure, such as good highways. An example was the large military investment in roads in Thailand in connection with the Vietnam War. Increase in demand, either domestic or foreign, may also stimulate a change in output mix toward greater intensity.

One of the great dangers with agricultural growth through area expansion is taking attention away from the eventual need for technological change to raise productivity of existing land. The land frontier as a principal source of agricultural growth ran out in India in the late 1950s. It almost ran out in Thailand in the late 1980s and is beginning to run out in much of Africa in the 1990s.

On one hand, where area expansion has been proceeding rapidly and yield-increasing technology neglected, there is a large nascent potential for such expansion through improved technology. On the other hand, the very complex institutional structures needed for such expansion may not be developed. Thailand is a very good example of such failure. Even though its crop yields are low by Asian standards, its agricultural growth rate has plummeted to well below the

Table 7.1

Average Annual Growth Rates of Production, Area Harvested, and Output Per Hectare of Major Food Crops, by Region and Subregion, 1961–1970 and 1971–1980

Country Group	Period	Average Annual Growth Rate			Contribution to Production Increase	
		Production /a	Area Harvested	Output Per Hectare	Area Harvested	Output Per Hectare
		(----------------------------------percent----------------------------------)				
Developing Countries	1961-70	3.6	1.1	2.5	30.0	70.0
	1971-80	2.9	0.6	2.3	20.0	80.0
(Excluding China)	1961-70	(2.9)	(1.5)	(1.4)	(51)	(49)
	1971-80	(2.6)	(0.8)	(1.8)	(32)	(68)
Asia	1961-70	3.8	0.5	3.4	13.0	87.0
	1971-80	3.3	0.5	2.8	16.0	84.0
(Excluding China)	1961-70	(2.7)	(0.8)	(1.8)	(31)	(69)
	1971-80	(3.1)	(0.9)	(2.2)	(30)	(70)
China /b	1961-70	5.2	-0.1	5.4	/d	100.0
	1971-80	3.4	-0.2	3.6	/d	100.0
South Asia	1961-70	2.7	0.8	1.9	29.0	71.0
	1971-80	2.7	0.7	2.0	25.0	75.0
East and Southeast Asia	1961-70	2.7	1.1	1.6	40.0	60.0
	1971-80	3.9	1.7	2.2	44.0	56.0
North Africa/Middle East	1961-70	2.4	1.2	1.2	51.0	49.0
	1971-80	2.6	0.7	1.9	26.0	74.0
Northern Africa	1961-70	3.3	1.4	1.9	43.0	57.0
	1971-80	0.9	1.5	-0.6	100.0	/d
Western Asia	1961-70	2.0	1.1	0.9	57.0	43.0
	1971-80	3.5	0.3	3.2	8.0	92.0

Sub-Saharan Africa	1961-70	2.2	2.4	-0.2	100.0	/d
	1971-80	1.6	0.8	0.8	50.0	50.0
West Africa	1961-70	1.1	2.2	-1.1	100.0	/d
	1971-80	1.9	1.1	0.7	61.0	39.0
Central Africa	1961-70	4.4	4.8	-0.4	100.0	/d
	1971-81	1.8	21.3	0.5	100.0	/d
Eastern and Southern Africa	1961-70	3.0	2.2	0.8	72.0	28.0
	1971-80	1.4	-0.3	1.6	/d	100.0
Latin America	1961-70	4.2	2.8	1.4	66.0	34.0
	1971-80	1.8	0.6	1.2	33.0	47.0
Mexico and Central America /c	1961-70	5.7	2.2	3.5	39.0	61.0
	1971-80	3.0	-0.2	3.2	/d	100.0
Upper South America	1961-70	4.6	3.7	0.8	82.0	18.0
	1971-80	1.8	1.8	0.0	100.0	0.0
Lower South America	1961-70	2.5	1.6	0.9	63.0	37.0
	1971-80	0.6	-1.3	2.0	/d	100.0

Sources: Food and Agriculture Organization of the United Nations (1976, 1980, 1982, 1984); People's Republic of China (various years); Republic of China (1983).

Notes: Negative rates also occurred of area during subperiods.

[a]The production dates exclude bananas and plantains, for which area estimates are not available.

[b]The data on Area for China are for area planted.

[c]Mexico and Central America includes the Caribbean.

[d]Negative. The contribution to the production increase is assigned totally to the other source of increase.

levels of land-short Asian countries as its land frontier vanished (Mellor, forthcoming).

Change in Product Mix

Change in the product mix toward commodities that give higher factor productivity has been an important component of agricultural growth in practically all developing countries that have experienced accelerated growth in their agricultural sectors (Mellor, forthcoming). This change in product mix is made possible by increases in international, as well as in domestic, demand. For the former, a favorable trade regime is necessary.

It is difficult to achieve more than a 2.5 to 3.5 percent rate of growth in the basic food staple sector, while countries with high agricultural growth rate achieve 4 to 6 percent rates of growth in the sector as a whole. Such high rates of growth are possible because of shifts in product mix toward commodities that provide a high value of output per acre and that are generally labor-intensive in their production. Those subsectors of agriculture can grow at rates comparable to those of the nonagricultural sector if effective demand increases at a comparable rate.

Product composition can be changed toward high-value, high-factor-productivity commodities by expanded exports. One of the best examples of this is the rapid growth in smallholder tea and coffee production in Kenya (Lele, 1991). At higher stages of development, exports of labor-intensive livestock products, such as pork and boned chicken from Thailand and Taiwan to Japan, and horticultural commodities, such as snow peas from Guatemala to the United States, provide scope for substantial increase in factor productivity (Mao and Chi, forthcoming; von Braun et al., 1989). The factor productivity in these export commodities is several times that in basic food staple production. The substantial additions to agricultural income provide an effective demand stimulus to the rural nonagricultural sector.

Rising incomes within a developing country also provide scope for shifting product mix in agriculture toward higher factor productivity commodities. The prime examples are increased consumption of livestock and horticultural commodities. Both of these allow greatly increased labor input and a raising of the productivity of labor in those activities as compared with the marginal activities that occur in a country of underemployed labor.

To meet the growth potentials from shifting product mix requires positive public action of the type associated with technological change and discussed in the next section. Those needs range from the institutional structures for research, input supply, finance, and marketing to massive public investment in physical infrastructure and education. The complexity of production and marketing needs associated with the greater perishability of many of the high-value products makes larger demands on each of these requirements than the basic food staple subsector of agriculture.

Technological Change

Sooner or later, yield-increasing technological change must displace area expansion as the basic engine of growth in the agricultural sector. A land area constraint on the means of growth is a key characteristic of agriculture (Mellor, 1966). That has already occurred in essentially all Asian countries and is increasingly occurring in Africa. Latin America has land frontiers, for example, the immense *cerrado* of Brazil, but that land generally has high operating costs. Technological change is also an important complement to increased intensification through change in the product mix. Maintenance of competitive position in nontraditional agricultural exports requires a research and development capacity. Expansion of high-value agricultural commodities for domestic markets in which demand elasticities are elastic also requires a substantial research and development capacity as well as the low transactions costs associated with improved rural physical infrastructure.

Traditional agricultures always experience gradual technological improvement, particularly in the face of population growth and increased pressures of population on land (Boserup, 1981). However, the productivity growth rate in traditional agricultures is rarely more than .5 percent per year. In developed countries with sophisticated research and extension systems, factor productivity may grow consistently year after year at close to 2 percent per year (Tweeten, 1990).

In developing countries that institute effective structures for agricultural research and extension, a substantial catching-up process is possible as the efficiency of modern science allows rapid progress of adaptive research. In those cases, factor productivity may increase at three or four times the long-term norm of around 2 percent, giving very rapid growth, at least for half a decade to a decade. The "green revolution" in Asia generally and in Indonesia specifically demonstrates the potentials for such catch-up growth rates, at least in relatively small areas.

Substantial acceleration of the growth rate in agriculture through technological change requires a complex institutional structure, significant parts of which must at least initially be provided by government. Thus, agricultural growth depends very much upon public sector activity.

KEY ELEMENTS IN TECHNOLOGICAL CHANGE

There are three key elements to technological change in the agricultural sector—institutions, physical infrastructure, and education. For each, broad participation is essential.

Agriculture is a relatively slow growth sector, as compared with the nonagricultural sector. In the latter, numerous countries achieve growth rates of 8 to 12 percent for a considerable period of time, while in agriculture relatively few countries exceed a 4 to 6 percent growth rate.

Thus, the importance of agriculture to growth rises not because of high growth rates, although there is a difference of a factor of two between slow growth rates and high growth rates in the agricultural sector, but rather because of the size of the sector. This has a very important implication. Since size makes the sector important, playing its full role requires that a high proportion of the agricultural sector be drawn into the development process. Thus, although not 100 percent of agriculture must be included, one cannot leave out major agricultural commodities or geographic areas or major subsectors of agriculture, such as the relatively smaller farmers.

The Institutions of Technological Change

Although an oversimplification, it is useful to think in terms of four classes of institutions for technological change: research and extension to generate and disseminate improved technology; input supply to feed output growth; marketing structures to exchange increases on outputs; and rural financial markets to finance expansion of the movable entrepreneurs.

Research and Extension

The agricultural research extension complex is the basic engine of accelerated agricultural growth. It is the system of modern science that allows acceleration in the agricultural growth rate sufficient to counterbalance accelerated population growth and to allow agriculture to play a positive role in leading overall economic growth. Just as population growth in developing countries is now far faster than the earlier development periods of contemporary developed countries, so, too, must science perform at a far faster pace if agriculture is to be important to development.

The rate of return to agricultural research is high—typically over 30 percent (Evenson, Pray, and Quizon, 1986). The underspending on research despite such high rates of return is due to lack of appreciation of its critical role despite the conceptualizations of modern economic growth theory and the drama of the green revolutions research breakthroughs. It may also be due to its placement in the public sector, where multiple objectives blunt the apparent importance of research. The high rate of return may also arise from the complexity of calculating the rate of return and hence lack of specific evidence as to the precise level of optimal expenditure on individual research systems and stations.

As a result of the latter factors, businesses and governments alike tend to use a rule of thumb of the percentage of total product for allocating funds to, and within, research. For developing countries the common recommendation is 3 percent of agricultural product to research, but many countries allocate less than 1 percent and some less than .5 percent (Oram and Bindlish, 1981). The same rule of thumb applied at the commodity level ranks commodities according to the level of recommended research expenditure. Analysis of such consonance between research expenditure and value of output shows many anomalies. Some are due to judgments with respect to the likelihood of research results given the conditions for growing the crop. Political circumstances and fortuitous forces are at work as well.

In practice, the agricultural research systems of developing countries are inefficient in their use of resources due to a range of administrative problems. Typically they spend the bulk of budget on personnel with consequent underallocation to such supporting services as vehicles and operating expenses for test plots. Such misallocation of resources arises, in part, from perceived problems of inadequate employment opportunity and consequent political and personal pressures to expand employment. It is also the result of inadequate understanding of the key role of research in agricultural growth.

It is also common to spread research resources too thinly over a multiplicity of commodities. In general, the procedures for setting priorities that would allow a concentration of limited resources where a critical mass would allow productive output and consequent political support are not in place, partly because of the difficulty of conceptualizing such an exercise.

There is generally inadequate integration of research and extension. Extension services tend to have inadequate technical competence and are disproportionately large. The latter arises from the importance of extension personnel in providing a government presence in the countryside in political systems that are still embryonic, poorly developed, and poorly represented in the countryside.

One of the most important current issues with respect to technology development is the appropriate division of effort between public and private sector activity. In developed countries, agricultural research and the dissemination of that information were initially largely a public sector activity. Now, considerable agricultural research is performed in the private sector. That is partly because of the change in the nature of technology. For example, hybrid seed varieties have become important in biological improvement; these must be replaced each year. Partly in response to the change in technology base, the legal frameworks have been modified to provide patent protection. Biological innovations are more easily patentable than was the case a few decades ago. The overburdening of public sectors in developing countries with activities best carried out in the private sector has reduced effectiveness in areas most suited to public activity. Thus, correctly diagnosing the appropriate division between public and private sector activities is important to the efficiency of each.

Inputs

Biological science innovation increases factor productivity in agriculture by increasing yields per acre of land. That increases per acre input requirements. In addition, developing countries are typically in tropical or subtropical areas in which rainfall is heavy, and often the soils are old; the two together cause low fertility. Thus, optimal rates of fertilizer application tend to be higher than in temperate-latitude developed countries.

In addition, as yields increase, not only the susceptibility but also the absolute losses from pest damage will increase. Thus, the inputs of pest control will increase as well. Even with the introduction of biological control methods, the quantity of complementary chemicals will be higher than in the previous initially very low or even zero levels of application. Finally, the percentage decrease in yields that comes from weed infestations will be greater with higher-yielding varieties, and at the same time labor cost will tend to rise as employment, both in agriculture and in nonagriculture, increases. As a result, inputs for controlling weeds are likely to become more important.

Thus, a key requisite of technological innovation in agriculture is development of institutional structures for providing rapidly increasing quantities of inputs. These structures are most efficiently operated largely in the private sector. However, it is essential that the government recognize the needs and monitor the extent to which the private sector is providing the necessary services.

There is a tendency in developing countries for the returns to working capital to be very high and for working capital to be scarce and expensive. As a result, the private sector is often reluctant to make the working capital investments in widely distributed inventories, particularly in areas in which the demand is unpredictable. In those circumstances, governments may have to play an important role in the initiation of purchased input use and, later, turn over those efforts to the private sector. The critical concern as the government initiates such activities is that the government not operate in a manner that reduces the profitability of the private sector. Subsidies to overhead costs when volume is low are self-eliminating and will not inhibit private operations in the long run, but more general subsidies inhibit essential private sector activity.

The current environmental concerns in developed countries spill over to the quite different problems of developing countries. In the latter, degradation—requiring more inputs—is the usual problem, not pollution—requiring less inputs. However, at low levels of education and with poor institutional structures inputs may be used inefficiently—a problem that deserves immediate attention and eventual remedy. In passing, greatly expanded future levels of nitrogen consumption in developing countries will use only a small fraction of the world's natural gas supplies. Reducing use of inputs in food production in developing countries is hardly the optimal immediate focus for environmentalists.

Fertilizer is the most financially important purchased input for agriculture and requires monitoring in three different areas. First, since it is produced by highly capital-intensive processes, it likely is and should be largely imported. It is important that foreign exchange controls not inhibit a high rate of growth in supply. Second, because the growth of demand is rapid and determined by complex factors that vary greatly across regions, regional distribution requirements are difficult to predict for any one year. It is important that immense amounts of credit be available to finance the stocking of fertilizer in a timely manner, on a broad geographic basis. Third, international fertilizer prices fluctuate enormously. Because of the impact of food production on overall economic growth, an effort to stabilize prices around a projected long-term moving average is sensible.

Marketing

In virtually all developing countries, there is an initial private sector providing marketing services. That private sector is, by definition, integrated into a national and indeed into an international market. Thus, it should be able to expand and respond to the stimulus of increasing production and factor productivity in agriculture. Government should monitor the activities of the private sector to be sure that it is performing effectively, that it is competitive, and that necessary complementary public investments are made. That requires substantial investment in physical infrastructure, not only in including all-weather roads, electricity, and telephone, all of which are essential to efficient and competitive private sector behavior, but also in seeing to it that adequate physical marketing facilities are provided. Governments also have an important role to play in providing regulations to ensure competitiveness, including weights and measures, and ensuring adequate marketing yards and other means of facilitating market access and transparency.

Traders in rural markets have always been vilified in populist movements. The statistical evidence is that they operate competitively, as demonstrated by margins that just cover their transaction costs of transport, storage, financing, and processing. The seminal corroborating study by Lele (1971) has been confirmed by numerous other studies over a wide range of time and space. These same studies also confirm that postharvest losses are also modest—for cereals about 6 percent—and not easily reduced. Lack of competition and low factor productivity arise when physical infrastructure is poor—one of the several reasons massive investment in rural infrastructure is necessary to accelerated agricultural growth.

Finance

The traditional financial system in rural areas, unlike that for agricultural marketing, is generally not integrated into a national grid. Thus, it is difficult to reform or tune the traditional financial markets to the needs of a dynamic, growing agriculture.

A dynamic, growing agriculture has immense, rapidly rising, uneven credit needs. This is because of rapid commercialization in input use and growth in the quantity and variety of output. During periods when technological innovation is proceeding rapidly in a particular region, the demand for credit to finance working capital in agriculture will quickly exceed the local capacity for savings. The supply of local finance is inelastic (Desai and Mellor, forthcoming; Rosegrant and Herdt, 1981). Under such circumstances, a nationally integrated financial market is essential to flow funds to other regions of accelerated technology change.

Conversely, when a particular burst of innovation has passed for a particular geographic area, the savings rate will rise. Marginal savings rates among agriculturalists tend to be on the order of 30 percent in a technologically dynamic circumstance with well-working financial markets. Thus, there is an important job of deposit mobilization. On balance, rural deposit mobilization is much greater than rural lending and comprises an important source of finance for growth of the nonagricultural sector.

Under these circumstances and in sharp contrast to marketing, new institutional forms are essential to the development of effective integrated national financial markets. The urban-based commercial banking system can play an important role in this context. However, in general, urban-based banks are reluctant to expand into rural areas dominated by small farmers. They envisage excessively high operating costs and are uncomfortable with the new forms of risk entailed in lending to small farmers. Typically, governments have to step in to force an opening of branch banks in rural areas. Ex-post rural banking systems usually turn out to be quite profitable, particularly because of the high rate of deposit mobilization.

A system of rural cooperatives can also provide effective competition for commercial banks utilizing a quite different set of highly knowledgeable local sources of management skills. Governments may have an important role to play in training managers for such institutions and in providing oversight.

Given the rural financial markets' need for new institutional forms and rapid expansion, it is not surprising that loan repayment rates are low. High overdues, the bulk of which is not bad debt, are due to misspecification of terms, including repayment periods that do not synchronize with the crop season; poor administrative supervision, which must be greater for illiterate farmers than for those who are better educated; unstable agricultural environment and hazards; undisciplined political systems that encourage nonpayment of debt; and management weaknesses that are generic to rapidly expanding institutions. These problems need to be solved while continuing to expand the rural financial system and its coverage, not by contracting the system.

The major dilemma of rural financial systems is reconciling the need for a dense system of branches with the need to hold down transaction costs. Additional branches add convenience while raising administrative costs. Rural people respond in borrowing and depositing more to the convenience of a branch than to the level of interest rates (Rosegrant and Herdt, 1981). Nevertheless, the elasticity of borrowing with respect to interest rates is elastic, while the elasticity for deposits is inelastic (Desai and Mellor, forthcoming). Thus, lending rates and hence transaction costs are important to the finance of technological advance. The dilemma is best resolved by expanding the density of lending by restraining interest rates and by enlarging the range of activities, certainly including mobilizing deposits. In addition to farmers, there is an immense need to finance working capital requirements of agricultural businesses. That need also offers opportunities to spread overhead costs of branches over a higher volume of business.

Infrastructure

In the last decade, a substantial number of studies have been made of the role of infrastructure in rural development. They consistently show that rural infrastructure is essential to rural growth (Ahmed and Hossain, 1990). Indeed, the role of physical infrastructure is much greater than one would expect by simply looking at the impact on direct transportation cost. The reason for that is that rural development requires complex institutions staffed by well-educated people. Such people and their families will in general refuse to live in isolated, rural areas. Thus, the provision of an all-weather road on which buses can ply, telephone, and electricity are essential to adequate institutional development for agriculture. It is also essential to achieving the low levels of information and transaction cost essential to well-operating markets (Ahmed and Hossain, 1990).

In developing countries, a high proportion of rural people are not located adjacent to all-weather roads and associated physical infrastructures and hence have higher transaction costs and a general lack of access to the institutions of development. That proportion is on the order of one-third to one-half in much of Asia and 90 percent in much of Africa. The total investment required to rectify that situation would be about $200 billion (Mellor, 1990). That would require $20 billion per year of investment, spread over ten years, one-quarter of which would be represented by food consumed in the labor-intensive processes. Building new roads is of little use if both old and new roads are not maintained, which is frequently the case. That will generally require building local government institutions, which in turn tend to be threatening to urban-based national governments. For that reason, national governments often prevent development of local governments. Thus, a coupled interaction of investment requirements and political institutions is difficult to achieve.

Education

Education, like physical infrastructure, requires immense public investment. In these two areas one measures urban bias, which must be corrected if agriculture is to play a leading role in development.

Because accelerated agricultural growth depends so much on institutional structures, not only is it important to have substantial intensity of higher education to provide the staffing for such structures, but it is also important that farmers be educated, in large part, through the secondary school system so that they will know how to develop, manipulate, and interact with such institutions and their educated staff. Returns to rural education are high (Sabot, 1989).

Initially, in the catching-up stage, technological advance in agriculture tends to come in forms that give substantial percentage increases in production, and it is accompanied by relatively simple input and management techniques. The initial "green revolution" fertilizer response—short, stiff-stemmed wheat and rice varieties—is an example. However, over time, a high growth rate is maintained by continual introduction of a substantial number of much smaller innovations which are more difficult to understand and to apply. Thus, the need for education rises rapidly as the technological process proceeds.

All of this is strongly reinforced by environmental concerns. In the face of complex modern agricultural and biological technology with relatively high-input levels, environmental destruction possibilities increase. First, there are likely to be increased specialization and therefore increased monocropping on individual fields as each field is used to its optimum use. Second, the high-input levels may cause leaching into groundwater and other destruction. In both these cases, sophisticated soil analysis and understanding of complex biological processes become important. In developed countries, there has been radical change toward environmentally sound practices. Application of needed change has moved relatively rapidly in developed countries because of the complex institutional support systems, ranging from simple extension education to complex soil-testing institutions and the ability of highly educated farmers to understand the need for, and to utilize, such institutions. In developing countries, both the requisite institutional structures and education of the farmers are embryonic at best. Thus, environmentally unsound practices are likely to continue for a long time, until the needed investments are made.

Rural education must be expanded to cover secondary as well as primary education. Primary education provides the tools for learning, and secondary education begins the process of learning itself. That need for secondary education grows rapidly with the increasing complexity and sophistication of agriculture.

As in the case of infrastructure, since the investment in education is very large, there is need to develop institutional structures, particularly at the local level, for raising the tax revenues for meeting those needs. Marginal tax rates at a given level provide less disincentive when the proceeds are for activities that local people want, particularly if those investments of tax monies shift the cost schedule for the agricultural sector in a favorable direction. Again, we have an argument for rural local government and face the dilemma of its threatening nature to urban-based political systems.

FOOD SECURITY AND POVERTY

In poor developing countries, a quarter to half of the rural population lies under the normally defined absolute poverty line (Mellor, 1990). Such absolute poverty is associated with inadequate food intake. People are so poor that even devoting 80 percent and more of their income to food, they still have inadequate calories for an active, healthy life.

The food security pyramid (Figure 7.4) depicts the complex processes involved

Figure 7.4
Food Security Pyramid

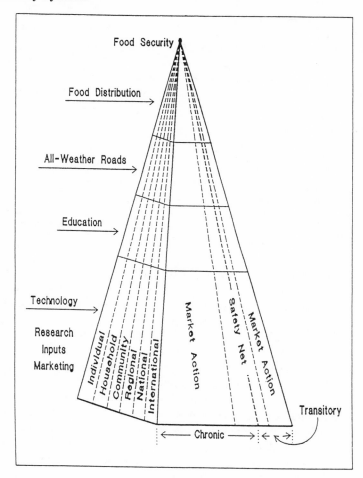

in dealing with absolute poverty and the accompanying food insecurity. This chapter is largely concerned with agriculture in the context of economic growth. But year-to-year changes in the food situation are critical to the survival of a high proportion of the population in developing countries; food security affects political stability and, hence, growth; and it is inseparable from poverty, the reduction of which is a prime objective of growth.

Food security is seen by virtually all development-oriented organizations as a major objective of development. Most institutions, for example, the World Bank, the Food and Agriculture Organization of the United Nations, and the International Fund for Agricultural Development, define food security as a circumstance in which all people at all times have sufficient food to lead a healthy

Table 7.2
Geographic Distribution of Poverty, 1990*

				Agricultural Potential	
Region	Total	Urban	Rural	High	Low
(numbers in millions, percentages in brackets)					
Africa	137	14	123	61 (50)	61 (50)
South Asia	350	70	280	140 (50)	62 (50)
East Asia/Pacific	31	5	26	6 (25)	20 (75)
Latin America	72	29	43	11 (25)	32 (75)
Near East	34	10	24	8 (33)	16 (67)
China	76	-	76	26 (33)	50 (67)
TOTAL	700	128	572	252	312

Source: Mellor (1990), 511.
*The distribution by rural and urban classification is based on a survey of country poverty studies.
   All poverty in China is grouped under rural poverty. The classification into agricultural potential
   is based on unpublished work by Broca at IFPRI.

and active life (Huddleston, 1990; Reutlinger and van Horst Pellekaan, 1986; Alamgir and Poonan, 1991). Such a broad but powerful definition conveniently divides itself into chronic aspects of food security and transitory aspects. Since absolute poverty is normally defined in terms of income required to provide food security (e.g., minimal caloric intake), food insecurity and absolute poverty are synonymous.

Chronic food insecurity describes the situation of those people who at least for significant periods of each year are food-insecure on a day-to-day basis. Such food insecurity manifests itself in the significant stunting of children. For example, the children of the poor in poor countries, due to food insecurity, are typically several inches shorter than the children of the urban middle classes at the same age. People who in many or even most years are food-secure but who become food-insecure in specific years of unusually unfavorable weather or civil strife are said to be victims of transitory food insecurity.

In round numbers, about 700 million people are in a state of chronic food insecurity in this, the last decade of the twentieth century (Table 7.2). Food insecurity is endemic in South Asia, where on the order of one-third to one-half of the populations are in a food-insecure state and compose roughly half of the food-insecure of the world. About one-fifth of the world's food-insecure are in Africa, where the proportion of the population in food insecurity is similar to that of South Asia. However, food insecurity either has been declining or is in an incipient state of decline in South Asia, while it has been increasing in Africa. Thus, within a decade there may well be more people in a state of chronic food insecurity in Africa than in Asia.

Another 10 percent of the food-insecure are in China, primarily in the low-production potential areas, while the proportion of the total population in a food-insecure state is about half that of South Asia. That is partly due to moderately higher per capita income and partly due to the radical land redistribution of the 1950s. The remaining fifth of the food-insecure are scattered in Latin America, North Africa, the Middle East, and Southeast Asia.

In addition to the 700 million people in chronic food insecurity, an additional 200 million people are close enough to the margin of chronic food insecurity that fluctuations in weather cause them to move back and forth across that line. Thus, we may speak of the total number of people in food insecurity as close to 1 billion.

With such massive dimensions to food insecurity, it seems unlikely that the more well-to-do people in the more prosperous countries would, year after year, provide transfer payment to lift so many people to food security on a long-term basis. The obverse is that solution to the food insecurity problem must come from bringing the mass of the food-insecure into the growth process. Incomes must be raised through broad processes of development, based on agricultural growth and the stimulus to nonagricultural growth that comes from rising farm incomes. The key to those processes is improved agricultural technology arising from modern agricultural research systems.

The centrality of broad participation in economic growth to food security is explicitly recognized by the International Fund for Agricultural Development, the Food and Agricultural Organization of the United Nations, and the World Bank (Alamgir and Poonan, 1991; Huddleston, 1990). Several of the bilateral foreign assistance agencies also have position papers that recognize this relationship between growth and food security (Maxwell, 1990). With that perception, the effort to reduce food insecurity largely takes the form of broad development efforts rather than specific food security projects.

Food insecurity and poverty are two sides of the same coin. People who are not poor allocate their income in such a manner as to be food-secure. They may, of course, not do so very efficiently, and they may suffer some malnutrition from a poor allocation of their food budget. But they do have adequate calories for an active and healthy life. The food-insecure have inadequate income to command adequate quantities of food.

In that context, there has been some controversy as to whether food insecurity is a problem of inadequate supplies of food or inadequate income for commanding the food (Sen, 1981). This is an unproductive and diverting argument. Of course, the poor do not have the purchasing power to obtain adequate food. However, the processes of increasing agricultural production and various direct and indirect effects of increased agricultural production provide the increased incomes and purchasing power that lift the poor to food security.

The food-insecure poor are primarily in rural areas. In Africa, roughly 90 percent of those who are so poor as to be food-insecure are located in rural areas; in Asia, the proportion is about 80 percent; and in Latin America, with much higher incomes and more differentiated economies, the proportion of the poor in rural areas is much lower but still on the order of 60 percent (Table 7.1). Many of the urban food-insecure have fled the countryside because of endemic food insecurity. Thus, the basic solution to food insecurity lies in the rural areas of the poor countries.

The distribution of the poor within rural areas relates to the level of development and instructs us as to the strategy for providing food security. In the very poorest countries, the poor are located with greater density in the rural areas with substantial agricultural production potential. Examples are the densely populated but agriculturally rich areas of the Gangetic and Brahmaputra basins of South Asia, the volcanic soils of Java, and the upland farming areas of western Kenya. In each case, both the overall rural population density and the density of the food-insecure poor are very high (Mellor, 1990).

Reducing poverty and increasing food security are a straightforward process in such agricultural-technology responsive areas. Not only does accelerated growth in agricultural production create many more jobs directly in agricultural production, but the expenditure of higher agricultural incomes creates substantial growth in employment in the expanding provision of nonagricultural goods and services. The high rural population densities reduce the cost per capita of provision of the physical infrastructure of all-weather roads, electrification, and telephones, which are so essential to rapid growth in rural nonagricultural employment.

Thus, we find that in middle-income developing countries, the poor are virtually not to be found in the good agricultural areas and instead are found largely concentrated in the poorer agricultural areas. In those countries the processes of development have lifted people in the more productive areas out of the absolute poverty that brings food insecurity. Thus, in higher-income Thailand, there is essentially no poverty or food insecurity on the rich soils of the Central Plain. Such poverty is largely concentrated in the much poorer areas of the northeast. In contrast, in the poor countries of India and Bangladesh, we find a substantial proportion, on the order of 60–70 percent, of the food-insecure concentrated in the rich alluvial areas of the major river systems and in the coastal areas (Table 7.1).

We can draw a conclusion that in the poor countries it makes sense to concentrate first on lifting people out of poverty and into food security in the richer agricultural areas, then, when those easier problems have been solved, to move to the more intractable problems of dealing with those on the poorer soil areas.

Children in particular and, to a lesser extent, women are disproportionately represented among the absolute poor and the food-insecure. The disproportionate representation of women arises partly from the general problem of maintaining adequate incomes in single-family-headed homes and also from discrimination against women, particularly as societies modernize and as women are restrained from taking full advantage of the modern institutions, such as for credit, and purchased inputs, which play such an important role in lifting people out of rural poverty.

Children are disproportionately represented among the food-insecure because the poor tend to have larger numbers of children than the more well-to-do and because large numbers of dependents bring greater poverty, at least in the short run. The problem of food-insecure children has two faces. There is the extraordinary humanitarian problem of small, defenseless people facing chronic hunger, with its debilitating effect on their physical and mental development. The other face is the creation of a new generation of people who are vulnerable to ill health and have not experienced the mental development that should occur with increased schooling.

Solution to the massive problem of food insecurity requires a combination of market-oriented development activities, public safety nets involving redistribution of income, and a complex mix of public and individual action. The complexity is simplified by Mellor's food security pyramid, depicted in Figure 7.4.

The current dimensions of food security are depicted by the broad base of the pyramid, representing the 700 million people in chronic food deficit and the 200 million who occasionally become food deficit in periods of unfavorable weather or other natural disaster. The aspiration of a food-secure future is represented by lateral and vertical contraction of the pyramid to the point of the pyramid at which time food insecurity has been eliminated.

The front face of the pyramid depicts in horizontal bands the actions to achieve food security. The vertical dimension is comprised of two segments representing chronic and transitory food insecurity. Each of those is further divided into the components to be treated by accelerated growth achieved through the operation of private enterprise and free markets in cooperation with complementary public activities and the components requiring direct public action to provide a safety net of income transfers. The side faces of the pyramid designate the continuum of action from the international arena through various levels of national organizations, both public and private, reaching the ultimate objective of the family and the individual child, woman, and man within the family.

Because of human disability and misfortune, it is unlikely that the ultimate objective of contracting the pyramid to the point of universal food security will be achieved entirely by market processes. Hence, specific public programs will continue to be necessary. But the objective of moving close to that point on the basis of development and growth, supplemented by public income transfers, is reachable.

The numbers of the food-insecure are so large that growth must be the primary instrument of food security. Thus, the bulk of the width of the pyramid, for both chronic and transitory food insecurity, is comprised of market-oriented growth activities. Those activities are much larger in total than what is depicted on the food security pyramid. The pyramid includes only the specific orientation of those efforts toward food security. Thus, as the pyramid compresses, the size of those activities specifically oriented toward food security may decline, while the general activity increases. Within the context of market-oriented growth, specific government programs will provide income transfers to reduce food insecurity.

Many types of effort contribute to increased food security. Some efforts have a direct effect while others, no less important in their impact, are indirect. Classes of such effort are depicted as horizontal bands on the pyramid, with those having the most direct effect near the top of the pyramid and those having the most indirect effect near the base. Each of those activities is pursued through international and national collectivities, as well as by family and individual effort, and so they slice across the pyramid in each direction.

The food security pyramid draws attention not only to the importance of a broad process of agricultural growth but also for the need to see that the process plays its role in reducing food insecurity. Thus, each activity needs to be monitored from that point of view. Does the food distribution system work effectively in areas where the poor are concentrated? Is intervention needed to ensure competition, low cost, and wide access? Are all-weather roads introduced in all food-insecure areas? Does education include not only basic skills but nutrition education to improve allocation of resources for the poor to achieve food security? Is the agricultural technology system adequately oriented to the crops and livestock important to food security because of their importance in consumption or in generating income for the poor?

Treatment of food insecurity requires sensible policy. That policy has five elements: First, the developing countries must pursue vigorous technological change in their agricultural sectors through research and its application and bring all people into an exchange economy through good rural infrastructure and universal education, at least through the secondary school level. Foreign technical and financial assistance can greatly speed those processes.

Second, an international mechanism is needed to help the poorer countries finance food flows to ensure against transitory food insecurity. Rehabilitation of the IMF Cereal Facility is the correct mechanism (Adams, 1983).

Third, open-trading regimes are essential. They facilitate increased incomes to developing countries as they specialize in commodities to which their resources are best suited. They also discourage excessive investment in low rate of return agriculture, which will be expensive to maintain when the bulk of the world has moved to food security.

Fourth, as we approach global food security, we can attach increased weight to approaches to agriculture that may increase the cost of production but preserve and enhance the physical and aesthetic qualities of the environment.

Fifth, as each nation approaches a state of food security, it must pursue policies that maintain flexibility to adjust agriculture to stagnating demand in the face of continued technological improvement. We must recognize that as developing countries move into a mature phase, they will not have a large block of followers moving into a high food consumption phase.

The greatest dangers to the hope of universal food security are (1) that the developing countries will not give the centrality to agricultural development that is essential to broadly participatory economic development and (2) that the developed countries will not use their food surpluses (per the next section) to foster the short-term transfers and the long-term increase in rural infrastructure and education that can be accelerated by the thoughtful use of food aid.

FOREIGN AID

Foreign assistance to developing countries was simple and effective in the 1950s and 1960s. Taiwan's spectacular development and the green revolution had strong roots in foreign aid (Mellor, forthcoming). At that time, foreign aid concentrated on the central physical infrastructure systems that are essential even to the feeder systems to rural areas and on technical assistance to agriculture. With the initial success of such foreign assistance in Asia, emphasis shifted to poverty abatement and then to even more specialized concerns with women, environment, and, more recently, narrowly defined ideological concerns. These recent efforts were reasonably well absorbed in Asia, where the basic process of development was well under way. However, in Africa, the cart was clearly put before the horse. Before the basic processes of development, particularly those for the agricultural sector, were under way, all sorts of specialized efforts were brought into play. Although the results are blamed largely on bad macro-policy, sectoral and subsectoral policies were quite bad as well. As a specialized example, most African countries have had more money spent on developing their agricultural research systems than is true with Asia, and yet the African systems have in general been quite unproductive.

Effective foreign assistance to an agriculturally based strategy has two basic thrusts. First is provision of technical assistance to develop the complex institutions, many in the public sector, needed to forward the agricultural sector. It must be kept in mind that agriculture with its lack of economies of scale fostering a smallholder agriculture needs institutional development from the public sector far more than the larger-scale industrial sector. Second is supplementing of public revenues. Because public expenditure is so important for development, particularly for the massive expenditures on infrastructure and education, public revenues are apt to be more inhibiting to development than lack of economywide savings. Thus, very poor countries, such as India, have savings rates in the 20–25 percent range. That is adequate if properly invested to provide a high growth rate. However, in a context in which a substantial portion of the economy is not monetized and in which taxation systems are not well developed, it is difficult to raise public sector revenues to the level needed for physical infrastructure and education to be expanded at the rate needed to complement private sector savings. Foreign assistance can provide technical assistance for institutional development, particularly for agriculture, and public sector revenues to allow rapid expansion of physical infrastructure, both in the trunk system and in the feeder system in the rural areas, and for the educational system.

Food aid has a particularly important role to play in foreign assistance. In most developed countries effective demand for food is growing little or not at all due to high incomes, while technological change in agriculture has been institutionalized to provide a steady rate of growth in production at around 2 percent. The resultant necessity for removing resources from agriculture overtaxes the political capacity to shift such resources. Note the lack of correlation between subsidies to agriculture and the rate at which resources are removed. Thus, food surpluses tend to be generated at a substantial level.

Concurrently, developing countries generate extraordinarily rapid rates of growth of food consumption once incomes begin to rise. This is because of the only modestly inelastic demand for basic food staples and extremely high demand elasticities for land-using commodities, such as livestock and concentrated feeds to livestock as well as horticultural commodities. Thus, virtually without exception, developing countries, particularly those doing well in agriculture, rapidly increase their food imports (Mellor and Johnston, 1984). Further, developing countries, in general, operate at a suboptimal capital labor ratio. They tend to underutilize labor in the production process. That is because of the dominance of import substitution policies.

Food aid in that circumstance can help redress an existing imbalance by providing the food to back up the wage goods for more employment-oriented growth (Mellor, 1976). The food aid can be project-oriented for data-intensive rural infrastructure or program-oriented with context shift and more employment-oriented policies.

REFERENCES

Adams, Richard H. 1983. "Role of Research in Policy Development: The Creation of the IMF Cereal Import Facility." *World Development Journal* 11, no. 7.

Ahmed, Raisuddin, and Hossain, Mahabub. 1990. "Developmental Impact of Rural Infrastructure in Bangladesh." International Food Policy Research Institute, Research report #84, October. Washington, D.C.

Alamgir, Mohiuddin, and Poonan, Arora. 1991. *Providing Food Security for All.* IFAD Studies in Rural Poverty #1. New York: New York University Press.

Anand, Sudhir. 1983. "Inequality and Poverty in Malaysia: Measurement and Decomposition." Washington, D.C.: World Bank.

Anderson, Jock R., and Hazell, Peter B. R., eds. 1989. *Variability of Grain Yields: Implications for Agricultural Research and Policy in Developing Countries.* Baltimore: Johns Hopkins University Press.

Bautista, Romeo M. Forthcoming. "Rapid Agricultural Growth Is Not Enough: The Philippines, 1965–80." In *Agriculture on the Road to Industrialization,* edited by John W. Mellor. Baltimore: Johns Hopkins University Press.

Berry, Albert. Forthcoming. "The Contribution of Agriculture to Growth: Colombia." In *Agriculture on the Road to Industrialization,* edited by John W. Mellor. Baltimore: Johns Hopkins University Press.

Bigsten, Arne, and Collier, Paul. Forthcoming. "Linkages from Agricultural Growth in Kenya." In *Agriculture on the Road to Industrialization,* edited by John W. Mellor. Baltimore: Johns Hopkins University Press.

Boserup, E. 1981. *The Conditions of Agricultural Growth: The Economics of Agrarian Change Under Population Pressure*. Chicago: Aldine.

von Braun, Joachim, Hotchkiss, David, and Immink, Marten. 1989. "Nontraditional Export Crop in Guatemala: Effects on Production, Income, and Nutrition." International Food Policy Research Institute, Research Report No. 73. Washington, D.C.

Celis, Rafael, and Lizano, Eduardo. Forthcoming. "Development in Costa Rica: The Key Role of Agriculture." In *Agriculture on the Road to Industrialization*, edited by John W. Mellor. Baltimore: Johns Hopkins University Press.

Chernichovsky, Dov, and Meesook, Oey Astra. 1984. "Poverty in Indonesia: A Profile." World Bank Staff Working Paper No. 671. Washington, D.C.: World Bank.

Desai, B., and Mellor, John W. Forthcoming. "Institutional Finance for Agricultural Development: A Cross National Study of Critical Issues." International Food Policy Research Institute, Research Report. Washington, D.C.

Dev, Mahendra. 1988. "Regional Disparities in Agricultural Labor Productivity and Rural Poverty in India." *Indian Economic Review* 23, no. 2.

Eicher, Carl, and Baker, Doyle. 1992. "Agricultural Development in Sub-Saharan Africa: A Critical Survey." In *A Survey of Agricultural Economics Literature*, edited by Lee H. Martin. Minneapolis: University of Minnesota Press.

Evenson, R.E., Pray, C., and Quizon, J. 1986. *Research and Extension Productivity and Income in Asian Agriculture*. Ithaca, N.Y.: Cornell University Press.

Hazell, Peter, and Bell, Clive. 1980. "Measuring the Indirect Effects of an Agricultural Investment Project on Its Surrounding Region." *American Journal of Agricultural Economics* 62, no. 1.

Hazell, P.B.R., and Röell, A. 1983. "Rural Growth Linkages: Household Expenditure Patterns in Malaysia and Nigeria." International Food Policy Research Institute, Research Report No. 41. Washington, D.C.

Hossain, M. 1988. "Credit for Alleviation of Rural Poverty: The Experience of Grameen Bank in Bangladesh." International Food Policy Research Institute, Research Report No. 65. Washington, D.C.

Huddleston, Barbara. 1990. "FAO's Overall Approach and Methodology for Formulating National Food Security Programs in Developing Countries." In *Food Security in Developing Countries*, edited by Simon Maxwell. Rome: FAO.

Johnston, Bruce F., and Kilby, Peter. 1975. *Agricultural and Structural Transformation*. New York: Oxford University Press.

Lele, Uma J. 1971. *Foodgrain Marketing in India. Private Performance and Public Policy*. Ithaca, N.Y.: Cornell University Press.

———. 1991. "Aid to African Agriculture. Lessons from Two Decades of Donors' Experience." Washington, D.C.: World Bank.

Lele, Uma J., and Mellor, John W. 1981. "Technological Change, Distributive Bias, and Labor Transfer in a Two-Sector Economy." *Oxford Economic Papers* no. 3 (November).

Mao, Yu-Kang, and Schive, Chi. Forthcoming. "Agricultural and Industrial Development of the Republic of China." In *Agriculture on the Road to Industrialization* edited by John W. Mellor. Baltimore: Johns Hopkins University Press.

Maxwell, Simon, Swift, Jeremy, and Buchanan-Smith, Margaret. 1990. "Is Food Security Targeting Possible in Sub-Saharan Africa?" *IDS Bulletin* 21, no. 3.

Meesook, Oey Astra. 1979. "Income, Consumption, and Poverty in Thailand, 1962/63 to 1975/76.'' World Bank Staff Working Paper No. 364. Washington, D.C.: World Bank.

Mellor, John W. 1966. *The Economics of Agricultural Development*. Ithaca, N.Y.: Cornell University Press.

————. 1976. *The New Economics of Growth—A Strategy for India and the Developing World*. Ithaca, N.Y.: Cornell University Press.

————. 1990. ''Ending Hunger: An Implementable Program for Self-Reliant Growth.'' In *The World Food Crisis: Food Security in Comparative Perspective* edited by J.I. Hans Bakker. Canada: Canadian Scholars' Press.

Mellor, John W., and Johnston, Bruce F. 1984. ''The World Food Equation: Interrelations Among Development, Employment, and Food Consumption.'' *Journal of Economic Literature* 22 (June): 22–43.

Mellor, John W., and Mudahar, Mohinder. 1992. ''Agriculture in Economic Development: Theories, Findings, and Challenges in an Asian Context.'' In *A Survey of Agricultural Economics Literature* edited by Lee H. Martin. Minneapolis: University of Minnesota Press.

Mellor, John W., et al. 1968. *Developing Rural India: Plan and Practice*. Ithaca, N.Y.: Cornell University Press.

Oram, Pl A., and Bindlish, V. 1981. ''Resource Allocation to National Agricultural Research: Trends in the 1970s (A Review of Third World Systems).'' ISNAR, The Hague, Netherlands.

Paulino, Leonardo. 1986. ''Food in the Third World: Past Trends and Projections to 2000.'' International Food Policy Research Institute, Research Report No. 52. Washington, D.C.

Rao, C.H. 1975. *Technological Change and Distribution of Gains In Indian Agriculture*. Delhi: Macmillan.

Reutlinger, Shlomo, and van Horst Pellekaan, J. 1986. *Poverty and Hunger. Issues and Options for Food Security in Developing Countries*. Washington, D.C.: World Bank.

Rosegrant, Mark, and Herdt, Robert W. 1981. ''Simulating the Impacts of Credit Policy and Fertilizer Subsidy on Central Luzon Rice Farms, the Philippines.'' *American Journal of Agricultural Economics* 63, no. 4.

Sabot, Richard. 1989. ''Human Capital Accumulation in Post-Green Revolution Pakistan: Some Preliminary Results.'' *Pakistan Development Review* 28, no. 4.

Schuh, G. Edward, and Brandao, Salazar P. 1992. ''The Theory, Empirical Evidence, and Debates on Agricultural Development Issues in Latin America: A Selective Survey.'' In *A Survey of Agricultural Economics Literature,* edited by Lee H. Martin. Minneapolis: University of Minnesota Press.

Sen, A.K. 1981. ''Ingredients of Famine Analysis: Availability and Entitlements.'' *Quarterly Journal of Economics* 96:433–64.

Siamwalla, Ammar. Forthcoming. ''Land-Abundant Agricultural Growth and Some of Its Consequences: The Case of Thailand.'' In *Agriculture on the Road to Industrialization,* edited by John W. Mellor. Baltimore: Johns Hopkins University Press.

Solow, R.M. 1963. *Capital Theory and the Rate of Return*. Amsterdam: North-Holland.

Tweeten, Luther. 1990. ''Implications for Agronomists Under Present Voluntary Supply Management Policies.'' *Journal of Production Agriculture* 3, no. 2 (April-June).

World Bank. 1988, 1989. *World Development Report*. Washington, D.C.: World Bank.
————. 1988–1989. *World Tables*. Washington, D.C.: World Bank.
Yu, Terry Y.H., and Lee, C.S. 1973. "Agricultural Technology and Income Distribution in Taiwan." Paper presented at the Seminar on Agricultural Development, Joint Commission on Rural Reconstruction, Taipei, Taiwan, December 10–14.

PART III

REGIONAL DEVELOPMENT EXPERIENCES

8

ECONOMIC POLICIES AND PERFORMANCE IN LATIN AMERICA

Vittorio Corbo

The purpose of this chapter is to review development policies, economic performance, and the determinants of economic growth in Latin America. The chapter is organized as follows. After the introduction, I review development policies since 1910. In the period up to World War II, economic policies in most Latin American countries were still guided by the classical theory of international trade. That pattern was disrupted by the Great Depression, a period during which Latin America responded to the economic upheaval by pursuing a strategy of important substitution. Growth was now to be led by import-substitution industrialization.

By the end of World War II, most countries in Latin America had accumulated substantial foreign reserves, while it seemed certain there would be a resurgence in world trade. The logical next step was to reduce the antiexport bias resulting from the trade policies that had been implemented in the previous fifteen years as a response to the crisis of the 1930s. Instead, as described in the next section, Latin America pursued and even intensified the import-substitution strategy, influenced in large part by the recommendations of the Economic Commission for Latin America (ECLA). When the increasing cost of the import substitution strategy, especially for the medium-sized and small countries of the region, could no longer be ignored, and the times seemed to call for a lessening of import substitution, most countries simply switched to another version of the same strategy—regional integration—ideally to be complemented by foreign aid. The first attempts at reducing the antiexport bias of economic policies took place in the 1960s. These attempts were followed by the Southern Cone countries in the 1970s. Their positive experience with some of their liberalization reforms was unfortunately overcome by an ill-fated stabilization program and, in Chile and Uruguay, by the severe external shocks of the 1970s. Another policy shift of a more fundamental character took place in the 1980s, when, following the hardships of the debt crisis one by one, countries in Latin America started to embrace market-oriented reforms. I then review economic and social performance in the region and analyze the main factors accounting for differences in growth performance. Finally, the main conclusions are presented.

ECONOMIC POLICIES IN LATIN AMERICA

The Period 1910–1945

Up to the Great Depression, economic policies in most countries in Latin America were very much shaped by classical trade theory, and those countries were still very open to international trade. Although some countries raised their average tariff levels in the 1920s, they did so in a moderate way and mainly for fiscal reasons. Further, most of them returned to the gold standard after World War I, and their macroadjustment was thus closely related to balance-of-payments adjustments (Furtado, 1985).

Critics of the prevailing free trade orthodoxy did, however, point to signs of growing protection in the most advanced countries (the United States and the European nations), but they did not have much influence in policy.

At this time, economic ideas were to be found in political writings or general essays on Latin America (Hirschman, 1961). However, some import substitution did develop, both naturally, as part of the normal development process following income growth, and more artificially, when the flow of imports was interrupted during World War I. Nevertheless, in general, trade policies were fairly neutral between incentives for the local and foreign market. International trade faced few restrictions, mainly in the form of low tariffs and export taxes on primary products. Also at that time, tax revenues came primarily from the foreign trade sector, and government expenditures were oriented toward the development of physical infrastructure. Macropolicies were mostly governed by the rules of the gold standard, and there was relative price stability. Capital inflows became important in the second half of the 1920s but fell substantially in 1929. Until that time, balance-of-payments crises were the exception.

The Great Depression sent many unfavorable shocks through Latin America's economies. First, as international commodity markets collapsed, export prices fell more than import prices, and the terms of trade in individual countries dropped between 21 percent and 45 percent (CEPAL, 1976). Second, the capital inflows that had become important up to 1928 had almost disappeared by 1929. Third, the collapse in export prices increased substantially the real burden of external debt.

A fourth factor was rising protectionism in the key industrialized countries, which made the prospects for world trade very discouraging. Protectionist pressures in this period resulted in the Smoot-Hawley tariff of 1930 in the United

States, the British Abnormal Importation Act of 1931, and the Ottawa, Commonwealth Preferences of 1932.

In light of these large external shocks and the lack of foreign financing, the Latin American economies were forced to adjust.

Adjustment took the form of a mix of aggregate demand policies, devaluation, and import restriction. To implement this type of policy, they abandoned the gold standard, imposed exchange controls and discriminatory trade restrictions (such as quotas, tariffs, and multiple exchange rate systems) on imports of consumer goods, and adopted countercyclical fiscal and monetary policies.[1] This set of policies has been called the model of domestically oriented growth. Import-competing manufacturing activities were given an advantage not only through protective trade policies but also through tax and credit incentives. Specifically, the dynamic growth element, instead of being the export sector as it was up to the eve of the Great Depression, was private and public investment in import-competing industries.

It should be noted that the initial choice of an import substitution strategy was more the end result of the countries' implementation of ad hoc policy measures designed to accelerate adjustment to the severe external shocks they were facing than a deliberate policy choice. Indeed, those countries that broke away from the gold standard while they followed active public expenditure policies (in particular Argentina, Brazil, Chile, Colombia, and Mexico) still pursued a fiscal policy aimed at achieving a balanced budget. This approach did not keep them, however, from running small deficits.

On the relative price side, three main factors were at work: (1) the world depression, with the resultant collapse in the prices of primary commodities; (2) widespread exchange controls and devaluations following the devaluation of the pound in September 1931; and (3) the multiple exchange rate system and an increase in the levels and dispersion of nominal tariffs, with effective rates of protection many times the nominal rates and increasingly a function of the state of fabrication. Grouping output into three categories—importables, exportables, and nontradables—the relative prices of importables and nontradables in terms of exportables increased. Within importables, the sharpest increases were for consumer durables.

Real exchange rates, exclusive of the tariff and nontariff effects for importables in terms of nontradables, show that large real devaluations took place in most of the large countries during the 1930s. If the effects of the tariffs and other constraints on trade (such as multiple exchange rate and import quotas) are added to these rates, the increased incentives to import substitution are seen to be even sharper. The nontradables sector expanded not only as a response to improvement in its relative price but also because government services and public investment in infrastructure (an important nontradable) grew. Not surprisingly, there was substantial government intervention in this decade, not only in economic management but also in important investment projects in physical infrastructure.

The creation of a domestic industry geared to the production of previously imported nondurable consumer goods and some raw material inputs obviously decreased imports of these goods. However, at the same time, imports of other raw materials and capital goods required for those same industries increased. To relieve the pressure on the external accounts, "nonessential" imports were restricted, a move that accelerated the process of import substitution and its costs. Finally, World War II created both a boom in the prices of mineral exports and a natural suspension in the flow of imports from industrial countries. These conditions also stimulated demand in the import-competing sector.

The Period 1945–1960

As the postwar period opened, most Latin American nations found themselves with substantial foreign reserves in their central banks (although there were convertibility problems with the pound sterling). Despite conflicting signals about the future evolution of world trade, the Marshall Plan and the creation of international institutions geared to avoid the trade wars of the previous twenty years provided positive indications of an expansion in world trade. It seemed that the stage was set for a reduction in the high level of protection of import-competing industries and in the discrimination against exportables that had evolved over the previous fifteen years.

However, an important initial condition had been built up during the previous decade. New industrialist and labor groups in the emerging manufacturing sectors strongly lobbied for the enactment of tariff protection to replace temporary natural protection; differentiated tariffs and multiple exchange rates were important elements in the arsenal of import substitution policies deployed in the 1945–1960 period. As is a common pattern in the early stages of import substitution, manufacturing output initially achieved substantial growth but started to decline when the "easy" import substitution phase was completed. One common result of these policies was slow growth in total exports and in manufacturing exports in particular: exports practically stagnated between the early postwar years and the beginning of the 1960s. This was especially the case for the Southern Cone countries (Argentina, Chile, and Uruguay), where protection was higher, and to a lesser degree for Brazil and Colombia.

Some exceptions to these policies were observed during this period. Thus, by the early 1950s, Mexico and Peru realigned their exchange rates and lifted import-repressing policies so as to increase incentives to foreign trade (Díaz-Alejandro, 1983). Peru, the most important exception, continued an export-led growth process until 1960, when ECLA's ideas began to be influential (Noguès, 1985).

At this time, however, a debate emerged over what long-term development strategy Latin America should follow. Initially, the debate was at the country level. On one side were the producers of exportables (agriculture and mining) and the traders of imported goods, who argued for reducing the bias of the trade regime against them. They were supported at the time by the mainstream economists of the region, who also favored a more balanced trade regime. On the other side were the leaders of the manufacturing associations, the new industrialists, and organized labor in the new manufacturing industries, all of whom advocated keeping and even intensifying the protectionism. Clear manifestations of this debate appeared in Argentina, Brazil, Chile, and Colombia.

In 1948, ECLA (then still temporary) was set up in the United Nations. It soon entered the debate. Consisting of a group of economists under the leadership of Prebisch, ECLA proposed a development strategy for Latin America that differed from the early recommendations of most economists that trade be liberalized. Prebisch (1950) presented what is called today the structural critique of the export-led growth model of the pre-1930 period. A central argument in Prebisch's thesis was that the main determinant of the rate of growth of per capita GDP was technical progress, a thesis few economists questioned. Prebisch also asserted that the international terms of trade of primary exports from peripheral countries had a secular tendency to deteriorate vis-à-vis their imported manufactured goods. He therefore concluded that countries needed to industrialize if they were to keep the fruits of technical progress. A second component of Prebisch's thesis was that import substitution manufacturing produced dynamic externalities.

Prebisch recommended that the state should promote industrialization through protection and investment in the infrastructure to support import-competing manufacturing. Prebisch's ideas had the most impact in Chile, the country that had called for the creation of ECLA and that became its home.

Receptivity to policies of import substitution industrialization and state intervention through production and regulation was intimately linked to political developments in the region. Popular movements and populist governments came to power in Chile, Brazil, and Argentina in the late 1930s and the 1940s. Political developments in these countries had a common theme of removing power from conservative agrarian oligarchies and vesting it increasingly in mass movements of urban workers. These latter groups made important alliances with the new industrialists against export-oriented landowners and foreign-owned mining companies. As a part of this scenario, programs of import substitution industrialization and state intervention built up strong institutional and political support.

By the early 1940s, Keynesian demand management policies were becoming fashionable in Latin American academic circles and in ECLA and soon started to influence government policies (Prebisch, 1947; Pinto, 1960). At a time when it was becoming increasingly difficult to keep balanced budgets, demand management to stabilize output provided analytical respectability for the expansionary demand policies starting in the late 1940s.

The expansionary demand policies and rapid use of the foreign reserves accumulated during World War II combined with increasingly restrictive trade regimes to produce accelerated inflation, balance-of-payments difficulties, and slow export growth in the early 1950s. By that time, ECLA was developing another argument for import substitution industrialization. It was based on a foreign trade gap that could be reduced only by decreasing import requirements through further import substitution.[2] Prebisch (1959a) postulated that the relation between the rate of growth of imports and the rate of growth of output (a total income elasticity concept) was substantially higher than the ratio of the rate of growth of exports to the rate of growth output. Therefore, without further access to external financing, the only way to increase output growth without a balance-of-payments crisis was to reduce the income elasticity of imports through further import-substitution industrialization. It was not considered that, given the industrialization of the previous thirty years, manufacturing exports, not to mention primary exports, could respond to price incentives.

These policies not only failed to halt the steady growth of imports but also led to the stagnation of exports and a series of other undesirable effects (Little, Scitovsky, and Scott, 1970; Balassa and associates, 1971; Bhagwati, 1978; Krueger, 1978). First, an inefficient, ever-growing bureaucracy emerged to enforce the often contradictory regulations enacted to support an overvalued currency.

Second, although the creation of a domestic industrial sector geared to the production of previously imported consumption goods led to a decline in imports of these goods, it simultaneously raised imports of the raw materials and capital goods required to produce consumption goods resulting in a greater dependence on importing. The availability of raw materials and capital goods became fundamental to the smooth functioning of the economy: if the supplies of foreign inputs were interrupted, not only would consumption levels fall as before, but unemployment and underutilization of the industrial capacity would result as well.

Third, there was a lack of a competition within the industrial sector: either the small size of the market precluded the existence of many efficient firms or, if very few firms were present, they did not compete among themselves. This was a more acute problem in the smaller countries of the region (Chile and Uruguay).

Fourth, resources were socially misallocated, as indicated by the substantial dispersion in the computed domestic resource cost of the different import-competing industries (Taylor and Bacha, 1973; Berlinski and Schydlowski, 1982; Bergman, 1970). This outcome was attributable mainly to the protectionist policies that closed the door on external competition and to the whole range of government intervention built up to promote industrialization.

Finally, in many cases, subsidized imports of capital goods (stemming mainly from the fact that they attracted the lowest rate in a multiple exchange rate system) led to factor price distortions that penalized employment.[3]

The proponents of the import substitution model probably did not clearly envisage the protective regimes that finally emerged. Indeed, their recommendations were designed to achieve a degree of industrialization as a precondition for future growth based on manufacturing exports. Over time, however, as the typically small and scattered industrial sector could not compete internationally, they sought and got higher protection. Political economy and rent-seeking considerations sustained these policies. In this connection, it is illuminating to make a comparison with the South Korean model, where the governments also intervened to promote industrialization. In Korea, however, while import restrictions (tariffs and nontariff barriers) were used as major protective devices, the government simultaneously provided important export incentives to compensate for the bias of the import regime. Therefore, the trade regime resulted in a bias against nontradables rather than against exportables. Indeed, one of the most careful studies of the system of incentives in Korea has concluded that it was equally attractive for a Korean producer to produce for sheltered local markets and for world ones (Westphal, 1978). This was hardly the case in Latin America. Even in Brazil, despite the export promotion strategy of the 1960s, there was still an important antiexport bias in the trade regime.

The Crisis of the Import Substitution Model

In the late 1950s and early 1960s, as a result of expansionary macroeconomic policies and a pronounced antiexport bias of trade policies, an important group of Latin American countries (Argentina, Chile, Colombia, Uruguay, Bolivia, and Brazil) were facing recurrent balance-of-payments crises and periodic outbursts of inflation. As a consequence, some of these countries entered into International Monetary Fund (IMF) agreements to obtain temporary financing while putting in place a stabilization program. Most of the time, the IMF-type recommendations called for control of aggregate expenditures and exchange rate adjustment and unification; not surprisingly, these recommendations were in direct conflict with the policies being followed.

A structuralist view of inflation was developed in response to the stabilization prescriptions of the IMF (Noyola, 1965; Pinto, 1960; Seers, 1962; Sunkel, 1958). (For an evaluation of the monetarist and structuralist views of inflation, see Corbo, 1974, chapter 5.) This new view proved very influential in delaying the implementation of the policies required to reduce inflation and the balance-of-payments deficits. The structuralist focus on supply response diverted attention from important ways of cutting inflation, such as achieving a permanent reduction in the public sector deficit and eliminating the monetization of government deficits (Harberger, 1964).

By this time ECLA was becoming increasingly concerned with the inefficiencies arising from import substitution at the country level and therefore recommended that Latin American countries needed to move on to a second stage of import substitution (Hirschman, 1961, pp. 18–19). Prebisch (1959a, 1959b) concluded that further import substitution would have to take place at a regional level.

With the intellectual leadership of ECLA and the support of the United States, a Latin American Free Trade Association (LAFTA) was created in 1961. However, reduction of the trade barriers within the region was to be negotiated commodity by commodity, and the industrialists in the highly protected manufacturing sectors were to play a central role as members of the country negotiating teams. These industrialists had vested interests in protecting the benefits that they had obtained from import substitution policies in their countries. Their benefits were being put in jeopardy by the regional integration. Not surprisingly, it proved very difficult to reach agreement on tariff reductions, except in the case of a small number of commodities whose production within the region was minimal.

In 1969, with the LAFTA initiative going nowhere, a subset of middle-sized LAFTA members formally approved an Andean Common Market Pact, an initiative that had actually first been launched in August 1966. In designing its rules of operation, members of the Andean Pact took into account many of the lessons learned from the LAFTA initiative. Tariffs and nontariff barriers were to be fully eliminated among member countries by the end of 1980; Chile and Colombia had advocated an even faster decline (Díaz-Alejandro, 1973). Instead of proceeding commodity by commodity, tariffs were to be reduced each year by 10 percent of the minimum ad valorem tariff then existing in Colombia, Chile, and Peru, which in no case was to exceed 100 percent. Thus, reduction of the tariffs was going to be automatic. The less-developed members (Ecuador and Bolivia) were, however, given more favorable terms.

Parallel with the general rule of automatic reductions, the Andean Pact called for the allocation of new manufacturing activities to individual countries to avoid duplication and to reap benefits from economies of scale. The result would be import substitution at a regional level. The countries were also to negotiate a common external tariff.

The politics of import substitution at a regional level proved much more difficult than that within a country, and the Andean Pact lost its dynamism in the second half of the 1970s. The final blow came when Chile, which had played a central role in the creation of the pact, withdrew from it after failing to obtain agreement on its proposals for sharply reducing the common external tariff and for lifting the pact's restrictions on direct foreign investment.

In the meantime, new developments were taking place on the analytic front, especially in the area of applied commercial policy. The concept of effective protection, which had been in the process of development since at least the early 1950s, became widely known to professional economists through the seminal paper of Corden (1966). His work was particularly important in terms of producing a framework for evaluating the effects of the tariff structures on value added, as well as the economic effects of different types of distortions. In addition, the difference between promotion and protection was made explicit. These developments in applied commercial policy were used to evaluate the trade regimes of developing countries. Interestingly enough, Macarios (1964), then the director of research at ECLA, had already used effective protection concepts to evaluate industrialization in Latin America critically.

The studies (an important set of them is summarized in Little, Scitovsky, and Scott, 1970; Balassa and associates, 1971; Bhagwati, 1978; Krueger, 1978) highlighted the large economic costs associated with the import substitution strategy and the strong antiexport bias that arose out of these policies. The costs were inversely related to size of the economy and directly related to the intensity of import substitution. To make matters worse, according to work by Krueger (1983), in general the strategy of import substitution also hindered the growth of employment.

As such, it is ironic that as early as 1950, Viner (1953), in a series of lectures delivered in Rio de Janeiro, had rejected most of the arguments for protecting import-competing industry and recommended eliminating the discrimination against exports and improving the operations of the price system. (See Furtado, 1985, for an evaluation of ECLA's reception of Viner's talk.) Nor was Viner's the only challenge in the region to ECLA's ideas. They were questioned both by some academics and by other economists in the public and private sectors.

One of the early critics was Roberto Campos (1961) in Brazil, who questioned the emphasis in favor of industry and against agriculture, the confidence shown in the theory that by substituting public initiative for private initiative, new resources would be created, and the assumption that inflation could be used to increase capital formation in a sustainable way. In particular, Campos stated that economic incentives are one of the main factors accounting for the economic performance of Latin America. Nevertheless, ECLA's thoughts on the role of the state in providing protectionism reigned supreme up to the early 1960s. With inflation a major problem in the region, rationalization of the protection system did not seem as pressing as stabilization.

Still, in the context of the stabilization programs, overvalued exchange rates were adjusted, and the multiple exchange rate system was eliminated or improved as ways to reduce part of the antiexport bias. However, as public sector deficits were not reduced, the overvalued exchange rate returned fairly quickly, and the antiexport bias remained. There were, however, a few more substantial departures from excessive import substitution policy, stimulated in part by the exposure of a new generation of economists to alternative schools of economic thought. In the late 1950s and especially in the 1960s, there was a substantial increase in the number of Latin Americans pursuing graduate studies in economics abroad, in both the United States and Europe. On returning to their countries, most of these newly trained economists contributed a marked improvement in the level of economic debate. In particular they called into question stabilization policies, trade policies, and the selection of public investment projects (Diz, 1966; Universidad de Chile, 1963; French-Davis, 1971).

The first major break from import substitution policies was initiated by Brazil in 1964, some sixteen years after Viner questioned this type of policy. This and subsequent policy initiatives in the direction of greater liberalization are discussed in the next section.

The Liberalization Attempts

As noted, while the rest of Latin America was still struggling to deepen import substitution, Brazil undertook a set of reforms designed to improve the functioning of its markets and the profitability of export activities. The measures included (1) a more realistic real exchange rate and elimination of most export taxes; (2) introduction of subsidized credit and tax incentives for export activities; (3) reduction of the public sector deficit and control of inflation; (4) development of a capital market; and (5) downward adjustment of real wages.

Later on, Colombia in 1967, Chile in 1964–1970, and Mexico made some attempt at reducing the extreme antiexport bias of trade policies.

The need to adjust to the second oil shock, especially when the easy option of foreign borrowing all but disappeared, resulted in a major reexamination of economic policies in Latin America. Not surprisingly, given the severity of the crisis that was developing, the 1980s saw a major change in policies all over Latin America.[4]

After 1982, countries in Latin America recognized their incapacity to continue financing large current account deficits. They also have recognized, one by one, the need for major policy reforms to enable them to achieve a sustainable current account deficit reduction with a higher level of output than otherwise, while creating the conditions for sustainable growth. Key among these reforms has been a comprehensive program of structural adjustment that addresses stabilization, efficiency, and growth objectives concurrently. There are two principal components to the reform programs being undertaken. One involves restoration of macroeconomic balances, with the emphasis on bringing the level of demand and its composition (tradables relative to nontradables) into line with the level of output and the level of external financing that can be mobilized on a recurring basis. In addition, the high rates of inflation and the external deficit must be reduced, objectives that usually require a credible and sustainable reduction in the public sector deficit. The other component aims at increasing efficiency and restoring growth, with the focus on creating more appropriate incentives, removing the constraints on factor mobility, and increasing saving and investment. A major component of these structural reforms has been a redefinition of the role of the state. This redefinition includes its role as producer, regulator, and distributive agent. Therefore, restructuring of public enterprises and privatization are key areas of reform.

These types of reforms were implemented in Mexico starting in 1983 but increasingly so since 1985, in Uruguay since 1984, in Bolivia since 1985, in Venezuela since 1989, in Costa Rica since 1985. Chile, a country that had made the most progress on structural reform before its own severe crisis of 1982–1983, starting in 1984 concentrated on creating a stable macroeconomic situation as a way of providing a framework for a sustainable expansion in tradable activities. While Brazil and Argentina are still struggling in controlling inflation, Peru and Nicaragua postponed the adjustment and have had the largest deterioration in social welfare. Lately, El Salvador and Honduras have also initiated major reform efforts.

In the implementation of these reforms, political resistance has been the greatest for the reform of the public sector, trade regime, and labor and domestic markets. Reforms of the public sector and of the trade regime have faced strong opposition from rent-seekers that have traditionally benefited from a larger public sector, suppliers of the public sector and the trade unions (Argentina and Brazil are good examples here), and the producer and employees of highly protected industries. Major progress has been achieved in controlling inflation in Bolivia, Costa Rica, Chile, and Mexico. Mexico, Costa Rica, Bolivia, Venezuela, and lately, El Salvador and Honduras have made major inroads in the liberalization of foreign trade. Good progress on restructuring the public sector and reducing the role of the public sector in production and distribution has been made in Bolivia and Mexico. However, achieving sustainable high growth in income per capita has been very difficult in most of the region. The debt overhang that accumulated in the period of easy spending of the late 1970s and early 1980s and the associated macroeconomic crisis of the 1980s have most likely played a negative role in setting the investment and growth response.

However, in spite of the difficulties encountered, there is an increasing acceptance in Latin America that to emerge from the current crisis, the reform effort had to be sustained. The eventual recovery of growth needs not only less distortionary policies but also more investment and higher savings. The eventual recovery of investment requires a stable and predictable macroeconomic situation where long-term commitments can be made (Serven and Solimano, 1992). On the other hand, higher saving to finance the higher investment requires a major fiscal effort (Corbo and Schmidt-Hebbel, 1991).

In the 1980s in Latin America there has emerged a consensus that included three key components: stabilization, a restructuring of the public sector, and the need to integrate with the world economy. In particular, it has become increasingly accepted that some otherwise desirable reforms could have even negative effect if the macroeconomic situation is not brought under control early on. Therefore, a credible and sustainable fiscal and public sectorwide reform effort is at the core of successful reform efforts. In this sense, Chile and Mexico have made the most progress on laying the foundation for the successful implementation of other efficiency-enhancing reform.

LATIN AMERICAN GROWTH RECORD

In this section we examine Latin America's growth record of the last fifty years. As Table 8.1 indicates, for the three decades ending in 1969, almost all countries in the region experienced a positive rate of growth of per capita gross domestic product (GDP). By the end of this period import substitution was well advanced, and the antiexport bias of trade policies was quite pronounced. However, in the high-income countries of Chile, Uruguay, and Venezuela, growth

Table 8.1
GDP Per Capita Growth

Country*		1941-49	1950-59	1960-69	1970-79	1980-89	1990
Low Income	Avrg.	2.7	0.9	2.1	1.4	-2.4	-2.5
	Stdv.	3.6	1.5	1.5	1.9	1.0	3.0
Haiti		0.2	0.7	-0.8	2.7	-1.4	-2.6
Nicaragua		4.2	2.4	3.6	-2.5	-3.8	-2.8
Guyana		...	...	...	0.7	-2.9	-6.1
Bolivia		0.6	-1.7	3.2	1.9	-3.0	-0.2
Honduras		1.5	-0.1	1.8	2.4	-1.0	-3.3
El Salvador		9.3	1.8	2.2	1.8	-2.6	1.4
Guatemala		0.3	0.5	1.9	3.1	-2.1	0.3
Peru		2.5	3.0	2.5	1.2	-2.1	-6.8
Middle Income	Avrg.	1.9	2.1	2.3	3.7	0.2	-0.5
	Stdv.	2.3	1.5	1.2	2.8	0.9	3.7
Dominican Republic		3.0	3.4	1.4	4.6	0.7	-6.8
Jamaica		...	...	...	-2.0	-0.5	2.6
Paraguay		0.6	-0.7	1.1	5.0	0.9	0.2
Ecuador		4.1	2.4	1.8	7.0	-0.1	0.0
Colombia		1.6	1.8	2.1	3.2	1.6	2.2
Costa Rica		4.7	2.8	2.2	3.3	-0.8	0.6
Panama		-2.2	1.8	4.8	1.9	-0.6	3.1
Brazil		1.6	3.6	2.8	6.1	0.8	-5.7
High Income	Avrg.	3.4	1.8	1.7	1.9	-0.8	0.1
	Stdv.	2.0	1.1	1.5	1.4	2.2	2.1
Uruguay		2.5	1.0	0.3	2.5	0.1	0.2
Argentina		2.3	0.8	2.8	1.3	-2.3	-1.4
Mexico		3.7	3.1	3.5	3.2	-0.3	1.7
Chile		1.5	1.3	1.9	0.6	1.9	0.3
Venezuela		6.7	2.9	0.0	-0.1	-3.4	3.2
Trinidad and Tobago		...	...	...	3.6	-3.4	-0.3
Barbados		...	...	...	2.1	1.5	-3.3
Latin America		...	...	...	3.1	-0.4	-1.7

Source: ECLA data files.
*Countries are classified by their 1990 GDP per capita at constant 1980 dollars.
Low Income Countries are those with a GDP per capita lower than US$ 1,000.
Middle Income Countries are those with a GDP per capita higher than US$ 1,000 and lower than US$ 2,000.
High Income Countries are those with a GDP per capita higher than US$ 2,000.

was already very low in the 1960s. Chile and Uruguay were paying the cost of a very protective trade regime that had isolated their small economies from the discipline of foreign competition. The star performer of this period was Brazil. Growth in Brazil initially originated from the integration of the local economy and, starting in 1964, from the economic reforms introduced (Carvalho and Haddad, 1981). Mexico's growth is also quite impressive, but this growth was pulled by an incredible expansion in the public sector that later proved to be unsustainable (Corden, 1991). Performance on the inflation front was also favorable (see Table 8.2). In the 1960s only Brazil and Uruguay achieved inflation

Table 8.2
Inflation Rate

Country*		1951-59	1960-69	1970-79	1980-89	1990
Low Income	Avrg.	13.5	3.3	14.0	687.0	3044.0
	Stdv.	26.2	3.2	6.7	1229.3	5011.3
Haiti		1.1	2.2	10.2	7.5	26.1
Nicaragua		...	...	19.4	3787.5	13490.9
Guyana		1.6	2.0	9.9	20.4	...
Bolivia		77.3	6.3	19.0	1113.7	18.0
Honduras		1.2	1.7	7.4	6.9	36.4
El Salvador		4.2	0.4	9.9	19.2	19.3
Guatemala		1.2	0.5	8.9	13.3	59.6
Peru		7.9	9.8	27.5	527.7	7657.8
Middle Income	Avrg.	8.3	9.1	14.8	70.6	233.8
	Stdv.	11.0	14.2	7.8	131.5	511.5
Dominican Republic		1.2	1.3	10.3	22.4	100.7
Jamaica		2.2	3.5	17.7	15.7	29.7
Paraguay		32.6	4.3	12.5	19.7	44.1
Ecuador		0.8	4.0	11.4	35.8	49.5
Colombia		7.4	11.2	18.5	23.5	32.0
Costa Rica		2.0	2.0	10.5	27.1	27.5
Panama		0.3	1.0	5.1	2.8	1.5
Brazil		19.8	45.8	32.7	417.6	1585.2
High Income	Avrg.	16.6	15.8	57.7	135.3	225.6
	Stdv.	14.7	16.8	60.9	252.1	458.2
Uruguay		15.6	50.1	58.5	64.8	129.0
Argentina		30.2	22.9	126.7	750.3	1343.9
Mexico		8.1	2.7	14.1	69.7	29.9
Chile		41.3	25.1	170.7	20.7	27.3
Venezuela		1.8	1.1	7.5	23.8	36.5
Trinidad and Tobago		2.5	3.0	11.9	11.5	9.5
Barbados		...	5.5	14.5	6.5	3.4

Source: ECLA data files.
*Countries are classified by their 1990 GDP per capita at constant 1980 dollars.
Low Income Countries are those with a GDP per capita lower than US$ 1,000.
Middle Income Countries are those with a GDP per capita higher than US$ 1,000 and lower than US$ 2,000.
High Income Countries are those with a GDP per capita higher than US$ 2,000.

levels above 30 percent per year. Inflation in Brazil was not a major hindrance on growth as mechanisms were introduced to protect the profitability of the tradable sector from stable inflation in the range of 30 percent per year (Table 8.2).

In the 1970s, economic performance improved, on average, for the middle-income and the high-income groups. The star performers of this decade were Brazil, Colombia, Ecuador, the Dominican Republic, Trinidad and Tobago, Paraguay, and Mexico. Among the large countries, Brazil was getting the fruits of the reforms implemented during the second half of the 1960s. Ecuador's growth was associated with a major expansion in government expenditures facilitated by the oil boom. Colombia continued its fiscal discipline, and thanks to a coffee boom, was collecting the dividends of a stable real exchange rate policy. Paraguay was in the middle of a construction boom pulled by the construction of the Itaipu dam. Mexico achieved its growth through a large and unsustainable expansion in the public sector funded by the oil boom and the access to foreign borrowing. On the inflation front (Table 8.2), Chile and Argentina achieved an average, for the decade, of over 100 percent per year. These results were the manifestation of a severe macroeconomic crisis that both countries suffered as a result of populist policies in the first half of the 1970s (Larraín and Meller, 1991; Sturzenegger, 1991).

The growth and inflation performance of the 1980s was very poor. This period has been called the "lost decade" of Latin America. In this decade, sixteen out of the twenty-three countries listed in Table 8.1 achieved negative growth in GDP per capita. The improvement in growth performance of the 1970s soon proved to be unsustainable. The increase in international interest rates and the drop in terms of trade of the early 1980s triggered the debt crisis of the early 1980s. As a result of the shocks and the reduced access to foreign borrowing, most middle-income and high-income countries entered into a deep recession. In the low-income countries, the political conflicts in Nicaragua and El Salvador and the associated collapse of the Central American common market submerged this region into a deep recession too. The best performance in the region was achieved by Chile, a country that, in the middle of the previous decade, initiated a deep transformation of its institutions and policies. On the other hand, Colombia continued its steady growth under very stable macroeconomic policies. The other countries were struggling to survive a deep macroeconomic crisis (Brazil, Argentina, Uruguay, and the Central American countries) or initiating a profound structural transformation (Bolivia and Mexico).

This was also the decade in which high inflation became more of a regional problem. In the middle of severe balance-of-payments crises, most countries went through large devaluations that in many cases triggered a devaluation-prices-wages spiral. The worst performers were Nicaragua, Bolivia, Argentina, and Peru. However, the increase in inflation was a manifestation of a regionwide macroeconomic crisis. Inflation, on average, accelerated in all the country groups. At the country level, inflation accelerated in sixteen out of twenty-three countries. On the positive side, Bolivia was successful in controlling its hyper-inflation, moving to an inflation rate between 10 and 20 percent per year. Chilean inflation was also sustained in the 30 percent range.

Now we examine the evolution of some indicators of human capital. For this purpose we examine the evolution of life expectancy and infant mortality data. Life expectancy is perhaps the most comprehensive indicator of the population's health status. It is the result of a large number of inputs that affect longevity in a complex and, as yet, not well understood way. Many of these inputs (e.g.,

Table 8.3
Life Expectancy in Years

Country*		1950-55	1955-60	1960-65	1965-70	1970-75	1975-80	1980-85	1985-90
Low Income	Avrg.	43.6	46.4	49.1	51.7	54.5	56.3	58.5	61.2
	Stdv.	5.2	5.6	5.7	5.5	5.5	5.3	5.4	5.2
Haiti		37.6	40.7	43.6	46.3	48.5	50.7	52.7	54.7
Nicaragua		42.3	45.4	48.5	51.6	54.7	56.3	59.8	62.3
Guyana		55.2	58.7	61.2	62.5	64.1	66.5	68.2	69.7
Bolivia		40.4	41.9	43.5	45.1	46.7	48.6	50.7	53.1
Honduras		42.3	45.0	47.9	50.9	54.0	57.7	61.9	64.0
El Salvador		45.3	48.6	52.3	55.9	58.8	57.4	57.2	62.2
Guatemala		42.1	44.2	47.0	50.1	54.0	56.4	59.0	62.0
Peru		43.9	46.3	49.1	51.5	55.5	56.9	58.6	61.4
Middle Income	Avrg.	53.6	56.7	59.5	61.7	63.5	65.5	67.9	69.3
	Stdv.	5.5	4.9	4.5	4.1	3.8	3.8	4.2	3.9
Dominican Republic		46.0	50.0	53.6	57.0	60.0	62.1	64.1	65.9
Jamaica		57.2	61.2	64.3	66.3	67.8	69.0	73.4	74.0
Paraguay		62.6	63.2	64.4	65.0	65.6	66.0	66.4	68.9
Ecuador		48.4	51.4	54.7	56.8	58.9	61.4	64.3	65.4
Colombia		50.6	55.1	57.9	60.4	61.6	64.0	67.2	68.2
Costa Rica		57.3	60.2	63.0	65.6	68.1	70.8	73.5	74.7
Panama		55.3	59.3	62.0	64.3	66.3	69.2	71.0	72.1
Brazil		51.0	53.4	55.9	57.9	59.8	61.8	63.4	64.9
High Income	Avrg.	57.7	60.9	63.2	64.7	66.3	68.2	69.9	71.0
	Stdv.	5.3	4.5	4.0	3.2	2.5	1.9	1.8	1.7
Uruguay		66.3	67.2	68.4	68.6	68.8	69.7	70.9	72.0
Argentina		62.7	64.7	65.5	66.0	67.3	68.7	69.7	70.6
Mexico		50.8	55.4	58.6	60.3	62.6	65.4	67.4	68.9
Chile		53.8	56.2	58.0	60.6	63.6	67.2	71.0	71.5
Venezuela		55.2	58.1	61.0	63.8	66.2	67.7	69.0	69.7
Trinidad & Tobago		57.9	62.4	64.8	65.7	66.5	67.5	68.7	70.2
Barbados		57.2	62.6	65.9	67.6	69.4	71.3	72.7	73.9

Sources: Statistical Yearbook for Latin America and the Caribbean; ECLA (1989).
*For country classification see Table 8.1.

adult literacy and access to clean water) are, by their nature, quite resilient to the economic cycle.

Life expectancy indicators show a marked improvement through time in all the countries of the region (Table 8.3). The improvement continued during the crisis years of the 1980s. The infant mortality figures (Table 8.4) also show a marked improvement through time in all the countries. The speed of the improvement is most marked in the case of Chile, which went from the fourth highest among the fifteen middle-income and high-income countries in the 1965–1970 period, to the third lowest of the group by the period 1985–1990. This shows that even during recessions the improvement in health indicators can continue with well-targeted programs aimed at the lowest-income groups in the population (Castañeda, 1992). For other countries, the steady progress in immunization and oral rehydration is the most likely reason for the continuing

Table 8.4
Infant Mortality, 1950–1990

Country*		1950-55	1955-60	1960-65	1965-70	1970-75	1975-80	1980-85	1985-90
Low Income	Avrg.	162.7	147.0	131.4	118.3	105.9	95.7	83.7	71.4
	Stvd.	37.8	35.3	33.9	31.0	28.4	26.7	26.9	25.6
Haiti		219.6	193.5	170.5	150.3	134.9	120.9	108.2	96.6
Nicaragua		167.4	148.3	130.9	114.8	100.0	92.9	76.4	61.7
Guyana		93.0	76.0	61.0	56.0	56.0	49.0	36.0	30.0
Bolivia		175.7	169.7	163.6	157.5	151.3	138.2	124.4	109.9
Honduras		195.7	172.0	147.2	123.7	100.6	89.8	78.4	68.4
El Salvador		151.1	137.0	122.7	110.3	99.0	87.3	77.0	57.4
Guatemala		140.6	131.1	119.0	107.6	95.1	82.4	70.4	58.7
Peru		158.6	148.2	136.1	126.3	110.3	104.9	98.6	88.2
Middle Income	Avrg.	104.0	91.6	79.6	69.9	61.0	51.3	44.1	39.4
	Stvd.	24.8	23.6	23.9	22.8	21.6	21.2	20.3	19.0
Dominican Republic		89.0	76.0	63.0	55.0	49.0	44.0	36.0	31.0
Jamaica		85.0	71.0	54.0	45.0	36.0	25.0	21.0	18.0
Paraguay		73.4	69.7	62.3	58.6	54.8	52.8	53.0	48.9
Ecuador		139.5	129.4	119.2	107.1	95.0	82.4	69.6	63.4
Colombia		123.3	102.2	84.5	74.2	66.9	59.4	53.3	48.6
Costa Rica		93.8	87.7	81.3	67.7	52.6	36.5	23.3	19.4
Panama		93.0	74.9	62.7	51.6	42.8	31.6	25.7	22.7
Brazil		134.7	121.9	109.4	100.1	90.5	78.8	70.7	63.2
High Income	Avrg.	107.3	87.4	77.0	67.2	57.9	47.1	38.8	34.1
	Stvd.	34.1	30.8	28.5	25.2	21.7	21.2	20.0	17.4
Uruguay		57.4	53.0	47.9	47.1	46.3	41.7	37.6	34.0
Argentina		65.9	60.4	59.7	57.4	49.0	40.5	36.0	32.2
Mexico		113.9	97.7	86.3	78.5	70.9	59.0	49.9	42.6
Chile		126.2	118.3	109.4	90.1	69.9	46.6	23.7	18.1
Venezuela		106.4	89.0	72.8	59.5	48.6	43.3	38.7	35.9
Trinidad & Tobago		149.4	132.2	117.0	105.0	93.5	84.3	74.5	65.0
Barbados		132.0	61.0	46.0	33.0	27.0	14.0	11.0	11.0

Sources: Statistical Yearbook for Latin America and the Caribbean; ECLA (1989).
*For country classification see Table 8.1.
**Annual number of deaths before the age of 12 months per 1,000 live births.

progress in the reduction of infant mortality. The life expectancy and child mortality data show that the increased availability of affordable, low-technology, lifesaving procedures permits increased progress even in hard times.

We now investigate the evolution of the illiteracy rates (Table 8.5), one of the measures of the level of human capital used in the next section. There are wide variations in the illiteracy rate across Latin American countries. Through time, most countries show a continuous improvement. Some deterioration appears in 1985. However, the data for this year are from a different source. Progress in school enrollment (not shown here) also continued through time. It could be argued that the recession may have had the most immediate impact on the quality of education rather than on school enrollment. We do not have quality-adjusted measures to test this hypothesis.

Table 8.5
Illiteracy**

Country*		Around			
		1960	1970	1980	1985
Low Income	Avrg.	52.1	41.7	29.8	29.2
	Stdv.	20.8	20.2	13.3	19.2
Haiti		85.5	78.7		62.4
Nicaragua		50.4	42.5		13.0
Guyana		12.9	8.4		4.1
Bolivia		61.2	36.8	18.9	25.8
Honduras		55.0	43.1		40.5
El Salvador		51.0	42.9	38.0	27.9
Guatemala		62.2	54.0	44.2	45.0
Peru		38.9	27.5	18.1	15.2
Middle Income	Avrg.	27.2	20.7	16.9	15.8
	Stdv.	8.4	10.1	8.5	6.0
Dominican Republic		35.5	33.0	31.4	22.7
Jamaica		18.1	3.9		
Paraguay		25.5	19.9	12.3	11.8
Ecuador		32.5	25.8	16.5	17.6
Colombia		27.1	19.2	12.2	17.7
Costa Rica		15.6	11.6	7.4	6.4
Panama		23.2	18.7	12.9	11.8
Brazil		39.7	33.8	25.5	22.3
High Income	Avrg.	16.4	11.8	8.7	6.9
	Stdv.	14.0	9.4	6.1	3.7
Uruguay		9.5	6.1		4.6
Argentina		8.6	7.4	6.1	4.5
Mexico		34.5	25.8	16.0	9.7
Chile		16.4	11.0	8.9	5.6
Venezuela		37.3	23.5	15.3	13.1
Trinidad & Tobago		6.6	7.8	5.1	3.9
Barbados		1.8	0.7	0.5	

Source: Statistical Yearbook for Latin America and the Caribbean; ECLA (1989); 1985 data UNESCO.
*For country classification see Table 8.1.
**As a percentage of population 15 years and over.

We also have a larger data base, which we use for our econometric analysis of the next section. The larger data base is taken from the Summers and Heston International Price Comparisons (IPC) project, and it is taken from Summers and Heston (1991). This data base includes indicators of macroeconomic performance and policies as well as indicators of human capital development. The regional indicators are presented in Table 8.6. When compared with Asia and the Organization for Economic Cooperation and Development (OECD) averages, the average growth performance of Latin America appears very poor. The dif-

Table 8.6
Basic Indicators

	AFRICA				ASIA				LATIN AMERICA				OECD			
	1960-69	1970-79	1980-84	1985-88	1960-69	1970-79	1980-84	1985-88	1960-69	1970-79	1980-84	1985-88	1960-69	1970-79	1980-84	1985-88
Per Capita GDP Growth (%) /a*	1.66	2.34	-1.51	-0.62	4.15	4.30	2.89	2.98	2.48	3.14	-2.28	-0.33	4.28	2.80	0.86	2.96
Population Growth (%)*	2.47	2.65	2.96	3.05	2.65	2.41	2.08	1.94	2.60	2.28	2.12	-0.43	1.05	0.81	0.58	0.51
Inflation Rate**																
Average (%)	4.50	12.58	20.28	19.32	12.30	11.90	23.86	14.27	10.26	29.73	58.52	216.10	4.01	10.89	13.84	7.81
St. Deviation	3.99	6.45	8.03	8.68	8.52	6.81	12.70	12.29	4.92	17.87	44.09	293.13	1.46	3.58	4.38	2.21
Rate of Growth** of Export to GDP Ratio (%)	2.20	2.95	0.44	0.63	3.45	5.13	0.55	2.24	0.63	3.28	1.78	2.35	1.60	2.29	4.13	-1.91
Trade Balance to GDP /b** Ratio (%)	2.98	6.65	10.09	5.77	3.68	3.21	4.77	0.03	0.97	2.29	2.63	1.19	0.89	1.32	1.18	-0.47
Total Trade to GDP /c** Ratio (%)	49.09	56.69	59.63	54.41	47.81	59.95	69.28	70.19	43.87	49.85	50.19	51.78	50.69	59.15	68.73	68.18
Investment to GDP /d* Ratio (%)	10.06	12.65	11.92	10.48	18.75	23.13	23.55	20.69	15.80	17.21	15.57	13.49	26.19	26.85	23.90	23.98
Government Expenditure /d* to GDP Ratio (%)	20.50	23.79	23.07	22.01	16.84	17.06	17.41	18.55	14.15	15.71	16.87	16.53	13.72	13.91	15.02	14.71
Direct Investment to /e** GDP Ratio (%)	1.05	0.63	0.55	0.40	0.26	0.52	0.55	0.44	1.74	1.06	0.72	0.69	0.36	0.23	-0.00	-0.32

Sources: *Summers and Heston (1991); Penn World Table (Mark 5), 1991; **World Bank Data Base.

aReal GDP per capita in constant dollars adjusted for changes in the terms of trade (1985 International Prices).

bDefined as (Import − Export)/GDP.

cDefined as (Import + Export)/GDP.

dReal Investment and Real Government share of GDP % in constant dollars (1985 International Prices).

eNet Direct Investment = Credits or net increase in liabilities − Debits or net increase in assets. First period is 1966–69.

Table 8.7
Social Indicators

	Africa	Asia	Latin America	OECD
Enrollment Ratio for Primary Education /a				
1960	42.57	82.31	84.85	109.58
1970	58.14	93.76	91.55	106.46
1985	75.07	98.15	102.55	102.13
Enrollment Ratio for Secondary Education /a				
1960	4.38	25.96	18.20	50.38
1970	9.79	38.78	29.00	70.63
1985	23.52	60.08	48.10	85.92
Infant Mortality Rate (Ages 0-1)				
1965	15.23	7.62	9.30	2.95
1985	11.11	4.40	5.51	1.29
Mortality Rate for Ages 0 through 4				
Average of 1965 and 1985	15.53	6.67	8.27	2.30

Source: Barro and Wolf (1989).
[a]Constructed as ratio of total students enrolled in primary (secondary) education to estimated number of individuals in the age bracket 6–11 (12–17) years.

ference in performance is more pronounced for the 1980s. The Latin American average performance is also poor for inflation and for the investment rate.

Social indicators, presented in Table 8.7, show a marked improvement in all regions. However, the improvement in primary enrollment and infant mortality is more pronounced in Latin America than in Asia.

DETERMINANTS OF LATIN AMERICA'S GROWTH PERFORMANCE

Determinants of Growth in GDP per Capita

This section presents some estimates of the effect on long-term growth of variables related to economic policies, factor accumulation, and the initial relative productivity gap of individual Latin American countries vis-à-vis the United States. Estimates are obtained using a panel data set where the individual observations are period averages for the main regressors.[5] The periods used are 1960–1964; 1965–1969; 1970–1974; 1975–1979; 1980–1984; and 1985–1988. The most robust determinants of growth are the investment rate, the initial relative productivity gap vis-à-vis the United States, the government expenditures to

GDP ratio, the primary school rate, the growth rate in terms of trade, and the two measures of macroeconomic stability (the inflation rate and the trade deficit). In most of the regression, the coefficients of these variables appeared to be statistically significant regardless of the inclusion of other variables. The black market premium rate also appeared to be negatively correlated with growth, but this result was more sensitive to the particular equation specification utilized. The overall fit of the regressions is quite good, and the regressions explain up to 55 percent of the variability of the five-year average rates of growth.

We present now the individual regression results. The first regression on Table 8.8 shows the importance of the terms of trade effect to explain the rate of per capita GDP growth in Latin American countries. In all the specifications presented in Table 8.8, the coefficient of the terms of trade variable was positive and highly significant, indicating that improvement in terms of trade will induce faster growth. A possible explanation for this result lies in the fact that in many of the Latin American countries in our sample the level of utilized capacity depends quite heavily on the export earnings and their import capacity to buy the intermediate inputs and capital goods. Therefore, an improvement in the terms of trade increases capacity utilization, and it shows up in a higher rate of growth. A similar argument was advanced by Díaz-Alejandro (1976, p. 238).

All the regressions in Table 8.8 show evidence of convergence of per capita GDP growth. That is, holding everything else constant, the countries with the lower level of per capita income growth have a higher rate than countries with a higher level of per capita income. Since the logarithm of productivity gap has a more straightforward interpretation than the level of productivity gap, in regression 2 we replaced the level by its logarithm; however, the overall fit of the regression and the significance of the rest of the coefficients were marginally lower in this case.

The human capital variable (proxied by the primary school rate) shows a positive and significant effect on growth in all the regressions. On the other hand, government spending on GDP has a negative and significant effect on growth in all the regressions of Table 8.8.

Regression 3 assesses the effect on long-term growth of macroeconomic instability. A stable macroeconomic framework can be described as one where inflation is low and predictable, real interest rates are positive but not too high, fiscal policy is stable and sustainable, the real exchange rate is competitive and predictable, and the balance-of-payments situation is perceived as viable (Corbo and Fischer, 1992). We consider two measures of macroeconomic instability: the inflation rate[6] and the trade deficit to GDP ratio. Both variables have negative and significant coefficients.

Regressions 5 and 6 assess the effect on long-term growth of trade openness. Two measures of openness were considered: the GDP share of total trade and the black market or parallel market premium. The first one tries to use a proximate effect of openness as a proxy for openness itself. The black market premium is directly related to changes in trade restrictions or in openness basically because

Table 8.8

Pooled Regressions for Growth Rate in GDP Per Capita, Five-Years Averaged Data for Latin American Countries, 1960–1988 (Inst. Variable Estimation)

	(1)	(2)	(3)	(4)	(5)	(6)	(7)	(8)	(9)
Constant	-0.019 (-0.643)	-0.079 (-1.781)	-0.016 (-0.436)	-0.012 (-0.374)	-0.018 (-0.497)	-0.01 (-0.447)	-0.011 (-0.274)	-0.026 (-0.848)	-0.02 (-0.638)
Investment Ratio in t	0.291 (1.517)	0.273 (1.309)	0.34 (1.967)	0.319 (1.798)	0.346 (1.976)	0.281 (1.360)	0.333 (1.959)	0.325 (1.772)	0.316 (1.761)
Investment Ratio in t-1	-0.258 (-1.611)	-0.239 (-1.367)	-0.307 (-2.073)	-0.294 (-1.926)	-0.311 (-2.076)	-0.276 (-1.579)	-0.309 (-2.106)	-0.289 (-1.835)	-0.291 (-1.862)
Productivity Gap Vis-a-Vis USA	-0.056 (-2.997)		-0.079 (-3.805)	-0.083 (-3.821)	-0.078 (-3.686)	-0.083 (-3.284)	-0.08 (-3.757)	-0.081 (-3.689)	-0.081 (-3.663)
Log Productivity Gap Vis-a-Vis USA		-0.016 (-2.470)							
Government Spending (x10E-2)	-0.119 (-4.457)	-0.123 (-3.820)	-0.073 (-2.350)	-0.078 (-2.406)	-0.074 (-2.345)	-0.101 (-1.930)	-0.073 (-2.374)	-0.083 (-2.542)	-0.084 (-2.575)
Primary School Rate	0.044 (2.901)	0.049 (2.555)	0.041 (3.178)	0.046 (3.306)	0.041 (3.072)	0.047 (2.822)	0.04 (2.903)	0.044 (3.312)	0.043 (3.089)
Growth Rate in Terms of Trade	0.208 (4.565)	0.199 (4.919)	0.188 (4.172)	0.185 (4.274)	0.19 (4.204)	0.201 (4.709)	0.179 (3.797)	0.186 (4.090)	0.177 (3.721)

Table 8.8 (continued)

	(1)	(2)	(3)	(4)	(5)	(6)	(7)	(8)	(9)
Inflation Rate			-9.96E-04 (-2.575)	-4.45E-03 (-1.487)		-7.03E-04 (-1.773)	-1.02E-03 (-2.723)		
Trade Deficit			-0.185 (-2.022)	-0.209 (-2.202)	-0.172 (-1.863)	-0.180 (-1.705)	-0.192 (-2.091)	-0.189 (-1.960)	-0.197 (-2.036)
Black Premium Rate				4.10E-04 (1.233)	-9.27E-05 (-2.925)				
Trade Ratio						0.008 (0.549)			
Assassinations							-0.002 (-1.278)		-0.002 (-1.176)
For High Inflation Countries Dummy for Invst. Ratio in t								-0.066 (-2.505)	-0.068 (-2.584)
Dummy for Invst. Ratio in t-1								0.062 (2.159)	0.062 (2.171)
Sample Size	100	100	100	100	100	100	100	100	100
Corrected R-squared	0.518	0.502	0.539	0.537	0.536	0.53	0.538	0.553	0.552

Note: t statistics in parentheses. The regressions also include time-period dummies for periods 1965–1969; 1970–1974; 1975–1979; and 1980–1984.

the premium reflects the excess demand for tradable and for foreign assets that is not satisfied by the official foreign exchange market. Thus, the greater the controls on the use of official foreign exchange, the larger is the premium on the black or parallel market exchange rate. The estimates of the regression 6 show that the coefficient of the share of total trade in GDP is positive but not significant. However, in the case of the black market premium rate, its coefficient in regression 5 is significant and negative, indicating that those Latin American countries with more foreign exchange restrictions have presented slower output growth.

The significant effect of the black market premium rate on growth depends on the presence of the inflation rate in the regression. When both variables are included in the specification (regression 4), both variables are not significant and the sign of the black market premium is positive, indicating that this variable could also represent some degree of macroeconomic instability more than the degree of openness of the economy. This caveat to use the black market premium as a proxy for openness arises from the fact that the demand for foreign exchange assets is also a function of the degree of political and macroeconomic instability. Thus, when the premium changes because the portfolio excess demand for foreign assets is affected by political or economic ''news'' or internal civil disturbances, it does undermine the usefulness of the premium as a measure of openness. Then, the premium may change due to speculation, even when there is no change in the degree of restrictiveness of the trade regime.

In general, the main reason macroeconomic factors matter for growth is through uncertainty. The literature has concentrated on two channels here. First, policy-induced macroeconomic uncertainty reduces the efficiency of the price mechanism. This uncertainty, associated with high inflation or instability of the budget or current account, can be expected to reduce the level of productivity and, in contexts where the reallocation of factors is part of the growth process, also the rate of increase of productivity. Second, temporary uncertainty about the macroeconomic situation tends to reduce the rate of investment, as potential investors wait for the resolution of the uncertainty before committing themselves. This second channel suggests that investment would be lower at times when uncertainty is high. In other words, countries with high inflation rates are expected to present not only a low level of investment rates but also small efficiency of their investment rates. This last point is assessed in regressions 8 and 9 through including interaction effects on investment rate variables in countries with average inflation rates in the period 1960–1988 over 30 percent per year. In both regressions, the coefficients are significant with the expected signs, which, together with the direct effect of the investment rates on growth, indicated that the Latin American countries with lower-average levels of inflation have showed faster growth.[7]

There are many reasons that the increase in the degree of openness should be associated with higher growth (Dornbusch, 1992). In particular, the new growth theories suggest a link between openness and the long-run rate of growth of output rather than a rise in the level of output. Grossman and Helpman (1992) and Romer (1986) suggest that this can occur through the favorable impact of openness on technological change. For example, openness to trade increases growth rate because it provides access to a variety of imported inputs that embody new technology. On the other hand, Krugman (1980) maintains that greater openness expands the size of market facing domestic exporters, thereby raising returns to innovation and thus enhancing the country's specialization in research-intensive production. However, the new growth theories also show that growth can be lowered by increased foreign competition or that it can be increased by import protection if protection promotes investment in the research-intensive sectors of the relevant country. Thus, the direction of the openness-growth relationship is an open question for empirical research, rather than a theoretical given. Finally, the roles of political variables on growth were investigated. Regressions 7 and 9 add as growth determinant the index of assassinations taken from Barro and Wolf (1989). The estimates indicate that the coefficient of this variable is negative but not significant.[8] A possible explanation of this result can be found in the fact that the role of political variables is confined to its possible negative effect on investment. This point is addressed in the next section.

Investment Rate Determinants

The second channel through which economic policies could affect growth is their effect on investment rates. Table 8.9 presents estimates of a number of pooled investment regressions. In all these regressions the dependent variable is the share of investment in GDP for each of the periods also used for the growth equations. Regression 1 presents the results of the simplest model. In this model the investment rate is explained in terms of an accelerator model augmented by a human capital variable, the share of government spending in GDP, and the productivity gap vis-à-vis the United States. In this equation the coefficient of the relative productivity gap vis-à-vis the United States and all the other coefficients are significant and with the expected signs. In particular, the significant coefficient on the growth rate in GDP per capita is consistent with the usual finding that accelerator-type investment functions perform well.

Similar to the results obtained on growth, both the human capital and the government expenditure on GDP present significant effects on investment rate in all the regressions of Table 8.9. Both effects on investment not only present the expected signs but also are significant at the 1 percent level.

In regression 2, we add the terms-of-trade variable. The terms-of-trade variable has a highly statistically significant coefficient; the inclusion of this variable not only indicates that improvements in the terms of trade are likely to make investment more attractive at home but also leaves the relative productivity gap as another variable that is significant at the 1 percent level. The importance of the terms-of-trade variable in the investment specification is directly reflected in

Table 8.9

Pooled Regressions for Investment Ratios, Five-Years Averaged Data for Latin American Countries, 1960–1988

	(1)	(2)	(3)	(4)	(5)	(6)	(7)	(8)	(9)
Constant	9.601 (3.984)	9.394 (4.246)	7.899 (3.050)	8.908 (3.904)	9.033 (3.992)	9.11 (4.061)	8.402 (3.414)	9.896 (4.458)	8.927 (3.528)
Growth Rate in GDP Per Capita	28.339 (2.846)	38.527 (4.354)	37.474 (4.120)	37.395 (4.276)	37.662 (4.291)	37.911 (4.304)	35.835 (4.157)	34.983 (3.996)	35.159 (3.858)
Productivity Gap Vis-a-Vis USA	-9.326 (-1.178)	-13.609 (-2.083)	-12.485 (-1.937)	-13.442 (-2.041)	-13.487 (-2.052)	-13.531 (-2.066)	-13.067 (-1.945)	-14.096 (-2.281)	-13.203 (-2.164)
Government Spending	-0.368 (-3.360)	-0.361 (-3.507)	-0.362 (-3.502)	-0.349 (-3.345)	-0.349 (-3.336)	-0.351 (-3.351)	-0.358 (-3.350)	-0.377 (-3.549)	-0.39 (-3.707)
Secondary School Rate	37.679 (2.260)	40.176 (2.809)	41.448 (2.776)	39.747 (2.741)	39.749 (2.749)	39.836 (2.768)	40.108 (2.665)	39.609 (2.887)	41.162 (2.908)
Terms of Trade Index		0.016 (3.921)	0.014 (3.633)	0.0153 (3.865)	0.015 (3.889)	0.015 (3.909)	0.014 (3.644)	0.014 (3.890)	0.013 (3.573)
Dummy for High Infl.			-1.358 (-1.825)						-1.301 (-1.817)
Inflation Rate				-0.115 (-1.549)			-0.879 (-1.954)	-0.111 (-1.676)	
Variance of Inflation					-0.058 (-1.543)				
Black Premium Rate						-0.009 (-1.504)	0.084 (1.772)		
Assassinations								-3.487 (-6.302)	-3.456 (-6.508)
Sample Size	120	120	120	120	120	120	120	120	120
Corrected R-Squared	0.272	0.305	0.315	0.304	0.303	0.301	0.308	0.356	0.364

Note: t statistics in parentheses. The regressions also include time-period dummies for periods 1960–1964; 1965–1969; 1970–1974; 1975–1979; and 1980.

the increment on the explanatory power for the investment rate by more than three percentage points.

Regressions 3, 4, and 5 assess the effect on the investment rate of macroeconomic instability reflected by three inflation measures: the inflation rate, the variance of the inflation rate, and a dummy variable for high-inflation countries.[9] Both the inflation rate and the variance of the inflation rate have similar negative effects on the investment rate; however, the negative relationship between inflation rate (or variance of the inflation rate) and the share of the investment is significant only at the 10 percent level. For observations with average inflation for a period of over 50 percent per year, the estimate of the dummy variable in regression 3 shows a more significant negative relationship with investment rate than that obtained with the other two measures of inflation. High inflation rates are associated with macroeconomic instability, and then this uncertainty about the macroeconomic instability tends to reduce the rate of investment, because potential investors wait for the resolution of the uncertainty before committing themselves. Thus investment would be lower at times when uncertainty is high or when countries with high inflation rates are expected to present low levels of investment rates. The results shown in regressions 3, 4, and 5 tend to sustain the hypothesis that the effect of the uncertainty, reflected by high inflation rates, on the investment rates is stronger in countries that have experienced higher inflation episodes, in particular, over 50 (or 30) percent per year.

As another measure of economic uncertainty, regressions 6 and 7 add the black market premium rate. This variable can be interpreted both as a measure of expectation of depreciation of the currency and as a crude index of distortions. According to Fischer (1992), the first interpretation may affect investment through several channels: first, it is more attractive to hold foreign assets when depreciation is expected; second, economic uncertainty is higher under such conditions; but third, for those who can obtain foreign exchange at official rate, foreign capital goods are cheap to import. Thus, while the first two channels suggest a negative relationship between the black market premium and investment rate, the third suggests the opposite. On the other hand, the second interpretation is that the black market premium serves as a general index of distortions and therefore of an unsustainable situation; then it is likely to be negatively correlated with investment.

In regression 6 the black market premium rate is the only measure of uncertainty or macroeconomic instability included. In this case its coefficient is negative and significant only at the 10 percent level. The coefficients of the other variables in the regression are significant and stable with respect to the estimates obtained from regressions 2 to 5. When another measure of macroeconomic instability, the inflation rate, is added together with the black market premium, both the inflation rate and the black premium rate are statistically significant; however, only the inflation rate presents the expected negative relationship with investment. This fact can be explained by the high collinearity between both variables because high-inflation countries are also countries that show high levels of black market premium, reflecting the level of uncertainty and instability of the economy.

Finally, regressions 8 and 9 include additional variables to control for constitutional changes and political stability. The coefficients of these variables were negative and strongly significant, helping to improve the explanatory power of the regression by around six percentage points. As Barro (1991) maintains, this negative relationship between investment and political instability (proxied by figures on number of coups, index of political rights, and political assassination) could involve the adverse effects of political instability on property rights and the linkage between property rights and private investment. However, the correlation could also reflect a political response to bad economic outcomes. From Tables 8.8 and 8.9, we observe that the political instability variable both is strongly negatively correlated with investment and does not appear to affect the rate of growth on GDP per capita significantly. The explanation would seem to be simple: the political instability affects the rate of investment directly and thereby the rate of growth indirectly. The political instability (proxied in Tables 8.8 and 8.9 by an index of political assassination) can be interpreted as affecting the rate of investment.

CONCLUSIONS

At the risk of oversimplification, it could be said that, up to World War I, economic policies in Latin America were based on comparative advantage. During that period, growth was led by exports. While industrialization in light manufacturing was progressing, it was the result of income growth rather than government intervention.

By the early 1920s, most had also returned to the gold standard and had put in place trade regimes that discriminated slightly against exports as a result of taxes on exports and mild tariffs on imports. When the Great Depression hit and the export and international capital markets collapsed, these countries intensified their import controls by increasing tariffs and instituting nontariff barriers to trade. Although some reduction in import restrictions took place in the second part of the 1930s and early 1940s, the trade regime in existence at the outbreak of World War II was biased in favor of import-competing manufacturing and against export activities.

As world trade resumed in the post–World War II period, Latin American exports grew, but at a slower rate than that for the world as a whole because of the antiexport bias. In addition, industrialization was already under way, spurred by import substitution stemming from the biases in the trade regimes and by the concomitant growth in income.

Although world trade was picking up at this time, many countries in Latin America were pessimistic about the possibility of returning to exported growth. This pessimism led to a first phase of import-substitution industrialization. This strategy was articulated by Prebisch at the ECLA, where he recommended import substitution industrialization as a development strategy.

As countries started to experience balance-of-payments and inflation problems and as the dynamism of the manufacturing sector was slowing down, once the easy import substitution phase has been completed, the import substitution model was beginning to be questioned. The proponents of the import substitution model had to modify their model. Their response in the late 1950s added a new twist to the structuralist theory. Now growth was being limited by the unavailability of foreign exchange. Given that import substitution had already been pushed too far, a new form of this strategy—regional integration—had to be pursued, preferably in combination with increased foreign aid. Economic planning would provide the coordinating framework for evaluating the policy options.

The first element in this policy prescription found expression in a movement toward regional economic integration, as ECLA had recommended in the late 1950s. The second element, based on the two-gap model of limits to growth, gave rise to the gap theory of foreign aid, given the virtual absence at the time of international capital markets for medium- and long-term capital flows and the pessimistic outlook on export growth.

Some countries did recognize the dangers and instituted reforms. The first was Brazil in the mid-1960s, followed soon thereafter by Chile in 1965 and Colombia in 1967. Somewhat later, in the mid-1970s, three Southern Cone countries—Argentina, Chile, and Uruguay—initiated a set of reforms oriented toward liberalizing their economies and controlling inflation. For a time their efforts proved quite successful, and they might well have worked had it not been for the substantial appreciation that resulted from ill-fated stabilization efforts and ill-advised capital inflow during the late 1970s. External shocks, particularly the oil price increases, the rise in international interest rates, and the subsequent worldwide recession, coming on top of the macro errors helped the collapse of the three economies.

Following the second oil shock and the debt crisis, the receptivity to reforms became more widespread in Latin America. Bolivia, Costa Rica, Mexico, and Venezuela became major reformers. Lately, El Salvador and Honduras have followed the same route. Key areas of reforms have been the public sector, the trade regime, and the regulation of domestic markets.

Latin America's growth performance up to the late 1960s did not provide any warning for the crisis that was about to unravel. However, problems were building up with the deterioration of the overall macroeconomic balances and the increasing cost of market interventions that had accumulated in the previous thirty years. The first oil shock surprised some of the countries of the region. But when the second oil shock came, easy access to foreign borrowing prolonged the use of the existing development model. The external shocks of the early 1980s detonated a crisis that had been in the making during the previous thirty years.

Sooner or later, the countries in the region recognized the need to carry out a profound transformation of their economic system to adjust to the crisis and to start a process of sustained growth while creating the conditions for a permanent reduction in poverty.

As a consequence of the external shocks and the policies and institutions developed in the previous thirty years, Latin America had in the 1980s its worst decade of the century. Only six out of the twenty-three countries in the region experienced a positive rate of growth in per capita GDP. The deterioration in inflation was just as dramatic. In sixteen out of twenty-three countries the inflation accelerated, and in five of the sixteen it reached over three-digit annual level for the decade as a whole.

Chile, Bolivia, and Mexico have progressed the most in the structural transformation of their economies. Among them, Chile is on a path to sustainable growth while Mexico and Bolivia are initiating a growth process after many years of much-needed and painful adjustment. These three countries are benefiting today from below 20 percent annual inflation and positive growth in per capita income. However, growth is still low in Mexico and Bolivia, and there is increasing demand in both countries to accelerate growth.

For quite a while, development economists had been advocating the need to restore the basic macroeconomic balances and to reduce distortions to get output close to its potential and to accelerate growth. However, only with the new insights of the "new growth theory" has a respectable theoretical base been developed to understand the channels through which better policies and factor accumulation affect not only the level of output but also its rate of growth.

From an analysis of the factors accounting for differences in growth performance we found that policies can affect growth directly through the law of motion for growth and indirectly through investment rates. With respect to the role of different variables we found that:

1. the change in terms of trade has a positive and significant effect on growth.

2. human capital variables have a positive effect on growth both through the growth equation and through a higher rate of investment. This result shows that public policy has an important role in promoting growth by enhancing the human capital base. The latter could be done through the direct provision of human capital for the low-income groups of the population or through creating an enabling environment that reduces distortions to the accumulation of human capital.

3. controlling for other factors, the share of government spending on GDP has a negative effect on growth and on investment rates. In general, government spending can enhance growth or hinder growth. Government spending may promote growth by providing essential public goods. However, it could create negative growth effects by wasting resources on programs with a low rate of return. Our results shows that on average, government spending has a strong negative effect on growth.

4. the black market premium is more a measure of macroeconomic instability than of the degree of openness.

5. political instability has a negative effect on growth through lower investment rates. This result confirms recent theoretical work on the role of uncertainty and the credibility of policies on investment (Serven and Solimano, 1992).

NOTES

1. By the end of 1933, all Latin American countries except Argentina stopped full service of their external debt. Argentina continued meeting its obligation only because most of its debt was held by Great Britain, which also happened to be its largest export market. But an emerging confrontation was developing with the increasingly restricted access of Argentinian exports to Great Britain.

2. This argument was derived from a comparison of the relations over time in individual Latin American countries between import and output growth, on one hand, and export and output growth, on the other. The rationale for the first type of calculation, after accounting for relative prices, is clear. However, the relationship between exports and domestic output growth could hold only in countries where exports were residual after satisfying the domestic market. The case hardly applied to most Latin American countries.

3. For another evaluation of the structuralist-ECLA type of policies, see Fishlow (1985).

4. For an assessment of the consensus on policy reforms, see Williamson (1990) and Vittorio Corbo and Fischer (1992).

5. This section draws on Corbo and Rojas (1993).

6. The variance of inflation rate was also considered, finding a negative and significant effect on growth. Since the general results do not change when the inflation rate is considered, we do not report the results in Table 8.4.

7. F-tests were carried out to test the null hypothesis that the investment rates and interaction effects coefficients were significantly no different from zero. The levels of significance of the F-test for regressions 8 and 9 were 0.13E-5 and 0.15E-5, respectively, rejecting strongly the null hypothesis.

8. We report only the result for the variable number of assassinations per million population per year (1960–1985). Other variables were also considered and were found not to have a significant effect on growth. These variables were index of civil liberties, index of political rights, and number of coups.

9. Average inflation rates of 50 and 30 percent per year in each five-year period were used as cutoff points. In both cases the coefficient of the dummy was significant. However, in the case of the 50 percent cutoff point, the coefficient was more significant, and the explanatory power of the regression was higher. In Table 8.5, we report only the results where the dummy takes a value of one when the country has an average inflation rate over 50 percent per year.

REFERENCES

Balassa, B., and associates. 1971. *The Structure of Protection in Developing Countries*. Baltimore: Johns Hopkins University Press.

Barro, R.J. 1990. "Government Spending in a Simple Model of Endogenous Growth." *Journal of Political Economy* 18: 23–25.

———. 1991. "Economic Growth in a Cross Section of Countries." *Quarterly Journal of Economics* (May).

Barro, R. and Wolf, H.C. 1989. "Data for Economic Growth in a Cross Section of Countries." Boston: National Bureau of Economic Research.

Bergman, J. 1970. *Brazil: Industrailization and Trade Policies.* London: Oxford University Press.

Berlinski, J., and Schydlowski, D.M. 1982. "Incentive Policies and Economic Development: Argentina." In *Development Strategies in Semi-Industrial Economies,* edited by B. Balassa. Baltimore: Johns Hopkins University Press.

Bhagwati, J. 1978. *Anatomy and Consequence of Trade Controls Regimes.* New York: National Bureau of Economic Research.

Campos, R. 1961. "Two Views on Inflation in Latin America." In *Latin American Issues,* edited by A.O. Hirschman. New York: Twentieth Century Fund.

Castañeda, T. 1992. *Combating Poverty. Innovative Social Reforms in Chile During the 1980s.* San Francisco: ICS Press.

CEPAL 1976. *America Latina: Relación de Precios del Intercambio* (Latin America: Terms of trade). Santiago, Chile: ECLA.

Corbo, V. 1974. *Inflation in Developing Countries. An Econometric Study of the Chilean Inflation.* Amsterdam: North-Holland.

Corbo, V., and Fischer, S. 1992. "Adjustment Programs and Bank Support Rational and Main Results." In *Adjustment Lending Revisited,* edited by V. Corbo, S. Fischer, and S. Webb. Washington, D.C.: World Bank.

Corbo, V., and Rojas, P. 1993. "Investment, Macroeconomic Stability and Growth: The Latin American Experience." Mimeo.

Corbo, V., and Schmidt-Hebbel, K. 1991. "Public Policy and Savings in Developing Countries." *Journal of Development Economics* 36 (July): 89–116.

Corden, M.W. 1966. "The Structure of a Tariff System and the Effective Protective Rate." *Journal of Political Economy* (August): 74: 221–37.

———. 1991. "Macroeconomic Policy and Growth." In Proceedings of the World Bank Annual Conference on Development Economics. Washington, D.C.: World Bank.

Díaz-Alejandro, C.F. 1976. *Foreign Trade Regimes and Economic Development.* New York: Columbia University Press.

———. 1983. "Stories of the 1930s for the 1980s." In *Financial Policies and the World Capital Market: The Problem of Latin American Countries,* edited by P. Aspe-Armella, R. Dornbusch, and M. Obstfelds. Chicago: University of Chicago Press.

Diz, A.C. 1966. "Money and Prices in Argentina, 1935–62." Ph.D. diss., University of Chicago.

Dornbusch, R. 1992. "The Case for Trade Liberalization in Developing Countries." *Journal of Economic Perspectives* 6 (Winter).

Dornbusch, R., and Wetzel, D.L. 1989. "Policy Determinants of Growth: Survey of Theory and Evidence." World Bank PPR WP#343.

French-Davis, R. 1971. "Economic Policies and Stabilization Programs, Chile 1952–69." Ph.D. diss., University of Chicago.

Fischer, S. 1992. "Macroeconomic Stability and Growth." *Cuadernos de Economía* 29 (August).

Fishlow, A. 1985. "The State of Latin American Economics." In *1985 Report,* edited by Inter-American Development Bank. Washington, D.C.: World Bank.

Furtado, C. 1985. *A Fantasia Organizada* (An organized fantasy). Río de Janeiro: Editore Paz et Terra S.A.

Grossman, G., and Helpman, E. 1992. *Innovation and Growth in the Global Economy.* Cambridge: MIT Press.

Harberger, A. 1964. "Some Notes on Inflation: In *Inflation and Growth in Latin America,* edited by W. Baer and I. Kerstenetzky. New Haven, Conn.: Yale University Press.

Hirschman, A.O. 1961. "Ideologies of Economic Development in Latin America." In *Latin American Issues: Essays and Comments*, edited by A.O. Hirschman. New York: Twentieth Century Fund.

Krueger, A.O. 1978. *Foreign Trade Regimes and Economic Development: Liberalization Attempts and Consequences*. Cambridge, Mass.: Ballinger Press for NBER.

———. 1983. *Trade and Employment in Developing Countries*, Chicago: University of Chicago Press.

Krugman, Paul. 1980. "Economies of Scale, Product Differentiation, and the Pattern of Trade." *American Economic Review*, December, pp. 950–59.

Larraín, F., and Meller, P. 1991. "The Socialist-Populist Chilean Experience: 1970–1973." In *The Macroeconomics of Populism in Latin America*, edited by R. Dornbusch and S. Edwards. Chicago: University of Chicago Press.

Little, I., Scitovsky, T., and Scott, M. 1970. *Industry and Trade in Some Developing Countries: A Comparative Study*. New York: Oxford University Press.

Macarios, S. 1964. "Protectionism and Industrialization in Latin America." *Economic Bulletin for Latin America* 9 (March).

Noguès, J. 1985. "A Historical Perspective of Peru's Trade Liberalization Policies of the 80s'." Mimeo.

Noyola, J. 1965. "El Desarrollo Económico y la Inflación en Mexico y Otros Paises Latinoamericanos" (Economic development and inflation in Mexico and other Latin American countries). *Investigaciones Economicas* 16, no. 4.

Pinto, A. 1960. *Ni Estabilidad ni Desarrollo: La Política del Fondo Monetario Internacional* (Neither stability nor development: The policy of the IMF). Santiago: Editorial Universitaria.

Prebisch, R. 1947. *Introducción a Keynes* (Introduction to Keynes). Buenos Aires: Fondo de Cultura Economica.

———. 1950. *The Economic Development of Latin America and Its Principal Problems*. New York: United Nations.

———. 1959a. "Commercial Policy in the Underdeveloped Countries." *American Economic Review Proceedings* 2 (May).

———. 1959b. *El Mercado Comun Latinoamericano* (The Latin American common market). New York: United Nations.

Romer, P. 1986. "Increasing Returns and Long-Run Growth." *Quarterly Journal of Economics* 105 (May).

Seers, D. 1962. "A Theory of Inflation and Growth Based on Latin American Experience." *Oxford Economic Papers* 39 (June).

Serven, L., and Solimano, A. 1992. "Private Investment and Macroeconomic Adjustment: A Survey." *World Bank Research Observer* 17 (January).

Sturzenegger, F.A. 1991. "Description of a Populist Experience: Argentine, 1973–1976." In *The Macroeconomics of Populism in Latin America*, edited by R. Dornbusch and S. Edwards. Chicago: University of Chicago Press.

Summers, R., and Heston, A. 1991. "The Penn World Table (Mark 5): An Expanded Set of International Comparisons, 1950–1988." *Quarterly Journal of Economics* 106 (May).

Sunkel, O. 1958. "La Inflación Chilena: Un Enfoque Heterodoxo" (The Chilean inflation: A heterodox approach). *El Trimestre Economico* (October–December).

Taylor, L., and Bacha, E. 1973. "Growth and Trade Distortions in Chile." In *Analysis of Development Problems,* edited by R.S. Eckaus and P.N. Rosenstein-Rodan. Amsterdam: North-Holland.

Universidad de Chile. 1963. *La Economia Chilena en el Periodo 1950–1963.* Santiago: Instituto de Economía.

Viner, J. 1953. *International Trade and Economic Development.* Oxford: Clarendon Press.

Westphal, L. 1978. ''The Republic of Korea Experience with Export-Led Industrial Development.'' *World Development* 6.

Williamson, J. 1990. *Latin American Adjustment: How Much Has Happened?* Washington, D.C.: Institute for International Economics.

9

AFRICA'S POSTINDEPENDENCE DEVELOPMENT EXPERIENCES

Tony Killick

During the course of the 1980s, the perception grew that the economies of Africa were in crisis. The progress that was made in the early years of independence faltered during the 1970s and ground to a halt in the following decade. Although we shall later question that judgment, there is today a widespread perception that Africa's postindependence development record has been one of failure. This chapter first examines the evidence on this, and the remainder of the chapter is taken up with examining explanations of this record. One section of the chapter centers around an econometric "sources of growth" study; another seeks to go beyond the econometrics to introduce a wider range of economic explanations, including the influence of incentive systems and state interventionism; the quality of macroeconomic management; and the effects of market failures. Then the chapter inquires beyond the boundaries of economics into the influence of historical, political, and institutional features and offers a summary and conclusion. The coverage is confined to Sub-Saharan Africa (SSA), excluding South Africa.

THE RECORD

Growth and Modernization

The central fact with which we must concern ourselves is the long-term slowness of economic growth in SSA, by comparison with other developing regions. Figure 9.1 shows that at the beginning of the 1990s per capita gross domestic product (GDP) was no higher than twenty years earlier, although we may also note that the Asian record stands out as truly exceptional. Nonetheless, if we leave aside the Middle East as a special case, the economies of Africa have failed to a special degree to meet the material aspirations of their peoples. Indeed,

Figure 9.1
Developing Countries: Real GDP Per Capita by Region (1970 = 100)

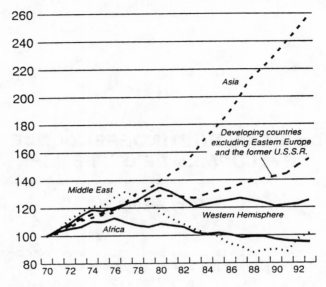

Source: IMF 1992, Chart 12.
Note: Composites are averages for individual countries weighted by the average U.S. dollar value of their respective GDPs over the preceding three years. The shaded area indicates staff projections.

the trend for low-income Africa over the last two decades is even worse when adjusted for the income-reducing effects of deteriorations in the commodity terms of trade.[1]

Table 9.1 throws further light on this. Statistically speaking, the trend in per capita income is the combined outcome of high and rising population growth rates and low gross national product (GNP) growth, with the former outstripping the latter from the early 1970s, although there was a modest revival of GNP growth in the latter part of the 1980s. In consequence of declining per capita incomes, private consumption levels have fallen, overall and for most subperiods, both for low-income SSA countries and for the region as a whole.

Parallel with this stagnation in living standards has been an, at best, halting progress with economic modernization, as is shown in Table 9.2. Comparing these trends with observed regularities of structural change during economic development, we see only gradual moves toward industrialization and away from primary production. We also see gross saving and investment rates remaining in 1989 about where they were in 1965 (if we can rely on the statistics), again in contrast to other developing regions. Partly in consequence of low saving rates, we see a far heavier dependence on aid receipts, relative to GNP, than in

Table 9.1
Trends in Economic Performance Indicators, 1965–1990

	1965–73	1973–80	1980–85	1985–90	1980–90	All low-income countries /b 1980–90
	(------------------------ percentage change per annum ------------------)					
1. Population						
(a) Total SSA /a	2.63	2.75	3.10	3.22	3.17	
(b) Low-income SSA /a	2.64	2.77	2.99	3.16	3.08	2.72
2. Total GNP						
(a) Total SSA /a	4.3	3.4	1.0	2.4	2.0	
(b) Low-income SSA /a	3.4	2.7	0.8	3.1	2.0	3.6
3. Private consumption per capita						
(a) Total SSA /a	-0.7	2.9	-1.3	-2.0	-2.2	
(b) Low-income SSA /a	-0.6	1.1	-0.8	-0.2	-0.5	-0.5
4. Prices (GDP deflator)						
(a) Total SSA /a	6.5	16.5	18.1	22.2	19.6	
(b) Low-income SSA /a	6.2	19.4	26.1	35.1	30.2	14.8
5. Export volumes						
(a) Total SSA /a	14.2	-0.2	-3.1	0.0	-0.7	
(b) Low-income SSA /a	-	0.9	-4.9	0.5	-1.8	0.8
6. Import volumes						
(a) Total SSA /a	3.8	7.9	-6.7	-1.8	-5.9	
(b) Low-income SSA /a	3.1	1.6	-3.0	1.0	-0.7	-3.2

Source: World Bank data bank.
[a]Excludes Nigeria.
[b]Excluding China and India.

Table 9.2

Comparative Economic Structures, 1965 and 1990

	SUB-SAHARAN AFRICA		East Asia & Pacific		South Asia		Latin America & Caribbean		All low & middle income countries	
	1965	1990	1965	1990	1965	1990	1965	1990	1965	1990
1. Average GDP size ($ billion)	0.82	4.79	-	-	-	-	-	-	4.56	34.02
2. Agriculture as % GDP	40	32	37	21	44	33	16	10	27	17
3. Manufacturing as % GDP	8	11 /a	24	34	15	17	23	25	21	-
4. Gross domestic investment as % GDP	15	16	22	37	17	21	20	19	20	26
5. Gross domestic saving as % GDP	14	13	23	35	14	18	21	24	20	27
6. Aid receipts as % GNP	-	9.6	-	0.8	-	1.6	-	0.4	-	1.4
7. Total external debt as % GNP	-	109	-	27	-	30	-	42	-	40
8. Share of primary products in exports	93	92	69	31	63	30	93	67	75	51
9. Urban population as % of total	14	29	19	50	18	26	53	71	24	44
10. Energy consumption per capita (kgs of oil equivalent)	74	103	164	553	90	205	579	1057	277	605

Source: World Bank (1992), Development Indicators.
[a]1989 figure.

the rest of the developing world,[2] aid that came in the form of concessional loans rather than grants contributed to the exceptionally large stock of external debt shown in Table 9.2, despite only slight access to world capital markets during the credit boom of the 1970s and since.

Perhaps the most significant indicators in Table 9.2, however, relate to the composition of exports and consumption of energy. The slow growth of energy consumption reflects not only the stagnation of living standards but the limited extent of modernization of the productive system. We feature Africa's export record prominently later, but note now the virtually unchanged reliance on primary product exports, a record that contrasts starkly with that of the other regions. For most of the African countries that came to independence heavily reliant on a limited number of commodity exports, that position had changed little by the beginning of the 1990s.[3]

These features, combined with small economy size (and therefore heavy reliance on international trade), have left SSA vulnerable to terms-of-trade shocks. The continuing dependence of large majorities of the population on rural sources of income also leaves the region's economies vulnerable to variations in the weather, as witness the famine of 1983–1984 and the more restricted one of 1991–1992.

There is other evidence of the slow pace of modernization. In agriculture, for example, average fertilizer consumption per hectare is estimated to have been a mere tenth of the average for all developing countries in 1989–1990, with the gap having tripled since the beginning of the 1970s (World Bank, 1992, Table 4), and yields for a number of crops are far below the developing country average.[4] Africa still awaits a green revolution.[5] There is also a widely noted technology gap in much of manufacturing. The slow pace of technological progress helps to explain why estimates show no improvement at all in total factor productivity in Africa during 1960–1987, against a trend rate of increase of 0.6 percent per annum for all developing countries, with a substantial decline in SSA in 1973–1987 (Boskin and Lau, 1990).

This record helps explain the population trends shown in Table 9.1. If population growth is seen as conforming to some version of the demographic transition model, it has continued to accelerate because the economic modernization associated with reductions in fertility has not yet occurred (although there are signs that the 1990s may reveal a turning point in Africa's population growth).

Taken together, the evidence just adduced leaves SSA in an unenviable position. Sixteen of the twenty countries with the lowest recorded per capita incomes are in SSA,[6] as are most of those classified by the United Nations (UN) as "least developed." The World Bank estimated that in 1985 nearly half (47 percent) of the population lived below the poverty line, a proportion exceeded only by South Asia (notably India). In that year SSA contributed a disproportionate 16 percent of the estimated total number of those living in poverty in developing countries, a share projected to double by the end of the century (World Bank, 1990, Table

9.2). Unfortunately, the data deficiencies are such that nothing general can usefully be said about trends in the size distribution of income.

Not only are African countries poor, but their poverty is persistent. A study based on a sample of sixty-three countries (ODI, 1988) examined trends in per capita incomes (measured in 1980 international dollars) over 1960–1985, placing countries into five income bands. It found that a third of the thirty-three sample countries that fell into the two lowest bands in 1960 had managed to raise themselves into higher bands, *but none of the SSA countries had achieved this.*

Macroeconomic Balances

In addition to stagnant incomes and slow modernization, Africa's economies have been marked by persistent macroeconomic imbalances and pressures. There has, for instance, been a chronic tendency toward unviable balance-of-payments deficits. This cannot be reduced to simple statistical demonstration, but note the following evidence:

- the cuts in import volumes during the 1980s, shown in Table 9.1.

- the frequency with which its African members have had recourse to International Monetary Fund (IMF) assistance, so that as of April 1992, twenty-two SSA countries had programs with the fund (with a further five ineligible because they were in arrears with repayments of earlier credits).

- SSA's current account deficit in 1973–1992 averaged 23 percent of export earnings—a proportion far higher than for any other developing region—and ended the period higher than it began.[7]

- SSA's international reserves are far lower than for any other region, averaging only 13 percent of annual imports in 1983–1991.[8]

Underlying these pressures was the poor export record already mentioned. This is illustrated further by the figures on export volumes in Table 9.1, showing the quantum of exports to have actually declined since the early 1970s. Indeed, although its exports remained heavily concentrated on primary products, even SSA's share of these world markets declined, as did its share in developing country commodity export earnings, although there is some evidence of a recovery in the later 1980s.[9]

Table 9.1 draws attention to another aspect of the pressure of demand on resources: significant and accelerating inflation levels, although here the intercountry differences are large enough to make the use of such averages suspect.

Given the low saving rates reported earlier (Table 9.2), such macroeconomic pressures are not surprising. Even though we have seen these to have been augmented by exceptionally large amounts of development assistance, the continent's access to private sources of world savings has been slight.

Social Welfare

It is with some relief that we can now turn to a range of indicators where there is more progress to report. The dearth of good data is particularly acute when it comes to social welfare, but Table 9.3 pulls some evidence together. To the extent that these figures are to be relied upon and with the exception of calorie supply, these all show substantial progress and help put the earlier evidence on poverty and stagnant living standards into context: the mortality improvements and accelerating population growth are inconsistent with economic catastrophe.

The demographic statistics are arguably the most fundamental welfare indicators of all and show Africans to be living longer, with the mean expectation of life having gone up by about a fifth over the years in question and with mortality rates down by nearly a third. Underlying these results are better public health provisions, with substantial improvements in ratios of doctors and nurses to the general population (Akeredolu-Ale, 1990, Table 5). Encouraging as these trends are, however, we see in the table that the mortality statistics have been improving even faster in other developing countries. Infant and child mortality remains much higher than in other developing regions. Twenty-five to thirty years after independence more than half the African population still has no ready access to health services, almost two-thirds lack supplies of safe water, and many continue to suffer from preventable diseases (UNDP, 1991, pp. 35–36). Moreover, the particularly virulent spread of acquired immunodeficiency syndrome (AIDS) in Africa threatens to undermine such social progress as has occurred.[10]

Africa's comparative disadvantage is starker in Table 9.3's figures on calorie supply. The statistics here are liable to particularly large error margins, but there is other evidence pointing to adverse nutritional trends.[11] Africa's poor agricultural record and its limited import capacity are the key factors here.

The school enrollment rates are also noteworthy, showing great improvements on the neglects of colonialism and more than matching the record of other low-income countries. Inspection of Table 9.3 reveals, however, that this improvement was not sustained into the 1980s, as budget constraints imposed themselves. It is also possible that the numerical progress recorded in the table was undermined by a decline in the quality of the education provided. Data on teacher-pupil ratios do not support this view, showing no deterioration, but the UN publication, *Africa Recovery* (April 1992, p. 13), noted a decline in real government expenditures and commented:

The declines in educational spending have directly translated into an erosion in the quality of schooling in much of Africa. Severe shortages of textbooks and other school materials became even worse as funds available for their purchase dried up. In many African countries, the whole infrastructure of support services—school inspection and supervision, in-service teacher education, school health services, and the maintenance of schools' furniture, equipment and physical facilities—has deteriorated. (p. 13)

Table 9.3
Trends in Social Welfare Indicators, 1965–1990

		1965	1973	1980	1985	% change since 1965	% change, since 1965 all low-income countries /b
1.	Crude death rates						
	(a) All SSA	22.5	20.1	18.3	15.2	-32	-39
	(b) Low-income SSA /a	22.7	20.4	18.8	15.8	-30	
2.	Infant mortality rate						
	(a) All SSA	157	138	125	105 /c	-32	-37
	(b) Low-income SSA /a	156	141	130	109 /c	-30	
3.	Life expectation at birth						
	(a) All SSA	42.0	45.0	47.2	51.3	+22	+25
	(b) Low-income SSA /a	41.9	44.6	46.6	50.5	+21	
4.	Per capita calorie supply						
	(a) All SSA	2034	1990	2112	2011 /d	-1	+13
	(b) Low-income SSA /a	1977	1963	2043	1968	-	
5.	Primary school enrolment ratios (% of relevant age group)						
	(a) All SSA	42	56 /e	77	65 /d	+55	+60
	(b) Low-income SSA /a	40	55 /e	66	63 /d	+58	
6.	Secondary school enrolment ratios						
	(a) All SSA	4.4	10.0 /e	15.8	18.2 /d	+314	+207
	(b) Low-income SSA /a	3.8	10.3 /e	14.3	14.9 /d	+292	

Source: World Bank data bank.
[a]Excludes Nigeria.
[b]Excluding China and India.
[c]1989 figures.
[d]1988 figures.
[e]1975 figures.

(Similar doubts about the quality of service surround the improvements in public health services reported earlier.) In any case, comparative enrollment statistics show that SSA's position remains a great deal worse than that of other developing regions.[12] Moreover, the economic value to the continent of this educational expansion has been reduced by a substantial outflow from among the best-qualified Africans to other regions and international agencies.

Moving beyond the indicators in Table 9.3, particular mention should be made of the plight of many African women. With the large-scale migration of young men to urban centers in search of wage employment, a great deal of the food farming is left to women, who also bear large families and look after the home and who are discriminated against in the design of agricultural policies and access to agricultural services.[13] They are discriminated against in education too, with a far larger discrepancy between male and female school enrollment rates than for other developing regions and poorer salaried job opportunities (UN, 1991, p. 190–95). Progress in reducing these discrepancies has been slow.

Finally, various symptoms of environmental deterioration should be mentioned, although there is little firm continentwide evidence or agreement on the extent of the resulting problems.[14] There appears, first, to have been a trend decline in rainfall in the Sahelian zone and parts of the Horn since the late-1960s—areas that were already short of water—and consequential land degradation. This is possibly a result of global warming, in which case it will presumably persist and worsen, but there is no scientific consensus about this. Relatedly, there is much concern about the southward spread of the Sahara, although here again there is little agreement on the extent and seriousness of this, nor are there firm data with which to settle the matter.

Further south, there is concern about the deforestation occurring in rain forest areas, notably in Ghana and the Côte d'Ivoire, although this appears less a direct result of logging than the work of farmers seeking to keep ahead of the loggers and to clear forest land for cultivation. Elsewhere, in savanna and other less wooded regions, areas are being cleared of trees in order to satisfy the growing demand—particularly emanating from the towns—for charcoal and fuelwood, with rural communities finding it increasingly burdensome to meet their own needs. Deforestation is only one of the environmental problems associated with urbanization, however; weak controls mean that Africa's cities have more than their share of air and water pollution.

Cautions

It is unfortunately necessary to qualify the generalizations just offered in two important ways. First, there is much that we cannot understand about SSA's socioeconomic situation because of inadequate data. There are often large gaps in countries' statistical coverage and many questions about the reliability of available data. Quite often there is little reliable demographic information, even about the size of the population. The extent and value of subsistence activities are usually estimated in most approximate ways. Even data on marketed food production are often little more than guesstimates. Fiscal statistics remain alarmingly poor. Data on international trade and capital movements are subject to large error margins.[15] We have no alternative but to use such statistics as are available, while trying not to put more weight on them than they will bear, but the reader will do well to retain a skeptical attitude toward statistical analyses of Africa's economic situation.

The second caution concerns the level of generalization involved in a survey of African experiences. As with any other geographical region, there are large differences in the resource endowments, structures, performances, and problems of the forty-five or so national economies within SSA. In particular, there is an ever-present temptation to slip from the poor *average* record of SSA economies to assuming that *all* have performed poorly or have similar problems. The temptation must be resisted. Figures 9.2 and 9.3 reveal that there has, in fact, been a considerable spread of experiences, at least as regards the growth of per capita income. Indeed, Figure 9.1 shows that for the whole period 1965–1990 nearly half of the countries recorded managed to achieve at least some increase in average incomes, and several managed long-term growth rates that were respectable by any standard. Comparison of Figures 9.2 and 9.3, however, shows the marked worsening during the 1980s reported earlier, with only a handful of countries sustaining significant income growth during that decade. Moreover, a number of the fastest-growing countries have only small populations, while the largest ones (Nigeria, Ethiopia, Zaire) feature among those that have stagnated or slipped back. A few of those believed to be among the worst performers, like Angola, Mozambique, and Sudan, do not feature in the diagrams at all because their statistics are too poor. There are also major differences between the situations of the oil-importing and oil-exporting countries. The Franc Zone arrangements place most Francophone West and Central African countries into a special category (see page 334), at least as regards their macroeconomic situations. Countries in the Sahelian zone and the Horn of Africa have a special vulnerability to uncertain rainfall. The fluctuating relationships between the giant economy of South Africa and its far smaller neighbors place them in a special category.

Nonetheless, there *are* many common characteristics and problems and substantial similarities in development experiences.[16] Inevitably, limitations of space impel us to pay more attention to the similarities than to the differences, but the reader should look out for overgeneralization.

Overall, and after all due caveats have been entered, the record surveyed is an unhappy one, both absolutely and by comparison with other developing countries. The high hopes that accompanied independence have been dashed. Many initially poor people have remained poor; some have slipped back. The promised modernization has faltered. The task of the remainder of this chapter is to explore the reasons for these disappointments, paying special attention to the comparative slowness of growth. Our central preoccupation is with the ques-

Figure 9.2
Change in Per Capita GNP, 1965–1990 (percent)

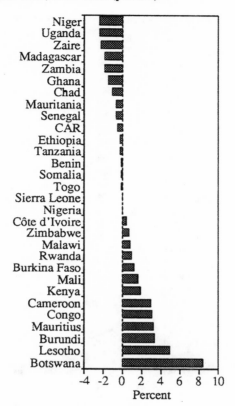

Source: World Bank, *World Development Report, 1992.*

tion, Why Africa? What in that continent's situation has produced such poor comparative results?

ACCOUNTING FOR STAGNATION

Econometric Results

Such an exploration forbids a narrowly quantitative approach; we must range more widely than that. We can nevertheless take an econometric study as our starting point, to provide pointers for exploration later. In the tradition of the growth accounting literature, an unpublished study by el-Farhan (forthcoming) has applied an OLS regression model to cross-sectional data on thirty-two SSA countries from 1960 to 1986 in order to test for the influences on GDP growth.[17]

Figure 9.3
Change in Per Capita GDP, 1980–1989

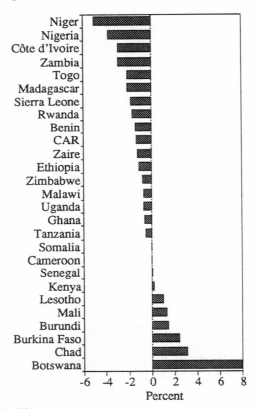

Source: World Bank 1991.

Her principal results are summarized in Table 9.4, where the years covered are also broken down into three subperiods.

With real GDP growth as the dependent variables, the explanatory variables (with expected signs in parantheses) were:

POP: Population growth rate ($+$ or $-$)

GDI: Gross domestic investment as percentage of GDP ($+$)

GOV: Government consumption expenditure as percentage of GDP ($-$)

ODA: Aid receipts as percentage of GNP ($+$)

LIT: Percentage of population who are literate ($+$)

INF: Rate of inflation (as measured by GDP deflator) ($-$)

XGR: Growth of volume of merchandise exports ($+$)

MGR: Growth of the volume of merchandise imports ($+$)

Table 9.4
Regressions for GDP Growth in African Economies

Period	Constant	POP	GDI	GOV	ODA	LIT	INF	XGR	MGR	TDS	POLIN	R^2	n	DW
Equation 1														
1960-69	-0.125	1.338 (2.050)**	0.145 (2.192)**	-0.098 (1.186)	0.175 (1.123)	-0.019 (0.708)	-0.291 (2.301)**	0.056 (1.638)	-	-	-	.62	26	1.8
1970-79	3.205	0.046 (0.067)	0.145 (2.226)**	-0.138 (1.294)	0.148 (0.863)	0.010 (0.379)	-0.106 (1.201)	0.147 (1.636)	-	-	-	.46	30	1.9
1980-86	-3.584	0.805 (1.211)	0.050 (1.869)*	-0.098 (1.202)	0.012 (0.254)	0.059 (2.442)**	-0.009 (0.300)	0.419 (5.923)***	-	-	-	.75	27	1.2
1960-86	1.027	0.126 (0.197)	0.118 (1.759)*	-0.049 (0.424)	0.005 (0.400)	0.014 (0.485)	-0.073 (1.027)	0.205 (2.142)**	-	-	-	.62	22	1.9
Equation 2														
1960-69	5.165	-	0.135 (2.124)**	-0.150 (1.959)*	-	-0.034 (1.378)	-0.058 (0.918)	0.060 (1.699)*	-	-	-0.128 (1.890)*	.39	31	1.8
1970-79	4.364	-	0.102 (1.594)	-0.078 (0.878)	-	0.007 (0.287)	-0.055 (0.609)	0.143 (1.741)*	-	-	-0.166 (1.593)	.50	30	1.8
1980-86	-1.845	-	0.058 (1.901)*	-0.055 (0.743)	-	0.062 (3.040)***	-0.014 (0.512)	0.367 (5.661)***	-	-	-0.047 (1.367)	.75	27	1.2
1960-86	1.607	-	0.135 (2.792)**	-0.074 (1.064)	-	0.008 (0.468)	-0.036 (0.904)	0.213 (3.577)***	-	-	-0.030 (0.546)	.72	27	1.6
Equation 3														
1970-79	0.992	0.134 (0.246)	0.203 (3.276)***	-	-	0.016 /a (0.557)	-0.017 (0.245)	-	0.147 (2.416)**	-0.680 (2.100)**	-0.150 (1.752)*	.69	31	2.1
1980-86	-1.511	0.211 (0.284)	0.190 (2.498)**	-	-	0.025 /a (1.050)	0.036 (1.263)	-	0.244 (3.005)***	-0.252 (1.693)	-0.085 (2.018)*	.52	30	1.8
1970-86	-0.905	0.043 (0.065)	0.233 (3.527)***	-	-	0.011 /a (0.429)	-0.028 (0.699)	-	0.206 (2.178)**	-0.420 (2.001)**	-0.067 (1.323)	.62	30	1.9

Source: el-Farhan (forthcoming).

Notes: Figures in parentheses are t-statistics.

*significant at 0.90 level

**significant at 0.95

***significant at 0.99

[a] In this equation this variable was lagged by one period.

TDS: Total debt servicing as percentage of GDP $(-)$

POLIN: An index of political instability $(-)$

This project was limited by many lacunae in the data. Even for the variables that could be included, all the doubts expressed earlier about the reliability of the statistics resurface in evaluating the results and deciding how much weight to place upon them. On the other hand, the results have reasonable overall explanatory value, most of the signs are "correct," and the equations are fairly well behaved. What, then, might we learn from them?

The strongest explanatory variable emerges as the growth of export earnings, with results at, or close to, the 90 percent significance level or better, with particularly significant results for the later years and with large coefficient values. It may be objected that export volume growth is also a major part of the dependent variable, biasing the results. However, in Equation 3, import growth (MGR)— a variable that might be thought of as having a deflationary effect on the growth of the domestic economy—is substituted for export growth, and here too the results are significant and with positive sign for 1970–1986 (data were inadequate for the 1960s). Equation 3 also introduces another balance-of-payments variable, the debt servicing ratio (TDS). This too yielded significant values, with the expected negative sign: debt servicing depresses growth. Taken together, these results point up the importance of the foreign exchange constraint described earlier, particularly, the adverse consequences of Africa's weak export record. A related variable that was also tested (not reported in Table 9.4) was changes in the commodity terms of trade, but, although it had the expected positive sign, this variable did not pass minimum tests of significance. More on this later.

A further highly significant explanatory variable was the investment rate (GDI), with positive signs and statistically significant explanatory values throughout. Such a result is, of course, in line with conventional growth models, but we give reasons later for being surprised about it.

A feature of el-Farhan's work is the inclusion of an index of political instability as an independent variable (see Equations 2 and 3).[18] For each of the subperiods, this turns out to yield moderately significant results, with a consistently negative sign. However, the significance of this variable disappears when the whole period is examined (see Equation 2), which might suggest that the negative effects of political turmoil are relatively short-lived and do not tell us much about the longer-term determinants of growth. On the other hand, this line of explanation runs contrary to the conclusions of economic historians such as Reynolds (1985, pp. 38–39) who have emphasized the strong negative influence on economic development exerted by political instability. It may well be that the real point here is that it is difficult to adequately capture the influence of political factors in an econometric study of this type.

Few of the other variables (including a number not reported) were statistically significant, but some of these "nil returns" are themselves interesting. The nonsignificant results from the population growth variable (POP) is noteworthy, for it contradicts those who emphasize the negative effects of Africa's high rates of population growth. In fact, Table 9.4 records this variable as having a *positive* sign. However, when the equation was reworked using the growth of per capita GDP as the dependent variable, the signs became negative (and the result was significant at the 90 percent level for 1980–1986).

The literacy variable (LIT) was included as a proxy for the stock of human capital. Given Africa's large initial disadvantage in this area (discussed later), it is puzzling that this variable produced generally nonsignificant results, although LIT is a highly imperfect indicator of human capital. Also noteworthy is that the share of GDP taken up by government consumption (GOV) yields nonsignificant results, although the signs are consistently negative, but again this ratio is a poor indicator of the effects of government interventions. Inflation emerges, with the predicted negative sign but low significance. Aid receipts (ODA) also emerge as without explanatory value. This may be partly because some of its positive investment-augmenting effects are captured separately by the GDI variable. However, the lack of significant explanatory value is consistent with the results of various other econometric studies that have specifically examined the correlation between aid and growth—an apparently damning result, which, however, is partly due to the fact that aid is partly allocated *because* of the hardships resulting from poor economic performance.[19] An attempt was also made to test for the influence of price distortions, as proxied by the difference between official and black market exchange rates, but this turned out to be of no explanatory value.[20]

Finally, note that, in common with most growth-accounting results, there remain large unexplained residuals. Of the results reported in Table 9.4, the largest R^2 for the whole period was 0.72 (Equation 2), with 0.75 the largest value for any of the subperiods (Equation 2, for 1980–1986). There remains a good deal the model has been unable to capture, of which the influences of technology, institutional factors, and the supply of high-level manpower are among the most plausible candidates.

BEYOND ECONOMETRICS

We return to the results previously reported as we go along, but now we must extend the search for explanations of Africa's economic record beyond the variables that readily lend themselves to quantification and testing. This takes us more directly into controversy, for there is a good deal of disagreement about the weight that ought to be attached to various frequently cited causes of SSA's substandard economic performance:[21]

- the influence of the world economic environment
- the influence of domestic policy mistakes
- the influence of sociological factors and political systems
- the influence of colonialism and Africa's initial underdevelopment

Influence of the External Environment

Expressed in its most general form, one school of thought emphasizes the negative influence of trends in the world economy and of industrial-country policies and is skeptical about the extent to which integration into world trade and payments is in the interests of Africa.[22] The argument runs as follows.

Almost all SSA economies are reliant on primary products as their chief exports, often on only a small number of such commodities. Such exports are, it is argued, (1) subject to a long-run trend decline in real prices and (2) prone to greater world price instability. The first of these characteristics, it is argued, means that SSA is particularly prone to adverse barter terms of trade, a tendency that is heightened by pressures from the IMF and World Bank (hereafter the IFIs) and other aid donors for African countries to increase their export volumes in the face of weak world demand—what has become known as the "fallacy of composition" argument. For a number of crops, the sluggishness in demand, it is suggested, is partly the result of industrial-country agricultural protectionism. The Organization for Economic Cooperation and Development (OECD) industrial protectionism also gets in the way of export diversification, through a cascading of protection levels, lowest for imported raw materials and highest for finished goods. In addition, commodity price volatility destabilizes export earning and import capacity, causing fluctuations in levels of capacity utilization, increasing economic uncertainties, aggravating the difficulties of macroeconomic management, and necessitating the retention of larger international reserves than would otherwise be necessary.

This school also stresses adverse features on the capital account of the balance of payments: Africa's limited access to world capital markets; the allegedly deleterious effects of direct investments by multinational corporations; the distorting and demoralizing effects of aid dependency; and the crippling effects of the external debt overhang.

Fortunately, there is empirical research with which to assess this line of argument, at least as regards its trading aspects. First, the particularly severe declines of the last decade have brought wider acceptance than formerly of the declining real commodity price thesis, although much hinges on how the discontinuous shifts in the long-run price series are handled in the econometrics. A substantial number of recent studies have confirmed the existence of a long-run downward trend and the desirability, therefore, of export diversification.[23]

Whether OECD agricultural protectionism is a significant price depressant for African exporters is more doubtful, for the main affected commodities are sugar, rice, and certain other grains. Since, overall, Africa is a minor net importer of sugar and a major net importer of cereals, it seems likely that its terms of trade benefit from the lower world prices resulting from OECD agricultural protectionism (although this is not true for a number of specific SSA countries).[24] Various Latin American and Asian countries are worse affected.

What, then, of the influence of export prices and the terms of trade? In such open economies, the importance of these variables can scarcely be doubted. Thus, a detailed econometric analysis of the sources of stagnation in SSA during the 1970s found an "extremely close relationship" between movements in export prices and average GDP growth (Wheeler, 1984, p. 1 and passim). A more recent analysis of SSA export performance (Svedberg, 1991, Tables 2.6, 2.7) similarly found terms-of-trade movements (up or down) to be the main influence on export earnings in eleven out of thirty-three countries in 1970–1985 (although in only one country during 1954–1969) and to have exerted a substantial influence in a further eight countries. The experience in the later-1980s was considerably worse (Ndulu, 1991, Table 28-3).

However, it is by no means clear that SSA as a region has suffered from worse terms of trade than some other developing regions. Figure 9.4 (section a) shows large fluctuations for the region as a whole but no clear downward trend. The movements shown there are partly influenced by the special experiences of Africa's oil exporters, but a similar absence of a downward trend is shown in Figure 9.4 (section b) relating to the region's middle-income oil importers. The (oil-importing) low-income countries shown in Figure 9.4 (section c) suffered a marked deterioration from the mid-1960s, although even within this group there have been variations.

Pickett (1990, pp. 229–34) attempted to assess the effects on GDP growth of long-run terms-of-trade trends for a sample of twenty low-income SSA countries from 1966–1986.[25] In all twenty the income effect of terms-of-trade trends were negative, but in most cases the effect was quite modest. Worst hit was Zambia (whose terms-of-trade index fell 70 percent between 1966–1973 and 1979–1986), with Mauritania and Zaire also hard hit. All three are minerals exporters. For the others, however, the computed income effects were relatively small, reducing estimated annual GDP growth by less than a third of a percentage point. It is likely that larger effects would have been found had the analysis been extended to the later-1980s and early-1990s, but Pickett's result is consistent with that of el-Farhan, reported earlier, who found that, although there was a positive association between the terms of trade and GDP growth, this was generally not significant.

For an analysis of the long run, it is, in any case, open to question whether we should view SSA countries as merely passive recipients of world prices. In the short run the small country assumption is appropriate but over a twenty- to thirty-year span the question becomes, Why have those confronting long-run downward trends in the real prices of their traditional exports not responded by diversifying? To a considerable extent the adverse terms-of-trade experiences of low-income SSA reflect an internal failure of response, in addition to external forces. To put it another way, many Asian countries had a better terms-of-trade experience over the same period because they reduced their dependence on commodity exports facing weak global demand (see Table 9.2). Thirty years later Kindleberger's (1962) comment about countries that complain about adverse terms of trade seems highly pertinent: "The complaint will be true, but the

Figure 9.4
Terms of Trade and Income Effect in Sub-Saharan Africa, 1961–1987

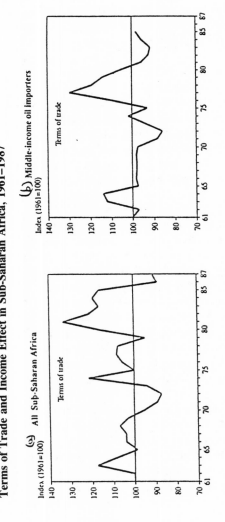

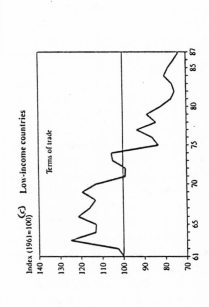

Source: World Bank (1989b), Fig. 1.8.

difficulty will lie not in the manipulation of its terms of trade by the world beyond its frontiers, but in its incapacity to transform'' (p. 103).

What of the "fallacy of composition" argument? There is no question that IFI-sponsored adjustment programs have been based on an export-led strategy and that in the short-to-medium term they have treated expansion of traditional exports as the fastest way of raising foreign exchange earnings. The seriousness of the danger of self-defeatingly large price-depressing effects depends crucially on the scale of commodity export expansion that can be linked to IFI programs. Bank staff members dismiss the "fallacy" argument by suggesting that SSA is a minor supplier on all but a few commodity markets, but this is an unsatisfactory response, both because SSA is actually a major world supplier of several commodities[26] and because it is necessary to examine the adjustment-induced expansion from *all* sources, not just from SSA.

Another line of response might be that the fallacy argument imputes to adjustment programs a potency that they do not possess, and we see later that it is indeed easy to exaggerate the effectiveness of such programs. However, they have had a significant effect in boosting exports; Ibrahim Elbadawi (forthcoming) and Koester et al. (1989, pp. 279–81) have shown that in at least one of the six cases they looked at (cocoa), the price-depressing effects of expansion were likely to produce negative returns to new investment in this crop, with coffee as a marginal case—a result that affects the design of adjustment in such countries as Côte d'Ivoire and Ghana.[27] All in all, the fallacy argument cannot be dismissed, although it is often exaggerated.

What, now, about the argument that industrial country protectionism has discouraged the export diversification that would reduce these risks? Here we can draw upon the results of a detailed study of protection facing SSA exports in the European Community, Japan, and the United States by Refik Erzan and Peter Svedberg (1991). This shows the usual escalation of tariff rates from unprocessed to finished goods and shows that SSA has not escaped the spread of nontariff barriers, but their overall conclusion is unequivocal:[28]

On the whole, SSA had a better deal in terms of both tariff and non-tariff protection. . . . This was in part due to special preferential treatment, especially in the EC [European Community], and in part a consequence of the commodity consequence of its exports, heavy in primary goods. . . . There was no compelling evidence suggesting that protection in the major industrial markets has been a significant constraint on SSA's export growth. In fact, we found evidence to the contrary. Some SSA countries have benefited from protection restricting (MFA)—and in some cases virtually barring (CAP)—other developing countries' exports. In cases where SSA's exports were subject to "hard core" barriers, they nevertheless had most often an advantage over other developing countries in market access. This finding rules out protection in the major markets as a cause of the poor *relative* export performance of SSA countries.'' (p. 123)

This brings us to the proposition that the earnings instability associated with the commodity composition of SSA's exports has depressed economic growth.

Although results differ according to the methods and models employed and sample and period coverage, empirical tests relating to developing countries as a whole have not pointed to strong conclusions.[29] However, a study by Kwabena Gyimah-Brempong (1991, pp. 815–28) limited to data from thirty-four SSA countries for 1960–1986 produces suggestive results. Employing a neoclassical growth equation, he finds export instability to have a negative and significant effect on GNP growth—a result that he finds robust with respect to alternative measurements and that is consistent with Gerald Helleiner's (1986) finding that growth in Africa is adversely affected by *import* instability. These results are also consistent with the findings of Jerker Edström and H. W. Singer (1992), based on data for a sample of eighty-five countries (i.e., not confined to SSA), of a statistically highly significant negative correlation between GNP growth and variability in countries' barter terms of trade.

In concluding this discussion, two brief comments can be offered concerning allegedly negative external effects on capital account transactions. The first relates to the possible deleterious effects of aid dependency. Table 9.2 has already shown reliance on aid to be far greater for SSA than other developing regions; this is also true when expressed relative to gross investment or to imports. Tony Killick (1991) surveys the evidence and shows there are major problems with excessive dependence, stemming from a proliferation of often poorly coordinated donors and projects, leading in the worst cases to a major loss of control by national governments over the composition and financing of public investment. However, this study also points out that, *despite its large absolute size*, various tests consistently find no significant correlation (positive or negative) between aid and growth in Africa, and we have already reported el-Farhan's similar finding. Were aid dependence to have a strongly adverse effect, we would expect it to show up in such studies.

The second comment concerns the adverse effect of the external debt overhang. El-Farhan, it will be recalled, found the debt servicing ratio to have had a significantly negative effect in the more recent years; others have made a similar connection between SSA's debt and economic performance.[30] To some extent, external factors played a part in this, notably the terms-of-trade trends already discussed, reduced access to world capital markets, and, to a modest extent, higher world real interest rates. However, domestic weaknesses aggravated this deterioration in the external environment. The central fact is that SSA's debt was, on average, acquired on far more favorable terms than was true of Latin America, in regard to both maturity and interest, as is shown by the following figures on the average terms on new loan commitments from all sources in 1980–1989:[31]

	Interest (%)	Maturity (years)
All Sub-Saharan Africa	5.3	23.0

Low-income SSA	3.4	29.0
Latin America & Caribbean	9.2	12.4

Most African countries simply did not enjoy the access to international capital markets to have borrowed on a large scale at high interest and medium-term maturities during the rapid expansion of Euromarket lending through the 1970s. Given the (average) terms on which they did borrow (chiefly OECD export credits plus concessional development assistance loans), that many of them should have run into debt difficulties reflects not only their export performances but also the apparently low rates of return on domestic investment—a judgment particularly valid for low-income borrowers.

Overall, then, various external forces have hampered the development of the economies of Africa. The strength of these retarding factors has varied from time to time and, of course, from case to case. Recent terms-of-trade trends have been particularly adverse. However, if we take a long-term view, the evidence runs against those who see a hostile world economic environment as the main reason for SSA's comparatively poor postindependence development record. This points us toward an examination of internal constraints on development, a task to which we now turn.

The Influence of Policy Deficiencies

Modern policy analysis stresses the importance for economic performance at the microlevel and sectoral level of the economywide policy environment. This is applicable to the SSA case. While there are disagreements about the nature and importance of the weaknesses, there is general agreement that in a large proportion of SSA countries postindependence policies (often building on colonial practices) created distortions and inefficiencies on such a scale as to contribute in a major way to the continent's unhappy development record. In examining this proposition, export policies make a natural starting point.

Export and Exchange Rate Policies

We earlier noted SSA's poor record on export volumes (Table 9.1). This led to declining world market shares, so that the region's share in total recorded world imports from developing countries fell from 14 percent in 1970 to 6 percent in 1990, with its share in world imports of primary products from developing countries also falling, from 33 percent to 13 percent over the same period.[32] There was a particularly notable failure to diversify into manufactured exports, so that between 1960 and 1985 Africa's share of total developing-country manufactured exports fell from 9.3 percent to 0.4 percent (Riddell, 1990, Table 2A.3). This performance was not only weak compared with that of other developing regions but also by comparison with Africa's own performance in earlier years, with trends in export volumes dominating the effects of world price

Table 9.5
Index of Real Exchange Rates in Selected African Countries (1969–1971 = 100)

Country	1973-75	1978-80	1981-83	1988-90
	(-----------------------1969-71 = 100-----------------------)			
Cameroon	133	172	125	156
Cote d'Ivoire	123	179	135	161
Ethiopia	108	156	149	134
Ghana	112	435	1250	116
Kenya	114	145	116	81
Malawi	106	118	106	97
Mali	147	200	152	127
Niger	125	179	135	87
Nigeria	132	233	244	54
Senegal	141	167	118	126
Sierra Leone	100	111	137	102
Sudan	132	172	135	220
Tanzania	118	145	196	60
Zambia	111	127	116	82
Unweighted mean of above	122	181	222	114
Median value of above	121	170	135	109
All Sub-Saharan Africa	119	161	145	–

Source: For 1969–1983: World Bank, *World Development Report, 1986*, Table 4.2. For 1988–1990: UNDP-World Bank (1992), Table 3.9.

Note: The real exchange rate is defined as the official exchange rate deflated by a ratio of the U.S. consumer price deflator to the domestic consumption deflator. A rise in the index indicates exchange rate appreciation. Data are three-year averages. Figures for the first three periods are inversions of the data given in the original. The data for the final period were linked to the previous entries by means of "chaining," giving rise to additional possible sources of inaccuracy resulting from differences in data series, and so on.

movements (Svedberg, 1991, pp. 16–25). Explanations of this deterioration can be sought by reference to price incentives and various nonprice factors.

Exchange rate policies deserve particular attention. The extreme case is represented by the countries of West and Central Africa that are members of the Franc Zone, which have had a nominal exchange rate that has not changed since 1948 (see "The Effects of the Franc Zone"). While not going to this extreme, most other SSA countries maintained "adjustable peg" policies, which led in practice to rather inflexible nominal rates during the 1960s and 1970s. At the same time (outside the Franc Zone) inflation was more rapid than in Africa's trading partners. This combination led to a major real exchange rate appreciation in a large proportion of the countries of the region during the 1970s. This is shown in Table 9.5, where each of the regional averages shows major appreciations during 1969–1971 to 1978–1980, and every one of the individual country entries also shows appreciations over the same period. The effect of overvaluation was in practice mitigated by the growth of parallel foreign exchange markets in many countries (although not in the Franc Zone because of currency convertibility), although this in turn gave rise to serious economic distortions. For example, in the early 1980s the parallel rate for foreign exchange in Ghana was twenty to thirty times the official rate, and a high proportion of all foreign exchange transactions was conducted through the parallel market, but the huge profits that could be made from access to imports at the official rate led to widespread corruption and other forms of rent-seeking. Similar, if less extreme, situations existed in many other SSA countries.

THE EFFECTS OF THE FRANC ZONE

Thirteen French-speaking countries are members of the Franc Zone, under which they have ceded substantial control over monetary and exchange rate policy and, to a lesser extent, fiscal policy to regional central banks in exchange for the advantages of a fixed nominal exchange rate (which has been pegged at 50 CFA francs to the French franc since 1948) and a currency convertibility guaranteed by France.

At least until the mid-1980s, these arrangements safeguarded against a number of the policy weaknesses experienced elsewhere on the continent. Franc Zone members did not suffer from the same problems of overvalued exchange rates, and their real exchange rates were a great deal more stable. Fiscal deficits were smaller, and monetary growth less expansionary. A number of studies have concluded that these differences benefited the economic performance of the participants. Until the later-1980s member-states had substantially faster rates of GDP and export growth, lower inflation, and less of a foreign exchange constraint. Indeed, so persuasive were the advantages that some (e.g., Collier, 1991, pp. 348–50) have urged similar arrangements for other SSA countries.

Others, however, now write of the Franc Zone as being in crisis. Certainly, much of the superiority in economic performance seems to have disappeared in the later-1980s, with Franc Zone countries beginning to show inferior growth and export records, overvaluation of real exchange rates emerging as serious in some countries (notably Cameroon and Côte d'Ivoire), and the system perceived as having operated to the advantage of the larger, richer African members at the expense of some of the poorest nations in the world.

There are a number of problems with the system as it has come to be practiced. Unlike earlier periods when the French franc was among the weaker of the OECD currencies, it has become stronger (and effectively linked to the deutsche mark) as a member of the European Monetary System. By contrast with the theory of how such currency unions should work, it has also become apparent that zone-member governments have been able to circumvent some of the regional central banks' monetary and fiscal controls to expand state spending, by accumulating large external debts, using public enterprises—and nonpayment of bills—as means of evading expenditure limits, and various devices for enlarging the government's share of total domestic credit.

The emergence of overvalued real exchange rates is particularly difficult to deal with within the constraints of the fixed peg to the French franc, implying the need for a degree of disinflation that governments may be unwilling or unable to impose (as the difficulties of Côte d'Ivoire demonstrate). Even more subversive, however, is the revealed willingness of governments to bend or evade rules upon which the long-term viability such a currency union depends. By the early-1990s there were growing doubts about the viability of the present system.

The disincentive effect of exchange rate overvaluation for exporters (and import-substituters) was often compounded by other factors. The narrowness of the tax base and the difficulties of enforcing direct taxes led many SSA governments to rely upon taxes on international trade. Some taxed exports heavily, either overtly or covertly through state marketing monopolies offering producer prices far below the local currency equivalent of world market levels.[33] Quite apart from the revenues accruing to the state through these means, there was additional "taxation" in the form of excessively high marketing costs on the part of the marketing monopolies.[34]

There was also implicit taxation of exporters resulting from high protection levels afforded local industry. Dean De Rosa (1990) shows low-income SSA countries to be exceptionally heavy protectors and estimates that liberalization would, on average, raise the price of exports relative to nontraded goods by between 15 and 34 percent (although he also found large intercountry variations). He estimates that the effects of this "taxation" were to reduce exports by similar proportions and to discourage export diversification.

With overvalued exchange rates, fiscal taxation, x-inefficiency by state marketing boards, and price biases induced by protectionism, the price disincentives against exporting were severe. Since there is abundant evidence that the farmers and entrepreneurs of Africa are price-responsive,[35] it is unsurprising that export performance lagged.

There is more to it than just price, however. For suppliers to be fully responsive to price movements, other conditions must be satisfied: supporting institutions and the basic infrastructure should be adequate; markets should be reasonably competitive and efficient; there should be ready supplies of raw materials and other inputs. All of these probably deteriorated in the 1960s and 1970s (and in some cases, through the 1980s). Export promotion services were weak, as was technology policy. There was a widely observed deterioration in the systems of transportation (particularly in road networks), communications, and marketing. This decay, in turn, almost certainly reduced market efficiencies, a decline further fostered by the protectionism just described, by instruments of financial repression (see later) and by price controls and other interventions fostered by a general distrust of market forces.

Poor agricultural performance and, in particular, inadequate import capacity starved exporters of needed raw materials, spare parts, and capital goods, leading to a vicious circle in which poor export performance induced import scarcities, which further undermined exports.[36] Shortages of imported consumer goods also weakened incentives, giving rise in extreme cases to apparently perverse supply responses. There is econometric evidence for this from Tanzania (Bevan et al., 1987), supported by anecdotal evidence from elsewhere on the continent.

It is not possible to quantify the impact of these nonprice constraints, but there is little doubt that they were serious in many countries. For example, a detailed study of trade performance in six SSA countries in each case concluded on the *joint* importance of price and nonprice constraints.[37]

Some measure of the significance of nonprice factors in limiting supply elasticities may be gauged from the rather muffled responses of exports to the improved price incentives of the 1980s. Leaving the Franc Zone to one side, in this period far more SSA governments adopted flexible exchange rate policies, and there were large depreciations. In consequence and despite continuing problems with the control of inflation, there have been major *real* exchange rate depreciations since the early 1980s, as can be seen from the two right-hand columns of Table 9.5, with the *median* values indicating an average fall of roughly a third over the 1978–1980 level. There has also been some action to abolish or reform some of the marketing boards.

Despite these changes, the response of exports has been sluggish, if in the desired direction. It appears that it was not until the late-1980s that a clear improvement in export volumes occurred, and even then data problems prevent us from being sure.[38] While it is doubtless true that protection, taxation, and the special problems of the Franc Zone continue to bias relative prices against exports, the slowness of response reemphasizes that it would be a mistake to attribute the poor results of earlier decades exclusively to price distortions. At the same time, there is accumulating evidence that exports are responding in countries that have acted decisively to improve incentives, including the development (from a tiny base) of some manufactured exports. In Ghana, for example, C.D. Jebuni et al. (1992) find a positive supply response of nontraditional exports to the improved exchange rate and other incentives introduced there after 1982, including a large expansion of manufacturers such as furniture, aluminium goods, and other processed goods, which expanded in real terms by more than fivefold in 1986–1990.

To sum up, we see the weak performance of the export sector—diminishing quantities often exacerbated by declining real world prices—as central to SSA's poor postindependence development record. Domestically originated price and nonprice disincentives contributed to this and left the continent with a major foreign exchange constraint. With heavily trade-dependent economies and imports predominantly made up of producer goods, which could not readily be replaced by local products,[39] this inevitably held back SSA's post-independence economic development. This was illustrated by el-Farhan's finding of strong and significant positive association between GDP growth and import volumes, reported earlier. Given the structure of the region's economies, policies that discouraged exports were about the worst possible choice.

Other Policy Failings

We will deal more briefly with the other ways in which past policy mistakes contributed to SSA's poor development record. A variety of failings deserve mention: policies that discriminated against agriculture; discouraged the development of the financial sector and private enterprise; neglected macroeconomic management; and assumed for the state a range of interventions and powers that it was incapable of using to public benefit.

We have already deployed evidence bearing on *agricultural neglect:* the stagnation of per capita food production (Table 9.3); the poor (predominantly agricultural) export record; evidence of low and relatively declining agricultural yields; the depression of the relative prices of tradable goods resulting from overvalued exchange rates and export taxation; high levels of industrial protection. To these can be added underresourced and inefficient research and extension services and underinvestment in rural infrastructures, contributing to a rising dependence on food aid and other imports. Although the (unreliable) official statistics probably overstate the seriousness of the relative decline of the sector and there have been large differences among African countries, the past overall weakness of agricultural performance has been widely recognized.[40] Policy weaknesses have by no means been the only cause of this, but they have aggravated more deep-seated weaknesses. Robert Bates has put the matter trenchantly (1991):

Governments intervened in markets that determined the incomes of farmers in ways that raised the prices that farmers paid for the goods they consumed, lowered the prices that farmers received for the goods they sold, and, while lowering the prices for farm inputs, conferred these benefits on but a small group of elite farmers . . . the agricultural policies of African governments violated the interests of most farmers. (p. 117)

Here again, we must note the large penalties attaching to such policy biases in economies still predominantly agricultural, with high proportions of the population still reliant on incomes derived from the rural economy.[41]

There is also ample evidence of *financial repression* in a high proportion of SSA countries (including within the supposedly liberalized Franc Zone):[42] administratively determined submarket interest rates; lending decisions based on political and other nonfinancial criteria enforced through direct controls over bank lending; and the use of state-owned banks and central bank powers to secure a disproportionate share of total credit for the public sector.[43] The interest controls, combined with inflation, led to negative real interest rates at levels comparable with those for Latin America and far below the rates for East and South Asia (Killick, forthcoming, Table 8.1). There is evidence too (though less comprehensive) that this set of policies led to a crowding out of the credit needs of the private sector, as well as contributing to low-productivity investments and retarding the development of the financial system.[44] With financial deepening an essential component of economic modernization, these "repressive" policies added yet further to the antigrowth biases of state interventions.

Fiscal weaknesses underlie a good many of the problems already discussed, although the inadequacy of public finance statistics prevents us from analyzing these with any refinement. Data on the deterioration in budget current account

Table 9.6
Gross Domestic Saving in SSA (as percentage of GDP)

	1972	1981	1987
Gross Domestic Saving	17.8	15.3	12.6
Fiscal Current A/C Deficit	-3.3	-5.9	-7.2
Private and Other Saving (Residual)	21.1	21.2	19.8

Source: World Bank (1989b), Table 8.1, p. 165.

deficits are set out in Table 9.6. These show a deteriorating trend and suggest that the decline in SSA's gross savings ratio is almost entirely attributable to the worsening budget deficits. The problems of financing these, in turn, contributed to the balance-of-payments and inflationary pressures already described. They also contributed to the difficulties that many of the region's countries had in servicing their external debts, reflecting their inability to mobilize through the public finances the transfers necessary if interest and amortization commitments on the externally held public (or publicly guaranteed) debt are to be honored.[45]

In addition to these macrolevel consequences, fiscal pressures have led to distortions and inefficiencies in public expenditure patterns. This has shown up in a number of ways: severe cuts in public investment programs because they are easier to reduce than current expenditures; a related underutilization of available aid through inability to provide local counterpart financing; what has become known as the "recurrent-costs" problem, meaning inadequate revenues to meet the intended standards of operation and maintenance of public services and infrastructure.[46]

These fiscal difficulties cannot all be attributed to policy failings. They are also the outcome of a small, inelastic tax base; large pressures for the provision of public services in the face of massive needs; and the generally depressed state of the domestic economy. But some of the difficulties have been avoidable. Revenue collection has often been inefficient or corrupt. Governments have been slow to reform palpably suboptimal systems. Revenues have also been depressed by the macropolicy mistakes already discussed, especially exchange rate overvaluation. Governments have too often slipped into the error of seeking to aid specific groups by providing general and costly subsidies. Expenditure planning has often been weak and excessively politicized, exacerbating the recurrent costs problem and resulting in low-productivity capital projects. Commitment to, and execution of, expenditure control has sometimes been weak, as is illustrated in the discussion on the Franc Zone.[47] In consequence of these conditions, government consumption expenditures, relative to GDP, have grown faster in SSA than in other developing regions.[48]

An illustration of the essentially expenditure-driven nature of fiscal difficulties is provided by evidence of the mismanagement of commodity booms (although this weakness is not confined to the governments of SSA). During temporary

Table 9.7
Share of Public Enterprises in Output and Investment

	Percentage Share of GDP at Factor Cost	Percentage Share in Gross Fixed Capital Formation
	1974-77	1974-77
Sub Saharan Africa	17.5	32.4
Latin America	6.6	22.5
Asia	8.0	27.7

Source: Short (1984).

commodity booms tax revenues rise, directly through export taxes and/or via increased levels of imports and economic activity. Faced with this windfall the government succumbs to the temptation to raise public sector spending (often in hastily contrived ways), increasing civil service salaries, initiating new capital projects, and expanding public services. When world prices and tax revenues return to more normal levels, the government finds it much harder to reduce expenditures accordingly than it did to expand them during the boom, leaving the budget in a weakened condition, with potentially grave consequences for inflation and the balance of payments. Such episodes are, for instance, well documented for Tanzania and Kenya, where the results of a coffee and tea boom in 1976–1977 eroded the mechanisms of treasury control over government spending so seriously that it took several years to restore control.[49]

The large-scale creation of various *public enterprises* and other parastatal agencies was a further symptom of the tendency to overextend the sphere of the state—see Table 9.7. A low standard of efficiency in public enterprises is not axiomatic,[50] and some have good track records. Nonetheless, there are a disquieting number of indicators of low efficiency in the SSA case. We have already cited the high administrative costs of agricultural marketing boards. R.E. Stren (1988) has shown how public agencies have failed to keep pace with the demand for transport, housing, and other urban services in African cities, with the consequence that private enterprises have sprung up to fill the vacuum. Killick's (1983b) survey of the economic performance of industrial public enterprises in Ghana, Senegal, Tanzania, and Zambia, although based on limited information, found generally substandard performance and found that it was difficult to point with confidence to any substantial achievements, except in the Africanization of the skilled and managerial labor force (p. 79).

There is evidence, too, of the perverse and harmful effects of state attempts to use *administrative controls* over prices, imports, and other variables and the rent-seeking to which they gave rise, although most of it is seriously dated.[51] A final example of the way in which the reach of the state exceeded its grasp relates to the poor results secured from the *development planning* that was so extensively adopted after independence. Here, too, the African experience has been surveyed

Figure 9.5
Rate of Return on Investment in Sub-Saharan Africa and South Asia

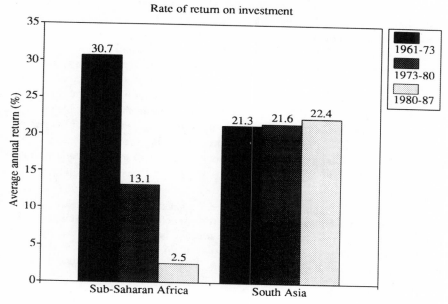

Rate of return on investment

Source: World Bank (1989), Fig. 1.9.

by Killick (1983a), utilizing cross-sectional and country case materials, concluding:

> While there are pitfalls in the way of a satisfactory assessment and there have also been positive achievements to cite, there is no doubt that the general outcome . . . has been negative. Limited success has been achieved in meeting plan targets, which have been biased towards over-optimism. Actual results show wide dispersions about target levels and planners seem impotent to modify more than marginally the impact of market forces. While country experiences have reportedly varied between the good (Ivory Coast) and the abysmal (Ghana and Senegal), all have failed in varying degrees to put their development plans into effect. (p. 57)

The various policy weaknesses described point up a pervasive weakness of the post-independence period: *the expansion of the economic role of the state beyond its capacity to operate efficiently.* Given the large share of the public sector in total investment and the sensitivity of the productivity of private investment to the economywide policy environment, it seems likely that this overexpansion contributed to the declines in the productivity of investment illustrated in Figure 9.5, although the foreign exchange constraint, itself partly due to policy weaknesses, made matters worse by reducing the utilization of capital (Ndulu, 1991, p. 289).

Its overexpansion, moreover, undermined the state as an instrument for economic change, by widening the gap between the expectations created and governments' ability to satisfy these expectations, alienating the people and creating what John Ayoade (1988) has called "states without citizens." Indeed, some of the chosen forms of state intervention themselves hastened the decline of the state, by spawning parallel markets, eroding the tax base, and diminishing those parts of economic life that came within the control of the center. Some governments have failed even to perform their most basic function, the provision of security to their peoples. Wars, civil and international, political instability, and breakdowns of the rule of law have brought great suffering to Africans—displacing many, forcing others to retreat into the subsistence economy or to operate in the twilight zone of the parallel economy, increasing the size of burdensome armies that become as much part of the security problem as safeguards against it.[52] To quote the UNDP (1991):

In several countries . . . problems have been compounded by political violence—cross-border conflicts, ethnic upheavals and civil strife. Angola, Burundi, Ethiopia, Liberia, Mozambique, South Africa and Uganda have suffered especially in this respect. By 1989 a combination of apartheid, social unrest and military skirmishes had created about six million refugees and 50 million disabled persons. Including the effect of natural disasters and difficult socio-economic conditions adds another 35 million displaced persons. (p. 36)

Richard Sandbrook (1991, p. 105) has estimated the number of civil war deaths in SSA in 1963–1987 at 4 million.

During the 1980s there were important changes within SSA in the economic role of the state. These came partly as a result of the sheer unviability of continuing as before, partly through the "conditionality" of the IMF and World Bank, and partly as a consequence of a general change in the intellectual climate.

Significant reforms were introduced in a substantial number of countries (in Ghana, Gambia, Nigeria, and Tanzania, to name but some): the liberalization of trade; the reform of the financial system; the deregulation of prices. In other areas, progress was more patchy in the privatization or rehabilitation of public enterprises and other institutional reforms; in the reform of taxation and control of public expenditure; in the reduction of industrial protection. It is probably a fair judgment that in only a few countries did reforms introduced in the 1980s comprise a decisive break with the revealed weaknesses of the past. This may explain the only slight improvement in SSA's economic performance in the most recent years of the period.

The policy weaknesses described above were far from being restricted to Africa. Many of the same mistakes were made in Asian and Latin America countries. What perhaps placed SSA in a special category was the slowness with which its governments responded to the clearly adverse consequences of the measures they had adopted. Why were dysfunctional policies kept in place for so long despite deteriorating economic results, even though governments' popularity, even legitimacy, was undermined by the resulting economic decline?[53] Why was it commonly left to the IMF and World Bank to initiate the eventual policy reforms? Why has progress with these been slow? To answer such questions, we need to go outside the frontiers of economics, to examine political, historical, and cultural factors.

BEYOND ECONOMICS[54]

The Effects of Personal Rule

We earlier quoted Bates to the effect that government policies in many SSA countries had violated the interests of most farmers. He went on to add that such a phenomenon calls for a political interpretation. Others agree on the centrality of political explanations of SSA's poor comparative economic performance. The World Bank (1989b)—in a passage inserted at the prompting of its African advisers—placed on the international agenda a view that had already attracted a good deal of intellectual support:

Underlying the litany of Africa's development problems is a crisis of governance. . . . Because the countervailing power has been lacking, state officials in many countries have served their own interests without fear of being called to account. In self-defence individuals have built up personal networks of influence rather than hold the all-powerful state accountable for its systemic failures. In this way politics becomes personalised, and patronage becomes essential to maintain power. The leadership assumes broad discretionary power and loses its legitimacy. Information is controlled, and voluntary associations are co-opted or disbanded. (pp. 60–61)

In an influential contribution based on a study of the operation of marketing boards, Bates (1981) offered his own political explanation. Writing broadly within the traditions of the public choice school, which sees those involved with the state as using it to maximize their own welfare, Bates sees governing groups as maintaining their positions by seeking coalitions of allies willing to support them in return for economic rents. He thus explains the exploitation of Africa's farmers in terms of a state dominated by an urban-based coalition of industry, commerce, and the public bureaucracy, to which is added a small elite of large-scale farmers.

Others have taken this view further, writing of the African state as predatory upon the economy, using its legal monopoly over the use of violence to maximize the "profits" of government. Jonathon Frimpong-Ansah (1991b, pp. 47–50; 1991a, p. 57) has developed such a model to interpret the recent history of Ghana and the persistence of dysfunctional trade policies in Africa. He sees the African state as taxing its prey (the economy) almost to the point of extinction, until the decay of the economy reaches crisis point and political change becomes inevitable. This, no doubt, is an extreme view, raising the question why the "predators" would see it in their interests to allow the economy to deteriorate to this degree, but it is a view that its author formed through an intimate personal experience of economic policy-making in Africa.

More influential among political scientists are models that present the state in terms of personal rule (e.g., Jackson and Rosberg, 1984; Sandbrook, 1985), where the position of the ruler and his or her government is maintained by patron-client relationships, based for the most part on familial and ethnic loyalties. Followers are rewarded with preferential access to loans, import licenses, contracts, and jobs. Institutional rules and constitutional checks and balances are swept aside by the competition for patronage and the struggle to maintain power. Rulers have themselves voted "president for life"; the dubious virtues of one-party rule become the official ideology; open political competition is banned or carefully delimited; and the distinction between the public and private domains becomes blurred.[55]

Governments that conform to this model are unlikely to care much about securing broad-based, long-term economic development. That is scarcely among their objectives. Sandbrook, for example, sees personal rule and the patron-client relationships that underlie it as destructive of capitalist development, with the pursuit of personal aggrandizement and short-term political advantage leading to economic irrationality. As rule becomes more personalized and power more concentrated, policies are apt to become less predictable, more arbitrary. Such states, he argues, become less and less capable "of maintaining the political, legal and economic conditions that a flourishing capitalism requires" (1986, p. 328). Thomas Callaghy (1984) and Janet MacGaffey (1988) have provided vivid accounts of the consequences of personal rule in the extreme form it has taken in Zaire and the consequential decay of the state. MacGaffey wrote:

In Zaire those with political position have used the power of their office to seize control of the economy . . . to acquire manufacturing, wholesale and retail businesses and plantations. However, they have neither managed their enterprises in a rational capitalist fashion nor invested their profits in expansion of their businesses and improved production. (p. 175)

The ruling class is not a true economic bourgeoisie; it is one that loots the economy and collapses effective administration. It is thus unable to exercise the control over production necessary to maintain its dominance and must resort to consolidating its position by participating in the more lucrative activities of the second [parallel] economy. (p. 172)

Fortunately, only a minority of African countries have been driven to the benighted condition of Zaire. We should not get carried away by the explanatory power of any single model of African politics. Here especially we must beware of overgeneralization. A few SSA countries have established democratic traditions (Botswana, Gambia, Senegal, and, more recently, Namibia). Even in the much larger number of states marked by personal rule, neither the extent nor consequences of this have been uniform across countries.

Nonetheless, what is particularly persuasive about the personal rule model is its ability to predict and explain a number of the policy weaknesses described earlier:

1. Emphasis on the appropriation and distribution of resources by the state, rather than on growth and wealth creation.

2. The growth of the state relative to the private sector, in order to maximize the opportunities for patronage and reward, including the creation of (often politicized and overmanned) public enterprises.

3. For the same reason, forms of intervention that provide the agents of the state with direct and discretionary control, as against operating impersonally through price incentives, for example, use of import controls instead of the exchange rate.

4. Inward-looking import substitution policies, to provide further opportunities for rewarding important urban groups; and the neglect of (politically unimportant) peasant farmers.

5. Financial repression and politicized credit allocation mechanisms, in order to have cheap loans to offer to supporters.

6. The growth of crony capitalism (as in Kenya and Zaire), to the frustration of genuine local entrepreneurial talent.

7. The persistence of antidevelopmental policies long after their ill effects have become apparent, because their primary function was to provide a system of rewards and maintain the ruler in power, rather than promote development per se.

Thus, for all the qualifications and cautions that are necessary in using it, the personal rule model appears to take us a considerable distance in seeking to answer the questions posed earlier.

The Influences of History and Social Structure

Personal rule and clientelist-based politics are not, of course, confined to Africa, but they do seem particularly pervasive there. Again, we must ask, Why? To take this further requires examination of the historical experiences and the social values and structures that underlie the political condition of the continent— treacherous territory for an economist. Various questions arise. How did history and social structure influence the economic policy choices that were made after independence? How are they connected to the spread of anti-developmental political systems? Above all, how do they help us to understand why SSA's development experience has been worse than that of other developing regions? What is different about Africa?

One feature that is different from, say, most of Asia is low population densities.[56] A number of writers see this characteristic as having far-reaching implications for contemporary political processes. In precolonial times, most

Africans were either pastoralists or cultivators with few obligations to feudal overlords or landlords. They hence enjoyed a degree of autonomy impossible in the highly regimented agriculture of precolonial Asian civilizations (Hyden 1986, p. 54), although this did not altogether prevent the development of centralized political systems, for example, in precolonial Nigeria and Uganda. The favourable land-labor ratio and the low carrying capacity of much of Africa encouraged dispersed settlements and voluntary migration in search of food, pasture, and trading opportunities (Hopkins 1986, p. 1479). These factors and the prevalence of premodern cultivation techniques meant low productivity in agriculture and the absence of a surplus with which to support a highly stratified or specialized society. In most cases the political unit remained the village or clan. Social obligations were determined by the ties of kinship.

Such social structures were, of course, modified by colonialism, for example, through the alienation of land and forced commercialization of agriculture, but they were rarely transformed by it.[57] A key feature of colonialism—covering not only Britain but France and other colonial governments—was their insistence that colonies should pay their way and not become a burden on the "home" budget. This led in the British case to "indirect rule" as a cost-effective way of governing an empire with a handful of personnel, committing the colonial authorities to supporting traditional rulers and the relations of production on which they depended, and often enhancing or even creating ethnic divisions.[58]

In principle, the French colonial philosophy was different, embodying the notion of the "assimilation" of colonial peoples, under which those who qualified became French citizens entitled to elect deputies to the French National Assembly. In practice, however, only a tiny proportion of colonial peoples achieved this status, partly because of a financially induced neglect of the educational system.[59] Many bureaucrats in the French territories still owed their position to the status they enjoyed in traditional society. The principle of the balanced budget was thus in conflict with the modernization of the French and British colonies alike. The position of territories colonized by Portugal was even worse, where tight budgetary restrictions were accompanied by little desire to modernize in any case (Mayer, 1990).

In the view of writers like Hyden, the survival of traditional social structures through the colonial period and the superficiality of any social "modernization" as a result of European rule make Africa unique in the developing world and impart a special character to the nature of its political organization. In urban areas immigrants continue to seek support from members of their tribe or village, and as a result urban dwellers continue to behave in ways more akin to those of villagers than an urban proletariat. Hyden calls this structure "the economy of affection" and views the role of ethnicity in African politics as closely tied to this perpetuation of links to the countryside. It results, he argues, in the vertical (ethnic), not horizontal (class), political groupings that characterize African society and in structures hostile to formal bureaucratic principles.

Without the power and authority of their imperial overlords and as the cement of anti-colonialism lost strength, postcolonial rulers lacked adequate legitimacy to rule over the ethnically diverse communities that had constituted the colonial state. Despite the grafting on of democratic forms during decolonization, the colonial state left a dominant legacy of authoritarianism and group rights, derived from the tradition of indirect rule and the cooptation of traditional authorities (Young, 1986).

Colonial borders that lacked geographical or ethnic integrity made matters worse, committing governments to the maintenance of artificial unions, sometimes in the face of considerable opposition. Expenditure on security was consequently an important component of the growing fiscal deficit, sometimes intensified by the impact of the cold war.

Inexperienced political leaders were thus faced with the daunting task of maintaining their authority and the integrity of their nations in the face of divided societies and fragile states. They sought to maintain their positions through a concentration of power reinforced by a system of rewards. This included an expansion of the welfare systems introduced in the last years of colonialism, using these selectively as a means of generating and rewarding public support.

A further legacy of British colonial administration in many territories was the practice of taxing cash crops, which newly independent governments took over and extended (Young, 1986).[60] Often lacking large mineral resources or alternative sources of revenue, the metropolitan insistence that colonies be self-financing meant that colonial administrations increasingly came to rely on the taxation of export crops, often through marketing board monopolies. This subsequently facilitated the urban bias that we have noted earlier as a common feature of postindependence SSA.

As nationalist pressures grew, however, the thrust of colonial policy changed. Increasingly it was felt that an imperial presence could be justified only in the name of social and economic development.[61] This led to grants and soft loans under the British Commonwealth Development & Welfare Acts and the French Fonds d'Investissement pour le Développement Economique et Social (FIDES) program. Moreover, in the decade after World War II commodity prices improved to the point that larger development expenditures could be reconciled with the fiscal constraints of the metropolitan powers. The operation of the marketing boards in the British colonies generated substantial revenues for the colonies, which enabled large increases in state expenditure. In the French colonies loans under the FIDES program enabled the colonies to run large deficits in their balance of payments (Fieldhouse, 1986, p. 14). There was a surge in development and welfare spending. Even in colonies like the Belgian Congo a tiny educational system was rapidly expanded to enroll 70 percent of school-age children by independence, with state outlays there rising elevenfold in 1939–1959 and tripling again by 1962.[62] Such experiences were to leave a lasting impression on the nationalist leaders who brought their countries to independence.

The colonial experience also had an influence on the new leaders' attitudes to the outside world (although this was less the case in former French colonies), many of whom agreed with Kwame Nkrumah's doctrine that political independence was meaningless without economic independence. From this it was an easy step to pursue a relatively closed-economy approach to development, the nationalization of foreign-owned companies[63] and a rapid Africanization that paid little heed to the consequences for efficiency.

Leaders of this type of persuasion were also easily impressed by authors, like Paul Baran (1957), writing in the tradition of what later became known as the dependency school, which had its roots in Latin America but made ready converts among African intellectuals.[64] Writers in this tradition viewed economic autonomy as the starting point and a way of breaking the cycle of underdevelopment that participation in the world economy was thought to induce. Countries that adopted this approach therefore had to rely on agriculture and trade as the chief means of generating funds for investment in structural transformation. The common emphasis on taxing the existing agricultural base to support industrialization and large-scale commercial farming meant that ideologically opposite regimes, in different parts of Africa, pursued similar developmental goals with similar policies, but with different degrees of coercion and openness to the world economy.

Even those who remained skeptical of the dependency position were influenced by the prevailing consensus in development economics.[65] This reinforced their own predilection for a process of development that depended on state-led expansion in many sectors of the economy. They agreed with a need for the structural transformation of their economies by forcing an increase in domestic capital formation, based on a combination of trade taxes and foreign borrowing. Surpluses generated in primary production could be used to fund industrialization, which was typically seen as the ultimate objective of economic development.

Planning was seen as a superior organizing principle of economic life to the unbridled operation of markets, just as India had earlier committed itself to securing development through five-year plans. Belief in planning was at its peak in the 1960s. France used indicative planning for its own economy and helped to transfer the system to its erstwhile colonies. The Soviet model also exerted a potent influence, not least through cold war diplomatic competition.

Returning to the questions previously raised, the argument here is that there was a conjuncture of demographic, social, and historical influences that made the African continent particularly fertile ground for the spread of clientelist-based political systems. Of course, political systems worldwide have elements of clientelism in them; what we are discussing here is a matter of degree. The contention is that conditions in postcolonial SSA encouraged rather extreme forms of this way of doing political business, often organized around the principle of personal rule. That such systems came into being in fragile nation-states reinforced the incentive to use patronage and a centralized authoritarianism to hold the state together. These factors combined with the experiences of late colonialism and various intellectual influences to result in many of the policy choices that hindsight now shows to have been antidevelopmental. We can add that the economic decline in many SSA countries, together with the excesses and unresponsiveness of authoritarian governments, in turn, added to the crisis of legitimacy. This resulted in many of the policy reforms noted earlier and, by the beginning of the 1990s, in often irrepressible movements for political reform.

The Influence of Rapid Population Growth[66]

Since it reflects a high-fertility culture related to the economic and social characteristics just discussed, we can here consider the hypothesis that rapid population growth helps to explain SSA's poor comparative development performance. We observed in Table 9.1 that SSA has the highest rate of demographic expansion among developing regions. Alone among them, the rate of increase has accelerated steadily, leaving the average in 1985–1990 at 3.2 percent per year. Individual countries had growth rates well above the average, for example, Zambia (3.7 percent); Kenya (3.9 percent); and Côte d'Ivoire (4.1 percent). Is it not likely that such extraordinary increases in numbers have retarded the pace of development?

Partly because of the intrinsic difficulties of tracing the interactions between demographic and economic variables, there is a dearth of direct evidence with which to test this hypothesis. However, we should recall here el-Farhan's results reported previously. These were (1) that growth of total GDP was *positively* associated with population growth but (2) that growth of per capita GDP was *negatively* correlated. This suggests that each increase in population results in some accretion to value-added but by an amount less than the previous average per capita level. However, (3) few of her results for the POP variable were statistically significant, so that, at most, the effects of demographic expansion were weak.

Various reasons can be hypothesized why population growth might retard average incomes. A high child dependency rate is a characteristic of a rapidly expanding population: output per active member of the labor force has to be shared among a larger number of mouths. This, in turn, is liable to depress saving and investment rates and to reduce growth in economies constrained by shortages of investable resources. Such a tendency may be reinforced from other directions. An expanding population and the young age structure that goes with it place pressure on the public provision of education, diluting the quality of the schooling that can be offered and/or diverting resources that might otherwise be invested in more directly productive ways. Rapid population growth is also likely to lead to accelerated urbanization, which will similarly absorb resources, because of the extra high-cost investments needed in urban infrastructure and services.[67]

If, for these reasons, net directly productive investment is reduced, this will likely slow down the rate at which technological improvements are embodied in the productive system. Expansion of the population may also lower productivities. Even if investment remains unchanged, the more rapid expansion of the labor force means that there will be less investment per worker, tending to lower output per worker. There will also be growing pressures on natural resources that are nonrenewable or that can be enhanced only with difficulty. While generally low population densities limit this problem, localized areas of high density, when combined with premodern cultivation techniques, lead to soil erosion in semidesert and dry bushland areas, such as the Sahel and parts of Kenya and Ethiopia.

We should not, in any case, restrict ourselves to inquiring into possible effects on economic growth. Development is about more than that, and there is prima facie reason for thinking that rapid population growth has negative influences on the quality of life. In particular, it bears especially hard on the poor, aggravating the problem of poverty. It is also likely to be associated with the social ill effects of open unemployment and rapid urbanization: shantytowns, crime, and drug abuse. Finally, Africa's high fertility rates are closely bound up with the generally low status of its women and the limited opportunities available to them.

At the same time, we should keep this in perspective, as el-Farhan's results remind us. Population growth has its most detrimental effects when there are already large pressures of population on resources. Although the pressures are growing, most SSA countries are still characterized by low densities, with agriculture commonly still operating at the extensive, rather than the intensive, margin.[68]

In such situations the expanding labor force associated with population growth can be thought of positively, as enhancing productive resources. In sparsely populated areas expanding numbers may permit economies of scale in the provision of public services,[69] although that is an argument to be treated with caution. There is also evidence to support the argument associated with E. Boserup, that growing population pressures in rural communities act as a stimulus for the introduction of improved standards of husbandry.[70] To the extent that her results signify genuine correlation, forces of this type presumably explain el-Farhan's positive association between the growth of population and total GDP.

To sum up, it would be unjustified to place large weight on demographic explanations of SSA's poor development experience. Indeed, the continent's rapid population growth is probably as much a result of the poor record as a cause of it. Nonetheless, the population explosion has surely made progress harder in already difficult conditions and has magnified the ill effects of the policy mistakes and other weaknesses discussed earlier. Moreover, densities are steadily rising and, with them, pressure on resources. D.K. Leonard (1986) has suggested that the mid-1980s were a threshold period during which the land frontier became an increasingly binding constraint, and resulting environmental damage became an increasingly serious problem. Presumably, for such reasons African governments have gradually moved from their former passivity to the adoption of measures to reduce fertility.

SOCIAL CAPABILITIES AND THE PROBLEMS OF CATCHING UP

Whatever the validity of these wider political and cultural factors, they do not alone explain Africa's comparative development experience. We need also to refer to a variety of conditions at the time of independence and to chronic weaknesses in economic structures, in respect of which the representative African country was at a serious disadvantage relative to other developing countries at the beginning of the 1960s.

At this point we should bring in further features of the colonial legacy. One was the heavy reliance on primary production and commodity exports and the consequentially tiny industrial base. Another was the poor state of the capital stock at the time of independence.

First, the physical infrastructure was often minimal. The chief capital investment was often a single railway line constructed to facilitate the transportation of agricultural produce or mineral ores to the coast for export. The cost of this investment meant that the colonial authorities were slow to build roads (Fieldhouse, 1986, p. 35). There were virtually no links between adjacent West African states. Even in 1976 the extent and quality of Africa's road network were significantly poorer than in Asia.[71] Other forms of infrastructure were poorly developed. Energy consumption per capita (measured in coal equivalent kilograms) was in 1960 only an estimated 76 compared with 356 for all low-income countries.[72]

Of much graver long-term significance was an acute shortage of educated and trained personnel, reflecting the slight development of the educational system until the last years of colonial rule. The number of people with advanced education was often negligible. There were few universities or even technical schools to provide industrial and managerial skills (Fieldhouse, 1986, p. 35). In consequence of these neglects, the proportion of people enrolled in tertiary education relative to the population aged 20–24 was in 1960 less than half of 1 percent in sixteen of the eighteen SSA countries for which estimates exist, compared with 2 percent for all low-income countries taken together, 4 percent for middle-income countries, and 17 percent for industrialized countries (World Bank, 1981, Annex Table 38). At independence the new states were still largely populated by people who were illiterate and innumerate. Despite the large educational expansion that has occurred since, Africa's relative disadvantage persists today, with substantially lower school enrollment rates than in any other developing region (World Bank, 1991, Table 29).

The new states were also, of course, poor, and it is tempting to include this condition as an explanatory factor, along the lines of poverty-trap models.[73] But while such models may indeed throw light on the special difficulties of low-income countries generally, they do not appear to help us explain the African case, since initial income levels were, on average, rather higher than in South and East Asia (always assuming that such comparisons are meaningful). The tiny initial size of the domestic market is more persuasive. Line 1 of Table 9.2 illustrates this by reference to the average value of GDP. A separate estimate for African and comparably sized economies suggests that even in 1988 their internal market for industrial goods was only around one-three-hundredth of the market in the average OECD country (Killick, forthcoming, Table 4.1). This has obvious implications for the possibilities of industrialization in the pervasive presence of economies of scale and underscores the shortsightedness of post-colonial attempts to industrialize on the basis of an inward-looking, import-substitution policy stance. A wholehearted open economy approach may have permitted a more sustainable industrialization, on the East Asian model. The constraint imposed by the small size of the domestic market has been made more intractable by the absence of effective regional cooperation on industrial policies and, indeed, the disintegration of some of the regional bodies created under colonialism.[74]

Low incomes and small economies, poor communications and infrastructure, and great scarcities of many kinds of skilled manpower—these are not conditions in which we can expect markets to operate very smoothly, even when policy interventions do not make things worse. The evidence points to often low levels of market efficiency at the time of independence (and through to the present time): dualistic labor and capital markets; the predominance of monopolistic or oligopolistic structures in manufacturing, banking, and parts of distribution and trade; incomplete markets for rural credit and insurance.[75]

How might we assess the impact of these initial conditions on SSA's weak comparative development performance? Modern growth theory particularly stresses the importance of knowledge and human skills as key influences on output growth and technological progress.[76] Consistent with this, Robert Barro (1991) has found the initial stock of human capital to have a substantial positive influence on economies' ability to catch up with more prosperous countries.[77] We have seen SSA to have been particularly disadvantaged in the supply of educated people, and the latest World Bank report on SSA (1989b, chap. 3) reemphasizes the centrality of larger and better investments in people if Africa's development record is to be improved (a task made more urgent by the rapid spread of the AIDS virus in Africa).

We can also posit an important role for industrialization in long-run development, along the lines of findings by Kuznets, Chenery, and others, in which case a combination of tiny domestic markets, a poor supply of skilled labor, and policies that discriminated against exporting can be seen as particularly crippling.

Flowing from these factors, Sanjaya Lall (1989) argues that industrialization in Africa has been crucially held back by shortages of what he calls ''industrial capabilities.'' This can be understood to refer to the skills, institutions, and organizational arrangements that will permit firms to utilize suitable technologies and deploy their resources efficiently. Lall argues further that such was the tiny base of indigenous industrial capabilities with which independent SSA started that the main determinant of industrial development has been the success of each country in mobilizing and deploying non-African industrial capabilities.

Lall, then, takes us in the direction of also looking beyond the availability of labor skills to the effectiveness of institutions. Although it is not a feature that can be readily demonstrated, the malign effects of incompetent or corrupted police forces and judiciaries, outdated laws, and hidebound or venal public administrations were surely considerable in parts of the region. There are also questions about the supply of entrepreneurship. The general view on this is that there is no such shortage, only a scarcity of economic environments that encourage the expansion of private enterprise.[78] However, it is probably a fair judgment that there has yet to emerge a strong *modern* entrepreneurial culture, of businesspeople with access to the know-how necessary to bring the needed modernization of the continent's productive systems.

This factor has combined with weaknesses in the institutional infrastructure, the low policy responsiveness of political systems, and, especially, poor education to exert a powerful drag on Africa's *technological base:* its ability to keep abreast with, and take advantage of, technological advances.[79] The technological base can be thought of as being determined by the availability of trained and experienced manpower familiar with modern technologies and in touch with contemporary advances, by the appropriateness of the institutional framework within which they work, and by the skills of the production workers who must convert new processes into output. Given the accelerating pace of change, the region's comparative technological disadvantage is perhaps an even greater problem in the late twentieth century than it was at the time of independence.

Lall's notion of industrial capabilities and the weakness of SSA's technological base can be related to Moses Abramovitz's (1989) use of the idea of "social capability" as a determinant of economies' ability to catch up: "One should say, therefore, that a country's potential for rapid growth is strong not when it is backward without qualification, but rather when it is technologically backward but socially advanced" (pp. 222–24). If we consider the relative positions of SSA and most Asian countries around 1960 with this proposition in mind, we would predict what happened in reality: slow African growth outstripped by Asia.

If we again contemplate the initial SSA condition of a predominantly primary production base, a sparse infrastructure, little trained labor, weak institutions, poorly functioning markets, and weak states, we might make another prediction: economic inflexibility, a low capability to adapt to changing needs.[80] This, too, seems to fit the facts, for there is accumulating evidence that the response of African economies to the adjustment programs of the World Bank has been sluggish by comparison with that of other developing countries. A World Bank evaluation of its experiences with structural adjustment programs (1989a) concluded that results were weaker in SSA (and in heavily indebted) countries. A.K. Mullei (1992) similarly found weak results; and Elbadawi's (forthcoming) study of the effectiveness of bank programs in SSA finds only weak statistical evidence of positive program impact on GDP growth, in contrast with results for other adjusting countries. Although the evidence on the short-run effectiveness of IMF programs in SSA is mixed,[81] we have referred earlier to the continent's chronic tendency to persistent balance-of-payments difficulties, which suggests that long-run effectiveness is low.

If we are right in suggesting that the characteristics of SSA economies result in inflexibility, their difficulties with stabilization and adjustment programs are easy to understand. This, in turn dampens long-run growth, because of the negative feedback from foreign exchange shortages (and perhaps inflation).

SUMMARY AND CONCLUSION

Summary

The argument of this chapter can be summarized in the following propositions:[82]

1. Notwithstanding poor data and considerable intercountry differences, SSA's post-independence record on economic growth, modernization, macroeconomic manage-ment, and, to a lesser extent, social welfare has been poor, when judged against the aspirations of its peoples and the achievements of other developing regions. The chapter has been directed to explaining this, particularly why SSA's performance has been generally inferior to that of other Third World regions.

2. Explanations have been sought from different directions. As regards *economic expla-nations,* only modest weight has been given to two commonly asserted sources of difficulty: a hostile world environment and rapid population growth. Even the overhang of external debt, which is strongly linked with the stagnation of the 1980s, is seen primarily as reflecting domestic weaknesses. Poor export performance and the factors contributing to that have been given pride of place, including past exchange rate overvaluation and other policy interventions that biased incentives against exports. The declining productivity and limited volume of investment have also been stressed, as have the adverse consequences of fiscal weaknesses and the overexpansion of the economic role of the state.

3. Economic explanations take us only so far, however, for they leave unanswered the question why antidevelopmental policies were adopted and allowed to remain in place for so long. To answer this we looked at *political factors.* Political instability is one source of difficulty, but we paid particular attention to "personal-rule" models of African politics. Such models seem able to predict quite a number of the policy weaknesses previously described, which increases their persuasiveness, although we point out the dangers of overgeneralizing about Africa's varied political reality. In any case, the personal rule model still leaves us with the question, Why Africa?

4. This search thus led us into the *historical and social* particularities of the continent, concluding that a conjuncture of demographic, social, and historical influences unique to SSA resulted in a situation ready-made for a more debilitating development of

clientelist-based political systems than in other regions. The fragility of postinde-pendence nation-states reinforced the incentive to use patronage and a centralized authoritarianism. These factors combined with the experiences of late colonialism and various intellectual influences to result in many of the policy choices that hindsight shows to have been antidevelopmental.

5. We finally drew attention to other comparative disadvantages with which SSA entered the 1960s, in terms of the stock of human and inanimate capital, technological ca-pacities, and institutional development, which together define the region's *"social capabilities"* for rapid economic development. We stressed the problems created by the smallness of the domestic market and the economic inflexibility that characterizes most SSA economies.

Conclusion

History, particularly the colonial inheritance, emerges prominently from this analysis. Major objections suggest themselves, however. If the initial conditions were so oppressive, how can it be that most indicators suggest relatively good economic performance in the 1960s and into the 1970s, with the worst coming later? Is it not implausible still to be blaming colonialism thirty years after independence?

A reasonable answer to the first part of this challenge is that the effects of weaknesses that can be traced back to the 1960s were gradual and cumulative and, among low-income countries, were for a while disguised by relatively favorable terms of trade (Figure 9.4). Poor export performance only gradually imposed a serious constraint on import capacity, and it was only from the later 1970s that worsening terms of trade laid bare the underlying fragility of the situation. Similarly, the seeds of fiscal deterioration were sown in the 1960s, but it was only later that these resulted in major deficits. It is also plausible to postulate a delayed reaction to poor public enterprise performance and other manifestations of the overexpansion of the state. The marginal productivity of capital began to decline in the 1960s, but it was only later that this became most serious.

That it is increasingly implausible to attribute Africa's economic ills to co-lonialism is obvious. Our argument restricts itself to the proposition that from neglects of colonialism and the ways it interacted with traditional social struc-tures, it could be *predicted* that Africa's new states would have great difficulties in sustaining a reasonable pace of economic development and that these con-ditions led to political systems incapable of responding adequately to economic crisis. It is therefore inappropriate to characterize the SSA experience as one of failure: sustained rapid development would have been extraordinary.

Viewing the situation in the early 1990s, there are a number of grounds for optimism. There have been important economic policy reforms in a number of African countries, and there is a general search for a better balance between the state and the private sector in economic life. The growth record has improved in some countries, despite adverse terms-of-trade movements.

There is also a strong public impetus for a fresh political start, rebelling against personal rule in favor of more representative and responsive modes of government. This holds out a prospect that there will be a break with the inflexibilities that exerted such a baneful influence during the preceding three decades. At the same time, it is implicit in our analysis that "policy reforms" without changes in underlying social and political realities are unlikely to bring fundamental solutions. Getting prices right and markets to work better is important but by no means all the story. Sandbrook (1991) has put the point persuasively:

Factional loyalties and patronage will continue to be the "glue" that holds many fissi-parous states together and permits governments to govern. Enlightened structural adjustment policies, recognising the importance of the state to economic recovery, will need to take account of these political exigencies. This will mean trading off some short-run efficiency to enhance governability. Public bureaucracies and public policies have legitimate, if unacknowledged, goals other than efficiency and distributional justice. What appears from an economistic viewpoint merely as "waste" or "mismanagement" may play a significant role in preserving order and some measure of unity. "Reform" in sub-Saharan Africa is a far more complicated business than many realize. (p. 111)

However, if these complications mean that fundamental change cannot be sustained and things will continue largely as before, then the prospects for the peoples of Africa are bleak indeed.

NOTES

I should like to acknowledge with gratitude the financial support of the World Bank for the preparation of this paper; the substantial help of Richard Ketley in assembling materials and preparing briefing notes on a number of the topics covered here; and the help of Parita Suebsaeng of the World Bank in providing special tabulations. I am also indebted for valuable comments on earlier drafts by Enzo Grilli, Gerald Helleiner, Adrian Hewitt, Douglas Rimmer, Mark Robinson, Christopher Stevens, and other colleagues at ODI, who have rescued me from rash judgments and helped to tighten the argument. The usual disclaimers apply.

1. See World Bank (1989b, p. 24), which calculates heavily negative income effects from terms-of-trade trends among low-income African economies from the mid-1970s, although the record is more mixed for the region as a whole.

2. See Killick (1991, Table 1) showing that in 1980–1988 aid to SSA was equivalent to 33 percent of investment (ten times as high as the average proportion for other developing countries) and 26 percent of imports (five times as high).

3. William Lyakurwa (1991, Table 5) shows that export concentration indexes actually went up during 1970–1985 in a majority of the African countries for which data were available.

4. Shamsher Singh (1983, Table 4) shows for 1978–1980 mean yields for coffee, rice, maize, sorghum, and ground nuts in SSA averaging less than half of those in other developing countries.

5. Thus, Hans Binswanger and Prabhu Pingali (1988) argue that many past agricultural

research failures in SSA have been due to a mismatch between technological strategies and farming systems. See also Dunstan Spencer (1986).

6. See World Bank (1992, Table 1).

7. Calculated from IMF (1992, Table A35). The average for 1988–1990 was an estimated 25 percent.

8. Calculated from IMF (1992, Table A43). The comparable averages for other developing regions were: Asia 32 percent; Western Hemisphere 26 percent.

9. Svedberg (1991, Table 15) shows SSA's share in world primary product exports to have fallen from 7.0 to 4.1 percent in 1970–1971 to 1984–1985, with its share in developing country commodity exports declining from 21.0 to 14.5 percent during the same years. However, the World Bank (1991, Table 2.4) shows a recovery of SSA shares in some of the main markets during the 1980s.

10. Jill Armstrong (1991) suggests that in the African countries where the human immunodeficiency virus (HIV) incidence is greatest, the resulting deaths were already, by the early-1990s, eroding past progress in reducing mortality rates and warns of the likelihood of far greater losses in coming years. See also Charles Becker (1990) for an admirably balanced survey of the demographic and economic impact of AIDS in Africa.

11. See E. O. Akeredolu-Ale (1990, pp. 17–18).

12. The World Bank (1992, Table 29) gives the following total enrollment rates for 1989:

	primary	secondary	tertiary
SSA	69	18	2
East Asia and Pacific	129	46	5
South Asia	90	38	
Western Hemisphere	107	50	18

13. See Christina Gladwin and Della McMillan (1989, pp. 356–59) for a brief survey of the evidence on this.

14. See A. T. Grove (1991) for a brief and balanced survey.

15. Thus Alexander Yeats (1990) finds large discrepancies between the trade statistics of African countries and those of their trading partners. There are particularly large discrepancies in data on intra-African trade, such that he concludes these cannot be relied upon to ''indicate the level, composition or even direction and trends in African trade.''

16. Thus, of the thirty-one SSA countries for which data on the growth of per capita GNP in 1965–1989 are available, the growth rate of twenty fell in the range of between +1.9 percent per year and −1.9 percent per year (see World Bank, 1991, Table 1). Also, underlying a number of the statistical presentations in this chapter is a large number of special tabulations, prepared from the World Bank's data base, which subdivided SSA into various alternative subgroups. These have been little used here because, by and large, the records of the various subgroups were similar.

17. See Hania el-Farhan (forthcoming). I am much indebted to her for allowing me to make use of her results and for valuable discussions of her work. Her study started with forty-five SSA countries, but thirteen had to be dropped because of data deficiencies. The precise number of countries covered by her various equations varied from test to test, and three explanatory variables had to be dropped from the tests for the earlier years, also because of unavailability of data. Besides those reported here, she also ran regressions that excluded Nigeria, as a large special case, and oil exporters, but these exclusions made little difference to the nature of the results.

18. This is a composite index, modifying an approach developed by T. H. Johnson, R. O. Slater, and P. McGowan (1984). It is based on the frequency of such events as foiled plots to overturn the government; unsuccessful coup attempts; successful coups; and civil or external wars, with weights attached to these of ascending value.

19. See Roger Riddell (1987, chap. 10) for a good survey of this literature; and Howard White (1992) for a valuable recent contribution.

20. This was so even after Franc Zone countries were excluded, on the ground that their currencies are convertible, eliminating, or minimizing divergences of the black market from the official rate.

21. See Thandika Mkandawire (1991, pp. 83–90) for a brief, trenchant statement of some of these controversies.

22. In addition to academics writing in the tradition of the dependency school, the UN Economic Commission for Africa is at best ambivalent on this issue. Thus, a well-publicized report (1989, p. 5) writes of external dependence and the openness that has contributed to it as having increased vulnerability to external shocks and to various resource leakages. While it goes on to reject a strategy of autarky, it favors only "a degree of openness."

23. See Enzo Grilli and M. C. Yang (1988) and Pier Ardeni and Brian Wright (1990), who, using different methods, both estimate a long-term trend rate of decline of 0.6 percent per year. Subsequent articles by James Boughton (1991) and D. Sapsford, P. Sarkar, and H. W. Singer (1992) also find a long-run trend decline. Andrew Powell (1991) suggests that the trend of real commodity prices is actually stationary but that primary products are peculiarly prone to discrete downward shifts. This reinterpretation of the data still points to the desirability of export diversification, however.

24. See Koester and Malcolm Bale (1990) for a review of the effects of the European Community Common Agricultural Policy on developing countries.

25. He actually examined twenty-one countries, but the data did not permit the estimate to be undertaken for Uganda. It appears that the columns of his Table 12.7 (p. 232), estimates of income effects, have been transposed, and the table should be read accordingly.

26. Svedberg (1991, Table 2.4) shows SSA to have supplied 30 percent or more of the world total in 1984–1985 in seven out of thirty-one selected primary commodities. This number would be substantially increased if the list were extended to more minor commodities.

27. In addition to cocoa and coffee, Koester et al. studied tea, cotton, sugar, and ground nuts.

28. See also Christopher Stevens (1990, p. 55) who argues that export diversification in Africa and other countries has been assisted by the terms of the Lomé agreements associating them with the European Community.

29. See Kwabena Gyimah-Brempong (1991, pp. 815–17) for a brief recent survey of this literature.

30. See Percy Mistry (1988, 1991); Joshua Greene and Mohsin Khan (1990); and a special issue of the *African Development Review* (December 1991) for discussions.

31. Sources: World Bank, *World Debt Tables, 1990–1991* and special tabulations. The figures for low-income SSA relate to 1981–1990 and exclude Nigeria.

32. I am indebted to Christopher Stevens for these figures, which are derived from the data base of the UN Statistical Office.

33. See P. T. Bauer (1963) for a classic critique of the economic effects of West African marketing boards.

34. This could reach extreme levels. Thus, in Tanzania, where there was limited fiscal taxation of exports, escalating marketing costs (in combination with currency overvaluation) absorbed increasingly large shares of the total local currency proceeds of commodity exports. Delphin Rwegasira (1984) provides the following figures on the percentages of world price being passed on to Tanzania's farmers:

	1969	1980
cashew nuts	70	35
coffee	81	45
cotton	70	45
tobacco	61	48

35. See T. Oyejide (1990) for a survey of the evidence.

36. Mohsin Khan and Malcolm Knight (1988) tested a model along these lines for a sample of thirty-four developing (not only African) countries and found a large, highly significant correlation between export volumes and the availability of imported inputs. See also William Lyakurwa (1991, p. 17).

37. Frimpong-Ansah et al. (1991, p. 8, chaps. 9–14). The six countries were Côte d'Ivoire, Ghana, Kenya, Nigeria, Tanzania, and Zimbabwe.

38. The IMF (1991, Table A24) and World Bank (1991, Table A9) provide the following contrasting estimates of SSA export volume growth rates (percent p.a.):

IMF		Bank	
1973–1982	−1.0	1973–1980	−0.2
1983–1987	2.2	1980–1987	−1.8
1986–1989	0.3	1986–1989	3.2

However, the IMF (1991) estimates the growth of export volumes for 1988–1991 at nearly 4 percent p.a.

39. William Steel and Jonathan Evans (1984, Table 12) provide the following mean end-use composition of the imports of seven SSA countries in 1978–1982 (percentages of total):

Consumer goods	20
Intermediate goods	49
Capital goods	32

See Benno Ndulu (1991, pp. 289–90) for further evidence on the seriousness of the import constraint.

40. See Vali Jamal (1988) for a dissenting view, however. These and other objections are briefly discussed in Killick (forthcoming, chap. 7).

41. An estimated 72 percent of the population of SSA still lived in rural communities as late as 1989; the equivalent figure for 1965 was 86 percent (World Bank, 1991, Table 31).

42. See Eric Nelson's (1991) study of the Senegalese case.

43. This evidence is surveyed in Killick (forthcoming, chap. 8). See also World Bank (1989c).

44. See, for example, C. C. Agu (1988); David Cole, Philip Wellons, and Betty Slade Yaser (1991); and James Hanson and Craig Neal (1985) on Nigeria; and Killick and F. M. Mwega (1990) on Kenya.

45. On this aspect see Gerald Scott (1991, pp. 186–87), who develops the concept of

the "capacity to transfer." For a general conceptual framework see Edmar Bacha (1990), presenting a three-gap model, where the third gap relates to the public finances, particularly in the face of large debt commitments.

46. On this, with a special focus on agriculture, see the collection of papers in John Howell (1985), particularly Howell's own introduction and the essay by Heller and Aghevli. It is often also said that social service expenditures are particularly at risk as a result of budget stringency and cuts introduced in adjustment programs, but the evidence suggests otherwise (Hicks, 1991), although the recurrent costs problem has certainly had serious effects on the supply of school teaching materials and drugs and other supplies for public clinics and hospitals.

47. ODI (1990) provides a succinct discussion of the issues. For fuller treatment of this complex subject, see S. Devarajan and J. de Melo (1987); P. Guillaumont, S. Guillaumont, and P. Plane (1988); Patrick Honohan (1990); Christopher Lane and Sheila Page (1991); Eric Nelson (1991).

48. As the following figures show, between 1960 and 1981 the share of government consumption in GDP increased by 47 percent in SSA as compared with 10 percent in East Asia and the Pacific, 30 percent in South Asia, and 22 percent in Latin America and the Caribbean (general government consumption as percent of GDP at current market prices):

	1960	1981
Africa South of the Sahara	9.7	14.3
East Asia and Pacific	11.2	12.3
South Asia	7.7	10.0
Latin America and the Caribbean	9.8	12.1

Source: World Bank (1984).

49. See D. L. Bevan, P. Collier, and J. W. Gunning (1990) for these case studies.

50. The evidence on the comparative efficiency of public enterprises is generally inconclusive—see Millward (1988).

51. On import controls see J. Clark Leith (1975), and on price controls see Killick (1973). Both are based on evidence from Ghana. Frederic Pryor (1990, pp. 316–17) provides some information on the operation of price controls in Madagascar.

52. Recall el-Farhan's finding of a negative and significant medium-term relationship between political instability and economic growth (Table 9.4). Note also Gyimah-Brempong's (1989) finding of a trade-off between military spending and economic growth in Africa, because of its depressing effect on investment.

53. In support of this proposition, el-Farhan (forthcoming, chap. 6) finds a statistically significant relationship that runs from GDP growth to political stability: the slower the growth, the greater the incidence of instability.

54. This section is much influenced by the work of my colleagues John Healey and Mark Robinson (1992), from which I have borrowed extensively. They provide an excellent survey of the literature on the political systems of Africa and their economic consequences.

55. Thus, it has been said of Malawi that "the private sector is alive and well—and owned by President Banda! " See Pryor (1990, chap. 4) for some supporting evidence.

56. As of 1960, population densities (per km^2) were estimated as follows, although

such averages, of course, conceal huge intercountry differences within each region (UN *Statistical Yearbook, 1975,* Table 2):

Africa	13
Asia	80
Latin America	15

57. D. K. Fieldhouse (1986) and A. G. Hopkins (1986) both note this feature.

58. In fact, ethnicity in modern Africa is viewed by some as a relatively modern creation, in which the experience of colonization played an important part. For a survey of approaches to ethnicity in modern Africa, see L. Vail (1986), who also presents case studies.

59. On this, see Fieldhouse (1986); E. Mortimer (1969).

60. This was not true of the French colonies, but after independence the governments of Francophone Africa were quick to notice the revenue potential of this source of taxation, which was, indeed, one of the few cost-effective sources available to nascent tax administrations.

61. See Fieldhouse (1986) for a detailed discussion of the conflicting pressures on the old imperial powers during this period.

62. Quoted in C. Young (1986, p. 32).

63. According to Sandbrook (1985, p. 136), between 1960 and 1974 more foreign firms were expropriated in Africa than in any other part of the world.

64. For a detailed discussion of the intellectual inheritance of post-independence African leaders see R. Sklar (1986).

65. This case is argued by reference to the Ghanaian case by Killick (1978, especially chap. 2).

66. For useful surveys of modern approaches to the population-development nexus see N. Birdsall (1988); World Bank (1984). On the African case see particularly Boserup (1985); F. T. Sai (1986, 1988); World Bank (1986).

67. Urbanization may occur in the absence of population growth, but the evidence from SSA suggests that much of its results from push factors in the rural areas, including the growing pressure of population on the land. Becker and A. R. Morrison (1988) found that only 8 percent of SSA's urbanization could be explained by urban pull factors. See also Sai (1986).

68. Note the following estimated population densities (per km^2) as of 1990, calculated from World Bank (1992, Table 1):

Africa	22
East Asia and Pacific	101
South Africa	222
Western Hemisphere	21

69. A desire to tap these was one of the explanations offered for the ill-fated creation of Ujamaa villages in Tanzania.

70. A major study of long-term trends in the Machakos district of Kenya undertaken at the Overseas Development Institute under the direction of Mary Tiffen found that agricultural productivity has more than kept pace with the rapid growth of population in that district and that environmental conditions have tended to be enhanced rather than degraded despite the emergence of high population densities there.

71. R. Ahmed and N. Rustagi (1987) provide data on the density of the road network for eleven SSA countries with a mean of 0.05 kilometers of road per km^2 of land area,

against figures of 0.35, 0.41, and 0.41 for Bangladesh, India, and Indonesia, respectively. They also show that in these three countries an average of 36 percent of their roads was paved, against a mean for the SSA countries of 14 percent.

72. World Bank (1981, Annex Table 6).

73. Such models are, of course, out of fashion, but recent econometric work by Barro (1991, p. 437) has found that GDP growth is positively associated with the initial level of per capita income when other explanatory variables are held constant.

74. There is a substantial literature on the history and modalities of regional cooperation in SSA. For useful recent contributions see Arthur Hazlewood (1991); O.E.G. Johnson (1991); Peter Robson (1990).

75. See, in particular, Uma Lele's (1988, pp. 196–204) exploration of market efficiency in Africa's present-day rural economies and of the implications of the remaining deficiencies for policy.

76. See, for example, the "Policy Forum" on this topic in *Economic Journal* 102 (May 1992): 598–632.

77. We should recall here, however, that el-Farhan got generally weak results from the inclusion of the literacy rate in her tests of the sources of SSA growth (Table 9.4), which conflicts with the view being argued here. However, the literacy ratio is such a poor proxy for the stock of human capital that the absence of statistically significant results is unsurprising.

78. For developments of this theme see Walter Elkan (1988) and Keith Marsden (1990).

79. See Paul Vitta (1990) for a discussion of the weaknesses of technology policies in SSA and of the obstacles to a strengthening of these.

80. For a development of this theme and of the proposition that flexibility is a rising function of economic development see Killick (forthcoming, chap. 3).

81. This is reviewed in Killick et al. (1991, pp. 15, 24).

82. There are a number of points of similarity between the following conclusions and the outcome of a comparison of Asian and African experiences in Winrock International (1991).

REFERENCES

Abramovitz, Moses. 1989. *Thinking About Growth*. Cambridge: Cambridge University Press.

Agu, C.C. 1988. "Interest Rates Policy in Nigeria and Its Attendant Distortions." *Savings and Development* 12, no. 1: 19–34.

Ahmed, R., and Rustagi, N. 1987. "Marketing and Price Incentives in African and Asian Countries: A Comparison." In *Agricultural Marketing Strategy and Policy Pricing*, edited by D. Elz. Washington, D.C.: World Bank.

Akeredolu-Ale, E.O. 1990. "The Human Situation in Africa Today: A Review." In *The Human Dimension of Africa's Persistent Economic Crisis*, edited by A. Adediji, S. Rashid, and M. Morrison. London: Hans Zell.

Ardeni, Pier Giorgio, and Wright, Brian. 1990. "The Long-Term Behaviour of Commodity Prices." *Working Paper* WPS 358. Washington, D.C.: World Bank.

Armstrong, Jill. 1991. "Socioeconomic Implications of AIDS in Developing Countries." *Finance and Development* 28, no. 4 (December).

Ayoade, John A.A. 1988. "States Without Citizens: An Emerging African Phenomenon."

In *The Precarious Balance: State and Society in Africa,* edited by Donald Rothchild and Naomi Chaza. Boulder, Colo.: Westview Press, chap. 4.

Bacha, Edmar L. 1990. "A Three-Gap Model of Foreign Transfers and the GDP Growth Rate in Developing Countries." *Journal of Development Economics* 32 (April).

Baran, Paul A. 1957. *The Political Economy of Growth.* New York: Marzani and Munsell.

Barro, Robert J. 1991. "Economic Growth in a Cross-Section of Studies." *Quarterly Journal of Economics* (May).

Bates, Robert H. 1981. *Markets and States in Tropical Africa.* Berkeley: University of California Press.

————. 1991. "Agricultural Policy and the Study of Politics in Post-Independent Africa." In *Africa 30 Years On,* edited by Douglas Rimmer. London: Royal African Society and James Currey, chap. 9.

Bauer, P.T. 1963. *West African Trade.* London: Routledge and Kegan Paul (reissue).

Becker, Charles M. 1990. "The Demo-Economic Impact of the AIDS Pandemic in Sub-Saharan Africa." *World Development* 18, no. 12 (December).

Becker, M.B, and Morrison, A.R. 1988. "The Determinants of Urban Population Growth in SSA." *Economic Development and Cultural Change* 36, no. 2 (January).

Bevan, D.L., Bigsten, A., Collier, P., and Gunning, J.W. 1987. "Peasant Supply Response in Rationed Economies." *World Development* 15, no. 4 (April).

Bevan, D.L., Collier, P., and Gunning, J.W. 1990. "Economic Policy in Countries Prone to Temporary Trade Shocks." In *Public Policy and Economic Development,* edited by M. Scott and D. Lal. Oxford: Clarendon Press.

Binswanger, Hans, and Pingali, Prabhu. 1988. "Technological Priorities for Farming in Sub-Saharan Africa." *World Bank Research Observer* 3, no. 1 (January).

Birdsall, N. 1988. "Economic Approaches to Population Growth." In *Handbook of Development Economics,* Vol. 1, edited by H. Chenery and T.N. Srinivasan. Amsterdam: North-Holland.

Boserup, E. 1985. "Economic and Demographic Interrelationships in Sub-Saharan Africa." *Population and Development Review,* 11, no. 3 (September).

Boskin, Michael, and Lau, Lawrence. 1990. *Post-War Economic Growth in the Group-of-Five Countries.* Stanford University: Center for Economic Policy Research.

Boughton, James M. 1991. "Commodity and Manufactures Prices in the Long-Run." *IMF Working Paper* 91/47 (May).

Callaghy, Thomas M. 1984. *The State-Society Struggle: Zaire in Comparative Perspective.* New York: Columbia University Press.

Cole, David C., Wellons, Philip A., and Yaser, Betty Slade. 1991. "Financial Systems Reforms: Concepts and Cases." In *Reforming Economic Systems in Developing Countries,* edited by M. Roemer and D. Perkins. Cambridge: Harvard University Press.

Collier, Paul. 1991. "Africa's External Economic Relations, 1960–1990." In *Africa 30 Years On,* edited by Douglas Rimmer. London: Royal African Society.

Cook, Paul, and Kirkpatrick, Colin, eds. 1988. *Privatisation in Less Developed Countries.* Brighton: Wheatsheaf Books.

De Rosa, Dean A. 1990. "Protection and Export Performance in Sub-Saharan Africa." Washington, D.C.: *IMF Working Paper* No. WP/90/83 (September).

Devarajan, S., and de Melo, J. 1987. "Adjustment with a Fixed Exchange Rate: Cameroon, Côte d'Ivoire and Senegal." *World Bank Economic Review* 1, no. 3 (May).

Edström, Jerker, and Singer, H. W. 1992. "The Influence of Trends in Barter Terms of

Trade and of Their Volatility on GNP Growth.'' Brighton: Institute of Development Studies, University of Sussex. Mimeo.

Elbadawi, Ibrahim A. Forthcoming. "Economic Performance and Effectiveness of Bank-Supported Adjustment Programs in Sub-Saharan Africa.'' *World Bank Working Paper*. Washington, D.C.

el-Farhan, Hania. Forthcoming. "Analysis of the Growth Performance of Sub-Saharan African Countries, 1960–1985.'' Ph.D. diss., School of Oriental and African Studies, London.

Elkan, Walter. 1988. "Entrepreneurs and Entrepreneurship in Africa.'' *World Bank Research Observer* 3, no. 2 (July).

Erzan, Refik, and Svedberg, Peter. 1991. "Protection Facing Exports from Sub-Saharan Africa in the EC, Japan and the US.'' In *Trade and Development in Sub-Sharan Africa*, edited by Jonathan H. Frimpong-Ansah, S.M. Ravi Kanbur, and Peter Svedberg. Manchester: Manchester University Press.

Faini, Riccardo, de Melo, Jaime, Senhadji-Semlali, Abdel, and Stanton, Julie. 1989. *Growth-Oriented Adjustment Programs: A Statistical Analysis*. Oxford: Queen Elizabeth House.

Fieldhouse, D.K. 1986. *Black Africa 1945–1980; Economic Decolonization and Arrested Development*. London: Allen and Unwin.

Frimpong-Ansah, Jonathan H. 1991a. "Sub-Saharan Africa and the International Trade System: Perspectives of Policy.'' In *Trade and Development in Sub-Saharan Africa*, edited by Jonathan Frimpong-Ansah, S.M. Ravi Kanbur, and Peter Svedberg. Manchester: Manchester University Press, chap. 4.

———. 1991b. *The Vampire State in Africa: The Political-Economy of Decline in Ghana*. London: James Currey.

Frimpong-Ansah, Jonathan, Kanbur, S.M. Ravi, and Svedberg, Peter, eds. 1991. *Trade and Development in Sub-Saharan Africa*. Manchester: Manchester University Press.

Gladwin, Christina H, and McMillan, Della. 1989. "Is a Turnaround in Africa Possible Without Helping African Women to Farm?'' *Economic Development and Cultural Change*, 37, no. 2 (January).

Greene, Joshua E., and Khan, Mohsin S. 1990. "The African Debt Crisis.'' *Special Paper No. 3*. Nairobi: African Economic Research Consortium.

Grilli, E.R., and Yang, M.C. 1988. "Primary Commodity Prices, Manufactured Goods Prices and the Terms of Trade of Developing Countries: What the Long Run Shows.'' *World Bank Economic Review* 2, no. 1 (January).

Grove, A.T. 1991. "The African Environment.'' In *Africa 30 Years On*, edited by D. Rimmer. London: Royal African Society and James Currey.

Guillaumont, P., Guillaumont, S., and Plane, P. 1988. "Participating in African Monetary Unions: An Alternative Evaluation.'' *World Development* 16, no. 5 (May).

Gyimah-Brempong, Kwabena. 1989. "Defense Spending and Economic Growth in Sub-Saharan Africa: An Econometric Investigation.'' *Journal of Peace Research* 26, no. 1 (February).

———. 1991. "Export Instability and Economic Growth in Sub-Saharan Africa.'' *Economic Development and Cultural Change* 39, no. 4 (July).

Hanson, James A., and Neal, Craig R. 1985. *Interest Rate Policies in Selected Developing Countries, 1970–1982*. World Bank Staff Working Paper No. 753. Washington, D.C.: World Bank.

Hazlewood, Arthur D. 1991. "Economic Integration: Lessons for African Recovery and Development." In *The Challenge of African Economic Recovery and Development*, Chap. 27, edited by Adebayo Adedeji. London: Frank Cass.

Healey, J.M., and Robinson, M. 1992. *Democracy, Governance and Economic Policy: Sub-Saharan Africa in Comparative Perspective.* London: Overseas Development Institute.

Helleiner, Gerald K. 1986. "Outward Orientation, Import Instability and African Economic Growth: An Empirical Investigation." In *Theory and Reality in Development*, edited by S. Lall and F. Stewart. London: Macmillan.

Hicks, Norman L. 1991. "Expenditure Reductions in Developing Countries Revisited." *Journal of International Development* 3, no. 1 (January).

Honohan, Patrick. 1990. "Monetary Co-Operation in the CFA Franc Zone." *Working Paper No. 389.* Washington, D.C.: World Bank.

Hopkins, A.G. 1986. "The World Bank in Africa: Historical Reflections on the African Present." *World Development* 14, no. 12 (December).

Howell, John, ed. 1985. *Recurrent Costs and Agricultural Development.* London: Overseas Development Institute.

Hyden, G. 1986. "African Social Structure and Economic Development." In *Strategies for African Development*, edited by R.J. Berg and J.S. Whitaker. Berkeley: University of California Press.

International Monetary Fund. 1991. *World Economic Outlook.* Washington, D.C.: IMF.

———. 1992. *World Economic Outlook.* Washington, D.C.: IMF.

Jackson, Robert H., and Rosberg, Carl G. 1984. "Personal Rule: Theory and Practice in Africa." *Comparative Politics* 16, no. 4 (July).

Jamal, Vali. 1988. "Getting the Crisis Right: Missing Perspectives on Africa." *International Labour Review* 127, no. 6.

Jebuni, C.D., Oduro, Abena, Asante, Yaw, and Tsikata, G.K. 1992. *Diversfying Exports: The Supply Response of Non-Traditional Exports to Ghana's Economic Recovery Programme.* London: Overseas Development Institute.

Johnson, O.E.G. 1991. "Economic Integration in Africa: Enhancing the Prospects for Success." *Journal of Modern African Studies* 29, no. 1 (March).

Johnson, T.H., Slater, R.O., and McGowan, P. 1984. "Explaining African Military Coups D'état, 1960–1982." *American Political Science Review* 78.

Khan, Mohsin S., and Knight, Malcolm D. 1988. "Import Compression and Export Performance in Developing Countries." *Review of Economics and Statistics* (May).

Killick, Tony. 1973. "Price Controls in Africa—The Ghanaian Experience." *Journal of Modern African Studies* (September).

———. 1978. *Development Economics in Action: Economic Policies in Ghana.* London: Heinemann Educational Books.

———. 1983a. "Development Planning in Africa: Experiences, Weaknesses and Prescriptions." *Development Policy Review* 1, no. 1 (May).

———. 1983b. "The Role of the Public Sector in the Industrialisation of African Developing Countries." *Industry and Development*, no. 7.

———. 1991. "The Developmental Effectiveness of Aid to Africa." In *African External Finance in the 1990s*, edited by I. Husain and J. Underwood. Washington, D.C.: World Bank.

————. Forthcoming. *The Adaptive Economy: Adjustment Policies in Low-Income Economies.* Washington, D.C.: World Bank.

Killick, Tony, Malik, Moazzam, and Manuel, Marcus. 1991. "What Can We Know About the Effects of IMF Programmes?" *ODI Working Paper No. 47.* London: Overseas Development Institute.

Killick, Tony, and Mwega, F.M. 1990. "Monetary Policy in Kenya, 1967–1988." *ODI Working Paper No. 39.* London: Overseas Development Institute.

Kindleberger, Charles P. 1962. *Foreign Trade and the National Economy.* New Haven, Conn.: Yale University Press.

Koester, Ulrich, and Bale, Malcolm D. 1990. "The Common Agricultural Policy: A Review of Its Operation and Effects on Developing Countries." *World Bank Research Observer* 5, no. 1.

Koester, Ulrich, Schafer, Hartwig, and Valdés, Alberto. 1989. "External Demand Constraints for Agricultural Exports." *Food Policy* 14, no. 3 (August).

————. 1990. *Demand-Side Constraints and Structural Adjustment in Sub-Saharan African Countries.* Washington, D.C.: IFPRI.

Lall, Sanjaya. 1989. "Human Resources, Development and Industrialisation, with Special Reference to Sub-Saharan Africa." *Journal of Development Planning,* no. 19.

Lane, Christopher E., and Page, Sheila. 1991. "Differences in Economic Performance Between Franc Zone and Other Sub-Saharan African Countries." *ODI Working Paper No. 43.* London: Overseas Development Institute.

Leith, J. Clark. 1975. *Foreign Trade Regimes and Economic Development: Ghana.* New York: Columbia University Press.

Lele, Uma. 1988. "Comparative Advantage and Structural Transformation: A Review of Africa's Economic Development Experience." In *The State of Development Economics: Progress and Perspectives,* edited by G. Ranis and T.P. Schultz. Oxford: Basil Blackwell.

Leonard, D.K. 1986. "Putting the Farmer in Control; Building Agricultural Institutions." In *Strategies for African Development* edited by R.J. Berg and J.S. Whitaker. Berkeley: University of California Press.

Lyakurwa, William M. 1991. "Trade Policy and Promotion in Sub-Saharan Africa." Nairobi: African Economic Research Consortium, *Special Paper No. 12.*

MacGaffey, Janet. 1988. "Economic Disengagement and Class Formation in Zaire." In *The Precarious Balance: State and Society in Africa* chap. 7, edited by D. Rothchild and N. Chaza. Boulder, Colo.: Westview Press.

Marsden, Keith. 1990. *African Entrepreneurs: Pioneers of Development.* Washington, D.C.: International Finance Corporation.

Mayer, Jean. 1990. "Development Problems and Prospects in Portuguese-Speaking Africa." *International Labour Review* 129, no. 4.

Millward, R. 1988. "Measured Sources of Inefficiency in the Performance of Private and Public Enterprises in LDCS." In *Privatisation in Less Developed Countries* chap. 6, edited by P. Cook and C. Kirkpatrick. Brighton: Wheatsheaf Books.

Mistry, Percy. 1988. *African Debt: The Case for Relief for Sub-Saharan Africa.* Oxford: Oxford International Associates.

————. 1991. *African Debt Revisited: Procrastination or Progress?* The Hague: FONDAD.

Mkandawire, Thandika. 1991. "Crisis and Adjustment in Sub-Saharan Africa." In *The IMF and the South,* edited by D. Ghai. London: Zed Books.

Mortimer, E. 1969. *France and the Africans, 1944–1960*. London: Faber and Faber.

Mullei, A.K. 1992. "A View from Africa." In *Policies for African Development*, edited by I.G. Patel. Washington, D.C.: International Monetary Fund.

Ndulu, Benno J. 1991. "Growth and Adjustment in Sub-Saharan Africa." In *Economic Reform in Sub-Saharan Africa*, edited by A. Chhibber and S. Fischer. Washington D.C.: World Bank.

Nelson, Eric R. 1991. "Monetary Management in Sub-Saharan Africa: Senegal." Bethesda, Md.: DAI. Draft, mimeo.

Overseas Development Institute. 1988. "The Rich and the Poor: Changes in Incomes of Developing Countries Since 1960." *ODI Briefing Paper*. London: Overseas Development Institute.

———. 1990. "Crisis in the Franc Zone." *ODI Briefing Paper*. London: Overseas Development Institute.

Oyejide, T. Ademola. 1990. "Supply Response in the Context of Structural Adjustment in Sub-Saharan Africa." *Special Paper No. 1*. Nairobi: African Economic Research Consortium.

Pickett, James. 1990. "The Low-Income Economies of Sub-Saharan Africa: Problems and Prospects." In *Towards Economic Recovery in Sub-Saharan Africa*, edited by J. Pickett and H. Singer. London: Routledge.

Powell, Andrew. 1991. "Commodity and Developing-Country Terms of Trade: What *Does* the Long-Run Show?" *Economic Journal* 101 (November).

Pryor, Frederic L. 1990. *Malawi and Madagascar*. New York: Oxford University Press.

Reynolds, Lloyd G. 1985. *Economic Growth in the Third World, 1850–1980*. New Haven, Conn.: Yale University Press.

Riddell, Roger C. 1987. *Foreign Aid Reconsidered*. London: James Currey and Overseas Development Institute.

———. 1990. *Manufacturing Africa*. London: James Currey and ODI.

Rimmer, Douglas, ed. 1991. *Africa 30 Years On*. London: Royal African Society and James Currey.

Robson, Peter. 1990. "Economic Integration in Africa: A New Phase?" In *Towards Economic Recovery in Sub-Saharan Africa* chap. 7, edited by J. Pickett and H. Singer. London: Routledge.

Rothchild, Donald, and Chaza, Naomi. 1988. *The Precarious Balance: State and Society in Africa*. Boulder, Colo.: Westview Press.

Rwegasira, Delphin G. 1984. "Exchange Rates and the Management of the External Sector in Sub-Saharan Africa." *Journal of Modern African Studies*. 22, no. 3 (September).

Sai, F.T. 1986. "Population and Health: Africa's Most Basic Resource and Development Problem." In *Strategies for African Development*, edited by R.J. Berg and J.S. Whitaker. Berkeley: University of California Press.

———. 1988. "Changing Perspective of Population in Africa and International Responses." *African Affairs* 87, no. 347 (April).

Sandbrook, Richard. 1985. *The Politics of Africa's Economic Stagnation*. Cambridge: Cambridge University Press.

———. 1986. "The State and Economic Stagnation in Tropical Africa." *World Development* 14, no. 3 (March).

———. 1991. "Economic Crisis, Structural Adjustment and the State in Sub-Saharan

Africa." In *The IMF and the South* chap. 6, edited by D. Ghai. London: Zed Books.

Sapsford, D., Sarkar, P., and Singer, H.W. 1992. "The Prebisch-Singer Terms of Trade Controversy Revisited." *Journal of International Development* 4, no. 3 (May–June).

Scott, Gerald E. 1991. "The African Capacity to Transfer." *Journal of International Development* 3, no. 2.

Short, R.P. 1984. "The Role of Public Enterprises: An International Statistical Comparison." In *Public Enterprises in Mixed Economies: Some Macroeconomic Aspects,* edited by R.H. Floyd, C.S. Gray, and R.P. Short. Washington, D.C.: International Monetary Fund.

Singh, Shamsher. 1983. "Sub-Saharan Agriculture: Synthesis and Trade Prospects." Washington, D.C.: World Bank, *Staff Working Paper No. 608.*

Sklar, R. 1986. "The Colonial Imprint on African Political Thought." In *African Independence; The First 25 Years* edited by G.M. Carter and P. O'Meara. London: Hutchison.

Spencer, Dunstan S.C. 1986. "Agricultural Research: Lessons of the Past, Strategies for the Future." In *Strategies for African Development* edited by R.J. Berg and J.S. Whitaker. Berkeley: University of California Press.

Steel, William F., and Evans, Jonathan W. 1984. *Industrialization in Sub-Saharan Africa: Strategies and Performance.* World Bank Technical Paper No. 25. Washington, D.C.: World Bank.

Stevens, Christopher. 1990. "ACP Export Diversification: Jamaica, Kenya and Ethiopia." *ODI Working Paper* 40. London: Overseas Development Institute.

Stren, R.E. 1988. "Urban Services in Africa: Public Management or Privatisation?" In *Privatisation in Less Developed Countries* chap. 10, edited by P. Cook and C. Kirkpatrick. Brighton: Wheatsheaf Books.

Svedberg, Peter. 1991. "The Export Performance of Sub-Saharan Africa." In *Trade and Development in Sub-Saharan Africa,* edited by J.H. Frimpong-Ansah. Manchester: Manchester University Press.

UNDP. 1991. *Human Development Report, 1991.* New York: Oxford University Press.

UNDP-World Bank. 1992. *African Development Indicators, 1992.* Washington, D.C.: World Bank.

United Nations. 1992. *Africa Recovery.* New York: United Nations, April.

United Nations. 1975. *Statistical Yearbook.* New York: United Nations.

United Nations. 1991. *World Economic Survey 1991.* New York: United Nations.

Vail, L. 1986. "Introduction: Ethnicity in Southern African History." In *The Creation of Tribalism in Southern Africa* edited by L. Vail. London: James Currey.

Vitta, Paul B. 1990. "Technology Policy in Sub-Saharan Africa: Why the Dream Remains Unfulfilled." *World Development* 18, no. 11 (November).

Wheeler, David. 1984. "Sources of Stagnation in Sub-Saharan Africa." *World Development* 12, no. 1 (January).

White, Howard. 1992. "What Do We Know About AIDS' Macroeconomic Impact? An Overview of the AIDS Effectiveness Debate." *Journal of International Development* 4, no. 2 (March–April).

Winrock International. 1991. *African Development: Lessons from Asia.* Adis Ababa: Winrock International Institute for Agricultural Development.

World Bank. 1981. *Accelerated Development in Sub Saharan Africa: An Agenda for Action*. Washington, D.C.: World Bank.

———. 1984. *World Development Report, 1984*. Washington, D.C.: World Bank.

———. 1986. *Population Growth and Policies in Sub-Saharan Africa*. Washington, D.C.: World Bank.

———. 1989a. *Adjustment Lending: An Evaluation of Ten Years of Experience*. Washington, D.C.: World Bank.

———. 1989b. *Sub-Saharan Africa: From Crisis to Sustainable Growth*, Washington, D.C.: World Bank.

———. 1989c. *World Development Report, 1989*. Washington, D.C.: World Bank.

———. 1990. *World Development Report, 1990*. Washington, D.C.: World Bank.

———. 1991. *World Development Report, 1991*. Washington, D.C.: World Bank.

———. 1992. *World Development Report, 1992*. Washington, D.C.: World Bank.

Yeats, Alexander J. 1990. "On the Accuracy of Economic Observations: Do Sub-Saharan Trade Statistics Mean Anything?" *World Bank Economic Review* 4, no. 2 (May).

Young, C. 1986. "Africa's Colonial Legacy." In *Strategies for African Development*, edited by R.J. Berg and J.S. Whitaker. Berkeley: University of California Press.

10

THE EAST ASIAN DEVELOPMENT EXPERIENCE

Colin Bradford, Jr.

THE NATURE AND DEGREE OF DYNAMISM

The principal reason for the widespread interest in the East Asian development experience is the degree of dynamism that has characterized it and the remarkable growth in East Asian exports to Organization for Economic Cooperation and Development (OECD) markets. Quite apart from the controversies that have surrounded debates about the *causes* of East Asian dynamism, the development experience of Korea, Taiwan, Singapore, and Hong Kong has drawn attention simply because of the *facts*.

We begin this survey by asking the question, How exceptional is the dynamic development experience of the newly industrializing countries (NICs) of East Asia? The term *newly industrializing countries* suggests that NICs are defined as dynamic, rapidly industrializing exporters of manufactures. This means that measures of gross domestic product (GDP) growth, industrialization, and manufactured goods exports would be good criteria for identifying which countries are the most successful as NICs.

Some years ago William Branson pointed out that it would be best to develop ex ante criteria for identifying NICs. We were concerned that the existing literature either tended toward tautologies by ex post reasoning (high-performance countries are countries that have done well) or by confusing association with causality (as was the case, e.g., in the 1987 *World Development Report,* which associated high growth with outward orientation). Branson suggested the use of a clustering algorithm (Hartigan, 1975) as a more objective means of establishing

Permission to publish this chapter was granted by the Organization for Economic Co-operation and Development.

which countries are NICs and which are next-tier NICs (Bradford and Branson, 1987, pp. 6–7.) The clustering algorithm technique essentially maps the distance between a given country's data set of designated variables and that of all other countries in the sample and orders the gaps in the country rankings of aggregate "distances" so as to derive different country clusters according to the combination of the designated variables.

An initial effort to apply this technique was undertaken by Wozencraft (1987). The average annual growth rates of four variables between 1965 and 1980 were used as criteria: gross domestic product (GDP), manufactured output, value added in manufacturing, and manufactured exports. These variables fit the definition of NICs as dynamic, rapidly industrializing exporters of manufactures. Wozencraft compiled data on twenty potential NICs from various regions and applied the clustering algorithm to the data. The procedure generated four distinct clusters from the data set of twenty countries. Three of the four East Asian countries constituted the first cluster (Korea, Singapore, and Taiwan), and Hong Kong, Indonesia, Malaysia, Thailand, and Brazil were in the second cluster. Countries from other regions (Europe, Latin America, and South Asia) were in the third and fourth clusters (Bradford, 1989a, pp. 124–26). This experiment seems to objectively establish the four East Asian economies as leading NICs from this sample of twenty potential NICs.

The question that arises now is, Do the four East Asian NICs maintain the position in the 1980–1990 period that the previous analysis revealed for the 1965–1980 period? Whereas we are unable to apply the clustering algorithm to the new data set, Table 10.1 presents the average annual growth rates for the 1960s, 1970s, and 1980s for GDP, manufacturing value added, and total exports. The rank ordering of the mean growth rates calculated from the new data set for the three variables, for the three decades, and for the four tiers reveals the same ordering of clusters with the three East Asian NICs in the top cluster and Hong Kong in the second cluster. Even though the average growth rates of all three variables have fallen in the 1980s compared with earlier decades, in most cases, the decline in growth rates in the East Asian NICs has been less than in the other country groupings.

As a result, we can conclude that the four East Asian economies are "hypersuccessful" NICs (Pack and Westphal, 1986, pp. 91, 125), outliers, or divergent cases, especially if compared with all developing countries, not just to a preselected group of potential NICs, as in Wozencraft. This exceptional performance by the four East Asian NICs over three decades distinguishes them and has led to the extensive literature and debate on the causes of their dynamic development experience. Because the most dynamic developing economies have achieved their success based on industrialization and trade, the debate has centered on the influence of industrial strategy and, pari passu, the relative roles of the state and the market and on whether trade has stimulated growth or dynamic growth has generated exports.

The purpose of this volume is to provide an analysis of development experience

Table 10.1

Average Annual Growth Rates*

	GDP			Manufacturing V.A.**			Total Exports		
	1961-70	1971-80	1981-90	1961-70	1971-80	1981-90	1961-70	1971-80	1981-90
	(-- percent --)								
First Tier									
Korea	8.68	8.61	9.32	13.50	15.68	11.80	30.12	20.33	10.98
Singapore /a	9.55	8.93	7.03	18.53	10.90	6.90	n.a.	7.79	10.16
Taiwan /b, /f	9.65	9.75	8.01	14.63	12.64	8.56	22.03	16.08	11.35
Mean Growth Rate	9.29	9.10	8.12	15.55	13.07	9.09	26.07	14.73	10.83
Second Tier									
Hong Kong /c	9.29	9.40	6.58	8.87	6.90	4.24	11.85	9.40	13.65
Indonesia	3.88	7.23	5.57	5.04	14.04	11.75	4.70	9.22	1.39
Malaysia /d	5.97	7.87	6.83	10.82	11.64	8.41	5.31	7.82	9.71
Thailand.	7.96	6.70	7.83	9.75	10.07	9.15	8.32	9.58	13.88
Brazil	5.99	8.54	1.58	6.95	9.45	-0.10	5.52	9.93	5.98
Mean Growth Rate	6.62	7.95	5.68	8.28	10.42	6.69	7.14	9.19	8.92
Third Tier									
Mexico	7.02	6.57	1.64	8.43	7.14	1.89	4.67	8.35	7.53
Turkey	5.65	5.19	5.32	7.75	4.99	7.08	9.51	3.88	21.27
Greece	7.78	4.68	1.44	8.94	6.11	0.47	17.57	11.44	5.05
Philippines	5.38	6.17	1.70	4.94	6.97	1.63	5.90	7.31	5.08
Spain /e, /f	7.53	3.46	2.86	7.40	n.a.	2.25	12.27	7.05	6.07
Colombia	5.23	5.49	3.44	5.13	5.99	2.76	3.10	5.71	6.19
Mean Growth Rate	6.43	5.26	2.73	7.10	6.24	2.68	8.84	7.29	8.53
Fourth Tier									
Yugoslavia /g	5.42	6.04	-0.56	2.80	8.05	-0.04	9.70	4.66	-0.45
Portugal /h	6.36	4.81	2.79	7.18	7.42	1.22	9.50	3.35	8.30
Egypt /g	4.70	8.00	4.74	4.79	8.83	3.66	1.12	7.16	3.25
Pakistan	7.19	4.69	6.37	9.86	5.51	7.24	7.45	1.59	8.09
India	3.86	2.99	5.57	2.79	4.02	7.29	2.79	7.73	5.71
Argentina /f	4.24	2.62	-1.29	3.59	1.62	-2.30	5.72	4.78	4.98
Mean Growth Rate	5.30	4.86	2.94	5.17	5.91	2.84	6.05	4.88	4.98

*See bottom of Table 10.3 for Sources and Notes.

**For the 1960s for all countries Manufacturing V.A. in current prices was deflated using the implicit GDP deflator.

in major regions and sectors along with economic thinking on development theories and strategies so as to provide a stimulating mixture of theory and actual performance. In examining the East Asian development experience, the literature of the last fifteen years has been unusual in the highly potent mixture of these various strands of theory and evidence. These success stories have mobilized the attention of the economics profession to come to grips with the reasons for their exceptional performance, not just document it. Interpreting the reasons for success in East Asia has provided a proving ground for different theoretical approaches to the dynamics of economic growth over the last fifteen years.

The next section provides a presentation of the standard neoclassical approach to the achievement of neutrality of incentives as between exports and imports and, using the same approach, argues that a proexport bias in the broad incentive structure (beyond the exchange rate) is more likely to explain the hypergrowth experience of the East Asian NICs. The discussion here has interesting parallels with that in chapter 2 by James Riedel in this volume. More empirical and historical evidence is given to substantiate the extraordinary performance of the East Asian NICs and to explain it. The third section reviews some of the recent theories of endogenously determined growth, which seem to be more consistent with the notion of growth-led exports (rather than export-led growth), which characterize the East Asian experience. The fourth section looks at OECD literature on the growth experience of OECD countries, which attributes considerable significance to national systems of technological innovation at both the micro- and the macrolevel as a contributory element to rapid growth. This systemic approach seems consistent with the main factors that appear to have been of determining importance in the East Asian cases. These sections together attempt to meet Robert Wade's enjoinder that the East Asian success stories "challenge economics to deploy—or invent—theories which will make the non-neoclassical facts of East Asia analytically tractable" (Wade, 1990, p. 345).

The final section provides a summary of the theoretical and experiential perspectives. It suggests that the systemic approach that has emerged more recently, assigning increasing prominence to processes of technological development and diffusion in explaining high growth experiences, is a more inclusive and realistic framework for capturing the full scope of contributing elements to the East Asian success stories. This wider framework provides a vehicle for other countries to draw useful ideas for initiating the complex process of faster growth without necessarily requiring the imitation of an East Asian "model" of successful development.

FROM EXPORT PROMOTION TO EXPORT PUSH

Trade Regime Types

To clarify alternative interpretations of East Asian success, this section examines two formulations of trade orientation. The theoretical underpinnings of both the unbiased or neutral concept of "export promotion" and of the export-biased concept, where the incentives to produce exportables exceed those for importables, labeled here as "export push," are presented. In the 1980s the neutral version was the dominant version and the one most clearly identified with the East Asian NICs. In a 1986 volume surveying current thinking on development strategies, Jagdish Bhagwati wrote:

Let me first clarify that, by EP Strategy, the literature now simply means a policy such that, on balance, the effective exchange rate for exports (EERx) is not significantly different from that for imports (EERm), so that the EERx is roughly equal to EERm. . . . This as it were *minimalist definition* of EP conforms closely to the actual experience of the successful East Asian export promoters. (Bhagwati, 1986, pp. 92–93, emphasis added)

The case studies referenced by Bhagwati in this paragraph are the NBER studies summarized in part in Bhagwati (1978). The data and country experience referred to are for the pre-1973 period (see Bhagwati, 1978, Table 7.1, pp. 185–90). I pointed out in a chapter in the same volume (Bradford, 1986) that the references to pre-1973 country experience in the literature published at the end of the 1970s put the interpretation of the NIC experience in the 1970s out of phase with the historical reality, which during the 1970s entailed more government involvement in export promotion. In the 1986 article, Bhagwati acknowledges that "perhaps we need to distinguish between EP regimes where EERx roughly equals EERm and the ultra-EP regimes where, instead, EERx is substantially greater than EERm" (Bhagwati, 1986, p. 93, acknowledgments and footnotes 1 through 4 on pages 102–3). Bhagwati returns to the subject of "export promoting trade strategy" in later writings referred to further on (Bhagwati, 1988; 1989, p. 94.)
    One of the reasons for the predominance of the neutral EP version is in the assumptions of the theoretical model used to expound the definitions of EP and import substitution (IS). A standard, perfect competition trade model with two traded goods is used in Bhagwati's 1978 definition of EP and IS (pp. 207–8). The result is that EP occurs when EERx = EERm at a free trade optimality point P*, and import substitution results when EERm > EERx, at a point P at the left of P* on a given production possibility curve. "Export push," where EERx > EERm, occurs at P to the right of P* on the same production possibility frontier (PPF). Because the model assumes perfect mobility and full employment of factors of production, the trade policy regime affects the output mix *along* a *single* production possibility frontier and does not contemplate *shifts* in the production possibility frontier.
    Disequilibria rather than perfectly competitive conditions are more likely to prevail in developing countries. These disequilibria are likely not only to affect the impact of the trade regime on the economy but to constitute a reason for the adoption of the trade regime. As Edmar Bacha has neatly shown, in conditions of surplus labor and structural balance-of-payments problems, it is impossible

Figure 10.1
Effective Exchange Rate for Exports and Imports and Growth

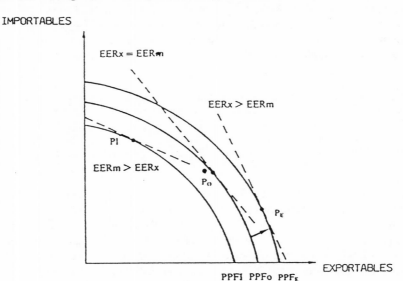

IMPORTABLES

EERx = EERm

EERx > EERm

PI

EERm > EERx

Po

Pε

EXPORTABLES

PPFI PPFo PPFε

to achieve equilibrium in goods markets, foreign exchange markets, and labor (factor) markets simultaneously (Arida and Bacha, 1984). As a result, an industrializing economy does not operate in reality at or along the competitive equilibrium PPF but on a lesser PPF.

Let us assume that in period t_o the economy begins with prevailing disequilibria that define the initial PPF as PPF_o, somewhere inside the competitive equilibrium PPF not shown, even though on average EERx = EERm at P_o (see Figure 10.1). Then, under import substitution trade policies, EERm > EERx. Because of increased protection, the economy experiences greater distortions than initially, and there is a shift in output *level* as well as output mix to a point P_I on a more constrained PPF called PPF_I. The economy is worse off at P_I than P_o not only because the product mix is distorted by the trade regime but because import-substituting policies overall would have a dampening effect on aggregate output. The output effect is due to the fact that more income is spent on domestically produced importables than would have been spent on cheaper imported goods, leaving less national income for the purchase of other output. This exposition fits with the general view that IS trade policies lead to worse economic performance.

The principal objective of an "export push" strategy is to increase the market share of the country's exports in foreign markets. This contrasts with the open neutral trade regime, which seeks to establish internal competitive market conditions to permit the country to be responsive to the growth in external demand for the country's exports, in which case the country's exports would be expected to grow at roughly the same rate as the growth of world trade.

Introducing a variety of incentives (credit policies, infrastructure development, fiscal subsidies, import rebates, and so on) to create a proexport bias can facilitate the capacity of firms to reap economies of scale and reach points on their cost curves below the world market price. These incentives are meant to enable firms to significantly increase their export shares in foreign markets. They would also encourage firms to operate at a much higher level of production than would have been possible if they were price takers under a neutral trade regime. This larger-scale production made possible by the introduction of export incentives would absorb idle resources (unemployed labor, unused productive capacity in input producing firms, capital that might have otherwise been invested abroad, and so on). The difference between the IS point in Figure 10.1 and the "export push" point is that import substitution, by definition, entails more costly production, and export incentives induce lower cost production relative to the neutral trade regime.

In addition to the foreign market share and scale objectives, a proexport bias regime may be used to achieve industrial upgrading, moving a country's productive structure up the technological scale from labor-intensive to capital-intensive to skill- and technology-intensive industries as the country's endowment base matures. By accelerating this process through the introduction of export incentives, there are likely to be productivity gains resulting from the shift in resources from older sectors into newer ones or older technologies to newer ones.

Hence, by biasing economic policies toward exports, an economy is potentially able both to move resources into higher productivity sectors and to utilize existing resources more fully. An export bias regime, therefore, can cause a shift to a point on a PPF that is farther from the origin than PPF_o. This possibility is shown by P_E on $PPF_E > PPF_o > PPF_I$ in Figure 10.1. Departing from realistic initial conditions in a developing country with underutilized resources and imperfect competitive conditions, the "export push" strategy can utilize productive capacity and factors of production both more fully and more efficiently than either EP or IS strategies and, therefore, move the economy to a higher production possibility frontier.

Structural Change and Investment

The theoretical idea of an export push regime that results in relatively higher output growth already contains explanatory dynamics just mentioned. But we can go further. The idea of moving resources to higher productivity sectors that lies behind the export push idea implies that shifts in the sectoral composition of output would be expected to accompany an export-push strategy. I had previously found (Bradford and Branson, 1987, chapter 1, pp. 7–9) an association of high rates of structural change in industry with the average growth rates of

Table 10.2
Industrial Structural Change Index

	1965-80	1975-92
	(--------in degrees-------)	
First Tier		
Korea	31.37	28.55
Singapore	48.32	45.53
Taiwan	n.a.	19.72
Mean	39.85	31.27
Second Tier		
Hong Kong	9.87	10.16
Indonesia	19.52	25.12
Malaysia	15.86	25.20
Thailand	17.69	20.17
Brazil	30.03	18.48
Mean	18.59	19.83
Third Tier		
Mexico	14.83	28.28
Turkey	23.20	14.92
Greece	13.56	6.21
Philippines	10.95	11.22
Spain	24.73	22.64
Colombia	10.90	9.46
Mean	16.36	15.46
Fourth Tier		
Yugoslavia	12.01	15.61
Portugal	21.61	12.00
Egypt	21.61	31.55
Pakistan	32.40	15.90
India	20.89	17.47
Argentina	15.90	17.35
Mean	20.74	18.31

Source: UNIDO (1985, 1991–1992).

value added in manufacturing (and other attributes defining the NICs), using an index of structural change based on shifts in the sectoral composition of output in sixteen manufacturing sectors between 1965 and 1980. Using this United Nations Industrial Development Organization (UNIDO) data for 1965 to 1980, Korea, Singapore, and Brazil were found to have the highest indexes of industrial structural change, roughly three times the world average for the period. We now have data for the 1975 to 1990 period and data for Taiwan (see Table 10.2).

The comparison of the 1975–1990 data with the 1965–1980 data is extremely interesting. It reveals that Korea and Singapore still have the highest indexes of structural change, though they decline slightly. We would expect the rates of structural change in manufacturing to slow down as the industrial sector matures. This is shown also in the European countries (Turkey, Greece, Spain, and Portugal) that also have declining indexes. The next-tier Asian NICs, on the other hand, have increased rates of structural change (Indonesia, Malaysia, and Thailand). This shows the catch-up dynamism of these three Southeast Asian economies that has characterized them in the 1980s. Hong Kong has decidedly lower indexes of industrial structural change, which is the result of the dominance of textiles and apparel in Hong Kong's production and trade. The manufacturing sector in Hong Kong actually decreased as a share of GDP from 1965 to 1990, from 24 to 18 percent, while textiles and clothing maintained a share of 40 percent of value added in manufacturing over the last twenty years (World Bank, 1992, Tables 3, 6). Over 35 percent of Hong Kong's total exports came from seven clothing and fabric sectors (three-digit level) in 1987–1988 (UNCTAD, 1990, p. 203.) In these respects, Hong Kong has a very different pattern from that of the other East Asian NICs.

The average indexes of structural change by cluster reveal that the rankings of countries according to growth in GDP, manufacturing value added, and total exports (Table 10.1) are associated with high rates of industrial structural change. Therefore, these data provide evidence that the East Asian NICs in particular (except for Hong Kong) and NICs as a category are characterized by high rates of structural change as measured by the UNIDO indexes of structural change. (The fourth tier is an exception.)

Structural change—changes in the composition of output—is achieved by investment—increases in productive capacity. Above-average indexes for structural change would be expected to be associated with above-average levels of investment as a share of GDP. Table 10.3 presents data for the 1966–1990 period on the average annual growth of gross domestic investment (GDI) and GDI as a share of GDP for the twenty developing countries in the Wozencraft clustering exercise. Over the thirty-year period the ranking of clusters by mean growth rates fits the original clustering pattern. Although the initial level of GDI-GDP shares does not fit the original ranking, the growth rates over the three decades tend toward the expected divergence. There are exceptions, but the pattern of investment growth and GDP shares reveals that on average high investment tends to be associated with high values of the five other variables analyzed thus far.[1]

Strategy

These data seem to confirm an investment-led, structural change process of industrialization that has led to exceptional rates of growth in GDP, value added in manufacturing, and total exports. Hong Kong is an exception in having low rates of structural change. But Hong Kong is also the country with the most laissez-faire regime. The issue that is posed by these data and that has been a major one in the literature is the degree of state intervention or strategic guidance that has been involved in the East Asian cases. The exceptional rates of change in the sector composition of output in the East Asian NICs suggest the presence of an active, visible hand of the public sector in accelerating the rates of sectoral change by supporting structural transformation. This implies that the states in Korea, Taiwan, and Singapore have played a positive role in supporting the industrialization process through policies that provided incentives to industries with export potential, facilitating investment and promoting exports.

The problem in much of the literature is that state intervention has been

Table 10.3
Gross Domestic Investment

	Average Annual Growth Rate			Share in GDP		
	1961-70	1971-80	1981-90	1961-70	1971-80	1981-9
	(------------------------------percent---------------------)					
First Tier						
Korea	21.98	10.91	12.64	17.53	26.42	30.1
Singapore /a	24.10	9.63	5.94	13.84	41.78	42.1
Taiwan /b, /f	14.83	12.59	5.18	16.63	26.01	21.8
Mean	20.31	11.04	7.92	16.00	31.40	31.3
Second Tier						
Hong Kong /c	10.42	13.10	3.57	20.22	30.00	27.9
Indonesia	8.50	13.85	10.39	8.99	17.57	31.3
Malaysia /d	8.59	11.08	7.28	15.72	25.44	30.6
Thailand	14.36	5.76	9.92	22.53	27.71	26.9
Brazil	6.50	9.54	-1.34	16.91	29.52	21.4
Mean	9.67	10.66	5.97	16.88	26.05	27.6
Third Tier						
Mexico	7.52	8.86	-2.01	19.85	28.47	23.2
Turkey	10.22	5.94	3.82	17.41	27.06	24.2
Greece	7.81	2.92	-2.53	25.12	31.59	20.8
Philippines	6.87	9.40	-3.72	19.92	27.45	19.9
Spain /e, /f	11.35	1.74	5.14	26.02	22.96	19.5
Colombia	4.91	5.05	1.29	19.22	21.42	21.3
Mean	8.11	5.65	0.33	21.26	26.49	21.5
Fourth Tier						
Yugoslavia /g	6.21	6.42	-7.19	31.10	20.82	19.9
Portugal /h	6.12	4.61	-1.36	18.51	36.80	30.8
Egypt /g	4.89	14.20	1.14	14.81	22.08	22.3
Pakistan	9.81	3.42	5.67	17.21	18.85	18.7
India	4.33	4.77	4.62	17.37	23.33	24.0
Argentina /f	4.39	3.70	-11.40	20.02	27.21	16.4
Mean	5.96	6.19	-1.42	19.84	24.85	22.0

Sources: 1961–1970 data in constant local currency from "World Tables, 1976," World Bank.
1971–1990 data in constant local currency from "World Tables, 1991," World Bank.
ªSingapore: No Total Exports data until 1975.
ᵇTaiwan: Source used for all data "Taiwan Statistical Yearbook, 1989."
ᶜHong Kong: 1971–1990 Manufacturing V.A. in current prices deflated using the GDP deflator.
ᵈMalaysia: Manufacturing V.A. data only until 1989.
ᵉSpain: for 1971–1990, Manufacturing data in current prices (1980–1986) deflated using the GDP
   deflator.
ᶠNo data available for 1990.
ᵍ1961–1970: Manufacturing V.A. includes Mining. 1971–1990: Industry V.A. instead of Manufacturing V.A.
ʰPortugal: for 1971–1990, Industry V.A. in current prices (1977–1987) deflated using the GDP
   deflator.

identified with inward-looking, import substitution policies and that trade liberalization and market orientation have been identified with outward-looking
regimes. The debate has centered around trade liberalization versus protectionism
and market-oriented regimes versus restrictive intervention and failed to even
consider the possibility that intervention and export orientation might go together
and might prove a more potent combination than the diads previously specified.
The third alternative has been missing from the mainstream debate.

T.N. Srinivasan's comment (1990) on Elhanan Helpman's paper "The Non-competitive Theory of International Trade and Trade Policy" at the first World Bank Annual Conference on Development Economics (1989) reveals this bipolar character:

Their new theory suggested a more active role for government policy in trade. In some cases it appeared to provide an intellectually respectable economic argument for such not-so-respectable policies as protection. Those die-hard development economists who were loath to give up their intellectual investment in an inward-oriented development strategy—despite mounting evidence of its failure—latched on to the new theory in hopes of salvaging their intellectual investment. . . . It is therefore essential to take explicit account of a country's policymaking and rent-seeking realities. The new theory has yet to take this step, and until it does the traditional arguments for limited or no intervention in trade will remain unchallenged. (pp. 217, 221)

Nancy Barry (1990), commenting on the same paper, made a different argument, which is consistent with the alternative formulations mentioned here:

The real success stories of the 1980s are Japan, the Republic of Korea, and Taiwan. We may try to rewrite that history, but it is clear these economies have several things in common. And one of them is that they have been *factor endowment makers—not factor endowment takers*. They have really sat down and said, "Where is the world going to be in the year 2000, where do we want to be in that world, and what are the pieces that we don't have that we need to get?" And that type of thinking has been in the context of using international competitiveness, present and future, as the litmus test. The strategies pursued place the East Asians apart from other developing economies—not in the level of government intervention but in the purposes of that intervention. (pp. 223–24, emphasis added)

If the essence of the process is investment-led structural change creating a dynamic growth path that generates exports of manufactured goods at high growth rates, then the notion of selective intervention by a government in ways that facilitate and accelerate the industrialization process would appear to be a logical interpretive theory for explaining the dynamic performance of the East Asian economies. This is a strategy-led, structural change, export push theory of dynamic development that represents an alternative to the open economy, internal liberalization version of outward orientation.

Strategy-led does not mean "picking winners" but rather an interactive relationship between the public and the private sector that yields concerted action between them. This notion postulates a "catalytic" state rather than a strong state, one that is flexible, adaptable, and committed to dynamic efficiency for the economy as a whole rather than politicized interventionism in response to rent seekers. Howard Pack and Larry Westphal (1986) call this "integrated decision-making" (p. 99).

In examining the activity of the Korean government, they indicate that it "achieved integrated decision making by acting as a central agent mediating among market agents, forcing and facilitating information interchange and ensuring the implementation of decisions reached. . . . The government has almost always consulted extensively with private agents. . . . The process of integrated decision-making has been a highly flexible one. . . . Priorities at all levels have been established and revised through continual monitoring related to implementation" (p. 99).

Wade, in his landmark book focusing on Taiwan (Wade, 1990), calls this governing the market (GM), which he juxtaposes with the free market (neoclassical) theory (FM) and the simulated free market theory (SM) of East Asian success, SM being instances in which government intervention has been used to approximate market prices when they are absent due to disequilibria and imperfections.

The GM theory, on the other hand, emphasizes capital accumulation as the principal general force for growth, and interprets superior East Asian performance as the result of a level and composition of investment different from what FM or SM policies would have produced, and different, too, from what the "interventionist" economic policies pursued by many other LDCs would have produced. Government policies deliberately got some prices "wrong" [see also Amsden, 1989, chapter 6], so as to change the signals to which decentralized market agents responded, and also used nonprice means to alter the behavior of market agents. The resulting high level of investment generated fast turnover of machinery, and hence fast transfer of newer technology into actual production. (p. 29)

What differentiates [the East Asian] efforts, above all, are a consistent and coordinated attentiveness to the problems and opportunities of particular industries, in the context of a long-term perspective on the economy's evolution, and a state which is hard enough not only to produce sizable effects on the economy but also to control the direction of the effects, which is a more demanding achievement. (p. 343)

There is a synergistic connection between a public system and a mostly private market system, the outputs of each becoming inputs for the other, with the government setting rules and influencing decision-making in the private sector in line with its view of an appropriate industrial and trade profile for the economy. (p. 5)

The catalytic state, functioning in this fashion, is capable of a proexport bias. Bhagwati recognizes this in his more recent book on protectionism:

In South Korea and Taiwan . . . the shift to the export-promoting strategy took place through a substantial reduction in overvaluation . . . and through the adoption of export incentives that offset and indeed outweighed the residual bias against exports by making the average incentive for exports (EER_x) greater than the average incentive to import (EER_m). Within this regime . . . selectivity of incentives continued to specific industries. . . . Moreover, these policy departures from fully free trade reflected a symbiotic relationship between an active government and the private sector. (Bhagwati, 1989, pp. 94–95)

Whereas Bhagwati had postulated EER_x greater than EER_m as ''ultra EP strategy'' earlier (Bhagwati, 1988, pp. 32 ff), this is the clearest statement by him identifying it with the East Asian NICs and as having positive results.

A neutral trade regime ($EER_x = EER_m$) is normally the preferred option in the literature. This regime requires trade liberalization (and exchange rate reform) to open the economy to world market prices. The idea is that without trade restrictions, internal market prices will equal international prices. The static efficiency gains from the optimal resource allocation resulting from market price signals replacing market distortions are supposed to account for the growth of exports. In an open, neutral trade regime, exports respond to world market *demand*. In the export-biased $EER_x > EER_m$ regime, exports are *supply*-driven.

The Relative Importance of Trade Liberalization

A practical problem with implementing the neutral trade regime in developing countries is that it requires more than the removal of trade restrictions to have optimal conditions prevail, given imperfect initial conditions. Financial liberalization to enable interest rates to reach world market rates is imperative to assure that capital is allocated efficiently and that capital-intensive techniques are not widely adopted due to repressed financial regimes. In the Korean case, it is well known that preferred credit schemes have been a major instrument for creating the proexport bias. The bank-based financial system in Korea (as opposed to a market-based financial system in Anglo-Saxon terms) (Fischer-Reisen, 1992) was more easily controlled by the government as a policy instrument to implement the investment-led strategy. Capital account and internal financial liberalization have a long and difficult road ahead in Korea because of the different nature of the bank-based system (Kang, 1992). But this kind of bank-based financial system does not necessarily create inefficiencies in circumstances where there are large information imperfections, if the banking system is in effect a quasi-internal organization within the industrial structure that compensates for the disadvantages of underdeveloped capital markets (see Lee, 1992; for the Taiwan story see Wade, 1990, chapter 6, pp. 159–94).

The evidence that import liberalization was the key force in generating the dynamic growth path of the East Asian NICs seems weak in light of the data on trade restrictions in Korea and Taiwan and in light of other factors contributing to growth apart from trade liberalization. Kwang Suk Kim, for example, identifies two periods of import liberalization in Korea: 1965–1967 and 1978–1990 (Kim, 1991, Table 15, pp. 59–63). The first episode was a ''jump'' whereas the second was a ''gradual multistage approach'' that was more continuous. The ''jump'' in the liberalization effort in 1966–1967 was principally in shifts in QRs while tariffs actually rose. There was no effective liberalization between 1967 and 1977. In the second period after 1977 both tariff and QR liberalization were undertaken together. Kim calculates that the overall degree of liberalization moved gradually from roughly 60 percent in 1977 to roughly 90 percent in 1990, when the average tariff rate was 14 percent (Kim, 1991, Table 15, p. 56; see also Dornbusch and Park, 1987, appendix). Kim concludes by pointing out that "the country not only delayed the promotion of import liberalization until it became somewhat confident in export expansion even *after* the shift to the export oriented policy, but has also been *cautious* in the promotion of liberalization" (p. 101, emphasis added). It does not appear that Korea was an example of trade liberalization-induced growth.

A somewhat similar pattern seems to have prevailed in Taiwan, where nominal tariff rates remained above 40 percent from the 1950s to the 1970s, reaching a maximum of over 55 percent in 1974 (Chen and Hou, 1991, Table 2, pp. 45–48). They declined gradually to just under 40 percent in 1979, at which time the tariffs schedule split into two parts: one for the United States, which declined to 20 percent by 1987, and one for the rest of the world, which declined to 32 percent. The effective real tariff rates ranged between 15 and 17 percent in the 1960s, between 11 and 12 percent in the 1970s, and between 7 and 9 percent in the 1980s (Chen and Hou, 1991, Table 2). This tariff history does not reveal a liberalization thrust that could be interpreted to be the engine of export-led growth. In fact, the authors fear that, rather, it has been an instrument for protection of "key industries" (p. 45).

Hong Kong and Singapore, as city-states with entrepôt traditions, have historically had open trade regimes. But they have had quite different histories in terms of the patterns of industrialization and trade. Hong Kong has had a laissez-faire government that had "no definite government industrial policy" (Chen, 1987, p. 355) and a fairly static structure of production dominated by textiles and apparel. Singapore, on the other hand, after breaking away from the Malaysian federation in 1965, launched a labor-intensive manufactured goods export drive emphasizing foreign direct investment through the 1970s and made deliberate efforts to upgrade the industrial structure in order to accommodate wage increases to fit the greater skill level of its population in the 1980s (Lim and Pang, 1991). Whereas Singapore has a very open financial regime to attract FDI and multinational corporations to make up for the lack of an entrepreneurial cadre, the government was highly centralized, played a major role in the development strategy, and exercised considerable control over the labor movement. In contrast to Hong Kong, sectoral diversification in Singapore was high. "As for direct export, both structural changes and growth rates are the highest in the years between 1966 and 1975 when there was a significant turn toward export-oriented industrialization" (Wong, 1989, p. 390, Table 13.6). Linda Lim and Eng Fong Pang conclude in their survey of FDI and industrialization in Malaysia, Singapore, Taiwan, and Thailand that "all four have developed with a strong role for the State, which is most interventionist in Singapore" (Lim and Pang, 1991, p. 30.) Stephan Haggard concludes in a similar vein: "Singapore thus falls squarely within the East Asian mold, with a relatively autonomous state, a highly centralized and interventionist economic policy making apparatus, a weakened left and a tamed labor movement" (Haggard, 1990, p. 115).

While both Hong Kong and Singapore have relatively open trade regimes, as can be seen from the previous discussion, they are on nearly opposite ends of the spectrum in terms of the role of the state. Trade liberalization by itself may not be the dominant conduit for the spread of market forces internally that was thought to be the key to the manufactured goods export drive of East Asia. Rather than envisioning open markets and strong states as opposing models, the East Asian experiences suggest the possibility of compatibility and, indeed, positive synergy between the two. An active government engaged in supportive policies consistent with the trade orientation is a potentially powerful combination, which seems to be evident in three of the four East Asian cases.

In retrospect, perhaps one of the deficiencies of the open economy trade liberalization, neutral regime thrust that became the orthodoxy in the 1980s was that by focusing on neutrality and the removal of distortions, its essential reformist thrust became negative, emphasizing what needed to be taken away, especially trade barriers. By looking at possibilities for export-bias and trade promotion industrialization, a wider array of elements comes into the picture and a more positive proactive attitude is taken. ("The governments of 'dos' generally produce economic performance superior to that produced by governments of 'don'ts' " [Bhagwati, 1989, p. 98]).

Historical Experience and Institutional and Cultural Coherence

The argument thus far is largely economic. The case for an investment-led structural change, proexport bias trade regime in which the state plays a catalytic role can rest on economic grounds alone. But additional evidence for explaining dynamic growth comes from the broader historical, cultural, and institutional setting.

Often overlooked in the economic studies of East Asian dynamism is the question of national security. The four East Asian NICs are quite special countries in terms of their historical experience. Korea is a divided country, and Taiwan in a juridical sense is not recognized by the world system as the sovereign national representative of the people of China. When the two city-states are added to this grouping, it becomes clear that these countries are really quite unique in their historical experience as integrated nation-states.

The insecurity that is felt by the South Korean government in the face of its adversary to the north, the insecurity that the Taiwanese government feels in relation to mainland China, the tenuousness of the situation in Hong Kong, and the degree to which Singapore also has shown signs of insecurity through its highly controlled cultural policy indicate that these four countries seem to be characterized as perceiving national security as a palpable reality. The governments of the four East Asian NICs have been able to use threats to national security as means of imposing control and discipline over their societies.

In the four East Asian cases, this preoccupation for national security has translated into a capacity to develop a national economic strategy to generate sufficient economic strength to face these security concerns. The existence of a national security threat provided the government with the opportunity of galvanizing the society on behalf of a disciplined economic effort for the achievement of national survival. As a consequence, development strategies have had a different meaning and a different impact in these societies than they have had elsewhere. First, it is clear that the development strategy was more than the normal humdrum of national economic policy; it is elevated to the highest level of political priority and commitment. Second, it has meant that it was possible, given this high priority, to achieve a strong coherence across a wider range of policy instruments than has been possible in most other national economic circumstances. Third, it provided the government with more capacity to achieve a greater degree of implementation of the strategy than might be possible in less threatening circumstances. Fourth, it has provided a consistent, stable economic policy framework over time that other governments with more vulnerability to changes in political climate have been unable to achieve. This stable policy framework is particularly useful in providing a constant mark for private sector development and planning.

This means that these four governments were in a very different position than most other governments. They were able to marshall a broad set of policy instruments behind a single objective, to implement a strategy to provide long-term stability, to galvanize the society on behalf of national objectives and to drive the entire economy and the society toward development. The missing elements in other developing countries have been urgency, the sense of crisis, the felt need that survival was threatened and that national security was a real concern.

In these circumstances, the choice of an export-led growth strategy seems to be quite logical. The two city-states had been entrepôts for a long time; they are major ports and trading cities at the crossways of the world's sea-lanes. Establishing an export-led growth strategy in Singapore and Hong Kong cannot be seen as a strange deviation from national character, but rather as something intrinsic to the very nature of these economies. Taiwan launched an export-led growth strategy to achieve financial security through massive external reserve accumulation, and Korea did so to enhance national power through exports of manufactured goods. In these cases, governments turned to economics rather than to military power as the vehicle for enhancing national security and used the perceived national security threat as a means of mobilizing society and achieving an unusual degree of development discipline.

This suggests examining the alternative configurations between different elements in the process of policy formation that may underlie the capacity of a society to marshall resources in behalf of a dynamic development strategy (Bradford, 1989b). It is useful to distinguish four major elements that define the institutional context within which development strategies are forged. The four elements are first, the national political leadership, the president of the country, and the power base that surrounds his leadership; second, the bureaucracy or government administration and the civil service class that controls the administrative apparatus of government; third, the private sector economy and how it is organized and its relationship to the state; and fourth, the polity or public, the society itself, and how it is linked to the state institutionally through elections or not. A key factor in determining the degree to which a society is able to mobilize its economic resources toward a single set of economic objectives is the degree to which these four elements are either autonomous from each other or fused into one another as a whole. This applies to each of the four elements. We can think of several different configurations on a continuum from autonomy to a fusion of these four elements.

Industrial democracies seem to be characterized by an institutional context in which the leadership, the bureaucracy, the economy, and the polity are relatively independent of each other: elections in OECD countries change the leadership; continuity is provided by the civil service; the private sector is independent from the state; and the polity holds the government in check through elections that make the leadership accountable to the public. The autonomy of each of the four elements provides the dynamic interaction that generates a given economic and societal direction. In OECD countries, this is generally an orderly process from the point of view of the institutional rules and framework that exist, but is a messy process from the point of view of direction and continuity because of the number of actors involved in the process and the amount of power that each has, which reduces the degree to which any single actor or authority can predominate within a pluralistic system.

At the other end of the spectrum, we have a situation that was exemplified by a communist regime whereby the leadership in essence came from the bureaucracy; the communist party was the bureaucracy, was the state; it was a one-party state situation in which the leadership essentially emerged out of the bureaucracy and was of it and led it, but through a process in which there is no real distinction between the political leadership and the civil service. Property ownership, the economy, and the state were one. Finally, the polity had no autonomy and no capacity to hold the leadership or the bureaucracy accountable to public interests.

The East Asian NICs have been somewhere between the industrial democracies and the communist system on the spectrum defining the institutional context, but they have been rather more toward the side of fusion than autonomy. In Korea, Taiwan, and Singapore the polity has not really, until very recently, had much autonomous influence on the leadership. The leadership has been able to direct the bureaucracy and control it, and the economic groups in the countries have been in a consensus arrangement with the leadership. The dominant economic groups are not divergent in their directional thrust from the orientation of the political leadership. A crucial element that was manifested in the success stories of East Asia was the degree of coherence in the institutional setting among the political leadership, the government, the administrative apparatus, the private sector, and the passive public. Structurally, these constitute the underlying in-

Figure 10.2
Ideal-Type Ideologies

	INDIVIDUALISM		COMMUNITARIANISM
1.	Individualism>Society Self interest Atomistic Equality of opportunity Contractual Adversarial	1.	Community>Individual Group interest Organic Sense of place Consensus Cooperative
2.	Property rights Free enterprise system Free trade Deregulation Separation of "church" and state	2.	Rights and duties of membership Ordered competition Managed trade Regulation Partnership business/government

3.	Market competition to define
	  and meet consumer desires
	Interest group competition to
	  yield public interest
		3.	Community need defined by
			  community thru government
			Market competition to meet needs
			Public interest separate from
			  private interest

4.	Limited State Conflict Checks and balances Piecemeal (a little for each) Short-run Soft/bureaucratic Skeptical public	4.	Active State (Catalytic) Coordination Authoritative Priorities (trade-offs) Planning (long-run) Efficient/competent Confidence of public
5.	Specialization Fragmentation Separate disciplines	5.	Holism Interdependence Interrelatedness

Source: Lodge and Vogel (1987). Figure 1.1, p. 11, substantially further elaborated by the author,
  is based largely, though not exclusively, on the text, pp. 10–23.

stitutional conditions that permitted a decisive direction to take hold in a *sustained*
fashion once a national security threat was either posed or perceived.

This institutional setting is influenced by prevailing social thinking. George
Lodge and Ezra Vogel (1987) see two "ideal-type" ideologies in the contemporary world, individualism and communitarianism. These ideologies have five
components: (1) the relationship of person and community, (2) institutional
guarantees, (3) the appropriate means of controlling production, (4) the role of
the state, and (5) the prevailing perception of reality. Figure 10.2 elaborates
these two types of ideologies in relation to the five components, building on the
work of Lodge and Vogel. The interesting thing about arraying the components

in this way is the degree to which the different elements are opposites (Richardson, 1992). Lodge and Vogel found that "when ideology is coherent and adapted to the relevant context, the roles and relationship of government, business and labor appear more effective in reaching solutions adapted to their environment than when there is ideological conflict and ambivalence. . . . [and that] in general, those countries with coherent communitarian ideology have been able to best adapt to [the] international competitive system" (Lodge and Vogel, 1987, pp. 303, 305). In their ranking of countries according to ideological coherence, they have Japan, Korea, and Taiwan at the top of the list of the nine countries in their study. This ranking of "ideological strength" or "degree of ideological coherence and adaptability" is found to be highly correlated with growth in real gross national product (GNP) per capita, percentage point change in export share of world market, and the investment-GDP share from 1965–1984 (Lodge and Vogel, 1987, Table 2.1 p. 307).

Not only does the communitarian mode of thinking and social organization correlate well with the data we have been using to identify the NICs, but the concepts of communitarianism characteristic of East Asia are consistent with the strategy-led, structural change, catalytic state, export push elements that emerge from the analysis of economic elements as major determinants of the dynamism of the East Asian NICs. The primacy of the group over the individual; cooperation, coordination, and consensus over adversarial relations; individualism and conflict; an active collaborative state over a minimalist government; and integration and interaction over fragmentation and specialization add elements of explanation to the economic analysis of East Asian success. Even though not strictly economic, they are integral parts of the causal story and reinforce the explanatory power of the economic elements highlighted here. They help explain the high savings-GDP ratios, the disciplined work force, and the consistency and continuity in economic policymaking characteristic of the East Asian NICs.

With this broader understanding of the range of explanatory variables, we return to the more strictly economic literature to see to what extent recent theorizing about endogenous growth, knowledge accumulation, and technological innovation captures some of the newer explanatory elements and is consistent with the foregoing analyses.

GROWTH-LED EXPORTS OR EXPORT-LED GROWTH: RECENT THEORIES

In recent years, there has been some reexamination in economics of our understanding of the growth process. Several issues are taken up by this relatively new literature that relate to each other and, more important for our purposes here, affect our thinking about economic policies affecting growth. One issue is the relative weight of the quantitative accumulation of factor inputs versus the qualitative improvement in factor inputs. The importance of human capital vis-à-vis physical capital is one dimension of this issue. Another issue is the importance of technological change and how it should be treated analytically. Whether technology is exogenously or endogenously determined is a crucial distinction. Still another aspect is whether export growth is supply-determined or demand-driven. This is a question of whether cases of dynamic growth are cases of growth-led exports or export-led growth.

The recent literature on these issues sheds light on the fundamental difference in conceptual perspective by which development strategies are formulated. The difference is between whether the process of strategy formulation is one of structural reform of the national economy for internal competitiveness that results in dynamic growth and an increased supply of exports or whether it is one of trade policy reform for international competitiveness that allows the economy to respond to external demand.

Helpman (1988) put the problem very well: "We need a theory that can address fundamental questions, such as: Does growth drive trade or is there a reverse link from trade to growth? Many authors have emphasized the role of free trade in promoting growth (see Bhagwati, 1978; Krueger, 1978). Nevertheless, there also exist arguments that trade policy was central in the promotion of fast growth in Japan and some of the NICs. Current theory is not suitable to deal in a satisfactory way with these alternative views" (p. 6).

Conventional models with diminishing returns to capital led to the hypothesis of convergence among countries. The idea is that wage rates and capital-labor ratios would converge since the rate of return on investment and the rate of per capita output growth are decreasing functions of the level of per capita stock. Since we have witnessed in the 1980s a world of divergent economic performance, with East Asia in ascendance and Latin America and Africa experiencing a "lost decade," a reexamination seems appropriate.

In a frequently referenced article, Paul Romer (1986) began with the point that if the assumption in conventional models of constant returns to scale in production held, then, of course, the output growth would be completely accounted for by the quantitative growth in factor inputs. The growth accounting work of Kendrick (1979) found the rate of growth of output to be between 1.06 and 1.30 times the rate of growth of inputs in the period from 1929 to 1969. This is evidence that the rates of growth of human and nonhuman, tangible and intangible inputs were not sufficient to explain the growth of output (Romer, 1986, p. 1013).

This suggests to Romer the possibility of a new formulation involving three assumptions. First, knowledge is viewed as a capital good with an *increasing* marginal product. Capital stock is assumed to be a composite good where the knowledge component has increasing returns to scale that outweigh the decreasing returns of the physical capital stock component. Second, technological change becomes endogenously determined like any other input with a price and a marginal product that determine its economic role, rather than exogenously given as it is in most models. Third, the returns to new knowledge cannot be captured only by the firm generating it but constitute an externality that can be reaped by other economic agents. This creates a divergence between social and private return that must be addressed.

These assumptions make major differences in how the growth process is understood and activated. They have been taken as the basis for further work by others. For example, Jaime de Melo and Sherman Robinson (1990) have formulated three types of knowledge externalities that help explain the dynamism of the growth process associated with high export-GDP and import-GDP shares. These are trade promotion externalities, import externalities, and export externalities. Trade promotion externalities are provided by governments through information services, market development advice, assistance in design and packaging, and so on that can be appropriated by firms with ambitions to export. Import externalities result from the learning opportunities that are possible from importing capital goods and intermediate goods with embodied technologies. Export externalities accrue from meeting international market standards, product quality specifications, quality criteria, and distribution and marketing challenges that, once achieved, can be generalized to other products and processes.

De Melo and Robinson find that when their model included measures of these externalities rather than relying solely on factor accumulation and exogenous technical change, it improved the fit of export-GDP and import-GDP with patterns of structural change in output and trade in Korea and Taiwan.

These results and the theoretical ideas behind them lead to a different concept of the benefits of outward orientation and openness to the world economy. The benefits of trade derived from this line of work are the knowledge generation and spillover effects generated by export experience, importing embodied technologies, and trade promotion linkages. The knowledge generation effects of trade complement the already extant stock of knowledge from internal sources— education, previous economic growth, science and technological development, research and development (R & D) promotion, and so on. If knowledge is critical to growth, as Romer argues, the fact that much of the world's stock of knowledge is in industrial countries creates an imperative for openness to trade as means of capturing knowledge from abroad and internalizing it. Romer (1989) in another paper finds, using a regression of ninety countries, that openness as measured by the export-GDP share leads to increases in the rate of technological change and higher marginal productivity of capital whereas exogenous increases in savings and investment are less potent in affecting these variables.

The conceptual innovation here is something more than putting the "A" term for the residual in the production function inside the parenthesis of the production function itself. It makes explicit the endogeneity of the knowledge generation process, the dynamic effects to be realized from it due to increasing returns, and the public good quality of knowledge that means that firms and institutions will have to devise strategies to capture the externalities. The endogeneity of the knowledge absorption process through openness generates dynamic national economic growth, which then yields rapid growth in the supply of exports. This is not the same as demand-driven, export-led growth that results primarily from getting internal market conditions to reflect international prices. In the new formulation, the internalization of knowledge spurs dynamic growth of the domestic economy, which provides the surplus supply of exports. Alice Amsden's (1989) analysis of Korea's success emphasizes learning as the major force for dynamic growth.

These new theories of growth suggest seeking technologies for sectors in which dynamic competitive advantage is being developed, developing reinforcing advantages for those sectors (credit, access to imports, infrastructure, coordinated plans for interrelated sectors) so that externalities and increasing returns are both generated and reaped, and facilitating marketing abroad for exports so that learning by doing is both encouraged and generalized. These activities imply having a sectoral strategy and a technology policy to support it, deliberately creating synergy and interactions through coordination efforts, and trade promotion and selective intervention to create a proexport bias. These theories suggest lines of action that are consistent with the strategy-led sectoral transformation, export push theory of dynamic growth. (For empirical evidence of the externality effect of exports in the nonexport sector and of increasing returns to scale in the East Asian NICs, especially Korea, see Sengupta, 1991.)

Helpman (1988) concludes: "The extremely fast growth of exports in some of the NICs give the impression that international trade plays an important role in the process. It can nevertheless be argued that the comovement of output and exports stems from internal sources that bring output growth, which induces in turn export growth. . . . Causality is from growth to trade rather than the other way around" (pp. 15–16). (For empirical evidence of the export-led growth hypothesis being rejected for ten potential NICs, including South Korea and Taiwan, see Chakwin, 1992.)

Recent thinking emphasizes the role of increasing returns to scale and sectoral technology strategies, and positive incentives for export production internally and export promotion externally indicate a complex process of dynamic industrialization and growth as the source of rapid growth in the exports of manufactures.

THE IMPORTANCE OF TECHNOLOGICAL INNOVATION PROCESSES LEADS TO A SYSTEMIC APPROACH

The foregoing discussion illustrates the degree to which major explanatory variables of dynamic growth have, until very recently, been left out of serious economic analysis of the East Asian success stories. As Simon Teitel and Westphal point out, "The existing relationship between technological change and industrial development is a field in which *practical* efforts have left analytical understanding behind" (Teitel and Westphal, 1990, p. 9, my translation, emphasis added). Not only has the place of technology in the traditional production analysis now been redefined to endogenize it within the production function, but the definition of international competitiveness involving the incorporation of technological change as a driving force has changed dramatically in international discourse.

A recent OECD report on technology and the economy (known as the TEP study), which is based on the experience of industrial countries, concludes that "competitiveness is now based increasingly on other factors than the cost of labour and other inputs and is waged by firms through non-price as well as through price factors; sound macro-economic policies remain a condition of competitiveness but cost indicators such as relative labour unit costs can no longer be considered as reflecting competitiveness or capable of predicting trade performance; comparative advantage based on very general economy-wide factor endowments began to give way from the 1960s; the competitiveness of firms is not exclusively of their own making: it is also an expression of domestic institutional and macro-social environments; it has a structural component and is supported by a wide range of externalities" (OECD, 1992, p. 321).

These understandings have led to new definitions. Several new terms of art connote the conceptual changes. "Structural competitiveness" is defined to stress "the interactive nature of the innovation process, the systemic features of technology, the learning processes associated with innovation, the vital importance of human capital, the significance of organisational and institutional factors in innovation and, of course, the central role of firms in competition" (OECD, 1992, p. 309). "Constructive competitive advantage" suggests that "competitiveness now depends on the successful establishment of systemic foundations for capturing the cumulative, learning and dynamic-increasing features of technological advance [and on] dynamic growth efficiency [rather than static allocative efficiency, the foundations of which] rest on the cumulative and dynamic increasing returns associated in combination with technology and . . . interactive and organisational factors" (OECD, 1992 p. 333).

The experience of the dynamic Asian economies suggests that many of the same factors highlighted in the analysis of the OECD economies were also of importance in the East Asian experience.

There is a difference between the studies that focus on OECD countries and those that focus on developing countries. The latter tend, in general, to converge on the effects of government trade and industrial policies, almost invariably joining the debate over export-oriented versus import-substituting industrialisation strategies and neglecting other determinants of technological development. Studies on OECD countries, on the other hand, usually look at innovation efforts, the functioning of labour and capital markets, industry-university ties, education systems and so on. The result has been a *schism* between the two schools, with each benefiting little from, and often ignorant of, the other. This schism has resulted in *incomplete* analyses of the industrialisation process in developing countries. (Emmerij, in Lall, 1990, p. 9, emphasis added)

Sanjaya Lall has analyzed the building of industrial competitiveness in *developing* countries. He argues that *both* firm-level technological capability (FTC) and national technological capabilities (NTC) are required (Lall, 1990, pp. 20ff).

FTC consists of investment, production, and linkage capabilities in addition to entrepreneurial and managerial capabilities. There is a high premium on process innovation and networking in order to incorporate new ideas into the firms' operations. NTC embraces a variety of elements that Lall draws from the economics literature on growth accounting, education and training, technology, incentives, and institutions. From this he develops a "three pronged approach, involving the interplay of capabilities, incentives and institutions" (pp. 26–30). After surveying the experience of ten developing countries (the East Asian NICs, Malaysia, Thailand, Brazil, Mexico, and Kenya), Lall concludes that "it is not one set of policies that matters to the exclusion of others, but the complex *interaction* of incentives, endowments, institutions and technological effort; a framework which concentrates on the interaction of these critical variables provides a fairly satisfactory explanation of industrial performance; success has depended on how (countries) *combined* incentives ensuing from trade and industrial policies with an adequate base of human capital, investments in technological learning and innovation, and institutions to overcome market failures in the technological system" (p. 59).

The lessons he derives from the historical experiences of the ten developing countries are the following. Export orientation is important for building up NTC but not without other ingredients such as human capital development, R&D tightly linked to the production process, a technology strategy, and even protection for technological learning. Whereas he sees the market incentives and skilled manpower as being sufficient for early stages of industrialization, upgrading and diversification require a technology strategy for channeling, matching, and diffusing technology.

Other analysts of technological innovation in the East Asian NICs have come to similar conclusions. "Technology policy in Taiwan is slowly moving from a stage of sheer technology importation and diffusion to technology development and innovation. Since the 1980s, emphasis has been on a comprehensive program to *upgrade* indigenous technological capabilities through improved research and development, institution building, and manpower planning. These efforts have taken place within the framework of the National Science and Technology Program, which aims at *integrating* science and technology policies with economic development strategy. At the implementation level, this has meant increased national R&D expenditures, mostly by government" (Dahlman and Sananikone, 1990, p. 220). As David O'Connor points out, "Judging from the Asian NIE experience, the appropriate government role changes as a country moves through different stages in its industrial development, and it also depends on such factors as the prevalent industrial structure" (O'Connor, 1991, p. 2). This active role for government in R&D and technological innovation has been complemented by heavy investment in education, training, and human resource development.

In Korea and Taiwan there has been a deliberate strategy for technology incorporation that has been an important feature of the "catch-up" thrust of these countries. "In large measure, the success of Taiwan's science and technology development program can be attributed to the fact that it was formulated *within* the context of a well-defined industrial strategy. . . . Whenever it has intervened, the Taiwanese government has focused it policies particularly on greater value-added industries to enhance Taiwan's international competitiveness, as in the 1980s when it targeted development of 'strategic' industries" (Dahlman and Sananikone, 1990, pp. 220, 210). "While governments invested in human capital formation, infrastructure development, and other preconditions for a broader advance, they selectively promoted the development of 'strategic' technologies and industries" (O'Connor, 1991, p. 14). A positive, facilitative, flexible, and selective role for government appears to be an essential ingredient of the East Asian success stories and is increasingly seen as critical to their performance.

It is quite clear from this brief survey of recent research that FTC and NTC depend on each other and that great capability in one without the other is not effective. The crucial nexus is the interaction of enterprises; educational, training, and research institutions; technological development; absorption and diffusion, communications networks; national policies; market incentives; resource endowments; and innovation strategies at a variety of levels and dimensions. This approach identifies sources of dynamic development in the private sector, in nonprofit institutions, in public policy, and, most important, in their effective, multiplicative, and synergistic interactions. In a word, though Lall does not use it, the approach is *systemic*.[2]

The OECD TEP study, even though it is focused on industrial countries, also finds that this *holistic* or *systemic* characteristic is critical for an effective approach to competitiveness. In echos from Lodge and Vogel, the TEP study finds "the only meaningful approaches to the relationship between technology and competitiveness are holistic. This is why the studies which have broken new ground and/or stirred significant public debate are those which have adopted such an approach" (OECD, 1992 p. 318). The TEP study then goes on to cite the well-known book by Michael Porter on the competitive advantage of nations in which he sets out his own definition of NTC (for sectors), involving four characteristics: factor conditions, demand conditions, related and supporting industries, and firm strategy, structure, and rivalry. The interesting point about Porter's typology, which is brought out in the TEP study, is its systemic character. The *interaction* among the four components is the key element making it a mutually reinforcing system. "The effect of one determinant is contingent on the state of others. . . . Advantages in one determinant can also create or upgrade advantages in others." Because of this systemic, interactive quality, TEP finds that "the linkages, mechanisms, and factors which *relate* different determinants one to another are of key importance" (OECD, 1992, p. 320).

With few exceptions the discussion of competitiveness in developing countries has yet to fully absorb the insights generated in this discussion of technology in advanced industrial countries. This foregoing analysis seems to make clear that the dichotomous mode of debate does not serve us well if we are looking for policy relevance. Just in the economic realm alone, we need a wider lens, a less discipline-driven approach that can capture the full range of factors and variables that affect firm-level and national competitiveness. Institutional capacity, human resource development, and organizational innovation are as important in determining the capacity of a country to manage technological change and integrate it into economic activity as are market incentives, macropolicies, and openness to international trade. It is not just that we have tended to ignore these aspects of development in the economic literature until very recently but that there has also been a tendency to specialize in such subjects so that their relationship with the rest of the elements of the economy have been, by and large, missed. As we have seen, the interactive aspect is crucial, and hence it is not just that more attention is needed to these new elements as add-ons to our inventory of development lessons but that the new elements must be fully integrated into a broader framework.

STRANDS IN THOUGHT: FROM THE 1960s TO THE 1990s

In sum, the theoretical and analytical literature has gone through several phases in dealing with the East Asian cases of successful export growth. The first phase, based on the experience up to 1973, emphasized the importance of outward orientation in explaining success. Outward orientation was defined as trade liberalization and exchange rate reform to permit domestic prices to reflect international market prices. This defines the neutral trade regime where the incentives to import are equal to the incentives to export and reflects the neoclassical economic view. In the 1980s a second strand of thought, based on the experience of the East Asian NICs in the late 1970s through the mid-1980s, emphasized the positive role of government in pushing exports through setting priorities, mobilizing resources, and involving private sector exporters. This interpretation fit the strategy-led, structural change interpretation and reflected the strategic trade theory (Helpman and Krugman) and the business school literature on the subject (Scott and Lodge, Porter). In the late 1980s and early 1990s, the third strand of literature emphasized the role of technological innovation and human resource development in industrial upgrading and catch-up in the more recent East Asian experience and reflects the literature in the OECD and elsewhere on a holistic or systemic approach. Nevertheless, throughout the entire period, the policy debate tended to be dominated by the supposed dichotomy between inward-looking interventionist import substitution and open economy, market-oriented outward orientation.

The first strand was more focused on markets, the second on the interaction of the public and the private sector, and the third on the diffusion of technological innovation processes throughout the economy. In practice, actual economic evolution in East Asia has undoubtedly consisted of all three of these elements together, with the proportions shifting over time. In addition these elements have received different emphases in each of the four East Asian NICs. The progression in thinking through these three phases has been toward an increasingly inclusive frame of reference. The first phase focused almost exclusively on the trade and exchange rate regimes. The second phase or strand added macroeconomic and industrial policies. The third phase is something of a synthesis, which includes the other two but goes beyond them by both adding additional elements and postulating the interaction of the various elements as the essential ingredient.

In the course of the intellectual evolution, there has been considerable debate between the market orientation of the neoclassical approach and the dirigisme orientation of the strategic approach. The strategy-led, supply-push approach did not so much follow from the neoclassical approach, as it has been a dissent from the mainstream (Bradford, 1986; Wade, 1990, esp. pp. 14–22). By contrast, the rent-seeking literature tended to identify rent seeking with inward-looking import substitution policies and to equate any government intervention with price distortions that favored protectionist importers over outward-looking exporters. This tended to negate the potential positive effects of strategies and selective intervention that generate yields from the interaction of elements.

In retrospect, the anti-intervention bias in the literature on outward orientation meant that those elements now recognized by the systemic approach and by the business-school literature on organizational aspects were missed by the conventional wisdom. The failure to take seriously the possibility of positive government intervention and conceive of a third alternative of a proexport bias regime excluded major causal elements from the analysis, which, in light of a longer time perspective and recent theorizing, seem more salient.

As a consequence of this kind of debate, policymakers trying to choose effective policies were confronted with an intellectual, if not indeed seemingly ideological, dialectic in which they had to choose between conflicting paradigms. Throwing the difference between the stylized outward-oriented, open economy, trade liberalization approach and the stylized inward-looking, rent-seeking, interventionist approach into high relief has not been helpful to policymakers and private sector agents seeking pragmatic guidance. The dialectical nature of the debate forced more focus than necessary on trying to replicate the East Asian "miracles" by choosing the right paradigm rather than trying to draw selectively lessons from a rich variety of experiences from the four different country histories at different times and adapt them to the prevailing international conditions, the structure of the country concerned, and the existing capacities of both the private and the public sector.

The increased attention in the 1990s on technology and the broader systemic approach spawned promises to provide a more eclectic array of variables, elements, institutions, incentives, and options from which a given country can draw in designing a development strategy to apply to the economic situation it confronts. Catch-up countries are then less in posture of hoping to replicate the exceptional performance of the NICs by adopting a model that supposedly caused it than they are in a posture of improving their growth performance by taking what is most applicable, effective, and feasible from the broad menu of elements the NICs demonstrated are relevant to the enterprise of dynamic growth. This is a much more pragmatic exercise, which hopefully can lead to stronger policy results by a larger number of developing countries in the 1990s than in the 1980s, when the East Asian NICs' divergent growth performance seemed remote from the grasp of most other developing countries.

NOTES

The views expressed in this chapter are those of the author alone and do not represent those of the OECD or its member countries. The author has benefited from the comments by Enzo Grilli, Michael Klein, James Riedel, Robert Wade, and John Williamson. The usual caveat strongly applies. The statistical assistance of Vim Doussis is gratefully acknowledged.

1. Similar conclusions were reached using a different set of data on a slightly different grouping of countries in Colin Bradford (1987, pp. 181–92).

2. As Lall (1990) says, "The whole area of policy making is under-researched . . . the recent obsession with trade strategies may have diverted attention away from such concerns, in the quest of the Holy Grail of a simple policy panacea that meets all needs of all developing countries. No such panacea exists" (p. 65).

REFERENCES

Afxentiou, Panos C., and Serletis, Apostolos. 1991. "Exports and GNP Causality in the Industrial Countries, 1950–1985." *Kyklos* 44, Fasc. 2: 167–79.

Amsden, Alice H. 1989. *Asia's Next Giant: South Korea and Late Industrialization*. New York: Oxford University Press.

Arida, Persio, and Bacha, Edmar. 1984. "Balance of Payments: A Disequilibrium Analysis for Semi-Industrialized Economies." *Pesquisa e Planejamento Economico*, 14, no. 1 (April 1984): 1–58. In *International Trade, Investment Macro Policies and History: Essays in Memory of Carlos F. Díaz-Alejandro*, edited by P. Bardhan, A. Fishlow, and J. Behrman. Amsterdam: North-Holland, 85–108.

Barry, Nancy. 1990. "Comment on Elhanan Helpman's Paper, 'The Noncompetitive Theory of International Trade and Trade Policy' " at the first World Bank Annual Conference on Development Economics (April 27–28, 1989). In *Proceedings of the World Bank Annual Conference on Development Economics 1989*. Washington, D.C.: World Bank, 223–25.

Bhagwati, Jagdish. 1978. *The Anatomy and Consequences of Exchange Control Regimes*. Cambridge, Mass.: Ballinger.

———. 1986. "Rethinking Trade Strategy." In *Development Strategies Reconsidered*, edited by John P. Lewis and Valeriana Kallab. Washington, D.C.: U.S. Third World Policy Perspectives No. 5, Overseas Development Council.

———. 1988. "Export Promoting Trade Strategy: Issues and Evidence." *World Bank Research Observer*, World Bank, Washington, D.C., 27–57

———. 1989. *Protectionism*. Cambridge: MIT Press.

Bradford, Colin I., Jr. 1986. "East Asian Models: Myths and Lessons." In *Development Strategies Reconsidered*, edited by John P. Lewis and Valeriana Kallab. Washington, D.C.: Overseas Development Council.

————. 1987a. "NICs and the Next-Tier NICs as Transitional Economies." In *Trade and Structural Change in Pacific Asia,* edited by Colin I. Bradford, Jr., and William H. Branson. Chicago: University of Chicago Press.

————. 1987b. "Trade and Structural Change: NICs and Next-Tier NICs as Transitional Economies." *World Development,* 15, no. 3: 299–316.

————. 1989a. "The NICs in the World Economy: Toward an Open World Economy in the Mid-1990s." In *A Dual World Economy,* edited by W.L.M. Adriaansen and J.G. Waardenburg. Rotterdam: Centre for Development Planning, Erasmus University.

————. 1989b. "The Reform Process in Socialist Economies: Toward a Framework for the Comparison of Economic Policy Reforms in an Open World Economy." Washington, D.C.: World Bank.

————. 1990. "Policy Interventions and Markets: Development Strategy Typologies and Policy Options." In *Manufacturing Miracles: Paths of Industrialization in Latin America and East Asia,* edited by Gary Gereffi and Donald L. Wyman. Princeton, N.J.: Princeton University Press.

Bradford, Colin I., Jr., and Branson, William H. 1987. "Patterns of Trade and Structural Change." In *Trade and Structural Change in Pacific Asia,* edited by Colin I. Bradford, Jr., and William H. Branson. Chicago: University of Chicago Press.

Chakwin, Naomi. 1992. "Exports and Growth: An Empirical Investigation of Causality." Ph.D. diss., New School for Social Research, New York.

Chen, Edward K.Y. 1987. "Foreign Trade and Economic Growth in Hong Kong: Experience and Prospects." In *Trade and Structural Change in Pacific Asia,* edited by Colin I. Bradford, Jr., and William H. Branson. Chicago: University of Chicago Press.

Chen, Tain-jy, and Chi-ming, Hou. 1991. "The Political Economy of Tariff Policy in the Republic of China on Taiwan." *Industry of Free China* 76, no. 5.

Collins, Susan M. 1990. "Lessons for Development from the Experience in Asia: Lessons from Korean Economic Growth." *AER Papers and Proceedings,* 80, no. 2 (May).

Dahlman, Carl J., and Sananikone, Ousa. 1990. "Technology Strategy in the Economy of Taiwan: Exploiting Foreign Linkages and Investing in Local Capability." Mimeo. Washington, D.C.: World Bank.

Dornbusch, Rudiger, and Park, Yung Chul. 1987. "Korean Growth Policy." *Brookings Papers on Economic Activity* 2: 389–44. (See appendix, "The Main Stages of Recent Economic History," 439–44.)

Durand, Martine. 1986. "Method of Calculating Effective Exchange Rates and Indicators of Competitiveness." OECD Department of Economics and Statistics, Working Paper No. 29, February.

Emmerij, Louis. 1990. "Preface." In *Building Industrial Competitiveness in Developing Countries,* edited by Sanjaya Lall. Paris: OECD Development Centre Studies.

Fischer, Bernhard, and Reisen, Helmut. 1992. "Towards Capital Account Convertability." *Policy Brief No. 4.* Paris: OECD Development Centre.

Haggard, Stephan. 1990. *Pathways from the Periphery: The Politics of Growth in the Newly Industrializing Countries.* Ithaca: Cornell University Press.

Hartigan, John A. 1975. *Clustering Algorithms.* New York: Wiley.

Helpman, Elhanan. 1988. *Growth, Technological Progress and Trade.* Cambridge, Mass.: NBER.

Helpman, Elhanan, and Krugman, Paul R. 1989. *Trade Policy and Market Structure.* Cambridge: MIT Press.

Kang, Moonsoo. 1992. "Monetary Policy Implementation Under Financial Liberalization: The Case of Korea." Paper presented at OECD Development Centre Seminar on "Financial Opening: Development Country Policy Issues and Experiences," Paris 6–7 July 1992.

Keesing, Donald B. 1967. "Outward-Looking Policies and Economic Development." *Economic Journal* 77 (June).

Kendrick, J. 1979. "Productivity Trends and the Recent Slowdown." In *Contemporary Economic Problems,* edited by W. Fellner. Washington, D.C.: American Enterprise Institute.

Kim, Kwang Suk. 1991. "Trade and Industrialization Policies in Korea: An Overview." Paper prepared for WIDER Conference: Trade and Industrialization Reconsidered, Paris, 31 August–3 September.

Kravis, Irving B., Heston, Alan, and Summers, Robert. 1982. *World Product and Income: International Comparisons of Real Gross Product.* Baltimore: Johns Hopkins University Press.

Krueger, Anne O. 1978. *Foreign Trade Regimes and Economic Development: Liberalization Attempts and Consequences.* Cambridge, Mass.: Ballinger.

———. 1990. "Asian Trade and Growth Lessons." *AER Papers and Proceedings* 80, no. 2 (May).

Lal, Deepak. 1985. *The Poverty of "Development Economics."* Cambridge: Harvard University Press.

Lall, Sanjaya. 1990. *Building Industrial Competitiveness in Developing Countries.* Paris: OECD Development Centre Studies.

Lee, Chung H. 1992. "The Government, Financial System, and Large Private Enterprises in the Economic Development of South Korea." *World Development* 20, no. 2: 187–97.

Lim, Linda Y.C., and Fong Pang, Eng. 1991. *Foreign Direct Investment and Industrialisation in Malaysia, Singapore, Taiwan and Thailand.* Paris: OECD Development Centre Studies.

Lodge, George C., and Vogel, Ezra F., eds. 1987. *Ideology and National Competitiveness: An Analysis of Nine Countries.* Boston: Harvard Business School Press.

Luedde-Neurath, Richard. 1986. *Import Controls and Export-Oriented Development: A Reassessment of the South Korean Case.* Boulder, Colo.: Westview Press.

de Melo, Jaime, and Robinson, Sherman. 1990. *Productivity and Externalities: Models of Export-Led Growth.* Washington, D.C.: World Bank.

O'Connor, David. 1991. "Technology and Industrial Development in the Asian NIEs: Past Performance and Future Prospects." Paper presented at Conference on the Emerging Technological Trajectory in the Pacific Rim, by Fletcher School of Diplomacy, Tufts University, 4–6 October 1991, OECD Development Centre, Paris.

OECD. 1992. "Background Report Concluding the Technology/Economy Programme (TEP)." Report by the secretary-general, Paris, May 1991, published as *Technology and the Economy: The Key Relationships.* Paris: OECD.

Pack, Howard, and Westphal, Larry E. 1986. "Industrial Strategy and Technological Change: Theory Versus Reality." *Journal of Development Economics* 22: 87–128.

Park, Yung-Chul. 1990. "Development Lessons from Asia: The Role of Government in South Korea and Taiwan." *AER Papers and Proceedings* 80, no. 2 (May).

Porter, Michael E. 1990. *The Competitive Advantage of Nations.* New York: Free Press.

Richardson, Michael. 1992. "East Asia Spurns West's Cultural Model." *International Herald Tribune,* 13 July 1992, Paris.

Romer, Paul M. 1986. "Increasing Returns and Long-Run Growth." *Journal of Political Economy* 94, no. 5: 1002–37.

———. 1989. *What Determines the Rate of Growth and Technological Change?* Washington, D.C.: World Bank.

Salvatore, Dominick, and Hatcher, Thomas. 1991. "Inward Oriented and Outward Oriented Trade Strategies." *Journal of Development Studies* 27, no. 3 (April).

Scott, Bruce R., and Lodge, George C., eds. 1985. *U.S. Competitiveness in the World Economy.* Boston: Harvard Business School Press.

Sengupta, Jati K. 1991. "Rapid Growth in NICs in Asia: Tests of New Growth Theory for Korea." *Kyklos* 44, Fasc. 4: 561–79.

Srinivasan, T.N. 1990. "Comment on Elhanan Helpman's Paper, 'The Noncompetitive Theory of International Trade and Trade Policy.' " Paper presented at the first World Bank Annual Conference on Development Economics (27–28 April 1989). Published in *Proceedings of the World Bank Annual Conference on Development Economics 1989.* Washington, D.C.: World Bank, 217–21.

Teitel, Simon, and Westphal, Larry J., comps. 1990. *Cambio Tecnologico y Desarrollo Industrial.* Buenos Aires: Banco Interamericano de Desarrollo y Fondo de Cultura Economica.

United Nations Conference on Trade and Development (UNCTAD). 1990. *Handbook of International Trade and Development Statistics, 1990.* Geneva: United Nations.

United Nations Industrial Development Organization (UNIDO). (1985, 1991/92). *Industry and Development: Global Report 1985* and 1991/92, New York: United Nations.

Wade, Robert. 1990. *Governing the Market: Economic Theory and the Role of Government in East Asian Industrialization.* Princeton, N.J.: Princeton University Press.

Wong, John. 1989. "The ASEAN Model of Regional Cooperation." In *Lessons in Development: A Comparative Study of Asia and Latin America,* edited by Seiji Naya, Miguel Urrutia, Shelley Mark, and Alfredo Fuentes. San Francisco: International Center for Economic Growth, ICS Press.

World Bank. 1987, 1992. *World Development Report.* New York: Oxford University Press.

———. 1976, 1991. *World Tables.* Washington, D.C.: World Bank.

Wozencraft, George. 1987. "Classifying the Rise of the New Industrializing Countries in the Context of Differentiated Development Patterns in the Third World." Senior essay, Yale University.

11

INDIA: ECONOMIC POLICIES AND PERFORMANCE

Vinod Dubey

India achieved independence on 15 August 1947 and embarked soon after on the path of planned economic development. Independent India was a poor economy with low per capita income, with large parts of the population exposed to disease, malnutrition, and food insecurity. A famine in Bengal in 1943 had resulted in about 3 million deaths.[1] Indian leaders, having won political independence, now sought to achieve economic independence and prosperity. The slow development of the country's economy and persistent poverty were seen as a direct result of colonial government and its laissez-faire policies.[2] Therefore, an active role for the state in promoting economic development was a basic tenet for the country's leaders. Further, under the influence of Soviet experience, state planning was seen as the major instrument for rapid economic development. A National Planning Committee under Jawaharlal Nehru's chairmanship had been set up in 1938 by the Congress party and produced a plan enshrined in a series of reports in the early 1940s.[3]

Since the first Five-Year Plan, produced in 1951, India has implemented a series of seven Five-Year Plans and has embarked on an eighth. There was a brief plan holiday characterized by annual plans in 1966, 1967, and 1968. The plans have had four interrelated goals: "(a) a suitable increase in the national income so as to raise the levels of living in the country; (b) rapid industrialization with particular emphasis on the development of basic and heavy industries; (c) a large expansion of employment opportunities; and (d) a reduction of inequalities in income and wealth and more even distribution of economic power."[4] Increased self-reliance was also a basic objective, stated explicitly only in the Third Plan. The aim was to achieve greater self-sufficiency with regard to agriculture and "basic industries like steel, fuel and power and machine-building capacity so that the requirement of further industrialization can be met mainly from the country's own resources.''[5]

A number of other stated objectives essentially followed from the major ones; for example, the objectives of developing small industries and of balanced regional development may be considered instruments for increasing employment and reducing inequality. The relative weight given the various objectives has varied during different plans, but there has been an underlying continuity in the basic economic philosophy and development strategy during the last forty years.

These objectives were to be achieved within a democratic framework and without recourse to violence. The aim was a peaceful revolution. Nehru spoke of it as a "third way" that combined the best from other existing systems—the American, the Russian, and others. The third way, however, failed to provide India either with rapid growth and structural change or with rapid social progress.

THE DEVELOPMENT STRATEGY AND ITS EVOLUTION

The development strategy that was first articulated in the Second Plan and that has dominated government thinking and policy-making till a major reorientation was started in 1991 rested on the following premises, which were tenaciously adhered to in the face of mounting empirical evidence that a number of them were "either misguided or inadequate or unrealistic."[6]

1. The achievement of a high rate of economic growth required a major increase in capital accumulation (and embodied modern technology). Increased capital accumulation required an increase in domestic savings. To increase savings, the vicious circle of low incomes-low savings-low investment-slow growth needed to be broken through government action. The primary focus of attention for achieving growth was, therefore, on increasing savings and investment and only secondarily on the efficiency of their utilization and allocation.

2. A pessimistic assessment of the country's export prospects resulted in import substitution being regarded as the prime means for achieving self-reliance. Self-reliance was equated with self-sufficiency, and considerations of efficiency and relative costs were often neglected in import substitution investments. The guiding principle of policy was that India should produce whatever it needs.[7]

3. Industrialization was essential for achieving rapid growth of income and employment. This required an emphasis on the development of heavy and basic industry that would produce the machines and intermediate inputs required to sustain economic growth.[8] It was recognized that the development of capital-intensive heavy and basic industries would absorb a large part of available investible resources and, for a period of time, not add much to the production of consumer goods or to employment. Therefore, during the transition small-scale and cottage industries and agriculture were to be relied on to produce the required wage goods and provide employment with relatively little investment.

4. The private sector and the market were viewed with suspicion. Traditionally in India the businessman and the profit motive were looked down upon. In an agricultural

economy with periodic crop failures, profits were considered as based on scarcity and misery. But more directly relevant was the view that the market mechanism could not be relied on for industrialization because (1) it would channel savings into the most profitable industries, which were not necessarily those with the highest priority (such as heavy industry) and (2) it would lead to high income and consumption by the rich and thus retard the growth of savings. The market (and the private sector), therefore, needed to be regulated and controlled in depth by the state to ensure that it functioned in the social interest. At the same time violent expropriation was ruled out, and it was recognized that the private sector and the market, suitably regulated, had an important role to play.[9]

5. The public sector would play a leading role in the achievement of national objectives for a number of reasons. First, the stated political objective was to establish "a socialistic pattern of society where the principal means of production are under social ownership and control." The public sector had to be in control of the "commanding heights" of the economy to ensure that "major decisions regarding production distribution, consumption and investment [are] made by agencies informed by social purpose."[10] Second, the public sector had to develop the capital goods and basic industries required to "convert growing savings into additional real investment."[11] They could not be developed by the private sector because (1) their output had to be sold at low prices (i.e., low profits) and (2) they were capital-intensive and had a long gestation period so that the private sector would be either unwilling or unable to undertake these investments. Third, a large public sector would also generate and mobilize resources for supporting further increases in public investment.[12]

In short, India's development strategy gave a leading role to the state and the public sector and emphasized heavy and basic industry development to the relative neglect of traditional industries; it had a strong import substitution (almost autarkic) bias to the neglect of considerations of comparative advantage and international competitiveness; and it had an interventionist and regulatory character in order to give a social orientation to the activities of the private sector. The "third way," instead of combining the best from other systems, appeared to have combined the worst. The result was a system of "command capitalism" in contrast to the objective of "market socialism."[13]

The strategy was fully developed and implemented in the Second Plan (1956–1961). Investment as a proportion of gross domestic product (GDP) increased sharply; the share of the public sector in total investment was raised as was the share of public sector plan outlays going to industry. However, the implementation of the strategy soon ran into three sets of interrelated problems. First, the acceleration of investment resulted in a sharp increase in imports and severe balance-of-payments difficulties. Second, it also led to increased demand for wage goods and pressure on prices. This focused attention on the relative neglect of agriculture. Third, the relatively slow growth of employment resulting from the emphasis on capital-intensive basic industry brought up questions of equity and the share of the benefits of development going to the weaker sections of the population. The problems were intensified by a series of external shocks. Wars with China and Pakistan (1962 and 1965, respectively) resulted in a sharp increase in defense expenditure, forced cutbacks in investment, and exacerbated inflationary pressures. Two disastrous harvests followed the failure of monsoon rains in 1965 and 1967. The country was in the midst of a full-fledged crisis, and Raj (1965) commented on the "atmosphere of discontent and gloom in the country." Five-Year Plans were replaced by a series of Annual Plans (1966–1969). Intense internal debate accompanied by interaction with the major aid donors resulted in a change in the agricultural strategy and a start toward a more liberal industrial and trade policy. A devaluation of the rupee in 1966 was accompanied by moves to exempt a number of industries from industrial licensing and significant liberalization in import licensing policy.[14] While the change in agriculture development strategy was sustained, the beginnings in industry and trade were aborted fairly early, and the relatively pragmatic approach of the Nehru years was replaced by a more radical approach toward the private sector. The nationalization of major commercial banks (1969), of general insurance companies (1972), and of the coal mines (1973) and a more restrictive policy toward large industrial houses under the Prevention of Monopolies and Restrictive Trade Practices (PMRTP) (1971) are indicative of this radical trend. Efforts were also made to strengthen the focus on poverty amelioration. "Garibi Hatao" (remove poverty) became the slogan of Indira Gandhi in the 1971 election. The approach to the Fifth Plan (1974–1979) was based on a strategy of "redistribution with growth," but its redistribution objectives were shelved following a harvest failure in 1972 and the international oil crisis of 1973. Consequently a significant attack on poverty through direct measures such as rural employment programs had to wait till the Sixth Plan (1980–1985).[15] The decade of the 1980s, roughly coinciding with the Sixth and Seventh Plans, was a period of reappraisal of the existing system of industrial and trade policy and the performance of the public sector. A large number of official committees were established, and following their recommendations, gradual and halting efforts to change the system were started.[16] However, the basic tenets of the established strategy were not challenged, actions taken being restricted largely to marginal changes. A new chapter appears to have begun in July 1991, when for the first time the issues in trade and industry were faced squarely and fundamental reorientation of the development strategy was attempted. The system of detailed regulation, licensing, and control is being replaced by a more "market-friendly" approach. The role of the public sector is being redefined. Considerations of efficiency, competitiveness, and comparative advantage are overriding the mindless worship of import substitution. For the first time, the objective of self-reliance is being understood positively as implying a strong competitive and more open economy rather than a highly protected, sheltered, closed economy.[17]

THE INSTRUMENTS FOR IMPLEMENTATION

The development strategy was implemented through a system of Five-Year Plans that stated priorities and objectives as well as indicative investment levels and allocations for the economy. The process of plan formulation also included the approval of projects and programs to be implemented in the public sector. The actual commitment of funds to these projects and programs was made in Annual Plans, which were integrated with the annual budget. Plan objectives were to be achieved through a comprehensive system of control, licensing, and regulations, impinging on all sectors of the economy. This system was only imperfectly integrated with the plans but was decisive in the implementation of the strategy. The areas covered by the framework include (1) industrial policy; (2) trade policy; (3) fiscal policy; (4) monetary policy; and (5) price controls and subsidies.[18] The following discussion indicates the policy and regulatory framework as it existed up to July 1991, when a fundamental reorientation was initiated.

Industrial Policy

The main instrument of industrial policy was a comprehensive system of licensing. The Industrial Development and Regulation Act of 1951, which initiated industrial capacity licensing, classified industries into three groups: those closed to the private sector, those where state ownership would increase but private sector would be permitted, and those open to the private sector. Prior government approval was required to establish new capacity, expand existing capacity by more than 5 percent a year or 25 percent over five years, manufacture a new product or change the input mix in an existing plant, and relocate a plant. Small firms with assets below $2 million generally did not need licenses. The system was used mainly to guide investment into so-called priority industries in line with plan objectives on expansion of capacity, location, and so on, as well as to control the volume of investment in particular industries in order to avoid waste of capital. According to Jalan (1991), "The license is granted after taking into account domestic demand in the future, existing capacity, foreign exchange implications, and other factors considered relevant" (p. 82). It is noteworthy that costs and competitiveness do not figure in the list. The criteria used were discretionary and not transparent. The relative weight given to different considerations changed from case to case at the discretion of the licensing authority. Capacity licensing was buttressed by control of foreign investment. Under the Foreign Exchange Regulation Act (FERA) of 1973, firms with over 40 percent foreign equity were very tightly regulated. In addition, the Monopolies and Restrictive Trade Practices Act imposed special restrictions on large firms and business houses with a view to contain the concentration of economic power.[19] A technology licensing policy aimed at increasing self-reliance in the capital goods industries and the indigenous generation of new technology strictly regulated technology imports, joint ventures, the employment of foreign technicians, and the import of capital goods. A restrictive approach to technology licensing contributed to a growing technology gap in Indian industry (Lall, 1987).

In addition there are strict regulations on industrial exit policy to protect the interests of labor and conserve capital. The 1976 amendment to the Industrial Development Act of 1947 made layoff, retrenchment, and closure illegal except with the prior permission of the government, in all establishments employing 300 (later 100) or more workers. Other laws, complex procedures, and interpretations of the concept of "public support" also make the closure of nonviable units a forbidding and protracted process. As a result, the number of so-called sick enterprises has increased to 120,000 in 1985 and 221,000 in 1990.[20] The restrictive exit policy also had a significant negative effect on total employment in large-scale industry.[21]

Strong support is given to small-scale industries because they are believed to "provide immediate large scale employment; they offer a method of ensuring a more equitable distribution of the national income and they facilitate an effective mobilization of resources of capital and skill which might otherwise remain unutilized. Some of the problems that unplanned urbanization tends to create will be avoided."[22] Government support to cottage and small-scale industries includes financial incentives (such as tax exemptions, price preferences, and subsidies), the provisions of infrastructure, and extension and marketing services, as well as restrictions on production by large-scale industry. The number of products reserved exclusively for production in small enterprises increased from 128 in 1971 to 844 in 1981 and remains at around that level. A Statement on Industrial Policy in 1977 went even further to state, "It is the policy of the government that whatever can be produced by small and cottage industries must only be so produced." The policy has not produced the intended benefits and has led to waste of resources and hampered industrial development. A World Bank research project (Little, Mazumdar, and Page, 1987) found that, on the average, small enterprises are neither more efficient nor more labor-intensive than medium-size or large enterprises. A study by Goldar (1988) also concluded that in those industries in which small-scale units are efficient, there is little difference in capital–labor ratios between small and large industries. In other words "where [small units] have substantial advantage in employment generation they are relatively inefficient, and where they are efficient, they do not have much advantage in employment generation." The Narasimham Committee (Government of India, 1985a) stated that "the policy of reservation has adversely affected the efficiency of investment, increased the cost structure of production . . . and has not ensured maintenance of quality standards" (p. 7). The objective of greater dispersal of industries by encouraging small units has also not been achieved. Because of considerations related to infrastructure, market, and supply of input, the bulk of small industry is located in the urban areas in proximity to large-scale industry.

Government interventions to support small-scale industries also suffer from weaknesses of administration and leakage. They have encouraged large firms to set up small units to benefit from the incentives and have led businesses to fragment production. According to the second census report of registered small-scale industrial units, 38.5 percent of the 582,000 units covered were reported to be "sick," with outstanding dues of Rs.26 billion. The bulk of these are considered to be unviable units. Further, a large number of ghost units exist essentially to benefit from special concessions such as preferred access to scarce raw materials and cheap credit. The concessions essentially have encouraged entry in an area where "there may already be too many cooks in the kitchen."[23]

The Trade Regime

A very restrictive import regime[24] provided "tailor made protection to support inefficient investments which are ordained in the pursuit of other objectives."[25] Primary reliance was placed on nontariff barriers, including import licensing, import "canalization," the "actual user" policy, and phased manufacturing programs requiring progressively greater import substitution from individual producers. Consumer goods imports were banned. Capital goods imports were classified into those that were "restricted" and those on Open General License (OGL). OGL capital goods could be imported without license by actual users, provided industrial licensing requirements were met. "Restricted" goods and items not specifically mentioned in the OGL list were subject to an import license. Intermediate goods were classified into Banned, Restricted, Limited Permissible, and an OGL category. Effectively, only items listed in the OGL category could be imported without license by "actual" users. The system was administered in a discretionary, ad hoc manner on the basis of two criteria: (1) the principle of "essentiality" and (2) the principle of "indigenous nonavailability." Each request for an import license required a "sponsoring agency" certifying essentiality of the item to be imported and a "clearing" agency certifying indigenous nonavailability. If domestic production of an item existed, the license could not be processed. In short, the domestic producer was given unlimited protection.

"Canalized" imports, which accounted for about half of total imports in recent years, came through sixteen designated organizations, which were the sole importer for products such as oil and oil products, steel, nonferrous metals, fertilizer, newsprint, sugar, cement, and edible oils.

The "actual user" policy disallowed imports for resale by intermediaries. The policy effectively discriminated against the import of capital goods by small and medium-size firms because of the large transaction costs of small import orders.

Phased Manufacturing Programs (PMPs) were associated with the grant of industrial licenses for products that require import of intermediate inputs and components and reflected an agreement by the producer to progressively increase the indigenous content. This resulted in a separate set of quantitative import controls for PMP firms, overriding the prevailing import regime.

India also has a system of very high tariffs. The average level of nominal tariffs was about 118 percent in 1989–1990, and if countervailing excise duties on imports are included, 142 percent.[26] The administration of tariffs is complicated by a large number of general and ad hoc exemptions specific to firms and industries and frequent and sometimes short-lived changes of duties of individual items for no discernible reason. Tariff collection rates (tariff revenue as a pro-portion of the value of imports) are extremely high (average 55 percent during 1986–1990) and have been increasing (average 34 percent in 1980–1985). World Bank studies indicate that the rising trend does not reflect a shift from quantitative restrictions (QRs) to tariffs during the gradual "liberalization" of the 1980s. Collection rates are highest on imports in the restricted list (i.e., subject to QRs) and lowest on items in the OGL list. These collection rates are much higher than those prevailing in other developing countries (Indonesia 7 percent, Brazil 9 percent, Mexico 8 percent, and Pakistan 25 percent). The normal escalation of tariffs with the stage of processing is observed.[27] However, the escalation is much less than in other developing countries because of very high tariff rates on capital and intermediate goods. Effective protection rates are high but show large variations between firms and industries. World Bank studies of effective protection rates for sixteen product groups indicate EPRs ranging from −16 percent for aluminum products to 162 percent for synthetic fibers and resins.

Export licensing exists to restrict exports of agricultural and manufactured products, to keep domestic prices below world prices, and to implement "can-alization" of some exports, as well as to support domestic regulation and controls. However, export policy was basically promotional, and with few exceptions export licensing has not been a serious deterrent to exports. There was an elab-orate and complicated system of export promotion, essentially for manufactur-ers.[28] A number of programs facilitated the access of exporters to imported inputs. Till recently a system of special import licenses for exporters (known as re-plenishment [REP] and imprest licenses) allowed the exporter to import certain raw materials up to a specified percentage of the value of exports. There was also a drawback scheme that allows the refund of customs duties on imports and indirect taxes included in the cost of domestically purchased raw materials. A cash compensatory support scheme compensated the exporter, in principle, for other domestic taxes. Another, limited scheme provided for duty-free imports of raw materials. An advance licensing scheme, introduced in 1978, also allows the duty-free import of specific raw materials for secured export orders. Profits from exports are exempt from income taxes, and concessional export credit is also provided. Some domestic inputs are also available at subsidized rates for export production. Controls are imposed to prevent diversion of materials to nonapproved uses. In recent years there was some liberalization of capital goods imports for export-oriented industries. Tariffs on such imports were reduced, and the import of some domestically available capital goods was also permitted.

The trade regime provided very high protection to the domestic producers and created a strong bias in favor of sales in the domestic market relative to exports. The numerous export promotion incentives only partially offset the discrimination against exports. World Bank studies based on ICICI data for 1986–1987 show that exporting firms had an average profitability rate of 13.2 percent on domestic sales and −17 percent on exports sales (without incentives) and −0.2 percent with incentives. Export profitability showed wide variations among different products.

Other Interventions

Industrial location policies to promote balanced regional development have been important. Initially the emphasis was on developing infrastructure and locating public sector plants in the less-developed states. In the 1970s 246 districts were classified as backward, and financial incentives were provided to industries locating in them. However, the policy also has a strong restrictive element. For example, location of industries is banned in the municipal areas of all towns and cities as well as specific areas around the twenty largest cities.[29]

Price controls are maintained for over sixty commodities (including fertilizer, paper, sugar, drugs, petroleum products, and, until recently, steel) with the object of controlling inflation, subsidizing consumption, or providing concessions to selected groups.[30] Prices are set by the government on the recommendations of the Bureau of Industrial Costs and Prices (BICP) for most controlled commodities, though the recommendations are not always accepted. While prices are generally set on a cost plus basis, the approach varies from commodity to commodity.

Money and Finance

Monetary and financial institutions and policies have been an important instrument for meeting the government's objectives of resource mobilization and allocation. As characteristic of other parts of the economy, the methods used for this have been based on direct intervention and control, particularly after the nationalization of commercial banks in 1969.[31] The banks were given targets to open new branches, particularly in rural areas. Between 1969 and 1990, 51,000 branches were opened, of which two-thirds were in rural areas and four-fifths in rural and semiurban areas. This resulted in a large increase in the mobilization of deposits (from 13 percent of GDP in 1969 to 38 percent in 1991). More broadly there has been a large increase in the financial intermediation of savings. Financial savings of households constituted 30 percent of total household savings in 1971, and the proportion increased to nearly 48 percent in 1987. In addition to the increase of bank branches, positive real interest rates, fiscal incentives, and growth in the variety of financial instruments available to the public were factors in this growth.

The resources mobilized through the financial institutions are partly channeled to designated priority sectors, mainly agriculture and small-scale industry (including transport and self-employed). These sectors accounted for 14 percent of total bank credit in 1969; the proportion now stands at 40 percent. Credit targets are set for individual sectors, and performance is monitored. For example, the target (and share of credit) for agriculture is currently 18 percent—which compares with 5 percent in 1969. Within agriculture there is a subtarget for small and marginal farmers. Lending to the priority sectors is at concessional interest rates and has negative effects on the profits of the banks. Further, the approach has encouraged the banks to meet the set targets, without paying adequate attention to the riskiness of the borrowers. This has led to an inevitable weakening of the banks' portfolio. At least 20 percent of the portfolio in agriculture and small industry is considered to be "infected." The Narasimham Committee (Government of India, 1991) points out that part of "the increase in priority sector credit would be on account of accumulated interest arrears which is added to the outstanding credit amount."[32] In addition to priority sectors, banks have been forced to lend to specific industries and enterprises—for example, sick industries—to protect employment. Portfolio quality has also deteriorated because of political and administrative interference in credit decisions.[33]

A second set of "directives" on bank investments aims to channel the mobilized resources to the public sector. The cash reserve ratio (CRR) that the banks need to maintain with the Reserve Bank of India has been raised from its traditional level of 7 percent to 8 percent, currently to 15 percent. Banks are further required to maintain a statutory liquidity ratio (SLR) in government bonds and approved securities and treasury bills. Instead of being used as a prudential liquidity safeguard, the SLR has been used "as an instrument for diverting part of the household sector savings mobilized by the banking system to finance public sector investment."[34] These devices preempt more than half the resources mobilized by the banking system, much of it for low-efficiency public investment. The average return on these funds to the banking system is 9.2 percent as against its average cost of funds of 8.7 percent.[35]

The policy of preempting funds for the public sector and directing credit at concessional rates to designated priority sectors has resulted in weakening the financial health of the banking system and a crowding out of lending to the private sector, outside the priority sectors. This crowding out becomes even more emphatic during periods of monetary restriction because the thrust of the measures falls on the 30 percent of bank portfolio that represent nonpreempted and nondirected credit.

The public sector-dominated banking system suffers from problems that are characteristic of most of the public sector in India. There is a lack of operational flexibility and internal autonomy in the day-to-day working, which has led to a lack of motivation and professionalism in staff and management. The expansion of branches, the diversification of functions because of the social orientation of banking, inefficient operation, and management, poor quality of manpower, and overmanning have resulted in rising costs, poor service, and a deterioration in the quality of record keeping and internal follow-up and control. Many of the banks are seriously undercapitalized given the quality of the portfolio.[36]

The Narasimham Committee has recommended against privatization of the banks. However, it has proposed the elimination of restrictions on private and foreign banks to increase competition and improve the efficiency of the system. It has also suggested an eventual elimination of directed and subsidized credit and a reduction of the SLR to reduce the preemption of bank resources by the public sector. The government has yet to act on most of these recommendations.

Interest rates are determined by the Reserve Bank, which issues directives fixing minimum and maximum deposit rates and lending rates. Interest rates have been kept positive in real terms during the 1980s. This has helped in mobilization of household savings within the financial system. However, interest rates play little role in the allocation of resources that has been determined by government directives. Concessional interest rates prevail for the government and priority sectors and within them to small borrowers. The interest rate varies with the size of loans, with the smallest loans carrying the lowest interest—contrary to normal banking practice. Since 1988 the Reserve Bank has moved to a system of setting floor rates for lending. However, the interest rate structure continues to be complex, with rates varying from a low rate of 4 percent for DRI advances to a minimum lending rate of 20 percent for lending for commodities coming within selective credit control. Currently, about 1 percent of the loans are at the DRI rate, about 17 percent are at 11.5 percent, and 52 percent are above the 20 percent minimum lending rate. The average lending rate on outstanding bank credit is 16.8 percent as against the announced "minimum" rate of 20 percent. If account is taken of nonperforming assets, the banks receive an average of 14.3 percent on their lending.[37]

Public Finance

With the state playing a leading role in development there has been a large increase in the share of the national income mobilized and spent through the government budget. Total central and state government expenditures have increased from around 15 percent of GDP in 1960–1961 to about 30 percent during 1985–1990 (Table 11.1). Tax revenues have grown from about 6.5 percent of GDP in 1950 to 12.0 percent in 1970 and 19.4 percent in 1989. The bulk of the increase in revenue has come from indirect taxes (mainly excise, customs duties, and sales taxes), which account for 84 percent of total tax revenue today as compared with about 63 percent in 1950 (Table 11.2). The share of direct taxes in total revenue has declined, as they have remained more or less stagnant at around 2.4 percent of GDP. By contrast customs duties have increased from around 1.3 percent of GDP in 1970 to 4.6 percent in 1989, and central government excise duties from 4.4 to 5.6 percent of GDP during the same period. The level of taxation is fairly high by international standards; countries with a similar per capita income have an average tax ratio of 12–13 percent (Government of India, 1992b, p. 19).

Traditionally, government current expenditures have been less than current revenue, that is, government savings have been positive. However, starting from the late 1970s, there has been an explosion of current expenditures (mainly

Table 11.1

Government Revenue and Expenditure (Central and State Governments and Union Territories)

	1960-61	1965-70	1970-75	1975-80	1980-85	1985-90
	(———————————————in % of GDP———————————————)					
1. Revenue Receipts	10.7	13.3	14.5	17.6	18.0	19.7
Tax	8.3	10.6	12.0	14.6	15.2	16.2
Non-tax	2.3	2.7	2.4	2.7	2.6	2.7
External Grant	-	0.1	-	0.3	0.2	0.2
2. Revenue Expenditure	9.4	11.9	13.8	15.8	18.3	22.3
Interest	1.3	1.7	1.7	2.0	2.7	4.0
Defence	1.5	2.6	2.5	2.7	2.7	2.8
Subsidies	0.6	0.9	1.0	1.8	2.6	3.6
Food	0.1	0.1	0.1	0.5	0.4	0.6
Fertilizer	n.a.	n.a.	n.a.	0.2	0.5	0.7
3. Revenue Surplus	1.2	1.3	1.7	1.8	-0.3	-2.5
4. Capital Expenditure	6.0	6.0	5.1	6.9	7.5	7.0
5. Overall Deficit	-4.8	-4.7	-4.4	-5.2	-7.8	-9.6
6. Primary Deficit (excludes interest)	-3.5	-2.9	-2.6	-3.3	-5.3	-5.6

Source: Bagchi and Nayak (1990) as in I. Ahluwalia (1991).

Table 11.2

India's Tax Structure (Center, States, and Union Territories)

	1950–51	1960–61	1970–71	1980–81	1990–91
	(————————percentage of total tax revenue————————)				
Direct Taxes	36.79	29.77	21.23	16.47	15.96
Corporation Tax	6.28	8.12	7.80	6.61	6.09
Income Tax	21.37	12.49	9.95	7.59	6.80
Indirect Taxes	63.21	70.23	78.76	83.53	84.04
Customs	25.07	12.59	11.03	17.18	23.48
Union Exise	10.78	30.83	37.0	32.76	27.88
Sales Tax	9.29	12.14	16.55	20.25	20.10

Source: Acharya (1988, Table 14.10); World Bank (1988).

compensation to government employees, interest of public debt, and subsidies), which has outstripped the growth of current revenue, and government savings have turned negative in the 1980s.[38] Government savings declined from 2.9 percent of GDP in 1975 to 0.7 percent in 1980 and −4.1 percent in 1989.

The major issues in the area of public finance are, therefore, the following. First, the growth of current expenditures has to be controlled by reducing and rationalizing subsidies and restraining the growth of the government wage bill and employment and efforts to contain interest payments.[39] Second, the effectiveness of public expenditure should be increased. Acharya (1988) points to large "illicit leakages from public expenditure programs." Public investment decisions, for example, may favor new plants as against consolidation and expansion of existing plants because of the greater scope for "commissions" on large foreign contracts. Such distortions result in significant reduction in the effectiveness of public expenditure. There is also significant scope for changing intrasectoral allocation, for example, toward primary education from higher education. Third, the tax structure has to be rationalized, by increasing the reliance on direct taxes and reforming the existing set of distortionary indirect taxes. A beginning in this direction was made by the government's Long-Term Fiscal Policy in 1985, which initiated an effort to simplify and bring stability to the tax system. The system of excise taxes was reformed through the introduction of a modified value added tax system (Modvat), and emphasis was placed on lower, "reasonable" tax rates, better administration, and a stability in the tax system. However, the reform ran out of steam during elections and changes in government in 1989–1991. The growth of a flourishing "black" economy in reaction to the system of bureaucratic intervention and control and to the very high, even penal, rates of taxation imposed up to the late 1970s has resulted in a situation where "an assessee's tax liability has less to do with his ability to pay and more to do with his ability to evade."[40] It has also led to widespread corruption, which not only results in lower revenue for the government but also higher expenditures. Another effort started in 1991 with the establishment of a Committee for Tax Reform headed by R.J. Chelliah. Its recommendations have focused on simplifying the tax structure, reducing exemptions and differentiation of tax rates, broadening the tax base and reducing tax rates, and strengthening tax administration. Fourth, there are important issues of federal finance, relating to the fiscal relationship between the state government and the central government. The constitutional allocation of responsibilities between the two makes the state governments responsible for agriculture, power, and the social sectors. This has meant an imbalance between their expenditure needs and revenue resources. The states have been dependent on large transfers from the center to carry out their responsibilities. This has militated against fiscal discipline. The financial performance of state public sector enterprises is significantly worse than that of the central government. Sales taxes are the major source of tax revenue for state governments. This poses an important hurdle in moving to a VAT-based tax system. Fifth, cost recovery in the provision of economic and social

Table 11.3
Central Government Public Enterprises

	1980-81	1985-86	1989-90	1990-91
Number	163	211	233	236
Capital Employed (Rs. billion)	182.07	429.65	848.69	1017.97
Gross Profit before Interest and Tax (Rs. billion)	14.18	52.87	106.22	113.59
Net Profit after Interest and Tax (Rs. billion)	-2.03	11.72	37.89	23.68
As % of Capital	-1.1	2.7	4.5	2.3

Source: Economic Survey (1991–1992).

services has to be strengthened. Recent studies by Mundle and Rao (1991, 1992) estimate that if implicit subsidies are taken into account, the ratio of subsidies to GDP was above 15 percent in 1987–1988. Of these about 60 percent were for economic services, and the rest for social services. The average cost recovery rate for economic services in 1987–1988 was 41 percent, and for social services, about 4 percent. The lowest cost recovery ratio (1.3 percent) was for education. About 60 percent of the subsidy for education was for secondary and higher education. About 35 percent of the total subsidies take the form of budget support to the public sector enterprises.

The Public Sector

Rapid growth of the public sector was the chosen instrument of rapid industrial development and mobilizing resources for investment. By the Industrial Policy Resolution of 1956, the private sector was excluded from industries considered to be of basic and strategic importance and from public utilities. As a result there was a large expansion of the public sector in these areas. In 1951, there were 5 public sector enterprises (PSEs) of the central government with an investment of Rs290 million. In 1990, the number of PSEs had increased to 236, and the total capital employed was over Rs1000 billion (Table 11.3). The public sector today has a monopoly or near monopoly in the production of coal, lignite, crude petroleum, nonferrous metals, telephones, and teleprinters. It produces half the nitrogenous fertilizer, three-fourths of the steel, and a fourth of the aluminum.[41]

The public sector has been characterized by gross inefficiency and has failed to achieve many of the expected social and economic objectives. In particular, it has failed to generate the financial surpluses that were expected to support further increases in public investment. The net profit of central government PSEs implied a rate of return on capital employed of -1.1 percent in 1980–1981 but increased to 2.5 percent in 1984–1985 and 2.3 percent in 1990–1991.[42]

The increase in net profits reflects largely the growing profits of the enterprises in the petroleum sector. For example, in 1989–1990 of the total profit of PSEs of Rs37.8 billion, over three-quarters were generated by the petroleum PSEs. The improved performance of PSEs in generating resources indicates only that their performance has "changed from worse to bad," but it remains pretty bad.[43]

A study of three industries in which there were both public and private enterprises showed that the social profitability as measured by the ratio of value added to gross capital employed was roughly twice as high in the private sector units.[44]

Another study comparing the profitability of a sample of large-scale private enterprises with public sector units between 1973–1974 and 1987–1988 found an average gross rate of return on total capital of 10 percent for public enterprises and 23 percent for private firms.[45]

There are many reasons for the poor performance of public enterprises. First, there is a contradiction between the two perceived roles for the public sector—generating profits for public investment and providing an incentive to invest to the private sector by making capital goods and basic inputs available at low prices (i.e., low profits). Neither objective has been achieved because the public enterprises in basic and heavy industry are high-cost producers. Second, many of the enterprises "became the instruments for meeting short term or ad hoc demands such as producing mass consumption goods, stimulating growth in economically backward areas, or for using locally available raw materials" (Jalan, 1991, pp. 195–96). In a number of cases these considerations led to poor investment decisions—inappropriate location, inappropriate technology, an irrational product mix, and imposed marketing arrangements. Third, the operational inefficiency of many public enterprises in India is very low. Political interference in day-to-day management, lack of autonomy, frequent changes in management, and overmanning together with strong trade unions lead to low productivity and high costs.[46] Finally, in the interests of maintaining employment the government took over a number of "sick" units from the private sector and has run them at a loss. This has extended the public enterprise sector into a variety of consumer goods industries (e.g., textiles) that are far removed from the "commanding heights" role of the public sector. It has also led to high losses. In 1989–1990 the nationalized PSEs made a loss of Rs4.8 billion, or a loss of 27 percent on capital employed.

From the beginning of the 1980s there has been much discussion of the failures of the public sector. A committee under Arjun Sengupta recommended changes in the organizational structure (e.g., holding companies), greater autonomy to management, and the institution of Memoranda of Understanding—contracts that set out mutually agreed performance targets for each undertaking. However, relatively few substantive changes resulted, and the reform of the public sector has still to come.

WEAKNESSES OF THE SYSTEM AND EFFORTS AT REFORM

The system of regulation, control, and protection that prevails in India is one of the most complex and opaque systems anywhere. Bhagwati and Desai (1970) and, more recently, Mohan and Aggarwal (1990) have pointed to the wartime origins of the main instruments of control. Doubtless this explains the very strong restrictive, as distinct from promotional, stance of the framework.[47]

The following characteristics and shortcomings of the system have been pointed out by academic work and government studies. First, the system is based on discretionary administrative decisions on a case-by-case basis. The principles underlying the decisions are so general and ad hoc that any decision can be justified by reference to one principle or the other. Second, the regulatory regime is complex, and the procedures for implementation are extremely cumbersome, leading to long delays and waste. This effectively put small and new entrepreneurs at a disadvantage. Third, the system has militated against competition and promoted inefficiency "by creating innumerable barriers to entry." Firms "fortunate to have been licensed to invest and produce have pre-empted share of the market by virtue of administrative action rather than economic competitiveness" (Government of India, Narasimham Committee, 1985, pp. 20, 21). Fourth, the policy regime has led to a fragmentation of capacity and plants of less than optimal size in many industries as the expected market was distributed among various applicants for investment licenses in the interest of encouraging competition and regional dispersal of industry.[48] Fifth, it has resulted in a large growth of rent seeking and directly unproductive activities as well as pervasive bureaucratic and political corruption. It also led to a burgeoning underground or parallel economy. "By the late 1960s the accumulation of 'black money'—from tax evasion on unrecorded production, black market transactions in scarce commodities, illegal payments for licenses and permits, bribes to avoid the application of controls, and illegal exports of foreign exchange and other goods—had become so extensive that it constituted a parallel economy."[49] Sixth, the flourishing corruption and growing parallel economy have led to a gradual weakening of the rule of law. The violation of one or the other innumerable economic controls and regulations became a part of accepted behavior, and this social attitude has spread to erode the respect for the law in general. Finally, the system resulted in excessive centralization of economic decisions with the central government at the expense of the state and local governments and stifled local and regional initiative and responsibility, adding to inefficiency and waste of resources.[50]

The industrial licensing system failed to channel investments in "desired directions." For example, despite reservation and subsidies the share of unregistered small industry in total manufacturing output declined from 46.3 percent in 1950–1951 to 37.3 percent in 1983–1984.[51] Within registered manufacturing over the same period the share of small enterprises in total production declined from 33 to 22 percent, and in total employment, from 36 to 33 percent. The policy of reservation for small industry also often had unintended effects. For example, restriction on the production of cloth by the textile industry did not benefit the handloom industry as was expected but led to the development of a powerloom sector. Similarly, despite MRTP, the degree of concentration with the large business houses has not declined. Total sales of the twenty largest business houses that were equal to 61 percent of the net domestic product of the private organized sector in 1972 increased to 87 percent in 1981 (Bardhan, 1984, p. 105). The failure of the system to attain stated objectives was recognized very early, but relatively little was done to dismantle and change the fundamental orientation of the system till July 1991. As early as 1969 the Industrial Licensing Policy Committee (the Dutt Committee) concluded "that the system had failed practically on all counts, whether it was regional dispersal import substitution or preventing concentration of economic power."[52]

A process of tinkering with the industrial licensing system to increase flexibility and fine-tune it toward specific ends has gone on for the last twenty years, with some acceleration in the 1980s. However, the fundamental orientation did not change. Reviewing the piecemeal liberalization of the industrial licensing policy during 1970–1988, Paranjape concludes that "the government policy in this matter has tended to take the shape of chopping and changing instead of the pursuit of a well defined strategy . . . there has been a persistent tendency to make bold announcements of changes in policy but modifying them with a number of conditions and exceptions. . . . Government has persistently shown an inclination even while taking steps towards liberalization, of maintaining adequate discretionary powers so that the politicians and the bureaucrats can continue to operate like toll gate keepers, and grant and receive favors."[53]

Review of the gradual changes in the trade regime leads to a similar conclusion. The changes up to 1991 were essentially in the nature of marginal shifts, with the only change of some significance being the relaxation of controls on the import of capital goods for export-oriented industries such as leather garments and diamond processing. The growth in the number of items under OGL since 1978 has consisted essentially of goods not produced in India. Items were regularly moved off the OGL list to more restricted categories whenever domestic products were available. It is estimated that unrestricted imports directly competitive with domestic production were less than 5 percent of total nonpetroleum imports or less than 4 percent of total imports in 1988. A survey in 1986 of thirty-two firms in the engineering industry, which was considered to be suffering from import competition, indicated that with the exception of machine tool producers the firms were not facing competition from OGL imports.[54] Trends in the ratio of import and domestic price index for manufactures also indicate that the relative price of imports has increased sharply in the 1980s, mainly because of the increase in tariffs relative to domestic excise taxes.

The practice of making small, specific changes in the policy regime has introduced an element of instability as well as complexity.[55] It has increased the scope for manipulation and corruption—changes are tailored and fixed to benefit specific interests and industries. In the context of export incentives, Jalan (1991) refers to "pressure lobbies," which have developed to protect, preserve, and enhance specific incentives. "Incentive bargaining becomes a more important determinant of profitability than the expansion of exports" (p. 115).

At the same time studies of decontrol in specific industries show a favorable outcome of policy changes. For example, up to 1982 the cement sector was highly regulated; prices were controlled, and a part of output was sold to government at concessional prices; restrictive capacity licensing mainly directed at MRTP companies was practiced, and there was a policy of freight equalization to ensure uniform prices throughout the country. When these policies were changed, in 1982, both investment and production increased; prices also increased significantly in the initial years but then stabilized and are at present competitive with international prices.

The question has to be asked as to why the system of intervention and control persisted for such a long time despite ample evidence that it led to inefficiency, waste, and corruption. In other words, why was Indian development policy "wittingly foolish?"[56] The basic reason related to the creation of vested interests that benefited from the system and stood to lose with change. As Bhagwati has argued, "The Indian regime of controls spawned its own interests . . . [it] created a business class that wanted liberalization in the sense of less hassle, not genuine competition. The bureaucrats . . . [got] enormous power that the ability to confer rents generates . . . politicians became addicted to the use of licensing to generate illegal funds. The iron triangle of business, bureaucrats and politicians was born around the regime."[57] It needed a financial crisis in 1991 to initiate a fundamental reorientation of economic policy.

GROWTH AND STRUCTURAL CHANGE

India's economic performance since independence is at best a mixed one. Performance as compared with stated objectives is dismal. Rapid growth, rapid industrialization, self-reliance, and the elimination of poverty have not been achieved. Forty years after the start of planned development India still remains one of the poorest countries in the world. There was, however, a marked acceleration in the pace of economic growth from that prevailing before. In the twenty-year period, 1931–1951, net national income increased by a total of 35 percent. Nearly half of the total increase in national income derived from agriculture.[58] In the succeeding twenty years, 1951–1971, NNP increased by 120 percent, with agriculture contributing 33 percent of the increment. Between 1900 and 1950 per capita GDP is estimated to have declined by about 5 percent.

Table 11.4
Growth of GDP

	1950–51 1959–60	1960–61 1969–70	1970–71 1970–80	1980–81 1988–89
Primary	2.7	1.5	1.7	2.6
(Agriculture)	(2.9)	(1.2)	(1.9)	(2.9)
Secondary	6.0	5.5	4.7	7.4
(Manufacturing)	(6.1)	(4.7)	(4.9)	(8.0)
(Registered)	(7.2)	(5.6)	(4.8)	(9.7)
(Unregistered)	(5.1)	(3.7)	(5.0)	(5.6)
Services	4.1	4.4	4.6	6.2
(Public Admin. and Defense)	(5.2)	(7.6)	(4.9)	(8.1)
GDP at Factor Cost	3.7	3.3	3.4	5.2

Notes: Least squares trend growth rates of GDP in 1980–1981 prices.
Primary includes agriculture, forestry and fishing.
Secondary includes mining, manufacturing, electricity, gas, water, and construction.
Services include transport, storage and communication, trade and hotels, banking, finance and real estate, public administration and defense, and other services.

Between 1950 and 1987 the increase in per capita GDP was 84 percent, despite the rate of population growth being higher.[59]

Economic growth has, however, been below plan targets as well as below levels achieved by many other developing countries. The growth and structure of GDP since 1950 are presented in Tables 11.4 and 11.5. Between 1950 and 1983 India's GDP growth rate averaged 3.6 percent per year—significantly below the average growth at GDP in developing countries of 5.2 percent. It was also the lowest among thirteen countries in South and East Asia (Sundrum, 1987). However, the growth of GDP accelerated to an average of 5.2 percent a year over 1980–1989, at a time when many other developing countries were facing increasing economic difficulty. In the 1980s India was among the most rapidly growing developing countries.[60]

India's performance has also been poor in terms of raising living standards and eliminating poverty. India today has the largest single concentration of the absolute poor—between 25 percent and 34 percent of the global poor live in India, according to the World Bank and the UNDP estimates, respectively. While there has been progress in education, health, and the status of women, India is still behind many other developing countries in indicators of social development. In 1980, among forty-six developing countries India ranked twentieth in real per capita income, thirty-second in life expectancy, nineteenth in infant mortality,

Table 11.5
Structure of GDP at Factor Cost (1980–1981 Prices)

	1950	1960	1970	1980	1990
	(-------------------in percent--------------)				
Primary	55.8	50.9	44.5	38.1	31.6
(Agriculture)	(48.7)	(45.8)	(39.7)	(34.7)	(29.5)
Industry	14.5	20.0	23.6	25.9	28.7
(Manufacturing)	(11.4)	(13.9)	(16.1)	(17.8)	(20.6)
(Registered)	(5.4)	(7.3)	(9.4)	(10.1)	(12.5)
(Unregistered)	(6.0)	(6.6)	(6.7)	(7.7)	(8.1)
Services	29.7	29.1	31.9	36.0	39.6
(Public Admin. & Defence)	(2.3)	(2.6)	(3.8)	(4.7)	(5.6)
TOTAL	100	100	100	100	100

Source: Computed from *National Accounts Statistics.* See Notes to Table 11.4.

and twenty-third in literacy (Dasgupta, 1990). For a nation aiming to establish a socialistic pattern of society and become a model for other developing countries, this was poor performance indeed. The expectation of life at birth has increased from 32 years in 1951 to 58.6 years in 1991, but it is still below that of countries like China (70), Sri Lanka (71), Thailand (66), and Philippines (64). Over the same period, infant mortality has decreased from 146 to 91 per 1,000 live births, but it is still much higher than in countries like China (29), Sri Lanka (19), Thailand (27), and the Philippines (41) and the average for low-income countries (69) (World Bank, 1992). While the percentage of literacy has gone up from 16.6 percent in 1951 to 43 percent in 1991, the absolute number of illiterates has been increasing, and female illiteracy levels are still unacceptably high.[61] In 1981, 82 percent of the rural females aged fifteen and over were illiterate as compared with 53 percent of the males.

The poor performance in ameliorating poverty, ill health, and illiteracy is partly the result of slow economic growth. However, it also reflects the relatively low priority given to the attainment of social objectives during the last forty years. In this area the gap between the government rhetoric and action has been particularly wide. In a comparison of actual public sector outlays with planned outlays during 1951–1990 Mohan and Aggarwal (1990) find the greatest under-achievement consistently was in the social services, comprising health, education, housing, and human resource development.

Given the size of the country, there are large variations in growth and social welfare indicators among different states. Between 1960 and 1979 the growth rate of state domestic product varied from about 5.5 percent for Punjab and Haryana to around 2 percent for U.P., Madhya Pradesh, and Bihar. In 1991 Kerala and Tamil Nadu had the highest literacy rates (91 percent and 64 percent, respectively) and the slow growing states just mentioned had the lowest (ranging between 38 percent and 43 percent).

Exports and Imports

The export pessimism underlying India's development strategy has been self-fulfilling, and the pursuit of import substitution behind unlimited protection has also constrained imports. The share of merchandise imports and exports in GNP (around 5 and 8 percent, respectively) is one of the lowest in the world. However, instead of increased self-reliance this has led to increased vulnerability to external shocks and a more fragile balance of payments.

India's export growth has been slower than that of developing countries and slower than the growth of world trade. Indian exports as a percentage of world exports declined from 2.1 percent in 1951, 1.2 percent in 1961, 1.0 percent in 1965, and 0.6 percent in 1970 to only 0.45 percent in 1987.[62] During the 1950s total exports stagnated. While there was a sluggishness in the world market for a number of traditional exports, analysis indicates that the stagnation reflected domestic factors—export controls and duties and relatively slow growth in production in the face of increasing domestic demand.[63] In the 1960s export growth picked up, largely because of two factors: (1) a large increase in export to the East Bloc countries and (2) an adoption of export subsidization policies on a large scale (fiscal concessions and import entitlement schemes in 1965–1966 covered 80 percent of Indian export earnings). The success of the export subsidization schemes demonstrated conclusively "that export earnings could be increased by making exports profitable."[64] However, because of the inward orientation of the policy framework, the relatively poor export performance continued. Between 1960 and 1987 total exports in real terms grew at an average annual rate of 4.4 percent, with manufactured exports increasing at 5.2 percent. The growth rate has varied, with sharp spurts during 1974–1976 and again in 1985–1989 and a period of virtual stagnation during 1979–1983. Export growth appears to be broadly correlated with changes in the real exchange rate. It depreciated between 1975 and 1978, appreciated during 1978–1984, and declined steeply during 1985–1990. Growth in export subsidies and the simplification of procedures, together with emerging excess capacities in many industries, also had a significant impact on export growth in recent years.

There has been debate on the relative importance of external demand and domestic structural constraints as against the inward-oriented investment and trade policies to explain India's inadequate export performance. In the early 1960s Manmohan Singh had shown that Indian exports were constrained by supply factors and not by external demand. Bhagwati and Desai (1970) and Bhagwati and Srinivasan (1975) showed conclusively the negative impact of domestic industrial and trade policy on export performance.[65] However, according to Nayyar, economic policies essentially accentuated basic structural problems, arguing that "it is misleading to suggest . . . that the policy regime provides the main explanation for overall economic performance . . . the domestic factors which constrain India's exports are the costs of production, the pressure of domestic demand and the infrastructural or sectoral supply bottlenecks which coupled with non price factors such as quality have adversely affected the competitiveness of exports."[66] The structural constraints listed by Nayyar essentially originate in distortions created by economic policy. For example, the main reason Indian industry is weak on "nonprice" factors like marketing and quality control is that producing for a captive, highly protected market, it can earn high profits without paying attention to these factors. Otherwise one is implying that Indian businessmen are inferior to those in Korea, Malaysia, Indonesia, and Thailand, developing countries with much better export performance than India.

A specific example of policy-related poor export performance is textiles. Between 1973–1974 and 1985–1986 India's share of world exports of textiles and clothing declined from 4.5 to 3.8 percent, while that of China increased from 4.5 to 14.6 percent and of Korea from 7.7 to 13.6 percent. Other exporting countries like Pakistan, Hong Kong, and Thailand also increased their share, India being the only major developing country exporter to lose market share (Jalan, 1992). In a study of textile exports to nonquota markets, Rajaraman (1990) found that "the market share of India relative to that of China has responded in a predictable way to movements in relative competitiveness, as measured by published data on exchange rates and price indices."

There has been a relatively more rapid growth of manufactured goods exports (Table 11.6). Manufacturing goods accounted for 40 percent of the total exports during the First Plan. The proportion increased to over 60 percent in 1975 and 72 percent in 1990. The growth of manufactured exports accounted for almost all of the increase in total exports between 1980 and 1990. The largest part of the increase in exports came from nontraditional manufactures such as gems and jewelry (share in total increment, 29 percent), chemicals (18 percent), garments (15 percent), engineering goods (12 percent), and leather manufactures (8 percent).

Export growth has not kept up with imports. Exports as a percentage of imports averaged a little over 80 percent over 1970–1979, declined to around 60 percent during 1980–1984, and barely held their own (59 percent) during 1985–1990. The merchandise trade gap has been rising very rapidly in absolute terms—from an average of $1.4 billion during 1975–1979 to $8.0 billion in 1985–1989. The rising merchandise trade gap is related both to internal and external developments—the gradual moves toward liberalization in the 1980s combined with the expansionary stance of macropolicy and international price developments. There was a virtual explosion of imports during 1977–1980, when imports increased from $6.5 billion to nearly $16 billion (or by 145 percent in three years), partly because of the sharp rise in import unit values (stemming from the second oil shock) but also reflecting a sharp increase in volume. During 1980–1985 both export and imports stagnated (total import growth over the five years was 9 percent, and export growth, 17 percent). During 1985–1990 both exports and

Table 11.6
Merchandise Exports

	1975-76	1980-81	1985-86	1990-91	Increase 1980-81 to 1990-91
		←———— million US $ ————→			
Primary	1817	3400	3108	3740	340
Fish	146	270	334	535	265
Tea	274	539	512	599	60
Iron Ore	247	384	473	585	201
Other	1150	2207	1789	2021	-186
Manufactures	2855	5067	5684	14383	9316
Chemicals	99	298	406	1781	1483
Leather Manufactures	264	473	629	1423	950

Table 11.6 (continued)

	1975-76	1980-81	1985-86	1990-91	Increase 1980-81 to 1990-91
			⟨——million US $——⟩		⟨————⟩
Textiles	652	1292	1026	1705	413
Garments	235	717	872	2252	1535
Gems/Jewelry	150	783	1228	2903	2128
Engineering Goods	477	1010	780	1978	968
Petroleum Products	-	10	425	523	513
Other Manufactures	978	479	318	1819	1340
Total (Customs)	4672	8467	8792	18123	9656
Statistical Discrepancy	156	-135	669	362	498
Total (B.O.P.)	4828	8332	9461	18485	10153

Source: World Bank Data Bank.

imports increased rapidly, with the trade gap fluctuating between $7 billion to $9 billion annually. The bulk (75 percent) of imports consists of petroleum, raw materials, and intermediate goods, and the rest consists of capital goods (18 percent) and food and consumer goods (7 percent) (Table 11.7).

Savings and Investment

India has succeeded in raising the rate of gross investment from an average of about 10 percent of GDP during 1950–1954 to over 18 percent in 1970–1974 and nearly 24 percent in 1984–1988 (Table 11.8). Reflecting the leading role of the state in the development strategy, public investment, which accounted for about a quarter of total investment in 1950, increased to about 46 percent of the total in 1960–1964 and has ranged between 40 percent and 50 percent since then. The sectoral distribution of investment is shown in Table 11.9. The growth in investment was financed primarily by an increase in domestic savings, indicating a high degree of success in resource mobilization. India has one of the highest domestic savings rates among low-income developing countries, though its performance is dwarfed by that of China. Gross domestic savings, estimated at 10.4 percent of GDP in 1950, averaged 16.6 percent in 1970–1974 and 21 percent in 1987–1989. The marginal rate of saving has been around 20 percent since the 1950s, though it increased to 26 percent during the 1970s. The "stagnation" of savings in the economy in recent years essentially reflects the fact that the average savings rate has increased to about the same level as the marginal rate of savings.[67] The increase in domestic savings reflected a relatively rapid growth of household savings after the 1970s, offset by a mediocre performance by the corporate sector and a poor performance by the public sector (Table 11.10). About 83 percent of the total domestic savings in 1988–1989 was by households, the rest being about equally divided between the corporate and the public sector.

Public savings as a percentage of GDP peaked at 4.9 percent of GDP in 1976, when public savings accounted for nearly a quarter of domestic savings. In that year, about 50 percent of the public savings originated in government, 14 percent in departmental undertakings like railways, and the rest in public enterprises. Since then the trend has been for government savings to decline both absolutely and relatively to GDP and for those of public enterprises to increase both relatively and absolutely, while those of departmental enterprises have tended to decline in relative terms. The savings of government turned negative in 1984, and the growing surplus of public enterprises was insufficient to compensate for the decline.

Public sector investment has consistently exceeded public sector savings, the difference being met by the savings surplus of the private sector and the inflow of foreign funds. The investment savings gap of the public sector was 1 percent of GDP in 1950–1951. It increased to about 4.7 percent in the 1970s and about 7.5 percent in the 1980s. The reliance on foreign savings has been small relative

Table 11.7
Merchandise Imports

	1975-76	1980-81	1985-86	1990-91	Increase 1980-81 to 1990-91
			million US $		
Food	1568	1348	1321	713	-635
Other Consumer Goods	510/a	378	452	853	475
P.O.L. /b	1417	6669	4054	5726	-943
Capital Goods	1080	2307	3337	4292	1985

Intermediate Primary	n.a.	1277	2156	4184	2907
Intermediate Manufactures	1510	3920	4744	8285	4365
Total Imports (Commerce)	6085	15899	16064	24052	8153
Statistical Discrepancy	-602	-7	1231	3000	3007
Total Imports	5483	15892	17295	27052	11160

Source: World Bank Data Bank.

[a]Includes "other imports," some of which may be intermediate goods.
[b]Petroleum and oil-related imports.

Table 11.8
Gross Domestic Capital Formation

	Total		Public	Corporate	Household
	*Adjusted	Non-Adjusted			
	(------------------as % of GDP at market prices---------------)				
1950-51	10.2	10.5	2.8	2.3	6.0
1960-61	15.7	15.9	7.0	3.3	5.6
1970-71	16.6	17.1	6.5	2.4	8.2
1980-81	22.7	20.9	8.7	2.5	9.7
1981-82	22.6	25.0	10.5	5.7	8.8
1982-83	20.6	22.9	11.3	5.7	5.9
1983-84	20.0	20.7	9.8	3.4	7.6
1984-85	19.6	21.1	10.8	4.4	5.9
1985-86	22.1	24.0	11.1	5.5	7.4
1986-87	22.1	24.7	12.5	5.7	6.5
1987-88	22.4	22.7	10.4	3.6	8.6
1988-89	23.9	23.9	9.9	4.2	9.8

Source: *National Accounts Statistics* (1989, 1991).
*The figures are adjusted for errors and omissions.

to GDP—averaging about 1.08 percent of GDP during 1951–1975. The proportion increased to 1.7 percent in 1980–1981, 2.8 percent in 1985–1986, and 3.3 percent in 1988–1989, largely reflecting deteriorating public savings performance. Foreign savings have, however, been important in financing the public investment program and imports. Foreign savings were equal to about 25 percent of the public sector's savings investment gap during 1951–1975, about one-third in 1980–1981, and about three-fourths in 1985–1986. Foreign aid (which was practically identical with foreign savings till the mid-1970s) financed about a third of total imports in the mid-1960s and about one-sixth in the mid-1970s.[68]

The rapid rise in total investment did not result in a commensurate increase in the growth rate of GDP because of higher incremental capital output ratios, largely reflecting growing inefficiency and waste from the inward-oriented development strategy and the licensing and control system (Table 11.11). However, a number of alternative explanations for the trend were advanced in India. One argument was that the increase in ICORs was exaggerated because of the upward bias in investment data resulting from (1) relatively faster rise in the prices of capital goods and (2) relatively faster growth of investment in inventories. However, even when allowance is made for these factors, ICORs are still high.[69] A second argument was that rising ICORs merely resulted from a rapid increase in investment while output would follow with a lag. However, the rise in ICORs was greater in the 1960s, when investment growth was slow (3 percent per year)

Table 11.9

Sectoral Distribution of Gross Fixed Capital Formation

	1950-51 1959-60	1960-61 1969-70	1970-71 1979-80	1980-81 1989-90
	(———in % at constant 1980-81 prices———)			
Agriculture	20.81	17.75	18.68	13.52
Mining and Manufacturing	22.18	24.44	26.02	30.08
Electricity, Gas and Water	4.48	8.93	10.98	14.16
Construction	1.47	2.34	1.92	2.06
Transport, Storage & Communications	14.22	15.60	12.75	12.83
Real Estate	20.68	14.54	13.07	11.00
Other	16.16	16.40	16.58	16.35
TOTAL	100.00	100.00	100.00	100.00

Source: Calculated from *National Accounts Statistics* (1989, 1991).

Table 11.10
Gross Domestic Savings

	Total	Public		Corporate	Households	
		Govt.	Public /a Enterprises		Total	Financial
	(--------------as % of GDP at market prices------------)					
1950-51	10.4	1.7	0.1	1.0	7.7	1.7
1960-61	12.7	2.2	0.4	1.7	8.4	2.8
1970-71	15.7	1.3	1.6	1.5	11.3	3.2
1980-81	21.2	1.9	1.6	1.7	16.1	6.3
1981-82	21.0	2.4	2.2	1.6	14.9	6.0
1982-83	19.1	1.6	2.8	1.6	13.1	7.2
1983-84	18.8	0.5	2.8	1.5	14.0	6.4
1984-85	18.2	-0.1	2.9	1.7	13.7	7.7
1985-86	19.7	-0.2	3.5	2.0	14.5	7.1
1986-87	18.4	-0.8	3.7	1.7	13.9	7.9
1987-88	20.3	-1.6	3.8	1.7	16.5	7.8
1988-89	21.1	-2.2	4.1	2.1	17.1	7.3
1989-90 /b	21.7	1.8		2.1	17.8	9.2

Source: National Accounts Statistics (1989, 1991), *Economic Survey, 1991–92.*
aIncludes savings of departmental and nondepartmental public enterprises. For 1960–1961 and 1950–1951 the savings of departmental enterprises are included in government savings.
bQuick estimates.

than in the 1970s, when it was more rapid (6.8 percent per year). A third line of reasoning pointed out that the increase in ICORs was an international phenomenon, and in this respect India was no different from other countries.[70] However, this was not true of all developing countries and still did not tackle the issue why Indian ICORs were relatively high. A fourth explanation was that the rise in ICORs was the result of intersectoral shifts in investment toward sectors with relatively high ICORs.[71] However, Sundrum (1987) and Ahluwalia (1985) demonstrate that a large part of the rise in ICORs was due to the rise within individual sectors and only a part of it was due to shifts in the pattern of investment. It has also been pointed out that rising ICORs within sectors may not reflect deterioration in efficiency. Chakravarty (1987) argues that the ICOR has risen in agriculture because with the new technology, agriculture requires much more capital resources, and it has risen in energy because "of the quality of resources (such as high ash coal), or because easily exploitable reserves may be getting somewhat exhausted." The recent decline in sectoral ICORs raises questions about this explanation for rising sectoral ICORs. ICORS have declined sharply in all the sectors (except construction and trade and hotels) in the 1980s as compared with the 1970s. The decline in ICORs in the 1980s may be traced

Table 11.11
Incremental Capital Output Ratios

	1950–51 1959–60	1960–61 1969–70	1970–71 1979–80	1980–81 1988–89
Primary	2.0	4.7	5.4	3.5
(Agriculture)	(2.0)	(6.0)	(5.1)	(3.1)
Secondary	4.2	6.0	7.7	5.5
(Manufacturing)	(4.3)	(7.0)	(6.9)	(4.0)
(Electricity, Gas & Water)	(16.3)	(15.2)	(18.5)	(15.7)
(Construction)	(1.2)	(1.5)	(3.1)	(4.1)
Services	6.1	5.7	5.3	4.2
(Transport, Storage, Comm.)	(12.8)	(14.6)	(8.8)	(6.5)
(Banking, Finance, Real Estate)	(10.0)	(9.8)	(6.2)	(5.0)
Average	3.9	5.7	6.2	4.7

Source: Computed from *National Accounts Statistics.*
ICOR—Average real investment as a share of value-added of factor cost in 1980–1981 prices in
   each period divided by growth of gross value-added at factor cost over corresponding period.

partly to improvement in productivity in individual sectors. For example, there
has been a significant increase in the efficiency of thermal power generation with
the average plant load factor increasing from 44 percent to 55 percent during
1980 to 1988. Similarly, productivity in coal mining has increased at 6 percent
per year since 1985 with a shift from low productivity, labor-intensive underground mining to open cast mining. Technical ratios in the railways also show
improvement. A more pervasive and general reason for increasing efficiency is
the gradual effort to rationalize and liberalize the system in the 1980s and higher-
capacity utilization, reflecting expansionary macroeconomic policies.

Population and Employment

Population remains a major long-run development issue. In 1991 the density
of population per square kilometer was 267, and it was 515 per square kilometer
of arable land. With declining mortality rates and relatively slower decline in
birthrates the population growth rate increased from 1.3 percent per year in

Table 11.12
Population

	1951	1971	1981	1991
	(---------------in millions-------------)			
Total Population	361.1	548.2	683.3	843.9
Growth Rate	1.25	2.20	2.22	2.11
Crude Birth Rate	39.9	36.9	33.9	30.5
Crude Death Rate	27.4	14.9	12.5	10.2
Infant Mortality Rate	146	129	110	91
Expectation of Life	32.1	-	-	58.6
Percentage of Urban Population	17.3	19.9	23.3	25.7

Source: Population and growth rate from census data *CBR, CDR* and *IMR* for 1971 and later from *Sample Registration System* (SRS) data.

1941–1951 to 2.0 percent in 1951–1961, and 2.2 percent in both 1961–1971 and 1971–1981 (Table 11.12). The growth rate in 1981–1991 is slightly lower, at 2.1 percent. The crude death rate has declined from 15.0 per 1,000 population in the 1970s to 9.6 per 1,000 in the 1980s. At the same time the crude birthrate has also declined from 37.2 to 29.9 per 1,000. The slow but steady decline in the birthrate can be largely credited to increased literacy, urbanization, and income growth, together with the government family planning program started in 1966. The program promotes contraception (including sterilization) through health and family welfare centers and provides advice and support. Sterilization is the most widely practiced method of contraception. The percentage of eligible couples protected, according to official statistics, which err on the optimistic side, has increased from 10.4 percent in 1970–1971 to 32.1 percent in 1984–1985. However, sterilization may soon be reaching the point of diminishing returns because of the success in reaching relatively older couples interested in termination. The emphasis on sterilization has meant that a large fraction of the family planning program's potential target—younger couples—has been virtually ignored. Hence in future, more reliance on temporary methods may be required.

There are large variations in the progress of the demographic transition among different states, with Kerala having reached near replacement levels of population growth, and the largest state, U.P., lagging significantly behind the national average. Following the 1991 census the government seems to be focusing on an intensification of the family planning efforts in areas of high fertility. Ninety districts with fertility rates over 39 per 1,000 have been selected as areas for concentration. The critical factor influencing the decline in fertility in Kerala appears to have been female literacy. The rising level of female literacy and a strengthening of the effect of female literacy on fertility over time accounted for

Table 11.13
Employment in Organized Sector

	1960–61	1970–71	1980–81	1988–89*
	(----------------------'000----------------------)			
Public Sector	7050	10374	15484	18515
Private Sector	5040	6696	7395	7470
TOTAL	12090	17070	22879	25985

Source: Economic Survey, various issues.
*Provisional.

almost all the decline in child-women ratios in Kerala between 1961 and 1981. However, there is still a tendency in India to consider the population issue more in terms of poverty, unemployment, and lack of access to medical services rather than one of women's education. In Kerala, in spite of poverty and growing unemployment, massive decline in fertility occurred because of the impact of female education. The elimination of illiteracy and the spread of female education is clearly of the highest priority not only for improving the quality of life but for tackling the population problem.

With rapid population growth the total labor force has increased by about 1.5 percent per year during 1951–1981. The percentage of the labor force dependent on agriculture has changed little—from 72.4 percent in 1951 to 69 percent in 1981. Of the total absolute increase in the labor force of 79.3 million during the period, agriculture absorbed 49 million (62 percent). Some of the increase in labor force in agriculture reflects increased labor requirements from expansion of irrigation, changing cropping patterns, and technology, as well as growth of production. However, part of it undoubtedly results from the relatively slow growth of employment in modern nonagricultural activities.

The modern organized sector currently employs only about 26 million people or about 10 percent of the labor force. Of these about 70 percent are employed in the public sector (Table 11.13). Total employment in the organized sector increased by 8.9 million between 1970–1971 and 1988–1989. Growth in public sector employment accounted for more than 90 percent of this increase. Slow growth in employment in the private organized sector results mainly from the relatively high and rising real wages and the restrictive labor legislation, which makes dismissing workers very difficult and "provides strong incentives to create additional employment outside the organized sector."[72]

The record of modern industry in generating employment is very poor. Total employment in manufacturing in the organized sector increased from 3.4 million in 1960 to 6.05 million in 1980 and 6.24 million in 1988, representing annual growth rates of 2.9 percent and 0.4 percent, respectively. Of the 2.85 million jobs added during 1960–1988, 52 percent were in public sector industry. Employment in unorganized manufacturing increased faster, growing at about 5.5 percent per year in the 1980s in contrast with stagnating employment in the organized sector. The slow growth of employment in the organized sector reflects mainly (1) the emphasis on heavy and basic goods industries in the public sector; (2) the distortions in the labor market, such as regulations making it very difficult to dismiss workers; and (3) increasing real wages. Real wage rates in manufacturing have risen sharply in the 1980s (34 percent) after being stable in the second half of the 1970s and increasing by 60 percent between 1950 and 1976.

National Sample Survey (NSS) data confirm that the bulk of employment growth has occurred outside the organized sector, much of it as self-employment in household enterprises and professions. According to the NSS for 1987–1988, 56 percent of the total work force consisted of self-employed persons, about 30 percent of casual workers, and only 14 percent of regular salaried and wage labor. Of the self-employed, the bulk are in agriculture. However, the number of self-employed workers in nonagricultural activities also exceeded the number of regular employees, mainly because of the predominance of self-employment in rural nonagricultural activities. Rural nonfarm employment now accounts for over 20 percent of the jobs in rural areas (Table 11.14). Studies indicate that regions with higher growth of agricultural production and incomes tend to have a faster growth of rural nonagricultural employment. However, there is also empirical support for the hypothesis that rural nonfarm activities are absorbing residual workers who cannot find adequate work in agriculture.[73]

Total labor force is projected to grow by nearly 80 million during 1990–2000, making employment a key issue for the future. The major proportion of the additional labor force is likely to find work in self-employment and as casual workers, to an increasing extent in nonagricultural activities. There is some concern about the continued ability of agriculture to absorb a large share of the increment in the labor force. The increasing pressure of population on land as reflected in the increase in the number of operational holdings (from 71 million in 1970 to 98 million in 1985) and in the number of marginal holdings of less than one hectare (from 36 million to 57 million over the same period) indicates the declining potential of agriculture as a provider of employment. The growth in marginal holdings puts an upward pressure on the supply of wage labor in agriculture since they provide insufficient employment and income for the household. The reduction in the size of larger holdings implied by the increase in the number of holdings results in a fall in the demand for wage labor, since the household can meet more of the labor requirements of a smaller farm. Together these tendencies put a downward pressure on rural wages, which increased by only 0.4 percent per year in real terms during 1950 to 1980. According to NSS data, agriculture absorbed about 49 percent of the absolute increment in workers

Table 11.14

Structure of Employment: Distribution of Person Days per Day of Persons of Age Five and Above, by Current Daily Activity

	Rural*	Urban*	Total*
	(-----in percent-----)		
I. Working and Non-Working Persons in Labor Force	100.00	100.00	100.00
a. Working on own farm	48.71	6.46	39.50
b. Working in household, non-farm enterprise	10.10	30.29	14.46
c. Working as regular wage labor in farm	2.78	5.59	2.30
d. Working as regular wage labor in non-farm	5.57	40.47	13.02
e. Working as casual labor of which	24.55	13.14	22.10
Agriculture	19.73	2.74	16.04
Non-Agriculture	4.11	9.97	5.39
f. Working as bonded labor	0.39	0.13	0.34
g. Not working but seeking/available for work	7.94	9.52	8.28
II. Working and Non-Working Persons in Labor Force as Percent of Total Population	43.09	37.60	41.77

Source: Computed from *National Sample Survey*, 38th Round (1983).
*For period January–December 1983.

between 1972 and 1983. The proportion declined to less than 10 percent between 1983 and 1988.[74] However, the precipitous decline in the share of agriculture in providing incremental employment partly reflects the disastrous drought of 1987, and the proportion is likely to be higher in the future.[75]

Rural unemployment rates have been around 90 percent of the labor force since the early 1960s while urban unemployment rates, though higher than in the early 1960s, have hovered around 10 percent of the labor force. With growing population and fairly stable participation rates, the number of unemployed has, of course, grown significantly in absolute terms. The relatively stable and low levels of unemployment revealed by NSS data on employment apparently contradict the much higher poverty ratios prevalent in urban and rural areas. The reason for the apparent anomaly between the unemployment and the poverty statistics is that the absolute poor have to work in order to survive and accept any work at pittance wages. As Papanek (1988) writes, "The poor simply cannot afford to remain unemployed. . . . That explains the very low rates of open unemployment recorded in surveys." Many of the unemployed belong to classes with assets and income to survive without working for a period of time.

Agriculture

At the time of independence and for the subsequent two decades, India had to more or less regularly import food grains to meet domestic requirements. Self-sufficiency in food grains in a normal crop year was attained in the 1970s. However, with growing population and little change in the proportion of population dependent on agriculture the per capita net domestic product in agriculture hardly changed between 1950 and 1980, increasing slowly thereafter.[76]

Development strategy in agriculture has evolved in two phases. During the first period, till the end of the 1960s, the policy consisted of "progress through democratic planning," with reliance mainly on institutional changes such as land reforms, cooperation, and community development to promote both social and economic development in the rural areas. At the same time there was a large increase in investment in irrigation. Land reform legislation aimed at the abolition of the "Zamindari System" (intermediary tenures), reforms of tenancy to provide security of tenure, the imposition of land ceilings and redistribution of surplus land to the poor, and land consolidation. Other than the abolition of intermediary tenures, these reforms were only imperfectly implemented.[77] The major beneficiaries were the large tenants who formed the basis of a new class of "bullock capitalists," who play an important role in the political economy of Indian development. Second, a community development program was started in 1952 to provide "a multipurpose extension apparatus for coordinating government action on all problems associated with low agriculture productivity."[78] They were to focus on all "social" factors associated with low productivity (e.g., basic education, credit and rural industries) and emphasized cooperation and self-help with the aim of "reconstructing" the village as the primary unit of economic and political action. Third, there was strong support for cooperative management of land and other resources. Cooperative farms were to be set up on the surplus land provided through ceiling legislation. In the period of transition to cooperative joint farming, universal coverage by service cooperatives was the aim. Cooperative joint farming was never implemented because of opposition within the Congress party, mainly from the landlords and the larger peasants. Very little land was also made available by the ceiling legislation.

During the 1960s there was a gradual shift from the community approach to a new agricultural policy of "progress through profit."[79] The earlier approach of developing agriculture with the mobilization of local resources and traditional inputs was replaced by a concept of a more capital-intensive agriculture using modern inputs focused on selected crops and areas. With the foreign exchange crisis during the Second Plan there was an urgent need to reduce imports and raise domestic production of agricultural goods. In 1959 a report on "India's food crisis and steps to deal with it" by a Ford Foundation team echoed thinking in the Food and Agriculture Ministry of giving priority to technology and scientific practices over institutional change to secure rapid increase in production. The approach was based on (1) "package programs" of improved practices and services and modern inputs in selected districts with assured water supplies and irrigation, that is, with the largest potential for rapid increase in production; (2) focus on the "economically progressive" farmers instead of the village as a unit; and (3) price incentives to farmers to encourage private investment in modern inputs. The approach of "selection and concentration" initially adopted for one district in each state was extended to another 100 in 1964–1965. The existing community development apparatus was now focused on production growth rather than the social transformation of the villages. The change in policy and the successful introduction of HYV seeds in the latter part of the 1960s led to the "green revolution," which allowed India to become self-sufficient in food grains in normal years.

Growth of agriculture GDP has been moderate (2.6 percent annually over 1950–1988) and scarcely faster than population. Growth has been significantly below plan targets, and the rate of growth after the green revolution has been almost the same as in the preceding years.[80] Growth has also been very uneven across regions and subject to wide fluctuations from year to year. Increasing yields have been the most important source of growth of production over the period as a whole. However, during 1950–1964 expansion of cropped areas contributed just over half of the growth in production. After 1965 area expansion accounted for less than one-fifth of the growth. Growth of production has been concentrated in a small number of food crops—rice, wheat, sugarcane, and rape seed/mustard. For the best performing crops, for example, rice and wheat, area increases were an important factor in growth as cropping patterns shifted in response to incentives and technologies.

The increase of production, particularly since the green revolution, has relied on increased use of HYV seeds, fertilizer, and water. The new technology, dependent, as it is, on irrigation, has not substantially affected rain-fed agriculture. The share of gross cropped area under irrigation did not increase between 1960 and 1970 (17 and 18 percent, respectively) but was 23 percent in 1980 and nearly 31 percent in 1989. However, as Vaidyanathan (1991) points out, there has been excessive concern with expanding the area under irrigation and neglect of the quality of irrigation. The problem relates primarily to the way irrigation facilities are managed. Fertilizer use increased from less than two kilograms per hectare of cropped area in 1960 to fourteen kilograms, thirty kilograms, and sixty-two kilograms in 1970, 1980, and 1988, respectively. HYVs covered 9 percent of the cropped area in 1970, 25 percent in 1980, and 31 percent in 1989. Total factor productivity analysis indicates important contribution to growth of irrigation, HYV seeds, and research and extension. It is estimated that in the case of food grains between one-fourth and one-fifth of the increase in output reflects an increase in the productivity (as distinct from the amount) of inputs. There has been some concern that the engine of growth—increased yields—is slowing down because of (1) increased coverage by HYV seeds and other modern inputs among both crops and geographical regions; (2) the slowing down of yield increases in the older green revolution areas like the Punjab and

Haryana; and (3) slowing down of irrigation expansion because the easily irrigated land has been developed. However, the concern may be a bit premature. First, there are still large areas, particularly in the center and the east, that have yet to adopt the current technology. Second, there has been excessive emphasis on a few key crops, mainly for irrigated regions. The new technology has not significantly affected rain-fed agriculture. The current need is to broaden the focus to cover rain-fed agriculture and a diversification of crops. A beginning in these directions is evident in the past few years. Third, there is significant room for the reform of existing government pricing, subsidy, and credit policies. Fourth and perhaps most important, it is necessary to break out of the self-sufficiency syndrome in agriculture and pay greater attention to comparative advantage and trade opportunities in agricultural products. World Bank studies of effective protection indicate that the crop-weighted effective protection for agriculture in the mid-1980s was −13 percent as compared with an average of 40 percent for industry. There were large variations, with items like groundnut and sugarcane receiving high protection and rice, cotton, and wheat receiving relatively large negative protection.

The government operates an extensive procurement and price support program covering about twenty commodities, of which wheat, rice, sugar, and cotton are the most important. The objectives are self-sufficiency in key crops, providing remunerative prices to farmers, safeguarding against famine, and stabilizing consumer prices. A wide range of instruments is used—support prices, monopoly procurement, compulsory levies, buffer stocks, restrictions on crop movement, and controls on imports and exports. The government also operates a public distribution system, which operates through a system of fair price shops and accounts for 13.5 percent of the market distribution of food grains. Subsidization of this program amounted to about $1.3 billion in 1989. The Food Corporation of India (FCI) is the main central government institution for procurement and distribution.

There has been a growing reliance on input subsidies, mainly for fertilizer, irrigation, electricity, and credit. These subsidies totaled about $6 billion in 1989. Over 40 percent of this was accounted for by fertilizer subsidies, a quarter by irrigation, and the rest by subsidized power. In addition credit on concessional terms is provided by financial institutions. This, together with unacceptable default rates (as high as 40 percent to 50 percent of all agricultural loans), results in an additional, large extra-budgetary subsidy. Much of the input subsidies go to the large farmers in the most prosperous states. A significant part of the fertilizer subsidy goes to inefficient fertilizer producers in the public and private sector. The irrigation subsidy reflects an increase in the operation and maintenance (O&M) expenditures, together with declining water charges collection. Revenues as a percentage of recurrent expenditures for irrigation declined from 22 percent in 1980 to 7.5 percent in 1988. The increase in O&M expenditures represents mainly increase in staff costs and does not represent improvement in the management of national assets.

The system of prices and subsidies played a positive role in the early years of the green revolution in encouraging the use of modern inputs, and the public distribution system, together with other efforts, has prevented famines even in disastrous rainfall years (e.g., 1987). However, the system's impact on costs, incentives, and market structure and its budgetary cost suggest a need for overhaul.[81] For example, the original rationale for the fertilizer subsidy—encouraging use of a modern input—no longer applies. Analysis by the NCAER shows that fertilizer use varies mainly with the percentage of irrigated area and HYV area and not so much with prices. This confirms that there is no need for a fertilizer subsidy to encourage demand for fertilizers.

The recent trend of an absolute decline in total investment in agriculture (a decline of 1.8 percent per year in the 1980s) is a matter for concern. The decline appears to result from (1) decline in public investments; (2) declining cost recovery in sectors like irrigation and power exacerbating the resource crunch in the public sector; and (3) a decline in private investment partly because of the decline in public investments (with which private investments are complementary) but mainly because of a diversion of resources into investment outside agriculture. The persistence of this decline would endanger future agricultural growth.

Industry

India today has a "sophisticated and diversified" industrial sector.[82] However, the share of manufacturing in GDP is less than in other industrializing countries. Further, in 1989 total value added in manufacturing is only about one-third of that of Brazil or China and about two-thirds of that of Korea.[83] India produces a large variety of industrial goods and exhibits a high degree of self-sufficiency in manufactured products. Imports account for only 5–10 percent of total domestic consumption of manufactures, varying from zero in the case of textiles to 25 percent in nonelectrical machinery.[84] The obverse of the high degree of self-sufficiency is a low export orientation. Manufactured exports have increased faster than total exports but are still low relative to production and to other industrializing countries. Only about 12 percent of manufacturing production was exported in 1978, and the proportion had declined to 7 percent in 1985.[85] The import intensity of industrial production was 10.6 percent in 1973–1974, 15.7 percent in 1981–1982, and 11.7 percent in 1987–1988 (Jalan, 1992, p. 192).

There has been a significant change in the structure of industrial production, with the share of consumer goods in value added declining from nearly 50 percent in 1951 to about 20 percent in 1990, that of capital goods increasing from 4 to 24 percent, and that of basic goods increasing from 20 percent to about 40 percent.

The average growth of value added in registered manufacturing industry declined from 7.6 percent during 1959–1965 to 5.5 percent in 1966–1979 and accelerated to 7.2 percent in 1980–1990. The three periods were marked by different trends in factor productivity. The relatively rapid growth in the first half of the 1960s was associated with high rates of increase in capital and labor and poor growth in productivity. The period of relative stagnation (1966–1979) was marked by slow increase in capital but relatively favorable growth in labor and stagnant and declining productivity. In contrast to both these periods, the 1980s have been characterized by only a modest growth in capital and stagnating employment, but significant growth in productivity (measured either by total factor productivity or partial capital and labor productivity) (Ahluwalia, 1991).

The acceleration of industrial growth and productivity in the 1980s is the result of three factors. First, the gradual reform of industrial licensing and trade policies such as simplification of procedures, reduction of barriers to entry and expansion of capacity, and easier access to imported capital goods and technology; more flexibility regarding the products that can be produced from installed capacity; and reduction of restrictions on large business houses had a favorable effect on growth. Studies of specific industries, for example, cement and textiles, confirm that changes in government regulatory policies provided a significant stimulus to investment and production. Second, there were an increase in public investment in infrastructure (its share in total public investment increased from 34 percent in 1965–1979 to around 45 percent in 1980–1989) and also an improvement in the technical ratios of efficiency in transport and power. The reduction in infrastructural bottlenecks eliminated an important constraint on industrial production. Third, the high and relatively stable levels of public investment and the much more expansionary fiscal stance in the 1980s contributed by raising demand for industrial products. With "resurgent demand conditions, the reorientation of the policy framework and the toning up at the infrastructure sectors enabled a supply response to the rising demands through productivity improvements."[86]

There has been a tendency to denigrate the acceleration of industrial growth in the 1980s by referring to it as "consumption-led" growth in contrast to the "investment-led" growth in the 1960s.[87] However, while the growth rate of consumption goods industries has accelerated and, within it, consumer durables have been the fastest-growing segment, (1) the growth rate of consumer nondurables industries is only about the same as the average rate of growth of total manufacturing; (2) the consumer durables segment was the fastest-growing sector even during the period of "investment-led" growth; and (3) the share of consumer durables in total production is less than 4 percent and in employment around 3 percent. Its contribution to the acceleration of output and the stagnation of employment in manufacturing is, therefore, unlikely to have been decisive.

Poverty

Eradication of persistent poverty was the basic objective of Indian planning. The attack on poverty was viewed in the First and Second Plans as having two components: rapid economic growth through industrialization and an agrarian transformation to mobilize and unleash the productive forces in the rural areas.[88] Rapid growth did not materialize, and the strategy for rural transformation was effectively given up with the change in the agricultural policies in the mid-1960s. Questions were raised in the late 1950s about the effect of planning on the "minimum levels of living," and a committee chaired by Mahalanobis, the author of the Second Plan, reported on the question in 1961. A perspective plan for achieving minimum levels of living was drafted in the Planning Commission in the early 1960s. The relatively low overall rate of growth of the economy and the international skepticism about the efficacy of "trickle down" of the benefits of growth eventually led to large-scale adoption of direct interventions to attack poverty. Currently the direct poverty amelioration strategy has several strands: (1) programs targeted at the poor with the aim of providing employment such as Integrated Rural Development Program (IRDP) and National Rural Employment Program (NREP); (2) targeted programs for providing social services like health and education to the poor; (3) programs focused on the most vulnerable/destitute sections, which require support through transfer payments; (4) programs focused on specific areas such as the Drought Prone Area Program, Hilly Area Development Program, and the Tribal Area Development Program; and (5) programs for technology and skill upgrading such as Training Program for Rural Youth in Self-Employment.

The IRDP, started in 1978–1979, is essentially a scheme for generating self-employment by subsidizing loans tied to the acquisition of productive assets (e.g., well, livestock, or a bullock cart) to eligible borrowers (the poor, defined by a household income criterion). It assisted 16.5 million families in the Sixth Plan and 10 million new families in the Seventh Plan. It has been officially estimated that the program helped 9.34 percent of the poor households to cross the poverty line in the past ten years. The program has been the subject of a number of evaluative studies.[89] It has been criticized because (1) it is too narrowly focused on credit, to the neglect of other factors responsible for poverty; (2) there are leakage and corruption and waste of resources; (3) a significant share of the benefits has gone to the relatively privileged among the poor (e.g., those with land) and to many nonpoor households; and (4) many of the investments financed are economically nonviable. Further, in many cases the benefits are not sustained over time. A small sample study by the World Bank in twelve districts in U.P. found that 75 percent of the families reported income gains exceeding 15 percent in the first two years after acquiring the asset. However, productivity deteriorated sharply in the third year, and at the end of the fourth year 40 percent of the beneficiaries had liquidated or lost their investment.[90] A significant problem derives from the fact that the program is driven by targets determined for each district by the government rather than by the demand for credit. The management challenge is also really large. The program is poorly managed and coordinated and suffers from shortage of trained and motivated staff. The number of bank branches involved in the program is roughly 52,000, and about 100,000 officials in 5,092 development blocks in 430 districts over the country administer the program.

The National Rural Employment Program, which replaced an earlier Food for Work program in 1978–1979, is financed jointly by the central and state governments to generate temporary wage employment in community infrastructure projects. It was supplemented by the Rural Landless Employment Guarantee Program in 1983, financed entirely by the central government. The schemes have been recently merged with the new Jawahar Rozgar Yojana. There is also an Employment Guarantee Scheme (EGS) run by the state government of Maharashtra. In 1987–1988 Rs.17 billion was spent in these programs to create 2.1 million man-years of work. The programs provide temporary employment. Despite being large in absolute terms, they are quite small relative to the overall employment needs of the economy. The quality and productivity of the rural infrastructure (e.g., roads, schools, reclamation) built by the programs have been questioned. Moreover, the benefits from the assets created are generally cornered by the relatively well-off in the rural areas. The EGS, set up by statute in 1977 and not dependent on annual budgetary allocations, is, however, considered to have made a significant contribution in certain drought-prone areas of Maharashtra, accounting for 10–60 percent of income of marginal households, according to different studies. Its significance lies mainly in its reliable provision of employment and income insurance.[91]

The Minimum Needs Program (MNP) provides public services to the poor, including rural primary health care, programs to eradicate illiteracy and raise school attendance, rural electrification roads, housing and drinking water, and sanitation and water supply facilities in urban slum areas. In 1987–1988 Rs.28 billion was spent on the MNP. Social service programs suffer from inadequate funding as well as weaknesses in program design, such as complex, top-heavy, and staff-intensive delivery systems. The issues concerning the MNP are the same as those facing the government's overall social sector programs. First, the programs are small relative to needs and short of funds.[92] Relative to GDP, the level of education expenditure is, for example, less than that for Thailand, Malaysia, Egypt, and Kenya. The same is true, to a lesser extent, of health expenditures. The low level of cost recovery (less than 2 percent in education and 3 percent in health services) needs to be increased to raise more resources, particularly since the better-off sections of the population derive substantial benefits. Second, there is a poor correlation between expenditures and needs both among states and within functional areas. Social spending in states with the lowest education and health indicators continues to be much below the national average. There is also scope for a significant shift in the expenditure toward services (like primary education and health services) that are more likely to benefit the poor. This partly results from the relatively low level of central government funding of programs in the social areas, which constitutionally are the responsibility of state governments. Only 10 percent of total public education spending derives from the central government, and efforts under the National Policy on Education (1986) to increase this share have had to be scaled down, given the tight budgetary situation. Third, the programs are poorly coordinated among too many different actors, and there are poor control of costs and large leakages of supplies. Thus, even the limited resources available are not being used effectively.

The Integrated Child Development Scheme (ICDS), started in 1975, is a nationwide program focused on the relatively backward areas, providing a package of basic health, nutrition, and preschool education services to a target group of children 0–6 years and pregnant and lactating women. The state governments are expected to provide the food component, which is expected to account for 60 percent of total ICDS outlay. The program gives priority to areas with higher health and nutritional needs. However, there is a lack of clarity of objectives. In some states it is viewed as a health and education program; in others, as a supplementary nutrition scheme. It also faces the usual management and efficiency problems that affect all government programs.

This range of programs, while suffering from problems of funding, design, and administration that reduce effectiveness, appears to have had a measurable impact on the conditions of the poor. Several recent studies of the trends in poverty in India have concluded that the programs are one reason for the decline in the poverty ratio in recent years.[93]

Studies of the trends of poverty in India have a long and distinguished history. Using a poverty line of 2,250 calories and NSS expenditure data, Dandekar and Rath (1971) estimated that 40 percent of the rural population and 50 percent of the urban population were below the poverty line. Bardhan (1974) found a sharp increase in the poverty ratio between 1960 and 1968, while Minhas (1974) found a decline between 1956 and 1967. Ahluwalia (1978) failed to find a clear time trend in the rural poverty ratio between 1956 and 1973, and Ahluwalia (1985) confirmed this judgment. It would appear that up to 1973, while there were large short-term fluctuations in the proportion of the population below the poverty line, there was no long-term tendency for the ratio to fall or to increase. However, there has been a trend decline in the poverty ratio since 1978. The debate now is not whether there is a decline in the ratio but about its magnitude. Minhas, Jain, and Tedulkar (1991), using the official poverty line, find that poverty ratio has declined from 55.25 percent in 1970–1971, to 46.46 percent in 1983, and 42.70 percent in 1987–1988. The Planning Commission, making questionable prorata, upward adjustments to the NSS data to make them consistent with the National Accounts statistics, has reported much lower poverty ratios of 37.40 percent for 1983 and 29.20 percent for 1988.[94] Kakwani and Subbarao (1990), using a different price deflator and a different statistical method for intrapolation of the grouped NSS data find a somewhat sharper decline in the rural poverty ratio than Minhas, Jain, and Tedulkar, with the percentage of rural poor declining from 59 percent in 1973–1974 to 45 percent in 1983 and 37.5 percent in 1986–1987.

While the trend decline in the poverty ratio is encouraging, poverty continues to be a major problem still awaiting a solution. There are a number of characteristics of the poverty problem that are of policy relevance. First, while the proportion of people living in absolute poverty has declined, according to Minhas, Jain, and Tedulkar (1991), the absolute number of poor is increasing, in both urban and rural areas.[95] The total number of the poor has increased from 308 million in 1970–1971 to 361 million in 1987–1988. Second, the bulk of the poor (80 percent) still live in the rural areas. However, between 1970–1971 and 1987–1988 the number of the urban poor has increased faster (56 percent) than that of the rural poor (10 percent).[96] Third, within the rural areas, agricultural labor and marginal landholders have a higher risk of poverty than do others.[97] Studies of real agricultural wages show only a small increase during the period of planned development. Fourth, there are wide regional variations in the poverty ratio, with the ratio in Bihar in 1987–1988 (64.87 percent) being over three times as high as in Punjab (17.97 percent). Six northern and eastern states (U.P., Bihar, Madhya Pradesh, West Bengal, Orissa, and Assam), with a little less than 49 percent of the total population, accounted for over 60 percent of the total number of people below the poverty line in 1987.

There has been much discussion of the factors underlying changes in the poverty ratio. Ahluwalia (1978) found a statistically significant inverse relation between rural poverty and agricultural growth for the country as a whole. However, at the state level the relationship held in some states but not in others. The important role of price changes has also been analyzed, for example, by Ghose (1989). It appears that a rise in prices of agricultural products relative to manufacturers increases rural poverty in the short run, reflecting reductions in real wages because of unanticipated inflation. Gaiha (1989) also reported that rural poverty and agricultural production were inversely related and that fluctuations in prices as measured by the cost-of-living index of agricultural laborers affected rural poverty. Ghose's results suggest that fluctuations in the relative price of agricultural products had a stronger effect on poverty than the fluctuations in agricultural output. Gaiha also found that in a number of states, like Kerala, Bihar, and U.P., "price fluctuations play more decisive role than the level of agricultural production in causing temporary changes in poverty." The policy implications of these studies—emphasis on increased agricultural production and stable prices as an important element of an antipoverty strategy—are in line with conventional wisdom.

The impact of the new agricultural technology on poverty was a matter of much debate. While it was recognized early that the new technology was scale-neutral, it was argued that since its adoption required resources, particularly credit and entailed risk, the benefits were confined mainly to large farmers.[98] The new technology was seen to generate more employment—a factor favorable to the poor. However, growing mechanization and the greater use of family labor with adoption of tractors tended to erode this favorable effect. It was also found from surveys that the increased profitability of agriculture was associated with increased landlessness in rural areas as large farmers resumed lands from tenants and purchased land from small farmers.[99] In fact, many of the early concerns about worsening conditions of the poor did not materialize. It was found that small farmers adopted the new technology with only a short lag. While relatively fewer small farmers used fertilizer, those who did used it more intensively (per unit of land area). The distribution of institutional credit remains skewed, but the access of small farmers to credit has improved.[100] Even the landless have benefited through increase in nonfarm employment in rural areas in ancillary and service activities and from lower food prices resulting from the increase in production. However, there has been a significant decline in the elasticity of employment with respect to agricultural output for the country as a whole. The demand for labor has increased less than the increase in output, and its seasonal distribution has changed. The growth in demand for labor has not been sufficient to significantly offset the depressing effect on real wages stemming from a rapid increase in the labor force in an environment of relatively slow economic growth. Thus, while all groups have shared in the benefits, the largest gains have accrued to the large farmers, the smallest to the landless. The evidence, therefore, supports the judgment that as a result of the green revolution, while poverty has declined, income distribution has worsened.

MACROECONOMIC BALANCES AND POLICY

India has been characterized by conservative macroeconomic management over most of the period since independence.[101] The government has tended to react without delay to external shocks and inflationary pressures with strong fiscal, monetary, and balance-of-payments adjustment measures. Thus, India has had relatively stable prices compared with other developing countries, with double-digit inflation in only eleven years of the forty-year period 1951–1991. The average annual rate of inflation (as measured by the GDP deflator) was 6.7 percent during 1956–1975, 7.5 percent per year during 1976–1979, and 8.2 percent per year during 1980–1989.

India adjusted quickly and successfully to the first oil shock, even though the economy was already in difficulty because of two successive poor harvests in 1971 and 1972, which depressed growth and generated double-digit inflation in 1972 and 1973.[102] The increase in oil prices had an impact equivalent to 1.9 percent. GDP was exacerbated by the rise of prices of other imports but was partially offset by the rise of export prices. The adjustment effort included (1) mobilization of external assistance, with gross aid flows increasing from 0.7 percent of GDP in 1972 to 1.2 percent of GDP in 1974 and 1.6 percent of GDP in 1975; (2) a restrictive domestic policy, which reduced disposable income by about 1 percent of GDP. Public fixed investment declined by 14.5 percent in 1974 and merely recovered to 1973 levels in 1975; (3) the real effective exchange rate depreciated by above 11 percent between 1972 and 1975 after the rupee was linked to the pound sterling in 1972. These measures led to a decline in imports (other than food) in volume terms. At the same time the stimulus to exports from demand restraint and the exchange rate was strengthened by additional incentives given to exporters. The volume of exports increased by 50 percent between 1973 and 1976. The current account deficit of about $1 billion in 1974 was converted into a surplus of the same magnitude in 1976. A sharp increase in current transfers, from remittances particularly from workers in the oil-exporting countries, played a significant but unexpected role in helping the turnaround. A series of good harvests in 1973, 1975, and 1977 also facilitated the adjustment. The overall result was that the adjustment to the oil shock was achieved with an acceleration in economic growth. The GDP growth in 1974–1978 was about 5 percent per year compared with the trend growth of 3.5 percent. A very successful effort at import substitution in oil was also initiated during this period by investment in oil exploration and production. The benefits of this program in the shape of a sharp reduction in the volume of oil imports, however, came only in the 1980s.

Adjustment to the second oil shock, 1979–1980, was, in a number of ways, in sharp contrast to the policies in 1974. The impact of the oil price increase was equivalent to 1.5 percent of GDP. However, because of other factors the current account deteriorated by 2.2 percent of GDP between 1979 and 1980 as compared with 1.4 percent between 1972 and 1974. Again, there was an effort to mobilize external finance. However, the external finance mobilized was of shorter maturity and on less concessional terms than during the first shock. For the first time significant borrowing from commercial sources was initiated, and an EFF agreement was reached with the International Monetary Fund (IMF). Second, the domestic policy stance was more expansionary, even though in 1979 the country had a disastrous harvest and wholesale prices increased by 17 percent. Public investment between 1979 and 1982 increased by 26 percent. This, together with a liberalization of the import policy on capital goods, resulted in the growth of nonoil imports by 56 percent between 1978 and 1983. The period was also marked by a slightly appreciated but essentially stagnant real effective exchange rate, prices in India rising faster than world prices. Exports stagnated in volume terms and increased quite slowly in value. Stagnation in workers' remittances was also in contrast with the first shock period. Consequently the current account deficit continued at around $2.8 billion during 1980–1984. The situation would have been worse but for the significant reduction in the volume of oil imports in this period as a result of the success of the policy of increasing domestic oil production initiated during the first oil shock.

The contrast between the adjustment policies of the first oil shock and the second points to the proximate causes of the current financial crisis in India. Until about the mid-1970s India followed a dirigisme, inward-oriented import substitution strategy together with conservative macromanagement policies. The development strategy did not achieve rapid growth or self-reliance, but the conservative macromanagement tended to keep the economy on an even keel. Around the mid- to late 1970s, for reasons related mainly to the domestic political economy, the conservative macromanagement was modified, with resulting macroimbalances.[103]

The change was initiated in fiscal policy, with a sharp increase in government current expenditures greatly exceeding the growth in revenues and resulting in large and growing current deficits. The growth in current expenditures resulted from three sets of forces. First, there was a view in certain parts of the government that, given the large idle capacity in industry and surplus labor in rural areas, a greater reliance on deficit financing would not be destabilizing.[104] Second, the political economy led to a growing pressure for rapid increase in public expenditures that ultimately could not be resisted. Bardhan (1984) points out that with planned development, three dominant classes had emerged—industrialists, rich farmers, and the professionals in the public sector. These classes operated as a loose and uneasy coalition, with each class pulling in different directions to attain its own interest. Since "none of them is strong enough to dominate the process of resource allocation one predictable outcome is the proliferation of subsidies and grants to placate all of them" (p. 61). Pressures for state subsidies built up also from a number of "demand" groups beyond the dominant coalition. These pressures proved increasingly difficult to resist because of the deinstitutionalization of the Congress party and state structures that accompanied Indira Gandhi's success, between 1969 and 1984, in centralizing power in her own hands (Rudolph and Rudolph, 1987, pp. 6–7). There was an erosion of the autonomy and professionalism of state institutions—"The independence, professional standards, and procedural norms of the Parliament, courts, police, civil service, and federal system gave way to centralization based on personal loyalty" (p. 7). There was a change also in the nature of the political leadership—"Nationalist politicians were succeeded by professional politicians and they in turn by a generation of political condottieri" (p. 8). A vast increase in public expenditures to benefit the "dominant coalition" and the "demand groups" was the inevitable outcome. Third, with time, the relatively small and manageable deficits incurred to finance the public sector investment program led to a gradual increase in the public debt. There was eventually a rapid growth of interest payments. In the 1980s the interest rate on new borrowings also increased as borrowing requirements became larger with growing public sector investment and government dissaving. Of the total increase in public sector current expenditures of Rs.875 billion between 1980–1981 and 1989–1990, 25 percent was accounted for by interest payments, about 30 percent by subsidies and net current transfers, and the remaining 45 percent by consumption expenditures (ways and means and salaries). The largest subsidies are for food and fertilizer, but there are a large number of smaller subsidies. The bulk of the benefit of subsidies flows to the more affluent sections of society.[105] The gross deficit of the public sector, which averaged 7.4 percent of gross national product (GNP) during 1975–1979, increased to 10.7 percent during 1980–1984 and 13.1 percent during 1985–1989. The ratio of central and state government debt to GDP rose from 49 percent in 1980–1981 to 66 percent in 1990–1991. Thus, trends were unsustainable, and

Table 11.15
Balance of Payments

	1975-76	1980-81	1985-86	1990-91	1991-92
	(----------------million US $----------------)				
Export of Goods	4,828	8,332	9,461	18,485	18,002
Import of Goods	-5,483	-15,892	-17,295	-29,804	-20,671
Net Non-factor Services	311	1,433	1,186	823	634
Net Factor Income	-191	356	-1,552	3,743	3,653
Net Current Transfers	470	2,860	2,305	2,000	2,685
Current A/C Balance	-65	-2,911	-5,395	-8,862	-3,003
Foreign Direct Investment	-	8	160	112	200
Official Grants	342	643	359	476	451
Net Medium and Long-Term Loans	1,352	1,425	2,545	2,926	3,532
Capital Flows NEI*	-558	1,370	1,984	3,578	1,973
Change in Reserves	-816	346	-548	1,770	-3,153
Errors & Omissions	-155	-200	474	..	..
Memo: Current A/C Balance as % of GDP	0.1%	1.7%	2.7%	3.1%	1.2%

Source: World Bank Data Bank.
*Includes IMF.

drastic action to control public expenditure and reduce public sector deficits was necessary to avoid a crisis.

The balance-of-payments developments reflected the growing fiscal imbalance (Table 11.15). Exports of goods and nonfactor services grew slowly at around 1.2 percent per annum during 1980–1985, when the real effective exchange rate appreciated slightly and remained stable. Imports of goods and nonfactor services increased at about the same rate as exports, and the current account deficit fluctuated at around $3 billion during 1980–1981 to 1983–1984 and then jumped to $6 billion in 1985–1986. In the second half of the 1980s export growth accelerated to about 12 percent per year because of an active exchange rate policy and increase in export subsidies. However, import growth averaged about 9.5 percent per year because of growing aggregate demand and some loosening of import restrictions. As a consequence, the current account deficit increased from $6 billion in 1985–1986 to about $10 billion in 1990–1991. Given the constraints on the growth of concessional aid, the large current account deficits led to relatively large increases in commercial borrowing, including short-term credits. Outstanding debt to private creditors increased from $2.5 billion in 1980 to $26.5 billion in 1990. Effectively, "commercial borrowings became a substitute for domestic savings to finance low productivity investments" (Jalan, 1991, p. 107).

Crisis and Reform

In 1990 things came to a head with the Gulf crisis, which increased the import bill and reduced workers' remittances and exports to Iraq and Kuwait. This, together with domestic political uncertainties, resulted in a downgrading of India's bonds by international credit-rating agencies, reduced access to external finance, and brought on a balance-of-payments crisis. Foreign exchange reserves had declined to about two weeks imports by the end of 1990. A new minority government came to office in June 1991 and in July embarked on a fundamental reorientation of economic policy, with the twin objectives of restoring macroeconomic stability and reversing the inward-oriented, international development strategy.

The program represents a fundamental reorientation of the development strategy followed since independence. The underlying premises were rejected, though the changes continue to be described as a continuation of the Nehruvian strategy. Self-reliance was interpreted in a positive sense, and its equation with self-sufficiency was rejected. Integration with the world economy was seen as desirable. The role of the public sector in development was to be narrower and focused primarily on economic and social infrastructure, and public enterprises would be required to pay their way. Foreign investment was to be encouraged, and the mass of regulation and controls set up for the private sector were to be abolished in favor of a more market-friendly approach. This last reflected the realization that government failure was, if anything, even more pernicious than market failure, which government intervention and investment had been designed to correct.

The stabilization measures included a significant exchange rate adjustment, increases in the interest rate, and action to increase revenue and cut expenditures to reduce the budget deficit. The government also announced its intention to reform existing trade and industrial and financial policies, increase the efficiency of public enterprises, and rationalize the tax system.

The trade reform measures taken so far have virtually eliminated QRs on intermediate and capital goods imports, lowered tariffs, and transformed the payments regime. While the maximum tariff has been lowered, tariffs still remain very high. The high reliance on customs for revenue purposes is proving a major hurdle to lowering tariffs. Export subsidies have been eliminated. The REP scheme was initially broadened into an Exim scrip scheme but later replaced by a more transparent dual exchange rate system in which exporters are allowed to sell 60 percent of their foreign exchange earnings in the free market. The stated objective is to move to convertibility of the rupee on trade account. The twenty-six import-licensing lists have been replaced by a negative list consisting of consumer goods, eight goods subject to "canalized" imports, and a fairly large miscellaneous group such as electronic goods, drugs, pesticides, and sixteen categories of goods reserved for small-scale production. The imports of all other goods are not subject to license. Most intermediate and consumer goods are not on the negative list, and their import is not subject to licensing restrictions. It is estimated that about 45 percent of the domestic production of manufactured goods is still protected by QRs. No new PMP agreements will be concluded, and the existing ones will be reviewed. The maintenance of infinite protection for consumption goods with the elimination of QRs for capital and intermediate goods poses the danger of inducing further uncompetitive production. The major thrusts of further reform should be (1) to eliminate the "tax" on exporters inherent in the dual exchange rate; (2) to further reduce the extent of reliance on QRs; and (3) to reduce the level of tariffs. The budget of 1993 includes measures in all these areas.

The reform of the industrial licensing and regulation system included the reduction of the number of sectors reserved exclusively for the public sector from eighteen to eight. Important areas like coal, oil, and mining of ferrous and nonferrous metals are still reserved exclusively for the public sector. Prior government approval is no longer required for investments except in eighteen "sensitive" sectors published in a negative list. The requirement for prior government approval for expansion, diversification, merger, and acquisition by large firms under the MRTP act has been eliminated. Measures to encourage foreign investment include the automatic approval of new investment of up to 51 percent of equity. The further deepening of the reform would require reduction in the sectors reserved for public investment, the reduction of licensing requirements in the "sensitive" industries (which include oil refining, wood products, alcoholic drinks, consumer durables, and hides and skins). The production of about 850 products still remains reserved for small industries. The whole small-industry policy needs review and reform.

The reform of the public enterprise sector is an important part of the government's agenda. Much greater use is to be made of memoranda of understandings to provide greater autonomy to existing public enterprises. It has been decided to review the portfolio of public sector investments with a view to concentrate them in areas of strategic importance requiring high technology and considered essential for infrastructure. Up to 20 percent equity in selected public enterprises is to be offered to public sector mutual funds and investment institutions, and privatization of some enterprises is under study. Chronically loss-making enterprises are to be referred to the Board of Industrial and Financial Reconstruction (BIFR) for restructuring for the formulation of rehabilitation schemes. A National Renewal Fund has been established to finance the cost of retrenchment or retraining of displaced workers.

Government has also decided to reduce and eventually eliminate budget support to the manufacturing public enterprises. If this decision can be made to stick, it could have a very major impact on the efficiency and survival of many inefficient and inviable enterprises. The World Bank estimates that during the 1980s the annual net financing needs of the departmental and nondepartmental public enterprises amounted to over 5 percent of GDP. During the four years 1988–1991, only about 50 percent of the investment of central government public enterprises was met from internal resources, 30 percent from budget transfers, and the rest from domestic and external loans and deposits from the public.

Progress in the restructuring of both the public and the private sector depends crucially on the government's success in reducing the existing barriers to labor retrenchment and the liquidation of assets. A beginning in this direction was made in 1985 by the institution of the BIFR to determine necessary measures for such enterprises. However, the effort made little headway. The legal and bureaucratic hurdles have been immense, and opposition of trade union and local and state governments has been very strong. A streamlining and refocusing of the BIFR process and a change in the legal framework and procedures for bankruptcy and winding up of enterprises are a high priority.

The program has had positive results in terms of mobilizing support from international financial institutions. Funds made available mainly by the IMF and World Bank helped increase reserves. There has also been an increase in interest of foreign investors in India, and a few significant ventures have been initiated. However, the more substantive results have yet to appear. Industrial production declined, and exports have stagnated. The inflation has also been slow to come down, partly because of expectations and the sharp increase in prices of agricultural goods. The slow response to the first year of the reform can be traced to several factors. First, for credibility the reforms have to be sustained for some time before public perception that the new regime is here to stay. While many changes may have been announced, things on the ground have frequently been slow to change. Bureaucracy and red tape still abound.[106] It is natural, therefore, for many investors to adopt a wait-and-see attitude. Second, the high levels of interest rate and the very strict import controls adopted as an emergency measure in the early days of the reform have naturally inhibited increases in production of manufactures and exports, requiring imported inputs. Third, the program is as yet incomplete. The most important weakness is the failure to come up with a credible program for facilitating retrenchment of labor and closure of unprofitable enterprises. This lacuna acts as a restraint on new investment, particularly by entrepreneurs who are already hindered with "sick" units. Fourth, the deterioration in the law-and-order situation in large areas of the country and the wide perception that the rule of law has been significantly eroded create a major hurdle for a smoothly functioning market economy. Local thugs, often with strong political backing, can introduce a significant block to the operation of competition between different firms by supporting one against the other. For example, raw material supply can be dislocated, labor troubles can be fomented, and customers can be frightened away. On the other hand, India has a dynamic entrepreneurial class, large supplies of skilled and unskilled labor, and the basic infrastructure to permit rapid response to reform once a credible approach to an "exit" policy has been established and the rule of law reinstated.

The reform program has been subject to strong criticism in debate in India.[107] The major criticisms are the following. First, it is argued that reform is being "dictated" by the international institutions. Bhagwati (1992) points out that the basic ideas behind the reform have been developed and advanced in India for some time. The dialogue with the international institutions may only have helped sharpen and focus these ideas. Second, it is argued that the reform is leading India into a *laissez-faire* economy, in which the state would have a minimum role to play. This again is a travesty of the facts. The problem in India has been that the state has taken direct responsibility for large areas of the economy and has imposed a regime of controls on the rest of the economy with the objective of promoting rapid development. In the process the resources and capabilities of the state have been overstretched: the objective has not been achieved, and in the process a large number of crucial activities have been neglected or weakened. The program requires the government to do more, not less, in crucial areas, like education and literacy, health, and economic infrastructure. It requires that the state get out of areas—manufacturing production, tourism, and so on—where experience shows that the state is not very efficient. The program also requires that the state change the instruments of regulation that it uses—direct discretionary, administrative interventions to be replaced by monitoring and regulation and the imposition of sanctions for violations of guidelines that operate in an automatic manner and not through discretionary decisions. Third, it is argued that the reform will lead to layoffs and a vast increase in unemployment. In this context it needs to be pointed out that to the extent that workers are employed at relatively high wages in inviable and inefficient "sick" enterprises surviving on budget support or on the basis of high protection, their employment disguises an inefficient and socially inequitable system of "social security." The perpetuation of this employment is at the expense of higher investment and more rapid growth of output and employment in the rest of the economy. The more efficient allocation of resources that would follow from the implementation of reform would result in more rapid increase in employment in the future. The transitional unemployment that would be generated obviously needs to be managed through negotiated separation packages, workers retraining programs, and provision of assistance for displaced workers to set up in self-employment activities, for example, small businesses. The implementation of an appropriate exit and restructuring policy would benefit the workers, including new entrants to the labor force, by increasing the employment elasticity, with respect to output in the organized sector over a period of time. The experience with trade liberalization in other countries does not show sharp increases in unemployment during the implementation of the reform program.[108]

CONCLUSION

The "third way" that India sought to follow after independence resulted in the country's lagging behind other developing countries such as China, Korea, and Taiwan, which started with fewer assets and more handicaps on the path to development. India's achievements were significant only when compared with those of the colonial past—a small increase in the rate of per capita income growth and the eradication of serious famines. However, they fell far short of the objective of eliminating poverty that motivated the drive for planned economic development. After forty years of effort, India still remains a poor country with major structural problems. The outcome is tragic because most analysts agree that India could have done much better.[109]

The relatively poor economic performance of India can be traced largely to the flawed development strategy that was adopted and the policy and institutional framework, relying primarily on government intervention, control, and regulation, that was erected for its implementation. The system achieved significant success in mobilizing resources for investment. However, it showed a poor record of allocating these resources in terms of equity and efficiency.

It has been argued that India's performance cannot be blamed on its development strategy because the Five-Year Plans were never really implemented because of (1) information and administrative weaknesses and (2) failure to establish a structure of incentives that would establish behavior patterns consistent with plan goals (S. Chakravarty, 1987, chap. 4, "Problems of Plan Implementation"). This argument skirts the fundamental issue: even if the plan objectives had been fulfilled in terms of the level and allocation of investment, given the policy of import substitution and self-sufficiency regardless of cost and efficiency, reliance on the public sector, and the battery of controls and regulations of private enterprise, resources would still have been wasted.

Another explanation of India's poor performance argues that the basic problem was that India tried to have an economic revolution without a social revolution. The existing social structure had negative effect on efforts to raise the growth rate. One version of this view (e.g., Mittra, 1977) argues that given the power of the landlords and the large peasants, government policy shifted domestic terms of trade in favor of agriculture. The implied shift in income, given the patterns of rural consumption and income distribution, led to a relative slow growth in demand for industrial goods and hence to excess capacity and slow growth of output. The tendency was aggravated by declining wages and increased "pauperization" in agriculture. The hypothesis is, however, not sustained by empirical evidence. The terms of trade did move in favor of agriculture until the 1960s, but the trend has been reversed since the mid-1970s.[110] Agricultural wages have reflected overall conditions of demand and supply of labor and show a very slow trend rate of growth. The view that Indian industrial stagnation resulted from a lack of effective demand was shown to be incorrect by careful empirical analysis (Ahluwalia, 1985).

It is sometimes believed that India's slow rate of growth can be traced to the country's commitment to a democratic form of government, which prevented the government from generating higher rates of savings and investment more in line with the levels attained in some countries with authoritarian governments. However, the experience of countries in Eastern Europe has shown that high rates of savings and investment are not enough to yield sustained rapid growth and rising standards of living in the absence of efficiency in resource use.

The Indian economy is poised for future growth at a significantly higher growth rate than was achieved over the last four decades, provided the reorientation of economic policies toward more neutral structure of incentives between exports and the domestic market, the emphasis on more efficient use of resources through greater reliance on market forces and competition as opposed to direct intervention and control, the focusing of state action in human resource development and infrastructure, and the achievement of macroeconomic balance is continued. Two important factors that would contribute to such an outcome are the availability of adequate financial support during the transition and an improvement in the economic performance of the industrial economies.

NOTES

1. Malenbaum (1962) characterizes India at independence as "a static economy in progress," a phrase apparently borrowed from Rao's article on "Changes in India's National Income," *Capital*, 16 December 1954. The estimate of deaths from the Bengal famine is from Sen, *Poverty and Famines, an Essay on Entitlement and Deprivation*, Oxford University Press, 1981.

2. Discussing India's arrested industrial development during the hundred years before 1950, Malenbaum concludes that "it is in this matter of the posture of Government, rather than in the nature of indigenous entrepreneurship that one must seek the reasons for India's limited industrial performance prior to 1950" (Malenbaum, 1962, p. 159).

3. An alternative "Bombay Plan" drafted by eight of the country's leading industrialists was published in 1945. It, too, called for an active state role and government intervention and control in the country's development.

4. Second Five-Year Plan (1956) p. 24.

5. Third Plan: A draft outline (1961) p. 11.

6. Bhagwati (1973, p. 5). For a later review of the premises see William Byrd (1990). It must be recognized that a number of these premises were in the mainstream of the development orthodoxy of the time. They became increasingly anachronistic only in the light of experience in India and elsewhere.

7. Indira Gandhi, in a speech to the All India Congress Committee in April 1969, said that "to the extent India depended on imports, its independence was compromised, encroached upon" (Frankel, 1978, p. 404). Also: "Indian Planners . . . were in reality operating on the assumption of a nearly closed economy" (Chakravarty, 1987, p. 12).

8. "It cannot be emphasized too strongly that unless steps are taken to augment rapidly the output of the means of production and to build-up the fuel and energy resources . . . the scale and pace of advance in the coming years will be inhibited" (Second Five-Year Plan, 1956, p. 28).

9. In a speech to Parliament in 1956 on the Second Plan, Nehru stated: "While I am for the public sector growing, I do not understand or appreciate the condemnation of the private sector. . . . I have no doubt that at the present stage in India the private sector has a very important task to fulfil, *provided always that it works within the confines laid down*" (Nayar, 1989, p. 203, emphasis added).

10. Second Five-Year Plan, New Delhi (1965, p. 23).

11. Chakravarty (1987, p. 12).

12. A 1966 statement by Indira Gandhi quoted by Nayar (1989, p. 351): "We advocate a public sector for three reasons: to gain control of the commanding heights of the economy; to promote critical development in terms of social gain or strategic value rather than primarily on considerations of profit; and to provide commercial surpluses with which to finance further economic development."

13. Robert E. B. Lucas, "India's Industrial Policy" (Lucas and Papanek, 1988,

p. 183). In a recent speech Finance Minister Manmohan Singh has characterized the system as "functionless capitalism."

14. See Bhagwati and Desai (1970, chap. 22).

15. See Chakravarty (1987, pp. 32–37) for an interesting survey of the evolution of the poverty amelioration strategy in India.

16. Among the government committees that reported on various aspects of the economy may be mentioned Report of the Committee on Controls and Subsidies, the Dagli Committee, 1979; Report of the Committee on Trade Policies, the Hussain Committee, 1984; Report of the Committee to Examine Principles of a Possible Shift from Physical to Financial Controls, the Narasimham Committee, 1985; and the Report of the Committee to Review Policy for Public Enterprises, 1984, the Sengupta Committee.

17. Prime Minister Rao in a speech to the All India Congress Committee stated: "The stage has now come when we could review our strategy. Import substitution cannot be an end in itself. . . . the criterion of self reliance today has to be not whether you can make whatever you need, but whether you can pay for whatever you need" (*The Hindu*, 9 May, 1992).

18. See Mohan and Aggarwal (1990) for a succinct survey of the complex and constraining nature of controls and regulatory policies.

19. "The MRTP clearance procedure has been more restrictive than the procedures for companies in general. Between 1982 and 1985 the approval rate of industrial license applications involving MRTP clearances (25%) was roughly half that of companies in general. . . . less than half of all applications by MRTP companies were decided within one year and many took two or more years" (World Bank, 1987, p. 87).

20. A unit is defined as sick if it has been registered for at least seven years, has accumulated losses equal to, or exceeding, its paid-up capital and free reserves, and has suffered cash losses in the current and the preceding year.

21. See P.R. Fallon and Lucas (1991).

22. Industrial Policy Resolution, 1956 (Sandesara, 1988).

23. Sandesara (1988).

24. The classic discussion still well worth reading is Bhagwati and Desai (1970, chaps. 15 to 21). See also Bhagwati and Srinivasan (1975), World Bank (1987), and Aksoy (1992).

25. Ahluwalia (1991, p. 28).

26. World Bank (1987, p. 128).

27. See World Bank (1987, p. 132, Table 4.3) for details.

28. Amaresh Bagchi (1981) points out that many of the export promotion schemes were started in the 1950s. He provides a list of eighteen separate schemes that were operating in the 1970s.

29. World Bank (1987, p. 143).

30. For example, 20–25 percent of the output of large paper firms was white printing paper to be sold to educational institutions at a fixed price, and sugar mills were required to sell 50 percent of output to the government at a concessional price for sale in "fair price" shops (World Bank, 1987, p. 92).

31. "Nationalization was a recognition of the potential of the banking system to promote broader economic objectives" (Government of India, Narasimham Committee, Report on the Financial System, 1991, p. 8).

32. Ibid., p. 28.

33. The Narasimham Committee (1991) refers in this context to IRDP: "In many

cases of IRDP lending banks have virtually abdicated their responsibilities. . . . and instead have tended to rely on lists of identified borrowers prepared by Government authorities.''

34. Narasimham Committee (1991, p. 25).

35. Speech by governor, RBI (*Hindu,* 27 February, 1992).

36. A recent scandal in which large sums of money were channeled to the stock market in contravention of Reserve Bank guidelines has spotlighted the weaknesses in the supervision and prudential regulation system.

37. Speech by governor, RBI (*Hindu,* 27 February 1992).

38. Mundle and Rao (1992) give data to show that the share of revenue expenditure in total expenditure increased from 53 percent in 1971–1972 to 70.46 percent in 1987–1988. Of the increase of 17.46 points over the period, 15.50 points were on account of compensation to government employees (3.60), interest (4.88), and subsidies (7.02).

39. It has been suggested that the government should sell the shares of public enterprises and use the proceeds to retire part of the public debt.

40. Acharya (1988).

41. See Lal (1988, Table 14.a).

42. B.R. Nayar (1989, Table 3).

43. Ahluwalia (1991, p. 24).

44. Lal (1988).

45. George Rosen (1992, p. 103).

46. S. Mulji (1990) thinks that ''the failure of the public sector has been due less to lack of resources, misguided investment and prior pricing policies than to bad management'' (p. 151).

47. Khatkhate (1992) states that ''the negative aspects with emphasis on don'ts rather than do's received greater prominence in fashioning the industry policy as well as the trade design.''

48. ''Licensing acted as a barrier to growth, specialization and the attainment of scale economies. In the nylon filament yarn industry, for example, eleven firms set up eleven plants with an average capacity of between a quarter and a tenth of those found in India's competitors'' (World Bank, 1987, p. 9).

49. As early as 1963, the Estimates Committee of Parliament listed twenty-five kinds of malpractices associated with the import-licensing system. The first Swaminathan Committee in 1963 examined licensing procedures and suggested not only their streamlining but also significant delicensing.

50. See, for example, Chelliah (1991b).

51. Unregistered manufacturing covers establishments employing fewer than ten workers with power or fewer than twenty workers without power (Sandesara, 1988).

52. Paranjape (1988, p. 2343). Paranjape was a member of the committee.

53. Paranjape (1988, p. 2356–57).

54. World Bank (1987, p. 134).

55. *The Economist,* London, in its Survey of India (4 May 1991) argued that ''the system remained substantially intact. In some ways it actually became more complicated . . . [the] reforms left the bureaucrats much in charge as before'' (p. 13).

56. Bhagwati in the 1992 Radhakrishnan lectures on ''India's Economy: The Shackled Giant'' speaks of ''the senseless adherence to policies that have been seen by others to have little rationale'' and ''the widely shared and justified perception that her policies have been wittingly foolish.''

57. For a succinct discussion of the vested interest thesis see Khatkhate (1991).

58. Malenbaum (1962, p. 75). Malenbaum's figures are for five-year periods.

59. Angus Maddison (1989, Table 1.3, p. 19). See also Sundrum (1987, pp. 33–34).

60. The current economic difficulties raise questions about the sustainability of this acceleration in the growth rate.

61. The total number of illiterates increased from 301 million in 1951 to 437 million in 1981. In the latter year 57 percent of the illiterates were women.

62. There was virtual stagnation of exports during 1951–1965. The value of total exports averaged $1.3 billion dollars in 1951–1955, $1.3 billion in 1955–1960, and $1.6 billion in 1961–1965.

63. See Bhagwati and Desai (1970, chap. 18).

64. Ibid., p. 429.

65. Manmohan Singh (1964); Bhagwati and Desai (1970); Bhagwati and Srinivasan (1975); Martin Wolf (1982).

66. Nayyar (1988). Jalan (1991) also reports on a study of the declining share of India in the world market for textiles, a trend that contrasted with the increasing share of its developing country competitors and in this context refers to "non price factors such as reliability and quality" as illustrating the role of microeconomic policies in explaining export success. However, he goes on to point out that for businessmen "indiscriminate protection over too long a period could lead to widespread inefficiency and a preference for the quiet life." Lack of attention to reliability and quality is essentially the result of the high protection and lack of competition.

67. Chakravarty (1987) gives marginal saving rates of 20 percent for the 1950s, 18.2 percent for the 1960s, 26.3 percent for the 1970s, and 21.4 percent for 1980–1984. Pandit (1991) argues that two factors affect the marginal savings rate in India: (1) rising marginal propensity to save with increases in the level of income and (2) constraints on the share of high-income-high-saving groups in the economy, which sets a low upper limit to the savings ratio. He estimates aggregate and household savings functions that show a rising marginal propensity to save and a falling income elasticity of savings.

68. Lipton and Toye (1990).

69. See Sundrum (1987, pp. 94–96).

70. Raj (1984).

71. Sundrum (1987) quotes Chakravarty that in 1976–1979 the "increase in the capital output ratio is due largely to shifts in this sectoral composition of aggregate investment and therefore cannot necessarily be interpreted as reflecting declining efficiency in the use of capital" (p. 95).

72. Visaria and Minhas (1991, p. 97). See also Fallon and Lucas (1991).

73. Vaidyanathan (1986); Hazell and Haggblade (1991).

74. Visaria and Minhas (1991).

75. Tyagi (1981) estimated an employment elasticity of 0.77 with reference to agricultural production for the 1970s. Rao (1975) estimated a figure of 0.75.

76. Dandekar (1988a).

77. See Frankel (1978) for discussion of the wide gap between the government's objectives and achievements in agrarian reform.

78. Frankel (1978, pp. 102–3).

79. See Walter C. Neale (1985).

80. Value added in agriculture increased by 2.4 percent per year during 1950–1964

and 2.6 percent per year during 1967–1988. The higher growth rate of GDP in the 1980s also appears in agriculture, the growth rate during 1980–1989 being 3.1 percent per year.

81. A World Bank study (1989a) points to "escalating costs . . . , FCI's inefficiency, inability to reach many of the poorer consumers in rural areas, market and trade controls which dampen producer incentives, financial problems threatening the sugar industry and constantly shifting procurement and distribution rules" (p. 33).

82. Balasubramanian (1984, p. 110).

83. World Bank (1992, World Development Indicators, Table 6). In 1970 manufacturing value added in India was four times as large as that in Korea and only 20 percent lower than in Brazil.

84. World Bank (1987).

85. Estimated from data in Kelkar and Kumar (1990).

86. Ahluwalia (1991, p. 197). Also C.P. Chandrasekhar (1988).

87. For example, Kelkar and Kumar (1990).

88. Bhagwati (1987) states, on the basis of his experience in the Planning Commission at the time, that rapid growth was perceived as "providing the only reliable way of making a sustained rather than a one shot impact on poverty."

89. See, for example, Sandeep Bagchee (1987); N.J. Kurien (1989); D. Bandopadhyaya (1988); Jean Dreze (1990); Indira Hirway (1988, 1991); World Bank (1989a).

90. World Bank (1989, p. 69).

91. Ibid., p. 119.

92. The public expenditure on social services and welfare increased from 5.3 percent of GDP in 1976 to 7.6 percent in 1984. Education and health absorb 70 percent of the total expenditure.

93. For example, Kakwani and Subbarao (1990, p. A-6); Ghose (1989, p. 318).

94. Minhas, Jain, and Jedulkar (1991) give a ratio of 57.33 percent for rural and 45.89 percent for urban population in 1970–1971 and 44.88 percent and 36.62 percent, respectively, in 1987. Official estimates for 1987 are 32.7 and 19.4, respectively, for rural and urban population. Datt and Ravallion (1992) estimate a poverty head count ratio of 38.66 percent for rural and 37.12 percent for urban population for 1988 based on NSS data. The difference in the ratio for rural areas as compared with that estimated by Minhas, Jain, and Jedulkar for 1987 is quite large and appears to derive mainly from the use of a different deflator. Also, 1987 was a year of severe drought. Both studies show a sharp decline in rural poverty between 1983 and 1987–1988.

95. Kakwani and Subbarao (1990) find that the number of rural poor declined from 265 million in 1973–1974 to 211 million in 1986–1987.

96. Datt and Ravallion (1992) find an even sharper trend toward higher poverty in the urban areas with indexes of poverty other than the head count ratio showing relatively higher percentage of poor in urban areas in 1987 and 1988.

97. Minhas (1975) found that in 1960–1961, 79 percent of the agricultural labor households were below the poverty line. Such households constituted 41 percent of the total number of poor in that year. In 1977–1978 agricultural labor householders accounted for about 44 percent of the poor in rural areas and marginal farmers for another third (Sundrum, 1987).

98. Frankel (1971).

99. For example see Gaiha (1985, 1989).

100. For an analytical survey of the literature see Singh (1990, chap. 5).

101. Joshi and Little (1989) consider India's macroeconomic policies to "have been

essentially conservative and cautious. . . . more Friedmanite than Keynesian.'' However, they also point out that ''in a subtle, creeping way, the micro-economic inefficiencies, acting in combination with political changes, have reduced macro-economic flexibility over time'' (p. 298). The definitive study of Indian macroeconomic policies is by Joshi and Little, *India: Crisis, Adjustment and Growth* (Oxford University Press: World Bank, 1993).

102. The following discussion of the period of the two oil shocks is based on M. S. Ahluwalia (1985b).

103. Reserve Bank of India (1991) describe the Indian debt crisis as essentially ''home made.''

104. Minhas (1988, pp. 121–31).

105. See Mundle and Rao (1991). Jalan (1991) quotes the example of Tamil Nadu, which provides a subsidy of Rs.2,650 on average for every agricultural pump set. About 91 percent of the subsidy went to large farmers.

106. As P.S. Jha (1992) writes, ''Further down the licence and permit Raj continues as if nothing has changed.'' For example, in thirty-four industries where foreign investment up to 51 percent has been made automatic, applications have to be approved in principle by the head office of the Reserve Bank, then in substance by the relevant branch office, and then scanned again at the head office for foreign exchange implications. Once approved, the investor has to comply with fifty-one industrial statutes, maintain sixteen separate registers, pay fourteen separate fees, and file 160 forms. He has to comply with sixty-seven provisions of the MRTP Act, 385 rules of the central exise collectors, eighty-one sections of foreign exchange regulations, and so on. All this is supervised by fifty-one inspectors, all with the power to stop production.

107. See Kohli (1989) for an excellent, though slightly dated, analysis of the sources of political support and opposition of liberalization in India. Examining the gradual and halting liberalization of the 1980s, he finds that ''concerted and direct opposition to the reforms has come from three quarters: the rank and file of the ruling party, the Congress; the left intelligentsia; and the organized working class in the public sector'' (p. 306).

108. Michaely, Papageorgieu, and Choksi (1991).

109. ''Nowhere else not even in Communist China or the Soviet Union, is the gap between what might have been achieved and what has been achieved as great as in India'' (''A Survey of India,'' *The Economist,* 4 May 1991, p. 3).

110. Swamy and Gulhati (1986) quote the Economic Survey, 1984, that the crude barter terms of trade defined as the ratio of agricultural commodity prices to manufactured product prices declined from 100 in 1970–1971 to 81.8 in 1980–1981.

REFERENCES

Acharya, S. 1988. ''India's Fiscal Policy.'' In *The Indian Economy: Recent Development and Future Prospects,* edited by R.E.B. Lucas and G.F. Papanek. Boulder, Colo.: Westview Press.

Acharya, S., and Associates 1985. *Aspects of Black Economy in India.* New Delhi: National Institute of Public Finance and Policy.

Agarwal, M. 1988. ''A Comparative Analysis of India's Export Performance, 1965–80.'' *Indian Economic Review* 23, no. 2: 231–61.

Ahluwalia, I.J. 1985. *Industrial Growth in India: Stagnation Since the Mid-Sixties.* Delhi: Oxford University Press.

————. 1991. *Productivity and Growth in Indian Manufacturing.* Delhi: Oxford University Press.

Ahluwalia, M.S. 1978. "Rural Poverty and Agricultural Performance in India." *Journal of Development Studies* 14, no. 3.

Ahluwalia, M.S. 1985a. "Balance of Payments Adjustment in India, 1970–71 to 1983–84." Mimeo. Report to the Group of Twenty-Four. UNDP/UNCTAD Project INT/84/021.

————. 1985b. "Rural Poverty, Agricultural Production, and Prices: A Re-examination." In *Agricultural Change and Rural Poverty,* edited by J.W. Mellor and G. Desai. Baltimore: Johns Hopkins University Press.

Aksoy, A.M. 1992. "The Indian Trade Regime." World Bank Policy Research Working Papers, WPS No. 989. Washington, D.C.: World Bank.

Bagchee, S. 1987. "Poverty Alleviation Programmes in Seventh Plan: An Appraisal." *Economic and Political Weekly* (24 January)

Bagchi, A. 1981. "Export Incentives in India: A Review." In *Change and Choice in Indian Industry,* edited by Amiya Kumar Bagchi and Nirmala Banerje. Calcutta: Center for Studies in Social Sciences.

Balasubramanian, V.N. 1984. *The Economy of India.* London: Weidenfeld and Nicolson.

Bandopadhyaya, D. 1988. "Direct Intervention Programmes for Poverty Alleviation: An Appraisal." *Economic and Political Weekly* (25 June).

Bardhan, P.K. 1974. "On the Incidence of Poverty in Rural India in the Sixties." In *Poverty and Income Distribution in India,* edited by P.K. Bardhan and T.N. Srinivasan. Calcutta: Ashish.

————. 1984. *The Political Economy of Development in India.* Oxford: Basil Blackwell.

————. 1988. "Dominant Proprietary Classes and India's Democracy." In *India's Democracy,* edited by Atul Kohli. Princeton; N.J.: Princeton University Press.

Bhagwati, J. 1973. "Indian Economic Policy and Performance: A Framework for a Progressive Society." Shastri Memorial Lecture, August. Hyderabad: Osmania University Press.

————. 1987. "Indian Economic Performance and Policy Design." Seventh Sir Purshottam Thakurdas Memorial Lecture, Bombay. *Journal of Indian Institute of Bankers,* 27.

————. 1988. "Poverty and Public Policy." *World Development* 16, no. 5.

————. 1992. "India's Economy: The Shackled Giant." Mimeo, Radhakrishnan Lectures, Oxford.

Bhagwati, J., and Desai, P. 1970. *India: Planning for Industrialization.* London: Oxford University Press.

Bhagwati, J., and Srinivasan, T.N. 1975. *Foreign Trade Regimes and Economic Development: India.* Delhi: Macmillan.

Bhargava, S., and Joshi, V. 1990. "Increase in India's Growth Rate: Facts and a Tentative Explanation. *Economic and Political Weekly,* Vol. 25, Nos. 48 and 69.

Blyn, George. 1983. "The Green Revolution Revisited." *Economic Development and Cultural Change,* 31 (March).

Byrd, W.A. 1990. "Planning in India: Lessons from Four Decades of Development Experience." *Journal of Comparative Economics* 14, no. 4.

Chakravarty, S. 1987. *Development Planning: The Indian Experience.* Oxford: Clarendon Press.

Chandrasekhar, C.P. 1988. "Aspects of Growth and Structural Change in Indian Industry." *Economic and Political Weekly,* November, Special Number.

Chelliah, R.J. 1991a. "The Growth of Indian Public Debt: Dimensions of the Problems and Corrective Measures." Mimeo. New Delhi: National Institute of Public Finance.

————. 1991b. *Towards a Decentralized Polity.* New Delhi: Fiscal Research Foundation.

Dandekar, V.M. 1988a. "Indian Economy Since Independence." *Economic and Political Weekly,* 23 April.

————. 1988b. "Population Front of India's Economic Development." *Economic and Political Weekly,* 23 April, 16 December.

Dandekar, V.M., and Rath, N. 1971. *Poverty in India.* Poona: Indian School of Political Economy.

Dasgupta, P. 1990. "Well Being in Poor Countries." *Economic and Political Weekly,* 4 August.

Datt, G., and Ravallion, M. 1992. "Growth and Redistribution Components of Changes in Poverty Measures." *Journal of Development Economics* 38: 275–95.

Dreze, Jean 1990. "Poverty in India and the IRDP Delusion." *Economic and Political Weekly,* 29 September.

Fallon, Peter R., and Lucas, Robert E.B. 1991. "The Impact of Changes in Job Security Regulations in India and Zimbabwe." *The World Bank Economic Review* 5, no. 3.

Frankel, F.R. 1971. *India's Green Revolution, Economic Gains and Political Costs.* Princeton, N.J.: Princeton University Press.

————. 1978. *India's Political Economy, 1947–1977.* Princeton, N.J.: Princeton University Press.

Gaiha, R. 1985. "Poverty Technology and Infrastructure in Rural India." *Cambridge Journal of Economics* 9, no. 3.

————. 1989. "Poverty, Agricultural Production and Prices in Rural India—a Reformulation." *Cambridge Journal of Economics* 13, no. 2.

Ghose, A.K. 1989. "Rural Poverty and Relative Prices in India." *Cambridge Journal of Economics* 13, no. 2.

Goldar, B.N. 1988. "Relative Efficiency of Modern Small Scale Industries in India." In *Small Scale Enterprises in Industrial Development: The Indian Experience,* edited by K.B.H. Suri. New Delhi: Sage.

Government of India. 1951. *First Five Year Plan, 1951–56.* New Delhi: Planning Commission.

————. 1956. *Second Five Year Plan, 1956–61.* New Delhi: Planning Commission.

————. 1961. *Third Five Year Plan, 1961–66.* New Delhi: Planning Commission.

————. 1964. *Report of the Industrial Development Procedures Committee* (T. Swaminathan, Chairman). New Delhi.

————. 1969. *Report of the Industrial Licensing Policy Enquiry Committee* (S. Dutt, Chairman). New Delhi.

————. 1970. *Fourth Five Year Plan, 1969–74.* New Delhi: Planning Commission.

————. 1976. *Fifth Five Year Plan, 1974–79.* New Delhi: Planning Commission.

————. 1978. *Report of the Committee on Import-Export Policies and Procedures* (P.C. Alexander, Chairman). New Delhi: Ministry of Commerce.

————. 1981. *Sixth Five Year Plan, 1980–85.* New Delhi: Planning Commission.

————. 1984a. *Report of the Committee on Trade Policies* (Abid Hussain, Chairman). New Delhi: Ministry of Commerce.

————. 1984b. *Report of the Committee to Review Policy for Public Enterprises* (A. Sengupta, Chairman).

————. 1985a. *Report of the Committee to Examine Principles of a Possible Shift from Physical to Financial Controls* (M. Narasimham, Chairman). New Delhi: Ministry of Finance.

————. 1985b. *Seventh Five Year Plan, 1985–90*, Vol. 1. New Delhi: Planning Commission.

————. 1991. *Report of the Committee on the Financial System* (M. Narasimham, Chairman). New Delhi: Ministry of Finance.

————. 1992a. *Final Report of the Committee on Tax Reform* (R.J. Chelliah, Chairman). New Delhi: Ministry of Finance.

————. 1992b. *Interim Report of the Committee on Tax Reform* (R.J. Chelliah, Chairman). New Delhi: Ministry of Finance.

Gulati, Ashok. 1989. ''Structure of Effective Incentives in Indian Agriculture: Some Policy Implications.'' *Economic and Political Weekly* 30 September.

Hanumanth Rao, C.H. 1975. *Technological Change and Distribution of Gains in Indian Agriculture.* Delhi: Institute of Economic Growth.

————. 1992. ''Agriculture: Policy and Performance.'' In *The Indian Economy: Problems and Prospects,* edited by Bimal Jalan. New Delhi: Viking.

Hanumanth Rao, C.H., and Rangaswany, P. 1988. ''Efficiency of Investments in IRDP: A Study of Uttar Pradesh.'' *Economic and Political Weekly,* 25 June.

Hazell, P.B.R., and Haggblade, S. 1991. ''Rural-Urban Growth Linkages in India.'' World Bank PRE Working Papers, WPS No. 430. Washington, D.C.: World Bank.

Hirway, Indira. 1988. ''Reshaping IRDP: Some Issues.'' *Economic and Political Weekly,* 25 June.

————. 1991. ''Poverty Alleviation Programmes in India: Past Experience and Future Directions.'' In *Poverty Reduction in India,* Report of a workshop held in July 1990, Development Cooperation Information Department, The Hague.

Jalan, Bimal. 1991. *India's Economic Crisis: The Way Ahead.* Delhi: Oxford University Press.

————. 1992. ''Balance of Payments, 1956–1991.'' In *The Indian Economy: Problems and Prospects,* edited by B. Jalan. New Delhi: Viking.

Jha, P.S. 1992. ''Cutting Red Tape: Question of Mindset.'' *Economic Times,* November 27.

Joshi, V., and Little, I.M.D. 1989. ''Indian Macroeconomic Policies.'' In *Debt Stabilization and Development,* edited by G. Calvo, R. Findlay, P. Kouri, and J. B. de Macedo. Oxford: Blackwell.

Kakwani, N., and Subbarao, K. 1990. ''Rural Poverty and Its Alleviation in India.'' *Economic and Political Weekly,* 31 March.

Kelkar, V., and Kumar, R. 1990. ''Industrial Growth in the Eighties: Emerging Policy Issues.'' *Economic and Political Weekly,* 27 January.

Khatkhate, D.R. 1991. ''National Economic Policies in India.'' In *National Economic Policies: Handbook of Comparative Economic Policies,* Vol. 1, edited by D. Salvatore. Westport, CT: Greenwood Press.

———. 1992. "India on an Economic Reform Trajectory." In *India, 1992*, edited by P. Oldenburg. New Delhi: Allied.

Kohli, A., ed. 1988. *India's Democracy: An Analysis of Changing State Society Relations*. Princeton, N.J.: Princeton University Press.

———. 1989. "Politics of Economic Liberalization in India." *World Development* 17, no. 3.

Kurian, N.J. 1987. "I.R.D.P.: How Relevant Is It?" *Economic and Political Weekly*, 26 December.

———. 1989. "Anti-Poverty Programme: A Reappraisal." *Economic and Political Weekly*, 25 March.

———. 1990. "Employment Potential in Rural India." *Economic and Political Weekly*, 29 December.

Kurien, C.T. 1989. "Indian Economy in the 1980s and on to the 1990s." *Economic and Political Weekly*, 15 April.

Lal, Deepak. 1988. "Ideology and Industrialization in India and East Asia." In *Achieving Industrialization in East Asia*, edited by Helen Hughes. Cambridge: Cambridge University Press.

Lall, Sanjay. 1987. *Learning to Industrialize: The Acquisition of Technological Capability in India*. London: Macmillan.

Lipton, M., and Toye, J. 1990. *Does Aid Work in India?* London: Routledge.

Little, I.M.D., Mazumdar, D., and Page, J.M. 1987. *Small Manufacturing Enterprises*. New York: Oxford University Press.

Lucas, Robert E.B. 1988. "India's Industrial Policy." In *The Indian Economy: Recent Development and Future Prospects*, edited by Robert E.B. Lucas and G.F. Papanek. Boulder, Colo.: Westview Press.

Lucas, Robert E.B., Papanek, G.F., and Gustav, F., eds. 1988. *The Indian Economy: Recent Development and Future Prospects*. Boulder, Colo.: Westview Press.

Maddison, A. 1989. *The World Economy in the 20th Century*. Paris: OECD.

Malenbaum, W. 1962. *The Prospects for Indian Development*. London: George Allen and Unwin.

Michaely, M., Papageorgieu, D., and Choksi, A. 1991. *Liberalizing Foreign Trade: Lessons of Experience in the Developing World*. Oxford: Blackwell.

Minhas, B.S. 1974. "Rural Poverty, Land Distribution and Development Strategy: Facts." In *Poverty and Income Distribution in India*, edited by P.K. Bardhan and T.N. Srinivasan. Calcutta: Ashish.

———. 1975. "Design of Economic Policy and the Phenomenon of Corruption: Some Suggestions for Economic Reform." *Journal of Social and Economic Studies* 3, no. 2 (September).

———. 1988. "The Planning Process and the Annual Budgets: Some Reflections on Recent Indian Experience." *Indian Economic Review* 22, no. 2.

Minhas, B.S., Jain, L.R., and Tedulkar, S.C. 1991. "Declining Incidence of Poverty in the 1980s: Evidence vs. Artifacts." *Economic and Political Weekly*, 6–13 July.

Mittra, A. 1977. *Terms of Trade and Class Relations*. London: Frank Cass.

Mohan, R., and Aggarwal, V. 1990. "Commands and Controls: Planning for Indian Industrial Development." *Journal of Comparative Economics* 14, no. 4.

Mulji, S. 1990. "Vision and Reality of Public Sector Management: The Indian Experience." In *Public Policy and Economic Development*, edited by M. Scott and D. Lal. Oxford: Clarendon Press.

Mundle, S., and Govinda Rao, M. 1991. "Volume and Composition of Government Subsidies in India, 1987–88." *Economic and Political Weekly*, 4 May.

———. 1992. "Issues in Fiscal Policy." In *The Indian Economy, Problems and Prospects*, edited by B. Jalan. New Delhi: Viking.

Nayar, B.R. 1989. *India's Mixed Economy: The Role of Ideology and Interest in its Development*. Bombay: Popular.

Nayyar, D. 1976. *India's Export and Export Policies in the 1960's*. Cambridge: Cambridge University Press.

———. 1988. "India's Export Performance, 1970–85: Underlying Factors and Constraints." In *The Indian Economy: Recent Development and Future Prospects*, edited by Robert E.B. Lucas and Gusaf F. Papanek. Boulder, Colo.: Westview Press.

Neale, Walter C. 1985. "Indian Community Development, Local Government, Local Planning, and Rural Policy Since 1950." *Economic Development and Cultural Change*, 33.

Oldenburg, P. 1990. "Land Consolidation as Land Reform, in India." *World Development* 18, no. 2.

Pandit, B.L. 1991. *The Growth and Structure of Savings in India*. Bombay: Oxford University Press.

Papanek, Gustav F. 1988. "Poverty in India." In *The Indian Economy: Recent Developments and Future Prospects*, edited by R.E.B Lucas and G.F. Papanek. Boulder, Colo.: Westview Press.

Paranjape, H.K. 1988. "Indian Liberalization: Prestroika or Salaami Tactics?" *Economic and Political Weekly*, Special Number, November.

Raj, K.N. 1965. *Indian Economic Growth: Performance and Prospects*. New Delhi; Allied.

———. 1984. "Some Observations on Economic Growth in India over the Period 1952–53 to 1982–83." *Economic and Political Weekly*, 13 October.

Rajaraman, I.L. 1990. "Textile Exports to Non-Quota Markets: Impact of Real Exchange Movements." *Economic and Political Weekly*, 31 March.

Rao, V.M. 1988. "Interventions for the Poor, Critical Discussions, Potentialities and Limitations." *Economic and Political Weekly*, Special Number, November.

Rao, V.M., and Deshpande, R.S. 1986. "Agricultural Growth in India, A Review of Experiences and Prospects." *Economic and Political Weekly*, Vol. 21, No. 38 and 39.

Reserve Bank of India. 1991. *Report on Currency and Finance 1990–91*. Bombay.

Rosen, George. 1992. *Contrasting Styles of Industrial Reform: China and India in the 1980's*. Chicago: University of Chicago Press.

Rudolph, L., and Rudolph, S. 1987. *In Pursuit of Lakshmi: The Political Economy of the Indian State*. Chicago: University of Chicago Press.

Sandesara, J. 1988. "Small-Scale Industrialization: The Indian Experience." *Economic and Political Weekly*, 26 March.

Sau, R. 1988. "The Green Revolution and Industrial Growth in India: A Tale of Two Paradoxes and a Half." *Economic and Political Weekly*, 16 April.

Sen, A.K. 1989. "Indian Development: Lessons and Non-Lessons." *Daedalus* 118, no. 4.

Sen, C. 1984. *"Essays on the Transformation of India's Agrarian Economy."* New York: Garland.

Singh, I.J. 1990. *The Great Ascent: The Rural Poor in South Asia.* Baltimore: Johns Hopkins University Press.

Singh, M. 1964. *"India's Export Trends and the Prospects for Self-Sustained Growth."* Oxford: Clarendon Press.

Srinivasan, T.N. 1991. "Reform of Industrial and Trade Policies." *Economic and Political Weekly,* 14 September.

Sundrum, R.M. 1987. *Growth and Income Distribution in India: Policy Performance Since Independence.* New Delhi: Sage.

Suri, K.B., ed. 1988. *Small-Scale Enterprises in Industrial Development: The Indian Experience.* New Delhi: Sage.

Swamy, D.S., and Gulhati, A. 1986. "From Prosperity to Retrogression: Indian Cultivators During the 1970s." *Economic and Political Weekly,* 21–28 June.

Tyagi, D.S. 1981. "Growth of Agricultural Output and Labour Absorption in India." *Journal of Development Studies.* 8, no. 1.

UNIDO. 1990. *India, New Dimensions of Industrial Growth.* Oxford: Blackwell.

Vaidyanathan, A. 1986. "Labour Use in Rural India: A Study of Spatial and Temporal Variations." *Economic and Political Weekly,* 27 December.

———. 1991. "Agriculture and the Economy: Causes and Consequences of Slow Growth." In *Economic, Society and Development,* edited by C.T. Kurien, E.R. Prabhakar, and S. Gopal. New Delhi: Sage.

Virmani, A. 1991. "Demand and Supply Factors in India's Trade." *Economic and Political Weekly,* 9 February.

Visaria, P., and Minhas, B.S. 1991. "Evolving an Employment Policy for the 1990s: What Do the Data Tell Us?" *Economic and Political Weekly,* 13 April.

Wolf, M. 1982. *India's Exports.* Oxford: Oxford University Press.

World Bank. 1989a. *India: An Industrializing Economy in Transition.* Washington, D.C.: World Bank.

———. 1989b. *India: Poverty, Employment and Social Services.* Washington, D.C.: World Bank.

———. 1987, 1992. *World Development Report.* Washington, D.C.: World Bank.

12

CHINA: SOCIALISM AND REFORM, 1950–1990

Gene Tidrick

OVERVIEW OF DEVELOPMENT, 1950–1990

China's economic history in the past forty years has been punctuated by sharp shifts in policy. Under Mao Tse-tung, campaigns of mass mobilization alternated with periods of adjustment. After Mao's death China launched sweeping reforms that reversed many of the policies of the previous quarter century, but the reform era, too, has been marked by sharp, though less convulsive, shifts in policy.[1]

The Maoist Years

The economy that the government of the new People's Republic of China inherited in 1949 was devastated by more than a decade of war. Agricultural and industrial production was well below peak prewar (1937) levels, and hyperinflation had destroyed the value of currency and financial assets. In the succeeding three years, the new regime carried out a massive redistribution of land and became involved in the Korean War, but it also brought prices under control and largely restored production to prewar levels. In 1953, therefore, the government felt in a position to launch the First Five-Year Plan and begin China's socialist transformation.

The First Five-Year Plan (1953–1957) followed the classic Soviet model. Development strategy was based upon rapid accumulation of capital extracted from agriculture and reinvested in heavy industry. High savings were generated through compulsory grain delivery at low prices combined with low wages, high prices, and high profits in largely state-owned industry. Profits were turned over to the state and reinvested according to a central plan. The plan controlled production and prices as well as investment.

The First Plan period was, in comparison with the Soviet First Plan under Stalin and subsequent Chinese experience, one of relatively gradual change. Following the radical land reform of 1949–1952, which had created some 100 million smallholdings, peasants were organized through successive stages into cooperatives, ostensibly on a voluntary basis. Forced collectivization came only in 1958, though compulsory grain delivery was established by 1954. Small-scale industries and services were also organized into cooperatives in this period and only later into communes and larger urban collectives. In large-scale industry and infrastructure, the government quickly established public ownership, central planning, and a thrust toward development of heavy industry. Growth was high during the First Plan. Real net material product rose by 9 percent per annum from 1952–1957, according to official statistics (SSB, 1990, p. 33).

The success of the First Plan prompted Mao to attempt a Great Leap Forward from socialism to communism in 1958. The Great Leap Forward added two distinctly Chinese dimensions to the Soviet model: mass mobilization of labor and reliance on moral, rather than material, incentives. The theory was that surplus agricultural labor could be tapped for labor-intensive construction projects and higher-value industrial activity. This concept had been applied in China for some 2,000 years (Perkins, 1988) and had become part of standard Western development economics (Lewis, 1954; Nurkse, 1955), but Mao applied it on an unprecedented scale. In a period of three months 753,000 collective farms were amalgamated into 24,000 "people's communes" with an average of 5,000 households and 10,000 acres. Rural labor was shifted from farming to large construction projects and small-scale industries such as the famous backyard furnaces. This was also the era of costless communal dining. Revolutionary enthusiasm in rural areas was matched by unrealistic central planning allocations. The share of heavy industry in total industrial output, which had risen steadily from 37 percent in 1952 to 45 percent in 1957, shot up to 53.5 percent in 1958 and to 66.6 percent in 1960 (SSB, 1990, p. 52). The accumulation rate (net investment as a share of net material product used), which had averaged an impressive 24.2 percent during the First Plan, was raised to 33.9 percent in 1958 and to 43.8 percent in 1959 (SSB, 1990, p. 38).

The full consequences of the Great Leap Forward became known to the outside world only years later. Grain output fell 15 percent in 1959 and 16 percent in 1960 and remained at the level for another year. The resulting famine is estimated to have caused 20 million to 30 million extra deaths during 1959–1961, mostly in the countryside.[2] The famine was due in part to drought and to failure to report the bad news in time for relief shipments to reach affected areas, but more fundamentally it was due to the diversion of resources to investment in industry. Industrial output more than doubled between 1957 and 1960 but then crashed in 1961, partly due to the abrupt withdrawal of Soviet assistance in 1960.[3]

The years 1963–1965 were a period of rehabilitation and adjustment. There was an attempt to return to the more centralized planning methods of the First Plan. The accumulation rate, which had plummeted to 10.4 percent in 1962, was held to an average of 22.7 percent. In agriculture, the commune system was not disbanded, but the basic accounting unit was shifted from the commune (5,000 households) to the production team (20–30 households), private sideline activities were permitted, and there was limited experimentation with production responsibility systems. By 1964 real income had recovered to the 1957 level and grew by another 17 percent in 1965, according to official statistics (SSB, 1990, p. 34). .

In 1966 the wheel turned again with initiation of the Cultural Revolution. In this period revolutionary Red Guards were encouraged by Mao to attack the bureaucracy and even party cadres; millions of intellectuals, technicians, and educated youth were sent down to the countryside; universities were closed; and moral incentives were extolled. Although Mao's attempt to promote "permanent revolution" was the best-known feature of the Cultural Revolution, an equally important and more enduring feature was the emphasis upon decentralization and regional self-sufficiency. Planning and "ownership"[4] of most industry were decentralized to the provincial and municipal levels (Wong, 1986). Each province was encouraged to become self-sufficient in heavy industry, and each locality in grain and simple consumer and producer goods. China thus replicated at the provincial—and in some products, right down to the brigade—level an inward-looking development strategy. Although the average population of a Chinese province (27 million in 1970) was equal to that of a medium-sized country, China forfeited many of the inherent benefits of its huge internal market. Also significant was "the Third Front" program of investment in remote regions of southwestern and western China aimed at creating a completely self-sufficient industrial base secure from foreign invasion (Naughton, 1988). This absorbed some 40 percent of China's total investment from 1964–1971.

In 1968 Mao called in the People's Liberation Army to suppress the Red Guards and restore order. There were periodic attempts thereafter to strengthen central planning, but conditions remained unsettled until Mao's death in 1976. In spite of the "Ten Years of Turmoil," as the period 1966–1976 is known in China, growth by official accounts averaged 6 percent per annum. But these figures must be treated with caution, not least because the State Statistical Bureau was virtually disbanded during the Cultural Revolution.

Development After Mao

In the two years following the death of Mao, Chinese economic policy showed signs of confusion. On one hand, ambitious development plans were formulated—the accumulation rate rose to over 36 percent in 1978—and there were campaigns against capitalist tendencies; on the other hand, China began the process of opening up to the outside world. Opening up mainly meant contracting for huge imports of capital goods from Japan and the West. A Chinese scholar commented, "If 1958 can be characterized as a year of excessive haste based on 'indigenous methods,' then 1978 was one of haste based on 'imported' methods'' (Liang, 1982, pp. 61–62; quoted in Johnson, 1990, p. 13). But in order to pay for these imports, China also began to expand exports. In current U.S. dollar terms, exports doubled between 1976 and 1979 (SSB, 1990, p. 602). Although opening up was not billed as a reform, it represented a significant break from Chinese practice under Mao.[5]

In December 1978, following Deng Xiaoping's consolidation of leadership, China launched a program of adjustment and reform that marked a sharp break with Maoist development strategy. The call for reform reflected profound disillusion with the excesses and hardships of the previous two decades. The adjustment half of the program was not new; it reflected the familiar need to reduce investment that was too large to be absorbed and threatened macroeconomic stability. But the underlying strategy of reform also implied lower investment. At the broadest level, the reform strategy was to rely on intensive growth—more productive use of resources—rather than extensive growth based on accumulation. With higher productivity, savings and investment could be lowered without sacrificing growth. The key was better (material) incentives, which would spur productivity growth and thereby both sustain output growth and permit high consumption, which in turn would provide the wherewithal to improve incentives, thus completing the virtuous circle of intensive growth. Material rewards linked to productivity were to replace controls in order to improve ''x-efficiency,'' to use Harvey Leibenstein's (1966) term, while markets were to supplement (but not supplant) planning in order to improve allocative efficiency.

This was the theory behind reform, though it was not articulated in these terms. It worked because of massive and easily removed inefficiencies in the economic system, especially in agriculture. There was no blueprint for reform. Above all it was pragmatic, experimental, and gradualist.[6] But once begun, reform took on a life of its own. Starting slowly with experimental household responsibility systems in agriculture, local authorities and peasants themselves took over and within three years effectively decollectivized agriculture. In nine years peasant consumption levels doubled, after two decades of no increase in per capita private consumption (Johnson, 1990, pp. 70–71). Reforms in industry and the urban sector came more slowly and fitfully, but increasing profit retention and gradual substitution of markets for planning led to significant changes. Between 1978 and 1989 or 1990:

- The share of gross output value of industry contributed by state-owned enterprises fell from 77.6 percent in 1978 to 56.0 percent in 1989 (SSB, 1990, p. 394).

- Employment in nonagricultural township and village-level enterprises increased by 65.4 million from 1978–1989, of which 38.9 million new jobs were in industry (SSB, 1990, p. 387).

- Total exports rose from $9.75 billion in 1978 to $62.1 billion in 1990. Manufactured exports increased from $4.5 billion to $46.2 billion in the same period (SSB, various years).

Table 12.1
China's Population and Income Growth, 1949–1990

Period		Population	National Income	National Income per capita
1949-52	Rehabilitation Period	2.4	8.9	6.3
1953-57	First Five Year Plan	2.0	14.9	12.7
1958-59	Great Leap Forward	0.0	-13.5	-13.5
1960-62	Aftermath of Great Leap Forward	2.5	14.7	11.8
1963-65	Adjustment Period	2.4	6.0	3.6
1966-76	Cultural Revolution & After	1.3	10.0	8.6
1977-78	Transition	1.4	8.4	6.8
1953-78	Prior to Reform	2.0	6.0	3.9
1979-90	Reform Period	1.4	8.4	6.8
1953-90	Total Average Growth	1.8	6.7	4.8

Sources: World Bank (1983, p. 76); SSB (various years).

- Government expenditure fell from 34.1 percent of gross domestic product (GDP) in 1978 to 21.9 percent in 1990 (World Bank, 1992a).
- Gross national product (GNP) in constant prices grew by 8.7 percent per annum from 1978 to 1990.

The course of reform was not smooth, as subsequent sections discuss. New experiments were regularly launched and reversed, and periods of reform alternated with reimposition of controls as macro imbalances appeared. The events of June 1989 in Tiananmen Square initially put the future of the entire reform program in doubt, but this now appears to have been only a temporary setback.

GROWTH AND STRUCTURAL CHANGE

Output Growth

According to official statistics, China has maintained a high, though fluctuating, growth rate for over forty years (Table 12.1). Despite a fall in output during the Great Leap Forward, net material product (NMP) grew at an average rate of 6.0 percent per year from 1952 to 1978. Growth accelerated to 8.7 percent per year during the reform period 1978–1989, giving an average annual NMP growth of 6.8 percent over the entire 1952–1989 period. Per capita growth averaged 4.9 percent, which implies that output per capita was about six times higher in 1990 than in 1952. Yet, China remains—again according to official statistics at official exchange rates—one of the poorest countries in the world with GDP per capita of about $350 in 1990.[7] How does one account for this apparent inconsistency? Has China grown as rapidly as official statistics show?

International comparisons, with attendant complexities of appropriate exchange rates, are discussed in chapter 13. At this point the focus is on growth of output in constant domestic prices. From this perspective there are several reasons for concluding that official statistics overstate the growth rate.

First, China's use of NMP rather than the more conventional GDP to measure output overstates the growth rate by around 0.5 percent per annum from 1957 to 1978.[8] This is because NMP excludes nonmaterial services, which, being considered nonproductive, were suppressed during this period. From 1978 both NMP and GDP estimates are available, and, owing to some catching up of the service sector, rates of growth of NMP and GDP were similar from 1978 to 1990.

Second, China's price structure, which has high relative prices for much (not all) of industry (Taylor, 1986; Rajaram, 1992), biases the growth rate upward. Using Indian price weights, which are hardly undistorted but more representative of other developing countries, the World Bank (1983, pp. 293–96) estimated that China's 1957–1979 NMP growth was 4.6 percent per annum compared with the official estimate of 5.4 percent. The official methodology of chain-linking different constant price series also biases growth rates upward, particularly for the early years when the industry-agriculture price ratio was especially high. Using 1980 rather than 1952 relative price weights, Gregory Chow (1985, p. 201) calculated that average growth fell from 6.0 percent during 1952–1978 to 3.9 percent. In per capita terms, the effect was even more dramatic—a fall from 3.9 to 1.7 percent (Johnson, 1990, p. 17).

Third, China's growth rate prior to 1978 is exaggerated because the normal gradual improvement in product quality, which one takes for granted in most economies and which is imperfectly reflected in their output statistics, failed to occur in China. With controlled and rigid prices, strict control over introduction of new products, and guaranteed sales of any output produced, Chinese industrial enterprises had little incentive to innovate or improve quality standards.[9]

Finally, assessment of China's growth performance should not ignore the verdict of the Chinese themselves that much of the officially reported growth, especially between 1957 and 1978, was an illusion.[10]

The above considerations apply to the prereform period, but post-1978 statistics also appear to overstate growth, mainly due to unreliable price deflators (Rawski, 1991).[11] We conclude that official statistics overstate China's growth rate during both the reform and prereform periods, though for different reasons. It is difficult to quantify the bias, but the fragmentary estimates just cited suggest that overall growth may have been exaggerated by as much as 2 percent per annum for the past forty years. This implies that rather than the nearly sixfold increase in real per capita income from 1952 to 1990 shown by the official statistics, the increase would have been slightly less than threefold. This is still a creditable performance, though less spectacular than the official record suggests.

Input Efficiency

Whatever the true rate of growth of Chinese output, growth was purchased at high resource or input cost. Throughout the Maoist period, China pursued a

Table 12.2
Accumulation Rate and Investment Rate

	Accumulation Rate	Investment Rate
1952	21.4	
1957	24.9	
1960	39.6	
1965	27.1	
1970	32.9	
1975	33.9	
1980	31.5	32.2
1985	35.0	38.6
1990	34.1	40.5

Accumulation Rate: Ratio of accumulation to national income used. National income used is national income produced (approximately equal to NMP) plus net imports. Accumulation is equal to national income used minus consumption; accumulation is therefore approximately equivalent to net investment, and the accumulation rate is approximately equal to the share of net investment in NMP.

Investment Rate: Ratio of gross investment to gross expenditure.

strategy of extensive growth based upon a high rate of accumulation of capital and mass mobilization of labor. The accumulation rate (roughly speaking, the share of net investment in net expenditure) rose from 21.4 percent in 1952 to 33.9 percent in 1975 and during the Great Leap Forward reached an unsustainable level of 40 percent (Table 12.2). This heavy investment yielded a low return even if one accepts the official output statistics. In the first years of reform a deliberate attempt was made to scale down the accumulation rate, but after 1984 it rose again. China's share of investment in total expenditures averaged about 31 percent from 1980 to 1984 and then rose to nearly 40 percent from 1985 to 1990. For most of the past forty years China has had one of the highest accumulation or investment rates in the world.[12]

High investment had a low return in the Maoist period because much of it was devoted to inherently low-yield activities, such as the Third Front investment in the late 1960s; because it largely led to replication of low efficiency or outmoded capital equipment;[13] and because the corresponding low consumption ratio provided insufficient incentives for workers, managers, and farmers to produce more efficiently. Or, from another perspective, the high investment rate was no substitute for better policies that would have generated growth at lower resource cost.

The effect of the extensive growth strategy can be captured by total factor productivity (TFP) estimates. TFP measures the relationship between output growth and a weighted average of input growth. In most fast-growing economies a large share (40 percent or more) of total output growth is unaccounted for by growth of capital and labor inputs. In China, estimates by Dwight Perkins (1988, p. 628) show that average annual TFP growth was actually negative over the entire period 1957–1976, but high (3.8 percent) from 1976 to 1985.[14] Growth

Table 12.3
Growth of Output by Sector

	Agriculture	Industry	Other	Total
	(--------------% per annum------------)			
NMP in 1970 Constant Prices /a				
1952-57	4.9	19.4	10.1	8.2
1957-79	2.3	10.8	3.9	5.3
1952-79	2.7	12.3	5.0	5.8
GDP in 1987 Constant Prices /b				
1978-90	5.6	10.8	9.2	8.7

Note on Coverage: Construction output is included in "Other," unlike in Tables 12.5 and 12.6, where construction is included in Industry. "Other" excludes nonmaterial services during 1953–1979.
[a]Double-deflated estimates from World Bank (1983, p. 72). These are more comparable to GDP figures than unadjusted official statistics.
[b]From World Bank unpublished estimates, based on official statistics.

in most of the Maoist period therefore depended almost entirely on high capital accumulation. In the early years of reform, a substantial portion of growth came from higher productivity. We have no TFP estimates for the overall economy in more recent years, but it is likely that TFP growth has been lower following the sharp increase in investment in the mid-1980s. Capital productivity certainly fell. The incremental capital output ratio (ICOR) rose from 3.75 during 1979–1984 to 5.17 during 1985–1990.[15]

Structural Change

China's sustained industrialization drive radically altered the structure of the Chinese economy. Real industrial output growth, according to official statistics, has averaged over 10 percent per annum for the past forty years (Table 12.3). Agriculture and services grew more slowly, especially during the Maoist period. Indeed, the main effect of reforms seems to have been to accelerate growth of agriculture and services, leaving industrial growth largely unchanged. Within industry, however, reforms shifted emphasis somewhat away from heavy industry.

High growth of industry, combined with high relative industrial prices, has led to an exceptionally high share of industry in GDP. For at least twenty-five years China's share of manufacturing has been about twice that of India and substantially above that of even Brazil and Korea, whereas the share of China's service sector has remained only about two-thirds as large as that of India (Table 12.4). Some idea of the effect of price distortions on these shares can be gained from the estimate of the World Bank (1983, pp. 293–94) that China's share of

Table 12.4
Structure of Production

	Per Capita Income 1989	Agriculture		Industry		Manufacturing		Services, etc.	
		1965	1989	1965	1989	1965	1989	1965	1989
	(----------------------------% of GDP----------------------------)								
China	350	40	27	37	52	(29)	(38)	23	27
India	340	44	30	22	29	16	18	34	41
Other Low-Income /a	300	44	33	17	28	8	14	31	39
Indonesia	500	56	23	13	37	8	17	31	39
Mexico	2010	14	9	27	32	20	23	59	59
Brazil	2540	19	9	33	43	26	31	48	48
Korea	4400	38	10	25	44	18	26	37	46

Source: World Bank, World Development Report 1991, except for China. Chinese figures for 1965 are own estimates based on World Bank (1983) methodology; 1989 figures are from SSB (1990, p. 32); manufacturing figures for both years are own estimates.
ªOther than China and India.
Definition: Agriculture includes agriculture, forestry, fishing, and hunting. Industry includes mining, manufacturing, construction, electricity, water, and gas. Services and so on include all other activities.

Table 12.5
Structure of Employment

	Agriculture	Industry	Services
	(-------------% of Labor Force----------)		
China			
1952	83.5	7.4	9.1
1965	81.6	8.4	10.0
1979	69.9	17.9	12.2
1989	60.2	21.9	17.9
India			
1989	74.0	11.0	15.0

Source: For China, SSB (1989, p. 109). For India, World Bank (1983, p. 75).

industry in GDP in 1979 was 47.1 percent, using Chinese prices, and 39.9 percent, using Indian prices. India's own share of industry in GDP in 1979 was 26.8 percent.

China's employment structure is more nearly like that of other developing countries than its production structure (Table 12.5). Over 80 percent of the labor force was still engaged in agriculture in 1965, and over 60 percent in 1989. The imbalance between production and employment shares implied a corresponding imbalance in sectoral productivity ratios. Output per worker in industry was nine times as high as output per worker in agriculture in China in 1965, though the ratio fell to 5.3 by 1989. The corresponding ratio for India in 1981 was 3.5. China's labor force continued to grow at 2.9 percent per annum from 1978 to 1990, compared with a population growth rate of 1.2 percent. This reflects entry from previous periods of higher population growth plus some increase in participation rates. Almost two-thirds of new jobs created during this period were outside agriculture, as nonagricultural employment grew at 5.6 percent per annum (4.7 percent in industry and construction and 6.6 percent in services). Although agricultural employment continued to grow at 1.6 percent per annum, China will soon reach a point, as the rate of growth of the labor force falls, when the absolute size of the agricultural labor force will also begin to fall.

AGRICULTURE

The organization of Chinese agriculture has been subject to frequent and far-reaching changes. In the Maoist years agriculture first underwent thoroughgoing redistribution of land (1949–1952), then collectivization into small units (mid-1950s), formation of gigantic communes as the basic collective unit (Great Leap Forward), and finally reestablishment of the production team (average size, thirty-five households) as the basic unit of collective agriculture. Along the way, small private plots, sideline activities, and rural markets were subject to cycles of toleration and suppression.

Collective agriculture, as practiced from 1962 until reforms started in 1979, was based on a system of production plans (including public works) and procurement quotas handed down from communes through brigades to production teams.[16] Each household, including those headed by the infirm or aged, was entitled to a basic minimum share of production team income. Remaining net team income was distributed on the basis of work points earned for undertaking collective farming. Work points were also earned by health workers ("barefoot doctors"), teachers, and party cadres.

The rationale for collective agriculture rested on three assumptions: there was surplus labor in agriculture, which could be mobilized for capital construction; there are large economies of scale in agriculture; and collectives are an effective way of providing basic needs and social security. The last of these assumptions was valid and underlay China's success in reducing mortality and expanding literacy (discussed later). But the other assumptions are questionable. Although surplus labor undoubtedly existed, this idea was hardly new to China, and most of the high-return, labor-intensive irrigation and other capital construction projects had long since been exploited (Perkins, 1988, p. 611). There are other ways to mobilize surplus labor (such as the corvee system), and subsequent Chinese experience has shown that sideline activities, which were largely suppressed, and rural industry would have provided higher returns to the surplus labor that did exist. As for economies of scale in agriculture, these are almost universally exaggerated. They are frequently offset by diseconomies of scale, and where economies exist, they can often be captured through equipment leasing or other means. The great fallacy is to assume that farm size must be large enough to internalize the minimum economic scale of the largest-scale activity.[17]

Collectivization suffered from one other great handicap: it provided inadequate incentives for production because, as Chinese critics put it, everyone was "eating out of one big pot." Redistribution of land, while contentious and bloody, at least provided the great majority of peasants with what they most wanted—land of their own. Peasants were also willing to enter into limited cooperative ventures. But forced collectivization more than offset any possible advantages of scale economies. The adverse effects of collectivization were compounded by irrational production planning and onerous procurement targets at the commune and brigade levels. The emphasis on "grain as the key link" imposed a costly target of self-sufficiency on localities. Provinces such as Shandong with a strong comparative advantage in cotton production were forced to reallocate land from cotton to grain production. In times of revolutionary fervor, there were even instances in which peasants were forced to fill in fish ponds to grow grain.

Under the circumstances, agriculture performed surprisingly well during the Maoist period. Irrigated area and chemical fertilizer use expanded after 1962, and modern high-yielding crop varieties were introduced (Lin, 1990, p. 155). Value added in agriculture grew by 2.7 percent per annum during 1952–1978 while population growth averaged 2.0 percent. China was thus able to feed approximately 22 percent of the worker's population with about 7 percent of the worker's arable land—a significant achievement. Nevertheless, by 1978 there were enormous allocative and x-inefficiencies waiting to be exploited.

Agricultural reforms introduced after 1978 were as far-reaching as earlier land redistribution and collectivization. There were four main elements of reform. First, household production responsibility systems were introduced, culminating in the virtual decollectivization of agriculture by the end of 1982. These allocated individual plots of land to households on a long-term leasehold basis (usually fifteen years). Second, agricultural markets were encouraged. Procurement quotas were reduced, and farmers were given a bonus for above-quota sales and permitted to sell surplus production in free markets. Village trade fairs were reactivated, and free urban markets gradually expanded. Third, quota purchase prices were increased by 20–50 percent. Combined with reduced quotas, bonuses for above-quota procurement, and the expansion of free market sales, this sharply improved the rural-urban terms of trade. Fourth, specialization of production according to local conditions was again permitted. These reforms constituted a clear break with Maoist agricultural organization.

The impact of the reforms was dramatic. Gross agricultural output increased by over 50 percent between 1978 and 1984 (7.6 percent per annum) and thereafter (1984–1990) slowed to the still highly respectable rate of 4.5 percent per annum (SSB, 1991, p.48). Real per capita consumption of agricultural residents increased by 67 percent from 1978 to 1984 (8.9 percent per annum) and by 26.5 percent (4.0 percent per annum) from 1984 to 1990 (SSB, 1991, p. 271). Studies of total factor productivity show that TFP in agriculture declined from 1958 to

1978 and then increased sharply after 1978. The studies attribute about half of increased agricultural output after the reforms to the introduction of the production responsibility system.[18]

The surge in agricultural incomes and productivity spurred an equally dramatic increase in rural nonagricultural production. Township and village enterprises (TVEs), as they were called after the abolition of communes and brigades in 1985, grew very rapidly. According to official statistics, the TVE share of gross industrial output increased from 9.1 percent in 1978 to 23.8 percent in 1989, an implicit real rate of output growth of nearly 23 percent per annum. Total TVE employment grew from 28.3 million to 93.7 million; 39 million of the additional 65 million jobs were in industry (SSB, 1990, pp. 387–88).[19] A caveat is in order, however, about the reliability of both output and employment data (Rawski, 1991). There is independent evidence that TVEs have grown extremely rapidly, though undoubtedly less rapidly than shown in the official statistics.

Despite these achievements rural reforms are incomplete.[20] Ownership and land tenure rights remain murky. Formal ownership of land is still vested in the collective, and individual leases have not always been honored. This has adversely affected agricultural investment and has led to a disproportionate amount of investment in rural housing for which individuals have clear ownership rights. Whether full private freehold is essential is debatable, but the need for clarification of ownership and land use rights is clear. Price and market reform also is incomplete. Quota procurement prices have been kept below market prices in an effort to reduce the fiscal costs of urban food subsidies, which amount to over 2 percent of GDP. In 1989 the government deferred part of the payment for compulsory grain deliveries, a serious setback to market reform. More recently, however, policy has begun to change. In 1991 the ration price of grain was increased by 67 percent (World Bank, 1992a, p. 18). Finally, complementary reforms are needed to provide social services and public goods. Some scholars have suggested that China's substantial achievements during the Maoist years in literacy, health, and poverty reduction have been jeopardized (Perkins, 1988, p. 610). While such concerns may be exaggerated, they are not unwarranted (discussed later). Similarly, irrigation and mechanization have declined somewhat. While this has often been a rational economic response, for example, in the decline of uneconomic triple-cropping, there are also reports of neglect of maintenance of productive irrigation systems. To the extent these problems exist, they point to a need to develop new institutional mechanisms to provide social services and public goods rather than to revert back to collective systems.

INDUSTRY

Prereform System

China's industrial organization was modeled on, but significantly different from, that of the Soviet Union.[21] As in the Soviet Union, Chinese enterprises were given production targets handed down from above and derived from an integrated plan based on material balancing. Material inputs were allocated by a supply agency, and outputs were distributed through a specialized agency at prices set by the price bureau. Employment and wages were controlled by a labor bureau. Consumer goods were rationed at controlled prices. All enterprise profits were handed over to the supervisory agency, and investment plans and funds were handed down. Planning was largely done in physical terms, with prices and money playing a passive or strictly accounting role.

China's planning system differed from that of the Soviet Union in important ways. First, planning was far less detailed in China, with a maximum of 837 centrally planned product categories compared with 65,000 in the Soviet Union. Less detail went with slacker plan targets, more uncertainty of supply allocations, and development of barter and other decentralized arrangements to make up for supply deficiencies. Second, planning was far more decentralized in China, leading to largely self-contained "cellular" subsystems at the national, provincial, and local level (Donnithorne, 1972). In addition, China had a large number of commune and brigade enterprises producing for the local market, in line with the Maoist strategy of "walking on two legs." These rural industries were meant to economize on transport costs and provide employment for surplus rural labor, which was generally not allowed to migrate to cities, while large-scale urban industry was to be the main instrument of structural transformation.[22] Third, in contrast to slacker production planning, China exercised tighter control over labor than other socialist countries. Workers were assigned jobs, typically for life. The work unit provided housing, grain rations, health care, and pensions. These mechanisms gave the party and the state enormous social control. Migration to urban areas was almost impossible without permission because grain and housing were essentially available only through the work unit. On pain of losing these benefits, workers also had to seek permission to marry and have children.

The Chinese planning system enabled China to mobilize high rates of surplus, to direct resources to priority sectors, and to generate a high rate of industrial growth. Heavy industry was favored and (in terms of gross output value) grew at 13.8 percent per annum from 1952 to 1978 while light industry grew at 9.3 percent. The share of heavy industry in the gross value of industrial output increased from 35 percent in 1952 to 57 percent in 1978. Control over migration and development of rural industry reduced infrastructural investment requirements and further augmented resources available for industrial investment.[23]

But the prereform planning system also had significant drawbacks. Both planner preferences and the incentive system were biased toward high investment. This investment hunger or expansion drive led, as in other planned systems, to a shortage economy (Kornai, 1980). This had several consequences. Above all, the enormous resources devoted to industry were used inefficiently. From 1957 to 1978, total factor productivity in industry was stagnant (Tidrick, 1986; Chen, et al., 1988); industrial growth was entirely accounted for by growth of capital and labor inputs, with rising labor productivity offset by falling capital productivity. Inefficiency at the aggregate level was mirrored by inefficiency in the use of energy and raw materials at the plant level. Furthermore, the system was biased against innovation and improvements in product quality. A significant part of output was either added to permanent inventories or discarded. While China produced a comprehensive range of industrial products, many of those products were uncompetitive in cost, quality, or technological level with those produced elsewhere. In addition, the heavy industry bias of industrial strategy yielded little advance in the urban standard of living. The average annual wage in state-owned units remained constant from 1957 to 1978, availability of basic consumer goods such as cloth expanded slowly, variety was limited, and urban living space in 1978 was only 3.6 square meters per person.[24] Finally, investment hunger led to periodic overinvestment and loss of macroeconomic control, even in the prereform system. This tendency, while emanating in the past from political decisions, was reinforced by enterprise incentives.

Industrial Reforms

Policy changes in industry after 1978 had two complementary elements: adjustment, which meant lowering the overall rate of investment and shifting emphasis from heavy to light industry, and reform. Reform in industry was less sweeping than in agriculture. The main objective of industrial reform was to improve the efficiency of the 84,000 state enterprises that produced 78 percent of industrial output in 1979[25] by decentralizing decisions, supplementing planning with market elements, and opening up the economy to foreign trade and investment. The continued dominance of planning and state enterprises was never questioned. But because reforms were incremental and uncoordinated, the effects were somewhat different than anticipated. The critical factor was that production, investment, and marketing decisions were partially decentralized without comprehensive price reform. Reforms took place in four main areas.

Enterprise Finance

Prior to reform, state enterprises handed over all profits and most depreciation allowances to the state. Working capital and investment funds for approved projects were provided as grants. These arrangements gave little incentive to improve efficiency or conserve capital. To enhance incentives and improve financial discipline, experiments in profit retention were introduced in 1979, along with a partial shift from capital grants to loans from the banking system. Profit retention schemes proliferated and spread quickly to most state enterprises.[26] During 1983–1985 profit retention schemes were replaced by a nationwide profit tax, and this, in turn, was partly supplanted by contract responsibility systems in the late 1980s.

These changes transformed the sources of investment finance. Before reform, nearly all state enterprise investment was funded through budget grants. By 1988 only 15 percent of state enterprise investment funds came from the budget while 24 percent came from bank loans, 40 percent from the enterprises' own funds, 9 percent from foreign investment, and 12 percent from other sources (Hussain and Stern, 1991a, p. 147). This loosened central control over investment decisions, but it largely failed to improve financial discipline, for several reasons.

First, the objective of most enterprises was expansion of benefits to workers and their families rather than profit maximization.[27] This led the authorities to keep tight controls over the use of retained profits and hence diluted the impact on incentives. Second, banks were not autonomous financial institutions but were heavily influenced in their lending decisions by local governments. The effect of shifting to bank loans was also weakened because principal repayments as well as interest were tax-deductible. Loan repayments were frequently renegotiated and delayed.

The most important reason reforms of enterprise finance failed to improve financial discipline was that profit retention rates were negotiable and "responsibility for profit and loss" extended only to profit, not loss. Rates of return varied widely across sectors and enterprises because of distorted prices and differing historical allocations of capital. Rather than level the playing field through price restructuring and charges on existing assets, the authorities negotiated profit retention rates for each enterprise. Even the uniform profit tax rate of 55 percent was modified for most large- and medium-scale state firms by an enterprise-specific adjustment tax to offset anomalies. Finally, loss-making enterprises continued to be financed through budget grants. It was only in the late 1980s that a bankruptcy law came into effect, and little progress has yet been made in disciplining loss-making state enterprises. In short, the reforms failed to establish a "hard budget constraint" for state enterprises. Moreover, the asymmetric treatment of profit and loss eroded government revenue by more than it reduced budget investment expenditure, thereby creating a serious problem of macroeconomic management.

Prices and Markets

Unlike other socialist economies, China had not restructured industrial prices since the mid-1950s. Although there was widespread recognition that prices were distorted, price reform was deferred because of concern over the effect on inflation, income distribution, and government revenue[28] and because the technical problems of determining an appropriate new price structure were too daunting. Initially, no consideration was given to reforming the price-setting mechanism, as opposed to restructuring administratively determined prices.

Rather than beginning, like Hungary, with comprehensive price reform and abolition of planning (Kornai, 1987), China developed a mixed planning and market system with two-tier pricing.[29] The original impetus came from decisions early in the reform period to reduce investment and to emphasize light, rather than heavy, industry. Plan targets for machinery and other producer goods were cut back, and government supply bureaus virtually abdicated responsibility for

Table 12.6
Structure of Industry

	1952	1957	1978	1985	1990
	(--------% of gross output----------)				
By Type of Ownership:					
State	76.2	80.1	77.6	64.9	54.6
Collective	3.3	19.0	22.4	32.1	35.6
(of which TVE)			9.1	14.6	20.2
Individual	20.6	0.8	-	1.8	5.4
Other				1.2	4.4
By Type of Industry:					
Light	64.4	55.0	43.1	47.1	49.3
Heavy	35.5	45.0	56.9	52.9	50.4

Source: SSB (1989, 1990).

marketing many goods that, for the first time, were in excess supply. Above-plan production was therefore marketed by enterprises themselves, often to rural industries that had previously had only limited access to state plan products. Self-marketing applied only to firms with excess supply, and above-plan prices were controlled. Gradually the share of self-marketed output expanded (Table 12.6), and the flexibility of prices for self-marketed output increased. In the system that emerged, some output was produced under the mandatory plan with controlled (low) prices for inputs and outputs, both of which were allocated, and the remaining output was produced under "guidance planning," or outside the plan, with inputs and outputs bought and sold at market prices. The reform model was one of "growing out of the plan" with an ever-shrinking share of output produced under the mandatory plan.

This system of two-tier pricing had several advantages. It enabled planners to protect priority sectors and projects;[30] it avoided the disruption of sharp changes in relative prices and revaluation of the existing asset stock; yet at the margin, market-determined prices equilibrated supply and demand and gave more appropriate signals for investment decisions (Byrd, 1987a).

Unfortunately, however, the system did not work as smoothly in practice as in theory. Because plan prices were separately controlled in each of the cellular subsystems, there were, in fact, multiple, rather than two-tier, prices for identical products, giving immense scope for arbitrage. In practice, too, the planning authorities could not ensure that allocated inputs matched output targets. There was therefore no neat separation into "low input—low output" and "high input—high output" pricing systems. Some firms found themselves having to purchase extra inputs at high market prices while selling output at low controlled prices and vice versa. More generally, shares of inputs and outputs subject to mandatory allocation were not fixed, and a great deal of enterprise effort was devoted to bargaining rather than to improving efficiency or expanding output in response to market signals. Thus, while two-tier pricing improved industrial performance, it failed to live up to its potential because it became entrenched as a semipermanent system rather than being used as a transitional device to facilitate growing out of the plan.

Much of the price reform that has taken place in China has been "price reform by stealth" (McMillan and Naughton, 1991). It is a clear instance of partial and uncoordinated reform having unintended consequences. The key elements were that production of consumer durables was highly profitable because plan prices were high and yet, due to pent-up demand and rising income, demand exceeded supply; investment by state enterprises was still fairly tightly controlled despite enterprise finance and management reforms; and looser controls over TVE and smaller state enterprise investment, plus the widening market for producer goods, facilitated TVE entry and expansion. The result in one consumer durable industry after another was that TVEs expanded output rapidly; the market became saturated; prices fell; and firms responded either by improving quality and efficiency or by withdrawing from production. The impact of tightening markets invariably increased enterprise attention to quality, customer preferences, and cost reduction (Byrd, 1987b). The process was untidy and undoubtedly took place at higher resource cost than would have occurred through a more coordinated approach to reform, but it generated rapid and broad-based growth and ultimately restructured many prices. It also showed that the dynamics of price and market reform, particularly the shift from a seller's to a buyer's market, may be as important as the ultimate achievement of rational prices.

Enterprise Management and Ownership

An early reform objective was decentralization of decision making. Enterprise managers, traditionally much weaker than their counterparts in other socialist countries (Granick, 1987), were given somewhat greater authority in the early 1980s, along with the introduction of profit retention. To a large extent, however, attempts to decentralize decision making to the enterprise level were intercepted by local authorities because of their control over bank lending and key inputs such as land and power allocation (Byrd and Tidrick, 1987). In addition, the tendency of managers to identify with worker interests led reformers to look for alternative ways to strengthen enterprise management and shift motivation toward profit maximization and production growth.

The result was a variety of contractual responsibility systems (CRS), with a common core of features: an explicit contract governing enterprise targets was drawn up between the enterprise manager and the supervisory agency; the manager was given greater authority over production decisions; his salary depended heavily upon meeting agreed upon targets; and the contracts were multiyear to avoid a short-term "ratchet effect" under which overfulfillment of targets would result in correspondingly higher targets in future (Byrd, 1991, p. 14). Some of these systems went to extraordinary lengths to mimic capitalist incentives within an overall framework of public ownership.[31] The CRS achieved some success in encouraging a business orientation and enhancing the independence of the director from both supervisory agency and worker pressure, but it did little to counter China's endemic bargaining culture, and it tended to undermine the tax system by including taxes in contract targets.

Following partial disillusionment with CRS and other reform efforts, reformers have increasingly turned their attention to ownership issues. Small private businesses were permitted in the mid-1980s. By 1990 their share of industrial output had grown to 5.4 percent. Most of this came from new entry, but leasing or even outright sale of very small state and collective units has also taken place, especially in retail commerce. The ownership debate has focused less on public versus private, however, than on creating new forms of public ownership consistent with market socialism. Experiments with distribution or sales of shares to workers or public institutions have been widely debated, and some shares have been sold on newly created stock markets, but so far no major changes have occurred.

Labor and Wage Reform

Labor and wages (along with land allocation) remain the least-reformed part of the system. For the most part, attempts to break "the iron rice bowl" of state enterprise employment have failed thus far.[32] Bonuses were restored in the initial stage of reform, but these were rarely linked to individual performance, becoming instead simply an addition to pay. Piecerate payment schemes have also been resisted. Three-year labor contracts were introduced, but these have not appreciably lessened security of employment. However, an ambitious new effort has recently been launched to extend labor contracting in some major cities. Finally, little progress has yet been made in delinking provision of housing and other social services from state enterprise employment, though state enterprises are now less likely to set up subsidiary collective enterprises for the sole purpose of providing employment to dependents of workers, and workers can no longer inherit jobs as they could in the early 1980s. TVEs are less burdened with egalitarian pay systems and permanent employment obligations (Byrd, 1992a, p. 9). Piecerate payment systems are commonplace, and TVEs have greater latitude in hiring, penalizing, or dismissing labor.

Results and Evaluation of Reform

Industrial reform has been partially successful in achieving its original aims. The overall rate of industrial growth has remained high—lower than the official estimate of 10.8 percent, no doubt, but still high, and probably as high as during 1957–1978, when the official estimate was also 10.8 percent per annum. The reforms also apparently succeeded in increasing total factor productivity, which had been stagnant from 1957 to 1978. Gary Jefferson, Thomas Rawski, and Yuxin Zheng (1990) estimate that TFP growth was 2.4 percent per annum in state industry and 4.6 percent in collective industry during 1980–1988.[33] In addition, disparities in factor returns and enterprise efficiency have been reduced during the 1980s. This tendency toward convergence provides some evidence that market reforms have induced stronger profit-seeking behavior and gains in efficiency (Jefferson and Xu, 1992). Thus, a prime objective of the reforms—a shift from extensive to intensive growth—appears to have been at least partly realized.

Notable structural change also occurred during 1978–1990 (see Table 12.6). The shift in emphasis from heavy to light industry resulted in an increased share of light industry in gross industrial output value from 43.1 percent in 1978 to 49.3 percent in 1990. Most of this shift took place in the early years of reform. More remarkable was the shift in the pattern of ownership. The share of state enterprises fell from 78 percent of industrial output in 1978 to 55 percent in 1990. This was due to the rapid growth of collective enterprises, especially TVEs, and of individual enterprises whose share of output went from zero in 1978 to over 5 percent in 1990. Other enterprises, including joint ventures of mixed (sometimes foreign) ownership, accounted for over 4 percent of output by 1990.

China's partial and incomplete reforms have also had important shortcomings and led to unanticipated problems. In particular, the uncoordinated reforms that led to rapid growth of nonstate enterprises eroded the monopoly profits of state enterprises as growing competition reduced the relative prices and many industrial goods. Average sectoral profit rates (profit plus tax/total capital) declined from 25.2 percent in 1980 to 16.8 percent in 1989, and the coefficient of variation across industries fell from 0.78 to 0.44 (Naughton, 1992). One consequence of the falling profit rate has been to reduce state revenues and create a problem of macroeconomic stability. This is discussed later. A second consequence has been to expose the extent to which, despite growing productivity overall, many state enterprises remain uncompetitive. This is reflected in growing state enterprise losses, which also contribute to macro instability. State enterprises' total losses rose from 1.0 percent of GNP in 1978 to 3.3 percent in 1990. State enterprises remain uncompetitive, largely because markets are still fragmented, prices are still controlled and give misleading signals, and they do not face a hard budget constraint that would pressure them to increase efficiency.[34]

China's industrial reform agenda remains daunting. First, price and market reform must be completed. The existing two-tier price system has improved price signals, but it perpetuates rent seeking and bargaining rather than stimulating a search for efficiency, and it undermines the fiscal system. In addition, some key prices remain controlled and distorted, though there were significant increases in many administered prices in 1990–1991 (World Bank, 1992a, p. 18).

Second, reform of factor markets has to catch up with reform of product markets. Urban land markets do not yet exist (Byrd and Tidrick, 1987), and labor markets, especially for state enterprises, are rudimentary. Despite reforms in enterprise finance, capital and financial markets still do not effectively reallocate funds horizontally. Enterprises are assigned mandatory quotas of low-interest government bonds and are offered very low deposit rates on surplus funds. Investments in new activities are also restricted, reinforcing tendencies to use retained earnings in existing lines of activity (World Bank, 1988b). Without better-functioning factor markets, reallocation of resources into more profitable lines of production will be slow.

Third, it is essential to create a hard budget constraint for state enterprises in order to increase enterprise responsiveness to price signals and improve enterprise efficiency. The task of hardening budgets is complicated in China because of the social responsibilities of state enterprises. Redundant workers stand to lose not only their job but their housing, pension, health, and education benefits as well. Clearing the way for loss-making enterprises to shed redundant labor therefore involves complementary reforms in housing and social security.

Finally, as in agriculture, clarification of ownership rights is needed. State enterprises are owned by the ''whole people,'' but this concept is so vague that it remains unclear who has the right even to dispose of existing assets. Schemes to distribute or sell shares in state enterprises to public financial institutions or local governments (World Bank, 1985) would improve accountability and incentives of state enterprise managers. Ultimately, however, reform of state enterprises may be insufficient. Experience of other countries suggests that state enterprises have been able to function as fully efficient commercial entities not only where they are themselves operated like autonomous private enterprises but where they are also subject to competition from private enterprises. Long-term improvements in industrial efficiency therefore imply a large expansion of private ownership.

FOREIGN TRADE AND INVESTMENT

For twenty years prior to reform, China's foreign trade was conducted according to a foreign trade plan. Domestic prices were insulated from foreign prices by an ''airlock system'' of cross-subsidized trade through twelve central foreign trade corporations (World Bank, 1985). The aim of trade policy was self-sufficiency. Imports were used to fill gaps in material balances, and exports were used to finance imports. Trade remained roughly balanced, and, following the split with the Soviet Union in 1960, China began to prepay its Soviet debt and resolutely avoided further foreign borrowing. From the late 1950s to early 1970s exports hovered around $2 billion per year. Between 1971 and 1974 China's exports more than tripled, in line with higher world prices and to accommodate imports of large-scale foreign technology such as fertilizer plants. An export drive during 1975–1978 further expanded exports. This expansion was helped by rapid development of new oil fields.

After 1978 China shifted more decisively from outwork to an ''open door'' policy. In a sharp break with past policy, China sought direct foreign investment, borrowed from international organizations and foreign commercial sources, and actively promoted exports.[35]

The impact of these changes has been dramatic. Starting from a low base of $9.75 billion in 1978, exports increased to $62.1 billion in 1990, an annual average growth rate of nearly 17 percent (Table 12.7). This was more than twice the rate of growth of world trade and raised China's share of world exports from 0.8 percent in 1978 to 1.9 percent in 1990.[36] Petroleum exports accounted for 35 percent of increased exports in 1978–1981, but they leveled off after that. The main source of export growth for the period as a whole was manufactures. China's share of developing country exports of manufactures increased from 6.4 percent in 1975 to 11.3 percent in 1987, making China the third largest developing country exporter of manufactures after Taiwan and Korea (Yeats, 1991, pp. 10–11). But export growth was not limited to manufactures. China's share of developing country foodstuff exports grew from 5.9 percent to 8.1 percent during the same period. China ranks second among developing country food exporters, after Brazil (Yeats, 1991, p. 13).[37]

China was also highly successful in attracting direct foreign investment. From 1979 to 1989 cumulative foreign investment amounted to about $19 billion, and the cumulative value of contracts signed was about $39 billion in over 27,000 contracts (SSB, 1990, p. 613). Net direct foreign investment averaged $2.5 billion per year during 1988–1990. About two-thirds of total direct foreign investment in recent years has come from Hong Kong, and more than one-third of total foreign investment was in Guangdong province. This reflects both the close cultural and communications links between Hong Kong and Guangdong and the policy of establishing special economic zones to attract foreign investment. Emphasis has been given to attracting foreign investment for export production, and by the end of the decade exports from foreign-invested firms reached nearly $4 billion.[38]

What accounted for China's strong export performance? Was it due to market-oriented reforms or to traditional directive planning? The answer is, some of both. As late as 1986–1987, 70 percent of exports were purchased at domestic prices under a mandatory plan at an average financial loss of over 10 percent based on the official exchange rate.[39] By the end of the decade, 55 percent of exports were outside the plan, but some of these were still licensed in order to prevent ''excessive'' exports of underpriced Chinese products. Thus, on the export side the trading system still substantially insulated the domestic price structure from world prices. Imports were more subject to market forces. By the end of the decade only 10 percent of imports were subject to the traditional rule that imports should be priced at a comparable level to domestic products adjusted for quality differences. The remaining 90 percent were priced at c.i.f. plus tariff and trading markup. But 45 percent of imports were still under license, and each time there was a balance-of-payments problem, the government tightened direct trade controls.

At the same time, however, financial incentives played an important role in trade expansion. One of the best indicators of this is that TVE exports, which are not part of the central trade plan, were U.S.$10 billion by 1989—nearly 20

Table 12.7
China: Foreign Trade, 1978–1990

	1978	1981	1984	1987	1990
	(-------------US\$ billion-----------)				
Exports	9.8	22.0	26.1	39.4	62.1
Mineral Fuels	1.3	5.2	6.0	4.5	5.2
Other Primary	3.9	5.0	5.9	8.7	10.6
Manufactures	4.5	11.8	14.2	26.2	46.2
Imports	10.9	22.0	27.4	43.2	53.4
Memo:					
China's share of world exports	0.8	1.2	1.5	1.7	1.9
Exports as share of GNP (\$)	4.6	7.9	8.7	13.0	17.0
Exports as share of GNP (constant 1980 prices)	4.9	7.9	7.2	8.6	9.5

Source: SSB (1990); World Bank statistics.

percent of total exports. Many specific measures improved export incentives in the 1980s. First, trade was decentralized. Authorized foreign trade corporations increased from 12 in 1978 to over 6,000 by the end of the decade. Competition among foreign trade agencies, in some cases even for planned products, provided extra incentives for production and nudged domestic prices in the direction of world prices. Although few enterprises were permitted to engage in foreign trade directly, an agency system working on commission provided a further link with world prices.

Exchange rate reform provided a second strong export incentive. Foreign exchange retention rights, shared between enterprises and supervisory agencies, were introduced in 1979 and gradually expanded to 44 percent of total export earnings by 1988. Rates varied by product, province, and for within- and above-plan earnings. In 1985 the government permitted retained foreign exchange to be traded in foreign exchange adjustment centers (FEAC). Despite continued licensing and periodic restrictions on the use of foreign exchange, the FEAC soon developed into a parallel foreign exchange market with a substantial premium (nearly 100 percent in 1987–1988). The combination of foreign exchange retention and the FEAC thus harnessed distortions and foreign exchange scarcity as a potent export incentive. The authorities also periodically devalued the yuan, from about 1.6 per dollar in 1978 to 5.2 per dollar at the end of 1990. Since average Chinese inflation was lower than that of major trading partners over the period, the real effective exchange rate depreciated by approximately 70 percent between 1980 and 1990, greatly enhancing the overall competitiveness of Chinese exports.[40]

A third export incentive, introduced in 1987 and generalized in 1988, is the foreign trade contracting system. This provided for very high marginal retention rates and liberalized the use of foreign exchange, thus providing a strong export incentive for provincial and local governments, with which contracts are concluded. Contracting has further decentralized export decision making (but to local governments rather than enterprises) and, by limiting central subsidies, has made these decisions more sensitive to profitability.

No account of China's trade success would be complete without reference to the Hong Kong connection. Hong Kong has contributed two-thirds of China's direct foreign investment, is the market for about half of China's exports (three-fourths of which are reexported), and supplies about one-third of China's imports (Sung, 1990, p. 255). Hong Kong firms have organized labor-intensive process industries that export to markets vacated by Hong Kong and other higher-wage economies. Almost 100,000 visitors per day enter China from Hong Kong, Macao, and Taiwan. Many are on business, but even those visiting relatives challenge attitudes associated with central planning. Apart from direct transfer of skills and technology, therefore, Hong Kong has provided an important "kindred model" for China's market-oriented reforms (Chen, Jefferson, and Singh, 1990). But Hong Kong's important contribution to China's development could not have taken place without receptivity on the Chinese side. In this sense, policy reform can be said to be the catalyst for activating the Hong Kong connection.

To what extent has growth of trade and foreign investment contributed to China's overall economic performance? That is, how efficient have trade expansion and opening up to the outside world been, especially in view of the role of mandatory planning in trade promotion? There are reasons for doubting whether the gains to the economy have been commensurate with overall growth of exports.

Not only have exports been subsidized on average, but the rate of financial subsidy has varied widely. In effect, each export good has been given its own implicit exchange rate. In 1983, these rates ranged from yuan 2.8 per dollar for petroleum products (which cost yuan 1.59 to produce) to yuan 5.34 for light chemicals. Foreign exchange retention rates have also been differentiated by products. It is difficult to know whether this differentiation, which was designed to offset domestic price distortions, resulted in an export structure that was justified in terms of China's resource endowment. Alexander Yeats (1991) has shown that the rank correlation of China's manufactured exports with labor intensity was high and statistically significant during 1986–1987, as were the rank correlations between China's manufactured export structure and those of Taiwan and India.[41] But Nicholas Lardy (1992) has argued, following leading Chinese authorities (Ma and Sun, 1988), that China overexported petroleum and energy-intensive products, particularly in the mid-1980s. Domestic energy shortages lowered production of labor-intensive manufactures that could have earned more foreign exchange.

Recent reforms, especially foreign trade contracting, have exacerbated the tendency to export the wrong products. These reforms have enhanced price responsiveness without reforming distorted domestic prices, increasing the likelihood of adverse selection. By concentrating decisions in the hands of local governments, they have also reinforced the tendency to concentrate on quantitative targets rather than the economic efficiency of exports (World Bank, 1990, p. 85). Finally, export retention and foreign trade contracting have encouraged provincial trade wars in which interior provinces producing raw materials at low, controlled prices refuse to supply these to established coastal industries because they neither benefit from higher domestic prices nor get credited with their indirect contribution to foreign exchange earnings.

In brief, lagging domestic reform, especially price reform, limits the benefits of trade expansion. Moreover, trade reform has gone about as far as it can productively go without domestic price reform; further decentralization of trade decisions could lead to increased exports of the wrong products.

It would be a mistake, however, to overemphasize the static allocative inefficiencies of China's trading system. Whatever allocative inefficiencies have been, they have been outweighed by the dynamic benefits of trade and investment expansion. Trade expansion is analogous to TVE growth in this respect, and it is perhaps no accident that TVEs have contributed so substantially to export growth. Foreign direct investment brought in new production, marketing, and management techniques and influenced domestic producers through competition and emulation. Vast imports of machinery and equipment and foreign licensing agreements contributed significantly to the growth and modernization of manufacturing. Equally important, the discipline of producing for export has almost certainly been a major source of total factor productivity growth and quality improvement. China must increasingly look to the efficiency of its trade to reap further benefits, but the process of learning to export on a vast scale in the 1980s, even if some of the exports were relatively high-cost, was an important factor in China's growth.

MACROECONOMIC POLICY

Prereform

The overriding objectives of macro management in the Maoist era were high domestic resource mobilization and stable prices. Inflation was particularly sensitive because hyperinflation in the late 1940s was one of the proximate causes of the collapse of the Nationalist regime.

Both the conventional macro instruments of fiscal and monetary policy and micro instruments such as pricing policy were directed toward achieving the two main objectives. Pricing policy, in particular, was subordinated to mobilization rather than allocation of resources. Low agricultural and mineral prices were used to mobilize a surplus from the primary sector. Basic wage goods were rationed at low prices. Low wages[42] and high prices of final industrial goods generated high industrial profits, which were transferred to the budget and then reallocated according to plan priorities. Unlike other socialist countries, China relied on direct transfer of industrial profits rather than a turnover tax as the main source of government revenue. In 1978 state enterprise profit remittances accounted for 55.6 percent of government revenue and 19.2 percent of GDP.

Money and credit policy was conducted through the standard socialist monobank system as an adjunct to physical planning, with the credit and wage plans tightly integrated with the physical output plan. Price controls and a conservative fiscal and monetary stance were used to prevent emergence of open inflation. There was a budget deficit in only nine of the twenty-six years from 1953 to 1978. Balance-of-payments management under Mao was as conservative as fiscal and monetary policy. In twenty of twenty-six years from 1953 to 1978 China ran a balance-of-trade surplus.

China's conservative macropolicy and detailed micro intervention were highly successful in reaching the main prereform objectives. The ratio of domestic savings to GDP had reached 33.2 percent in 1978, one of the highest in the world, and the average annual increase in the retail price index was 0.5 percent from 1957 to 1978. Growth was also high, and balance-of-payments crises were unknown before 1978. But even in this highly controlled economy, there was a business cycle with sharp fluctuations in the accumulation rate,[43] and success in resource mobilization was purchased at a high cost in efficiency and technological development.

Reform of Macro Management

Macroeconomic management changed dramatically after 1978. Not only was macropolicy reoriented to support reform, for example, by lowering the investment rate in order to promote intensive growth, but macropolicy instruments were themselves reformed. The objective of macro management reform was to develop indirect policy instruments to manage an increasingly decentralized system. But in the process of shifting from direct controls to indirect levers, inflation and, to a lesser extent, balance-of-payments problems emerged, creating at least the appearance of conflict between reform and macro stability.

Fiscal Reform[44]

Profit retention and other enterprise reforms were intended to lead to a balanced reduction in budget revenue and expenditure as enterprises used retained profits and bank borrowing to take over responsibility for investment finance. Unfortunately it did not work out that way.

Government revenue declined from 34.4 percent of GNP in 1978 to 19.9 percent in 1990—a remarkable 14.5 percentage points decline (Table 12.8). Revenue from enterprises fell by 16 percentage points of GNP, more than the decline in total revenue. In 1978 enterprise taxes and profit remittances accounted for 60 percent of budget revenue, in 1990 only 23 percent. Expenditure fell by an almost equally remarkable 12.2 percentage points of GNP, from 34.1 percent

Table 12.8
China: Government Revenue and Expenditure, 1978–1990

	1978	1981	1984	1987	1990	Change 1978-90
	(-----------------% of GNP---------------)					
Total Revenue:	34.4	29.0	26.4	22.7	19.9	-14.5
Revenue from enterprises	20.6	16.1	11.2	6.3	4.6	-16.0
Profit Remittance	19.1	15.1	9.9	0.4	0.4	-18.7
Profit Taxes	1.5	0.9	1.3	5.9	4.1	2.6
All Other Taxes and Revenues	13.8	12.9	15.2	16.4	15.3	1.5
Total Expenditure and Net Lending:	34.1	30.2	27.9	24.8	21.9	-12.2
Current Expenditure	19.3	22.4	19.8	18.1	17.4	-1.9
Administrative	1.4	1.5	2.0	1.6	1.8	0.4
Defense	4.7	3.5	2.6	1.9	1.7	-3.0
Culture, Education, Health	3.1	3.6	3.8	3.6	3.5	0.4
Economic Services	5.0	3.5	2.9	2.3	2.2	-2.8
Subsidies	3.2	7.7	5.9	5.9	5.5	2.3
Daily Necessities	2.2	6.4	4.5	2.6	2.2	0.0
Agricultural Inputs	0.0	0.5	0.1	0.0	0.0	0.0
Enterprise Losses	1.0	0.9	1.2	3.3	3.3	2.3
Other	1.9	2.6	2.7	2.8	2.8	0.9
Development Expenditure	14.9	7.8	8.0	6.7	4.4	-10.5
Budget Balance:	0.3	-1.2	-1.5	-2.1	-2.0	-2.3
Memo: Net Yield from Enterprises	19.6	15.2	10.0	3.0	1.3	-18.3

Source: World Bank (1992a).

to 21.9 percent. This brought China's budget shares down to a level much more typical of other developing countries than in 1978.[45]

The sharp drop in expenditure (12.2 percentage points of GNP) was mainly due to a decline in development expenditure (10.5 percentage points), partly reflecting the declining financial intermediation role of government. Current expenditure also fell by 1.9 percentage points. Defense expenditure was reduced by 3 percentage points as China demobilized 1 million men.[46] But subsidies increased from 3.2 percent of GNP in 1978 to 5.5 percent in 1990 and were even higher during the intervening period. In the early stage of reform, urban food prices were insulated from producer price increases by subsidies, but these subsidies were gradually reduced from 6.4 percent of GNP in 1981 to 2.2 percent in 1990. Meanwhile, however, subsidies for enterprise losses increased from 1.0 percent of GNP in 1978 to 3.3 percent in 1990. The combined effect of lower enterprise tax and profit remittances and increased subsidies to loss-making enterprises therefore amounted to a fiscal revolution. The net yield from enterprises fell from 19.6 percent of GNP in 1978 to only 1.3 percent in 1990.

Part of the reduction in budget revenue and expenditure was deliberate. Enterprises retained profits, and bank borrowing funded an increasing share of industrial investment, thereby reducing both the revenue and expenditure sides of the budget. But this accounted for only about one-third of the fall in revenues from enterprises. Profit retention and loan repayments were only about 5 percent of GNP in 1988 and 3.9 percent in 1989 (Naughton, 1992). The decline in revenue from enterprises was unintended and came mainly from the erosion of state enterprise monopoly profits due to industrial policy reforms. Increasing competition lowered average industrial profits by 8.4 percentage points of GNP between 1980 and 1989. The number of loss-making enterprises increased as well, putting additional pressure on expenditure through higher enterprise subsidies.

Difficulties in designing a uniform tax system for industry in the absence of price reform compounded the revenue loss from reform of enterprise finance. Bargaining firm by firm gradually eroded the revenue base. In addition, many of the profit retention schemes, including the CRS, reduced revenue elasticity by creating low or zero marginal tax rates. This also imparted a procyclical bias to the tax system (Blejer et al., 1991, p. 29).

Many of these problems were mirrored in center-provincial fiscal relations (Bahl and Wallich, 1992). China's taxes are collected at lower levels of government and funneled upward. Contract responsibility systems established between provinces and the center during the 1980s displayed many of the same features as enterprise CRS: bargaining, low or zero marginal tax rates, and gradual erosion of the central revenue base.[47] Moreover, lower-level governments negotiate tax rates and contracts for their enterprises and have an incentive to reduce taxes (shared with higher levels) and substitute ''voluntary'' contributions or to create new enterprises outside the budget altogether (Gordon and Li, 1991, p. 205).

The net result of fiscal-related reforms has been to reduce revenue by more than expenditure obligations and to complicate cyclical fiscal policy. This has led, among other things, to underfunding of infrastructure investment and a resort to ad hoc levies to counter inflationary pressure. More systematic fiscal reform is needed to secure a reliable and elastic revenue base.

Financial Sector and Monetary Policy

From the early 1980s China began to reform financial institutions[48] to complement agricultural and industrial reforms. Specialized banks were created to take over some functions of the People's Bank of China (PBC), which had operated as a monobank. The PBC itself became a central bank in 1984. The specialized banks have a national network of branches extending from the provincial to the local level. Since 1986 two universal banks have been established, along with a number of provincial banks. Nonbank financial institutions, such as investment trusts and financial companies formed by enterprise groups, were also created. Finally, some steps have been taken to establish markets for government and enterprise securities, and rudimentary stock exchanges have been established to market shares in a few enterprises.

Table 12.9
China: Macro Indicators, 1979–1980

Year	Real GDP Growth (% per annum)	Current Account Balance ($ billion)	Inflation Rate (% per annum)	Investment Ratio (% per annum)	Money and Quasi- money Growth (% per annum)
1978	-	0.2	0.7	33.4	
1979	7.2	1.0	2.0	34.8	
1980	7.9	1.0	6.0	32.2	
1981	4.5	3.0	2.4	29.2	
1982	8.7	6.5	1.9	29.7	
1983	10.1	4.7	1.5	30.3	
1984	14.5	2.8	2.8	32.2	
1985	13.0	-11.4	8.8	40.1	17.1
1986	8.4	-7.9	6.0	40.4	29.3
1987	11.2	0.1	7.3	39.2	24.2
1988	10.8	-3.8	18.5	39.7	21.0
1989	3.9	-4.5	17.8	39.2	18.4
1990	4.9	11.9	2.1	39.2	28.0

Source: SSB and World Bank data.

China's financial sector has expanded rapidly in both scope and complexity, though it remains far less deep and sophisticated than that of India. Moreover, some of the new financial institutions are not deeply rooted. Commercial banks remain under the sway of local and other governments and lack the independence needed to operate as true financial intermediaries. While household deposits, helped by generally positive real interest rates, grew spectacularly (from 7.1 percent of national income in 1978 to 39.5 percent in 1989), there are questions whether this represents true financial deepening or monetary overhang with enormous inflationary potential.[49] In any case, the large volume of liquid assets held by households and the shift toward a market economy have significantly increased the importance of household expectations for macropolicy. In particular, inflationary expectations potentially have a large impact on the inflation rate (Hussain and Stern, 1991a, p. 135).

The macro consequences of creating a central bank in 1984 have been disappointing. Open inflation has emerged as PBC has been unable or unwilling to restrain credit and money expansion (Table 12.9).[50] From 1984 to 1990 the average growth of money and quasi-money was 22.9 percent per annum. The forces driving monetary expansion have been the erosion of budget revenue and the rise in the investment rate again after 1984. Although the budget deficit has been relatively small (about 2 percent of GNP), the central investment plan has hardly changed. Central plan investment was 9 percent of GNP in 1978, but after an initial reduction in the early 1980s, it rose again to 8 percent of GNP in the latter half of the decade. Finance of public investment has increasingly been shifted from the budget to bank credit. With a large part of mandated central investment pushed off-budget, the public sector borrowing requirement was about 7 percent of GNP (Naughton, 1991, p. 210). The pressure for an accommodating credit and monetary expansion was heightened by credit claims from the rapidly expanding nonstate enterprise sector. The overall investment ratio rose from around 30 percent during 1980–1984 to around 40 percent during 1985–1990.

Credit and monetary growth has also been subject to sharp swings. Faced with excessive demand for credit, PBC has followed a stop-go policy. Weaknesses in financial sector and other reforms have contributed to the problem. PBC sets credit ceilings, which are disaggregated downward through bank branches, but local governments have been able to pressure branches to disregard ceilings. Equally important, government authorities have been able to ensure that state enterprises under their control are spared during credit crunches, thus throwing a disproportionate share of the adjustment burden onto the dynamic nonstate sector. Unable to enforce credit restraint on state enterprises and unwilling to tolerate a short-term cut in the growth rate, PBC has time and again prematurely relaxed credit in order to sustain growth.[51] The effect on prices was dampened in 1985 by a large trade deficit (5 percent of GNP), but as the trade deficit was reduced and inflationary expectations mounted, inflation accelerated in the late 1980s. By 1988 the retail price index was increasing by 18.5 percent, and the market price of consumer goods by 30.3 percent. At that point the authorities not only cut credit expansion but also reimposed direct investment controls and some price controls.

Macropolicy and Reform

The emergence of inflation and balance-of-payments deficits has created pressure to reverse reforms. Particularly in 1988–1989, loss of macro control led to reimposition of direct price and investment controls and tightening of import licensing. Chinese critics of reform (and even some reformers) have interpreted inflationary pressure to mean that there is an inherent conflict between reform and macro stability. This perception has become a self-fulfilling prophecy. Each balance-of-payments or inflationary crisis provokes not only a tightening of credit but also a partial reversal of reforms. Thus China has increasingly embarked on a stop-go cycle of reform and buoyant growth alternating with reversal of reform and slowing of growth.

In reality, macro instability is due more to incomplete reform rather than to reform per se. In addition it is due to bad policy stemming from overemphasis on growth. Inflation associated with relative price changes during 1978–1984 was minimal, and the higher inflation from 1985 onward owed little to relative price changes (Naughton, 1991). Acceleration of inflation was due mostly to the sharp increase in investment and the associated credit expansion. Macro instability owes more to the abandonment of adjustment than to enactment of reform.

Further reforms are needed, however, to enable the authorities to use indirect instruments of macro control. First, fiscal reform is needed to provide a secure and elastic revenue base for remaining central government expenditure. Second, within the financial sector, steps must be taken to enhance the autonomy and commercial orientation of banks. Finally and most fundamentally, two reforms are needed to lay the microeconomic foundation for macroeconomic control.

First, price reform is essential, for without that, decentralized decision making will lead to inefficient investment and trade decisions. Ultimately, real resource flows will lead to price restructuring—this has already happened to some extent—but this is a costly way to rationalize prices. Second, a hard budget constraint for enterprises is essential to impose financial discipline. Otherwise, enterprises will not be sensitive to prices or feel responsible for profit and loss, so that investment hunger and demand for imports will be hard to check through indirect means.

Macro stability will also require a shift in policy that accepts the rationale for the initial program of adjustment and reform: lower investment that pays for itself through higher efficiency. A corollary is that measured growth may also be somewhat lower, but the quality of growth, for example, in better-quality products and greater responsiveness to user demand, will be higher. Some of China's most important advances in the quality of growth came in the early 1980s when a deliberate cutback in investment (creating a recession by Chinese standards) led to the creation of buyer's markets and a marked change in enterprise behavior. China's growth fetish is the biggest obstacle to reform, which in turn would provide the most secure underpinning for economic transformation and macro stability.

POVERTY AND SOCIAL INDICATORS

The common perception is that Maoist China was very successful in reducing poverty and inequality and improving social indicators. This is correct. Progress in reducing dire poverty and improving life expectancy, health, and literacy was tremendous, though success was marred by the catastrophic Great Leap Forward. There is also a common perception that many of the gains of the Maoist era have been jeopardized or reversed by reforms since 1978. This, broadly speaking, is not correct. The gains of the previous quarter century have mostly been preserved, and most social indicators continue to improve. The incidence of poverty declined dramatically after 1978. Nevertheless, some social safety nets have deteriorated and raise questions about the sustainability of past gains.[52]

Gains in health, nutrition, literacy, and other indicators of quality of life have been dramatic (Table 12.10). Life expectancy has nearly doubled since 1952 (from thirty-six to seventy years) and is close to the average in industrialized countries (74.5 years); fertility and mortality rates have both fallen; and adult literacy has increased from 14 to 73 percent since 1952. Growth of per capita consumption prior to reforms was relatively slow—1.8 percent per annum in rural areas from 1952 to 1978 and 2.9 percent in urban areas, compared with per capita national income growth of 3.9 percent per annum. Improvements in social indicators in the Maoist era came less from the overall growth of consumption than from improved distribution and subsistence security provided through rural collective and urban social welfare measures. Collectives provided for minimum basic needs in grain, medical services ("barefoot doctors"), and

Table 12.10
China: Social Indicators, 1952–1990

	1952 /a	1965	1978	1990
Life Expectancy at Birth (years)	36	54	64	70
Infant Mortality Rate (per 1000)	175	90	37 /c	29
Birth Rate (per 1000) /b	37	38	18	22
Death Rate (per 1000) /b	17	10	6	7
Rate of Natural Increase (per 1000) /b	20	28	12	15
Calories per capita	1917	1929	2441	2639
Rural per capita Consumption Index /b	100	125	158	333
Urban per capita Consumption Index /b	100	137	213	381
Adult Literacy Rate (%)	14	50	66	73

Sources: [a]All 1952 data are from Table 13.1 except for per capita consumption indexes and demographic data.
[b]SSB various years.
[c]Banister (1987, p. 116).
All other figures are from World Bank, *World Development Report,* various years.

education for most of the rural population, while subsidized grain rations plus medical, education, and other social services (often provided through the work unit) assured urban residents of a basic subsistence floor.

The 20 percent of the population living in urban areas was much better protected than rural residents. On average, the consumption level in urban areas was 2.5 times that of rural areas (SSB, 1990, p. 273), but this ratio excluded subsidies and income in kind such as health care and much of the value of urban housing (Perkins, 1988, p. 640). By unofficial estimates, urban workers enjoyed incomes (including subsidies) four to six times those of the average peasant in the late 1970s (Matson and Selden, 1992, p. 704). Moreover, urban wages and benefits were largely uniform throughout the country, whereas rural incomes varied according to the resource base of the production team. For the most part, only urban areas benefited from state subsidies, and while poorer rural areas shared welfare gains, these were at a lower level than in more prosperous rural areas. The urban bias of Chinese policy under Mao is shown most starkly by the famine after the disaster of the Great Leap Forward. Up to 30 million people may have died. The national death rate, according to official statistics, more than doubled from 11.98 in 1958 to 25.43 in 1960, but the increase was much lower in urban areas (from 9.22 to 13.77) than in rural areas (12.50 to 28.58) because urban areas were favored in grain distribution.

Despite a pronounced urban bias and the Great Leap Forward disaster, the Maoist system of basic needs provision was highly successful by international standards in improving social indicators. It was natural, therefore, to fear that economic reforms, while sharply increasing the average growth rate of consumption, might undermine the gains that had been achieved. Concern focused on three areas: population growth, health and mortality, and income distribution and poverty. Each of these is discussed in turn.

China's success in reducing fertility rates came late and relatively abruptly. Population policy changed direction frequently during the 1950s and 1960s, but in the early 1970s a renewed and concerted attempt by the government to reduce family size was launched. By that time huge improvements in mortality rates and in education of girls, two of the main correlates of fertility decline, had prepared the way for China's demographic transition. A combination of incentives, education, and coercion helped reduce the crude birthrate from 33.4 in 1970 to 23.0 by 1975. In 1979 a one-child-family campaign reinforced pressures from the government to reduce fertility, but reforms may have reduced the effectiveness of the campaign. First, leverage over family reproduction decisions has (fortunately) declined somewhat with government relaxation of grain rationing, migration, and detailed control over rural households. Second, the demise of communes with their old-age security system has increased the incentive for peasant households to have at least one son, the traditional source of security in old age. Crude birthrates have risen slightly, but pressures from local officials to enforce strictly a one-child-family policy, combined with the traditional preference for male children, have led to reported cases of female infanticide. China shares with India the dubious distinction of having one of the world's worst gender ratios (Sen, 1990), but China's ratio appears to have worsened since the late 1970s (Banister, 1987, p. 40). The obvious direction of policy in order to promote a voluntary small-family outcome is to relax official pressure for one child and to develop an alternative social security mechanism.

An increase in crude death rates from 6.21 in 1979 to 6.69 in 1986 has caused concern and led to suggestions that deteriorating health services under reform may be responsible. Rural health services have changed significantly. The number of "barefoot doctors" and other part-time health workers has declined with the abolition of communes and the work-point system. Similarly, the rural health insurance system, which covered 85 percent of the rural population in 1979, has been largely replaced by a full-fee-for-service system. (There were always some fees even under the commune system.) This change has adversely affected the level and distribution of health care, though rising incomes may have reduced the impact somewhat (Hussain and Stern, 1991b, pp. 292–93). To what extent are deteriorating health services responsible for the rise in mortality rates? Athar Hussain and Nicholas Stern (1991b) have shown that about 80 percent of the increase is accounted for by a change in age structure, but some is also due, as Judith Banister (1987) has shown, to an increase in infant mortality rates. Banister estimates that infant mortality rose from a low of 37.2 in 1978 to 50 in 1984. Since this rise predates the widespread introduction of the household responsibility system, which was completed in 1982, the link between reforms and rising infant mortality remains a puzzle. Moreover, according to official statistics the crude death rate has started to fall (with some fluctuations) since 1986.[53] Clearly, however, access of poorer rural residents to health services has deteriorated under the reforms.

China's achievements in creating a more egalitarian income distribution under Mao also appeared to be threatened by economic reform. Maoist observers predicted that emphasis on development of the coastal regions, expansion of private enterprise, abolition of communes, and the introduction of bonuses and other forms of wage differentiation would increase regional and personal income inequality. On balance, however, income distribution seems not to have been much affected by reform.

To appreciate why this is so, it is important to understand the nature of income distribution in Maoist China. Within the urban sector, abolition of property and rental income combined with an egalitarian wage policy greatly compressed urban incomes. Similarly, in rural areas, first land reform and then collectivization virtually eliminated property income and narrowed intrapersonal income differentials within each locality. But large average income differentials remained between localities and regions. In 1979 distributed collective income per capita in Shanghai Province (which has a large rural area surrounding the city) was 4.6 times that of Guizhou Province. Leaving aside the predominantly urban provinces, the ratio of distributed collective income for Jilin Province was 2.5 times that of Guizhou (World Bank, 1983, p. 84). Differences were even greater at the county, commune, and production team levels. In addition, China had a large urban-rural gap, and this increased during the prereform era because restrictions on migration prevented an equilibrating movement of labor from poorer to richer areas (Matson and Selden, 1992). Because of regional rural differences and the urban-rural gap, overall income distribution was similar in China in 1979 (Gini coefficient of 0.33) to that in Pakistan and Sri Lanka (also 0.33) and only slightly better than in India (0.38) (World Bank, 1989, p. 94).[54]

Reform permitted the creation of private wealth and the emergence of some rich households, but these were offset by other shifts between broad groups. The urban-rural gap was reduced after twenty-five years of widening; rural per capita income grew by 6.4 percent per annum from 1978 to 1990, compared with 5.0 percent in urban areas. Within rural areas the Gini coefficient in 1988 was about the same as it had been in 1978 (Matson, and Selden, 1992, p. 704; Khan *et al.,* 1992, p. 70).), though it had first improved during the early 1980s and then deteriorated again.

Focusing on poverty rather than income distribution reveals more clearly the dramatic changes brought about by reform. The incidence of poverty (share of population below the poverty line) fell from 28 percent in 1978 to 9.2 percent in 1985 (Table 12.11). The largest gains came in rural areas, where the incidence fell from 33 percent in 1978 to less than 12 percent in 1985. Income gains in rural areas were broad-based, reflecting gains from relaxing limits on migration and sideline activities and from rural industrialization, as well as from higher agricultural production. But remote upland areas with poor resource bases have not benefited nearly as much from reforms. Absolute poverty in China is now

Table 12.11
China: Poverty Indicators

	1978		1985		1990	
Total Population (million)	963		1059		1143	
Urban	172	(17.9%)	251	(23.7%)	302	(26.4%)
Rural	790	(82.1%)	808	(76.3%)	841	(73.6%)
Average per capita Income (1978 yuan)						
Urban	--		557		685	
Rural	134		324		319	
Poverty Line (yuan/year)						
Urban	--		215		319	
Rural	98		190		275	
Incidence of Poverty (million)						
Total	270	(28.0%)	97	(9.2%)	98	(8.6%)
Urban	10	(4.4%)	1	(0.4%)	1	(0.4%)
Rural	260	(33.0%)	96	(11.9%)	97	(11.5%)

Source: World Bank (1992b).

concentrated mostly in these remote, resource-constrained areas, and little progress has been made in reducing this hard-core poverty since 1985 (World Bank, 1992b).

China's experience under reform has been that there is no large trade-off between growth and equity or between market-based reforms and equity and social development. China's experience supports David Morawetz's (1977) conclusion that the distribution of benefits of growth depend more on the original distribution of assets than on transfers and social programs. Nevertheless, some new institutions and policy changes are needed to preserve the access to health and other services achieved under Mao and to reach remote areas almost untouched by development.

NOTES

The author is grateful to William Byrd for extensive comments on successive drafts; to Shahid Javed Burki, Enzo Grilli, Peter Harrold, and Shahid Yusuf for comments at a later stage; and to Anne Auchter, Manisha Singh, and Indira Sharma for assistance.

1. For general surveys of the prereform period see Alexander Eckstein (1975), World Bank (1983), and Carl Riskin (1986). For the reform period see Harry Harding (1987), Dwight Perkins (1988), Elizabeth Perry and Christine Wong (1985), James Dorn and Xi Wang (1990), D. Gale Johnson (1990), and Peter Harrold (1992). For a Chinese perspective see Muqiao Xue (1986).

2. This estimate is from Ashton *et al.* (1984). A.K. Sen (1990) argues that famine of this magnitude could take place only in a nondemocratic country. Democracy and a free press have been critical in preventing famine in India since 1943. Bad weather contributed to the fall in output in 1959 but was not responsible for the disorganization and prolonged impact on agriculture that followed. For a summary account of agricultural

development in China see Lardy (1983), Perkins and Yusuf (1984), Johnson (1990), and Justin Lin (1990). See also Kenneth Walker (1984) on grain procurement policies.

3. Statistics during this period are suspect, but there is independent evidence of an unsustainable expansion of industrial output, much of it unusable.

4. State-owned enterprises at every level of government are technically owned by the "whole people," but many of the attributes of ownership accrued to the level of government to which the enterprise reported and handed over profits (Granick, 1990). Collectives and commune and brigade enterprises were not owned by the "whole people."

5. There had been episodes of large imports of technology from the West under Mao, but this was the first time prolonged imports had been proposed. See Gene Tidrick (1986). Despite the significance of this first opening to the outside we do not follow Perkins (1988, p. 627) in counting 1977–1978 as part of the reform period.

6. The pragmatism is reflected in Deng's maxim: "It doesn't matter whether a cat is black or white so long as it catches mice."

7. The World Bank (1991) shows India (at $340 per capita) and China ($350) ranked twentieth and twenty-first, respectively, from the bottom of a list of 124 countries.

8. Subramanian Swamy (1989, p. 55) estimates that nonmaterial services were 6.0 percent of Chinese GDP and 11.6 percent of Indian GDP in 1978. If nonmaterial services were 8 percent of GDP in China in 1952, the average growth rate of GDP would have been 5.5 percent (rather than 6.0 percent for NMP) during 1952–1978.

9. For example, the Liberation brand truck, which is still produced, is a copy of a Soviet model based on a U.S. model from the 1930s (Tidrick, 1986, pp. 17–18). The same arguments apply to India, though to a lesser extent. For example, India still produces the Ambassador car, which is based on the mid-1950s Morris Oxford.

10. According to official statistics, per capita consumption increased by 77 percent from 1952–1978 (57.6 percent in rural areas and 112.6 percent in urban areas). Johnson (1990, pp. 18–19) questions the reliability of per capita consumption figures on the grounds that the percentage of consumption expenditure devoted to food barely declined (from 58.4 to 56.7 percent) for urban residents from 1957–1981 and actually increased for rural residents. This is inconsistent with the stable and low income elasticity of demand for food generally found in expenditure studies and implies that real consumption growth was much lower than shown in the official statistics.

11. Rawski (1991) has shown that growth of the chemical and machinery industries is overstated during the 1980s, in part because of unreliable price deflators in an inflationary era with dual pricing. Adjusting for apparent inconsistencies between physical and value data of just those two sectors, he finds that average annual growth of all industry (excluding village industry) would be reduced by two percentage points, from 10.8 to 8.8 percent during 1980–1985. In the case of township and village enterprises (TVEs) Rawski found evidence of widespread confusion between current and constant price data, as well as some outright falsification of output data by local authorities.

12. This may turn out to be partly a statistical quirk. If, as some unpublished work at the World Bank suggests, China's GDP is underestimated by around 55 percent, then official statistics probably overestimate the investment ratio because most of the measurement error is in noninvestment items. Investment as a share of GDP would then have been something like 25 percent in the late 1980s—still high, but within the range to be expected of rapidly growing Asian economies. Revised national accounts and investment shares would probably not change total factor productivity growth estimates significantly,

however, because there is no presumption that the bias in official accounts has been changing systematically over time.

13. This is reflected in China's energy-to-output ratio. In 1979 China's energy consumption per dollar of GNP was more than 2.5 times that of other developing countries (World Bank, 1983, p. 126).

14. Perkins's estimates by period are as follows: 1953–1957 (4.1 percent); 1957–1965 (−1.4 percent); 1965–1976 (0.6 percent); 1976–1985 (3.8 percent).

15. Calculated from 1987 constant price data.

16. In 1978, 800 million rural people were organized into 52,780 communes (about 15,000 people per commune), each of which had an average of thirteen brigades, which were, in turn, comprised of seven to ten production teams averaging thirty-five households each (Johnson, 1990, p. 25).

17. Another common fallacy is to assume that minimum economic farm size is that which provides a specified income level to a household engaged in full-time farming. This ignores what will happen to the vast numbers who would be displaced from the land if all holdings were consolidated into units of "economic" size. It also ignores the possibility of supplementing household farm income through off-farm activities, on "sub-economic" holdings. For a survey and overview of farm size and productivity, see Hans Binswanger, Klaus Deininger, and Gershon Feder (1993 forthcoming).

18. The studies are Lin (1986, 1987); John McMillan, John Whalley and Li Jing Zu (1989); and Guanzhong James Wen (1989). These are summarized in Johnson (1990, pp. 33–38).

19. See William Byrd and Lin (1990) and Byrd and Alan Gelb (1990) for a review of the role of TVEs.

20. See Johnson (1990, pp. 89–100) for a good discussion.

21. For a comparison of Chinese and Soviet planning, see David Granick (1987) and Gene Tidrick (1987).

22. This is similar to the division of labor between small- and large-scale industry in India.

23. As noted earlier, this advantage was partly squandered by heavy investment in industry in remote areas.

24. Real per capita consumption of nonagricultural residents increased by 68 percent from 1957–1978, according to official statistics (SSB, 1990, p. 274). Some increase occurred because of higher labor force participation rates, but the aggregate figures are suspect (Johnson, 1990, p. 17).

25. The rest was produced by about 100,000 urban collective, 171,000 commune, and 580,000 brigade enterprises (World Bank, 1983, p. 121).

26. See Tidrick and Jiyuan Chen (1987) for an analysis of early reforms and Byrd (1992b) for case studies of enterprises under reform.

27. For a discussion of the enterprise objective function, see Byrd and Tidrick (1987), and for a particular case, see Byrd and Tidrick (1992).

28. The state budget relied heavily on profit remittances from state enterprises. High industrial prices, especially on final products, helped generate high profits and high state revenue. Industrial price reform therefore posed a fiscal problem. Ironically, by failing to reform prices and taxes simultaneously (e.g., by substituting a value added tax for profit remittances), China ultimately saw its fiscal base erode anyway (see "Foreign Trade and Investment").

29. This was commonly referred to as mandatory and guidance planning. See Barry Naughton (1990) for a discussion of guidance planning.

30. The principles were similar to those guiding priority foreign exchange allocation in India and many other developing countries.

31. Under the asset management responsibility system, for example, candidates "bid" for the enterprise director position. Bids consist of a development plan for the enterprise with associated profit projections, which become the targets against which performance is evaluated, with a large part of salary dependent on the change in asset value (discounted profit flow) that is achieved (Byrd, 1991, pp. 19–20).

32. On wage and employment reform see Byrd and Tidrick (1987) and Andrew Walder (1986).

33. TFP growth accounted for 28 percent of total output growth in state industry and 27 percent in collective industry.

34. TVEs do face a hard budget constraint because local governments do not have the means to subsidize loss-making enterprises.

35. The most up-to-date account of China's trade reforms is Lardy (1992). See also World Bank (1988a, 1990).

36. China's ratio of exports to GNP was very low in 1978 (4.6 percent) even by large country standards. The ratio increased to 17.0 percent by 1990, but this partly reflects the effect of exchange rate changes, which lowered the dollar value of GNP. As Lardy (1992) has pointed out, trade ratios for China are hard to interpret for this reason. An alternative measure—the ratio of exports of goods and nonfactor services to GNP, all in 1980 constant prices—grew from 4.9 percent in 1978 to 9.5 percent in 1990.

37. Nearly half of China's food exports go to Hong Kong. In 1990, China's food exports were $6.6 billion, and food imports $4.5 billion.

38. To prevent loss of foreign exchange from investment in highly protected domestic industries, China imposed a foreign-exchange balancing requirement on foreign investors. This was modified in the late 1980s to permit joint ventures to trade foreign exchange on the free market (Foreign Exchange Equilization Centres) to meet balancing requirements.

39. The average financial loss was even higher in some years, reaching 30 percent in 1988. Unless stated otherwise, all figures are from Lardy (1992).

40. A study by the World Bank (1992a) shows the real effective exchange rate index in December 1990 as 31.9 (1980 = 100), where a fall signifies depreciation. Official policy is to unify the exchange rate through gradual depreciation of the official rate.

41. The latter was true for both 1986–1987 and 1975–1977, suggesting that China successfully exploited its comparative advantage even during the period of centrally planned trade.

42. Urban wages were low by international standards and remained roughly constant from 1957–1978, but the consumption level of urban residents averaged about 2.5 times that of rural residents. Migration controls prevented convergence of urban and rural incomes or the emergence of wage-gap unemployment.

43. For eight years in a row between 1957 and 1965 the accumulation rate changed annually by more than four percentage points, with a range from 10.4 to 43.8 percent.

44. Useful analyses of fiscal reform are included in Mario Blejer *et al.* (1991), Hussain and Stern (1991), Naughton (1992), and World Bank (1988b).

45. In the mid-1980s the average revenue share was 16.7 percent for low-income countries and 25 percent for middle income countries. The corresponding expenditure

ratios were 22.8 percent and 29.5 percent (Blejer *et al.* 1991, pp. 23–25). In India in 1990 consolidated government revenue was 19.6 percent of GDP, and expenditure was 30.3 percent.

46. According to national statistics China's military expenditure was 1.7 percent of GNP in 1990 and India's was 3.3 percent of GDP. UNDP (1992, pp. 166–67) estimates military expenditure for 1989 as 3.7 percent for China and 3.3 percent for India.

47. India also faces difficult issues of center-state fiscal relations, but these stem mainly from an overly rigid assignment of revenue bases and a mismatch between revenue and expenditure responsibility. Generally, India has managed center-state fiscal relations better than China.

48. On these issues see Blejer *et al.* (1991), Naughton (1991), Christine Wallich (1990), World Bank (1988b), and Oktay Yenal (1989).

49. See Blejer *et al.* (1991, pp. 19–21) for a good discussion of monetary overhang and repressed inflation. They conclude that the preponderance of evidence suggests that both of these are relatively small.

50. As Yenal (1989, pp. 9–10) has pointed out, PBC did not lack adequate technical instruments to control the money supply.

51. There is a strong correlation between growth of credit and growth of industrial output (Blejer *et al.* 1991, p. 17).

52. Useful sources on poverty and social issues include Perkins (1988), Jim Matson and Mark Selden (1992), World Bank (1983), Dean Jamison *et al.* (1984), and Riskin (1986). The most recent and comprehensive source is World Bank (1992b).

53. The infant mortality rate given in Table 12.10 is based upon World Bank statistics and may differ from other estimates.

54. See Azizur Khan *et al.* (1992) for a discussion of more recent data. These results are summarized in chapter 13.

REFERENCES

Ashton, B., *et al.* 1984. "Famine in China." *Population and Development Review* 10, no. 4.

Bahl, Roy, and Wallich, Christine. 1992. "Intergovernmental Fiscal Relations in China." World Bank Policy Research Working Paper, WPS no. 863. Washington, D.C.: World Bank.

Banister, Judith. 1987. *China's Changing Population*. Palo Alto, Calif.: Stanford University Press.

Binswanger, Hans P., Deininger, Klaus, and Feder, Gershon. (1993 forthcoming), "Power, Distortions, and Reform in Agricultural Land Markets." In *Handbook of Development Economics*, Vol. 3, edited by Jere Behrman and T.N. Srinivasan. Amsterdam: North-Holland.

Blejer, Mario, *et al.* 1991. "China: Economic Reform and Macroeconomic Management." International Monetary Fund Occasional Paper, no. 76. Washington, D.C.: International Monetary Fund.

Byrd, William. 1987a. "The Impact of the Two-Tier Plan/Market System in Chinese Industry." *Journal of Comparative Economics* 11, no. 3: 295–308.

———. 1987b. "The Role and Impact of Markets." In *China's Industrial Reform*, chap. 10, edited by Gene Tidrick and Chen Jiyuan. New York: Oxford University Press.

———. 1991. "Contractual Responsibility Systems in Chinese State-Owned Industry:

A Preliminary Assessment." In *Advances in Chinese Industrial Studies*, Vol. 2, 7–35.

————. 1992a. "Chinese Industrial Reform, 1978–89." In *Chinese Industrial Firms Under Reform*, chap. 1, edited by William Byrd. New York: Oxford University Press.

————, ed. 1992b. *Chinese Industrial Firms Under Reform*. New York: Oxford University Press.

Byrd, William, and Gelb, Alan. 1990. "Township, Village, and Private Industry in China's Economic Reform." World Bank Country Economics Department Policy, Research, and External Affairs Working Paper, no. 406. Washington, D.C.: World Bank.

Byrd, William, and Qingsong, Lin, eds. 1990. *China's Rural Industry*. New York: Oxford University Press.

Byrd, William, and Tidrick, Gene. 1987. "Factor Allocation and Enterprise Incentives." In *China's Industrial Reform*, chap. 4, edited by Gene Tidrick and Chen Jiyuan. New York: Oxford University Press.

————. 1992. "The Chongqing Clock and Watch Company." In *Chinese Industrial Firms Under Reform*, edited by William Byrd. New York: Oxford University Press.

Chen, Kang, Jefferson, Gary H, and Singh, Inderjit. 1990. "Lessons From China's Economic Reform." World Bank Country Economics Department Socialist Economies Reform Unit Research Paper, no. 5. Washington, D.C.: World Bank.

Chen, Kuan, *et al.* 1988. "Productivity Change in Chinese Industry: 1953–85." *Journal of Comparative Economics* 12: 570–91.

Chow, Gregory C. 1985. *The Chinese Economy*. Cambridge, Mass.: Harper and Row.

Donnithorne, Audrey. 1972. "China's Cellular Economy: Some Economic Trends Since the Cultural Revolution." *China Quarterly* 52: 605–19.

Dorn, James A., and Xi, Wang, eds. 1990. *Economic Reform in China*. Chicago: University of Chicago Press.

Eckstein, Alexander. 1975. *China's Economic Development*. Ann Arbor: University of Michigan Press.

Gordon, Roger H., and Li, Wei. 1991. "Chinese Enterprise Behavior Under the Reforms." *American Economic Review* no. 2: 202–6.

Granick, David. 1987. "The Industrial Environment in China and the CMEA Countries." In *China's Industrial Reform*, chap. 5, edited by Gene Tidrick and Chen Jiyuan. New York: Oxford University Press.

Granick, David. 1990. *Chinese State Enterprises: A Regional Property Rights Analysis*. Chicago: University of Chicago Press.

Gupta, S.P., *et al.*, eds. 1991. *Development Experiences in China and India*. New Delhi: Allied Publishers Limited for Indian Council for Research on International Economic Relations and London School of Economics.

Harding, Harry. 1987. *China's Second Revolution: Reform After Mao*. Washington, D.C.: Brookings.

Harrold, Peter. 1992. "China's Reform Experience to Date." World Bank Discussion Paper, no. 180. Washington, D.C.: World Bank.

Hussain, Athar, and Stern, Nicholas. 1991a. "Macroeconomic Consequences of the Chinese Enterprise Reforms." In *Development Experiences in China and India*, edited by S.P. Gupta *et al.* New Delhi: Allied.

Hussain, Athar, and Stern, Nicholas. 1991b. "On the Recent Increase in Death Rates in China." In *Development Experiences in China and India,* edited by S.P. Gupta *et al.* New Delhi: Allied.

Jamison, Dean, *et al.* 1984. *China: The Health Sector.* Washington, D.C.: World Bank.

Jefferson, Gary H., and Xu, Wenyi. 1992. "Assessing Gains in Efficient Production Among China's Industrial Enterprises." World Bank Policy Research Working Paper Series, no. 877. Washington, D.C.: World Bank.

Jefferson, Gary H., Rawski, Thomas G., and Zheng, Yuxin. 1990. "Growth, Efficiency and Convergence in China's State and Collective Industry." World Bank Country Economics Department Socialist Economies Reform Unit Research Paper, no. 1.

Johnson, D. Gale. 1990. *The People's Republic of China 1978–1990.* International Center for Economic Growth, Country Study Number 8. San Francisco: ICS Press.

Khan, Azizur Rahman, *et al.* 1992. "Household Income and Its Distribution in China." University of California, Riverside, Working paper in Economics No. 92–3.

Kornai, Janos. 1980. *Economics of Shortage.* 2 vols. Amsterdam: North-Holland.

———. 1987. "The Dual Dependence of the State-Owned Firm in Hungary." In *China's Industrial Reform,* chap. 13, edited by Gene Tidrick and Chen Jiyuan. New York: Oxford University Press.

Lardy, Nicholas R. 1983. *Agriculture in China's Modern Economic Development.* New York: Cambridge University Press.

———. 1992. *Foreign Trade and Economic Reform in China. 1978–1990.* New York: Cambridge University Press.

Leibenstein, Harvey. 1966. "Allocative Efficiency vs. 'X-Efficiency.' " *American Economic Review* 56: 392–415.

Lewis, W. Arthur. 1954. "Economic Development with Unlimited Supplies of Labour." *The Manchester School,* vol. 22.

Liang, Wensen. 1982. "Balanced Development of Industry and Agriculture." In *China's Search for Economic Growth: The Chinese Economy Since 1949,* edited by Xu Dixin *et al.,* Beijing: New World Press.

Lin, Justin Yifu. 1986. "Measuring the Impacts of the Household Responsibility System on China's Agricultural Production." Department of Economics, University of Chicago.

———. 1987. "Household Farm, Cooperative Farm, and Efficiency: Evidence from Rural De-Collectivization in China." Working Paper no. 503. Economic Growth Center, Yale University.

———. 1990. "Institutional Reforms in Chinese Agriculture: Retrospect and Prospect." In *Economic Reform in China,* chap. 7, edited by James Dorn and Wang Xi. Chicago: University of Chicago Press.

Ma, Hong, and Shangqing, Sun. 1988. *Studies on China's Price Structure.* Shanxi: Shanxi People's Publishing House and the Chinese Social Sciences Publishing House.

Matson, Jim, and Selden, Mark. 1992. "Poverty and Inequality in China and India." *Economic and Political Weekly* 27, no. 14: 701–15.

McMillan, John, and Naughton, Barry. 1991. "How to Reform a Planned Economy: Lessons from China." University of California, San Diego.

McMillan, John, Whalley, John, and Zu, Li Jing. 1989. "The Impact of China's Economic Reforms on Agricultural Productivity Growth." *Journal of Political Economy* 97, no. 4: 781–807.

Morawetz, David. 1977. *Twenty-Five Years of Economic Development 1950 to 1975.* Washington, D.C.: World Bank.

Naughton, Barry. 1988. "The Third Front: Defence Industrialization in the Chinese Interior." *The China Quarterly* 115 (September).

———. 1990. "China's Experience with Guidance Planning." *Journal of Comparative Economics* 14: 743–67.

———. 1991. "Why Has Economic Growth Led to Inflation?" *American Economic Review* 81, no. 2.

———. 1992. "Implications of the State Monopoly over Industry and Its Relaxation." *Modern China* 18, no. 1 (January).

Nurkse, Ragnar. 1955. *Problems of Capital Formation in Underdeveloped Countries.* Oxford: Basil Blackwell.

Perkins, Dwight Heald. 1988. "Reforming China's Economic System." *Journal of Economic Literature* 26, no. 2: 601–45.

Perkins, Dwight, and Yusuf, Shahid. 1984. *Rural Development in China.* Baltimore: Johns Hopkins University Press.

Perry, Elizabeth, and Wong, Christine, eds. 1985. *The Political Economy of Reform in Post-Mao China.* Cambridge: Harvard University Press.

Rajaram, Anand. 1992. "Reforming Prices: The Experience of China, Hungary, and Poland." World Bank Discussion Paper, no. 144. Washington, D.C.: World Bank.

Rawski, Thomas G. 1991. "How Fast Has Chinese Industry Grown?" World Bank Country Economics Department Socialist Economies Reform Unit Research Paper, no. 7. Washington, D.C.: World Bank.

Riskin, Carl. 1986. *China's Political Economy.* New York: Oxford University Press.

Sen, Amartya. 1990. "More Than 100 Million Women Are Missing." *The New York Review of Books,* 20 December, 61.

State Statistical Bureau of the People's Republic of China (SSB). Various years. *China Statistical Yearbook.* Beijing: China Statistical Information and Consultancy Service Center.

Sung, Yun-Wing. 1990. "The China-Hong Kong Connection." In *Economic Reform in China,* chap. 12, edited by James Dorn and Wang Xi. Chicago: University of Chicago Press.

Swamy, Subramanian. 1989. *Economic Growth in China and India: A Perspective by Comparison.* New Delhi: Vikas Publishing House.

Taylor, Jeffrey R. 1986. "China's Price Structure in International Perspective." Center for International Research Staff Paper, no. 22. Washington, D.C.: U.S. Bureau of the Census.

Tidrick, Gene. 1986. "Productivity Growth and Technological Change in Chinese Industry." World Bank Staff Working Paper, no. 761. Washington, D.C.: World Bank.

———. 1987. "Planning and Supply." In *China's Industrial Reform,* chap. 8, edited by Gene Tidrick and Chen Jiyuan. New York: Oxford University Press.

Tidrick, Gene, and Jiyuan, Chen, eds. 1987. *China's Industrial Reform.* New York: Oxford University Press.

UNDP. 1992. *Human Development Report 1992.* New York: Oxford University Press.

Walder, Andrew G. 1986. *Communist Neo-Traditionalism: Work and Authority in Chinese Industry.* Berkeley: University of California Press.

Walker, Kenneth R. 1984. *Food Grain Procurement and Consumption in China*. London: Cambridge University Press.

Wallich, Christine I. 1990. "Recent Developments in China's Financial Sector: Financial Instruments and Markets." In *Economic Reform in China*, chap. 6, edited by James Dorn and Wang Xi. Chicago: University of Chicago Press.

Wen, Guanzhong James. 1989. "The Current Tenure System and Its Impact on Long-Term Performance of the Farming Sector: The Case of Modern China." Ph.D. diss., Department of Economics, University of Chicago.

Wong, Christine. 1986. "Ownership and Control in Chinese Industry: The Maoist Legacy and Prospects for the 1980s." In *China in the 1980s*, U.S. Congress, Joint Economic Committee. Washington, D.C.: Government Printing Office.

World Bank. 1983. *China: Socialist Economic Development*, Vol 1. Washington, D.C.: World Bank.

————. 1985. *China: Long-Term Development Issues and Options*. Baltimore: Johns Hopkins University Press.

————. 1988a. *China: External Trade and Capital*. Washington, D.C.: World Bank.

————. 1988b. *China: Finance and Investment*. Washington, D.C.: World Bank.

————. 1989. *India: Poverty, Employment and Social Services*. Washington, D.C.: World Bank.

————. 1990. *China: Between Plan and Market*. Washington, D.C.: World Bank.

————. 1991. *World Development Report, 1991*. New York: Oxford University Press.

————. 1992a. *China: Reform and the Role of the Plan in the 1990s*. Washington, D.C.: World Bank.

————. 1992b. *China: Strategies for Reducing Poverty in the 1990s*. Washington, D.C.: World Bank.

Xu, Dixin, *et al.*, eds. 1982. *China's Search for Economic Growth: The Chinese Economy Since 1949*. Beijing: New World Press.

Xue, Muqiao. 1986. *China's Socialist Economy*, 2d ed. Beijing: Foreign Languages Press.

Yeats, Alexander J. 1991. "China's Foreign Trade and Comparative Advantage." World Bank Discussion Paper, no. 141. Washington, D.C.: World Bank.

Yenal, Oktay. 1989. "Chinese Reforms, Inflation and the Allocation of Investment in a Socialist Economy." World Bank Asia Region Internal Discussion Paper Series, Report No IDP 52. Washington, D.C.: World Bank.

13

THE LARGE ECONOMIES: A COMPARISON OF CHINA AND INDIA

Gene Tidrick and Vinod Dubey

China-India comparisons have a well-established place in development studies.[1] The reasons are obvious. China and India are the two most populous countries on earth; together they account for nearly 40 percent of the world's population. Both have ancient civilizations and were among the most developed areas of the premodern world, but by the time they emerged from their long periods of colonial rule (India) and semicolonial dependency (China) around 1950, they were among the poorest societies on earth.

The similarity of initial conditions at mid-century invited comparison of subsequent experience (see Table 13.1). Per capita gross national product (GNP) levels were similar—fifty dollars for China and sixty dollars for India.[2] China's agriculture was more productive than India's, but India was ahead in industry and had a more developed infrastructure (power and transport) network. Partly reflecting its higher agricultural output, China was somewhat healthier and better fed than India, though India was slightly ahead in education.

The main interest in comparisons of China and India, however, was ideological. The two giants of the developing world were seen as the testing ground of two competing social systems: communism versus democracy, a command versus a mixed economy. China's revolutionary and authoritarian regime conducted vast social experiments—the Great Leap Forward, the Cultural Revolution—while India, the world's largest democracy, remained committed to democratic socialism and evolutionary policies. Both countries followed a version of the Soviet development model based on planning, high rates of saving and investment, and emphasis on development of industry for the domestic market, but India retained a mixed economy with a large private sector and continued to rely on market institutions, albeit heavily influenced by state intervention. The contest

Table 13.1
China-India Comparisons Around 1950

	USSR around 1928	Japan around 1936	China 1952	India 1950
GNP - billion (1952 $)	35	22.6	30	22
GNP per capita (1952 $)	240	25	50	60
Population - million	147	69	575	358
Birth rate (per 1,000)	44	31	37	38
Death rate (per 1,000)	20	18	17	24
Natural increase	24	13	20	14
Number of persons dependent on agriculture per acre of cultivated land	0.2	1.6	1.9	0.6
Paddy rice yield (ton per ha)	2.2	3.6	2.5	1.3
Wheat yield (ton per ha)	0.8	1.9	1.1	0.7
Foodgrain production (kg per capita)	-	-	285	195
Industrial Output Per Capita				
Coal (kg)	273	604	96	97
Pig iron (kg)	22	29	2.8	5
Crude steel (kg)	29	n.a.	2	4
Electric power (kw)	0.01	0.10	0.005	0.01
Cotton spindles (units)	0.05	0.17	0.01	0.03
Cement (kg)	13	63	4	9
Transportation				
Railways (km per million population)	-	-	50	153
Highways (km per million population	-	-	226	1094
Social Indicators				
Life expectancy (years)	-	-	36	32
Calories (per capita)	-	-	1917	1540
Literacy (per cent)	-	-	14.3	16.7
Students enrolled in higher education (per million of population)	-	-	440	1659

Source: Eckstein (1975, p. 214); World Bank (1983, pp. 43, 98); Swamy (1989, pp. 45–46).

was viewed not just in terms of growth and industrialization but also of eradicating mass poverty and slowing population growth.

The summary judgment of most scholars as of the late 1970s was that China had won the growth race (though by how much was in dispute) and more successfully reduced poverty, but at considerable human cost. At the same time, as ideological fervor waned and with the evidently greater success of Japan and the Asian newly industrializing countries (NICs) and Chinese condemnation of its own Maoist past, interest in China and India shifted to a different set of issues. The question then increasingly became which country could more successfully reform its economy to accelerate growth and become more internationally competitive. Attention shifted, too, to the particular lessons for other developing economies of differing reform strategies and specific policies.

This chapter draws on the preceding country surveys to compare Chinese and Indian economic development since 1950. The first section summarizes the country experiences of China and India analyzed in chapters 12 and 11, respectively. The next two sections compare the strategies of development and economic performance in the two countries. The final sections attempt to answer some larger and more difficult questions. What are the prospects for reform and future development? What lessons do Chinese and Indian experiences hold for each other and for other developing countries?

OVERVIEW OF COUNTRY EXPERIENCES

China

Immediately after consolidating power in 1949, the new communist government introduced a sweeping land reform and set about transforming the economy along classic Soviet lines. In 1958 Mao Tse-tung introduced the first radical departure from the Soviet model, the Great Leap Forward, which sought to accelerate China's transition from socialism to communism. The result was disastrous, leading to famine and collapse of industrial output. Following a period of rehabilitation in the early 1960s, however, Mao in 1966 launched the Cultural Revolution, a radical program of "permanent revolution" based on mass mobilization, high accumulation, and reliance on moral incentives. In China the period from 1966 until Mao's death in 1976 is known as the "Ten Years of Turmoil."

Despite the disruptions of the Great Leap Forward and the Cultural Revolution, China's economic performance was impressive in terms of overall growth; improvements in health, nutrition, and other social indicators; and creation of a broad industrial base. The main instruments of transformation in Maoist China were communes in agriculture, material balance planning in industry, and macroeconomic policies that linked agriculture and industry to generate a high rate of accumulation.

Communes, with collective production and collective distribution supplemented by work points, were very successful in redistributing income and providing for basic needs at the local level. They were far less successful in raising average agricultural production because they rested on false assumptions of significant economies of scale in agriculture and large amounts of surplus rural labor that could be mobilized for capital construction. More important, collective agriculture provided inadequate incentives for production.

China's industrial planning system, which was initially modeled on that of the USSR but which differed in many ways from Soviet central planning, enabled China to build up a broad base of heavy industry. But industry was also very inefficient, technologically backward, and unable to supply the variety, quality, and appropriate mix of products wanted by industrial users or final consumers.

Macroeconomic policy was directed mainly toward achieving high domestic resource mobilization and stable prices. Pricing policy, the chief instrument and main link between sectoral policy and macropolicy, was subordinated to mobilization rather than allocation of resources. Compulsory procurement of agricultural and mineral products at low prices was used to extract a surplus from the primary sector. Basic wage goods were rationed at low prices to keep urban wages low and stable, while final industrial goods prices generated high industrial profits, which were all transferred to the budget for reallocation through the plan. The whole interlocking system generated large surpluses, which were invested to restructure the economy, but despite obvious success in providing basic needs and social services, the Maoist system largely failed to raise average living standards.

In 1978 China started a program of reform that, with many changes and fluctuations, still continues. The main elements of reform were decollectivization of agriculture, greater use of prices and markets rather than planning, greater reliance on collective and private enterprises at the expense of state enterprises, an open-door policy for trade and investment, and the introduction of orthodox, indirect macropolicy instruments to supplant Soviet-type direct controls. The process of reform is incomplete, but the results in terms of growth, efficiency, export performance, and improved living standards have been dramatic. At the same time, prices have become less stable, and provision of social services less secure. Nevertheless, there appears to have been little trade-off between growth and equity.

India

India's development strategy gave a leading role to the state and the public sector while preserving a large, but highly regulated, private sector. This "third way" of state-led development began under Jawaharlal Nehru but intensified in the 1970s under Indira Gandhi. In the 1980s some (very modest) relaxation of state regulation began, and it was only in 1991 that major reversals of past policy started.

Public sector investment was the chosen instrument of industrial development and resource mobilization, and public sector enterprises now dominate not only the commanding heights but some of the lesser hills and a few valleys of industry and finance as well. But the public sector has largely failed to achieve its original aims. Public enterprises have neither generated large profits for public investment nor provided low-cost capital goods and basic inputs to the private sector. Operational efficiency has been low, and public enterprises have been asked to bear major social responsibilities, such as regional development and taking over sick private firms. The result is that apart from the petroleum sector and a few other exceptions, public enterprises make losses and have contributed to India's fiscal problems.

State-led development of private industry has also had several shortcomings. The main instrument of control over the private sector was industrial licensing, whose aim was to prevent wasteful duplication of investment but which shielded industry from competition and led to high costs and a large technology gap in Indian industry. Strict labor regulations have contributed to a growing number of "sick" enterprises, with an attendant drain on the government budget, and have also reduced the growth of employment in large-scale industry. Small-scale industry promotion, particularly the reservation of over 800 products for small-scale production, largely failed to achieve its objectives. To the extent that small-scale industry was more labor-intensive, it was not competitive; and to the extent it was competitive, it neither provided more employment nor needed special protection.

Trade policy reinforced control over the private sector. It was premised on export pessimism and consisted of a complex array of quantitative restrictions on imports and some of the highest tariffs in the world. The trade regime strongly favored production for the domestic market and, along with reluctance to depreciate the exchange rate, resulted in slow export growth.

Monetary and financial policies and institutions were important instruments for resource mobilization and allocation, especially after the nationalization of banks in 1969. India developed a deep and sophisticated financial system but has been more successful in mobilizing financial resources than in allocating them efficiently.

With the state playing the leading role in development, the share of national income mobilized and spent through the government budget has increased markedly. The main defects of this process were that expenditure grew faster than revenue, leading to an unsustainable fiscal deficit by the end of the 1980s; current expenditure grew faster than revenue, producing first a decline and then negative government savings; and the government has become too dependent on distortionary indirect taxes, especially import duties.

In agriculture, government policy gradually evolved from a community approach, with emphasis on land tenure reform, to support for technological development and profitability in farming. The "green revolution" in the late 1960s was a major policy success, bringing about self-sufficiency in grain production. Although fears that the new technology of the green revolution would perversely worsen poverty were not realized, overall agricultural growth has remained little higher than population growth so that poverty, especially in rural areas, has declined very slowly.

Overall, India's performance on growth and poverty alleviation has been disappointing compared with that of many other developing countries, despite better than average mobilization of domestic savings. This reflected the inefficiency of India's discretionary administrative system and the high costs of an inward-oriented development strategy. During the 1980s, however, the rate of gross domestic product (GDP) growth increased due to limited reforms and the growth of domestic demand. After 1985, export growth also rose due to export-promotion measures and depreciation of the real effective exchange rate, but imports also grew rapidly, fueled by growing domestic demand and limited liberalization of import restrictions. By the end of the 1980s it was increasingly evident that the higher growth rate of GDP was based on unsustainable fiscal and current account deficits. In 1991 a balance-of-payments crisis prompted the introduction of far-reaching reforms, along with stabilization measures. The reforms, which are still unfolding, liberalized trade and foreign exchange payments, deregulated industrial investment, and began to reduce the role of the public sector in production.

DEVELOPMENT STRATEGY

There are many similarities between the development strategies of China and India. In the first twenty-five to thirty years after 1950, both countries relied on capital accumulation as the engine of growth. With plentiful labor and scarce land and capital, the obvious way out of poverty and low productivity seemed to be to accumulate capital as rapidly as possible and transfer the large pool of low-productivity labor in agriculture to higher-productivity industry. Investments were made in irrigation and fertilizer to improve agricultural productivity, but the largest share of investment went into industry and associated infrastructure. Since the domestic market was large and prospects for exports seemed limited, development strategy was also inward-looking. Priority was given to heavy industry in order to lay the basis for self-sufficient industrialization. In both countries, however, there was a conscious dualism in industry. Labor-intensive rural industry (in China) and small-scale or cottage industry (in India) were meant to provide employment for surplus agricultural labor at low capital cost while the bulk of investment went into large-scale, mostly heavy industry, which was to be the main source of structural transformation. In both countries, too, agriculture was the main source of investible surplus, which was mobilized mainly indirectly through the pricing mechanism of high industrial prices and low agricultural prices.

In both countries the state was the main agent of development, and socialism was the accepted ideology. There were differences, of course. In China, Karl Marx was the theoretician and the Soviet Union was the model. State (or collective) ownership was virtually complete, and central (later decentralized and multilevel) planning determined investment and production decisions. In India, Laski and Mahalanobis were the theoreticians and Fabian socialism was the model. State ownership was confined mainly to the commanding heights of the economy, but the private sector was heavily regulated through investment and import licensing, directed credit, and price controls. In both countries, the market was viewed with distrust and seen as antithetical to development and to equity. In China, this led to efforts to abolish or suppress market allocation. In India, distrust of the market led merely to extensive regulation and intervention.

Although highly interventionist at the microlevel, both countries were relatively orthodox and even conservative in macromanagement. The "macro madness" leading to rampant inflation in Latin America was as abhorrent and incomprehensible to both as the interventionist "micro madness" of China and India was to the Latins.[3] India accumulated relatively little external debt, and most of that on concessional terms, even in the wake of the two oil crises of the 1970s. China had almost no external debt at the end of the 1970s. Both countries tried to keep budget deficits and inflation low (China more successfully).

Finally, China and India both stressed egalitarian development. This was reflected in programs of land reform, food and other price subsidies, and wage and price controls. Egalitarianism tended to be selective in both countries, however, with a distinct urban or wage earner bias. Lifetime employment in the public sector, once a job was obtained, was perhaps the most secure property right in either country, while food and housing subsidies are limited to urban residents in China and disproportionately favor urban residents in India.

Disillusionment with the strategy of development also spread in both countries toward the end of the 1970s. The extensive growth strategy had yielded disappointing growth in living standards, and even higher accumulation was needed to offset rising ICORs. Equally important, the obvious success of Korea, Taiwan, and other newly industrializing economies pointed to the need for reevaluation of the Chinese and Indian approaches to development. Indeed, emphasis on the differences that had dominated earlier comparisons between China and India—central planning versus mixed economy, revolution versus gradualism, communism versus democracy—began to seem misplaced. Seen in the broader context of the developing world as a whole, similarities between China and India seemed more pronounced than differences. The lesson of broader international experience seemed to be that less interventionist and more outward-looking strategies have been more successful. While there might be doubts about the applicability of the Korean-Taiwan model of export-led growth to countries as large as China and India, it was obvious that far more scope existed for export expansion than the latter two countries had allowed for. In 1975 China (population 925 million) had manufactured exports of $1.9 billion, and India (600 million) had manufactured exports of $1.3 billion. But Taiwan (population 16 million) had manufactured exports of $4.0 billion; Korea (33 million) $3.5 billion; and Hong Kong (4.3 million) $4.6 billion.

Both China and India shifted their development strategy toward growth of productivity (intensive growth) rather than capital accumulation (extensive growth); export promotion; and loosening of state control over decision making. The strategic reorientation was not complete; export promotion did not mean a complete shift to outward-looking development, for example, because incentives still favored production for the domestic market. But the direction of change was clear.

Despite broad similarities of strategy, China went further than India on almost every dimension. China had higher investment and lower productivity growth, heavier market intervention and state control, and more radical policies to promote equality and social change. Similarly, China went further and faster in the 1980s to reverse past policies: to promote exports, increase efficiency, and reduce state control over decisions. This is not to say that China is now less controlled

Table 13.2
China-India Growth Comparisons

A.   Official Sources

	1952-78	1978-90	1952-90
China			
National Income at Comparable Prices	6.0	9.4	6.7
Population Growth	2.0	1.4	1.8
National Income per capita	3.9	6.8	4.8
India			
GDPFC (1980-81 constant prices)	3.9	4.8	4.1
Population Growth	2.2	2.0	2.1
GDP per capita	1.6	2.7	2.0

B.   Unofficial Sources Compared

	Period	China Official	China Unofficial	India Official	India Unofficial
Chow (1985) - Rebased rates	1952-78	6.0	3.9	3.9	
World Bank (1983) - Chinese growth at Indian prices	1957-79	5.4	4.6	3.5	
Swamy (1989) - Constant 1970 purchasing power parity prices for both countries	1952-65	5.4	3.3	3.7	3.5
	1965-78	6.6	4.8	4.0	4.0
	1978-86	8.9	8.8	3.8	5.3
	1952-78	6.0	4.0	3.9	3.8
	1952-86	6.7	5.1	3.8	4.0

or inward-looking than India, because China had further to travel. But China has consistently embraced policies more fervently and shifted direction more quickly and sharply than India.[4]

PERFORMANCE

Growth

The level of GDP (or GNP) per capita and the rate of growth of GDP are the most common and comprehensive measures of economic performance. But international comparisons are always difficult and, in the case of China and India, particularly hazardous. Consider the following. Real output growth measured in constant domestic prices and using official national statistics has consistently been higher in China than in India. From 1950 to 1990 China's real output growth per capita has averaged 4.8 percent per annum compared with 2.0 percent for India (Table 13.2). This implies that in thirty-eight years China's output per capita has increased by a factor of six while India's has merely doubled. Given approximately equal starting points at mid-century ($50 per capita for China and $60 for India), China's output per capita should now be 2.4 times that of India. However, the most recent World Bank estimates of per capita GNP for the two countries are (in 1990 dollars) $370 for China and $360 for India (Table 13.3). Given growth rate differentials, this is inconsistent not only with mid-century estimates but also with earlier World Bank estimates for 1976 of $410 for China and $150 for India.

Table 13.3
China-India Per Capita GDP/GNP Comparisons

		1976	1980	1985	1990
A.	GDP per capita				
	Current dollars (WDR)	1976	1980	1985	1990
	China	410	290	310	370
	India	150	240	270	350
	Constant 1979 dollars				
	(World Bank 1983)	1950	1957	1979	
	China	117	143	256	
	India	122	137	191	
B.	Purchasing Power Parity				
	Kravis (1981) - 1975 dollars	1950	1965		
	China	294	879		
	India	328	472		
	Ratio	0.90	1.86		
	Penn/UN (Summers and Heston, 1988; 1988; UNDP, 1992) - 1980 dollars	1980	1985	1989	
	China	1619	2444	2656	
	India	614	750	910	
	Ratio	2.69	3.26	2.92	
	World Bank (1992)	1990			
	China	1950			
	India	1150			
	Ratio	1.70			
	Swamy (1989) - 1970 dollars	1952	1965	1978	1984
	China	101	122	171	315
	India	154	181	232	292
	Ratio	0.66	0.67	0.74	1.08

Only partial reconciliation of these differences is possible. Socialist national accounting estimates are prone to overestimate real output growth and underestimate inflation and, as noted in chapter 12, most scholars believe that China's growth rates are overestimated for several reasons: they are based on growth of material product, which excludes many services, and are biased upward by choice of base year, price distortions, and misreporting. Part B of Table 13.2 shows several independent unofficial estimates of China's growth rate, all of which are lower than official estimates.

Per capita dollar comparisons are notoriously unreliable, even when averaged over three years as they are in World Bank statistics. The official exchange rate may not be in equilibrium and in any case covers only traded output. China's official exchange rate depreciated faster over much of the 1980s than that of India, thus reducing the dollar per capita income gap despite higher constant price growth rates in China. Without more information there is no way of knowing which year is more representative of differences in level of output. Moreover, even if exchange rates are in equilibrium in both base and end years, higher growth rates may be needed to stay in the same relative position internationally if growth is concentrated in sectors whose relative prices are declining. There is some evidence that this occurred in China.

The only theoretically acceptable way to make international comparisons of GDP levels and growth rates is to use the same price weights for output in the countries being compared. Several such estimates have been made for China and India, but because they are based on either small samples or broad aggregates, the result differs widely (Part B of Table 13.3). The study of purchasing power parity (PPP) done under the University of Pennsylvania/United Nations (UN) international comparisons project (Summers and Heston, 1988) estimates that the ratio of Chinese to Indian output on a PPP basis in 1985 was 3.26, compared with Subramanian Swamy's estimated ratio of 1.08 (Table 13.3).[5] It seems likely that the former is too high and the latter too low, but resolution of differences must await a more definitive study.[6]

There is yet another way of comparing growth and levels of output: comparison of physical output of major and relatively homogeneous commodities over time. Table 13.4 presents the result of such a comparison by Swamy (1989, pp. 58–59). This suggests that, starting from relatively equal output per capita in 1952, China achieved a level of output per capita approximately twice that of India by the late 1970s and slightly increased that margin by the mid-1980s. Note, however, that this comparison makes no allowance for quality differences and that the sample is heavily weighted toward standard or homogeneous goods and totally excludes services.

What, in summary, can be said about comparative levels of output and rates of growth in China and India? The preponderance of evidence suggests that Chinese output per capita, starting from a point slightly below that of India in 1952, had reached a level 1.5 to 2 times that of India in 1990. This would mean that China's per capita output growth averaged 3.6–4.4 percent per annum from 1952 to 1990, compared with the official estimate of 4.8 percent and India's officially estimated rate of 2.07 percent. Of the 1.6–2.4 percentage points higher rate of per capita output growth in China, 0.3 points represented lower population growth and 1.3 to 2.1 points represented higher growth of aggregate output.

Contrasting official growth rates by sector and time period, there were two main factors in China's higher growth rate: industrial sector growth throughout 1952–1990 and growth of all sectors from 1978 to 1990 (Table 13.5). The upward bias in China's official growth rate is primarily due to overestimation of industrial growth or to associated weighting problems. Thus, while China's industrial growth rate was higher than India's, the gap was less than official statistics show. China's agriculture and all other sectors grew at rates similar to those in India prior to China's reform and at significantly higher rates thereafter.

Savings, Investment, and Efficiency

Although both countries stressed capital accumulation as the engine of growth from about 1950–1980, China consistently achieved a higher level of both do-

Table 13.4
Ratio of Outputs Per Capita—China to India

PRODUCT		1952	1957	1978	1986
	1 Rice	1.27	1.26	1.39	1.49
	2 Wheat	1.54	1.68	1.05	0.88
	3 Foodgrains	1.50	1.55	1.41	1.41
	4 Oil Seeds	0.50	0.48	0.33	0.85
	5 Tea	0.81	0.20	0.31	0.33
	6 Milk	0.01	0.01	0.03	0.06
	7 Meat	3.33	4.18	6.69	10.15
I.	FARM OUTPUT	1.29	1.43	1.56	1.64
	8 Cotton Cloth	0.49	0.48	0.80	0.83
	9 Sugar	0.16	0.21	0.27	0.46
	10 Paper and Boards	1.73	0.77	2.96	4.36
	11 Light Bulbs	0.76	1.01	2.53	2.54
	12 Bicycles	0.43	0.65	1.65	4.22
	13 Radios	0.83	1.16	3.97	14.58
	14 TV Sets	0.00	1.26	0.59	2.70
	15 Sewing Machines	0.91	1.04	15.76	24.55
II.	LIGHT INDUSTRIAL	0.51	0.58	2.41	4.43
	16 Coal	1.07	1.89	4.14	3.79
	17 Crude Oil	0.64	2.18	6.10	3.00
	18 Electricity	0.76	1.07	1.70	1.74
	19 Natural Gas	0.10	0.18	3.32	1.51
III.	ENERGY	1.03	1.91	4.65	3.45
	20 Steel	0.80	1.60	2.17	2.78
	21 Cement	0.45	0.70	2.26	3.22
	22 Fertilizers	1.53	0.72	2.18	1.68
	23 Machine Tools	1.87	4.37	1.36	1.20
	24 Motor Vehicles	0.01	0.18	1.35	1.51
	25 Tractors	0.14	0.28	1.62	0.42
	26 Rail Wagons	0.54	0.77	0.99	1.03
IV.	HEAVY INDUSTRIAL	1.11	1.27	2.47	2.01
V.	TOTAL OUTPUT	0.96	1.04	2.22	2.73
MEMO:	Population Ratio	1.57	1.59	1.47	1.38

Source: Swamy (1989, pp. 58–59).

mestic savings and investment. China's accumulation ratio[7] was 24 percent in the first Five-Year Plan period and averaged 33 percent in the decade of the 1970s. India's investment ratio (investment as share of GDP), by contrast, was about 10 percent in the early 1950s and then rose steadily to over 22 percent by the end of the 1970s. In the 1980s China deliberately restrained investment to about 30 percent of GDP in the early part of the decade but then reversed its policy and raised investment to a phenomenal 40 percent of GDP in the latter half of the 1980s. India's investment share remained fairly steady at around 22 percent throughout the 1980s. Foreign savings (equivalent to the current account deficit) was on average negligible for China throughout the past forty years, though in the 1980s China alternated between current account surplus and deficit with the deficit reaching just over 4 percent of GDP in 1985. India depended on foreign savings equivalent to 1–2 percent of GDP during much of the first

Table 13.5
Comparative Sectoral Growth Rates

	1952-78 /a	1978-90	1952-90
	(--------------% per annum-------------)		
China			
Agriculture	2.7	5.6	3.6
Industry	12.3	10.8	11.8
Other	5.0	9.2	6.2
Total	5.8	8.7	6.7 /b
India			
Agriculture	2.5	2.9	2.6
Industry	5.9	5.9	5.9
Other	4.7	5.7	5.0
Total	3.9	4.8	4.1

Source: China: Table 12.3 from chapter 12. India: *National Accounts Statistics.*
[a]For China, period is 1952–79.
[b]Alternative unofficial estimate of Chinese total growth 1952–90 = 5.47% to 6.2%.

three decades after 1950, rising to an (unsustainable) average of 3 percent in the second half of the 1980s.

China's higher growth rate was mainly due to higher investment. Indeed, available estimates suggest that China's capital and other resource use was less efficient than India's, so China needed somewhat higher investment in order to achieve a comparable growth rate.[8] This is reflected in China's poor total factor productivity performance. Swamy (1989, p. 127) estimates that the TFP growth rate was −0.5 in China from 1952–1981 compared with +1.1 percent in India from 1950–1980. Dwight Perkins (1988, p. 626) also estimates that China's TFP growth was negative from 1957–1976. However, both China and India have increased TFP growth in the 1980s.

By international standards both China and India were relatively inefficient prior to 1980. Average TFP growth for nineteen fast-growing developing countries was 2 percent per annum for the period 1950–1975 (Swamy 1989, p. 128), and TFP growth typically accounts for 25–50 percent of total growth in fast-growing economies. Both countries (especially China) were therefore atypical prior to 1980, mirroring their strategy of extensive growth. In the 1980s, however, China's balance between extensive and intensive growth became more typical of fast-growing economies, with a ratio of roughly 67:33.

One other important point should be noted. Correcting for relative prices, India's real investment was less than the ratio of investment to GDP would suggest whereas China's real investment may have been even higher than indicated by the investment ratio. Because of high protection of its capital goods industry, India's equipment prices are among the highest in the world (De Long and Summers, 1990; Ettori, 1992), whereas China has traditionally kept equip-

Figure 13.1
Export Performance, China and India

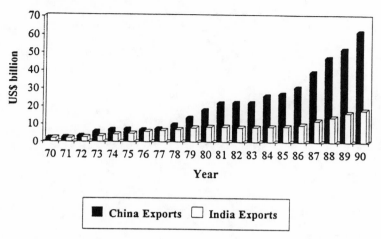

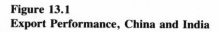

ment prices relatively low (Taylor, 1986; Rajaram, 1992). This suggests that India's disappointing (by international standards) growth yield from its relatively high investment ratio may have been mainly due to relative price distortions rather than to low productivity in real terms. For China, one can draw the opposite conclusion. The productivity of Chinese investment in real terms was even lower than conventional measures suggest.

Foreign Trade

One area in which China has unambiguously outperformed India is in growth of exports. Starting from comparably low levels of total exports (about $2.2 billion) in 1970, China completely outpaced India, especially in the 1980s (see Figure 13.1). By 1990 China's merchandise exports were $62 billion, compared with India's $18.5 billion.

The contrast is equally marked for exports of manufactures. India exported more manufactures than China in 1965 (Table 13.6). Indeed, India accounted for 14.3 percent of total developing country exports of manufactures, and China accounted for 13.1 percent in 1965. In the following decade both countries fell behind economies such as Korea, Taiwan, and Hong Kong, whose exports of manufactures exploded. India's share of developing country exports of manufactures fell to 4.5 percent, and China's to 6.5 percent. But whereas India's share continued to decline, China managed in subsequent years to expand its share of a rapidly growing world market.

China's success depended on three main factors. First, China made a deliberate decision to open up to the outside world and used traditional central planning mechanisms (mandatory targets and cross-subsidies) to expand exports. Second,

Table 13.6
Major Developing Country Exporters of Manufactures, 1965–1987

	1965	1975	1980	1983	1985	1987
	(--------------------value in US$------------------)
Taiwan (China)	130	3,990	16,169	20,996	28,237	49,632
Korea, Republic of	72	3,448	12,669	16,604	19,509	39,020
China (PRC)	554	1,896	7,712	9,899	13,022	28,420
Hong Kong	861	4,560	13,163	14,558	16,592	24,037
Mexico	145	1,951	4,480	6,446	9,483	14,636
Singapore	57	1,442	5,143	7,141	8,683	13,990
Brazil	132	1,452	5,206	6,413	8,776	10,844
Malaysia	24	476	3,010	3,847	4,786	7,466
India	607	1,331	3,877	3,591	4,160	6,666
Thailand	36	349	1,606	1,874	2,496	5,455
Philippines	72	358	2,149	2,569	2,960	3,800
Indonesia	10	66	466	948	1,357	3,277
Pakistan	108	436	990	1,121	1,218	2,246
All Developing	4,238	29,787	98,119	117,280	147,253	250,711
Memo: Share of total (%)						
China	13.1	6.4	7.9	8.4	8.8	11.3
India	14.3	4.5	4.0	3.1	2.8	2.7

Source: Yeats (1991, pp. 10–11).

in the 1980s trade decisions were increasingly decentralized and export incentives improved through devaluation, foreign exchange retention, and other devices. At the margin, better incentives were critical to export expansion. Third, China reversed its previous policy and tried to lure direct foreign investment, particularly for export production. In this it was highly successful, attracting $2.5 billion of net foreign investment per year by the late 1980s.

India began to improve export incentives significantly only after 1985, when it began to depreciate the real effective exchange rate and to strengthen mechanisms for providing exporters with imported inputs at world prices. This raised export growth. Only after 1990 did India begin to reduce the high level of protection for production for the domestic market, which acts as a tax on exports. Until 1991, India provided a fairly hostile climate for foreign investment. Direct foreign investment in India averaged about one-tenth the Chinese level in the late 1980s.

China's exports grew faster than India's, then, because China moved earlier and more strenuously to promote exports and attract foreign investment for export production.[9] China was also less constrained than India in using subsidies to offset domestic price distortions. While China's subsidy policies may have led to promotion of inefficient exports, it is likely that the overall import-substitution bias of Chinese prices is less than India's. That is, the domestic resource cost of saving a dollar of foreign exchange through import substitution is higher than that of earning foreign exchange through exporting, but the relative gap is probably higher in India. Thus, China may not only have expanded trade faster than India but may also have deployed resources more efficiently in doing so.

One additional advantage that China enjoys, of course, is proximity to Hong Kong. Hong Kong provided two-thirds of China's foreign investment and has played an important role in organizing production and marketing of China's exports. But whatever advantages proximity to Hong Kong conferred on China, these were not decisive in China's superior performance. Advantages have to be exploited and do not occur without effort. China failed to take advantage of the Hong Kong connection prior to 1980 just as Mexico failed to take advantage of proximity to the massive U.S. market until recent years. Moreover, India has assets of its own, including nonresident Indians, which it has not yet fully tapped. Proximity to Hong Kong was an advantage for China, but this was not sufficient and probably not even necessary to China's success in export expansion.

Social Indicators and Equity

Both China and India have emphasized eradication of poverty and egalitarian development. While social indicators have improved significantly in both countries, China has been more successful on every front: life expectancy is higher in China, infant mortality rates are lower, birthrates have fallen more dramatically, and nutrition levels and adult literacy are significantly higher (Table 13.7).

These figures mask large regional differences within each country, however. The state of Kerala in India, for example, has an infant mortality rate (IMR) of 29, which is lower than the Chinese national average and that of most Chinese provinces, whereas Xinjiang in China has a higher IMR (146) than Uttar Pradesh in India (143), both of which are higher than the average IMR in Ethiopia or Mozambique. Similar regional disparities occur in literacy rates. Purchasing power parity income differences explain much but by no means all of the regional variations in IMR and literacy in each country, but the relationship is stronger in China (Howes, 1992). In India Kerala's social indicators in particular and, to some extent, those of southern India generally are better than predicted as the basis of income differentials.

Comparisons of poverty levels are difficult and contentious even within a single country over time, let alone between countries, but most international observers agree that poverty remains a more serious problem in India. According to UNDP (1992, p. 132) estimates, 410 million people were below the poverty line in India in 1990, equivalent to 48 percent of India's population and 34 percent of all people below the poverty line in developing countries. (India's share of population of developing countries was 21 percent in 1990.) In China, UNDP estimates that 120 million people lived below the poverty line: 10.5 percent of China's population and 10 percent of all those below the poverty line in developing countries. (China's population share is 28 percent of the developing world.) The overwhelming majority of the poor live in rural areas: 83 percent in China and 78 percent in India.

Table 13.7
Comparative Social Indicators, 1952–1990

	1952 /a	1965	1978	1990
China:				
Life Expectancy at Birth (years)	36	54	64	70
Infant Mortality Rate (per 1000)	175	90	37 /c	29
Birth Rate (per 1000) /b	37	38	18	22
Death Rate (per 1000) /b	17	10	6	7
Rate of Natural Increase (per 1000) /b	20	28	12	15
Calories per capita	1917	1929	2441	2639
Adult Literacy Rate (%)	14	50	66	73
India:				
Life Expectancy at Birth (years)	32	45	51	59
Infant Mortality Rate (per 1000)	190	150	n.a.	92
Birth Rate (per 1000) /b	38	45	34	30
Death Rate (per 1000) /b	29	20	13	11
Rate of Natural Increase (per 1000) /b	14	25	21	19
Calories per capita	1540	2021	2021	2229
Adult Literacy Rate (%)	17	30	36	52

Sources: ᵃAll data are from Table 13.1 except for demographic data.
ᵇDemographic data are from national statistics. For India, demographic data in 1978 column are for 1980.
ᶜBanister (1987, p. 116).
All other data are from World Bank, *World Development Report*, various years.

UNDP estimates of Indian poverty are higher than those of most Indian sources. The most careful Indian study (Minhas, Jain, and Tedulkar, 1991) shows the proportion of the population below the poverty line declining from 56.3 percent in 1970–1971 to 48.1 percent in 1983 and to 45.9 percent in 1987–1988. The absolute numbers of poor people under this estimate rose from 308 million in 1970–1971 to 361 million in 1987–88. Official statistics, which make inadequate adjustment for cost-of-living differences, estimate the share of population below the poverty line as 37 percent in 1987–1988.

A recent World Bank (1992) study of poverty in China estimates that 98 million people (8.6 percent of the total population) were below the poverty line in 1990, down from 270 million (28 percent of the total population) in 1978. Most of the fall in poverty took place in the early 1980s. Since 1985 the absolute number of poor has hardly changed, due to the concentration of hard-core poverty in remote and resource-poor upland areas.

Growth and distribution both affect poverty. In China, the proportion of people in poverty declined significantly with rapid growth of rural consumption in the

1980s (Matson and Selden, 1992). In India, significant reduction in poverty has been achieved only when the growth rate exceeded 5 percent. But in both India and China poverty is concentrated regionally, and in India landless rural laborers are disproportionately represented among the poor. In China, landlessness is not a factor. There are few, if any, landless laborers. Rather, entire rural communities remain poor because they live on land of very low quality.

In popular conception, one of the most striking differences between China and India is the distribution of income. Although China's income distribution is better than that of India, the differences are much less than generally supposed. As explained in chapter 12, China's overall distribution of income was not greatly different from that of India around 1980 (Gini coefficient of 0.33 for China and 0.38 for India) because the commune system did not equalize incomes among rural localities and because there was a large urban-rural gap in living standards (World Bank, 1983, p. 94).[10] China does, however, have relatively greater income equality than India and most other countries within the urban sector, though not necessarily within the rural sector. Gini coefficients for urban incomes range from 0.148 to 0.289 in twenty-eight provinces, with most coefficients clustering around 0.20. In urban areas in India, Gini coefficients ranged from 0.247 to 0.387. In rural areas within Chinese provinces and Indian states the respective ranges were 0.195 to 0.281 in China versus 0.201 to 0.346 for India (Hussain, Lanjouw, and Stern, 1991, pp. 20–21).

Broadly speaking, what was achieved in China under Mao was to take an income distribution similar to (or worse than) that of India and to reduce incomes of the richest 10 percent and raise incomes of the poorest 10 percent. This was done, at the upper end, by confiscation of land and other property and, at the lower end, through grain rationing and public provision or subsidy of other basic needs. Major urban-rural or interprovincial differences were left intact, but within a given area the most visible extremes of wealth and poverty were sharply compressed. Since reforms, some of these policies have been reversed, but the overall distribution of income seems to have remained fairly stable.

ASSESSMENT OF PERFORMANCE

Previous sections have stressed the similarities of development strategy of China and India. What, then, accounts for the differences in performance?

Two strategic differences of approach are especially important. First, China underwent a radical land reform. India introduced much more limited land and tenancy reform, often with unintended effects of reducing security of tenure (Matson and Selden, 1992, p. 705). Collectivization in China was disastrous economically (and in terms of human suffering), but the early redistribution of land and the postcollective household responsibility system provided both strong incentives for production and an equitable distribution of assets, which in turn provided a secure base for relatively equitable distribution of the benefits of growth.

Table 13.8
Comparative Educational Development, 1985

| | Public Spending on Education (% of GNP) | | | | Gross Enrollment Ratios (%) | | |
	Total	Primary	Secondary	Higher	Primary	Secondary	Higher
China	3.3	1.3	1.4	0.6	118	39	1.7
India	3.0	0.8	1.4	0.6	92	41	9.0
Indonesia	3.7	2.3	1.0	0.3	118	42	6.5
Korea	3.4	1.9	1.1	0.3	96	75	31.6
Thailand	3.6	2.1	0.8	0.4	97	30	19.6

Source: Tan and Mingat (1989, pp. 9, 57).

The second strategic difference was in the realm of education. China provided and largely enforced universal primary education. India failed to provide, and certainly failed to enforce, universal primary education.[11] Table 13.8 tells the basic story. Public spending on education as a share of GNP was similar in China and India and not much different from that in other rapidly developing Asian economies.[12] But India's public spending on primary education was extremely low by Asian standards and also in comparison to spending on secondary and higher education. Indian enrollment ratios shown in Table 13.8 are misleading. Many children are enrolled who never or only sporadically attend primary school, and about half drop out before completing five years of primary education.

The importance of primary education is well established. Economic rates of return to primary education are high, income distribution is correlated with the distribution of education attainment (''human capital development''), and fertility is negatively correlated with female educational levels. India's failure to provide universal primary education has been very costly in terms of growth, distribution of income, and human development.

China has provided for universal primary education but has universally low enrollment in higher education. This, too, has undoubtedly taken its toll in terms of China's technological development. Both China and India, therefore, have unusual educational structures. India's structure, while not quite a cylinder, is effectively a narrowly based and only slowly tapering pyramid. China's structure is a broad-based pyramid that narrows sharply at the top.

Apart from specific differences of approach toward land reform and education, China has been generally more radical than India. Maoist China in particular underwent thorough and repeated revolutionary upheaval, leaving few of the old institutions and little of the social structure intact. India has followed a more evolutionary path. This has meant that China has generally made faster progress—and more spectacular errors—than India, which during the first thirty years of independence limped along steadily at the ''Hindu rate of growth.'' India's inherent conservatism has prevented it either from realizing the high rates of growth of China and other countries in East and Southeast Asia or from falling into a debt trap and macro disorder like many countries in Africa and Latin America.

In other respects, however, India got the worst of both worlds: the inefficiency of socialism and the inequality of capitalism. The Indian government intervened massively in production, but it maintained a democratic structure and shied away from coercive social revolution—not only radical land reform but even compulsory primary education. Because it was less harsh, India's success in capital accumulation (the only route to high growth under inefficient production) was less than that of China.

Despite China's radical tradition under Mao, its subsequent approach to reform has been relatively gradualist. India, starting later, has followed an even more gradualist reform path, but both China and India are gradualists by the standards of "big bang" reforms in countries such as Mexico and Poland. One reason is that, unlike in Mexico and Poland, reform began before systemic collapse. Because the system had not evidently failed, there was both intellectual and vested-interest opposition to any reform, but for the same reason prospects for successful reform without disruption were enhanced. It is significant that the one area in which China did reform radically was agriculture, where the system was perceived to have failed.

One lesson of China's experience with reform is that gradual reform can work. Another lesson is that radical reform in one area (agriculture in China) can be productive even if not accompanied by radical reforms elsewhere. This proposition is not universally accepted. The debate over incremental versus comprehensive reform is similar to the 1950s debate over unbalanced versus balanced growth. Since everything depends on everything else, anything short of a big push (balanced growth/radical reform) is held bound to fail. But interdependency, as Albert Hirschman (1958) showed, does not mean that everything must be done simultaneously. Linkages between investments or policies mean that once one change is introduced, the next steps needed are obvious. Thus, Chinese agricultural reform paved the way for other reforms not only by proving that removing big bottlenecks produces results but also by creating pressure for further reforms such as lifting restrictions on rural industry and reducing urban grain subsidies. Much of the price reform that has occurred in China has not been deliberate reform but an ad hoc response to pressures created by other reforms.

A third lesson of Chinese and Indian reform is that timely partial reform is preferable to delayed comprehensive reforms. Countries differ, and the dynamics of reform are important, but the experience of China versus the Soviet Union and India versus Africa suggests that half a loaf is better than none, even if failure to make any policy changes paves the way for system collapse and more radical reform later.

A fourth lesson of China's experience is that it is much better to launch reform before large macroeconomic imbalances appear (Harrold, 1992). Deep macroeconomic crisis forces a country to take stabilization measures that typically cause short-term output losses. This can delay or obscure the supply response to reform and undermine political support. In this respect, India began its reforms in 1991 from a more disadvantageous position than China in 1979. Because India faced a balance-of-payments crisis, it had to deflate more than China. It would have been better if India had started serious reforms before entering a balance-of-payments crisis, but it is unlikely that reforms would have begun if there had been no crisis.

None of this means that gradual or partial reform is necessarily preferable. Radical reform in selected areas can be highly productive, as in Chinese agriculture. Moreover, partial reform brings its own problems. Attempts to reduce micro interventions in China and, to a lesser extent in India have undermined macro control. Similarly, agricultural reform has undermined Chinese social security mechanisms. The proper response to these problems, as argued in chapter 12, is not to reverse reforms but to extend them.

Both China and India face a similar reform agenda and similar obstacles to further reform. First, both countries need to restructure relative prices in order to improve resource allocation. In both countries price restructuring aggravates fiscal imbalance. Reducing protection in India will deprive the central government of tariff revenue, which currently amounts to nearly 4 percent of GDP. Restructuring industrial prices will further deprive China of its principal source of government revenue, enterprise profits. Fiscal reform (a reduction in subsidies and a shift to a new tax base) is essential in both countries and is impeded by central-local fiscal relations and the income distribution implications of fiscal and relative price changes.

Second, both China and India need to impose a hard budget constraint on state enterprises and on provinces and states, respectively, in order to enhance price responsiveness and macro stability. In both cases this also implies a need to reconsider ownership patterns—greater competition between private and commercially oriented state enterprises, if not full privatization.

Finally, both countries need to reform or create new institutions to provide economic services and social security. In India, this means better targeting of social welfare programs, and in China it means creation of many of the institutions, such as urban housing markets and financial institutions, that already exist in India.

PROSPECTS

Only the foolhardy would try to predict the future course of Chinese and Indian development, but each country has important assets.

China has a demonstrated capacity for rapid growth under a variety of political conditions. In recent years China has been able to exploit opportunities in agriculture and services that had been suppressed in the Maoist era. Many more such opportunities and niches remain. In particular, the large and broad-based state enterprise sector has enormous potential for productivity growth and technological improvement. Maoist China provided another potentially important legacy—an egalitarian distribution of assets and mass literacy, as well as a clean sweep of old cultural and institutional impediments to growth. At the same time, revolution in China destroyed many institutions that must be rebuilt, and others, which never existed, must yet be created in order to make a market economy work and to preserve the social gains of the Maoist era. One of the lessons China must learn from India is the importance of institutions in promoting development. Finally, the vast network of overseas Chinese, including those in Hong Kong, provide a window on the outside world, which China has already learned to exploit to promote integration with the world economy.

India also has many advantages: a strong set of market institutions, a dynamic private sector, a large supply of well-educated engineers and managers who speak English and interact easily with foreigners, and its own large diaspora of nonresident Indians who can facilitate integration into the world economy. At the same time, India is handicapped by many attitudes, such as indifference to the importance of universal primary education, which will have to change in order to assure broad-based and rapid development. In addition, India's pluralism leads to more social and political conflict than in China. For better or for worse, India has less capacity for radical change than China. The amplitude of policy shifts and of economic progress is therefore likely to be less than in China.

NOTES

1. See, for example, Swamy (1973), Wilfred Malenbaum (1982), Robert Dernberger and Richard Eckaus (1988), Swamy (1989), Malenbaum (1990), S.P. Gupta *et al.* (1991), and George Rosen (1992).

2. These are the commonly accepted estimates given by Alexander Eckstein (1975). The base years are 1952 for China and 1950 for India, the first normal postwar and postpartition years, respectively. Swamy (1989, p. 45) estimates that on a purchasing power parity basis (1970 dollars) Indian per capita income was 50 percent higher ($154 versus $101 in 1952). World Bank (1983, p. 301) comparisons using Indian prices estimate that Indian per capita GNP was less than 5 percent higher than China's in 1952.

3. The terms originated with Deepak Lal.

4. On balance, India is still less controlled than China, especially since the 1991 reforms. But China is more outward-looking.

5. The Penn/UN studies yield very high results for Chinese output compared with most other studies. In 1980, the Penn/UN estimates are two to seven times as high as any other estimates (Taylor, 1986, p. 21).

6. Unpublished work under way at the World Bank has provisionally estimated that the level of Chinese GNP was underestimated by about 55 percent by official statistics in 1987, but this does not resolve the problem of international comparisons.

7. See chapter 12 for definition. Although this is a net measure, it is approximately equal in percentage terms to the share of gross investment in GDP.

8. At official rates of growth, China's ICOR was about 5.2 from 1952–1978 and 4.0 from 1978–1990, compared with India's decadal ICORs of 3.9 (1950s), 5.7 (1960s), 6.2 (1970s), and 4.7 (1980s). But adjusting for overestimation of growth rates, Swamy (1989,

p. 118) estimates overall ICOR's for 1952–1985 of 5.7 for China and 4.5 for India. This is consistent with other evidence on China's relative inefficiency. China's inventory ratio (share of GDP) was very high by international standards prior to 1978 (World Bank, 1983, p. 80); China's energy consumption per person in 1979 was 3.3 times that of India (World Bank, 1983, p. 176); and total factor productivity growth was negative in China during much of the 1952–1978 period.

9. One measure of India's lesser orientation to world markets is that 19.3 percent of India's exports in 1989 were still directed to the Soviet Union and Eastern Europe, compared with 6.5 percent of Chinese exports to the same markets. The absolute level of exports to the socialist countries was almost identical.

10. More recent work on China by Azizur Khan *et al.* (1992) reaches a similar conclusion about the ranking of China and India, though the numbers are different. Some of the main conclusions of this work were that China's rural inequality is about average by Asian standards—lower than Southeast Asia, higher than Taiwan and South Korea, and, surprisingly, nearly as great as India; China's urban inequality is low by Asian standards; subsidies and income in-kind (especially employer-provided housing) increase the inequality of urban incomes in China; overall income inequality is lower than in India but greater than in Taiwan and South Korea; and the main source of overall income inequality in China remains the urban-rural gap.

11. Myron Weiner (1991), in a stinging indictment, attributes Indian failure to enforce universal primary education and to eliminate child labor to the unwillingness of the Indian elite to permit fundamental change of the social order.

12. There is a great deal of local government support for education in China that is probably not captured by these statistics. In both countries there is also private spending on education: in India for private schools and in China through cost recovery for public primary education.

REFERENCES

Banister, Judith. 1987. *China's Changing Population*. Palo Alto, Calif.: Stanford University Press.

Chow, Gregory C. 1985. *The Chinese Economy*. Cambridge, Mass.: Harper and Row.

DeLong, J. Bradford, and Summers, Lawrence H. 1990. "Equipment Investment and Economic Growth." National Bureau of Economic Research Working Paper, no. 3515. Cambridge, Mass.: National Bureau of Economic Research.

Dernberger, Robert F., and Eckaus, Richard S. 1988. "Financing Asian Development 2: China and India." The Asia Society Asian Agenda Reports, no. 8. Lanham, Md.: University Press of America.

Eckstein, Alexander. 1975. *China's Economic Development*. Ann Arbor: University of Michigan Press.

Ettori, Francois M. 1992. "Measure and Interpretation of Effective Protection in the Presence of High Capital Costs: Evidence from India." World Bank Policy Research Working Paper, WPS no. 873. Washington, D.C.: World Bank.

Gupta, S.P., *et al.*, eds. 1991. *Development Experiences in China and India*. New Delhi: Allied Publishers Limited for Indian Council for Research on International Economic Relations and London School of Economics.

Harrold, Peter. 1992. "China's Reform Experience to Date." World Bank Discussion Paper, no. 180. Washington, D.C.: World Bank.

Hirschman, Albert O. 1958. *The Strategy of Economic Development*. New Haven, Conn.: Yale University Press.

Howes, Stephen. 1992. "Purchasing Power, Infant Mortality and Literacy in China and India: An Inter-Provincial Analysis." Suntory-Toyota International Centre for Economics and Related Disciplines, CP no. 19. The Development Economics Research Programme, London School of Economics.

Hussain, Athar, Lanjouw, Peter, and Stern, Nicholas. 1991. "Income Inequalities in China: Evidence from Household Survey Data." Suntory-Toyota International Centre for Economics and Related Disciplines, CP No. 18. The Development Economics Research Program, London School of Economics.

Khan, Azizur Rahman, *et al*. 1992. "Household Income and Its Distribution in China." University of California, Riverside, Working Paper in Economics No. 92–3.

Kravis, Irving B. 1981. "An Approximation of the Relative Real Per Capita GDP of the People's Republic of China." *Journal of Comparative Economics* 8, no. 1: 60–78.

Malenbaum, Wilfred. 1982. "Modern Economic Growth in India and China: The Comparison Revisited, 1950–1980." *Economic Development and Cultural Change* 45–84.

———. 1990. "Review Article: A Gloomy Portrayal of Development Achievements and Prospects: China and India." *Economic Development and Cultural Change* 38: 391–406.

Matson, Jim, and Selden, Mark. 1992. "Poverty and Inequality in China and India." *Economic and Political Weekly* Bombay, 27, no. 14: 701–15.

Minhas, B.S., Jain, L.R., and Tedulkar, S.C. 1991. "Declining Incidence of Poverty in the 1980s: Evidence vs. Artifacts." *Economic and Political Weekly*, 6–13 July.

Perkins, Dwight Heald. 1988. "Reforming China's Economic System." *Journal of Economic Literature* 26, no. 2: 601–45.

Rajaram, Anand. 1992. "Reforming Prices: The Experience of China, Hungary, and Poland." World Bank Discussion Paper, no. 144. Washington, D.C.: World Bank.

Rosen, George. 1992. *Contrasting Styles of Industrial Reform: China and India in the 1980s*. Chicago: University of Chicago Press.

Summers, Robert, and Heston, Alan. 1988. "A New Set of International Comparisons of Real Produce and Prices: Estimates for 130 Countries, 1950–1985." *Review of Income and Wealth* Series 34, no. 1: 1–26.

Swamy, Subramanian. 1973. *Economic Growth in China and India 1952–1970*. Chicago: University of Chicago Press.

———. 1989. *Economic Growth in China and India: A Perspective by Comparison*. New Delhi: Vikas Publishing House.

Tan, Jee Peng, and Mingat, Alain. 1989. "Educational Development in Asia: A Comparative Study Focussing on Cost and Financing Issues." World Bank Asia Region Internal Discussion Paper Series, Report No. IDP 51. Washington, D.C.: World Bank.

Taylor, Jeffrey R. 1986. "China's Price Structure in International Perspective." Center for International Research Staff Paper, no. 22. Washington, D.C.: U.S. Bureau of the Census.

UNDP. 1992. *Human Development Report 1992*. New York: Oxford University Press.

Weiner, Myron. 1991. *The Child and the State in India*. New Delhi: Oxford University Press.

World Bank. 1983. *China: Socialist Economic Development,* Vol 1. Washington, D.C.:
    World Bank.
———. 1991. *World Development Report, 1991.* New York: Oxford University Press.
———. 1992. *China: Strategies for Reducing Poverty in the 1990s.* Washington, D.C.:
    World Bank.
Yeats, Alexander J. 1991. ''China's Foreign Trade and Comparative Advantage.'' World
    Bank Discussion Paper, no. 141. Washington, D.C.: World Bank.

14

NORTH AFRICAN REGIONAL DEVELOPMENT EXPERIENCE

Richard Pomfret

The countries of North Africa provide a fascinating source for comparative study of development experience in the second half of the twentieth century. From some similarity in initial conditions they have pursued diverse development strategies, from the Arab socialism of Gamal Abdel Nasser's Egypt (and to a lesser extent Algeria) to the more outward-oriented strategies of Tunisia and Morocco. The resulting outcomes have differed, but perhaps even more surprising is the commonness of the problems facing these four economies in the early 1990s. They are all trying to implement liberalization programs in response to mounting external debt, while unemployment or inflation (or both) is increasing and is accompanied by internal political uncertainty (especially the rise of Islamic fundamentalists ready to challenge the entire concept of economic development).

The starting point in each case is clearly delineated by a major political change. In Egypt the 1952 revolution ended the monarchy, and especially after Nasser's assumption of power in 1954, an independent economic policy was pursued. The French protectorates over Morocco and Tunisia and Spanish rule over part of Morocco ended in 1956. Algeria, which had been integrated into France, experienced a bitter struggle for independence, which was achieved in 1962.

With per capita incomes ranging from $131 to $176 in the mid-1950s (Table 14.1) the North African countries could be classified as lower-middle-income countries.[1] They all had outward-oriented economies, with the Maghreb countries (Morocco, Algeria, and Tunisia) focusing on primary product exports to France and the Egyptian economy based on cotton exports.[2] By 1989 they had achieved significant improvement in income levels and in other indicators such as life expectancy but still ranked as lower-middle-income countries. As a group their performance was better than some other African countries (e.g., Ghana), but significantly worse than the East Asian newly industrializing economies (NIEs)

Table 14.1
North Africa, Basic Economic Data

	GNP Per Capita		Population		Life Expectancy at Birth		Adult Literacy			
	Mid 1950's	1989	1960	1989	1960	1989	1960	1970	1985 Total	1985 Female
	(--US dollars--)		(-millions-)				(-------percent--------)			
Algeria	176	2230	10.3	24.4	47	65	10	26	50	37
Egypt	133	640	25.9	51	46	60	20	..	44	30
Morocco	159	880	11.6	24.5	52	61	14	28	33	22.
Tunisia	131	1260	4.2	8	48	66	16	24	54	41

Source: Bhagwati (1966, p. 11); *World Development Report* (1991, pp. 204–5); *World Tables* (1980).

(among the NIEs both Taiwan and South Korea were significantly poorer than Tunisia or Egypt in the mid-1950s). Moreover, in the 1980s in all four countries, mounting political dissatisfaction reflected a growing sense that the economy was failing to meet expectations, especially in providing work for the rapidly growing labor force. Thus, the economic performance from the 1950s to the late 1980s has been respectable but not outstanding.

The first four sections analyze the development experience of each economy separately, although there are cross-references to the other countries. The next section attempts to draw lessons from the different strategies adopted in the 1960s and 1970s. Then the chapter considers why all four countries ran into serious economic problems in the 1980s, manifesting themselves in growing external debt and an increasing dependence on nonmanufactured exports. One theme arising in the individual country sections and stressed in the section on the lack of NIEs in North Africa is the question of why, despite declared intentions to emulate the NIEs' development strategy based on manufactured export expansion, none of the North African countries has yet succeeded in becoming a second-generation NIE. This leads into the discussion in the final section of the future prospects of these countries, which are all currently undertaking reform programs intended to stimulate the private sector by opening up the economy.

EGYPT

During the nineteenth century, Egypt, although formally part of the Ottoman Empire, enjoyed considerable local autonomy. A brief attempt by local strongman Muhammad Ali to promote industrial development during the 1820s was upset by the imposition of free trade policies upon Egypt by the European powers after 1841. For the next century the Egyptian economy was integrated into world trade as a classic example of monoculture (Issawi, 1961). The commercialization of the economy around long-staple cotton exports destroyed the old social relations, but the lack of domestic linkage effects meant that a diversified economy was not created. Failure to diversify left the economy vulnerable to supply-side constraints (the movement to marginal land in the twentieth century) and to adverse demand-side developments (falling world income and the development of synthetic fibers in the 1930s). Egyptian per capita income is believed to have fallen by about a fifth between 1910 and 1945 (Issawi, 1961, p. 16).

The political consequences of the economic problems were similar to some Latin American reactions to the 1930s: a gradual shift away from reliance on international trade and a more general mistrust of the market mechanism. Some import duties were introduced in the 1930s, but the process was delayed by the war-induced boom of the early 1940s. More dramatic changes followed the 1952 revolution, Nasser's assumption of the presidency in 1956, and the establishment of Arab socialism in 1961–1963.

The development strategy introduced between 1952 and 1963 was a classic import-substituting industrialization strategy. Licenses were required for all imports after 1952, and then in the early 1960s a government monopoly over all foreign trade was established. The government used its trade monopoly to control domestic currency prices of all traded goods and hence to create a surplus that could be channeled to capital goods industries. Exports were practically ignored; the commodity markets in Alexandria were replaced by a new system "remarkable only for its complexity and inefficiency" (Hansen, 1991, p. 200).

Economic growth accelerated from the mid-1950s, and gross domestic product (GDP) was growing by over 5 percent per year between 1959 and 1965, reversing the stagnation of the first half of the twentieth century. The mobilization of resources for industrial development clearly played a part. Also, the construction of the Aswan Dam with Soviet aid and land reform provided a boost to the agricultural sector. By 1963 or 1964 economic growth was slowing down. Agricultural output grew faster than population during the 1950s and most of the 1960s, but by the end of the decade this relationship was being reversed as the benefits of increased arable land from the Aswan Dam approached their limits. Nasser had also done rather well at currying foreign favor, with PL480 wheat aid coming from the United States, financial aid for the Aswan Dam and other projects from the USSR, and commercial credit from European sources (especially Italy). After 1967 the economy was in deepening crisis as the growth rate slowed, the balance-of-payments deficit widened, and food riots became more common.

The causes of Egypt's economic troubles are disputed. Bent Hansen (1991, p. 4) emphasizes the quasi-permanent state of war between 1963 and 1973, from the Yemen War to the last Arab-Israel War. The 1967 defeat leading to the closure of the Suez Canal and the loss of oil fields hurt foreign exchange earnings. Also, Hansen (1991, p. 198) refers to a tacit U.S.-USSR agreement not to bid up aid to Egypt after 1965–1966. Despite these adverse external developments, however, the key constraints appear to be policy-induced domestic economic shortcomings.

Egypt's economic growth between 1954 and 1967 was a standard import-substitution boom. Much of the growth consisted of replacing imports in branches of the economy where import/total supply ratios were high in the early 1950s, for example, metals, petroleum refining, fertilizers, chemicals, and paper (Girgis, 1977, pp. 57, 61). The import-substitution took place behind highly distorted prices. Hansen and Karim Nashashibi (1975) estimated effective rates of protection (ERPs) for several branches of the economy in the mid-1960s and found all industries except cement had high ERPs, ranging up to 600 percent for iron and steel and 250 percent for tires, while the main export crops (cotton, rice, and onion) had negative ERPs. Thus, resources were being directed from agriculture to industry, and the large dispersion of ERPs within industry provided strong incentives for resource misallocation.

The best measure of resource misallocation is the estimates of domestic resource costs (DRCs) calculated by Hansen and Nashashibi (1975, p. 311) for various products in the mid-1960s. The DRC for iron and steel was LE4.80 per dollar saved, while for cement the DRC was LE0.31; sixteen times as many domestic resources were needed to produce a dollar's worth of iron and steel as a dollar's worth of cement. In general, DRCs were much lower for Egypt's export goods and, within the industrial sector, lower for cement, tires, and fertilizers and high for automobile assembly, pulp and paper, and iron and steel. In sum, Egyptian resources were grossly misallocated by insulating the economy from world prices and hence providing no incentive for producers to pursue Egypt's comparative advantage—which was clearly not in capital-intensive products like iron and steel or paper.

By discriminating in favor of import substitutes, Egypt's development strategy ironically contributed to the balance-of-payments crisis of the late 1960s. Initial import substitution was concentrated in goods where Egypt's comparative disadvantage was smallest, but once import/total supply ratios had been reduced to minimal levels in these goods, the only way forward was to produce more complex or less-suited import substitutes. This led to an increased demand for imported inputs; Maurice Girgis (1977, p. 66) estimated the ratio of imported inputs to total output to be 0.068 in 1954 and 0.164 in 1969. Meanwhile, the distorted relative prices provided little incentive to exporters, and declining agricultural growth was associated with reduced self-sufficiency in key crops (e.g., wheat, maize, beans, and vegetable oils).

By emphasizing capital-intensive industries, the import-substitution policy also failed to create employment for the rapidly growing population. One aspect of this failure was that the government's guarantee of public service employment for any graduate of secondary or higher schools, which had been introduced in 1964, turned into a massive bureaucracy-creating scheme. Apart from failing to provide employment, the excessively capital-intensive industries also embodied obsolete technology and seldom operated at the optimal scale (Mabro and Radwan, 1976).

In 1974 Anwar Sadat reacted to the economic problems by the *infitah*. The private sector was encouraged, foreign investment was invited to Egypt, and trade policy was liberalized. In none of these dimensions, however, was there much success. In particular, the trade regime remained restrictive as bureaucratic delay proved to be a major nontariff barrier. Also, the more protected industries were adept at preventing significant reduction of their trade barriers.

Nevertheless, the Egyptian economy did perform rather well during the mid- and late 1970s. The oil crisis and the return of the Sinai oil fields helped boost export earnings.[3] The demand for Egyptian workers in the Arabian oil states led to significant labor migration and workers remittances.[4] U.S. aid also became significant as Egypt and Israel dominated the total and the U.S. administration strove for a balance between the two recipients. Finally, tourism picked up with peace between Egypt and Israel. In 1980–1981 Egypt's foreign exchange earnings consisted of 22 percent in loans and grants, 21 percent in oil, 22 percent in workers' remittances, 9 percent in nonfactor services (mainly tourism), 7 percent direct foreign investment, 6 percent Suez Canal revenues, 3 percent other factor income, and a mere 10 percent from exports of manufactures and agricultural products. Meanwhile, as the degree of food self-sufficiency continued to fall, Egypt became the world's largest recipient of food aid in the mid-1980s. In sum, the post-1974 boom rested heavily on oil and aid, while the *infitah's* goal of stimulating manufactured and agricultural exports was not being achieved.[5]

Over the three decades after Nasser's assumption of power, the Egyptian economy has performed reasonably well, but the basis was extremely fragile. Total factor productivity fell during the 1960s (Hansen, 1991, p. 161), and the main sources of growth were the extension of cultivated land in the 1960s and the increase in the investment/output ratio from 14 percent in 1954 to 31 percent in 1981–1982 (Hansen, 1991, p. 21), only to collapse back to 19 percent by 1986–1987. The emphasis on extensive growth and failure to sustain intensive growth is typical of centrally planned economies (CPEs), and, albeit on a smaller scale than in the CPEs, Egypt's post-1952 etatist and autarckic policies underlie the country's economic malaise. Also, as in the CPEs, Egypt's economy proved difficult to reform piecemeal. The *infitah* did not attract foreign investors because the economy remained entwined in red tape. Despite a statement of intent to liberalize trade, vested interests restricted the practical extent of trade barrier reduction. The public sector grew rather than shrank as the government continued to guarantee employment to graduates. Price controls remained pervasive, and partial loosening succeeded only in making a few entrepreneurs/arbitragers rich, while failing to stimulate the economy more generally.

The symptoms of economic failure became more pronounced during the 1980s, especially as world oil markets softened.[6] Unemployment appears to have risen substantially, although the data are complicated by the presence of school-leavers waiting to take up their guaranteed positions in the public service (Hansen, 1991, p. 182). Inflation crept up from an average 3 percent per year in 1963–1973, to 11–14 percent in 1973–1980, 24 percent in 1986, and an estimated 40 percent in 1991. Foreign debt rose from $21 billion when Mubarak assumed power in 1981 to $44 billion in 1986, when repayment had to be rescheduled. With International Monetary Fund (IMF) support Egypt embarked on a reform program in 1987, replacing the multiple exchange rates with a two-tier system, raising agricultural prices,[7] and putting pressure on state enterprises to reduce losses. Fear of domestic unrest, however, dampened the pace of reform. Renewed negotiations with the IMF dragged on through 1989 and 1990.

MOROCCO

When Morocco gained independence in 1956, the Alawi dynasty, which had ruled before the imposition of the Franco-Spanish protectorate in 1912, returned to power. Since then Morocco has remained a monarchy, in which the state's legitimacy derives both from the king's position as temporal leader and and from his religious role as "commander of the faithful." The monarchy traces an unbroken existence back to the ninth century, and historical claims underlay territorial disputes with Mauritania and Algeria (up until the early 1970s) and over the Western Sahara. Continuity has also been underlined by the long reign of the present ruler, Hassan II, who came to the throne in 1961.

European administration had a profound impact on the economies of Morocco, Algeria, and Tunisia. In all three, traditional, largely nonmonetized economies were transformed. European farmers occupied the best land and produced export crops that had previously been of minor importance but were known by the Europeans to grow well under Mediterranean conditions, with fruit and vegetables being especially important for Morocco, wine for Algeria, and olive oil for Tunisia. Light industries, which often threatened traditional handicraft activities, were introduced. Mineral resources were exploited, especially iron ore, phosphates, and certain nonferrous metals. Modern transport networks were constructed to support these activities. In each country, independence was accompanied by large-scale emigration by the European colonists, leaving the modern sector as a partly empty shell.

Thus, at independence the Moroccan economy was primarily rural, exporting agricultural goods to Western Europe. The monarch replaced the departing French elite by a Moroccan aristocracy of landowners and attempted to maintain economic and social stability. On the international plane, King Hassan has played the role of an Arab moderate, cultivating good relations with Western countries, including the United States, and with the Arab states of the Gulf. In economics, the crucial link was with France, the destination for over half of Moroccan exports at independence. When France joined the European Community (EC) in 1957, the Treaty of Rome promised special relations with Morocco and Tunisia, and association agreements in 1969 formalized the preferential access of their exports to EC markets. In practice, the preferential trading arrangements with the EC have ensured duty-free access for Moroccan manufactured exports and preferential treatment for her agricultural exports to the EC (Pomfret, 1986).

The Moroccan government used the country's privileged position at or near the top of the EC's pyramid of preferential arrangements with nonmember countries in order to maintain the economic status quo based on agricultural exports. In the long run, however, this strategy was doomed. The EC's position has always been to give member-country agricultural producers priority in supplying internal demand, and the preferred external trading partners receive first option in supplying the gap between internal demand and supply. With high support prices under the Common Agricultural Policy (CAP), EC self-sufficiency has been steadily increasing, and countries like Morocco are left negotiating for a share of a diminishing cake.

The problem of EC self-sufficiency was less apparent in the 1960s, when the CAP was introduced and initially applied to ''northern'' agricultural products such as grains, dairy products, and meat. During the 1970s the CAP was gradually extended to cover ''Mediterranean'' products such as fruit and vegetables, olive oil, and wine, and the consequences of concentrating on a handful of agricultural exports (oranges, tomatoes, and potatoes) to a single market began to emerge.[8]

The situation became disastrous for Morocco when three Mediterranean countries joined the EC in 1981 and 1986. Of all nonmembers, Morocco's bundle of agricultural exports most closely resembled that of the three new members (especially Spain), so that Morocco would be most adversely affected by the surge to EC self-sufficiency in Mediterranean products (Pomfret, 1981).

In sum, Morocco's development strategy based on maintaining the status quo and relying on agricultural exports to the EC was initially favored by the special trading arrangements, but in the long run had little prospect. By the late 1980s it was clearly a dead end, and Morocco had ceased to place much hope on having a privileged relationship with the EC. The last gasp was Morocco's 1987 application for EC membership, which was quickly rejected.

Apart from agricultural land, Morocco's major natural resource is phosphates. In 1974–1975 Morocco enjoyed a windfall when phosphate prices quadrupled and earnings from phosphate exports increased five times (Figure 14.1). The phosphate boom also made Morocco appear to be a good credit risk to foreign lenders at a time when interest rates were low, so that the second half of the 1970s saw a huge increase in available resources. Part of these went to an increase in government services, including military expenditure associated with the Western Sahara, but a large part also went to investment. Public investment expenditure increased from 1 billion dirhams in 1973 to 2 billion in 1974, 4 billion in 1975, 8 billion in 1976, and 10 billion in 1977 (Claasen, 1990, Table C7).[9]

The development strategy continued to favor irrigation agriculture, and funds were used to complete existing dam projects and to initiate three new dams. Within agriculture the major change was to promote sugar beet production in order to reduce the sugar import bill. Import substitution was also carried over to industry, where, in addition to the sugar refineries, cement plants, and petroleum refineries, fertilizer and vegetable canning factories were built in the second half of the 1970s. The new factories were supported by tariff protection and by an extension of nontariff barriers to imports, for example, by 1980, 66 percent of imports required licenses, compared with 22 percent in 1972 (Bertola and Faini, 1991, pp. 275–76). By World Bank estimates, the distorted system of incentives to industry resulted in an effective rate of protection of +25 percent for manufactures sold in the domestic market and of −17 percent for exports in 1978 (Roe, Roy, and Sengupta, 1989, p.29).

Thus, Morocco was a latecomer to the import-substituting industrialization strategy adopted by Egypt a decade and a half earlier. The outcome was even more disappointing in Morocco, where the stimulus to growth was short-lived. It is difficult to believe that Morocco had no projects that could yield returns over the low and even negative real rates of interest in the late 1970s, but the projects actually chosen were capital-intensive projects with poor returns and little foreign-exchange earning potential. As in Egypt, the projects failed to generate much employment, and with fewer safety valves they probably increased income inequality more in Morocco than in Egypt.

A combination of events contributed to economic disaster at the beginning of

Figure 14.1
Phosphate Rock Prices, 1961–1990

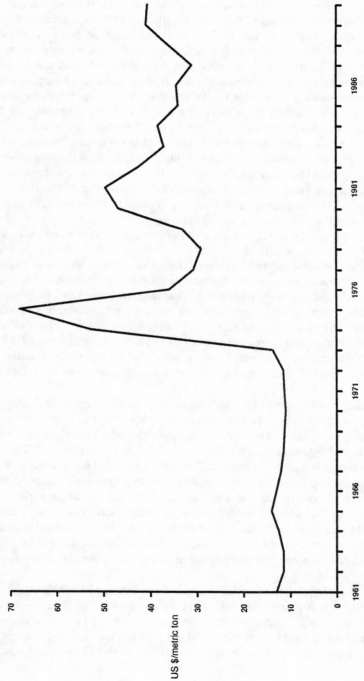

US $/metric ton

Source: International Financial Statistics Yearbook (1991).

the 1980s. The 1980–1981 drought was among the worst of this century, recession in Western Europe reduced workers' remittances and tourism earnings, expenditure on the Western Sahara war increased, and aid from Saudi Arabia was cut back in 1982. Combined with higher interest rates, these adverse events placed Morocco in the middle of the 1982 debt crisis. Nevertheless, the fundamental reason for Morocco's economic troubles was not external chance[10] but the development strategy selected in the 1970s. Phosphate prices fell from their peaks and were depressed through most of the 1980s. Thus, borrowing on the assumption that the 1974 prices represented new long-term levels was misguided. Even worse, spending the windfall gains and the borrowed money to finance inappropriate projects created no possibility of having funds to service the foreign debt if phosphate earnings failed to grow. The final outcome was accelerated by higher interest rates and other adverse developments of 1980–1982, but the fundamental problem arose from investing in projects whose financial (and social) return was less than the cost of capital.

The Moroccan government did try to encourage manufactured exports during the 1970s, but in a halfhearted way. Duty-free access to the EC provided an incentive for domestic and foreign producers to use Morocco as an export platform.[11] Morocco permitted foreign investment but made it unattractive by placing stringent requirements for Moroccan participation. Likewise, trade was liberalized by allowing remission of duty on imported inputs if the final product was exported, but the effect was muted by the delays and red tape that made it burdensome to locate processing activities in Morocco (Sharpston, 1975). In this setting foreign investors stayed away, and local entrepreneurs focused on the domestic market, with the net result that manufactured exports failed to take off.

Faced with declining earnings from primary product exports and meager manufactured exports, Morocco found it impossible to meet its import bill and debt-servicing obligations. The external debt, which had grown from $1.8 billion in 1975 to $11.3 billion in 1983, was rescheduled in 1983, and an IMF-sponsored restructuring was undertaken. Initial measures included liberalization of foreign investment legislation to allow majority foreign ownership, reduction of tariffs and export controls, and privatization of nonstrategic state enterprises. Nevertheless, the IMF standby arrangement was terminated in June 1986, because the 1985 budget deficit was larger than promised and the government had failed to raise state-sector prices. A new standby arrangement negotiated in December 1986 called for more dramatic reforms aimed at ending the current account deficit in 1987.

Over the first thirty years following independence, Morocco's economic performance has been modest. Following slower growth than Tunisia and Algeria during the 1960s and early 1970s, Morocco experienced a brief investment-led boom in the second half of the 1970s but then fell into a debt crisis and almost stagnant per capita income during the first half of the 1980s. Economic reform in the second half of the 1980s was thus undertaken in an atmosphere of incipient unrest (e.g., the January 1984 Casablanca riots against price increases).

TUNISIA

Tunisia, which had been a French protectorate since 1881, achieved independence at the same time as Morocco. The economic structure was fundamentally similar, but the resulting political order was different as a leader of the opposition to French rule, Habib Bourguiba, gained power. Bourguiba had initially advocated reformist measures and then been increasingly radicalized during the French period. After independence Bourguiba concentrated on consolidating his personal rule, and he became president for life until a bloodless coup deposed him in November 1987.

Economic policies after independence initially had some similarity to those of Egypt and Algeria, as the regime tried to reform agriculture (rather than turning the French estates over to a local elite as in Morocco) and to promote industry by import substitution.[12] The agricultural reforms disappointed hopes of achieving food self-sufficiency, and the import substitution policies were limited by the small domestic market. The preindependence private ownership was replaced by state ownership, initially (1956–1961) for nationalist reasons to preserve an industrial base when the colonial owners left, but after 1962 as an ideological desire for collectivization. Faced by mounting economic crisis, the cooperative movement was dissolved in September 1969. Unlike Algeria, Tunisia did not have oil exports to fall back upon for financing economic experiments.

Tunisia, like Morocco, had preferential access to EC markets, which was confirmed by a 1969 association agreement. In the agricultural sector, this was of less value to Tunisia, because her dominant export, olive oil, was a product in which the EC was already approaching self-sufficiency (unlike oranges). Agriculture's importance has declined steadily, from 24 percent of GDP in 1960 to 20 percent by 1970 and 14 percent after the drought of 1981–1983, where it has remained into the 1990s. Olive oil exports to the EC remain sufficiently important for the government to have negotiated a special arrangement after the EC's second enlargement, but agriculture has not been central to Tunisia's development strategy.

Starting in the early 1970s, Tunisia took advantage of the duty-free access to EC markets for its manufactured exports. In 1972 legislation encouraged direct foreign investment and reduced obstacles to firms wishing to use Tunisia as a base for supplying the EC with labor-intensive goods. The response was rapid, because the lags in establishing labor-intensive activities are short. Manufactured exports grew rapidly, primarily as a result of foreign investment in clothing, electronics, and other light industries. Manufactured goods accounted for over a third of Tunisian exports by 1977, compared with 19 percent in 1970, and clothing alone accounted for over 15 percent (from close to zero in 1970). The contrast with Morocco, which had no major manufactured export in 1977 (textiles, accounting for less than 4 percent of the total, were the leading manufacture), was stark. The difference in export performance was the main explanatory variable for the difference in growth in per capita incomes, with Tunisia a high performer and Morocco no better than mediocre (Pomfret, 1986, p. 57, 1990, p. 286). By the early 1980s Tunisia's per capita income was more than double Morocco's, despite starting from a lower level at independence a quarter century earlier.

Tunisia was widely regarded as a success story of the 1970s and considered a leading candidate to be a second-generation NIE. In the 1980s, however, the country lost its economic way as growth slowed and current account deficits mounted, culminating in a balance-of-payments crisis in 1986, when oil prices fell. The economy recovered in 1987–1988, led by exports and tourism,[13] which peaked in that year, but then the current account returned to deficit in 1989–1990.

Two possible explanations, neither very convincing, for the Tunisian turnaround are the political situation and oil. The Bourguiba regime became increasingly authoritarian and unpredictable during the 1980s, with rumors that the president for life was becoming senile. Unrest was forcefully repressed in 1987, including several executions of Islamic fundamentalists charged with plotting an Iranian-style revolution. In November Bourguiba was replaced by General Ben Ali, who initially increased political freedoms but in 1989–1990 returned to a personalized authoritarian government by manipulating elections. The argument is made that the deteriorating political situation and uncertainty deterred foreign investment, but it is unclear whether Tunisian rule has been any more authoritarian than that of some other NIEs.

Production in Tunisia's major oil field began in 1969 and expanded through the 1970s and early 1980s. Oil exports peaked in 1985, and since then its proven reserves have been falling. Growing oil exports plus the phosphate boom in the mid-1970s (phosphates are Tunisia's largest mineral export, but less important than in Morocco) may have had "Dutch disease" implications. The booming oil and mineral exports led to currency appreciation, which reduced the competitiveness of manufactured exports. This slowed down the process of diversification and left the economy exposed to the sluggish phosphate prices of the 1980s and the oil glut of 1986.

The years 1980–1984 saw a gradual deterioration in Tunisia's economic position. Despite a falling growth rate, both private and public consumption continued to grow at rates more appropriate to the 1970s growth rates. Gross domestic saving fell from 24 to 20 percent of GDP, and with investment remaining at 30–32 percent of GDP, the resource gap widened. This was reflected in a steady increase in imports, despite virtually stagnant exports, and a 1980–1984 cumulative current account deficit of $3.3 billion. Despite some moves to restrict demand in 1985–1986, the growing external debt contributed to the balance-of-payments crisis in 1986, when external debt service accounted for 9 percent of GDP. A large devaluation and favorable conditions in foreign markets contributed to an export boom in 1987–1988, and domestic devaluation reinforced the improvement in the balance of payments. Nevertheless, the recovery was not firmly based, reflecting continuing high incremental capital output ratios (i.e., low productivity of investment), which is a measure of the extent to which Tunisia failed to institutionalize an efficient growth path in the 1970s.

ALGERIA

Algeria was completely incorporated into France (and thus part of the EC in 1957) before a guerrilla war led to independence in 1962. The modern sector of the economy was highly specialized; in 1960, the last year of French rule before output collapsed, out of total exports worth 2,746 million francs, wine accounted for 895 million and oil for 800 million (Norbie, 1969). After independence, the immediate emigration of over a million foreign (mainly French) settlers plunged the economy, especially the commercial agriculture sector, into chaos. The first three years after independence were devoted to economic reconstruction, and, despite references to Algerian socialism, there was no clear development strategy. Politically these years under Ben Bella's leadership were dominated by power struggles, culminating in Houari Boumedienne's accession to power in June 1965.

Before independence the Algerian economy had been characterized by private ownership, and the Ben Bella regime transformed it into a mixed economy. The immediate postindependence issue was how to deal with the large farms owned by expatriates who had fled. Many of these farms had been spontaneously occupied by farm workers, and in 1963 the government legitimized workers' self-management by a series of decrees. In practice, however, the rules governing self-managed farms were too complex for an illiterate peasantry, and the Office Nationale de la Reforme Agraire soon controlled all decisions (Bennoune, 1988, p. 106). In other moves establishing state control, many Algerian-owned service activities were nationalized in 1963, and the cereals board, several financial institutions, and a hydrocarbon company were set up in 1964. Foreign trade was restricted, and capital controls were introduced.

Under Boumedienne the public sector came to dominate the economy. By 1978 the only parts remaining under private ownership were the traditional agricultural sector and some small-scale manufacturing and retail operations. Foreign-owned enterprises were nationalized. The government controlled all foreign trade and most domestic wholesale and retail trade, as well as all utilities, transport, and the financial system. Following the 1971 "agrarian revolution" Algerian landlords were expropriated, and over the rest of the decade 5,980 cooperatives were established, joining the 2,071 "self-managed" farms in a state sector controlling 3.5 million hectares (half of the total cultivated land, but by far the better half).

The development strategy that evolved during the 1960s and implemented most vigorously between 1970 and 1978 was import-substituting industrialization. The 1967–1969 three-year plan established the priority of creating basic industries such as steel, machinery, chemicals, construction materials, and petrochemicals. Trade was brought under government control, and industrial enterprises were gradually nationalized and amalgamated until eighteen socialist industrial enterprises became the prime vehicles of industrialization during the last Boumedienne years. During the two four-year plans investment was increased (so that it grew by 18.4 percent a year in real terms during the 1974–1977 period—Heidarian and Green, 1989, p. 250), while current consumption was restricted, and the investment was directed overwhelmingly into industry.

Until his unexpected death in December 1978, Boumedienne ran an austere socialist society based upon state-run agricultural and rapid industrialization. Neither the heavy industries nor the collectivized agriculture yielded appreciable benefits. Capital was wasted on low-yielding, capital-intensive projects, inappropriate to Algeria's factor endowments. The failure of the agricultural sector, deprived of capital and lacking motivation, was even more pronounced. Despite converting 150,000 hectares of vineyards to cereal, vegetable, and fruit production, Algeria's self-sufficiency in food declined precipitously. From being a substantial net food exporter in 1966, Algeria moved to a small deficit in 1967–1969, a larger deficit in 1970–1973, and a huge net import of food in 1974–1977.[14] Nevertheless, unlike Egypt in the 1950s and 1960s, Tunisia in the 1960s, or Morocco in the 1970s, Algeria was able to pursue its import-substituting industrialization policies for two decades without much questioning.

The Algerian economy was kept afloat by oil and natural gas exports, which came to account for almost all of exports. Not only did oil and gas revenues finance the rapid increase in domestic capital formation during the 1970s, but also private consumption expenditure became increasingly dependent upon oil revenues from the 1960s to the mid-1980s (Heidarian and Green, 1989). This development was acceptable to the government, in part because oil exports were not restricted to a geographically limited market, so that dependence on French or EC markets was reduced. Thus, although Algeria enjoyed preferential access to EC markets similar to that of Morocco and Tunisia, the government remained unconcerned by declining agricultural and wine sales or by failure to develop manufactured exports. The inefficiency cost of import-substituting industrialization was almost certainly along the same lines as in Egypt (but less documented for Algeria), but there was little pressure to change track as long as export revenues and per capita incomes increased.

Colonel Chadli Bendjedid became president in 1979 and consolidated power in the next two years. Chadli soon dismembered the eighteen large industrial enterprises created by his predecessors. By the mid-1980s the Chadli government was pursuing more flexible policies than its predecessor, encouraging private enterprise, and attempting to modernize the bureaucracy. In the 1985–1989 five-year plan greater emphasis was placed on agriculture and water supply, while responsibility for implementation was decentralized from the central planners. After years of conflict with international oil companies, the government reformed the oil exploration code in 1986 to try to attract the companies back. Reforming efforts were intensified after the 1985–1986 fall in oil prices, but the government's success at keeping foreign lenders and domestic constituents happy was at the expense of rising inflation and continued foreign borrowing. A wave of strikes in September 1988 was followed by riots in which 160 people died in six days.[15]

Following the riots and the brutal army response, Chadli tried to turn popular discontent to his advantage by instigating sweeping political reforms. Chadli hoped to rally popular support for further economic reforms while forcing the military and other leaders to the sidelines. A December 1987 land reform had broken up the 3,173 state farms, but the rights of the cultivators were clarified only in November 1988. Among the state enterprises, which accounted for 80 percent of nonhydrocarbon industrial output, viable enterprises were granted increased autonomy in 1988 and, after the 1989 banking reform, allowed to choose their bank.[16] The detailed regulation of interest rates was relaxed, and banks were granted some autonomy. Meanwhile, the restrictions on the heavily regulated private sector continued to be loosened.

Chadli's gamble on political reform failed to pay off. In the first multiparty elections, the regional elections of June 1990, the Islamic party (the FIS) took first place, with 55 percent of the votes. Chadli continued to hope that political and economic reforms would be rewarded by popular support, but this judgment was again confounded by FIS success in the first round of the general election in December 1991. Before the second round, when the FIS would have won by a landslide, Chadli resigned in January 1992. The succeeding military junta canceled the second round and then declared a state of emergency in February when hundreds of FIS supporters were killed or wounded and thousands imprisoned. In March 1992 the FIS was formally banned, and local councils controlled by the FIS were dissolved, ending the brief flirtation with democracy. The political uncertainty was underlined by the assassination of the new president, Muhammad Boudiaf, in June.

Despite the political setbacks, the government has continued with economic liberalization. The tourism trade, which had lagged far behind that of the other North African countries, was stimulated by legislation permitting foreign companies to manage hotels.[17] Between July 1990 and March 1991 the overvalued exchange rate was reduced by over 50 percent. The availability of foreign exchange was liberalized at the same time. State-owned firms are being granted greater autonomy prior to privatization and a Western-style financial system, including an independent central bank, is being created. Although the reform program has yet to show clear economic benefits, it has encouraged greater generosity by aid donors.[18]

Algeria's external debt has mounted, and private lenders have become increasingly nervous about the perceived political risk. Nevertheless, in March 1992 (on the same day as the FIS was banned!) they put together a debt-refinancing package, which allowed Algeria to avoid formal rescheduling. Algeria is, however, clearly near the end of the line, and there is some evidence that the lead creditor banks acted only under strong pressure from the French and Italian governments.[19] The Algerian government has accepted since 1989 some IMF supervision of the economic reform process, although the IMF's role is less formal than if a rescheduling had occurred.

SIMILARITIES AND CONTRASTS IN THE 1960s AND 1970s

There are two big differentiating features among the four North African countries' economic experiences since the 1950s. First, it mattered whether they had oil or not. Second, they adopted diverse economic policies.

Oil provided the basis for Algeria's higher per capita incomes throughout the 1960s, 1970s, and early 1980s and also helped to save Egypt and Tunisia from serious economic trouble in the late 1970s and early 1980s. To some observers, these were mixed blessings because fundamental reforms were delayed. Also, booming oil exports by appreciating the currency and therefore reducing nonoil exports may pull resources away from activities that have good long-term growth potential. This Dutch disease scenario can come close to concluding that it is better not to have plentiful natural resources, but that is surely too extreme. Morocco, with some coal and natural gas but minimal oil reserves and therefore a large net energy importer, was hurt by the energy crises and made significantly worse off in 1980–1982 by the second oil shock. Algeria and, to a lesser extent, Tunisia and Egypt were advantaged by their oil exports, even if they failed to take full benefit by using the oil rents to develop activities in which their long-term comparative advantage lay.

Policy differences explain much of the divergent performance of Egypt, Morocco, and Tunisia (Algerian performance was dominated by oil). Tunisia's outward-oriented policies of the 1970s produced the most successful nonoil-driven economic performance in the Arab world. Egypt's attempt to mobilize resources by import-substituting industrialization reaped only short-term benefits but, together with land reform, produced some economic gains in the early 1960s. Morocco's conservative strategy of preserving the landed aristocracy encountered growing problems as export demand in the EC dwindled, while overregulation hurt manufactured exports in both Morocco and Egypt.

These two differentiating features explain much of the variation in economic performance between the mid-1950s and the 1980s captured in Table 14.1. The Algerian economy grew fastest because of its fortunate resource endowment, while Tunisia outpaced Morocco and Egypt because of its superior economic policies. Despite these differences, by the mid-1980s, all four countries were facing similar problems of mounting external debt combined with rising domestic unrest driven by disappointment at the economic performance. In sum, even the more successful North African countries had failed to establish economies in which growth is self-sustaining and which could weather shocks (as the East Asian NIEs rode out oil price changes or exchange rate realignments).

WHY ARE THERE NO NIEs IN NORTH AFRICA?

It is easy to explain the failure of Algeria, Egypt, and Morocco to become newly industrializing economies in terms of their faulty development strategies. This explanation works less well for Tunisia, although we can resort to ad hoc explanations to explain the failure to maintain the momentum established during the 1970s. There are also some region-wide explanations why North Africa did not emulate East Asia, of which human resource and financial constraints may be highlighted.

Rapid population growth (2–3 percent) means that output has to grow rapidly to enable per capita incomes to increase. The age distribution of the population also works against achieving high savings rates. Even more important, however, the North African countries have failed to make good use of their human resources by investing in human capital formation.

The illiteracy figures in Table 14.1 reveal continuing high levels of illiteracy in all North African countries, especially among females. Despite declarations of the universal right to education ever since the 1923 constitution, Egyptian governments have not committed enough resources to education. Hansen (1991, pp. 228–32) describes Egypt's educational achievement under Nasser and Sadat as "unimpressive." Enrollment rates have increased since 1960 but remain unsatisfactory, especially in rural areas and among girls. Meanwhile, with the gradual decline since 1961 in the share of GNP going to education, "the quality of education has been declining at all levels" (Hansen, 1991, p. 245).[20]

Morocco also wastes potential human talent. Eighty percent of the economically active work force is male. Literacy rates have crept up since independence, but remain abysmally low (Table 14.1). Morocco's female illiteracy rate of 78 percent is exceeded by only ten countries, all of them significantly poorer. Algeria and Tunisia have a better record in promoting literacy but still have high illiteracy rates, especially for females, given their income levels. All four of the countries are classified among the forty lower-middle-income countries by the World Bank, and Tunisia and Algeria have above average income levels within this group (Algeria is the second highest); ranked within the group by female illiteracy, Morocco is second, Egypt third, Algeria sixth, and Tunisia seventh.

Human capital formation is also hampered by the high emigration rates of all four countries. The big Maghreb population in France dating from the colonial era facilitates continuing labor movement. The large Egyptian labor migration to the Gulf in the 1970s and early 1980s has already been referred to. Thus, people in all four countries, especially the more educated people, are well aware of opportunities elsewhere. Poor national economic performance can be exacerbated by a brain drain, and this has almost certainly happened in postindependence Maghreb and in Egypt since the early 1970s. While it is difficult to document precisely the educational achievement of the emigrants relative to the people who remain, the act of voluntary migration itself suggests a better-informed and more dynamic worker.[21]

Financial repression, although common among developing countries, appears to be especially severe among the North African countries. Among the twenty-four countries surveyed by Alberto Giovannini and Martha de Melo (1991), for example, the Maghreb countries stand out by the extent to which their government revenue benefited from financial repression during the early 1980s (Egypt was not in the sample); the savings from paying artificially low domestic interest rates, rather than world interest rates on government debt, are estimated to have amounted to 12 percent of Tunisia's central government revenue in 1981, 16 percent in Algeria, and 21 percent in Morocco. The mechanism was to require commercial banks to hold government bonds as reserves; the commercial banks held 55–56 percent of the total domestic government debt in each of the three countries (no other country in the sample had a share over 50 percent, and most were below 25 percent).[22]

As the governments' financial imbalances deteriorated, financial repression provided a breathing space with respect to the financing of deficits, but at the cost of propping up an inefficient financial system. Banks matched low interest rates on their assets by paying low interest rates on their deposits, which reduced the incentive to save (and required strict capital controls to prevent savers from seeking higher returns outside the country).[23] The excess demand for capital at the low interest rates had to be dealt with by credit rationing, leading to familiar problems of capital not being allocated to the most socially desirable uses. These problems became more acute during the 1970s and early 1980s as nominal interests changed very little but inflation accelerated (Bechri, 1989, p. 377).

In sum, the North African countries have a relatively poor record in investing in human capital, especially by neglecting opportunities to invest in girls' education and to include women in the labor force. They have also failed to create financial systems that mobilize savings and efficiently allocate them among potential investors.

RECENT DEVELOPMENTS AND FUTURE PROSPECTS

For the first time since the Egyptian revolution and the Maghreb countries' independence, the late 1980s saw economic policy convergence among these four countries. The underlying pressure for reform is recognition that existing economic structures are not producing desired results, but the external debt crises highlight the need for international competitiveness. Meanwhile, the diminishing importance of preferential access to EC markets and the depressed oil market have reduced the relevance of alternative methods to earning foreign exchange in the past.

Special relations with the EC have been a cornerstone of Morocco's development strategy and were important to Tunisia's manufactured export boom during the 1970s. Relying on continued privileged access to EC markets has become increasingly unattractive since the second enlargement of the EC. As the EC became more self-sufficient in agricultural products, especially the "Mediterranean" goods produced in North Africa, a preferential share of external supplies approaches a preferential share of nothing (Pomfret, 1986, p. 84). Favored access to EC markets for manufactures also becomes less significant as the EC's external tariffs have been reduced in successive rounds of multilateral trade negotiations. The North African countries are still relatively leniently treated with respect to quota-restricted textile and clothing exports to the EC but are being squeezed between calls from within the EC for more protection and pressure from developing countries in the Uruguay Round negotiations to phase out the Multifibre Arrangement.

Partly in frustration with the prospect of ever again getting a positive response from the EC on requests for meaningful preferential trading arrangements, Algeria, Morocco, and Tunisia joined Libya and Mauritania in forming the Arab Maghreb Union in February 1989. The intention is to eventually create a customs union, but trade among the member countries is small, and their economies appear competing rather than complementary. The Arab Maghreb Union is unlikely to provide a significant stimulus to economic diversification and growth.

The oil price increases of the 1970s shielded Algeria, and later Tunisia and Egypt, from the necessity to make economic reforms before the early 1980s. Falling oil prices during the 1980s had a bigger negative effect, to the extent that these countries had become reliant on oil-related revenue to cover their imports and as a government revenue source. Phosphate prices played a similar role in Morocco, although the denouement came earlier. The 1990–1991 Gulf War provided a brief windfall gain to the oil exporters, but the long-term prospect for higher oil prices is not promising.

The most important pressure for policy change in the 1980s was the growing external debt (Figure 14.2). Although the magnitudes varied, in all four countries the cause of the debt expansion during the 1980s was an inability to pay for a growing import demand, because primary product export earnings were stagnant or declining and because none of the North African countries has sustained long-term growth in manufactured exports. Morocco and Egypt were forced to reschedule their external debt, and Algeria and Tunisia avoided rescheduling only by drawing on standby facilities with the IMF/World Bank. The common feature was to introduce the multilateral institutions into the policy-making process, which contributed to standardization of the packages adopted. In all four cases, however, the governments recognized the need for economic reform and went more or less willingly down the path toward economic liberalization.

The main constraint on rapid policy reform is fear of popular unrest. This reaction to short-term pain is, of course, a problem in all countries whose

Figure 14.2
Public/Publicly Guaranteed Long-Term External Debt (Millions of U.S. dollars outstanding at end of year)

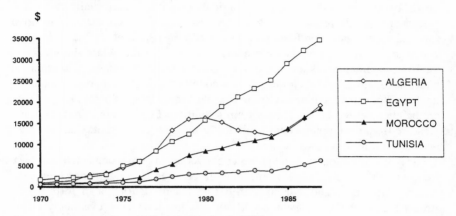

Source: International Financial Statistics Yearbook (1991).

governments seek to introduce dramatic reforms, but in North Africa it is exacerbated by the presence of an obvious and potent focus for discontent. All four countries have experienced the growing influence of Islamic fundamentalism, at least since the assassination of Sadat in 1981. The fundamentalist support is fueled by economic dislocation, especially measures adding to the already high youth unemployment.

In all four countries governments moved cautiously toward reform in the mid- and late 1980s. The process has been accelerated in the early 1990s by a mixture of frustration with the effects of partial reform and continued pressure from the multilateral institutions.

For Egypt the Gulf War, which hurt tourism and raised security concerns, had a silver lining because of international support for Egypt's role in opposing Iraq. The slow speed of implementing reforms since the May 1987 agreement with the IMF had led to long-running negotiations between the IMF and Egypt through 1989 and 1990. Meanwhile Egypt's debt continued to mount and by the end of 1989 was, in absolute amount, the sixth highest among developing countries.[24] After the Gulf War, however, official debts were effectively halved in return for adoption of an IMF-backed comprehensive liberalization program. In 1991 credit and Forex markets were reformed, state enterprises were privatized, and a plan to increase tax revenue by 40 percent was initiated.

Algeria had mixed success with economic reform in the second half of the 1980s and accelerated its reform process in 1990. Despite the much-needed reemphasis on agriculture and decentralization during the 1985–1989 plan period, the government failed to maintain macroeconomic control. Initially, substantial cuts in domestic demand by raising taxes, cutting public expenditure, increasing administered prices, and tightening credit policy limited the current account deficit to 3.5 percent of GNP despite the oil price drop in 1986 and brought it close to equilibrium in 1987. The economic and social costs of external adjustment, however, were high as per capita income fell in both years (Roe, Roy, and Sengupta, 1989, p. 24). Subsequently, spending for subsidies increased from 2.1 billion dinars in 1987, to 22 billion dinars in 1990, and over 50 billion in 1991.[25] Meanwhile, Algeria's external debt almost doubled from under $14 billion in 1984 to $26 billion in 1989, leading to greater external pressure for reform. The 1990–1991 Gulf War provided a small windfall in higher oil prices, which allowed Algeria to pay off some short-term debt,[26] but the long-term options are few and unattractive. In October 1991 the commerce minister announced price increases of up to 200 percent for staple goods, but whether such measures can be sustained in the face of rising urban unrest remains to be seen.

Morocco's debt problem is more long-standing than that of the other North African countries.[27] At first sight the government has had some success in cutting the budget deficit, from 11.6 million dirham in 1986 to a 0.8 million dirham surplus in 1990 (see Figure 14.2). This has been achieved in part by significant tax reforms, including introduction of a value-added tax and income tax reform, which have boosted the tax yield, but also by an increasing reliance on loans. Of the 31.7 billion dirham in state revenue in 1986 only 6.2 billion came from loans, but by 1990 18.4 billion out of a 66.2 billion total came from loans.[28] Trade and exchange rate policies were also changed dramatically during the 1980s. The real exchange rate depreciated by 25 percent between 1982 and 1987. Most imports were freed from quantitative restrictions, and maximum duties were reduced from 100 percent in 1984 to 45 percent in 1987. Manufactured exports did respond, and the current account deficit was reversed in 1987 and 1988, but this success was not sustained, as a deficit equal to 3.5 percent of GDP occurred in 1989. The proximate causes were higher international interest rates and food prices, but the economy was susceptible to these shocks because it had not diversified sufficiently during the 1980s. The Gulf War's effect on oil prices accentuated this vulnerability.

Tunisia's economic history during the 1980s was a fainter version of the Moroccan picture. Tunisia started from a far more positive position in 1980, mainly because of its superior policies in the previous decade and much smaller debt. Although the authorities pursued unsustainable policies in the first part of the decade, they avoided a debt problem on the Moroccan scale. Nevertheless, there are similarities. Tunisia has undertaken important reforms, including financial reforms in 1985 and 1987 (raising interest rates) and the introduction of a value-added tax in 1988, but remains vulnerable to shocks.

The regional picture in the early 1990s is remarkably similar as all four countries are implementing systemic reforms (see Table 14.2), which will make

Table 14.2
GDP and Population, Selected Years, 1950–1990

	GDP at Market Prices				Population			
	Algeria	Egypt	Morocco	Tunisia	Algeria	Egypt	Morocco	Tunisia
	(------- million 1980 US$ ------)				(------------- millions -------------)			
1950	9,401	4,058	5,871	1,833	8.8	20.5	9.0	3.3
1955	10,989	5,024	6,873	2,094	9.7	23.0	10.1	3.6
1960	17,639	6,902	7,056	2,604	10.8	25.9	11.6	4.2
1965	17,387 /a	10,015	8,386	3,360	11.9	29.4	13.3	4.6
1970	23,678	11,851	10,995	4,293	13.7	33.1	15.3	5.1
1975	31,351	14,114	13,766	6,431	16.0	36.3	17.3	5.6
1980	42,347	22,913	18,821	8,742	18.7	41.5	19.4	6.4
1985	54,444	31,951	22,131	10,733	21.7	47.6	22.1	7.1
1989	55,061	35,047	26,690	11,678				
1990					25.3	54.1	25.1	8.1

Source: World Bank data files.

[a] Algeria's GDP fell to 12,250 in 1962.

their economies more responsive to market forces. This follows current thinking on economic development, insofar as trade policy reform alone is insufficient, and intuitive support for the importance of markets and the inefficiency of state enterprises is forthcoming from the collapse of Soviet-style economies. The outcome of these reforms is difficult to predict, partly because there are few precedents but also because it depends critically upon implementation, especially upon whether governments can maintain macroeconomic control during the t ransition to a more market-oriented economy. More than in most countries, the North African governments must be concerned about the short term because their positions are not secure and the Islamic opposition groups provide an obvious focus for disaffected members of the population.

NOTES

I am grateful to Sonia Keda for her contribution as a research assistant.

1. Libya, with a per capita income of $90 was significantly poorer and more economically backward until oil exports became significant during the 1960s. Since then Libya's economic history has been dominated by petroleum, which for its small population yields a much higher per capita income ($5,310 in 1989) than the other North African countries. Mauritania is also sometimes included with the North African countries (like Libya, it is a member of the Arab Maghreb Union) but is excluded from the present comparison; Mauritania's small population (less than 2 million in 1989), low per capita GNP (estimated by the World Bank at $500 in 1989), and negative economic growth over the last quarter century make it significantly different from the countries studied.

2. In contrast to the extensive literature on Egypt, there is little available on the economic history of the Maghreb countries, especially in English. The two-volume study by Samir Amin (1966; shorter English translation in Amin, 1970) and the two books by Andre Tiano (1967, 1968) contain the most thorough accounts of the colonial and early postindependence periods. Charles Issawi (1982) places North African economic history between 1800 and 1980 in the broader context of the impact of European expansion on the area from Morocco to Iran. More recent economic and political surveys of the postindependence Maghreb are by Wilfrid Knapp (1977) and Richard Parker (1987).

3. The huge short-term impact of the Camp David peace agreement on the structure of Egyptian production is clear from the 1975 and 1980 mining shares in the following table.

Table 14.3
Composition of GDP

	1965	1970	1975	1980	1985	1990
	(-------percentage shares at current prices-------)					
Algeria						
Agriculture	15	11	12	10	10	12
Manufacturing	11	15	9	9	12	11
Mining	12	15	22	29	22	20
Const. & Utilities	10	11	15	16	17	17
Services	51	48	42	36	39	40
Morocco						
Agriculture	23	20	17	18	17	16
Manufacturing	16	16	17	17	19	18
Mining	4	3	9	5	4	3
Const. & Utilities	8	7	9	10	10	12
Services	49	53	48	51	50	51
Tunisia						
Agriculture	22	20	21	16	17	16
Manufacturing	9	10	10	14	14	17
Mining	3	6	11	14	12	8
Const. & Utilities	12	8	8	9	9	7
Services	54	57	50	48	49	52
Egypt						
Agriculture	29	29	29	18	20	18
Manufacturing	27		17	12	14	
Mining		28	3	19	9	30
Const. & Utilities	6		7	6	6	
Services	44	42	44	45	51	52

Source: Calculated from World Bank data files.

4. Data on workers' remittances are unreliable, but the number of Egyptians working abroad, primarily in the Arab oil-exporting nations around the Gulf, is commonly believed to have peaked around 1983 at something like 3.25 million; the number of people employed in Egypt at that time was about 12 million.

5. This is even clearer by the 1990s. Hansen (1991, p. 153) observes that "in relation to GDP, commodity exports, apart from oil, have almost disappeared."

6. Oil prices fell in 1986, but the inflow of workers' remittances peaked a few years earlier, and the negative impact is usually dated from 1982. Between 1982 and 1987 deteriorating terms of trade reduced Egypt's export earnings by 50 percent. The consequences were exacerbated by the extent to which the government had become dependent on oil for revenue, so that when it tried to maintain a high level of domestic demand by expansionary fiscal policies in 1982–1986 in the face of diminishing oil revenues it had to cover the twin deficits by inflationary finance as well as foreign borrowing.

7. Discrimination against agriculture had already been reduced in the first half of the 1980s (Hansen, 1991, p. 177). The Egyptian government appears to have been willing to proceed with reforms it had already embarked upon, but not to accelerate the process in response to external pressure. Also, some of the 1987–1988 reforms were undermined by actual practice; the real exchange rate appreciated during these years, and despite the declared objective of stimulating private investment, nearly 75 percent of net new credit was allocated to the public sector during the 1988 fiscal year.

8. In 1978 Morocco signed a number of agreements to sell citrus fruit and phosphates

to the USSR, but this market never assumed significant proportions (Pomfret, 1986, p. 109).

9. Emil-Maria Claasen (1990, pp. 99–101) argues that the investment boom was inaugurated before the phosphate boom, but this is disputed by Mateus (1988, p. 6) and several contributors, including myself and I. William Zartman (1987).

10. There is some evidence that external events were favorable for Morocco over the period 1974–1986. Andre Raynauld (1990) estimates the impact of three external shocks on the current account net of official transfers (CANOT) for five African countries, and Morocco turns out to have been relatively lucky: terms of trade gains were equal to 30.1 percent of CANOT, while the adverse effects of higher interest rates and depression in the world economy amounted to only 0.4 percent and 10.6 percent, respectively. Thus, external events contributed a net 19 percent *improvement* in Morocco's current account. Raynauld concludes that "Morocco is a clear case where the external shocks had nothing to do with the deterioration of the current account" (p. 13).

11. There are some quantitative restrictions, notably on textiles and clothing, but they have not proven a significant barrier to Moroccan exports. In fact, given the Multifibre Arrangement, some of Morocco's potential competitors are much more restricted in EC markets. Morocco benefited from this relative ease of access to increase textile and clothing exports to the EC during the 1970s, but by far less than other Mediterranean suppliers (Pomfret, 1982).

12. The import-substituting industrialization policies of the 1960s are described and evaluated in Mustapha Nabli (1981).

13. The 1988 tourism boom was led by Libyans. In 1989 the Libya-Egypt border was reopened, and many Libyans then chose to visit Cairo rather than Tunisia. The 1986 crisis had also been exacerbated by special considerations (the oil price fall and the severe drought, which cut agricultural output by over a fifth), but the long-term trend was a deteriorating current account of the balance of payments.

14. Average annual exports of foodstuffs fell from 931 million dinars (1966) to 717 (1967–1969), 736 (1970–1973), and 612 (1974–1977), while imports rose from 731 (1966 and 1967–1969) to 925 (1970–1973) and 4,049 (1974–1977) (Bennoune, 1988, p. 216).

15. These are the official figures for the deaths in "Black October"; widely accepted unofficial estimates are much higher.

16. Before 1989 each enterprise was allocated a bank with which it had to conduct all its financial business.

17. This met with an immediate decision by Accor, the world's largest hotel group, to build a 740-bed Sofitel hotel and then by a joint venture involving Daewoo of South Korea to build a Hilton hotel on the outskirts of Algiers. Both hotels opened in 1992.

18. In the EC aid package for 1992–1996 Algeria's increase was larger than that of Morocco or Tunisia. The World Bank has been an active supporter of the reform program, and its lending to Algeria is forecast to reach $3 billion during the first half of the 1990s, up from $1.4 billion in 1985–1989.

19. Economist Intelligence Unit, *Algeria* no. 1 (1992). The two governments not only pressured their domestic banks, but the French finance minister also telephoned U.S. cabinet members Baker and Brady to bring U.S. creditor banks into line (as a quid pro quo for French cooperation in refinancing arrangements in Latin America).

20. Hansen (1991, p. 232) estimates the share of GNP spent on education to have been 4.7 percent in 1950, 5.2 percent in 1961, and 4.1 percent in 1983. The post-1961

decline has been at a time when the number of students has been increasing at all levels and has led to shortages of classrooms, materials, and qualified teachers.

21. One of the most conspicuous groups of Egyptian workers in the Gulf states has been teachers. This fact partly reflects the low spending on schools in Egypt but also represents a cost to Egypt, which has paid for the teacher training and lost the services of trained teachers.

22. In Tunisia this percentage rose rapidly over the 1970s, from 5 percent in 1974–1975 to 35 percent in 1976 and over 50 percent by 1979 (Bechri, 1989, p. 393), which may be symptomatic of the insecure basis of the export-led growth of the 1970s described in the section on Tunisia. Tunisia's near neighbor, Malta, had a similarly successful 1970s but foundered in the early 1980s because of lost macroeconomic control; the Maltese government addressed mounting inflation by real appreciation of the currency, which discouraged exporters and quashed the export-led growth, which had been among the highest in the world during the 1970s.

23. Perhaps the most direct negative effect on saving is the disincentive for overseas workers to remit their savings. Indeed, they may hold their relatives' savings in overseas bank accounts, making capital controls rather porous. A third feature that could be added to the list of the reasons there are no NIEs in North Africa is the low savings rates, but these appear as much policy-induced as anything (by the late 1980s gross domestic savings were very low in Morocco and Egypt, at 11–14 percent of GDP in both countries, because public sector savings were negative).

24. World Bank, *World Development Report 1991*, pp. 244–45. As a percentage of GNP Egypt's external debt was greater than that of any of the five more indebted countries and was exceeded only by six Sub-Saharan African countries and Jordan.

25. The substantial real depreciation of the currency, which started in 1986 and accelerated after 1989, exposed the size of many subsidies, whose financial costs had previously been hidden by an overvalued exchange rate.

26. The short-term debt problem led to two policy changes after November 1989. All imports of under $2 million had to be paid for in cash unless financed by official credit, and all new short-term borrowing requests had to be reviewed by a committee chaired by the central bank. Both measures add to the financial repression that is described.

27. Morocco is included in the category of the fifteen heavily indebted countries in international statistics. Compared with the other North African countries, Morocco's external debt is smaller in absolute terms than that of both Egypt and Algeria and smaller relative to GNP than Egypt's debt. As a percentage of exports of goods and services, however, it is the highest in the region.

28. Economist Intelligence Unit, *Morocco: Country Profile, 1991–1992*, pp. 36–37. World Bank sources estimate that by 1989 domestic debt by the central government was equal to 37 percent of GDP, and this buildup had almost all occurred since 1983. As government debt dominates banks' balance sheets more and more and in the absence of variable interest rates or a well-developed separate capital market, the supply of funds to private sector borrowers is drying up, especially for new or risky projects (see section on the lack of NIEs).

REFERENCES

Amin, Samir. 1966. *L'Economie du Maghreb*. Paris: Editions de Minuit.
———. 1970. *The Maghreb in the Modern World—Algeria, Tunisia, Morocco*. Harmondsworth, UK: Penguin.

Bechri, Mohamed. 1989. "The Political Economy of Interest Rate Determination in Tunisia." In *The New Institutional Economics and Development: Theory and Applications to Tunisia*, edited by Mustapha Nabli and Jeffrey Nugent. Amsterdam: North-Holland, 375–403.

Bennoune, Mahfoud. 1988. *The Making of Contemporary Algeria, 1830–1987: Colonial Upheavals and Post-Independence Development*. Cambridge, UK: Cambridge University Press.

Bertola, Giuseppe, and Faini, Riccardo. 1991. "Import Demand and Non-Tariff Barriers: The Impact of Trade Liberalization—An Application to Morocco." *Journal of Development Economics* 34: 269–86.

Bhagwati, Jagdish. 1966. *The Economics of Underdeveloped Countries*. London: Weidenfeld and Nicolson.

Claasen, Emil-Maria. 1990. *Macroeconomic Policies, Crises, and Growth in the Long Run: Morocco, 1967–85*. World Bank.

Giovannini, Alberto, and de Melo, Martha. 1991. "Government Revenue from Financial Repression." *Discussion Paper No. 489*. London: Centre for Economic Policy Research.

Girgis, Maurice. 1977. *Industrialization and Trade Patterns in Egypt*. Tubingen: J.C.B. Mohr.

Hansen, Bent. 1991. *The Political Economy of Poverty, Equity, and Growth: Egypt and Turkey*. Oxford: Oxford University Press for the World Bank.

Hansen, Bent, and Nashashibi, Karim. 1975. *Foreign Trade Regimes and Economic Development: Egypt*. New York: Columbia University Press for the National Bureau of Economic Research.

Heidarian, Janshid, and Green, Rodney. 1989. "The Impact of Oil Export Dependency on a Developing Country: The Case of Algeria." *Energy Economics (UK)* 11 (October): 247–61.

International Monetary Fund. 1991. *International Financial Statistics Yearbook*. Washington, D.C.: International Monetary Fund.

Issawi, Charles. 1961. "Egypt Since 1800, A Study in Lop-sided Development." *Journal of Economic History* 21 (March): 1–25.

———. 1982. *An Economic History of the Middle East and North Africa*. New York: Columbia University Press.

Knapp, Wilfrid. 1977. *North West Africa: A Political and Economic Survey*. Oxford: Oxford University Press.

Mabro, Robert, and Radwan, Samir. 1976. *The Industrialization of Egypt, 1939–1973*. Oxford: Clarendon Press.

Mateus, John. 1988. World Bank Discussion Paper. Washington, D.C., World Bank.

Nabli, Mustapha. 1981. "Alternative Trade Policies and Employment in Tunisia." In *Trade and Employment in Developing Countries: Individual Studies*, edited by Anne Krueger, Hal Lary, Terry Monson, and Narongchai Akrasanee. Chicago: University of Chicago Press.

Norbie, O. 1969. "The Economy of Algeria." In *The Economics of Africa*, edited by Peter Robson and D.A. Lury. Evanston, Ill.: Northwestern University Press, 471–521.

Parker, Richard. 1987. *North Africa: Regional Tensions and Strategic Concerns*. New York: Praeger, for the Council on Foreign Relations.

Pomfret, Richard. 1981. "The Impact of EEC Enlargement on Non-Member Mediterranean Countries' Exports to the EEC." *Economic Journal* 91 (September): 726–29.

————. 1982. "Trade Effects of European Community Preferences to Mediterranean Countries: The Case of Textile and Clothing Imports." *World Development* 10 (October): 857–62.

————. 1986. *Mediterranean Policy of the European Community*. London: Macmillan for the Trade Policy Research Centre.

————. 1987. "Morocco's International Economic Relations." In *The Political Economy of Morocco*, edited by I. William Zartman. New York: Praeger, 173–87.

————. 1990. "Export Promotion in the Mediterranean Basin." In *Export Promotion Strategies: Theory and Evidence from Developing Countries*, edited by Chris Milner. Hemel Hempstead, UK: Harvester Wheatsheaf, 285–301.

Raynauld, Andre. 1990. "The Impact of External Shocks on the Current Account." *Atlantic Economic Journal* 18 (March): 1–14.

Roe, Alan, Roy, Jayanta, and Sengupta, Jayshree. 1989. *Economic Adjustment in Algeria, Egypt, Jordan, Morocco, Pakistan, Tunisia, and Turkey*. EDI Policy Seminar Report No. 15. Washington, D.C.: World Bank.

Sharpston, Michael. 1975. "International Subcontracting." *Oxford Economic Papers* 36 (March): 94–135.

Tiano, Andre. 1967. *Le Maghreb entre les Mythes—L'Economie Nord-africaine depuis l'Indépendence*. Paris: Presses Universitaires de France.

————. 1968. *Le Développement Economique du Maghreb*. Paris: Presses Universitaires de France.

World Bank, 1980. *World Tables*. Washington, D.C.: World Bank.

————. 1991. *World Development Report*. Washington D.C.: World Bank.

Zartman, I. William, ed. 1987. *The Political Economy of Morocco*. New York: Praeger.

PART IV

THE MAIN LESSONS

PART IV

THE MAIN LESSONS

15

DEVELOPMENT POLICIES AND DEVELOPMENT PERFORMANCE

Helen Hughes

LONG-RUN TRENDS IN GROWTH AND DEVELOPMENT

This half century has seen the most dramatic improvement in global living standards ever experienced. Until classical times the rate of per capita income growth was almost imperceptible. From the Middle Ages to the middle of the eighteenth century European countries grew at perhaps 0.3 percent per annum (Snooks, 1990). When the Industrial Revolution ushered in the age of accelerating technological change, national income growth rose to more than 1 percent per annum, and by the end of the nineteenth century it was more than 2 percent for many industrial economies (Grilli, 1994). But since the late 1940s, rises in per capita incomes have been as unprecedented as they were unexpected. Initially, the most rapid gains were made in the advanced industrial countries, but by the 1960s it was evident that Japan was catching up with the other industrial countries. A mere twenty years later, a few developing countries had bypassed lagging industrial economies and all the centrally planned economies of Eastern Europe. Progress, however, has been uneven. Some developing countries, not necessarily the poorest ones, have been stagnating. In some, per capita income has even been falling, so that uneven growth among developing countries had become as much a feature of development as high growth rates. But overall, there have been marked growth and development since the 1950s, with substantial poverty alleviation and hence improved income distribution.

Some broad regional patterns have emerged from the experience of the last thirty years. At the end of World War II, the most advanced and highest-income developing economies were clustered in Latin America, while many of the poorest were in East Asia. By the beginning of the 1990s the highest-income developing economies were Singapore, Hong Kong, and Taiwan. The Republic

Table 15.1
Average Annual Real Rates of Growth of GNP Per Capita of Developing Economies by Region, 1965–1990 (percent)

East Asia /a	5.2
South Asia	1.9
Middle East and North Africa	1.8
Latin America and the Caribbean	1.8
Sub-Saharan Africa	0.2

/a   Including Northwest Asia and Southeast Asia.

Source: Grilli (1993).

of Korea was devastated by war in the 1950s. In 1960 it had a per capita income of $80 ($560 in 1992 prices). In 1992 its per capita income was $5,400. This was well ahead of countries such as Brazil (per capita income of $2,680 in 1992), which had been one of the leading developing countries in 1960 (World Bank, 1992a). Per capita income growth, was of course, not only an East Asian phenomenon. In Africa, Botswana grew rapidly. In the Mediterranean, Malta was an outstanding performer.

The leading developing economies of East Asia (including China since the 1980s) clearly dominate growth performance, doubling their per capita income every decade from the 1960s. Per capita income growth has been more rapid than in other regions because rapid economic growth has damped down population growth. The large, very low-income countries of South Asia, after a very slow start in the 1950s and 1960s, improved their performance markedly in the 1970s and 1980s, edging ahead of the resource-rich countries of the Middle East and North Africa and of the Latin American countries. In addition to Botswana, a handful of other Sub-Saharan countries have had positive per capita income growth rates (Lesotho and Mauritius), but in most of the Sub-Saharan region, growth rates were reminiscent of the Middle Ages, and in some countries per capita incomes declined between 1965 and 1992 (World Bank, 1993).

Interpreting Growth and Development

The developing country experience since World War II thus covers a vast spectrum. It has been described and analyzed by country and region from a variety of objective and subjective viewpoints. Marxist-Leninist paradigms, stressing "structural" characteristics and the direct role of the state in economic management, had a profound impact on the evolution of thought about development (Little, 1982; Lal, 1984). The economic collapse of centrally planned countries, together with a revelation of the social and political excesses they perpetrated in the name of equity, has changed the ideological climate on the Left, but structuralist views of development, particularly those embedded in the use of econometric and modeling techniques to explain growth, have persisted. At the other, "only prices matter" extreme, support for the operation of markets has often ignored the case for public intervention established by classical economists (Sylos Labini, 1994).

While significant components of the development debate focused on ideological postures, a great deal of analytical and empirical work has remained in mainstream economics, and this strand of analysis has contributed most to the understanding of development in terms of intracountry and intercountry changes. National data and international comparability have improved, enabling hypotheses of considerable depth to be postulated about development processes. These have led to a broad consensus about the principal determinants of development. It seems that the policy frameworks that countries adopt and their implementation are critical for all countries from the least developed to the most advanced. The principal characteristics of policies conducive to growth have also been identified. Human resource development, macroeconomic stability, and openness to world trade are the key components. If these policies are appropriate, governments can concentrate on infrastructure and industry-specific issues in sectoral policies.

The Role of Government

Since policies are crucial, the nation-state, implicitly or explicitly, is the essential actor in growth and development. The policy framework that influences development is not narrowly economic. A nation's capacity to maintain external security is important. The desperate poverty of countries such as Afghanistan, Mauritania, and Vietnam makes it clear that development does not take place when resources are devoted to waging war. Internal security—personal safety and the rule of law—is essential if economic activities are to flourish. Good governance, ill-defined though the concept may be, is essential to growth.

Social and cultural factors and their reflection in political processes clearly affect development. If these processes were better understood, growth could be accelerated in many countries. Attempts to identify such relationships, particularly in slowly growing countries such as those of Sub-Saharan Africa, are highly commendable (Killick, 1994). But research and hypotheses linking cultural and political relationships and growth are necessarily country- or, at best, subregion-specific. Generalizations linking a Buddhist-Confucian ethic to growth, for example (Chen, 1989), are not valid over time and between countries. The Republic of Korea was regarded as a "basket case" in the 1950s; in the mid-1960s, with changed economic policies, it became a "tiger." Botswana and Malta do not share a Buddhist-Confucian culture. Societies tend to select out of their culture those traits that policy frameworks encourage. Social and cultural research results thus cannot be broadly applied. Political reforms require a country-specific framework.

Economic hypotheses, in contrast, are concerned with rules of economic behavior that have proved robust across widely differing economic and social systems. The problems of centrally planned economies were clarified only by the application of mainstream economic tools to the empirical analysis of "socialist economies." While "initial conditions" such as natural and human resource endowment, levels of per capita income, geographic location, size of land area, and population influence economic growth and development, the process is neither simply related to such "conditions" nor random (Riedel, 1988). This is why empirical research has been able to discern general relationships between economic policies and growth.

Creating a Policy Framework

The issue that emerges out of the ideological debates about development is not whether governments have a role in development, but what sort of role they should play. Economic agents—individuals, households, and enterprises—respond to explicit and implicit signals given by prices and regulations to produce, consume, save, invest, and participate in the international economy. In most economic areas market prices, reflecting international competitive conditions, provide the best guide available. Where "natural" monopolies, externalities, or policy distortions exist, however, returns to society are not identical with returns to individuals. Government intervention becomes necessary to ensure that social and private economic returns converge. Defense expenditures are an important "public good" in many developing countries, although they are rarely subjected to scrutiny. So are expenditures on education, health, and waste disposal. Some national and international markets are monopolized by private interests.

The recognition (or suspicion) of market failure has led to a great deal of government intervention in the economy, often on an ad hoc basis, on the assumption that governments (public servants and politicians) represent public interest better than markets. In its extreme form, government intervention took the form of central planning (China, Cuba, and Vietnam), but "statist" approaches were also strong in the "mixed" economies of India and other South Asian countries. But regulators, like entrepreneurs, make many errors. Unlike entrepreneurs, they are not wiped out by their losses but often keep subsidizing failed projects. The empirical analysis of the effects of direct government intervention in the economy remains an important research area because at present those who argue that the costs of direct intervention are high (Hughes, 1994b forthcoming) differ sharply from its advocates (Amsden, 1979, 1989, 1993; Wade, 1990).

A government can improve the information available to economic agents and thus reduce economic risk by clearly enunciating medium- to long-term development objectives and strategies. Although most developing countries had mixed economies with limited state participation in the production of goods and services, in the 1950s detailed economic plans modeled on central, physical planning were de rigeur. Multilateral and bilateral aid agencies encouraged (and sometimes required) national economic plans as a context for their assistance. Such planning consumed vast amounts of scarce professional resources. The outcomes bore little resemblance to the plans. Centrally planned and statist economies persisted with planning that led neither to growth nor to equity, but most developing countries, particularly those with serious growth objectives, transformed planning into indicative strategy statements and budgetary targeting of public infrastructural investment. These "indicative" plans were used to stimulate debate and generate the political support essential to the introduction and implementation of policies necessary for rapid growth. Economic policy discussions were used to make growth targets explicit and rational, demonstrating how reformed economic policies would contribute to them.

In most nation-states it is not difficult to agree on the main targets for development. Rising living standards are desired by all. Few dispute that poverty alleviation is desirable. Difficulties, however, arise when broad objectives are broken down into specific policies and the ensuing resource allocations required are made explicit. Countries do not start from a clean slate in formulating policies. Existing policies favor some groups, enabling them to reap large financial benefits by exploiting "economic rents" created by various subsidies. Infrastructure—roads, power, urban facilities, education, and health provision—is often skewed toward urban and high-income groups. The formulation of economic strategies and determination of policies is consequently an intensely political process. Little economic change occurs without cost, and those who bear the costs rarely benefit in the short term. Those who become displaced or dispossessed oppose change, while those who will gain in the long run cannot foretell the advantages from which they will benefit. Entrepreneurs, trade unionists, public servants, and others who enjoy monopolistic advantages, whether for historical reasons or as a result of distorted policies, are reluctant to give up their "rents." The greater the policy distortions and the more direct the intervention that takes place, the greater will "rent seeking" be and the higher its cost in terms of productivity and competitiveness (Krueger, 1974).

Ideological conflicts based on varying hypotheses about the process of development are highly divisive, particularly between extreme followers of public intervention and reliance on market forces. Although only a small group may benefit from such economic policies as protection or financial repression, these policies may be passed off as representing a growth orientation. But if growth does not occur, or if it is so skewed that it does not lead to poverty alleviation, governments have to repress popular demands for more open and successful policies. In many Latin American and African countries, empty development rhetoric has thus encouraged political repression and the isolation of elites from the majority of the population. Countries' political maturation has been delayed. Some authoritarian governments have been able to persuade the majority of the population to support policy changes that were inimical to the immediate interests of powerful groups because the benefits of growth were soon seen to outweigh the costs. Where growth has been rapid, sustained, and equitable, governments have moved toward democratic modes. Some countries, notably India in recent years, but also countries as disparate as Mauritius and Costa Rica, have been able to combine economic rationalism with democracy.

HUMAN RESOURCES

Putting people at the center of development has been an important practical and theoretical advance in the development debate since the 1950s. When Schultz pointed to the economic importance of education in 1963, human capital was largely ignored in growth models. Since then it has become clear that human capital is as crucial to growth as physical and financial capital. The impacts of growth on poverty alleviation and income distribution, within the household and within the community more generally, have become important areas of analysis. Poverty alleviation and movement to more equitable income distribution not only are important in their own right but have positive feedbacks on growth through consumption, savings, and investment.

Population

No simple relationship between population growth and economic growth exists (National Research Council, 1986). Rapid population growth has been associated with rapid economic growth in some circumstances, but so has low population growth. Different situations require different remedies, but whether implicit or explicit, population policies are core human resource policies.

In broad terms, economic development leads to a "demographic transition" from rapid to low population growth. The fall of mortality rates is followed by declining fertility rates. Longevity, one of the best indicators of welfare, rises. Rapid growth stimulates the demographic transition. It can also be assisted by health policies (reducing death rates, particularly of children), education policies (improving access to schooling, particularly for women), employment policies (making opportunities for women to work outside the home), social policies (such as those affecting age at marriage), and population planning policies.

Rapid population growth, particularly if it takes the form of immigration, stimulates growth because migrants are self-selected, highly productive groups that strengthen economic activities. The post–World War II experience of Hong Kong is an example. But high population growth rates are very costly in terms of health and education budgets. Instead of deepening human capital by improving health services, keeping children at school longer, and providing better education at all levels, expenditures are spread thinly over ever-increasing numbers of children. Similar considerations apply to health expenditures. Rapidly rising productivity is needed in areas such as agriculture (or exports to provide balance-of-payments income for agricultural imports) to satisfy food requirements. Keeping up with a rapidly rising demand for jobs is difficult. Capital and technology have to be diluted instead of being increased per worker. The small islands of the South Pacific are microcosmic examples of how rapid population growth can threaten economic growth (Cole, 1993).

Global population exploded after World War II, doubling in the last fifty years to more than 5 billion people. Only 600 million or so of these people live in high-income, industrial market economies. The bulk of the world's population is in developing countries, with more than 70 percent in Asia. India and China alone account for over 2 billion.

Population density varies greatly among and within countries, but Bangladesh already has about 750 people per square kilometer. Similar densities exist in Central Java and the river valleys of China and India. This compares with some 400 people per square kilometer in the Netherlands, the most densely settled industrial country. High population densities have high environmental costs. Despite broad commitment to population planning, the young structure of the population arising from past rapid growth means that, on conservative assumptions, the world's population is likely to rise to more than 11 billion people before a "stationary" population is approached in the year 2050 (World Bank, 1992b). Economic motives for emigration from lower- to higher-income regions and countries are already exerting strong internal and international pressures. High population growth beyond that forecast, apart from pressures on productivity, employment, and public expenditures, would be likely to exacerbate migration problems.

Education and Health

Education has objectives beyond economic growth, but growth releases resources for education, and favorable education policies stimulate productivity. At early levels of development, the highest private and social returns accrue to primary education (Psacharopoulos, 1991). The majority of developing countries have reached 100 percent primary school enrollment. The rapidly growing countries of East Asia and Malta have emphasized not only access to education but also its quality. Hong Kong and Singapore introduced many innovative practices to lower the cost of schooling. For example, schools were used for two shifts of children during the day and for adult education in the evening.

Poverty is the principal cause of low educational attainment. In lagging countries less than half the boys and a quarter of the girls of primary school age are enrolled. Cultural factors are also influential, particularly in the education of girls. The Melanesian countries of the South Pacific and some Muslim countries of the Middle East have lower enrollments of girls than their per capita incomes warrant.

Expanding secondary and postsecondary vocational education is the next important step in human resource development, yet vocational education has generally been neglected, reflecting the bias of education expenditures to middle- and upper-income groups. In many countries vocational education is largely left to the private sector, though governments sometimes contribute training subsidies or tax exemptions. These are common mechanisms in Latin American countries. The rapidly growing East Asian countries, in contrast, have established, or are establishing, high-quality, secondary-level vocational schools that enable their graduates to absorb concentrated mixes of on-the-job and formal training at the postsecondary level.

Private returns are usually highest for academic secondary and tertiary education. The wealthy groups in the majority of societies have captured most of the benefits of education by lobbying for expenditures on academic high schools and universities. A "brain drain" often results as youngsters from middle- and upper-income families are educated at public expense and then emigrate to benefit from high salaries in higher-income countries while their home countries continue to be starved of highly skilled labor (Bhagwati and Partington, 1976). Equitable education policies would charge the full costs of such tertiary education to parents. Scholarship programs could offer opportunities to talented children from lower-income groups. As incomes rise, a society can choose to widen access to education, but an equitable progression is rare.

Health policies, like education, are key human resource policies for development, and, like education, their objectives go beyond economic issues. Access to water of reasonable quality and to sanitation (Behrman and Deolalikar, 1988) is often the most important, albeit indirect, component of health policies. Such services are frequently skewed in favor of middle- and high-income urban groups. Education, particularly for girls, is an important input into health policy because women determine the quality of nutrition and hygiene in households. Education for women is an important correlate of population planning. Broadly based elementary health services that have eradicated such killer diseases as measles and malaria and reduced the impact of minor injuries and ailments have been the sources of principal improvements in health (World Bank, 1993). Sophisticated hospital services, on which most health funding has been spent, have been much less effective in improving health. Sophisticated health services should be based on "user pays" charges to enable them to be expanded to meet effective demand without crippling budgets.

Urban housing policies targeted at low-income groups have improved health as well as contributing to the rise of living standards more generally in several countries. They have also contributed to growth through stimulus to construction, though most analysts have failed to recognize the effects on the economy (Young, 1992). But for many years housing policies failed to meet their objectives. In many instances, public housing followed the worst practices of industrial countries. Costly high-rise buildings became unlivable within a few years of construction. Public housing expenditures usually subsidized middle- and upper-middle-income groups. New approaches to slum improvement and minimum cost site and service preparation in the 1970s involved people's being housed in housing developments. Private ownership was combined with public intervention in land allocation, that is, in the monopoly component of housing. Utilizing publicly owned land for housing by providing titles and improving access to property rights stimulated private investment. Public housing tenants were transformed into owners, releasing capital and improving maintenance. In Singapore and Hong Kong, public and private investment in housing made a substantial contribution to growth as well as to welfare.

Environment

The environmental dimensions of living standards have only belatedly come to concern industrial, as well as developing, economies.

The hard core of environmental degradation in developing countries is poverty. Poor people impoverish marginal soils, cut down forests for fuel and pasture, and hence destroy watersheds. They pollute water supplies. The first priority in environmental concerns in developing countries is therefore the reduction and elimination of poverty. Environmental policies, like population policies, can therefore not be separated from growth policies.

As countries' per capita incomes and productive capacities rise, cleaning up pollution arising from past and present practices becomes practicable. Empirical evidence suggests that the demand for environmental "goods" is highly income-elastic. Technological innovation is stimulated so that technology becomes more environmentally benign and the costs of environmental cleanup and enhancement fall. Environmental improvement becomes a rising component of growth (Low, 1992).

Traditionally, even in open industrial economies, bureaucrats favored control and regulation approaches to environmental policies over the use of pricing that reflected scarcity and social values. Risks of noncompliance, it was thought, were reduced. Increasingly this attitude is being seen as inappropriate. The full costs of eliminating pollution have to be built into production costs and consumption prices. Relevant technologies are making this possible not only in agriculture and manufacturing but also in services such as transport. In Singapore the use of pricing policies to regulate urban motor vehicle use contributed to making it a "garden city."

Environmental policies necessarily rely on government inputs because they involve large "externalities." Education, absence of infectious diseases, and clean air all have benefits that cannot be captured by the suppliers of these services. But while government intervention in the form of infrastructural expenditures and, in some cases, regulations is necessary, environmental sustainability has to be increasingly embedded in the price system.

Employment

Increasing the productivity of farmers, farm workers, and those in "informal" employment at the same time as new formal productive employment opportunities are created is an essential component of growth and the only way to improve living standards economywide. How well each policy component is designed and how well the components fit together depend on the economic policy framework as a whole. Attempts to subsidize through protection employment in sectors such as manufacturing fail to stimulate growth in the medium to long run because they have to be paid for by taxing other sections of the economy. Measures that limit labor mobility and fragment and delay the evolution of labor markets also discourage growth in employment. Barriers to informal sector activities, for example, by laying down formal sector conditions for service industries such as hairdressing and food stalls, severely impede work force participation. Policies favoring capital over labor and encouraging the premature introduction of capital-intensive technologies have the same effect. Credit subsidies and shift loadings are examples of policies that, despite rhetoric that gives employment a high priority, create a strong bias against the creation of jobs.

Poverty and Income Distribution

Poverty alleviation and equitable income distribution have been a major policy focus of countries such as India since the 1950s, but because national policies have not delivered growth, poverty persists. In many Sub-Saharan African countries, close to 50 percent of the population is still living in absolute poverty. At the other end of the spectrum, in the rapidly growing countries of East Asia, the "absolutely poor" are only some 10 percent of the population. The reduction and elimination of absolute poverty (defined in terms of minimal standards of nutrition, clothing, housing, and access to public services) are, accordingly, a prime development target.

The measurement of poverty, particularly across countries, is fraught with many difficulties. Nutrition standards, for example, are notoriously unreliable. On balance, however, it seems clear that development has been successful over the last thirty years in reducing both the number of people living in poverty and their proportion in the world's population. Physical welfare indicators, notably the years of life expected at birth, have been rising in all regions (Streeten, 1994).

Improving the distribution of the benefits accruing to growth is even more difficult to measure (Ravallion, Datt, and Chen, 1992). Much argument about how improved distribution is to be achieved has taken place. Impatient to achieve positive social results quickly, some economists have favored the redistribution of wealth and income (Chenery et al., 1974). But countries that chose this approach (Tanzania, Jamaica, Cuba) achieved neither equity nor growth. China and Vietnam showed that equality of income can be achieved at a very low standard of living for the majority of the population. But the disparity between the majority and the elite was considerable in China and Vietnam and grew over time. For example, the remuneration scales in Chinese universities in the 1970s were far wider than in more advanced developing or industrial countries. The "basic needs" approach, which is essentially redistributive, also stalled development. In China the rule of the "iron pot," that is, universal entitlement to basic needs regardless of work inputs, undermined initiative and the productivity of workers and managers. Total factor productivity was low and grew very slowly. With biases against agriculture, a concentration of investment on capital-intensive manufacturing, the neglect of service industries, and high military expenditures, standards of living were frozen at very low levels. Reforming these economies is proving very difficult.

Direct attempts to reduce poverty in "target" populations have had little economywide impact, even where they have been effective. A rural credit program designed by the Grameen Bank in Bangladesh for poor rural women has had some income-raising effects (Rahman, 1991). Its subsidy element, moreover, is relatively modest. But so is the impact. A similar concentration of institutional and financial effort on the construction of rural roads would probably have led to much greater, more extensive, and more sustained increases in low incomes in the rural areas of Bangladesh. Macroeconomic and trade policy reform would have been even more effective.

Many well-intentioned direct interventions, for example, through food subsidies, usually lead to food policy distortions that slow growth and entrench poverty. Middle-income, rather than low-income, groups absorb most of the benefits. Similar outcomes usually follow attempts to subsidize power, transport, and other public services. Unless "users pay," sources of maintenance and investment funds for public utilities dry up so that services cannot be maintained and extended.

The empirical analysis of trends in income distribution has made it clear that rapid growth does not necessarily lead to a worsening distribution of income before income distribution improves, as Kuznets (1955) argued. The worsening of income distribution that has occurred in some countries was a result not of growth but of economy-distorting policies. Rapid growth is essential for poverty alleviation and improved income distribution (Fields, 1989). Positive trends in the rapidly growing countries of East Asia contrast sharply with the poor and worsening income distribution experience of many Latin American, Mediterranean, and Sub-Saharan African countries. With policies targeted toward rapid growth, "trickle down" from growth works very well. Even low-income countries can alleviate poverty markedly by removing policy-created distortions. For example, in India and Indonesia, improved agricultural policies, by raising farm productivity and output, lowered the ratio of rural people living in poverty between the 1970s and 1980s (Ravallion and Datt, 1991; Booth, 1993). Rapid growth in Thailand led to a decline in the people living in poverty from 57 percent in 1963 to 21 percent in 1988 (Medhi, 1992). But if policies are inappropriate (as discussed later), the little growth that occurs is likely to concentrate the benefits in the hands of small middle- and upper-income groups.

MACROECONOMIC POLICIES

Macroeconomic policies have long been the sleeper of economic development. Where inflation has been low, exchange rates have been stable, and interest rates have encouraged savings and investment so that economic growth has been rapid and sustained, macroeconomic policy has attracted relatively little attention. But in slowly growing and stagnating countries inflation was high, the exchange rate was overvalued so that it had to be constantly depreciated, savings fled the country, imports poured in while exports stagnated, and external borrowing exploded. By the 1980s it had become clear that macroeconomic policies were a key input to growth (Hughes 1985; Fischer, 1993). Empirical research established that macroeconomic (and trade) policies had a greater influence on performance in sectors such as agriculture and industrialization than specific sectoral policies (Krueger, Schiff, and Valdez, 1988). In East Asia the importance of stable macroeconomic environments was recognized from the 1950s, but in Latin America and many other developing countries, only in the 1970s did high inflation begin to be seen as an impediment to growth (Corbo, 1992).

Fiscal Policy

The gathering of revenues and their spending is at the core of macroeconomic performance. The tax system has to be efficient, and it has to be seen to be equitable if revenues are to meet recurrent and developmental needs. Traditionally, income taxes were regarded as "progressive," and indirect taxes as "regressive," but income taxes proved easy to avoid and evade. In most developing countries income taxes have been in the main paid by wage and salary earners in the formal private enterprise and public sectors. Political failure to tax upper-income groups has thus been the underlying problem in fiscal weakness in many countries. The bulk of revenues came from indirect taxes. Value-added taxes that impact on consumption rather than savings and investment and that are difficult to evade on large consumption expenditures have become increasingly popular and effective (Harberger, 1990). Unless budgets are essentially balanced so that deficits are used only at the margin (together with borrowing for clearly identified productive uses), to stimulate economic activity in times of recession, undue pressure is placed on monetary and financial policy. Fiscal balance has thus been a central policy in the most rapidly growing economies in the world (Hong Kong and Singapore). Fiscal reforms were initial components of Taiwan and the Republic of Korea's turns to rapid development in the late 1950s and early 1960s, respectively. Taiwan, in particular, has maintained balanced budgets since that time. Most developing countries have improved the efficiency and effectiveness of tax gathering over the years. Petty corruption, endemic in large, ill-paid bureaucracies, has been reduced and in some cases eliminated as bureaucratic efficiency rose while numbers declined. Reform has mostly been a slow process, but some countries have taken dramatic steps. In Indonesia, for example, the entire Customs Service was replaced overnight by a private Swiss firm to end customs collection problems.

Containing budget deficits is inherently difficult and particularly difficult in developing countries. Rapidly growing populations demand high recurrent expenditures on education and health. Public investment needs in social and physical infrastructure are vast. In many countries "statist" approaches to development critically weakened fiscal systems. It was argued that the private sector was not established and mature enough to undertake major investments in manufacturing or in public utilities such as energy. The state had to control the "commanding heights of the economy" (in India) if the public was not to be exploited by monopolies. Employment needs and the exigencies of political patronage expanded public sectors regardless of efficiency, even in rapidly growing economies such as the Republic of Korea, but particularly in South Asia and in African countries where statism had a strong hold. Most state enterprises were not efficient, needing inputs of recurrent as well as investment funds, undermining budget income to which they were supposed to contribute from their profits. The most egregious costs of statism have, of course, been identified in centrally planned developing countries such as China and Vietnam.

When reduction of public sector investment to reduced costs of production and lower pressure on budgets became a policy issue in the 1980s, reforms were difficult to introduce. Staff and workers in public enterprises that were to be privatized did not want to be part of the cost reductions required. Whereas the rapid growth of the private sector had swamped public sector employment in rapidly growing countries such as Indonesia, Malaysia, and Thailand, so that many public sector employees voluntarily found employment opportunities elsewhere, in slowly growing countries they clung to their employment privileges, making cost reduction and privatization very difficult.

The expenditure effects of fiscal policy also led to unequal income distribution. Total infrastructural expenditures were limited by per capita incomes and by the efficiency of tax collections and expenditures. The skewing of public expenditures toward middle- and upper-income groups occurred not only in education and health but also in power supply, transport, and urban facilities. Extravagant infrastructural expenditures in countries such as the Ivory Coast or the Philippines undermined the fiscal base.

Monetary Policy

Management of the money supply is closely related to the fiscal balance. Some of the countries unable to balance their budgets relied on unduly restrictive monetary policies to prevent inflation. Real interest rates had to be high in such situations, although high interest rates discouraged investment. "Hot" money flowed into such countries, overvaluing the exchange rate. Since exchange rate devaluations fueled inflation, overvalued exchange rates were maintained, but this led to further distortions and difficulties, notably in Chile and Argentina in the 1970s.

More commonly, inflation was implicitly or explicitly chosen to make up for fiscal weakness. Instead of taxing upper-income groups, the money supply was expanded, domestic private sector borrowing was crowded out by government borrowing from the financial system, and in the 1970s, with a highly liquid international capital market, it became possible to stave off reform by borrowing abroad. Periodically, inflation got out of hand. Budgets were balanced, but at the cost of growth. When the International Monetary Fund came to the rescue, it was blamed for cutting back economic activities. Low-income groups bore the brunt of the "stop" measures in "stop/go" economies unwilling to increase effective taxation, and the fund was blamed for this too. Political turbulence was typically encouraged by fiscal and monetary imprudence. After decades of high inflation resulting from highly distorted policies that gave benefits to selected groups at the cost of the economy as a whole, macroeconomic reform was extremely difficult. By the end of the 1980s only Chile and Mexico had clearly emerged onto a growth path.

High inflation severely distorted resource allocation and utilization. International competitiveness was eroded directly by overvalued exchange rates. Inevitable devaluations were accompanied by speculation, and inflation soon led to further exchange overvaluation. The overvaluation of exchange rates was a constant problem in many developing countries. It was institutionalized in Francophone West Africa, allegedly to stabilize the economies by tying local currencies to the French franc. But the currencies were tied at an overvalued level, retarding exports while encouraging imports. High inflation was avoided at the expense of stagnation.

High inflation was a major cause of unequal income distribution in many countries. The rich were protected, particularly where financial instruments were indexed. Factory workers in protected manufacturing were favored by wage indexing. But the incomes of the poor, particularly of rural people, urban underemployed, the old, the disabled, and the sick, declined. In extreme cases, inflation was a systematic substitute for fiscal discipline, transferring incomes from low-income groups to the government. Effective domestic demand was undermined, with negative impacts on effective demand as well as equity.

Financial Policies

Macroeconomic policies not only determined the overall price levels but also had microeconomic effects on the relative use of capital and labor. Repressed financial policies were widely followed (McKinnon, 1973) until the 1980s. They often originated in ideological convictions that high interest rates were usurious. Low interest rate policies suited governments that relied heavily on bank borrowing to supplement their revenues. In inflationary periods, real interest rates became very low or even negative. Domestic savings were discouraged as capital flight grew. Cheapening the price of capital encouraged the substitution of capital for labor. It also discouraged the intensive use of capital. Machines were substituted for additional workers, but they lay idle much of the time (Bautista et al., 1981). Shift work, which would have lowered the cost of putting additional people into the work force, was rare despite the scarcity of capital in real terms.

Adjustment

The boom and bust cycles of many of the developing economies outside Asia were encouraged by stop/go policy stances, by the roller-coaster petroleum price changes of the 1970s, and by the low-cost international capital flows to which petroleum price increases contributed. The amplitude of macroeconomic swings became greater than it had been in the 1960s. An awareness of the costs of stop/go policies rose as attention was devoted to the analysis of the problems that made adjustment urgent (Edwards, 1984, 1989; Corbo and de Melo, 1987). The 1981–1982 recession, when industrial countries sought to conquer inflationary trends, had a "scissors" effect. The demand for imports fell while debt service obligations rose with an increase in real interest rates. In many countries these balance-of-payments difficulties finally led to the realization that far-reaching reforms were necessary.

Initially "adjustment" was seen as being imposed by the international economy, that is, by recession in industrial countries. As analysis proceeded, however, it became clear that adjustment was needed mainly to overcome domestic policy distortions (Balassa, 1982). Outside Asia the 1980s became a bitter period of coming to terms with the effects of stop/go policies. High indebtedness was the symptom, but weak fiscal and monetary policies and distorted financial and trade policies were the cause of the internal and external difficulties.

Many countries moved to reform policies. A great deal of discussion about the format of reforms and their sequencing in the "real" (goods) sectors and the financial sectors ensued. Some analysts opted for rapid reform on all fronts, while others favored a gradual, sequenced reform process. It soon became evident that the latter was often too slow to be effective.

The leading Asian countries had little fundamental macroeconomic reform or adjustment to undertake in the 1980s. They were able to take advantage of the rapid recovery in industrial countries, particularly in the United States, to continue to expand their economies by maintaining stable macroeconomic policies and relying on the continuing exploitation of changing comparative advantage. The Philippines was a notable exception. It had adopted severely distorted trade and macroeconomic policies from the 1950s, had acute adjustment problems in the 1980s, and has been slow to reform its policies even in the 1990s. Indian and other South Asian countries maintained macroeconomic balance and slowly began to reform trade and financial policies. The market was allowed more play. China, following its neighbors, tried to adopt a prudent macroeconomic stance to contain the grave inflationary pressures of a reforming, centrally planned economy, but it has had to resort to stop/go management because it lags in fiscal, financial, and monetary reforms and has barely begun to reform its trade regime (Tidrick, 1994.

Logically it seemed that since goods markets took longer to adjust than financial markets, trade policies should be adjusted before financial policies, and then exchange rate policies could follow. But it soon became clear that political commitment was an essential component of reform and that fiscal policies had to be improved if reforms were to gain broad support. For governments, the relative political ease of undertaking reforms was more important than the technicalities of sequencing them. In practical terms financial reforms were relatively easy to implement, and they were therefore usually the first to be undertaken. Governments intent on reform moved where they could.

Overall, reform was slow and halting in the 1980s, particularly in countries with the most distorted policies that needed adjustment most. The principal lesson that emerges from the adjustment experience of the 1980s is the importance of adopting appropriate macroeconomic policies that introduce minimal distortions in the first place, thus avoiding the need for adjustment.

TRADE POLICIES

While the importance of macroeconomic policies has been reflected in the development literature only since the middle of the 1980s, trade policies, because of their linkage with industrialization, have been a central development theme since Rosenstein-Rodan's pioneering article on development in 1943. Trade—and its absence—has hence been a central theme of development from the 1940s.

Industrialization

The economic development debate was off to a bad start with an "industrialisation" thesis that postulated that developing economies would be perpetually at a disadvantage in the world economy. Their terms of trade for traditional exports would decline, and they could not compete with industrial countries in the production of manufactured goods, either for domestic consumption or for export. Center and periphery arguments that linked the fates of developing economies to progress in industrial countries through a declining terms-of-trade hypothesis followed. The central conclusion was that high protection for manufacturing was necessary for growth. This view was not only widespread in developing economies, notably in South Asia and Latin America (Prebisch, 1950; Raj and Sen, 1961), but also strongly supported by Marxist developing economists from industrial countries.

Prebisch succeeded in mobilizing Latin American economists to support protectionist policies through the United Nations Economic Commission for Latin America (ECLA) (Corbo, 1992). He then organized support from other developing countries through the United Nations. Two specialized agencies, the United Nations Conference on Trade and Development (UNCTAD) and the United Nations Industrial Development Organization (UNIDO), were created to further high-protection industrialization policies and to seek redress from industrial countries for their alleged continued colonial practices in international trade. Heady images of rapid employment growth, balance-of-payments surpluses, and national economic self-sufficiency dominated economic thought in most developing countries.

The thesis did not reflect empirical reality even at the time of its formulation. It was by no means clear that there was a long-term secular decline in the terms of trade of primary products exported by developing economies from 1870 to 1960 (Grilli and Yang, 1988), particularly if quality improvements in manufactures were taken into account. It was also not evident that the "infant industry" argument—that industries in developing countries needed high tariff (and other) protection while they learned how to compete with industrial countries—was valid. As a practical demonstration of the competitiveness of manufactures in developing countries, economies as disparate as the Philippines (shoes), Brazil and Argentina (shoes and clothing), Costa Rica (clothing), and Hong Kong (clothing, toys, and other labor-intensive goods) were exporting manufactures in the early 1950s. With the exception of Hong Kong, which did not adopt protectionist industrialization policies, these countries had lost their exports of manufactures by the end of the 1950s as their protectionist policies raised costs of production.

It is still being argued that a period of infancy is necessary to enable industries to become competitive (Amsden, 1993), but empirical evidence indicates that infant industries do not become internationally competitive with time. In many developing countries some forty years of protection have failed to deliver international competitiveness. Protected infant industries did not lead the export drive in Taiwan or the Republic of Korea. The more recent exporters in Southeast Asia have also shown that new exporters were stimulated by exclusion from the local market rather than by privileged access to it (Suphachalasai, 1989; Saad, 1992). In the Philippines thirty years of infant industry protection failed to recover the relative efficiency that labor-intensive industries had in the 1950s.

Protectionism advanced in most developing economies in the 1950s and 1960s, but its negative impacts soon became evident. Hong Kong's strong growth in the 1950s was noted in East Asia. Although Singapore's entrepôt activities were different from Hong Kong's (importing manufactures and exporting raw materials), it followed Hong Kong's success when it left the Malaysian Federation in 1965 by turning to exports. Taiwan, a basket case in the 1950s with runaway inflation and repeated balance-of-payments crises, opted for stability and openness in the 1950s when the United States threatened to cut its nonmilitary aid. As export-oriented groups in Taiwan were not strong enough to reduce protection or end financial repression, Taiwan countered these by regulation. The Republic of Korea followed Taiwan's approach in broad terms in the 1980s. Taiwan finally embarked on trade and financial liberalization in the 1980s, and Korea followed in the 1990s.

The evidence of the high costs of protection began to emerge in many developing countries in the early 1970s (Little, Scitovsky, and Scott, 1970; Balassa and Associates 1971; Donges, 1974). But it took a further ten years of empirical research to demonstrate the costs of protection and the benefits of trade for development sufficiently to encourage widespread trade liberalization as part of the adjustment process in developing countries.

As soon as protection was introduced, costs of production were raised so that there was pressure to escalate import controls and tariffs further. Manufacturers also wanted reduced competition in domestic markets, often succeeding in having restrictions placed on entry into production and on production expansion. Costs remained high and qualities of output low in such situations, limiting economies of scale and the benefits of internal competition. India failed to industrialize efficiently despite its large domestic market. Where internal competition emerged despite attempts to contain it, for example, in nondurable goods industries in Brazil, production costs did become internationally competitive.

High costs of production meant a bias against agriculture as consumer goods and manufactured inputs became more costly. Protection for manufactures was often accompanied by depressed prices for agricultural goods, further subsidizing manufacturing and associated industries and their urban environments. Investment in infrastructure became biased toward urban areas. Productivity and employment in rural areas stagnated, apparently justifying a "labor holding" view of a dual agricultural/industrial developing country model. Agricultural development, so necessary for economies at low-income levels (Mellor, 1994), was delayed, often for decades, except in the Republic of Korea and Taiwan, where protection for industry was offset, and Indonesia, Malaysia, and Thailand, where the bias against agriculture was relatively low. The turning of the internal terms of trade against agriculture was a key element in retarding development in South Asia until the late 1960s, when policies changed, in such areas of Latin America as northeastern Brazil, and, until very recently, in Sub-Saharan Africa. Wherever the majority of the population lived in rural areas, highly protective industrialization policies were the principal cause of the persistence of poverty.

Agricultural exports could not compete internationally. The share of developing economies, notably Latin American countries, in world trade in agricultural products, fell. Large South Asian countries could not grow enough food for their rising populations or produce enough exports to pay for food imports. By the 1970s, many Mediterranean countries from Turkey to Egypt and those of Sub-Saharan Africa had also followed the Latin American model.

Macroeconomic imbalances were exacerbated as the subsidies implicit in protection (directly or through revenues foregone) weakened fiscal systems and financial policy and put an intolerable burden on monetary policy.

Employment in manufacturing is inherently relatively small (except in city-states in the early period of labor-intensive import substitution). The emphasis of protection on import substitution for middle- and upper-income demand for artificial fibers, "white goods," motor vehicles, and similarly capital-intensive products reduced it further. The substitution of capital for labor flourished as tax "holidays" were added to credit subsidies and escalating tariff schedules that generally exempted capital goods from import duties. Employment creation languished, particularly where "informal," admittedly often low-quality, small-scale manufacturing for the mass market was discouraged because of its competitive threat to high-technology, large-scale, capital-intensive firms. High manufacturing costs restricted domestic market expansion, limiting the benefits of economies of scale and further dampening the expansion of employment.

Some developing economies, such as Brazil and India, had strong balance-of-payments reserves at the end of World War II. These deteriorated sharply as protection was introduced. Foreign exchange became critically short. Foreign exchange saving was stressed as a reason for protection, usually regardless of domestic resource costs of domestic production. Protection meant a further overvaluation of exchange rates. With a protectionist trade regime, black market rates underestimate total, as distinct from balance-of-payments exchange rate, overvaluation. Imports are further encouraged, and exports are discouraged.

Protected economies became more, not less, dependent on international trade than open economies. Because protection was skewed in favor of import substitution of consumer goods bought by middle- and upper-middle-income groups in most countries and because final products were more highly protected than intermediate inputs, the demand for imported inputs into manufacturing grew rapidly. The pressure on the balance of payments rose accordingly, leading to severe administrative rationing of foreign exchange by central banks and departments of industry and trade. Rent seeking and corruption were encouraged. Imports of inputs into manufacturing could not be cut off as imports of final goods such as motor vehicles had been in previous times of balance-of-payments stringency because the employment of a highly vocal urban labor force was now at stake. "Foreign exchange" shortages became endemic, particularly in countries that had resorted to external borrowing for macroeconomic purposes.

Exports of Manufactures

In the 1950s most developing countries were exporters of (often only one or two) primary goods and importers of manufactures and services. By the 1980s this was no longer the case. Developing countries had diversified their agricultural and mineral exports and moved into manufactures and services (mainly tourism). Fuels had become major imports for many developing countries, as had food. While Southeast and South Asian countries reduced their grain imports as they developed their agricultural sectors, many Sub-Saharan African countries are now food importers. The developing countries' share of world trade fell during the 1950s and 1960s but rose again in the 1970s with the shift to exports of manufactures and services.

East Asian countries—Hong Kong, Taiwan, the Republic of Korea, and Singapore—have been leaders in exploiting their comparative advantage in ample labor supplies by exporting labor-intensive manufactures, mainly to industrial countries but also to other developing countries.

As skills and wages rose in the principal exporting countries, labor-intensive production shifted to Malaysia, Thailand, and Indonesia, while in the four "tiger'' countries, enterprises gradually moved to greater skill, capital, and technology intensity. Singapore developed a ''triangle'' with Malaysia and Indonesia to smooth and accelerate the transition. In the middle of the 1970s, Macau and Hong Kong investors began to shift production, informally, to China, where, despite low productivity, labor costs were low and labor-intensive production was thus competitive if the bureaucratic mire of Chinese officialdom could be avoided. When China ''opened its door'' to economic relations with the world (Tidrick, 1994), informal foreign investment in China accelerated rapidly, with Taiwanese investors becoming active. By the early 1990s some 5 million workers in China were estimated to be employed by ''overseas Chinese'' investors. Formal direct investment, in contrast, grew slowly and mainly went into import substitution (Yang, 1993). Trade policy reforms finally began to free up the very considerable Indian export potential in the 1990s. Except in Sub-Saharan Africa, many other developing countries also diversified their exports, moving into manufactures, but, with the exception of Chile and Mexico, on relatively small scales. East Asian countries dominated the exports of manufactures from developing countries from the 1950s to the 1990s with almost 70 percent of total developing country exports. Industrial country producers and markets adjusted as developing countries expanded their exports and trade in manufactures among developing countries also increased (Panoutsopoulos, 1992).

Declining barter terms of trade were feared for labor-intensive manufactures as volumes of exports grew rapidly. In the 1970s it was believed that the tigers' experience could not be replicated (Cline, 1982; Streeten, 1982), but the income and price elasticity of demand for labor-intensive goods was high. As exporters became more efficient, they were able to drop their prices, deliberately worsening their barter terms of trade but making their profits out of rising volumes. The countries benefited from rapidly rising income terms of trade.

The expansion of trade after World War II began in the industrial countries, fueling their economic growth. The Dillon, Kennedy, and Tokyo Rounds of multilateral trade negotiations under the General Agreement on Tariffs and Trade (GATT) auspices reduced barriers to trade substantially in manufactures. Each negotiation was more complex than the previous one and hence more difficult to conclude. The most recent negotiations, the Uruguay Round, by attempting to include agricultural and service products, has been the most difficult of all. By the 1970s there was some backtracking in the trading framework. Clothing and textiles became protected in industrial countries. The protection was institutionalized, creating an interest group among national and international bureaucrats that, together with clothing and textile manufacturers (and rent beneficiaries in developing countries), has been able to maintain high trade barriers in this industry. Footwear protection was not institutionalized, and it was hence substantially reduced in the early 1980s. Industrial country cartels (in steel and chemicals) and some managed trade with centrally planned economies reduced the efficiency of international trade. Antidumping actions have become a common protectionist mechanism in industrial countries. Overall, however, world markets are still more open than at any previous time in history. Trade has consistently grown faster than production, enabling open countries to benefit from low costs of imports, economies of scale, and competitiveness. The greatest barriers to trade, despite the liberalization movement of the 1980s, remain in developing countries.

The combination of macroeconomic stability and openness makes it possible for countries to exploit their ample resources—minerals, agricultural land, unskilled labor, capital or technological skill—through exports and to make up for the resources they lack. Countries' resources bases change as they develop. They move up a skill, capital, and technology ''escalator'' that enhances productivity and hence incomes. Countries with rapidly growing exports overcome balance-of-payments problems. They can afford to import the goods they need and to service debt created by borrowing for private and public investment. In small economies labor-intensive exports can make a marked contribution to employment. The multiplier effects, particularly through informal sector employment, can have a major impact on an economy.

Regional Arrangements

When protectionist policies began to run into trouble in the early 1960s, Prebisch (1959) argued that the smallness of the markets of individual countries was a principal cause of inefficient industrialization. Stimulated by the creation of the Economic Community (EC) and arguments for cooperation among developing countries as a means of offsetting industrial country dominance of the world economy, many regional integration arrangements among developing economies were formed. Following the Prebisch arguments, they were designed to create protection for regionwide industries that required economies of scale and to substitute regional trade for global trade.

Regional economic arrangements range from preferential trade areas, through customs unions with free internal trade and a common external tariff against the rest of the world, to fully integrated common markets that have full freedom of movement of factors of production (labor and capital), as well as goods and services. Common markets lead to common macroeconomic, human resource development, and other policies and hence tend toward total economic and political integration.

The arguments for regional arrangements initially lay in the benefits that could be reaped from a free trade area in a world of barriers to trade. It was soon evident, however, that regional arrangements could lead to trade diversion in contrast to trade creation. In protectionist regional arrangements trade diversion dominated, reducing, rather than enhancing, income growth. It also led to an unequal distribution of income between those benefiting from protection and those who had to pay for it through high input and consumption goods costs.

The more successful the regional arrangements were, the worse their ultimate failure. The collapse of the Central American common market, which had gone furthest in trade diversion, exemplified all the costs of protection complicated by the difficulties of allocating the few benefits and many costs among the various national members. Some thirty developing country regional arrangements have been established, though some only on paper. Almost all have collapsed (Balassa and Stoutjesdijk, 1976; Vaitsos, 1978). Some arrangements failed in part because they included countries with different political systems and at different stages of development, but essentially the "second best" nature of regional trade arrangements, compared with multilateral liberalization, was the principal cause of failure.

The Latin American Free Trade Area (LAFTA) has been one of the few to survive. Until the unilateral national liberalization of the 1980s in Latin America, trade had been mainly among branches of the transnational corporations established in the various countries in the region. Although this represented trade diversion, it enabled some economies of scale to be reaped so that costs of production fell below the very high levels of small-scale production in individual countries, though they remained substantially above international prices. LAFTA trade was relatively small and capital-intensive. It did not lead to the efficiency and employment gains of East Asian worldwide exports.

The main regional arrangement success among developing countries has been the Association of South East Asian Nations (ASEAN). But ASEAN is essentially not an economic arrangement, but a strategic political alliance. Economic integration rhetoric has mainly been reflected in preferential trade arrangements in products in which the countries had little trade. A proposal for an ASEAN Free Trade Area (AFTA) is not regarded as urgent. Regional trade among developing countries has grown rapidly throughout East Asia (more rapidly than in LAFTA), despite the absence of a regional trade arrangement, because trade barriers are relatively low by developing country standards. The rapidly growing countries are expanding their markets for raw materials, importing low-cost manufactures, and supplying capital goods to other countries in the region. These trade developments are clearly more efficient than regional trade arrangements.

Much of the renewed impetus for regional arrangements has emerged from the discrimination increasingly evident in European and North American arrangements. It has also been argued that multilateral negotiations had become so complex that it would be easier to liberalize trade from a regional base. But the Uruguay Round difficulties did not result from the scale of the negotiations but from the intransigence of agricultural protectionists in the industrial countries. Despite its initial liberal trade posture, the EC's evolution has demonstrated that, as trade theory predicts, compared with open multilateral trade, regional trade arrangements tend toward trade diversion and trade discrimination. These are not sufficiently offset by income gains to benefit either the member countries or those outside a regional arrangement. The North American Free Trade Area has already adopted discriminatory measures against the rest of the world.

SECTORAL POLICIES

Where economywide macroeconomic, trade, and human resource policies established a stable and open environment so that market prices by and large reflected international competitive market prices, resource allocation within and among sectors was reasonably efficient, and so was resource utilization. Such environments were marked by low inflation, foreign exchange rate equilibrium and stability, balanced budgets, and external accounts. Rapid growth and rising equality of opportunity followed. Political openness developed. More commonly the principal economywide policies were marked by distortions. These created pressure groups for their maintenance but also for measures to offset them. Farmers, urban entrepreneurs, workers employed in protected or other rent-creating industries wanted to maintain or increase their share of national income through monopolistic prices and rents. So did public servants whose power bases lay in distorted policies. Consumers, environmentalists, and lower-income groups (or more often socially concerned groups acting on their behalf) were usually able to mount only weak opposition to such demands.

Some sectoral policies have therefore emphasized and supported the distortions created by economywide policies. Tariffs, tax holidays, subsidized credits, and limits on the entry by new entrepreneurs (and hence on competition) were constantly enhanced to meet pressure group demands. But once it was recognized that protection harmed the economy, policies that would weaken protection were introduced, mainly in the form of offsets to protection and export incentives. Exemptions from import restrictions and tariffs on inputs into exports (or tariff drawbacks) were, however, the only effective countermeasures. Credit subsidies, privileged monopolistic access to domestic markets, tax holidays for profits on exports, and similar measures that sought to raise the profitability of exports vis-à vis protected domestic production created further distortions and rent seeking and were often ineffectual (Herderschee, 1991). Countries giving tax holidays competed with each other, creating high levels of revenue foregone. The stimulus they gave investors appeared to be negligible (Guisinger, 1985). Monopolies led to price and/or quality controls and regulations to protect consumer interests and thus to further distortions.

At early stages of development bureaucrats often considered that they were better equipped than private sector entrepreneurs to "pick winners," that is, enterprises that would succeed. They argued that this would save scarce resources that would otherwise be wasted in bankruptcies. Picking winners and supporting them by tariffs, credit subsidies, tax holidays, and other measures became a prime activity in planning agencies, boards of investment, departments of industry, and trade and development banks. But these officials were increasingly responding to "market failure" created by distorting macroeconomic and trade policies and the changes in them. Prices facing entrepreneurs were often not a guide to international competitiveness. Hong Kong never tried to pick winners. In Singapore, picking winners that turned out to be costly failures (silk and cameras) led to a stress on allowing the market to lead bureaucratic interventions (Hughes, 1994a forthcoming). In most developing countries, however, it was not until the 1980s that it was recognized that bankruptcy is a cheap and efficient method for clearing out inefficient producers. Not only is free entry into production essential for efficiency; so is exit.

Because fiscal and monetary policies had been stabilized in Taiwan and the Republic of Korea, offsets to protection in the form of tariff exemptions proved to be sufficient to stimulate exports in spite of the high costs of industrial regulation and financial regulations introduced to counter distorting policies. Many developing countries introduced elaborate incentives and interventions to avoid policy reforms. Intervention did not deliver high growth. On the contrary, it further weakened economies and worsened income distribution.

Public investment in production led to technical and economic inefficiency. Operating conditions are inherently more stable in infrastructural activities than in manufacturing, but many of the public enterprises in energy, transport, and other service activities were also very inefficient. Once established, state enterprises were difficult to dismantle. Their managers and workers formed very strong interest groups. Privatization was made costly. Some countries began to reduce government ownership in the 1960s, encouraging competing private enterprises to surround and engulf state enterprises. Privatization accelerated in the 1980s, but in many developing economies public sectors are still considerable.

In sectors against which economywide policies created a bias, producers' pressure groups tried to offset "negative" protection. Agriculture was the main sector affected. Farmers could not compete against imports or exports while industry was protected and the exchange rate overvalued. Macroeconomic instability and protection for industry should have been ended. But politically and bureaucratically this was rarely possible. Where protection discriminated against agriculture, typical offsetting policies included subsidies for manufactured inputs, notably fertilizers and other chemicals, reduction of import taxes on machinery, increased tariffs on competing imports, and minimum "floor" prices. Low-cost credit was made available to some farmers, but they were generally the well-off ones. Such government services as quality seed supplies or improved breeds of animals were subsidized. But if there was some concern for consumers (or for potential urban protesters), maximum output prices, compulsory government acquisition, and similar measures were also introduced, creating a web of conflicting incentives.

Each sector—transportation, energy, communications, housing—created its own plethora of regulations, partly to try to improve the functioning of markets but mainly as a result of pressure from interest groups. With interest group pressures, regulations frequently became excessive, increasing costs for other sectors.

Entrepreneurs had to live with the actual prices that faced them, distorted or not. Whether they invested in a sector or took their capital abroad—legally or illegally—depended on those prices. For a social evaluation of the net effect of the main economywide and sectoral policies, a cost/benefit analysis in an economywide equilibrium context was necessary. Such investigations were costly, and the skills required for them were scarce. For most heavily regulated countries with significant distortions, time series of the "net" market prices facing entrepreneurs and of social prices are not available. Careful analysis of policy impact on economic outcomes can thus not be undertaken. For example, it is by no means clear whether price signals to exporters in Taiwan and the Republic of Korea have given them positive subsidies or merely introduced neutrality. An enormous data and estimation effort would be needed to test such hypotheses.

IDEOLOGY, THEORY, GROWTH, AND DEVELOPMENT

Rapid growth has been achieved only by countries with a population of less than 350 million out of a total developing country population of some 4.5 billion people. It is sobering to consider that had China and India stressed the operation of private enterprise and markets in a context of exploiting comparative advantage, macroeconomic stability, and corresponding infrastructural investment from the early 1950s, both would now be middle-income countries, and they would have largely eliminated absolute poverty. The adoption of similar policies in Latin American countries would have seen most of these countries caught up with at least the lower ranks of the market-oriented industrial economies. If African countries had taken growth policy paths, they could have substantially improved their living standards instead of dropping back to medieval growth paths.

If the role of economists is to demonstrate that what works in practice is theoretically possible, then development economists have been busy. Ideology has played a negative role in growth and development. In its extreme form, Marxist-inspired development economics, encompassing protectionism, statism, and intensive regulations to correct "market failures," substantially reduced growth. The perception that trickle down did not work so that development policies had to focus on basic needs was not borne out in practice. The ideological emphasis on basic needs may have had some positive results in some cases, but it delayed the movement for economic reform and hence poverty alleviation by at least a decade.

The positive contribution of economics in rapidly growing countries has been through the use of a broad range of analytical tools, sometimes in a static, partial equilibrium context, though increasingly with dynamic, general equilibrium dimensions. The use of such tools in the analysis of fiscal efficiency, the causes and effects of inflation, the role of trade, and the importance of social policies underpinned the policy reform movement of the 1980s. It seems likely that future insights into development and hence into further policy improvement are more likely to come from more careful empirical work and associated incremental improvements in well-established, mainstream "boxes of economic tools," rather than in major outbreaks of theory.

NOTE

I am grateful to Ruel Abello for assistance in preparing this chapter and to Heinz Arndt, Enzo Grilli, Jim Riedel, and David Robertson for comments.

REFERENCES

Amsden, A. 1979. "Taiwan's Economic History: A Case of *Statisme* and a Challenge to Dependency Theory." *Modern China* 5, no. 3: 341–80.

———. 1989. *Asia's Next Giant: South Korea and Late Industrialisation*. New York: Oxford University Press.

———. 1993. "Structural Macroeconomic Underpinnings of Effective Industrial Policy: Fast Growth in the 1980s in Five Asian countries." United Nations Conference on Trade and Development Discussion Paper No. 57.

Balassa, B. 1982. "Structural Adjustment Policies in Developing Countries." *World Development,* 10, no. 1: 114–36.

Balassa, B., and Associates. 1971. *The Structure of Protection in Developing Countries.* Baltimore: Johns Hopkins University Press.

Balassa, B., and Stoutjesdijk, A. 1976. "Economic Integration Among Developing Countries." *Journal of Common Market Studies* 14: 37–55.

Bautista, R., Hughes, H., Lim, D., Morawetz, D., and Thoumi, F. 1981. *Capital Utilization in Manufacturing.* Oxford: Oxford University Press.

Behrman, J.R., and Deolalikar, A.B. 1988. "Health and Nutrition." In *Handbook of Development Economics,* Vol. 1, edited by H. Chenery and T.N. Srinivasan. Amsterdam: North-Holland.

Bhagwati, J., and Partington, M., eds. 1976. *Taxing the Brain Drain.* Amsterdam: North-Holland.

Booth, A. 1993. "Counting the Poor in Indonesia." *Bulletin of Indonesian Economics Studies* 29, no. 1: 53–83.

Chen, E.K.Y. 1989. "Trade Policy in Asia." In *Lessons in Development: A Comparative Study of Asia and Latin America,* edited by S. Naya, M. Urrutia, S. Mark, and A. Fuentes. San Francisco: International Center for Economic Growth, 55–76.

Chenery, H.B., et al. 1974. *Redistribution with Growth.* London: Oxford University Press.

Cline, W. 1982. "Can the East Asian Model of Development be Generalised?" *World Development* 10, no. 2: 81–90.

Cole, R., ed. 1993. *Pacific 2010: Challenging the Future.* Canberra: National Centre for Development Studies, Australian National University.

Cole, R., and Hughes, H. 1988. "The Fiji Economy, May 1987: Problems and Prospects." *Pacific Policy Papers No. 4.* Canberra: National Centre for Development Studies, Australian National University.

Corbo, V. 1992. "Development Strategies and Policies in Latin America: A Historical Perspective." Occasional Paper No. 22. International Center for Economic Growth. San Francisco: ICS Press.

Corbo, V., and de Melo, J. 1987. "External Shocks and Policy Reforms in the Southern Cone: A Reassessment." DRD Discussion Paper No. 241. Washington, D.C.: Development Research Department, World Bank.

Donges, J.B. 1974. "Conditions for Successful Import Substitution and Export Diversification in LDCs: A Summary Appraisal." In *The International Division of Labour Problems and Perspectives*, edited by H. Giersch. Kiel: Institut fur Weltwirtschaft.

Dubey, V. 1993. "India: Economic Performance and Prospects." In *The International Division of Labour Problems and Perspectives*, edited by H. Giersch. Kiel: Institut fur Weltwirtschaft.

Edwards, S. 1984. "Structural Adjustment Policies in Highly Indebted Countries." In *Developing Country Debt and Economic Performance*, Vol. 1, edited by J. Sachs. Chicago: University of Chicago Press.

———. 1989. *Real Exchange Rates, Devaluation and Adjustment*. Cambridge: MIT Press.

Fields, G. 1989. "Changes in Poverty and Inequality in Developing Countries." *World Bank Research Observer*, 4: 167–85.

Fischer, S. 1993. *Does Macroeconomic Policy Matter? Evidence from Developing Countries*. Occasional Paper No. 27. International Center for Economic Growth.

Garnaut, R.G., and Clunies-Ross, A. 1983. *The Taxation of Mineral Rents*. London: Oxford University Press.

Grilli, E. 1994. "Long-Term Economic Growth, Income Distribution and Poverty in Developing Countries: The Evidence." In *Economic Development*, edited by Enzo Grilli and Dominick Salvatore. Westport, CT: Greenwood Press.

Grilli, E., and Yang, M. 1988. "Primary Commodity Prices, Manufactured Goods Prices and Terms of Trade of Developing Countries: What the Long Run Shows." *World Bank Economic Review* 2, no. 1: 1–47.

Guisinger, S. 1985. "Investment Incentives and Performance Requirements: A Comparative Study of Country Policies." In *Investment Incentives and Performance Requirements: Patterns of International Trade, Production and Investment*, edited by S. Guisinger. New York: Praeger.

Harberger, A.C. 1990. "Principles of Taxation Applied to Developing Countries: What Have We Learned?" In *World Tax Reform: Case Studies of Developed and Developing Countries*, edited by M. Boskin and C. McLure, Jr. San Francisco: ICS Press, 25–48.

Herderschee, H. 1991. "Incentives for Exports: A Case Study of Taiwan and Thailand." Ph.D. diss., National Centre for Development Studies, Australian National University, Canberra.

Hughes, H. 1985. *Policy Lessons of the Development Experience*. Occasional Paper No. 16. New York: Group of Thirty.

———. 1994a forthcoming. "An External View." In *Challenge and Response: Thirty Years of the Economic Development Board*, edited by L. Low, T. Muntteng, T.K. Yam, and S.T. Wang. Singapore.

———. 1994b forthcoming. "Was There an East Asian Miracle?" In *Global Change and Transformation: Economic Essays in Honor of Karsten Laursen*, edited by L. Stetting, K.E. Svendsen, and E. Yndgaard.

Hughes, H., and You Poh Seng, eds. 1969. *Foreign Investment and Industrialization in Singapore*. Canberra: ANU Press.

Killick, T. 1994. "Africa." In *Economic Development*, edited by Enzo Grilli and Dominick Salvatore. Westport, CT: Greenwood Press.

Krueger, A. 1974. "The Political Economy of the Rent Seeking Society." *American Economic Review* 64, no. 1 (June): 291–303.

Krueger, A., Schiff, M., and Valdez, A. 1988. "Agricultural Incentives in Developing Countries: Measuring the Effects of Sector and Economy-Wide Policies." *World Bank Economic Review* 2, no. 3: 255–72.

Kuznets, S. 1955. "Economic Growth and Income Inequality." *American Economic Review* 45, no. 1: 1–28.

Lal, D. 1984. *The Poverty of Development Economics*. London: IEA, Hobart Paperback 16.

Lewis, W.A. 1954. "Economic Development with Unlimited Supply of Labour." *Manchester School of Economic and Social Studies* 22, no. 2: 139–91.

Little, I. 1982. *Economic Development: Theory, Policy, and International Relations*. New York: Basic Books.

Little, I., Scitovsky, T., and Scott, M.T. 1970. *Industry and Trade in Some Developing Countries: A Comparative Study*. New York: Oxford University Press.

Low, P. ed. 1992. *International Trade and the Environment*. World Bank Discussion Paper No. 159. Washington, D.C.: World Bank.

McKinnon, R. 1973. *Money and Capital in Economic Development*. Washington, D.C.: Brookings Institution.

Medhi, K. 1992. "Contributions of Agriculture to Industrialisation: The Case of Thailand." Paper presented at the Conference on the Making of a Fifth Tiger? Thailand's Industrialisation and Its Consequences, 7–9 December, Australian National University.

Mellor, J. 1993. "Agriculture." In *Economic Development*, edited by Enzo Grilli and Dominick Salvatore. Westport, CT: Greenwood Press.

National Research Council. 1986. "Rapid Population Growth and Economic Development: Policy Questions." U.S. National Academy of Sciences Report. Washington, D.C.: National Academy Press.

Neary, P., and van Wijnbergen, S. 1986. "Natural Resources and the Macroeconomy: A Theoretical Framework." In *Natural Resources and the Macroeconomy*, edited by P. Neary and S. van Wijnbergen. Cambridge: MIT Press.

Panoutsopoulos, V. 1992. "The Growth of Exports from Developing Countries: Export Pessimism and Reality." In *The Dangers of Export Pessimism: Developing Countries and Industrial Markets*, edited by H. Hughes. San Francisco: ICS Press.

Prebisch, R. 1950. *The Economic Development of Latin America and Its Principal Problems*. New York: United Nations.

———. 1959. "International Trade and Payments in an Area of Coexistence: Commercial Policy in the Underdeveloped Countries." *American Economic Review* 49, no. 2: 251–73.

Psacharopoulos, G. 1991. *The Economic Impact of Education: Lessons for Policy Makers*. International Center for Economic Growth Publication. San Franciso: ICS Press.

Rahman, R. 1991. "An Analysis of Employment and Earnings of Poor Women in Rural Bangladesh." Ph.D. diss., National Centre for Development Studies, Australian National University, Canberra.

Raj, K.N., and Sen, A.K. 1961. "Alternative Patterns of Growth Conditions of Stagnant Export Earnings." *Oxford Economic Papers* 13, no. 1: 43–52.

Ravallion, M., and Datt, G. 1991. *Growth and Redistribution Component of Changes in Poverty Measures: A Decomposition with Application to Brazil and India in the 1980s.* LSMS Working Paper No. 83. Washington, D.C.: World Bank.

Ravallion, M., Datt, G., and Chen, S. 1992. "New Estimates of Aggregate Poverty Measures for the Developing World, 1985–1989." Washington, D.C.: World Bank, Population and Human Resources Department.

Riedel, J. 1988. "Economic Development in East Asia: Doing What Comes Naturally?" In *Achieving Industrialization in East Asia,* edited by H. Hughes. Cambridge: Cambridge University Press, 1–38.

Rosenstein-Rodan, P. 1943. "Problems of Industrialization in Eastern and Southeastern Europe." *Economic Journal* 53: 202–11.

Saad, I. 1992. "The Impact of Trade Reforms and the Multifibre Arrangement on Indonesian Clothing and Textile Exports." Ph.D. diss., National Centre for Development Studies, Australian National University, Canberra.

Schultz, T.W. 1963. *The Economic Value of Education.* New York: Columbia University Press.

Snooks, G. 1990. "Economic Growth During the Last Millenium: A Quantitative Perspective for the British Industrial Revolution." *Working Papers in Economic History, No. 140,* Australian National University.

Streeten, P. 1982. "A Cool Look at Outward-Looking Strategies for Development." *World Economy* 5, no. 2: 159–70.

———. 1994. "The Social Dimensions of Development." In *Economic Development,* edited by Enzo Grilli and Dominick Salvatore. Westport, CT: Greenwood Press.

Sung, Y.W. 1991. *The China-Hong Kong Connection: The Key to China's Open-Door Policy.* Cambridge: Cambridge University Press.

Suphachalasai, S. 1989. "The Effects of Government Intervention and the Multi-Fibre Arrangement on the Thai Clothing and Textiles Industry." Ph.D. diss., National Centre for Development Studies, Australian National University, Canberra.

Sylos Labini, P. 1994. "The Classical Roots of Development Theory." In *Economic Development,* edited by Enzo Grilli and Dominick Salvatore. Westport, CT: Greenwood Press.

Tidrick, G. 1994. "China." In *Economic Development,* edited by Enzo Grilli and Dominick Salvatore. Westport, CT: Greenwood Press.

Vaitsos, C.V. 1978. "Crisis in Regional Economic Cooperation (Integration) Among Developing Countries: A Survey." *World Development* 6, no. 6: 719–69.

Wade, R. 1990. *Governing the Market: Economic Theory and the Role of Government in East Asian Industrialization.* Princeton, N.J.: Princeton University Press.

World Bank. 1985. *China: Long Term Issues and Options.* Baltimore: Johns Hopkins University Press.

———. 1992a. *World Development Report 1992.* New York: Oxford University Press.

———. 1992b. *World Population Projections 1992–93: Estimates and Projections with Related Demographic Statistics.* London: Johns Hopkins University Press.

———. 1993. *World Development Report 1993.* New York: Oxford University Press.

Yang, G. 1993. "China's Foreign Direct Investment and Manufactured Exports." Ph.D. diss., National Centre for Development Studies, Australian National University, Canberra.

Young, A. 1992. "A Tale of Two Cities: Factor Accumulation and Technical Change in Hong Kong and Singapore." In *NBER Macroeconomics Annual 1992,* edited by O. Blanchard and S. Fischer. Cambridge: MIT Press.

SELECTED BIBLIOGRAPHY

Bardham, Pranab. 1993. "Economics of Development and the Development of Economics." *Journal of Economics Perspectives* 7 (Spring): 129–42.

Bauer, P.T., and Yamey, B.S. 1957. *The Economics of Underdeveloped Countries.* Chicago: University of Chicago Press.

Bhagwati, J.N., and Ramaswami, V.K. 1963. "Domestic Distortions, Tariffs and the Theory of Optimum Subsidy." *Journal of Political Economy* 71 (February): 44–45.

Bradford, Colin I., Jr. 1986. "East Asian Models: Myths and Lessons." In *Development Strategies Reconsidered,* edited by John P. Lewis, and Valeriana Kallab. Washington, D.C.: Overseas Development Council.

———. 1987. "NICs and the Next-Tier NICs as Transitional Economies." In *Trade and Structural Change in Pacific Asia*, edited by Colin I. Bradford, Jr., and William H. Branson. Chicago: University of Chicago Press.

Chenery, Hollis, and Syrquin, Moshe. 1975. *Patterns of Development: 1950–1970.* London: Oxford University Press.

Chenery, Hollis, and Srinivasan, T.N., eds. 1989. *Handbook of Development Economics* 1. Amsterdam: North Holland.

Corbo, V. 1992. "National Economic Policies in Latin America." In *Handbook of National Economic Policies,* edited by D. Salvatore. Westport, Conn.: Greenwood Press.

Corbo, V., and Schmidt-Hebbel, K. 1991. "Public Policy and Savings in Developing Countries." *Journal of Development Economics* 36 (July): 89–116.

Domar, E.D. 1957. *Essays in the Theory of Economic Growth.* New York: Oxford University Press.

Dorfman, Robert. 1991. "Review Article: Economic Development from the Beginning to Rostow." *Journal of Economic Literature* 29 (June): 573–91.

El-Agraa, A. M., ed. 1988. *International Economic Integration.* New York: St. Martin's Press.

————. 1989. *The Theory and Measurement of International Economic Integration.* New York: St. Martin's Press.

Flemming, M. 1955. "External Economies and the Doctrine of Balanced Growth." *Economic Journal* 65 (June): 241–56.

Grilli, E., Kregel, J., and Savona, P. 1982. "Terms of Trade and Italian Economic Growth: Accounting for Miracles." *Banca Nazionale del Lavoro Quarterly Review* 143 (December): 395–416.

Grilli, E., and Yang, M.C. 1988. "Primary Commodity Prices, Manufactured Goods Prices, and the Terms of Trade of Developing Countries: What the Long Run Shows." *World Bank Review* 2, no. 11: 1–47.

Hirschman, A.O. 1958. *The Strategy of Economic Development.* New Haven, Conn.: Yale University Press.

Hughes, H., and Krueger, A.O. 1984. "Effects of Protection in Developed Countries on Developing Countries." In *The Structure and Evolution of Recent U.S. Trade Policy,* edited by R. Baldwin and A.O. Krueger. Chicago: University of Chicago Press.

Kaldor, N. 1957. "A Model of Economic Growth." *Economic Journal* 67 (December): 591–624.

Killick, Tony. 1978. *Development Economics in Action: Economic Policies in Ghana.* London: Heinemann Educational Books.

————. 1983. "Development Planning in Africa: Experiences, Weaknesses and Prescriptions." *Development Policy Review* 1, no. 1: 1–24.

Kuznets, S.S. 1955. "Economic Growth and Income Inequality." *American Economic Review* 45 (March): 1–28.

————. 1966. *Modern Economic Growth: Rate, Structure and Spread.* New Haven, Conn.: Yale University Press.

Lewis, W.A. 1954. "Economic Growth with Unlimited Supplies of Labor." *Manchester School* 22 (May): 139–91.

————. 1984. "The State of Development Theory." *American Economic Review* 74 (March): 1–10.

Little, I.M.D., Scitovsky, T., and Scott, M. 1970. *Industry and Trade in Some Developing Countries.* London: Oxford University Press.

Mellor, John W. 1966. *The Economics of Agricultural Development.* Ithaca, N.Y.: Cornell University Press.

Mellor, John W., and Johnston, Bruce F. 1984. "The World Food Equation: Interrelations Among Development, Employment, and Food Consumption." *Journal of Economic Literature* 22 (June): 22–43.

Nurkse, R. 1953. *Problems of Capital Formation in Underdeveloped Countries.* Oxford: Blackwell.

Pomfret, Richard. 1981. "The Impact of EEC Enlargement on Non-Member Mediterranean Countries' Exports to the EEC." *Economic Journal* 91 (September): 726–29.

————. 1982. "Trade Effects of European Community Preferences to Mediterranean Countries: The Case of Textile and Clothing Imports." *World Development* 10 (October): 857–62.

Prebisch, R. 1950. *The Economic Development of Latin America and Its Principal Problems.* New York: United Nations.

Riedel, J. 1984. "Trade as an Engine of Growth, Revisited." *Economic Journal* 94 (June): 56–73.

———. 1990. "The State of Debate on Trade and Industrialization in Developing Countries." In *The Direction of Trade Policy,* edited by C. Pearson and J. Riedel. Oxford: Basil Blackwell.

Rosenstein-Rodan, P.N. 1943. "Problems of Industrialization of Eastern and South-Eastern Europe." *Economic Journal* 53 (June–September): 202–11.

Salvatore, D. 1983. "A Simultaneous Equations Model of Trade and Development with Dynamic Policy Simulations." *Kyklos* 36, no. 1: 66–90.

———. 1989. *African Development Prospects: A Policy Modeling Approach.* New York: Francis and Lewis for the United Nations.

———, ed. 1992. *Handbook of National Trade Policies.* Westport, Conn.: Greenwood Press.

———, ed. 1994. *Protectionism and Welfare.* New York: Cambridge University Press.

Salvatore, D., and Hatcher, T. 1991. "Export and Growth with Alterative Trade Strategies." *Journal of Development Studies* 27 (April): 7–25.

Schumpeter, J. A. 1934. *The Theory of Economic Development.* Cambridge: Harvard University Press.

Singer, H.W. 1950. "The Distribution of Gains Between Investing and Borrowing Countries." *American Economic Review, Papers and Proceedings* 40 (May): 473–85.

Streeten, Paul, 1979. "From Growth to Basic Needs." *Finance and Development* 16, no. 3: 28–31.

Streeten, Paul, and Jolly, Richard, eds. 1981. *Recent Issues in World Development.* Oxford: Oxford University Press.

Sylos-Labini, P. 1983. *Il Sottosviluppo e L'Economia Contemporanea.* Roma-Bari: Laterza.

———. 1984. *The Forces of Economic Growth and Decline.* Cambridge: MIT Press.

Tidrick, Gene, and Jiyuan, Chen, eds. 1987. *China's Industrial Reform.* New York: Oxford University Press.

World Bank. 1992. *Proceedings of World Bank Annual Conference on Development Economics.* Washington, D.C.: World Bank.

INDEX

ABOUT THE CONTRIBUTORS

COLIN BRADFORD, JR. is Head of Research Programme at the OECD Development Centre in Paris where he has been since 1990. Before joining the OECD, Dr. Bradford was for two years the senior staff member in charge of the international outlook work of the Strategic Planning Division at the World Bank while on leave from Yale University. While at Yale for ten years, he was Associate Professor on International Economics and Management in the School of Management, Associate Director of the Yale Center for International and Area Studies, Director of Graduate Studies in International Relations, and a member of the Economics Department and the Yale Economic Growth Center. During the 1980s, Dr. Bradford was also a research associate of the National Bureau of Economic Research (NBER) in international economics.

VITTORIO CORBO is Professor of Economics at Catholic University of Chile, and has taught at several institutions in Canada and the United States. He served at the World Bank from 1984 to 1991, where his last position was Chief of the Macroeconomic Adjustment and Growth Division. Dr. Corbo has written and edited eight books in the fields of macroeconomics, economic adjustment and development strategies. He has also written over 80 articles in specialized professional journals and books and has presented his research at seminars in the leading universities in the United States andother countries. Currently he is an adviser to the Santander Group, and a frequent consultant to the World Bank, the IDB, UNDP, SIDA, the Harvard Institute for International Development, the Japanese Foundation for Advanced Studies in International Development and numerous governments.

VINOD DUBEY currently lives in Allahabad, India, where he is associated with the Indian Society of Economic Research and is on the Board of Editors of the *Indian Journal of Economics*. He retired from the World Bank in 1990 as the Director of the Economic Advisory Staff, and was Director of the Country Policy Department (1985–87), Senior Advisor on Adjustment lending (1984) and Chief Economist Europe, Middle East and North Africa (1975–83). He has published in the *Indian Economic Journal*, the *Journal of Regional Science* and the *Economic Journal*, among others, and was the coordinating author of the World Bank's study entitled, *Yugoslavia: Development and Structural Change* (1975).

ALI M. EL-AGRAA is Professor of International Economics and European/American Economics at Fukuoka University, Japan. He was previously Senior Scholar and Lecturer in Economics at Khartoum University, Sudan, Senior Lecturer in Economics at the University of Leeds, UK, and Visiting Professor of International Economics and Middle Eastern Economics at the International University of Japan. He has also taught at Fudan University in Shanghai, and has been awarded a lifetime Academic Citizenship by Wuhan University in China. He has published widely, and one of his books, *The Economics of the European Community*, is used by many universities all over the world. He is a member of several Journal Editorial Boards, is a consultant to many organizations, was a Committee member of the International Economics Study Group (UK), and is the Chairperson of Fukuoka International Forum.

ENZO GRILLI was until recently Director of Development Policy at the World Bank. He is now an Executive Director of the Bank. Heis also Professorial Lecturer of Economics at Johns Hopkins University in Baltimore and Visiting Professor at Bocconi University in Milano. He has published extensively on trade, growth and economic development issues. His books include: *The European Community and the Developing Countries* (1993), *The New Protectionist Wave* (1990), and *Italy at the Cross Roads: Stagnation or Growth* (1985). His articles are published in such journals as the *European Economic Review*, *Banca Nazionale del Lavoro Quarterly Review*, *The World Bank Economic Review*, *The Journal of International Money and Finance*, *Weltwirtschaftliches Archiv* and *The World Economy*.

HELEN HUGHES is Professor Emeritus of the Australian National University and Professor of Economics at Melbourne University where she directs a full employment in mature economies project. She has worked with the World Bank for fifteen years. She has published widely on the role of trade in development, industrial policies, the role of labour, international capital movements, theimportance of macroeconomic policies and the factors leading to sustainable development. Professor Hughes' special expertise is in the East and Southeast Asia.

TONY KILLICK is Senior Research Fellow and former Director of the Overseas Development Institute, London; and Visiting Professor of the University of

Surrey. His principal interests are in the areas of economic policies in developing countries, and in the ways in which the policies of international agencies impinge upon developing countries. He has a special interest in the economies of Africa. His books include studies of the economies of Ghana and Kenya, a two-volume study of the policies of the IMF, an ''informal textbook'' on adjustment policies in low-income countries, and a forthcoming study of the flexibility of national economies.

JOHN MELLOR is President of John Mellor Associates, a policy consulting firm. He is author of the book, *The Economics of Agricultural Development*, and has won several prizes for quality of research in that area. He has written or edited prize winning books on development strategy, agricultural price policy, African development policy, and poverty, as well as hundreds of scholarly papers. He was Chief Economist of the United States Agency for International Development; built the International Food Policy Research Institute into the premiere institute in its field; won the Wilhuri International Prize (Finland) and The Presidential Award (United States) for his contribution to the reduction of hunger; is Chairman of the Board of a U.S. food distribution company; is a fellow of the American Academy of Arts and Sciences, The American Association for the Advancement of Science, and the American Agricultural Economics Association; and a past member of the Board on Agriculture, National Academy of Sciences. He served for many years on the faculty of Cornell University, and for short periods at the Indian Agricultural Research Institute, Balwant Rajput College, and the American University Beirut. He has served on numerous national and international commissions.

RICHARD POMFRET is Professor of Economics at the University of Adelaide in Australia. He was previously at Johns Hopkins University (Baltimore, Bologna and Nanjing), Fudan University (Shanghai), Concordia University (Montreal) and the University of Kiel (Germany), and has been consultant to the United Nations (ESCAP), World Bank, Arab Monetary Fund, ASEAN and the European Community. His publications include seven monographs in the fields of international trade and economic development, three textbooks on International Trade, Development, and Canadian Economic History, and numerous journal articles.

JAMES RIEDEL is Professor of International Economics at the Paul H. Nitze School of Advanced International Studies of Johns Hopkins University and a consultant to the World Bank and other organizations. Among his recent publications are *Economic Crises and Long-term Growth in Turkey* (1993) and *The Direction of Trade Policy* (1990) as well as recent articles in such journals as *The Economic Journal*, *The World Economy* and *Weltwirtschaftliches Archiv*.

DOMINICK SALVATORE is Professor of Economics at Fordham University, consultant to the United Nations in New York and the Economics Policy Institute in Washington, and the author of *International Economics* (3rd ed., 1993). He has authored or edited 31 books, including *Protectionism and Welfare* (1993), *Handbook of National Trade Policies* (Greenwood Press, 1992), *The United States-Japan Trade Problem* (1991), and *African Development Prospects* (1989). He has published over 60 articles in the leading economic journals and presented his research in numerous universities in the United States and abroad. He is co-editor of the *Journal of Policy Modeling*, and *Open Economies Review*, and associate editor of *The American Economist*.

PAUL STREETEN is Professor Emeritus of Economics of Boston University and a Consultant to the UNDP on the Human Development Report. He is editor and the chairman of the Board of *World Development*. He is an Honorary Fellow of Balliol College, Oxford and of the Institute of Development Studies, Sussex. He has honorary degrees from the Universities of Aberdeen and Malta. His most recent books are *Development Perspectives*, *First Things First*, *What Price Food?*, *Beyond Adjustment*, and *Mobilizing Human Potential*. He is working on global interdependence, human development and poverty.

PAOLO SYLOS LABINI is Professor of Economics at the University of Rome, La Sapienza, and a member of the Accademia Nazionale dei Lincei, of the Académie Européenne des Sciences, des Arts at des Lettres of Paris and of the Academia Europaea of London. He is the author of a number of books, including *Oligopoly and Technical Progress* (1993), *Trade Unions, Inflation and Productivity* (1974), *The Forces of Economic Growth and Decline* (1984), and *Economic Growth and Business Cycles—Prices and the Process of Cyclical Development* (1993).

GENE TIDRICK is Lead Economist for the Southern Africa Department of the World Bank. His previous experience within the Bank includes seven years on China, three on India and five on East Africa. He has also served as an economic adviser to the governments of Tanzania (with Harvard Institute for International Development) and Kenya (with UNDP), and taught at Williams College. Books and monographs which he has edited or co-authored include *China's Industrial Reform* (1987); *Productivity Growth and Technological Change in Chinese Industry* (1986); *China: Long-Term Issues and Options* (1985); and *Accelerated Development in Sub-Saharan Africa* (1981).